DOCTOR WHO
ON LOCATION

DOCTOR WHO
ON LOCATION

Richard Bignell

Reynolds & Hearn Ltd
London

To Andrew Pixley
A great friend, researcher and fellow factophile with
whom I have spent many happy hours discussing
the production minutiae contained within the reams
of dusty BBC documents. Thank you for your
unceasing faith in this project and for being a
never-ending source of encouragement.

To David J Howe
For your generosity at the beginning of this
project and for convincing me that it was a goal
worth pursuing.

First published in 2001 by
Reynolds & Hearn Ltd
61a Priory Road
Kew Gardens
Richmond
Surrey TW9 3DH

A CIP catalogue record for this book is available from
the British Library.

ISBN 1 903111 22 6

Designed by Paul Chamberlain.
Cover design by Paul Vyse.

Printed and bound in Great Britain by Biddles Ltd,
Guildford, Surrey.

CONTENTS

ACKNOWLEDGEMENTS

Paul Allen, Peter Anghelides, BBC Written Archives Centre, Keith Barber (Malvern Library), Alan Barnes, Keith Barnfather, Christopher Barry, C M Bayliss (Hammersmith and Fulham Archive), Jeremy Bentham, Tony Bianchi, British Newspaper Library, Michael E Briant, Herbert Brooking (Sunbury and Shepperton Local History Society), Estelle Carter, John Challis, Spencer Chapman, Bill Chesneau, Geoffrey Cheshire, Timothy Combe, Arthur Cox, Patrick Cooke, Bernard Cribbins, Christopher D'Oyly John, Ann Davies, Ron and Dorothy Davis (Egham-by-Runnymede Historical Society), Raquel Ebbutt, Michael Elwyn, Peter Epstein, Nicholas Evans, Michael Ferguson, Peter Finklestone, Sharon Ford, Sue Garland (Guinness Brewing Ltd), Gary Gillatt, John Gleeson, Geoff Glover, Ian Gordon, Carmen Gomez, Ann Grant, David Guest, John Hills-Harrop, Margot Hayhoe, Highgate Literary and Scientific Institution, David J Howe, Frank Howe, David Jamieson (Circus Friends Association), John and Sue Jenkinson, Caroline John, Nicholas John, Anne Jones (Museum of Farnham), B T Keane (Cricklewood Archive), Julian Knott, Janet Lear, David Leboff, Michael Leeston-Smith, Barry Letts, Snowy Lidiard-White, Robin Llewellyn, Brenda Loader, Michael McStay, David Maloney, Judy Marsh, Derek Martin, Richard Martin, Derek Martinus, Peter Moffatt, Richard Molesworth, Bryan Nolan, Andrew Pixley, Justin Richards, Elfan ap Rees, John Rendle, Adrian Rigelsford, John Ringham, Pennant Roberts, Steve Roberts, Joan Rosaire, Jan Vincent-Rudzki, Gary Russell, Paddy Russell, Ian Rutter, Howard Salter, Stephen Scott, Derrick Sherwin, Julia Smith, Rachel Speake (Evesham Library), Andrew Spokes, Sheila Steafel, Isobel Stokes, Peter F Thorogood, Donald Turtle, Alexandra Tynan, Paul Vanezis, Stephen James Walker, Antony Webb, Marcus D F White, Martin Wiggins, John T Williams (Margate Local History Museum) and Mark Wyman.

Every effort has been made to identify the copyright holders of the photograhs contained in this book. Any mistakes or omissions will be rectified in future editions.

Special thanks to:

Stephen Carter
For all the tremendously detailed work you've done helping me to track down so many of the London locations. A location hunter who's willing to follow the clues to the bitter end!

David Brunt
For providing the answers to so many questions.

The **Goodfellows of Kklak!** and the guys in the **RT Chatroom** for helping to keep my sanity almost intact over the months.

Marcus Hearn and **Richard Reynolds**
For being so enthusiastic about this project.

PUBLISHERS' NOTE

While many of the locations listed in this book are accessible or visible to the public, many are also situated on private property. The inclusion of these filming sites within the pages of this book should not be taken as a permission to trespass. The author and publishers of Doctor Who On Location accept no responsibility for any legal action that may result from unauthorised access to private property.

FOREWORD

I was always very fond of Star Trek, but at the same time disappointed that so many of the planets Captain Kirk and his crew visited were obviously built from bits of polystyrene in a studio. On the rare occasions the Enterprise deposited its crew in a genuine outdoor location it always seemed to be the same bit of desert. One particular rock appeared over and over again. I became quite fond of it, and even wrote it a fan letter. It never replied.

Since browsing Richard Bignell's exhaustive guide to Doctor Who locations I realise that the Time Lord's excursions were just as rare during the 1960s. When I became Doctor Who in 1987 I was lucky to appear in a lot of adventures that took us out of the studio, and relieved that – contrary to popular belief – the programme didn't only shoot in quarries.

I have long since resigned myself to the fact that the Doctor Who fans I meet at conventions know more about my episodes than I've forgotten. My memories of shooting on location are a jumble of freezing winters and baking summers, nerve-jangling pyrotechnics and bafflng dialogue. But through it all I had the pleasure of working with my two travelling companions, Bonnie Langford and Sophie Aldred, and guest stars and crew-members too numerous to mention.

In my first year we filmed some episodes in a dilapidated Butlins camp that was soldiering on with knobbly knees competitions and wet t-shirt contests while we were filming. I wanted to stay there but they put me up in a hotel, which wasn't half as much fun. My second series was shot during the glorious summer of 1988 – the Cybermen and Daleks looked their best glinting in the sunlight.

My memories are all sunny, although fans from outside Britain still ask me, 'Why is it always raining on the planets you visit?' ■

Above: Sylvester McCoy and Sophie Aldred outside St Mary's House, Bramber, during the recording of Silver Nemesis in 1988.

Sylvester McCoy
London, September 2001

PREFACE

Locations and Dates

Information in this book on both the location sites and dates when filming occurred have been compiled wherever possible from existing production documentation held in the BBC archives or within private collections.

The primary document used for sourcing the location details has been the official Film Diary/Schedule/Itinerary or OB Schedule drawn up for each production. However, for a number of stories, no copies of these documents are currently known to exist. The stories affected are:

The Dalek Invasion of Earth*
The Chase
The Myth Makers*
The Massacre of St Bartholomew's Eve*
The Gunfighters
The Savages*
The Highlanders*
The Faceless Ones
The Tomb of the Cybermen
The Abominable Snowmen
The Enemy of the World
Fury from the Deep*
The Mind Robber
The Invasion
The Krotons
Spearhead from Space
Doctor Who and the Silurians
Terror of the Autons
The Mutants
The Seeds of Doom (Athelhampton OB only)
The Pirate Planet
Shada

* indicates that no production file is known to exist in the BBC archives

For those stories indicated above, locations and filming dates have been gleaned from other official production documentation, scripts, local newspaper coverage etc.

It should be stressed that for much of this work, the dates and details given are for what was scheduled to take place and that technical problems, poor weather and other events could heavily affect precisely what was performed when. Where interview anecdotes or other paperwork has shown a deviation from the planned schedules, details have been adjusted accordingly.

As building and land ownership often changes over the years, all locations, wherever possible, have been referred to under their original designation at the time the relevant filming for the programme occurred. Where it has been possible to do so, street numbers relating to the premises have been given in the description to assist any would-be location hunters, together with indications in the main text or footnotes as to the current usage of certain locations. However, some sites have radically altered over the years or have even been demolished entirely, but the details given in the descriptions should be sufficient to find the locations with the minimum of investigation.

Shooting Schedule

Production dates listed as, for example, 4-9 September indicate that the scenes were shot at some indeterminate date between those two points. Dates marked as 4/5 September indicate that the respective scene was filmed over a period of two days.

Some scene descriptions at the end of episodes conclude with two numbers, ie 2/3. This indicates that the location scene made up part of the episode's cliffhanger and was reprised and sometimes extended in the following episode.

Location descriptions are sometimes appended with a letter – ie Camden Deep Shelters – D. These letters are often those noted in the production documentation to indicate the different areas within a single location due to be used for filming.

Glossary of Terms Used

▸▸ **CSO** – Colour Separation Overlay, a BBC term for the Chromakey process whereby a plain coloured background (usually blue or yellow) can be electronically replaced with an image from another camera.

▸▸ **Film Shot List** – A listing that breaks down each film sequence into separate shots and camera angles. Usually looked after by the director's assistant (latterly called the production assistant), who notes slate (shot) numbers against each sequence, together with various continuity comments to ensure that the adjoining shots match as seamlessly as possible.

▸▸ **Foreground Model** – A scale model placed close to the camera, usually aligned with the background landscape, which gives the illusion of a much larger structure in the distance.

▸▸ **Glass Shot** – A sequence shot through a sheet of glass that has been painted to either augment or mask areas of the location beyond.

▸▸ **Jabolite** – A trade name for expanded polystyrene, used to create anything from snow to giant statues.

▸▸ **Recce** – Reconnaissance. Usually referring to a pre-filming visit made by production personnel to one or more potential location sites.

▸▸ **Telecine** – A pre-filmed insert shot, usually either a location scene or a model sequence. These telecine sequences were usually played during the studio recording sessions so that they could be transferred onto the main studio tapes along with the interior scenes for final editing. Also known by the abbreviation TK.

▸▸ **Telesnaps** – Between 1947 and the late 1960s, ex-RAF photographer Albert John Cura took off-screen photographs of various television productions from an HMV flat-screen monitor. These photographs were then made available to the BBC for their own records, as well as to actors and production personnel as a permanent reminder of their television work. The Doctor Who production office made regular use of Cura's services, availing themselves of his 'Single Coverage' package, for which he would provide, from each transmitted episode, 60-70 shots supplied as a set of contact miniatures together with ten 2" x 2_" glossy enlargements, as chosen by the producer. Cura's charge for this service was initially £2 12s 6d per episode until 1 March 1964, when the cost rose to £3 13s 6d, by which time the BBC Drama Group alone were spending over £1300 a year on telesnaps.

Transmission and Production Order

The stories listed in this book are all presented in their original transmission order. However, from Day of the Daleks onwards, production teams would sometimes produce stories in a different order than that ultimately presented on screen so that the production could tie in with the availability of certain actors or locations. A good example of this comes with the first three stories of the tenth season. Although transmitted in the order The Three Doctors, Carnival of Monsters and Frontier in Space, Carnival and Frontier were made first followed by The Three Doctors. The order was chosen as the production of the tenth anniversary story had to fit in with Patrick Troughton's other work commitments.

Episode Designation

When Doctor Who began production in 1963, each weekly instalment of the programme was given its own on-screen title. This practice continued until the 1966 story The Savages, when the individual titles were dropped and the designation 'Episode 1', 'Episode 2' etc was used. 'Episode' became 'Part' from the start of The Time Warrior in 1974, a designation which remained (with the sole exception of Destiny of the Daleks in 1979) until the end of Survival in 1989. In order to maintain the historical accuracy of the text, the terms 'Episode' are used for all stories up to and including The Green Death, with 'Part' being used thereafter for all subsequent stories. Exceptions are The Ice Warriors and Destiny of the Daleks, as noted above. ■

INTRODUCTION

Producer John Nathan-Turner once described taking Doctor Who out on location as 'a massive military manoeuvre.' He wasn't far wrong. The production of any television programme is a difficult and challenging task at the best of times, but when the decision is taken to move the action out of the controlled environment of the studio into the unpredictable 'great outdoors', the process can suddenly become far more complex.

For a programme like Doctor Who, the production initially revolved around two permanent figures, the producer and the script editor. The producer's role was best summed up by the official job description – he assumed 'ultimate responsibility for a series of programmes – artistically, editorially and financially' and, as such, he or she was in overall control of the finished product. Working closely with the producer was the script editor[1], who bore the responsibility for the commissioning and editing of the series' scripts and for ensuring that what they contained could effectively be realised within the budget assigned to the programme.

Once a script had been agreed and commissioned, the producer would then have the responsibility of assigning an appropriate director to the production, while the rest of the team, such as the various designers, assistant floor manager, camera crews, director's assistant and so on, would be directly allocated to the production by the department organiser within the BBC. This would usually be arranged on the basis of whoever was going to be free at the time, although on occasion producers would directly discuss with the organiser which personnel were potentially available, so that the most effective team could be assembled.

In a modern television drama, the production team will often be assigned a locations manager, someone whose sole task it is to track down suitable filming sites, negotiate for their use, get the relevant per-

missions to film from the police and any other interested parties, sort out parking for the toilets, catering vans and production personnel, book the hotel rooms, make the travel arrangements etc.

At the time of Doctor Who's production, however, a locations manager was an unknown luxury at the BBC and so virtually all of this responsibility fell squarely on the shoulders of the director's right hand man (or woman), the production assistant (a title later changed to production manager in 1981[2]). Time was always short on Doctor Who, and as directors would often be too busy in the early stages of a production with casting and other issues, the task of finding suitable filming locations (among numerous other duties) would become the responsibility of the production assistant.

Reviewing the scripts, the director and production assistant would decide in advance what location requirements the story called for. Usually, the production assistant would then begin to seek the most prominent of those requirements, which would often centre around the largest establishment in the script, such as a castle, a mansion house or a power station. Once the primary site had been found, efforts would then be made to find any secondary locations within the same general area, thus keeping any necessary travelling time down to a minimum. Usually, this process would involve the production assistant having to travel many miles by car over a period of several days.

Once a set of potential locations had been found, the director would then assess their suitability, either by examining photographs taken by the production assistant during the recce or, on occasion, by visiting the suggested locations for themselves.

Following the confirmation of the locations, and having gained all the necessary permissions and having agreed the fees payable to the respective owners, one of the next

major tasks assigned to the production assistant would be to assemble a highly important document, variously known as the Film Diary, Film Schedule, Film Itinerary or, latterly, the OB (Outside Broadcast) Schedule. In general, this document would provide precise instructions as to what events would be occurring on each day while the team was out on location. Details of each filming site would be listed together with information on which artistes would be required on the various days and what scenes were scheduled to be completed. The purpose of the diary was to ensure that everyone in the team (which could number anything up to 60 people) would know precisely where and when they should be at any given moment.

Once completed, this document would be circulated not only to all the members of the production team, but also the various department heads within the BBC responsible for providing transportation, publicity etc.

Yet, with all the planning in the world, Murphy's Law still inevitably holds true – 'If something can go wrong, it will go wrong.' During location filming on Doctor Who over the years, the various production teams made use of literally hundreds of different locations and had to cope with a seemingly never-ending catalogue of problems, all of which had to be overcome in order to get the programme 'in the can'. ∎

FOOTNOTES

1. Prior to the beginning of the sixth season of Doctor Who, this position was known by the title of story editor.

2. This change occurred from the production of Season 19 onwards, beginning with Four to Doomsday. From this point on, the director's assistant also changed title and became known as the production assistant.

'I know London and it isn't like this...'
Barbara – The Dalek Invasion of Earth

WILLIAM HARTNELL

THE FIRST DOCTOR

THE REIGN OF TERROR
(tx 8 August to 12 September 1964)

The Story

The TARDIS lands just outside Paris in 1794, at a period shortly after the French Revolution. The Doctor, his granddaughter Susan and fellow travellers Ian Chesterton and Barbara Wright become separated. They soon find themselves involved in the plans of the mysterious English spy, James Stirling, who is posing as Lemaitre, the governor of the Conciergerie prison. The travellers desperately try to avoid being caught up in Robespierre's violent reign of terror and are only able to make their way out of Paris when Robespierre is shot and sent to the Conciergerie.

The Locations

1. Isle of Wight Farm, over the Misbourne Road, Gerrards Cross, Bucks[1]
2. White Plains, Tilehouse Lane, Denham Green, Bucks

Shooting Schedule

EPISODE 2

▶▶ Doctor walks across field
Isle of Wight Farm **//** 15 June 1964
▶▶ Doctor walks down country lane
Isle of Wight Farm **//** 15 June 1964
▶▶ Doctor walks down country lane
Isle of Wight Farm **//** 15 June 1964
▶▶ Doctor walks up poplar-lined lane
White Plains **//** 15 June 1964
▶▶ Doctor walks down country lane
Isle of Wight Farm **//** 15 June 1964

The Facts

In order to convey the sense of the Doctor's journey through the French countryside en route to Paris, a single day of location work using a 35mm camera was planned, marking the very first use of exterior filming on Doctor Who. At the request of Hungarian director

Henric Hirsch, production assistant Timothy Combe was dispatched to find a location containing something identifiably French, namely, a row of poplar trees. These were eventually located at White Plains, a nursing home in Denham.

Timothy Combe (production assistant): 'I travelled miles trying to find those poplar trees. I had a hell of a job! Every now and then you'd find some poplars, but in the time of the French Revolution you couldn't have them going along a road. So I managed to find some located alongside a track and we shot the Doctor walking along.'

All the brief scenes showing the other parts of the Doctor's journey were filmed on the same day, a short distance away at Isle of Wight Farm, Gerrards Cross.

Above: The Doctor (Brian Proudfoot) walks through the cornfield at Isle of Wight Farm, completing the first ever location scene filmed for the programme.

Above right: The Doctor (Brian Proudfoot) walks through the poplar-lined driveway of White Plains at Denham.

None of the location work featured William Hartnell himself, who was busy with the first day's rehearsal on the fourth episode of The Sensorites, A Race Against Death. Instead, his place was taken by Brian Proudfoot, who had spent most of the previous Friday practising Hartnell's walk. His work as Hartnell's double on this occasion would earn him a fee of five guineas.

As soon as the unit had wrapped and returned to London, Combe wrote to both Mrs Shakespeare at White Plains and Mrs Gordon at Isle of Wight Farm to thank them for their assistance. Mrs Shakespeare was duly paid five guineas, while Mrs Gordon was sent a cheque for ten guineas, as the unit had spent most of the day at the farm and had also made use of her telephone.

Comment

After a total of nine months spent exclusively in the studio, Doctor Who finally broke free from the confines of Lime Grove, Ealing Film Studios and Television Centre. But rather like a child taking its first tentative steps, this initial use of location filming was an extremely low-key affair – a single day's work filming the back of William Hartnell's double. As the series had already got along quite well thus far without the need for any location material, had the footage not been included in The Reign of Terror, it's hard to say that it would have been missed. And yet even these few brief scenes add a sense of distance and weariness to the Doctor's journey.

THE DALEK INVASION OF EARTH

(tx 21 November to 26 December 1964)

The Story

The TARDIS lands in a derelict London several years into a full-scale invasion by the Daleks. Meeting up with a small band of resistance fighters, the Doctor learns that the Daleks have set up a huge mining operating in Bedfordshire, intent on destroying the Earth's magnetic core with a bomb and replacing it with a drive system which will enable them to pilot the planet like a giant spaceship. Ian manages to block the bomb in the shaft and the resultant explosion destroys the Daleks and their control centre.

The Locations

1. Hammersmith Bridge, Queen Caroline Street, Hammersmith, London, W6
2. Butlers Wharf, Southwark, London, SE1
3. 'A' Warehouse, St Katherines Dock, London, E1
4. Irongate Wharf, St Katherines Way, London, E1
5. White City Underground Station (Metropolitan Line), Wood Lane, Shepherd's Bush, London, W12[2]
6. Albert Embankment, London, SE11
7. Westminster Bridge, Westminster, London, SW1
8. Whitehall, London, SW1
9. Trafalgar Square, London, SW1
10. Royal Albert Hall, Kensington Gore, Kensington, London, SW7
11. Albert Memorial, Kensington, London, SW7
12. Palace of Industry, Engineers Way, Wembley, Middlesex
13. John's Hole Quarry, Stone, Kent
14. Third Way, Wembley, Middlesex

Shooting Schedule

EPISODE 1

▸▸ **Roboman commits suicide and TARDIS materialises**
Hammersmith Bridge – South Bank //
27 August 1964

▸▸ **Doctor, Susan, Ian and Barbara leave the TARDIS**
Hammersmith Bridge – South Bank //
27 August 1964

▸▸ **Establishing shot – Riverside warehouse**
Butler's Wharf // Date Unknown

▸▸ **Doctor and Ian enter the warehouse**
St Katherine's Docks // 25 August 1964

▸▸ **Barbara sees dead Roboman in river**
Hammersmith Bridge – South Bank //
27 August 1964

▸▸ **Ian falls through warehouse door**
St Katherine's Docks // 25 August 1964

▸▸ **Barbara follows resistance fighter into Underground**
White City Station // 25 August 1964

▸▸ **Barbara follows Tyler and Susan through passage**
White City Station // 25 August 1964

▸▸ **Two Robomen patrol the docks**
Irongate Wharf // Date Unknown

▸▸ **Roboman appears at the top of the staircase**
Hammersmith Bridge – South Bank //
27 August 1964

▸▸ **Dalek emerges from River Thames (1/2)**
Hammersmith Bridge – North Bank //
27 August 1964

EPISODE 3

- ‣ **Barbara, Jenny and Dortmun see Daleks on bridge**
  Embankment // 23 August 1964
- ‣ **Daleks crossing Westminster Bridge**
  Westminster Bridge // 23 August 1964
- ‣ **Dalek examines Embankment steps**
  Embankment // 23 August 1964
- ‣ **Barbara and Jenny wheel Dortmun across bridge**
  Westminster Bridge // 23 August 1964
- ‣ **Barbara and Jenny wheel Dortmun down Whitehall**
  Whitehall // 23 August 1964
- ‣ **Daleks patrol around Trafalgar Square**
  Trafalgar Square // 23 August 1964
- ‣ **Barbara, Jenny and Dortmun see Daleks at Memorial**
  Royal Albert Hall // 23 August 1964
- ‣ **Daleks patrol around Albert Memorial**
  Albert Memorial // 23 August 1964
- ‣ **Barbara and Jenny wheel Dortmun around Albert Hall**
  Royal Albert Hall // 23 August 1964
- ‣ **Dortmun is killed by the Daleks**
  Palace of Industry // 23 August 1964

EPISODE 4

- ‣ **Slaves pull railway truck in quarry**
  John's Hole Quarry // 28 August 1964
- ‣ **Barbara drives the dustcart out of the museum**
  Palace of Industry // 23 August 1964
- ‣ **Dustcart crashes through Dalek cordon**
  Third Way // 23 August 1964

EPISODE 6

- ‣ **Prisoners stream from mine and attack Daleks**
  John's Hole Quarry // 28 August 1964

The Facts

When the decision was taken to film the Daleks on location, it was thought necessary to make various adjustments to the design of their casings, to enable them to move smoothly over the rougher terrain that they would have to negotiate. As a result, designer Spencer Chapman specified the construction of enlarged fenders which would conceal a new pedal-driven arrangement and larger pneumatic tyres.

The most difficult scenes to film were those surrounding the flight across London of Barbara and freedom fighters Jenny and Dortmun as they try to avoid the patrolling Daleks. To create the impression of a deserted London, the scenes were shot early on the morning of Sunday 23 August 1964, when the city traffic would be at its quietest. The actors required for the scenes were called to Television Centre between 4.30 and 5.00 am to

Left: The production team get ready to film around the Duke of Cambridge's statue in Whitehall on 23 August 1964.

prepare for the shoot and, for the most part, all the planned sequences were completed without problems, although several rather drunk partygoers were encountered en route. Some evidence of city activity is apparent in certain shots, however, such as when a vehicle passes along the far side of Trafalgar Square. A shot of Barbara and Jenny pushing Dortmun past the entrance to the National Gallery was also filmed in the square.

Nick Evans (Dalek): 'It was a bit of a business getting out of the Dalek machines and there was never anyone about to help you get out if you wanted to go for a pee. So at one point during the filming, there was this procession of Daleks that had found themselves a grating in Trafalgar Square and were queuing up to position themselves over it. It relieved the day, if I can put it like that!'[3]

With the scenes in central London completed, the production team then moved to Wembley, to film Dortmun's death and the dustcart smashing the Dalek cordon, both of which were shot outside some of the remaining buildings from the 1924/5 British Empire Exhibition.

The scene of Dortmun facing the Daleks was filmed outside the Palace of Industry, the long shadows across the road being cast by the nearby Wembley Arena. Filming continued on the other side of the estate, where the Dalek cordon was set up outside the remains of HM Government Pavilion on Third Way and the dustcart was seen travelling down the road and smashing through the patrol.

The sequences of the Dalek's Bedfordshire mine

Right: The Daleks outside the London Planetarium during the publicity photoshoot for The Dalek Invasion of Earth on Thursday 20 August 1964.

were filmed at John's Hole chalk quarry in the small village of Stone, just outside Dartford, which featured a railway tunnel running under the A226, which would double as the mine entrance.

Richard Martin (director): 'I remember my cameraman Peter Hamilton, who had been a pilot in the war, standing on the precise lip of the quarry with a hundred foot drop beneath him.'

Unused Locations

The Mall, London – Reporting on the central London Dalek photocall held the previous day, the Daily Mail of 21 August 1964 indicated that it had originally been intended to film sequences (presumably for the flight sequence in Episode 3) in the Mall, with Buckingham Palace in the background. The newspaper reported that this had been cancelled because of concern over the potential traffic problems it may have caused.

Comment

As the first major location shoot for the programme, the filming done for The Dalek Invasion of Earth is a bit of a mixed bag. The filming in London is largely very effective, especially the scenes of eerily creaking cranes and Robomen walking along the docks in the first episode. Strangely, the slight let-down is the showpiece flight through London by Barbara, Jenny and Dortmun. You never really get to see the Daleks on Westminster Bridge as you do in the famous photographs – a lost opportunity.

THE CHASE

(tx 22 May to 26 June 1965)

The Story

Intent on destroying the Doctor, the Daleks begin to follow the TARDIS in a time ship of their own. Tracked first to the desert planet of Aridius, the travellers narrowly make an escape and are pursued to the Mary Celeste, New York and the World's Fair in Ghana before finally landing on the jungle planet of Mechanus. There, they are captured by the robotic Mechonoids who subsequently engage in a fierce battle with the Daleks. With both Daleks and Mechonoids destroyed, Ian and Barbara return to London in the Daleks' time ship while Steven Taylor, another prisoner of the Mechonoids, hides on board the TARDIS.

The Locations

1. Camber Sands, Camber, East Sussex
2. Garage behind Studio 3A/B, Ealing Film Studios, Ealing, London, W5

Shooting Schedule

EPISODE 1

▸▸ **TARDIS arrives on Aridius**
  Camber Sands // 9 April 1965
▸▸ **Travellers POV of Aridius**
  Camber Sands // 9 April 1965
▸▸ **Ian and Vicki cross the dunes**

Camber Sands // 9 April 1965
▸▸ **Ian and Vicki continue their exploration**
Camber Sands // 9 April 1965
▸▸ **Doctor and Barbara's post-sandstorm POV**
Camber Sands // 9 April 1965

EPISODE 2

▸▸ **Daleks on Aridius**
Camber Sands // 9 April 1965
▸▸ **Dalek on patrol**
Camber Sands // 9 April 1965
▸▸ **Dalek falls into trap**
Camber Sands // 9 April 1965

EPISODE 6

▸▸ **Ian and Barbara arrive back in 1965**
Ealing Film Studios // 10 May 1965
▸▸ **Ian and Barbara in London**
Photographs // 6 May 1965

The Facts

During a brief period of absence for director Richard Martin in early March 1965, producer Verity Lambert met with the design department to agree the details of their involvement with The Chase, and had confirmed with them that the schedule for the production would not involve any location filming. Once Martin returned to the production however, he indicated that he felt that there was a need to shoot a few brief sequences of location footage, which would only require minimal input from the story's two designers.

To represent the desert sands of Aridius, the production team travelled to one of the most expansive stretches of beach and dunes available along the south coast, Camber Sands. Prior to the crew's arrival, Camber resident Laurence Nesbitt was paid a total of £2 to dig and shore up two holes in the sand, 6ft deep by 5ft wide.

The first hole was required for the planned climax to the opening episode, The Executioners, where a Dalek, buried by the storm, rises from the sands. The original plan was to bury a full-sized Dalek on location and then pull it clear of the sand by attaching a connecting rope to the back of a moving vehicle. However, when the effect was attempted, the weight of the sand bearing down on the Dalek rendered it immovable and the attempt to produce it as a live action effect was duly abandoned. The transmitted sequence was filmed later as a model effect.

The second hole was prepared for the Doctor and Ian's Dalek trap in Episode 2, The Death of Time. Unfortunately, the shot of the Dalek falling into the hole was filmed during the day, while the surrounding studio shots were all recorded in a night-time setting making the transition between the film and studio material obvious.

Left: Attaching a rope to the front of a full-sized Dalek in the aborted attempt to pull it from the sand during the filming of The Chase at Camber Sands on 9 April 1965.

As the location filming at Camber Sands was being conducted on the same day that the second episode of The Space Museum, The Dimensions of Time, was being recorded in London, neither William Russell nor fellow cast-member Maureen O'Brien were available to travel to East Sussex. Their places were taken by David Newman and Barbara Joss and the footage was later overdubbed with the voices of the main actors.

Photographed Locations

The final sequence of Ian and Barbara arriving back home in 1965 was achieved using a montage of still photographs showing the couple enjoying themselves around various London landmarks. The photographic shoot[4], which began from Television Centre at 2.00 pm on Thursday 6 May, was presided over by Douglas Camfield, who had worked on a number of previous Doctor Who stories as both production assistant and director. As well as the photographer, only actors William Russell and Jacqueline Hill were required once they had finished their morning's rehearsals for the second episode of The Chase, The Death of Time. As planned, the itinerary was:

Car from TC to:-
1. HOUSES OF PARLIAMENT /
   WESTMINSTER BRIDGE AREA
   Shoot Lion-heart sequence – Big Ben – Pair on Bridge – Pair at fruit stall – Pair drinking Coca-Cola.

Above: Director Michael Leeston-Smith (on ground, with pipe) prepares to direct Alan Haywood as Hector at Fresham Ponds on 27 August 1965.

Taxi to: –

2. TRAFALGAR SQUARE
Nelson's Column – both feeding pigeons – Ian with pigeons on head – Barbara with pigeons on arm – Barbara paddling in fountain – Ian posing with Nelson's lions.

Taxi to: –

3. PICCADILLY CIRCUS / REGENT STREET
Eros – Traffic – Theatres – Cinemas – Pair eating ice cream – Pair window-shopping.

Taxi to: –

4. HYDE PARK (QUEENSWAY STATION)
Police phone box sequence – Round Pond sequence – Boats – Ducks – 'Health and Strength' statue – Leaping sequence – Serpentine – Fishing – Rowing – Running for bus.

END

During the photographic session, a five-shilling tip was paid to a stallholder, 2/6 went on fruit, 2/- on peanuts and 3/- on hotdogs.

In the end, the final 23" sequence as broadcast was composed of 26 different photographs:
Trafalgar Square – Ian and Barbara with pigeons, on lion statue, walking on wall.
Albert Embankment – Ian and fish statue, Barbara on Embankment, Ian looks shocked.
Kensington Gardens (Black Lion Gate), Bayswater Road – Ian and Barbara with Police Box
Regent Street – Ian and Barbara catch bus.

Comment

A minimalist approach was taken to the location filming on The Chase – only a few brief inserts were included in the story – and yet it works extremely well. The vast sand dunes of Camber, dotted with various mysterious black statues, really do help to create a sense of a barren and arid world. Strangely, it seems to work so well because it's all in black and white. When the programme returned to the same location 21 years later for The Trial of a Time Lord, the dunes didn't look half as alien when seen in colour and on video.

THE MYTH MAKERS

(tx 16 October to 6 November 1965)

The Story

Landing not far from the city of Troy, the Doctor is mistaken for the god Zeus and taken to the Grecian encampment. Forced to admit his mortal status, the Doctor is told to invent a way for the Greek army to breach the Trojan defences. Meanwhile, the Doctor's companions Vicki and Steven are taken to Troy where Steven assumes the identity of a Greek soldier named Diomede, while Vicki is treated kindly by King Priam and his infatuated son, Troilus. The Doctor 'invents' the concept of the wooden horse with which the Greeks invade Troy. Vicki chooses to stay with Troilus while a wounded Steven is helped back to the TARDIS by the Doctor.

The Locations

1. Frensham Little Pond, Frensham, Surrey
2. Ham Polo Club, Petersham Road, Ham, Middlesex

Shooting Schedule[5]

EPISODE 1

▸▸ **Hector fights Achilles**
Frensham Little Pond // 27 August 1965
▸▸ **Hector fights Achilles (remount)**
Frensham Little Pond // 30 August 1965
▸▸ **City of Troy (model shots)**
Frensham Little Pond // Date Unknown
▸▸ **Steven passes Greek patrol near camp**
Frensham Little Pond // 1 September 1965

EPISODE 3

▸▸ **Paris kills Cyclops**
Frensham Little Pond // 1 September 1965
▸▸ **Paris kills Cyclops (remount)**
Frensham Little Pond // 2 September 1965
▸▸ **Trojan soldiers look up at horse**
Frensham Little Pond // 1 September 1965

▶ Wooden horse (model shots)
Ham Polo Club // Date Unknown

EPISODE 4

▶ **Troilus fights Achilles**
Frensham Little Pond // 27 August 1965
▶ **Troilus fights Achilles (remount)**
Frensham Little Pond // 30 August 1965
▶ **Troilus fights Achilles (remount)**
Frensham Little Pond // 2 September 1965
▶ **City of Troy (model shots)**
Frensham Little Pond // Date Unknown
▶ **Troilus on plain**
Frensham Little Pond // 31 August 1965
▶ **Troilus on plain (remount)**
Frensham Little Pond // 1 September 1965

The Facts

As well as the main shoot at Frensham Ponds, a brief model shot of the Trojan Horse was also completed at Ham Polo Club in Middlesex. At the time, director Michael Leeston-Smith was a keen player at Ham Polo Club (having beaten Prince Charles on one occasion) as well as being an owner of several ponies.

John Woods (designer): 'Michael Leeston-Smith lived around that way and he'd seen a spot down there where we could set up the Trojan Horse and have a little bit of terrain behind it, which was quite interesting. It was a sandy area and we took the model down there and did a simple little shot which was inserted into the production, to give it a sense of scale. The rest of the model filming was done at Ealing.'[6]

For the first time on *Doctor Who*, use was made of a glass shot on location to represent the city of Troy. John Woods again: 'Something else I remember about The Myth Makers is that we did a glass matte shot – something virtually unheard of in the BBC at that time. It was a high-angle establishing shot of the interior of Troy, with people moving about within the walls. I got a scenic artist to paint a suitable picture of Troy based on visuals from the British Museum on a big sheet of glass and took it up to the main location at Frensham Ponds. This was an area with very alien-looking sands and there had been some burning going on up there, clearing of land and so on, so it looked terrific. We erected this sheet of glass in front of the camera, which we locked off in the usual way, and put the finishing touches to the painting, blending it in with the rough terrain. Then the actors were positioned so that they could be seen through the unpainted parts of the glass, off in the distance, moving about as required. It wasn't 100 per cent effective, but considering the time and the facilities and the money we had, and the fact that people weren't generally au fait with things like glass

Left: A publicity shot from The Massacre of St Bartholomew's Eve, showing Jackie Lane and the cobbled-together police box.

shots, it worked quite well enough. It was just a quick shot, sufficient to get the message across.'[7]

Ouch!

The location filming for The Myth Makers was plagued by small accidents. On the first day, both Cavan Kendall and Alan Haywood had to be treated for minor injuries gained during the filming of the opening fight sequence between Hector and Achilles. Haywood's right hand was treated for a graze sustained from the shield he was holding, while Kendall had grazes and blisters on his right hand and elbow as well as on his feet. A couple of days later, on 31 August, actor James Lynn sustained a cut to his hand from his prop sword.

Comment

Apart from a single photograph of the location filming taking place, there is no other visual record of what the exterior material in this story would have looked like as the episodes themselves have long since disappeared and no footage or off-screen telesnaps are known to exist. It's a great pity, as The Myth Makers is a wonderfully scripted story.

THE DALEKS' MASTER PLAN

(tx 13 November 1965 to 29 January 1966)

The Story

Following the death of Space Security Service agent

Right: Jackie Lane runs across Windmill Road on Wimbledon Common while being filmed from the back of the soft-suspensioned 2CV camera vehicle.

Mark Cory, the TARDIS crew meet up with Bret Vyon. During the mission to locate Cory, Vyon has learned enough to advise Mavic Chen, the Guardian of the Solar System, to mobilise a force against the Daleks. But Chen has joined forces with the Daleks and has helped them with the development of the Taranium Core, the power device for their latest weapon, the Time Destructor. The Doctor steals the core and is relentlessly pursued by the Daleks until they are destroyed by their own weapon.

Photographed Locations

1. Hammersmith Park, South Africa Road,
   Shepherd's Bush, London, W12

Shooting Schedule

EPISODE 8

➤➤ TARDIS lands on cricket pitch
   Hammersmith Park // 25 October 1965

The Facts

During the course of October 1965, permission was sought from the Greater London Council to take some photographs in Hammersmith Park (backing onto Television Centre) of the small scale TARDIS standing on the grass for the sequence of the landing at Lords Cricket Ground in Episode 8, Volcano.[8] Agreement was duly reached and the photographs were taken on Monday 25 October, for which the GLC were paid 19 guineas.

THE MASSACRE OF ST BARTHOLOMEW'S EVE

(tx 5 February to 26 February 1966)

The Story

Arriving in Paris in the year 1572, the Doctor decides to pay a visit to apothecary Charles Preslin, while Steven stays behind and meets up with a friendly group of Huguenots. Meanwhile the Catholic Queen Mother, Catherine de Medici, is secretly planning to massacre all the Parisian Protestants. Steven is shocked to find that the Doctor has apparently taken on the guise of the hated Abbot of Amboise, who is executed by the Catholics when a plan to assassinate the Protestant Admiral de Coligny goes wrong. While searching for the TARDIS key, Steven is relieved to find that the Doctor is safe and well, the Abbot being the Doctor's doppelgänger, and they leave as the horrendous massacre begins. Landing on Wimbledon Common, Dorothea Chaplet stumbles into the TARDIS and, as the police approach, the Doctor is forced to dematerialise.

The Locations

1. Windmill Road, Wimbledon Common,
   Wimbledon, London, SW19

Shooting Schedule

EPISODE 4

➤➤ **Dodo runs towards the TARDIS**
   Windmill Road // 7 January 1966

Left: Director Christopher Barry and his team prepare to shoot a scene with Peter Purves during the filming of The Savages.

⏵ **Woman sees TARDIS dematerialise**
Windmill Road **//** 7 January 1966

The Facts

Only two brief location inserts were required for the final moments of The Massacre of St Bartholomew's Eve. The first showed Dorothea 'Dodo' Chaplet (Jackie Lane) running across Wimbledon Common and entering the TARDIS while the second captured the reactions of a dog-walking woman as she sees the TARDIS dematerialise.

The shots of Jackie Lane running across the common were achieved by mounting the camera in the back of a Citroen 2CV, a vehicle often used during the 1960s and 70s for tracking shots due to its fold-back canvas roof and soft suspension.

Jackie Lane: 'The common was virtually deserted and it is, of course, quite large, so it was really all over before word got around. The only problem I had was having to jump across a ditch which was, unfortunately, too wide, so I fell into it. I suppose this made it more realistic, although I did end up with very grubby stockings!'[9]

As filming on Wimbledon Common occurred on the same day that the penultimate episode of The Daleks' Master Plan (The Abandoned Planet) was being recorded in studio, director Paddy Russell found herself unable to utilise the Doctor Who police box prop, as it was due to make an appearance in a scene being recorded that evening. As a result, another BBC police box had to be pressed into service. The condition of this prop was rather poor, however, with one side of the box having to be replaced with a wooden sheet roughly painted with an approximation of the panels and windows.

Comment

The location footage for The Massacre of St Bartholomew's Eve is short and to the point, simply used to help introduce the new companion, Dodo. As the final episode no longer exists in the BBC archives, it's impossible to know, but one hopes that the replacement police box prop used on Wimbledon Common wasn't seen too closely on screen.

THE GUNFIGHTERS

(tx 30 April to 21 May 1966)

The Story

Arriving in Tombstone in the year 1881, the Doctor visits the notorious Doc Holliday in a bid to cure his chronic toothache. The travellers discover that Holliday is engaged in a bitter feud with the Clanton family and the Doctor is soon arrested by lawman Wyatt Earp. The feud comes to a head when Pa Clanton hires the gunslinger Johnny Ringo, the two sides facing it out at the famous gunfight at the OK Corral. Leaving America, the TARDIS lands on a seemingly barren world. A savage figure observes its arrival from the crest of a nearby hill.

Above: A savage attacks Steven (Peter Purves) and Dodo (Jackie Lane) in a scene filmed at the Callows Hill Sandpit on 1 May 1966.

The Locations

1. Callow Hill Sandpit, Callow Hill, Virginia Water, Surrey

Shooting Schedule

EPISODE 4

▸▸ **Savage appears on TARDIS monitor**
Callow Hill Sandpit // 1 May 1966

The Facts▸▸

The Gunfighters featured only one sequence shot on location, which was used to close the final episode as a savage, played by John Raven, appears unobserved on the TARDIS monitor. Although it appears in The Gunfighters, the scene was actually shot by Christopher Barry along with the other location scenes he directed for The Savages.

Comment

With only one location scene included in The Gunfighters, there's very little to say about it – except that what remains is the only location footage left from the filming of The Savages.

THE SAVAGES

(tx 28 May to 18 June 1966)

The Story

Landing on an unnamed planet, the Doctor is surprised to find that he has been expected by the intelligent Elders and is treated as an honoured guest. Meanwhile, Steven and Dodo encounter the planet's other inhabitants, a race of seemingly primitive savages, before being taken to the city. While on a tour, Dodo stumbles into an advanced laboratory and discovers that the Elders' way of life is maintained by draining the life-force out of the savages and transferring it to themselves. Jano, the Chief Elder, then subjects the Doctor to the machinery but. As well as his life-force, however, Jano begins to take on the Doctor's other characteristics, including his mannerisms and conscience. The altered Jano turns to the savages for help and together they destroy the transference machinery. Steven decides to stay behind and become the new leader of the now united savages and Elders.

The Locations

1. Callow Hill Sandpit, Callow Hill, Virginia Water, Surrey[10]
2. Shire Lane Quarry, Chalfont St Peter, Buckinghamshire[11]

Shooting Schedule

EPISODE 1

▸▸ **TARDIS materialises**
Bedford Square // 22 May 1966
▸▸ **TARDIS on planet surface**
Callow Hill Sandpit // 1 May 1966
▸▸ **Steven starts to become worried about the Doctor**
Callow Hill Sandpit // 1 May 1966
▸▸ **Steven searches calling for the Doctor**
Callow Hill Sandpit // 1 May 1966
▸▸ **Dodo sees savages and tells Steven**
Callow Hill Sandpit // 1 May 1966
▸▸ **Steven and Dodo attacked by savages and meet Exorse**
Callow Hill Sandpit // 1 May 1966
▸▸ **Exorse patrols the craters**
Shire Lane Quarry // 29 April 1966
▸▸ **Nanina sees Exorse on patrol**
Shire Lane Quarry // 29 April 1966
▸▸ **Exorse waits for Nanina to come close to him**
Shire Lane Quarry // 29 April 1966
▸▸ **Exorse captures Nanina with his light gun**
Shire Lane Quarry // 29 April 1966

EPISODE 3

▸▸ **Edal meets Exorse in the scrublands**
Callow Hill Sandpit // 27 April 1966
▸▸ **Chal shows Steven the entrance to the city**
Callow Hill Sandpit // 27 April 1966

EPISODE 4

▸▸ **TARDIS dematerialises**
Callow Hill Sandpit // 1 May 1966

The Facts▸▸

To save time on location, Ewen Solon had his aged make-up for Chal applied at Television Centre. Reportedly, Solon then offered Jackie Lane and one of the make-up assistants a lift to the location in his car. Getting lost en route, Solon stopped the car and asked directions from a passing cyclist who, unperturbed by the alien make-up, gave the requested directions and then continued on his way, much to the amusement of Solon's two passengers.

Comment

The Savages is a relatively straightforward tale containing a twist on the theme of vampirism and requiring little in the way of location work. As no episodes of the story exist in the BBC archives, it's difficult to tell how effective the exterior scenes were, but the production photographs and telesnaps that remain all indicate that Christopher Barry maintained his usual high standard.

THE WAR MACHINES

(tx 25 June to 16 July 1966)

The Story

Landing near the newly completed Post Office Tower in London, the Doctor is suddenly overcome by a feeling of alien menace within the building. Visiting the Tower, the Doctor meets Professor Brett, controller of a new self-thinking computer called WOTAN which is about to link up with many other units throughout the world to form a super computer. WOTAN begins to develop a life of its own and, taking Brett and other humans under its hypnotic control, develops armed War Machines with which to subjugate mankind. With time running out, the Doctor captures a War Machine and reprogrammes it to destroy WOTAN.

The Locations

1. Bedford Square, Bloomsbury, London, WC1
2. Conway Street, Fitzrovia, London, W1
3. Covent Garden, Strand, London, WC2
4. Royal Opera House, Bow Street, Strand, WC2
5. Ealing Film Studios Backlot, Ealing Green, Ealing, London, W5
6. Charlotte Street, Fitzrovia, London, W1
7. Gresse Street, Fitzrovia, London, W1
8. Cornwall Gardens/Cornwall Gardens Walk, South Kensington, London, SW7
9. Berners Mews, Fitzrovia, London, W1
10. Maple Street, Fitzrovia, London, W1

Shooting Schedule

EPISODE 1

▸▸ **TARDIS materialises**
Bedford Square // 22 May 1966
▸▸ **Policeman walks by TARDIS**
Bedford Square // 22 May 1966
▸▸ **Doctor and Dodo head off towards the Tower**
Conway Street // 22 May 1966
▸▸ **Doctor arrives by taxi at Royal Scientific Club**
41 Bedford Square // 22 May 1966

EPISODE 2

▸▸ **Ben walks to Brett's warehouse**
Covent Garden // 26 May 1966
▸▸ **Ben walks to Brett's warehouse**
Royal Opera House // 26 May 1966

EPISODE 3

▸▸ **Army arrives at Brett's warehouse**
Ealing Film Studios // 25 May 1966
▸▸ **War Machine attacks army outside warehouse**
Ealing Film Studios // 25 May 1966

EPISODE 4

▸▸ **Machine attacks telephone box and moves off**
Charlotte Place // 22 May 1966
▸▸ **Machine crashes through dustbins**
Gresse Street // 22 May 1966
▸▸ **Couple runs away through alley**
Berners Mews // 22 May 1966
▸▸ **Trap is prepared as Doctor and Sir Charles arrive**
Cornwall Gardens // 26 May 1966
▸▸ **The Machine is caught in the trap**
Cornwall Gardens // 26 May 1966
▸▸ **Doctor neutralises the Machine**
Cornwall Gardens // 26 May 1966
▸▸ **War Machine heads towards PO Tower**
Berners Mews // 22 May 1966
▸▸ **Machine arrives at PO Tower**
Maple Street // 22 May 1966
▸▸ **Doctor paces outside TARDIS**
Bedford Square // 22 May 1966
▸▸ **Ben and Polly run to and from the TARDIS**
Bedford Square // 22 May 1966
▸▸ **TARDIS dematerialises**
Bedford Square // 22 May 1966

The Facts

The idea to centre a story around the imposing structure of the nearly completed Post Office Tower came directly from the production office and was suggested to writer Ian Stuart Black as a suitable hook on which to hang a new present-day story.

Although it would feature heavily in the story, it was ultimately decided that there wasn't a vast amount of filming needed at the Tower itself as the majority of

Above: Two policeman observe the filming at Cornwall Gardens Walk on 26 May 1966.

the location material being planned was designed to make use of the maze of streets and alleyways surrounding the building.

Following a recce to the Tower on 26 April 1966, the BBC contacted B Hogben at the General Post Office, requesting permission to take a small crew of six to the building on Sunday 22 May in order to take a few shots around the base of the Tower, as well as using the upper levels as a high filming platform for the planned TARDIS materialisation site in Portman Square.

The General Post Office responded to the BBC's letter on 5 May, turning down the request as the planned filming date fell on the first weekend after the Tower's official public opening and there were concerns about the possible disruption the filming would cause.

By 10 May, director Michael Ferguson's plans were

beginning to take shape. A letter was sent to the Superintendent of Marylebone Lane Police Station, requesting his agreement to filming being conducted in his area of jurisdiction on Sunday 22 May.

'Filming will take place from approximately 10.00 am to 5.00 pm in Berners Mews, Newman Passage, Fitzroy Square, Charlotte Place and Bedford Square. The producer would like to put up a police box in Bedford Square for a short time, and at some time during the day, one of the actors will be in police uniform as he walks towards the police box. Other shots will be of 'Dr. Who' or his deputy, a mechanical man and a 'Dalek' computer running up and down these passages.'

M E Carter to the Superintendent,
Marylebone Lane Police Station – 10 May 1966

For the Episode 1 sequence of the Doctor arriving at the Royal Scientific Club by taxi, the production team hired a genuine black cab and paid the driver, W Busell, £2 for his trouble.

Two other London 'locations' that appear in Episode 4 of The War Machines are Tottenham Court Road, seen as a back-projection behind War Machine 9 as it makes its way to the Post Office Tower, and Great Queen Street, Holborn, seen as the deserted road when police make their 'keep off the streets' announcement.[12]

During the shooting, permission had been gained from several people to use their premises as filming platforms in order to obtain a number of high-angle shots required by Ferguson, and on 6 June production assistant Noel Lidiard-White authorised the payment of facility fees to the various parties concerned.

George Wimpey and Co Ltd, Hammersmith
Grove, W6 – £10 10s 0d
Filming of TARDIS materialisation in Bedford
Square from Centre Point building – Episode 1
Mr Kline, 'Duke of York' Public House, Charlotte
Place, W1 – £2 2s 0d
Filming of War Machine's attack on man in tele
phone box – Episode 4
Mrs Lessing, 50F Cornwall Gardens, SW7 – £2 2s 0d
Filming of War Machine getting caught in
Doctor's trap – Episode 4

Unused Locations

Portman Square – Michael Ferguson's original intention was to film the materialisation of the TARDIS in Portman Square, just off Baker Street, to the west of the Post Office Tower, but when the Post Office declined the BBC permission to film the required opening shot from the top of their new building, the venue was switched to Bedford Square and the

Left: The Doctor (William Hartnell) and Sir Charles Summer (William Mervyn) approach a captured War Machine at Cornwall Gardens Walk.

sequence was filmed from the top of the Centre Point building in Tottenham Court Road.

Fitzroy Square – The existing production paperwork for The War Machines indicates that it had been intended, for reasons unknown, to split the scenes around the TARDIS over two different locations – Bedford Square being used for the majority of the shots and Fitzroy Square for the Episode 1 sequences of the Doctor and Dodo exiting the TARDIS and setting off towards the Tower.[13] However, there is no evidence that any material was actually filmed in Fitzroy Square, situated close to the base of the Post Office Tower.

Newman Passage – The scene of the couple running away from a War Machine in Episode 4 was originally intended to be filmed in Newman Passage, but on the day, this location was swapped to Berners Mews.

Several shots of other Machines rampaging around London were planned to have been seen as Machine 9 made its way to the Post Office Tower. Among the planned shots was a sequence showing Machine 4 in front of the Houses of Parliament.

Comment

One of the most pleasing aspects of the filming done for The War Machines is the fact that we get to see William Hartnell himself on location. The First Doctor stories that utilised exterior filming were few and far between and all too often Hartnell wasn't required to attend the shoots, so the fact that we see him walking to the Post Office Tower and playing an active part in the neutralisation of the War Machine in Cornwall Gardens is a rare treat.

THE SMUGGLERS

(tx 10 September to 1 October 1966)

The Story

Landing on a beach in 17th century Cornwall, the Doctor and his companions Ben and Polly meet churchwarden Joseph Longfoot who, trusting the Doctor, imparts a mysterious riddle. The conversation is overhead by Cherub, one of a gang of pirates lead by Captain Samuel Pike, seeking a treasure to which the riddle is the key. Meanwhile, the local squire is secretly smuggling contraband with the help of Pike. Caught in the middle, the Doctor's party helps Josiah Blake, a member of the King's Revenue, thwart both the pirates and the Squire's plans.

The Locations

1. Nanjizal Bay, Nanjizal, Cornwall
2. St Grada Church, Grade, Cornwall
3. Church Cove, Cornwall
4. Farmland between Helson and Wendron, Cornwall[14]
5. Trethewey Farm, Trethewey, Cornwall
6. Bonny Mary, Newlyn Harbour, Newlyn, Cornwall
7. Bosistow Cliffs, Nanjizal, Cornwall

Shooting Schedule

EPISODE 1

▶▶ **Cave and beach seen on TARDIS scanner**
Nanjizal Bay // 20 June 1966
▶▶ **Travellers leave TARDIS and climb cliff**
Nanjizal Bay // 19 June 1966
▶▶ **Ben's POV of the church**

St Grada Church // 21 June 1966
▸▸ **Kewper sends Tom to see Joseph Longfoot**
Trethewey Farm // 22 June 1966
▸▸ **Pirate signals others as they come inland**
Church Cove // 21 June 1966
▸▸ **Pirates signalling**
Farmland Nr. Helston // 21 June 1966
▸▸ **The unconscious Doctor is loaded onto a cart**
Trethewey Farm // 22 June 1966
▸▸ **Doctor taken down to the longboat and rowed away**
Church Cove // 21 June 1966
▸▸ **Kewper welcomes the Squire to the Inn**
Trethewey Farm // 22 June 1966
▸▸ **Doctor is brought aboard The Black Albatross**
Bonny Mary // 23 June 1966

EPISODE 2

▸▸ **Kewper leaves the Inn**
Trethewey Farm // 22 June 1966
▸▸ **Kewper goes to his boat on the beach**
Church Cove // 21 June 1966
▸▸ **Kewper boards The Black Albatross**
Bonny Mary // 23 June 1966
▸▸ **Pike and Cherub leave The Black Albatross**
Bonny Mary // 23 June 1966

EPISODE 3

▸▸ **Kewper and the Doctor escape from The Black Albatross**
Bonny Mary // 23 June 1966
▸▸ **Pike and Squire talk by house gates**
Nr. Helson // 21 June 1966
▸▸ **Cherub secretly watches Pike and the Squire**
Trethewey Farm // 22 June 1966
▸▸ **Blake tries to prevent Kewper leaving the Inn**
Trethewey Farm // 22 June 1966
▸▸ **Pike tries to find Cherub**
Bonny Mary // 23 June 1966
▸▸ **Blake mounts his horse and rides away**
Trethewey Farm // 22 June 1966
▸▸ **Kewper gallops through the gates of the Squire's house**
Farmland Nr. Helston // 21 June 1966
▸▸ **Cherub grabs Tom outside the Inn**
Trethewey Farm // 22 June 1966
▸▸ **Squire and Kewper mount their horses**
Farmland Nr. Helston // 21 June 1966
▸▸ **Blake gallops through countryside**
Nr. Bosistow Cliffs // 20 June 1966

EPISODE 4

▸▸ **Blake is thrown from his horse**
Nr. Bosistow Cliffs // 20 June 1966

▸▸ **Pike tells Spaniard to find Cherub**
Church Cove // 21 June 1966
▸▸ **Blake and soldiers head towards the beach**
Nr. Bosistow Cliffs // 20 June 1966
▸▸ **Spaniard and Daniel find the TARDIS**
Nanjizal Bay // 20 June 1966
▸▸ **Blake's men arrive at the top of the cliffs**
Bosistow Cliffs // 20 June 1966
▸▸ **Divided into two, Blake's party climb down the cliff**
Nanjizal Bay // 20 June 1966
▸▸ **Polly is chased into the cave**
Nanjizal Bay // 19 June 1966
▸▸ **Blake leads his men into the cave**
Nanjizal Bay // 20 June 1966
▸▸ **The Doctor, Ben and Polly enter the TARDIS**
Nanjizal Bay // 19 June 1966
▸▸ **TARDIS dematerialises**
Nanjizal Bay // 20 June 1966

The Facts

The original assistant floor manager assigned to The Smugglers was Margot Hayhoe, who had just finished her training in the job by trailing Lovett Bickford on the previous story, The War Machines.

Margot Hayhoe: 'The next story was one set in Cornwall, with lots of filming on beaches which all sounded very exciting. I think I might have got as far as sitting in the production office for a day and then I got a telephone call to say that another show, a thriller called Breaking Point which was being directed by Douglas Camfield, needed an AFM as it was just about to go filming. Apparently, the original AFM on Douglas' production team had been discovered wandering around Shepherd's Bush Green in a dazed condition after smoking some naughty substance that we don't talk about, and he was promptly sacked!'

As a result, The Smugglers ended up having three AFMs. Tony Gilbert took on the role during the location filming, while John Hansen and Maggie Saunders took up the position for the studio recording.

As soon as the first day's filming at Nanjizal Bay was complete, William Hartnell, Michael Craze (Ben) and Anneke Wills (Polly) were released from the shoot to enable them to join the rehearsals for Episode 3 of The War Machines which were due to begin the following day. Any further shots featuring the Doctor were accomplished using Gordon Craig, who doubled for Hartnell on 22 and 23 June.

The brief shot of St Grada Church in Episode 1 was obtained on the morning of Tuesday 21 June. While the rest of the cast and crew made their way to Church Cove to film the shots of various pirates passing signals, Julia Smith and her camera team of Jimmy Court and Keith Hopper formed a separate unit and diverted to the small village of Grade to film the single point-of-view shot.

All the horses used in the production were hired from the Rose Hill School of Riding in Penzance. John Ringham, who played the King's Revenue man Josiah Blake, was required to spend part of his location time mounted on horseback. Ringham wasn't comfortable with horses and this was confirmed during filming at Trethewey Farm on Wednesday 22 June, when the Episode 3 sequence showing Blake mounting his horse and galloping away was rehearsed just prior to filming.

John Ringham (Blake): 'The scene ended with great urgency, involving me wearing a hat with a large black feather in it, rushing to the horse, mounting it and riding off. The horse stood there, very nervous, with a full film crew with all their equipment bustling about constantly. Julia called for a rehearsal. We played the scene and I then rushed for the horse, big black feather waving about close to the animal's face, and with some difficulty, I mounted it. The horse had had enough. It bucked viciously and struck out with its legs. Equipment went flying and I – very, very aware of the hard concrete waiting for me – stayed on the horse from sheer willpower and terror. Someone must have grabbed the reins because the horse began to settle and I slid weak-kneed to the ground. If I'd been thrown, something would have broken.'

Problems also arose with the scene of Blake's horse galloping across the countryside. The scene was filmed in a large oblong field which sloped upwards for much of its length and then appeared to gently slope away. Unsure about whether he could carry off the galloping scene, Ringham was replaced for the sequence by stuntman Derek Ware. The plan was for Ware to ride the horse diagonally across the field, while being filmed by the camera placed in another corner. Not feeling that a rehearsal was necessary, Ware suggested going for a take and began his gallop across the field. On reaching the crest of the natural slope, Ware had just begun to descend, when both rider and horse suddenly and abruptly disappeared from view. Fearing an accident, the crew began to run across the field, but, as they approached the slope, the horse suddenly reappeared and started grazing, apparently unharmed. Not so Ware, who rose covered from head to foot in manure. Unbeknownst to the production team, an extensive midden was situated just out of view on the other side of the slope. Ware and the horse had galloped straight into it.

The scenes set on the deck of Pike's ship, the Black Albatross, were all filmed on board a 50-foot motor fishing vessel called Bonny Mary, owned by Donald Turtle of Penzance. On the evening of Wednesday 22 June, designer Richard Hunt and his scenic team arrived at Newlyn Harbour to convert the bow of the Bonny Mary to that of a 17th century privateer, the plan being to film on board while the vessel sailed between Newlyn Harbour and Najizel Bay.

Donald Turtle: 'The next morning, the fish workers gaped in disbelief at the vessel moored alongside the fish market. When everyone arrived, male and female, the man in charge asked me what toilet facilities were aboard, which was met by a roar of laughter from the fish workers who overheard the conversation. He explained to me that there must be some kind of toilet provision, and so he went off to buy a couple of buckets from a local hardware store. When all was safely assembled aboard, I steamed out of the harbour, slightly embarrassed by a few catcalls, knowing full well what was awaiting us. Cruising on a river or travelling in a large vessel is one thing, but venturing into the open Atlantic with a swell running in a fishing boat is quite another. Very soon, most of the participants were looking green. The weather was seriously interrupting the filming, so I eventually got the boat into a lee bay and they finished the filming there. I was impressed by the courage of the actors, weathering out the difficulties quite well.'

Julia Smith (director): 'We left Newlyn Harbour and it seemed fairly calm in the bay, but when we got out further, oh brother… It was drizzling and all the actors were sitting there with plastic capes on over their costumes and the pirate captain, who was quite a dandy, had a hood over his beautiful ringlet wig. And this picture sticks in my mind of a bright green face peering out from under the hood, being sick over port!'[15]

On conclusion of the filming, Julia Smith asked Turtle if he would like to keep the set dressings onboard his vessel instead of his £70 fee, but the offer was declined.

Drafted in to help the production were two Penzance Sea Cadets, Terry Hawes (15) and Ted Rogers (16), who were used to row the Lyonesse, a gig borrowed from the Penzance Sea Rangers which would appear as the longboat of the Black Albatross.

One of the biggest problems faced by the production team was finding a suitable building to double for Kewper's Inn, as most properties had too many windows to look authentic. Eventually, a suitable Grade II listed cattle barn was located at Trethewey Farm, owned by Donald Trewern.

Donald Trewern: 'There were several interruptions and frustrations during shooting. The passage of the helicopter to and from the Isles of Scilly and the swarming of one of my son's beehives could be counted as trials and tribulations, and I doubt if the chaps preparing the set really enjoyed spending an hour 'planting' bracken fronds and foxgloves in the manure heap. Nor did the continuity girl appreciate it when she stepped off terra firma into two feet of cow muck!'

While filming was being conducted at the farm, Trewern shot a colour 8mm home movie of the production in progress.

The shooting schedule for Wednesday 22 June indicates that the original intention had been to film at Trethewey Farm in the morning and then move onto Bosistow Cliffs, above Nanjizal Bay, in the late afternoon. Three sequences had been planned for the afternoon change of location – a brief shot of Tom riding along on Kewper's horse for Episode 1, Cherub peering through the bushes for Episode 3 and a longer scene featuring Pike and Cherub for Episode 2 as they make their way to see the Squire. As written, after climbing to the top of the cliffs, Cherub, with the aid of a mirror, helps Pike dress in his 'fine togs', namely a frock coat and ringlet wig,

while concealing Pike's spike with the aid of a scarf. Ultimately, the afternoon filming on the cliff tops was abandoned. The shot of Cherub looking through the bushes was achieved at Trethewey Farm[16] while the other two sequences were dropped altogether. The Episode 2 scene of Pike and Cherub leaving the Black Albatross, filmed the following day, was rewritten to incorporate material about the potential reaction to Pike's spike.

Comment

The Smugglers is yet another story that has long since been destroyed. And that's a crying shame, for the story marks the first occasion when the programme used locations outside London and the Home Counties (and therefore the first time a Doctor Who crew had stayed away from London overnight). The existing telesnaps indicate that Julia Smith, a native of Cornwall herself, certainly made the most of her time on location, shooting some wonderful material around Nanjizal Bay and Church Cove, and the decision to film on board a real boat was indeed a brave one. ∎

FOOTNOTES

1. Although the Isle of Wight Farm still exists and is indeed still owned by the Gordon family, much of the area used for the filming of The Reign of Terror has since been obliterated by the construction of the M25 motorway.

2. The station was used up until 25 October 1959 when it was destroyed by fire. Never used again, it was finally demolished in the early 1970s.

3. A Book of Monsters, David J Howe, p.85

4. Due to the brevity of the sequence, it is impossible to tell if Ian's point-of-view shot of White City Underground Station (opposite Television Centre) is a done using a short filmed sequence or a still photograph. The likelihood is that the shot was achieved using a photograph taken either at the beginning or the end of the 6 May photoshoot.

5. No film diary or schedule is known to exist for this story so the exact filming order is not known. The shooting schedule has therefore been constructed using all the available information in the production and contributor files to form the most likely sequence of events.

6. The Frame #23 and 24, p.68

7. The Frame #23 and 24, p.68

8. The film schedule for the story indicates that this sequence was originally intended to be shot in its entirety on Stages 3A/B at Ealing Film Studios on the morning of 8 October 1965.

9. DWM #157, p.14

10. Unfortunately, no documentation exists in the BBC archives indicating precisely which two locations were used during the production of The Savages. The only surviving paperwork remaining is a brief memo relating to the final sec-

onds of The Gunfighters, stating that the image of a savage on the TARDIS scanner was filmed on Sunday 1 May at Virginia Water. Evidence from the Egham-by-Runnymede Historical Society indicates that the only existing sandpit at Virginia Water at the time was that at Callows Hill, which had been used as a filming location in 1959 during the production of Hammer's The Stranglers of Bombay. Over the years, the site has been used for landfill before being grassed over.

11. As above, there is no actual documented evidence as to the location of the second quarry used during the filming of The Savages. However, on examination of contemporary Ordnance Survey maps of the area, director Christopher Barry has been able to identify the Shire Lane quarry as the location in question with a reasonable degree of certainty.

12. Although the camera zooms in at this location, it is unclear whether this is actual film footage taken on location or simply a still photograph of the street.

13. The intention had been to follow the Doctor and Dodo's journey over four or five shots, ending up with them entering the main doors of the Tower itself.

14. Production documentation indicates that the afternoon of Tuesday 21 June was to have been spent at a venue featuring 'open countryside and possible stables' near Helston, the exact location to be decided. The recollection of the unit's coach driver was that these sequences took place at a farm off the B3297 road between Helston and Wendron.

15. Doctor Who Autumn Special 1987, p.18

16. As seen in Donald Trewern's home movie footage.

PART TWO

'Look, I know Scotland when I see it...'
Jamie – The Mind Robber

PATRICK TROUGHTON

THE SECOND DOCTOR

THE HIGHLANDERS
(tx 17 December 1966 to 7 January 1967)

The Story
The TARDIS lands in Scotland, 1746, during the aftermath of the battle of Culloden. Captured by a small band of Scottish rebels, the Doctor agrees to help their wounded laird, Colin McLaren, but while Polly and McLaren's daughter, Kirsty, are away fetching water, the Doctor, Ben and the surviving Highlanders are arrested by the English Lieutenant, Algernon Ffinch. The prisoners are given into the custody of Gray, a corrupt solicitor, who has been illegally shipping slaves to the West Indies via a stolen ship, the Annabelle. The Doctor manages to get arms to the Scottish prisoners, who escape and set sail for France with the vessel's real captain, MacKay. With all his clansmen aboard the Annabelle, Jamie joins the TARDIS crew.

The Locations
1. Frensham Ponds, Frensham, Surrey

Shooting Schedule

EPISODE 1
▸▸ Alexander fights Redcoat and carries wounded Laird
   Frensham Ponds // 15 November 1966
▸▸ TARDIS materialises
   Frensham Ponds // 14 November 1966
▸▸ Doctor's party finds cannon
   Frensham Ponds // 14 November 1966
▸▸ Ffinch and soldiers approach cottage
   Frensham Ponds // 15 November 1966
▸▸ Alexander is killed as he attacks soldiers
   Frensham Ponds // 15 November 1966
▸▸ Polly and Kirsty arrive back and see the soldiers
   Frensham Ponds // 14 November 1966
▸▸ Sergeant's POV – Polly on hillside
   Frensham Ponds // 14 November 1966

▸▸ Polly and Kirsty pursued by soldiers
   Frensham Ponds // 14 November 1966
▸▸ Polly falls into a pit
   Frensham Ponds // 14 November 1966

EPISODE 2
▸▸ Ffinch and the soldiers arrive
   Frensham Ponds // 14 November 1966
▸▸ Ffinch falls into the pit
   Frensham Ponds // 14 November 1966

EPISODE 4
▸▸ TARDIS dematerialises
   Frensham Ponds // 21 November 1966

Above: A sequence of telesnaps showing how the location filming at Frensham Ponds appeared on-screen.

The Facts

For his opening scenes, actor Michael Elwyn was required to fire a pistol while mounted on horseback. Concerned that the noise might alarm his steed, Elwyn was assured that the horse had been trained not to react and that all would be fine. When the time came to film the scene of Alexander leaving the cottage and charging at the English soldiers, Elwyn fired his pistol and the horse promptly panicked and bolted.

Shooting in November meant that advantage could be taken of the early sunset, allowing director Hugh David to shoot several night sequences, including all the scenes around the pit and the original ending to the story with the TARDIS departing without Jamie.

The final scene of the story was of the TARDIS' departure from the Culloden moors. Originally this had been shot on 14 November 1967 with Jamie being left behind in Scotland, but in the week following the two-day location shoot, producer Innes Lloyd asked actor Frazer Hines if he would be willing to stay in Doctor Who. Hines agreed and, as a result, a return trip was made to Frensham Ponds on Monday 21 November to re-film the closing scene.

Comment

Although the use of location material is fairly small in The Highlanders, it's noteworthy that Hugh David never countenances trying to fool the audience into thinking that he can achieve the battle of Culloden with the tiny handful of actors and extras available to him. Wisely, the story opens a short distance away from the carnage and focuses on the small band of fleeing Highlanders. As David himself noted in a 1986 interview, the use of a few explosions and background sound effects achieved the illusion of the distant battle without any real expense being incurred.

THE UNDERWATER MENACE

(tx 14 January to 4 February 1967)

The Story

The TARDIS lands on an extinct volcanic island and the travellers are soon captured and taken to the subterranean city of Atlantis, where they are held as potential sacrifices to the fish god, Amdo. Before the sacrifice can be made, they are rescued by Professor Zaroff, who is reputedly working to raise Atlantis from the depths. In reality, the insane Zaroff plans instead to drain the sea into the molten core of the planet, causing the Earth to explode. The Doctor manages to breach the city walls, which floods Atlantis and drowns Zaroff, while the rest of the population escape.

The Locations

1. Winspit Quarry, Worth Matravers, Dorset

Shooting Schedule

EPISODE 1

▸ **TARDIS arrives**
  Winspit Quarry // 13 December 1966
▸ **Establishing Shot – Volcanic Island**
  Winspit Quarry // 12 December 1966
▸ **Exploration of beach and caves**
  Winspit Quarry // 13 December 1966

EPISODE 4

▸ **Jamie and Polly emerge from the caves**
  Winspit Quarry // 13 December 1966
▸ **Doctor, Ben, Jacko and Sean emerge from the caves**
  Winspit Quarry // 13 December 1966

The Facts

On 23 November 1966, production assistant Norman Stewart contacted the BBC's finance department:

'Could you please pay a facility fee to John S Strange of Westmanton, Worth Matravers, Dorset, who has agreed, after some discussion, to let us film on a section of the Dorset coast which he owns. He normally does not allow filming to be done there as he does not want it publicised, but as the filming will be done in winter, and the actual spot will probably be unrecognisable, he has granted permission.'

John Strange was subsequently paid a total of 15 guineas for the use of his land.

The location was reused 13 years later for the rocky terrain of Skaro in Destiny of the Daleks, featuring the same set of caves explored during the opening episode of The Underwater Menace.

To avoid taking the full-sized police box prop on

Far left: The miniature TARDIS prop on the shoreline next to Winspit Quarry, Worth Matravers.

Middle: Polly (Anneke Wills) stands outside the caves in Winspit Quarry during the first episode of The Underwater Menace.

Left: The Doctor (Tom Baker) and Romana (Lalla Ward) walk past the same caves 13 years later in Destiny of the Daleks.

location, a three-foot miniature TARDIS built by the Uxbridge-based Shawcraft Models was pressed into service.

Comment

It seems strange that the production team should have travelled out as far as Dorset to shoot the few brief shoreline and cave scenes for The Underwater Menace when there must have been suitable locations closer to London. That said, the existing telesnaps do give the impression that Winspit was ideal for representing the volcanic island with its craggy appearance and deep caves.

THE MACRA TERROR

(tx 11 March to 1 April 1967)

The Story

The TARDIS arrives on a planet inhabited by a seemingly happy and well-run human colony. However, the rebellious Medok informs the Doctor that the colony has in fact been infiltrated by giant crab-like creatures, the Macra, who have subjugated the colonists and are putting them to work in gas mines deep beneath the planet. There, they source the toxic gas vital for the Macra's survival. Under the Doctor's direction, Ben destroys the gas pumps, killing the Macra and freeing the colony.

The Locations

1. Associated Portland Cement Manufacturers Quarry, Houghton Road, Dunstable, Bedfordshire

Shooting Schedule

EPISODE 1

▸▸ Ola and guards chase Medok as TARDIS appears
APCM Quarry // 15 February 1967

EPISODE 4

▸▸ TARDIS dematerialises (cut)
APCM Quarry // 15 February 1967

The Facts

On 5 January 1967, production assistant Christopher D'Oyly-John telephoned Mr P St Clare Grondona of Associated Portland Cement Manufacturers Ltd in London and asked if he could have permission to recce a number of the company's quarries around the Swanscombe area of Kent. Arrangements were duly made and by the end of the following week, the decision had been reached that the ideal location would be, not one of the company's quarries in Kent as previously thought, but one situated in Dunstable.

'I am writing in confirmation of our telephone conversation this morning. We would like to film a short sequence for the 'Dr Who' serial in your Dunstable quarry on Wednesday 15 February 1967, between 9.30 am and 5.00 pm. The unit would consist of approximately 30 people.

'We will require to take two Land Rovers containing camera and technical equipment to the far end of the quarry. Also we would be most grateful if you could transport the 'Police Box' on your railway line to the quarry end. Will it be possible, please, if there are any odd technicians cars, to park them at the top of the quarry opposite your works offices?

'There is a small gully leading to the footbridge over the A5 and we thought perhaps this would be a good place to park our caterers van and the coach in which the artists will be transported.

'During the action of the sequence, the actors will have to run across the clay and mud. Would it be possible for some sort of washing facilities to be laid on for their use?

'As I mentioned, our Facilities Department will be contacting you regarding a suitable fee.[1]

'Finally, in case the 15th February proves to be impossible weatherwise, we plan to hold Thursday 16 February as a standby day, in which case the same arrangement will exist.'

Christopher D'Oyly-John to C J Millest – 16 February 1967

One of the items paid for by the production was a £3 3s 0d bottle of brandy, used to help combat some of the cold winds which blew through the quarry during the filming.

Most of the filming done at Dunstable was achieved using a single 35mm camera, although a 16mm hand-held camera was taken along too, contributing 38 feet of silent footage to the finished production.

Ouch!

At 1.25 pm actor Danny Rae, who was playing one of the guards, was filming a shot requiring him to run towards the camera and then out of frame. As this shot was being filmed, Rae's right foot hit a patch of uneven ground, which caused him to slightly sprain his ankle. As the injury was only slight, Rae was able to continue with the rest of filming.

Comment

Once again, The Macra Terror features a location sequence that's almost entirely superfluous to the story itself, and one that could have easily been altered to a studio-based setting had director John Davies so desired. It's also somewhat surprising that the scene of the TARDIS dematerialising at the end of the story was actually shot but never used. One can only wonder if the location filming would have been dropped from the production had Shawcraft, the company responsible for building the single Macra creature, revealed earlier that it was going to cost over £500 (the price of a small car in 1967) to construct.

THE FACELESS ONES

(tx 8 April to 13 May 1967)

The Story

The TARDIS lands on the runway of Gatwick Airport in 1966. The Doctor's curiosity is soon piqued after Polly witnesses someone being murdered in a hangar owned by Chameleon Tours, an airline company whose young passengers have mysteriously been going missing. With the aid of a police inspector, Crossland, and a concerned relative named Samantha Briggs, the Doctor discovers that the passengers are being kidnapped by the Chameleons, an alien race who have lost their physical identity due to a gigantic explosion. Able to assume the characteristics of the captured humans, the Chameleons are outwitted by the Doctor on their storage satellite and are convinced to release those they have taken from Earth.

The Locations

1. Gatwick Airport, Gatwick, Surrey
   - Air Courier's Apron
   - Passenger Concourse
   - Main Car Park

Shooting Schedule

EPISODE 1

▸▸ TARDIS lands, Crew chased by a Policeman
Air Courier's Apron // 13 March 1967

▸ Police get TARDIS, Crew hide from Policeman
Air Courier's Apron // 17 March 1967

▸ Polly escapes, Ben watches Police and TARDIS
Air Courier's Apron // 17 March 1967

▸▸ Doctor, Jamie and Polly under aircraft
Air Courier's Apron // 17 March 1967

▸ Polly is kidnapped
Air Courier's Apron // 17 March 1967

▸▸ Ben walks to Chameleon Tours hanger
Air Courier's Apron // 17 March 1967

▸ Blade takes Chameleon up escalator
Passenger Concourse // 10 March 1967

▸ Blade takes Chameleon to Medical Centre
Passenger Concourse // 10 March 1967

EPISODE 2

▸▸ Policemen search concourse
Passenger Concourse // 10 March 1967

▸ Jamie walks through concourse
Passenger Concourse // 10 March 1967

▸▸ Ann goes to Chameleon Tours kiosk
Passenger Concourse // 10 March 1967

EPISODE 4

▸ Jamie gives ticket to Ann
Passenger Concourse // 10 March 1967

EPISODE 6

▸ Concourse loudspeakers during announcement
Passenger Concourse // 10 March 1967

▸▸ Police search hangers and offices
Air Courier's Apron // 17 March 1967

▸▸ Meadows escapes from policeman
Main Car Park // 14 March 1967

▸▸ Jean and Sam begin searching cars
Main Car Park // 14 March 1967

▸▸ Jean knocks out Meadows and finds body in car
Main Car Park // 14 March 1967

▸▸ Bodies in car park. Sheath removed from Jenkins
Main Car Park // 14 March 1967

▸▸ The airport gets back to normal
Pass. Concourse/ AC Apron // 10 March 1967

▸▸ Ben and Polly say goodbye
Air Courier's Apron // 13 March 1967

The Facts

The original pre-production title for this serial was The Chameleons, but the title had been changed to The

Faceless Ones by 7 March.

The final location sequence to be filmed at Gatwick was for the closing moments of Episode 6, as the Doctor's party are taken back to the apron and they say goodbye to Polly and Ben. The sequence underwent a number of changes from what was initially planned in both the script and the filming schedule. Originally, it was planned that the Commandant would accompany the Doctor and his companions in the black Zodiac that takes them out to the apron. As scripted, the action and dialogue ran:

HIGH ANGLE car approaching camera – stops – door opens.
TRACKING SHOT DR WHO steps out of car – TRACK OUT with DR WHO to include COMMANDANT and GROUP.
Doctor: This will do quite nicely, thank you.
Commandant: Surely there's somewhere else I could drop you?
Doctor: No thanks.
Commandant: But, I say…
DR WHO shakes COMMANDANT'S hand and exits Frame L.

To avoid contracting guest star Colin Gordon just to say 11 words on location, the scene was rescripted to eliminate the Commandant's character. The Doctor's dialogue was thus adjusted to, 'This will do quite nicely, my thanks to the Commandant.'

The same sequence was also to feature Samantha Briggs kissing Jamie goodbye after they leave the Ford Zodiac. This scene appears never to have been filmed on location, however; indeed, the transmitted episode features this farewell scene recorded in studio on the air traffic control set.

Unused Locations

London Airport – The script was originally written with the idea that London Airport (now known as London Heathrow) would be the filming location; in fact, several references to 'London Airport' remained in the final rehearsal scripts. On Thursday 9 February, production assistant Richard Brooks approached both the British Airport Authority and, in particular, Field Aircraft Service Ltd, requesting general permission to film the main block of Episode 1's location sequences around their hangars and concrete apron at London Airport on Wednesday 8 March. Additionally, a request was made to the BAA to allow a cameraman to film some of the action from a 35-foot observation tower, situated on a grassed area in front of the Field Aircraft Service's hangar.

Permission to shoot the required scenes was duly granted but within a few days problems began to arise

which would preclude the location being used.

'Unfortunately, however, we have been obliged to make rather drastic alterations to our plans and shall not, after all, be able to film at London Airport at all. This has been brought about by extensive script re-writing which will inevitably put our overall costs a good deal higher than originally thought. This, together with the charges for filming at London Airport, will stretch our programme budget much further than can reasonably be expected.'

Richard Brooks to Mr Duncan, British Airports Authority and A R Putt, Field Services Ltd – 21 February 1967

By way of thanks for the help that had been offered by the staff at Field Services Ltd, the production team sent them two sets of tickets for recordings of The Rolf Harris Show that was being produced at the Television Theatre in London.

The final cost for using the facilities at Gatwick Airport amounted to £190 for the BAA and £252 10s 0d for Air Couriers Ltd.

Comment

Without a doubt, the storytelling of The Faceless Ones is greatly aided by the opportunity to actually film in a working airport, not only in the passenger terminals, but also out on the airport aprons as well. The establishment of a realistic 20th century setting was very important for the story as this was only the second time in Doctor Who's history that an alien invasion had occurred in a contemporary setting – the other being The War Machines, which supposedly happens on the exactly the same day that the events in The Faceless Ones are taking place at Gatwick Airport.

THE EVIL OF THE DALEKS
(tx 20 May to 1 July 1967)

The Story

The TARDIS is stolen from Gatwick Airport by Kennedy, a mercenary carrying out the orders of Edward Waterfield, apparently a dealer in Victorian antiques. Tracking the TARDIS to Waterfield's shop, the Doctor and Jamie are knocked unconscious and transported back 100 years to the Canterbury home of Theodore Maxtible, who, together with Waterfield, has captured the time travellers under orders from the Daleks. The Doctor is forced to put Jamie through an experiment to identify the 'human factor' – in reality, the Daleks are using him to identify the qualities that contribute to their own ruthlessness. With the information they need, the Daleks destroy Maxtible's house and return to Skaro,

Above: On 21 April 1967, cameraman John Baker prepares to film the high-angle opening shots from The Evil of the Daleks. This scene, showing the theft of the TARDIS, was filmed outside the BBC's OB Transport Base at Kendal Avenue.

but the Doctor manages to introduce the human factor to three Daleks, precipitating a devastating civil war.

The Locations

1. Grim's Dyke House, Old Redding, Harrow-Weald, Middlesex[2]
2. BBC OB and Transport Base, Kendal Avenue, London, W3
3. Warehouse Lane, off Macfarlane Road, Shepherd's Bush, London, W12

Shooting Schedule

EPISODE 1

▸▸ **TARDIS driven away on lorry**
Kendal Avenue // 21 April 1967
▸▸ **Kennedy listens to radio**
Grim's Dyke House // 20 April 1967
▸▸ **Kennedy speaks to Bob Hall**
Grim's Dyke House // 20 April 1967
▸▸ **Doctor and Jamie by petrol pumps**
Kendal Avenue // 21 April 1967
▸▸ **Kennedy calls Waterfield**
Grim's Dyke House // 20 April 1967
▸▸ **Hall drives from the airport**
Kendal Avenue // 21 April 1967
▸▸ **Doctor and Jamie arrive at warehouses**
Warehouse Lane // 21 April 1967

EPISODE 3

▸▸ **Victoria moved inside house**
Grim's Dyke House // 20 April 1967
▸▸ **Jamie and Kemel meet**
Grim's Dyke House // 25 April 1967

EPISODE 4

▸▸ **Jamie and Kemel fight**

Grim's Dyke House // 25 April 1967
▸▸ **Dalek places handkerchief**
Grim's Dyke House // 24 April 1967
▸▸ **Kemel leads Jamie out of axe room**
Grim's Dyke House // 25 April 1967
▸▸ **Daleks inspect Victoria**
Grim's Dyke House // 24 April 1967
▸▸ **Jamie and Kemel attack Dalek and are trapped (4/5)**
Grim's Dyke House // 24 April 1967

EPISODE 5

▸▸ **Remains of destroyed Dalek**
Grim's Dyke House // 24 April 1967

The Facts

Having decided on the use of Grim's Dyke House to represent Maxtible's Canterbury home, production assistant Timothy Combe also needed to find a suitable spot to film the shots of Kennedy sitting on a fence, speaking into his walkie-talkie for Episode 1. While recceing the house, Combe had noticed a suitable field backing onto the stables at the rear of the building. During the day, Combe had visited the local pub, the Red Lion, and established that the field belonged to Eric Massey, himself a film cameraman. A deal was struck and Massey was paid a half-day's facility fee for the use of his property. The shots of Griffith Davies as Kennedy were the first to be completed on the morning of Thursday 20 April and took at least an hour and a half to complete.

Unusually for Doctor Who, the main filming location was chosen more for its internal features rather than its external appearance, which only featured as a single photographic establishing shot (see Photographed Locations). One of the main areas used in the house was the Minstrel's Gallery where the Daleks hold Waterfield's daughter Victoria. The climax to the episode featured Jamie and Maxtible's mute servant Kemel climbing up to the gallery via a rope to find a Dalek waiting in ambush for them. To save themselves, Jamie and Kemel loop the rope around the Dalek and force it over the edge of the gallery. To ensure that no damage was done to the building's fixtures and fittings, the shot of the Dalek crashing through the balustrade and falling to the ground was later accomplished at Ealing Film Studios on Thursday 27 April.

The final set of scenes to be filmed at Grim's Dyke were those showing the fight between Jamie and Kemel in Episodes 3 and 4, all of which were accomplished during a period of evening work between 5.00 pm and 2.00 am. The London Borough of Harrow was paid £120 for the use of Grim's Dyke House.

Initially, both Michael Craze and Anneke Wills were contracted to work on the first two episodes of The Evil

Left: The exterior of Grim's Dyke House, which appeared as Maxtible's mansion in The Evil of the Daleks.

of the Daleks. When the decision was made to write them out earlier, producer Innes Lloyd hoped to persuade Pauline Collins (who appeared as Samantha Briggs in The Faceless Ones) to stay on and become the new companion, but the offer was declined. By now, the casting of Victoria Waterfield for Evil was well under way, and it's reasonable to suppose that at this stage there was no intention of her being an on-going character. On Monday 3 April 1967, two days after Episode 1 of The Faceless Ones had been recorded, a second audition for the role was being held by director Derek Martinus with Paula Challoner and her sister Carla. A week later, on 10 April, a further six actresses were auditioned – Celestine Randall, Elizabeth Knight, Gabrielle Drake, Tracy Rogers, Lans Traverse[3] and Denise Buckley. Following the audition, Buckley was offered, and duly accepted, the role of Victoria. However, for reasons unknown, on 13 April, only seven days before location filming was due to begin at Grim's Dyke, Innes Lloyd issued a memo confirming that the part would be played by Deborah Watling instead. On 19 April, a letter was sent to Buckley's agent, Scott Marshall Ltd, confirming that she would no longer be needed. It was also agreed that her full fee of £189 for all six episodes of her cancelled contract would still be paid.

The film schedule for the story indicates that the original intention had been to record the Dalek voices on location on both 20 and 24 April. Both voice artist Peter Hawkins and a lip microphone were listed among the requirements for the two days, but both were subsequently crossed out prior to the filming taking place.

The narrative of The Evil of the Daleks followed directly from The Faceless Ones, with the Doctor and Jamie searching for the missing TARDIS. To avoid the cost of returning to Gatwick Airport for a few brief sequences, the opening scenes were completed outside the BBC's own Outside Broadcast and Transport Base at Kendal Avenue in West London. As both Troughton and Hines were busy with the final rehearsals of Episode 4 of The Faceless Ones, the morning of Friday 21 April was devoted to filming all the shots not requiring the two main actors. Arrangements were made to collect the two actors by taxi from St Helen's Church Hall and transport them to Kendal Avenue. Following lunch, the six remaining shots requiring the two stars were filmed, some of which were achieved using a specially hired 25-foot platform crane from SGB.

Two weeks prior to the shoot, assistant floor manager David Tilley contacted the BBC's Prop Master with a list of requirements for the Kendal Avenue filming. The requested items were:

- 1 Large size TARDIS Police Box – Complete.
- 1 Fully pract. Lorry, open type with tailboard at rear (this to report as above and be loaded with

Above: Telesnaps showing the interior corridor and the Minstrel Gallery of Grim's Dyke House, as seen in Episodes 3 and 4.

TARDIS at Movement Control then go to location).
- Large quantity of 1_" diam. rope for securing TARDIS to above lorry.
- 1 Clipboard with driver's sheet/log.
- 1 Cheque (Graphics)
- 1 Sign (Re: Gatwick Airport) / Scenery
- 2 Signs 'Leatherbarrow'[4] for lorry / Graphics
- Ear piece radio (for Bob Hall)
- 1 Fully pract. Ford Anglia estate car approx. 6 years old (battered about for Bob Hall)
- 1 Fully pract. London taxi cab

As soon as work was completed at Kendal Avenue, the cast and crew moved to Warehouse Lane, a small row of garages and warehouses built into the arches of a bridge carrying London Underground trains, in the shadow of the BBC's Television Centre.

Location Facts

Grim's Dyke House – The main location chosen for The Evil of the Daleks was Grim's Dyke House, a Grade II listed building in Harrow Weald, Middlesex. The house, designed by Norman Shaw (who also designed the New Scotland Yard building), was originally built in 1870 for the Victorian Painter, Frederick Goodall. Later, in 1890, it was purchased by the librettist, Sir William Schwenck Gilbert of Gilbert and Sullivan fame, who lived in the house until his death in 1911. During the 1960s, the house was used as a location for a number of different television series such as The Saint, The Champions, The Avengers and Randall and Hopkirk (Deceased); it also featured in the films Curse of the Crimson Altar and Cry of the Banshee. In 1970, Grim's Dyke was designated a building of special architectural and historical interest and the house was converted into a hotel.

Photographed Locations

On Tuesday 25 April, a BBC photographer attended the location filming at Grim's Dyke House. Night-time photographs of the exterior of the house were taken for use during Episode 3 as well as shots of Deborah Watling in costume, which would be used to create the painting of Victoria's mother seen in Maxtible's house in Episode 2.

Comment

Director Derek Martinus' decision to fake his opening Gatwick Airport footage was a clever and cost-effective method of dovetailing into the closing narrative of The Faceless Ones. Having already seen the TARDIS being driven about on a lorry around various hangars and offices in the previous story, viewers would have had no reason to question that the footage had actually been shot miles away. Likewise, Martinus' interior use of Grim's Dyke House is also interesting, giving the action within Maxtible's residence a dimension that would not have been achievable within the confines of the television studio.

THE TOMB OF THE CYBERMEN
(tx 2 September to 23 September 1967)

The Story

On the planet Telos, an archaeological team led by Professor Parry manages to uncover the lost tomb of the Cybermen. The TARDIS arrives just as a crew member is electrocuted at the entrance doors and, despite initial suspicion regarding the travellers, the Doctor manages to gain entry to the tomb. However, behind the expedition are Kaftan and Eric Klieg, who hope to reactivate the Cybermen so that their Brotherhood of Logisticians can join forces with them. The reactivated Cybermen prove uncontrollable and, with both Kaftan and Klieg dead, the Doctor struggles to contain the unleashed threat.

The Locations

1. Gerrards Cross Sand and Gravel Quarry, Wapsey's Wood, Oxford Road, Gerrards Cross, Buckinghamshire

Shooting Schedule

EPISODE 1

▶▶ **Parry's party excavates tomb doors**
Gerrards Cross Quarry // 12 June 1967
▶▶ **Parry's party meets the Doctor, Jamie and Victoria**
Gerrards Cross Quarry // 12 June 1967

EPISODE 4

▶▶ **Doctor, Jamie and Parry watch Toberman**
Gerrards Cross Quarry // 12 June 1967

The Facts

The doors of the Cybermen tombs were represented on location by the use of a small foreground model placed approximately six feet in front of the camera.

At the time of filming The Tomb of the Cybermen, Frazer Hines was aged 22 and inclined to chat up

Left: Preparing to shoot the opening scenes of The Tomb of the Cybermen at Gerrards Cross on 12 June 1967.

some of his female co-stars. But it didn't always go quite as he expected.

Shirley Cooklin (Kaftan): 'Obviously I knew all the cast. I was married to the producer and I'd go along to the bar after studio recordings. However, come the day of filming, I was wearing a lot of false hair, as well as the make-up. Frazer was a bit of a lad for the girls and his eyes lit up when he saw me, and he started making moves in my direction. So I said to him, "Frazer! It's Shirley!" The penny then dropped and you should have seen his face!'[5]

Comment

As with the footage of Camber Sands in The Chase, the location material shot at Gerrards Cross for The Tomb of the Cybermen looks extraordinarily effective. But this isn't just down to the use of atmospheric black and white film; it's down to Morris Barry's direction and Peter Hamilton's superb camerawork. The opening shot of the camera following Toberman's feet to the edge of the precipice to see the rest of the expedition far below is a simple but remarkably inventive piece of camerawork, as is the lengthy 25-second shot of all the team members clambering up the bank and past the camera as they endeavour to reach the newly revealed tomb doors. The location material doesn't last long, but its inclusion is a valuable addition to the story.

THE ABOMINABLE SNOWMEN

(tx 30 September to 4 November 1967)

The Story

Landing in Tibet in 1935, the Doctor pays a return visit to the nearby Detsen monastery after a gap of 300 years. When he arrives, he is accused by explorer Professor Travers of murdering his colleague. Proving his innocence, the Doctor learns from the monks that the mysterious Yeti have become increasingly aggressive and soon he discovers the reason why – the Yeti are really robots controlled by Padmasambhava, the High Lama, who has been taken over by the formless Great Intelligence. Using the Lama, whose life has been prolonged by hundreds of years, the Intelligence seeks a way to gain a physical form. The Doctor manages to expel the Intelligence from Earth, thus allowing his old friend to finally die.

The Locations

1. Nant Ffrancon Pass, Gwynedd, North Wales

Shooting Schedule

EPISODE 1

▸▸ Travers and John attacked at campsite
Nant Ffrancon // 4 September 1967

Above: The Yeti are mollycoddled whilst filming around the TARDIS continues at Nant Ffrancon.

▸▸ Doctor walks from the TARDIS
Nant Ffrancon // 4-9 September 1967
▸▸ Doctor sees Detsen monastery
Nant Ffrancon // 4-9 September 1967
▸▸ Doctor finds footprint
Nant Ffrancon // 4-9 September 1967
▸▸ Creature watches the Doctor
Nant Ffrancon // 4-9 September 1967
▸▸ Doctor discovers John's body
Nant Ffrancon // 4 September 1967
▸▸ Jamie and Victoria find footprints around TARDIS
Nant Ffrancon // 5-8 September 1967
▸▸ Jamie and Victoria follow tracks to cave
Nant Ffrancon // 5-8 September 1967

EPISODE 2

▸▸ Jamie and Victoria escape from the cave
Nant Ffrancon // 5-8 September 1967
▸▸ Yeti chases Jamie and Victoria
Nant Ffrancon // 5-8 September 1967
▸▸ Jamie and Victoria meet Travers
Nant Ffrancon // 5-8 September 1967
▸▸ Travers, Jamie and Victoria arrive at monastery
Nant Ffrancon // 5-8 September 1967
▸▸ Three Yeti arrive
Nant Ffrancon // 4-9 September 1967

▸▸ Yeti begins to approach monastery
Nant Ffrancon // 4-9 September 1967
▸▸ Two Yeti depart
Nant Ffrancon // 4-9 September 1967

EPISODE 3

▸▸ Travers watches three Yeti
Nant Ffrancon // 4-9 September 1967
▸▸ Two Yeti move off to the monastery
Nant Ffrancon // 4-9 September 1967
▸▸ Travers follows the two Yeti
Nant Ffrancon // 4-9 September 1967
▸▸ Doctor and Jamie encounter three Yeti
Nant Ffrancon // 4-9 September 1967

EPISODE 4

▸▸ Yeti leaves the monastery
Nant Ffrancon // 4-9 September 1967
▸▸ Doctor and Jamie climb the mountain
Nant Ffrancon // 4-9 September 1967
▸▸ Travers watches Songsten and the Yeti by the cave
Nant Ffrancon // 4-9 September 1967
▸▸ Doctor and Jamie discover a Yeti outside the TARDIS
Nant Ffrancon // 4-9 September 1967
▸▸ Travers watches Songsten and Yeti leave the cave
Nant Ffrancon // 4-9 September 1967
▸▸ Doctor removes Yeti sphere and enters the TARDIS
Nant Ffrancon // 4-9 September 1967
▸▸ Doctor and Jamie fight to stop the Yeti activating
Nant Ffrancon // 4-9 September 1967
▸▸ Doctor begins to trace sphere signal
Nant Ffrancon // 4-9 September 1967
▸▸ Doctor and Jamie escape from the Yeti
Nant Ffrancon // 4-9 September 1967

EPISODE 5

▸▸ Travers and the Doctor observe two Yeti
Nant Ffrancon // 4-9 September 1967

EPISODE 6

▸▸ Travers and Ralpachan make towards the cave
Nant Ffrancon // 5-6 September 1967
▸▸ Travers and Ralpachan head back to the monastery
Nant Ffrancon // 5-6 September 1967
▸▸ Heading back to the TARDIS, Travers sees a real Yeti
Nant Ffrancon // 4-9 September 1967

Left: Patrick Troughton is interviewed by Glyn Owen for the BBC's local news programme Wales Today on 6 September 1967.

The Facts

The Abominable Snowmen is believed to be the first Doctor Who story to feature location footage shot on 16mm, as opposed to 35mm, film.

Barring a couple of brief shots involving Travers' dead companion John (played by Yeti actor Reg Whitehead), no real filming was done over the first two planned days of the schedule due to the high winds blowing down the Nant Ffrancon valley. This meant that the required scenes couldn't be completed by 8 September, when the crew were scheduled to finish, and an extra day had to be spent on location. Film cameraman Peter Bartlett attempted to speed up the rate at which the required shots were achieved by removing the camera from its tripod and placing it on his shoulder, which enabled him to move around the action freely and gain the best possible shots in the least amount of time.

All the location material in The Abominable Snowmen was originally scripted to be recorded in the studio.

On Wednesday 6 September, the cast and crew were visited by a production team from the BBC's local news programme, Wales Today. The two-minute 16mm film report appeared on the following day's programme and featured an interview with Patrick Troughton conducted by reporter Glyn Owen.

One original reel of 16mm location material from Episode 2 exists in the BBC archives. The footage, which retains the original sound, includes a slightly longer version of the scene where Travers, Jamie and Victoria run down the mountain towards the monastery, at the end of which Deborah Watling slips on the ground, out of shot. Two separate reels of 8mm colour ciné footage taken on location also exist from the story, taken by director Gerald Blake and Frazer Hines.

Ouch!

While filming up in the mountains, director's assistant Judy Shears suddenly felt a desperate need for the toilet. With the team too far away from the unit vehicles, Shears wandered round the location and found a conveniently secluded bolder further up the mountain, but as she walked around the back, her foot plummeted down a concealed hole, giving her a severe bruise down the back of her leg.

Comment

One of the criticisms sometimes levelled against the location filming of The Abominable Snowmen is the apparent lack of snow in the Himalayas. In fact, the foothills surrounding the real mountains are not snowy at all. As such, the Snowdonia location around the Nant Ffrancon Pass provides a dramatic backdrop to the story and it's a relief that Gerald Blake didn't choose to follow the script suggestion of shooting the entire story in the studio. It's on location that the Yeti really come into their own, looking big and menacing against the wind and the grey rocks. From the footage that still exists, it looks like Blake made an excellent

Above: Victoria (Deborah Watling) spots a huge footprint outside the TARDIS at the beginning of Episode 1.

Above right: The Doctor (Patrick Troughton) and Jamie (Frazer Hines) wonder how to get into the TARDIS in Episode 4.

THE ENEMY OF THE WORLD

(tx 23 December 1967 to 27 January 1968)

The Story

Landing on the beaches of Australia, the Doctor, Jamie and Victoria immediately come under attack from three assailants before they are rescued by Astrid Farrier. Taken to see Giles Kent, it is explained that the Doctor looks identical to Salamander, a man whom many believe is positioning himself to be a future dictator of the world. Doubling for Salamander, the Doctor discovers the true nature of his corruption and that he has been in league with Kent himself. Exposed, Salamander makes for the TARDIS, pretending to be the Doctor, but the ruse fails and Salamander gets sucked out into space.

The Locations

1. Climping Beach, Climping, Littlehampton, West Sussex
2. BBC Villiers House, The Broadway, Haven Green, Ealing, London, W5
3. Walpole Park, Ealing, London, W5

Shooting Schedule

EPISODE 1

▸▸ TARDIS arrives, watched by Anton
Climping Beach // 5-8 November 1967
▸▸ Doctor's party attacked and rescued by Astrid
Climping Beach // 5-8 November 1967
▸▸ Helicopter lands outside Astrid's bungalow
Climping Beach // 5-8 November 1967
▸▸ Hovercraft arrives outside Astrid's bungalow
Climping Beach // 5-8 November 1967
▸▸ Doctor's group escape from bungalow
Climping Beach // 5-8 November 1967
▸▸ Doctor's group hide in a ditch
Climping Beach // 7 November 1967

EPISODE 2

▸▸ Jamie in park
Walpole Park // 9 November 1967

EPISODE 4

▸▸ Guards on fire escape outside Kent's office
Villiers House // 9 November 1967
▸▸ Guards on ground outside Kent's office
Villiers House // 9 November 1967

EPISODE 5

▸▸ Guard chases Astrid
Climping Beach // 7 November 1967

EPISODE 6

▸▸ Jamie helps the 'Doctor' into the TARDIS
Climping Beach // 5-8 November 1967

The Facts

'I didn't know whether the Martians had landed, were about to land, or were going to land. I didn't even know if the Martians were involved. But there were men running around in bizarre, coloured suits, occasionally trying to shoot each other. This was the scene when I arrived on the location of a BBC film unit on Clymping Beach.[6] They were there to shoot the first episode of the next series of 'Dr Who', to be screened in December.

'Most of the production was 'hush-hush' but apparently the series is to be entitled The Enemy of the World. It takes place in 2018 and West Beach is supposed to be Australia.

'Considering the fact that there was a cold wind blowing and everyone was huddled to the eyebrows in sweaters and coats, I don't think anyone present had imagination that would stretch to part of our beach being Australia.'

So wrote journalist Roy Arber in the 11 November 1967 edition of the Littlehampton Gazette following his visit to the location on Tuesday the 7th.

The location filming utilised two large pieces of hardware, namely a helicopter and a hovercraft, both of which appeared in the 9'16" of film material included in the first episode.

The hovercraft was loaned to the BBC by Mr K R Morgan[7] of Worthing, a retired naval architect who had designed and built the vehicle himself. However, during filming on Monday the 10th, the hovercraft was caught by a cross wind which blew it onto the pebble beach, damaging the underside. Technical problems with the hovercraft continued for the remainder of the location shoot.

Originally, two of the hovercraft killers were scripted with the names Tibor and Otto. By the time of the programme's transmission, these names had been changed to the more Australian-sounding Rod and Curly, although the location article in the Littlehampton Gazette sites the name of Rhys McConnochie's character as still being Tibor, indicating that this change of

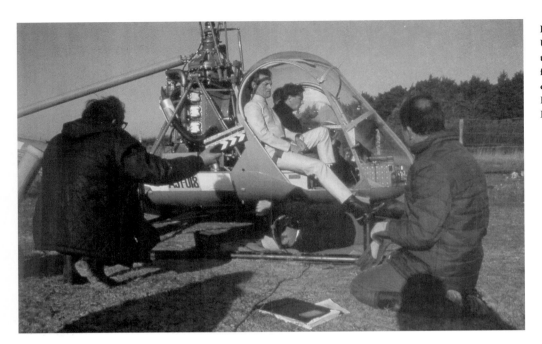

Left: The Hiller
UH-12 helicopter
takes off, filmed
from underneath by
cameraman Fred
Hamilton in
Episode 1.

names happened quite late in the day.

Like the hovercraft, the helicopter, a Hiller UH-12[8], was written into the script at the suggestion of director Barry Letts, who felt that it would provide a more exciting beginning to the story. While on location, Letts mentioned to the film cameraman, Fred Hamilton, that he'd wished he'd arranged for a gyroscopic camera mount to be available so that he could obtain shots of the action on the ground from the helicopter as it swooped up into the air. At this, Hamilton agreed to attempt to achieve the same shots with a hand-held camera.

Barry Letts: 'They took the doors off the helicopter and Fred, tied by a rope, sat on the floor with his feet on one of the skids. I sat in the seat on the other side of the pilot to balance him a bit. We took off at rather an alarming angle, got to about 20 feet in the air and landed again. The pilot said sorry and off we went once again and got a very good shot of Rhys McConnochie firing at the escaping heroes as the helicopter swooped up into the air. However, the pilot later revealed that the reason for his erroneous take-off was that he hadn't accurately allowed for the unbalanced weight of Fred Hamilton and the film camera and had very nearly side-slipped the helicopter straight back into the ground, which would have certainly resulted in the deaths of all three on board.'

Letts objected to the idea of Curly and Anton, the 'hovercraft killers', getting away with their wickedness, and so their demise, in Astrid's helicopter as it explodes, was at his instigation. The effect was achieved, not with the real helicopter, but by obtaining the rights from Eon

Productions to use four feet of 35mm test model footage from the James Bond film, From Russia With Love.[9]

The closing scenes of Episode 6, showing Salamander making his way back to the TARDIS, despite being scripted for filming during the day were switched to night shooting.

John Hills-Harrop (film recordist): 'There was a night shoot involved with that story which required some quite wide shots looking up from the beach. The general weather situation was quite bad on that shoot, so I was wearing an all-over black oilskin suit. The problem was that the shot we wanted was so wide that we couldn't get a microphone in anywhere. So after a certain amount of chatting between myself and Fred, we agreed that if I stood in a certain position, I could actually be in shot with the microphone because the scene was being back-lit and with my black oilskins on, the camera simply couldn't see me. Plus, if I stayed where he put me, I was also useful for hiding one of Fred's lamps! Fred decided that he didn't want to carry any of his filming kit any further than he had to. We had a Land Rover at the top of the beach, which was covered with pebbles. Wheeled vehicles and pebbles don't go too well together and he managed to get it stuck. I can't remember whether he got it out of the way before the tide came in.'

One unscheduled 'actor' used during the filming on Monday 6 November was Nigel Burtwhistle, a 17-year-old pupil from the nearby Westdown Tutors School in Climping who was presented with the opportunity to 'stand in' as the guard who pursues

Right: The helicopter take-off, as seen on-screen.

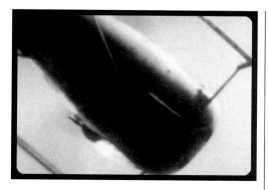

Astrid across a field in Episode 5.

One seeming location that didn't actually exist was Astrid's beachside bungalow, seen in the first episode. Instead of utilising a real building, director Barry Letts and designer Christopher Pemsel planned the layout of the studio set for the interior of the bungalow and, in advance of filming, had a window and a couple of wall flats constructed which were then taken down to Climping. The structure was erected near the beach and the camera placed inside, looking out of the window, to create the impression of a genuine building.

As Troughton, Hines and Watling couldn't be on hand for all four days' filming at Climping Beach (due to rehearsals for the fourth episode of The Ice Warriors), scenes of the Doctor/Salamander, Jamie and Victoria in long shot were achieved with the actors' doubles for this story, Peter Diamond, Richard Halifax and Sarah Lisemore, the wife of production assistant Martin Lisemore.

Barry Letts: 'Sarah, Richard and Peter represented our heroes whenever they were far enough away from camera for us not to twig. Patrick, Debbie and Fraser, for example, did not go up in the helicopter. We saw their doubles run over, get in and be borne away. Then we cut to the close shots of the real actors inside. In fact, I remember that we intended to do the closer shots inside the chopper in a mock-up in the studio, but it was so palpably a fake that we had to have an extra day's filming at the helicopter's home base, in the actual machine, with a blue skycloth as a background draped over the side of a prop van.'

For one long shot of the Doctor climbing into Astrid's helicopter, Troughton was replaced by director's assistant, Patricia Stern.

Walpole Park, situated immediately behind Ealing Studios, was used to film a brief shot of Richard Halifax (who doubled for Frazer Hines) walking towards a park bench. This short piece of film was later used in the studio during the recording of Episode 2 on 9 December as a back-projection for a scene involving Jamie meeting up with Victoria and Astrid at a park in Hungary. Several brief shots were then filmed around the nearby Villiers House, a BBC-owned building, which negated the need to pay any extra facility fees.

Comment

For the first and only time in Doctor Who's history, the TARDIS lands in Australia. Naturally unable to afford the tickets to film the opening antipodean scenes, Barry Letts decided to shoot all the beach sequences in the more domestic setting of West Sussex. However convincing or otherwise the sand dunes at Climping may have been, no doubt viewers' eyes were diverted by the use of a hovercraft and, for the first time on the programme, a helicopter – two rather flashy modes of transport for a programme that hadn't seen anything much more exotic than a dustcart up to this point. Letts certainly gets this tale of political double-dealing off to a very impressive start.

THE WEB OF FEAR

(tx 3 February to 9 March 1968)

The Story

Escaping from a strange web in space, the TARDIS lands in a seemingly deserted London Underground to discover that the Great Intelligence has invaded the capital, strangling the city with a nebulous fungus and its reactivated robot Yeti. The Doctor, Jamie and Victoria meet up again with Professor Travers who, together with his daughter Anne, is working with the army to defeat the alien menace. The Doctor discovers that the whole invasion has been set up to lure him to Earth so that the Intelligence can drain him of his knowledge. The Doctor sabotages the Intelligence's mind-draining machine, but Jamie's noble interference ruins the Doctor's plans, sending the Intelligence back into space.

The Locations

1. T J Poupart Ltd, Sheldon Street, Covent Garden, London, WC2[10]
2. Ealing Film Studios Backlot, Ealing Green, Ealing, London, W5

Shooting Schedule

EPISODE 4

▶ **Lethbridge-Stewart, Blake and Soldiers move up street**
TJ Poupart Ltd – Yard // 17 December 1967

▶ **Soldiers stop at road junction and enter alley (cut)**
TJ Poupart Ltd – Yard // 17 December 1967

▶ **Soldiers battle Yeti in yard**
TJ Poupart Ltd – Yard **//** 17 December 1967
▶ **Soldiers battle Yeti in yard**
TJ Poupart Ltd – Yard **//** 14 January 1968
▶ **Lethbridge-Stewart, Blake and Soldier**
Ealing Film Studios Backlot **//** 20 December 1967

The Facts

The main location showpiece of the story was to be the army's over-land battle with the Yeti that would take up nearly a quarter of Episode 4. The location chosen for this sequence was the area around the yard of T J Poupart Ltd, one of the main traders in Covent Garden. The cast and crew arrived on location at 8.30 am on the morning of Sunday 17 December 1967 with filming due to begin at 9.00 am, utilising two 35mm cameras and one hand-held camera. However, by the time dusk had fallen during the afternoon, the sequence was still not complete. So two days later, on Tuesday the 19th, production assistant Gareth Gwenlan wrote to Mr Heath, the Transport Manager at Poupart, to ask if the production team could make use of their facilities again on Sunday 14 January 1968. Permission was duly granted and the same team returned to the location to complete the scenes, with the exception of cameraman Alan Jonas and sound recordist Jack Gatland, who were replaced by Jimmy Court and Les Collins respectively. Jeremy King also replaced Colin Warman as one of the attacking Yeti. A two-page listing held in the production file for the story indicates how much of the sequence still remained to be filmed on 14 January, with some 34 shots scheduled to be completed over a total of 12 different set-ups.

Nicholas Courtney (Colonel Lethbridge-Stewart): 'I do remember having to calm [director] Douglas Camfield down on one occasion because we were using a lot of real equipment like bazookas, rifles and such and at one point, as he was trying to get the shots in quickly, Douglas discovered he'd positioned me directly behind a bazooka. If I'd stayed there, I'd have had my middle blown out. When this suddenly dawned on him, just in time, he got a bit edgy.'[11]

One location insert left intact in the script, but never transmitted, is a 19-second scene intended to be shown after the Doctor convinces Captain Knight to take him to the surface for some vital spares. As scripted, the scene an as follows: LETHBRIDGE and his MEN are running along a side street. As they approach a road junction, LETHBRIDGE halts them. He peers cautiously up and down. He gives a signal and they all sprint across the road and enter an alley opposite.

Unused Locations

Natural History Museum – The original intention

Above: Stuntman Tim Condren surrounded by two Yeti at P J Poupart's Yard, Covent Garden, on 14 January 1968.

was to shoot all the opening scenes showing the reactivation of the Yeti at the Natural History Museum during the evening of Monday 18 December (later moved to Thursday 21 December), once the building had closed to the public. It was estimated that the required scenes would be completed within a period of four to six hours, and a six-seater chauffeur-driven car was duly organised to transport the actors from Television Centre at 5.00 pm, drive them to the museum, and then collect them again shortly after midnight. Actor Desmond Cullum Jones was contracted to appear in these scenes as a commissionaire, but his role was terminated when the decision was taken to shoot all the museum scenes in the more controlled environment of Ealing Studios on 3 January 1968.[12]

As a result, two alterations were made to the script of Episode 3. During Travers' conversation with the Doctor in the laboratory, the script was amended from 'I gave one of the Yeti to the Natural History Museum' to '…a private collector named Silverstein' – though neither version was used in the transmitted episode. In a later scene, when Knight is briefing the Doctor, the script indicates that photographs of the museum would have been seen among the slides projected during the sequence. Due to the loss of the episode, it is no longer possible to state whether these slides were replaced with other landmarks (see Photographed Locations). However, Knight's dialogue was amended to delete a direct reference to the museum.

Aldwych Underground Station – On 7 November 1967, Gareth Gwenlan wrote to K G Pope, the Chief Press Officer of the London Transport Board, to formally ask permission to film at two locations on the Underground network. The first was the platform and a section of the tunnel at Aldwych Station on

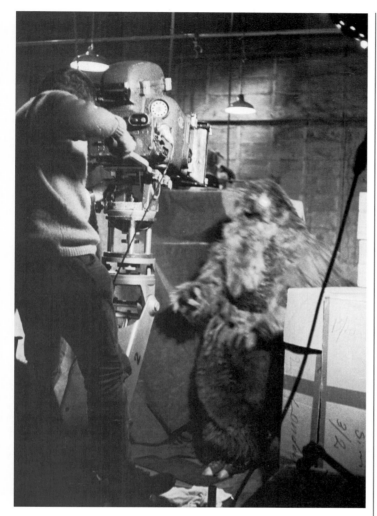

Above: The Yeti attack from Episode 4 of The Web of Fear is shot at Ealing Film Studios on 20 December 1967. Filming began in Covent Garden.

Friday 15 December.

Aldwych had been built as a small off-shoot of the Piccadilly line, but within ten years of its opening in 1907, its usage had fallen to such a point that one of its two platforms was taken out of service. Subsequently, the tunnel leading to Platform B was closed and the rails lifted, and later Platform A began operating only during peak times.[13] When the original lifts needed replacement in 1994, it was decided that the £3 million cost couldn't be justified and the station was finally closed. However, due to its unusual position at the dead end of a short spur line, Aldwych has found itself being used by many television and feature film crews needing to shoot in the London Underground. In recent years, the station has featured in such films as Patriot Games as well as the BBC's own production of Neil Gaiman's fantasy, Neverwhere.

Covent Garden Underground Station – The second location on the London Underground that the BBC hoped to use was the exterior of the booking hall and the gate of Covent Garden Station, the filming of which was slated to be done between 8.30 and 11.00 am on Sunday 17 December, the one day that the station would be closed during the week to the public.

Photographed Locations

On 28 December 1967, Gareth Gwenlan wrote an internal memo to Hugh Tosh asking him to supply photographs of any six of the following London landmarks which would be used during Captain Knight's slide briefing during Episode 3:

- Steps of St Paul's Cathedral
- Lions at Trafalgar Square
- Buckingham Palace
- Tower Bridge
- Westminster Abbey
- Tower of London
- Admiralty Arch
- Courtyard of the Houses of Parliament
- Downing Street

Gwenlan's memo continued: 'The object is that we shall later superimpose a Yeti on each photograph but it is absolutely essential that the London scene should look completely deserted. I should be grateful if you could complete the stills by Monday 15th January and as soon as they are ready I will arrange a photograph session for the Yeti.'

Comment

One of Douglas Camfield's greatest strengths as a director was his handing of action sequences, into which he would inject vast amounts of energy and excitement, and it seems that this was also the case for the one location sequence which finally made it into The Web of Fear – a sequence which took a full two days to film. It's interesting to speculate how different the final story might have looked if all Camfield's location plans had come to fruition. David Myerscough-Jones' studio sets are of such a high quality that it may well have looked no different at all.

FURY FROM THE DEEP

(tx 16 March to 20 April 1968)

The Story

Landing in the sea off the English coast, the travellers are arrested after they are seen tampering with a gas

Left: Filming at a cold and wet Botony Bay for Fury from the Deep.

pipeline belonging to the Euro Sea Gas Organisation (ESGO). Concerned by the unexplained fluctuations in the gas pressure, employees of the company appeal to Chief Robson to examine the cause of the problem – a problem that he steadfastly refuses to acknowledge. The Doctor discovers that the pipeline is being blocked by sentient seaweed, which is gradually taking control of ESGO staff-members. Accidentally discovering the weed's aversion to high-pitched noise, the Doctor manages to defeat the invasion by means of Victoria's amplified screams. Traumatised by the experience, Victoria elects to stay behind while the Doctor and Jamie continue their travels.

The Locations

1. Botony Bay, Kingsgate, Kent
2. Red Sands Sea Fort, Thames Estuary
3. Denham Aerodrome, Tilehouse Lane, Denham Green, Buckinghamshire

Shooting Schedule

EPISODE 1
▸▸ TARDIS lands on the sea
Botony Bay // 5 February 1968
▸▸ Doctor, Jamie and Victoria arrive on beach
Botony Bay // 4 February 1968

EPISODE 2
▸▸ Gas burning off at pipeline
Denham Aerodrome // 12 February 1968

EPISODE 3
▸▸ Robson watches Maggie Harris walk into the sea
Botony Bay // 6 February 1968

EPISODE 4
▸▸ Harris talks to Robson on beach
Botony Bay // 6 February 1968

EPISODE 5
▸▸ Robson carries Victoria out of base to mini-moke
Botony Bay // 4 February 1968
▸▸ Robson drives Victoria to helicopter
Botony Bay // 4-6 February 1968
▸▸ Monitor – Robson's helicopter takes off
Botony Bay // 4-6 February 1968
▸▸ Robson talks to the Doctor on the RT
Botony Bay // 4-6 February 1968
▸▸ Robson looks around while flying the helicopter
Botony Bay // 4-6 February 1968
▸▸ The Doctor and Jamie race to the helicopter
Botony Bay // 4-6 February 1968
▸▸ Robson turns the helicopter
Botony Bay // 4-6 February 1968

➤ **Robson's helicopter descends towards the rig**
Red Sands Sea Fort // 4-6 February 1968

➤ **Doctor's helicopter veers towards the rig**
Red Sands Sea Fort // 4-6 February 1968

➤ **Doctor and Jamie leave the helicopter**
Botony Bay or Denham Aerodrome // 4-6 or 12
February 1968

EPISODE 6

➤ **Doctor, Jamie and Victoria escape from the rig**
Botony Bay or Denham Aerodrome // 4-6 or 12
February 1968

➤ **Helicopter hovers some distance from the rig**
Red Sands Sea Fort // 4-6 February 1968

➤ **Doctor, Jamie and Victoria make for
Robson's helicopter**
Botony Bay or Denham Aerodrome // 4-6 or 12
February 1968

➤ **Foam covered rig**
Red Sands Sea Fort // 4-6 February 1968

➤ **Doctor's helicopter takes off from rig**
Botony Bay // 4-6 February 1968

➤ **Doctor, Jamie and Victoria in cockpit**
Botony Bay or Denham Aerodrome // 4-6 or 12
February 1968

➤ **Doctor's helicopter veers dangerously towards the sea**
Red Sands Sea Fort // 4-6 February 1968

➤ **Doctor tries to gain control of the helicopter**
Botony Bay or Denham Aerodrome // 4-6 or 12
February 1968

➤ **Helicopter levels out**
Red Sands Sea Fort // 4-6 February 1968

➤ **Doctor smiles confidently at Jamie and Victoria**
Botony Bay or Denham Aerodrome // 4-6 or 12
February 1968

➤ **Doctor and Jamie leave Victoria on the beach**
Botony Bay // 6 February 1968

➤ **Monitor – Victoria waves goodbye**
Botony Bay // 6 February 1968

➤ **TARDIS leaves**
Botony Bay // 5 February 1968

The Facts

One of the first problems faced by the production team working on Fury from the Deep was to find a suitable location that could represent the off-shore ESGO gas platform, which would appear as the foam-covered nerve centre of the weed monster's attack in the final two episodes of the story. Following a meeting between director Hugh David and his production assistant Michael Briant, it was decided that one possible solution to the problem could be found in the abandoned sea forts located in the Thames estuary.

Designed by Guy Maunsell, the army sea forts had been constructed to protect the estuary from German attack during World War II. Built in 1943 at Gravesend in Kent, a total of three forts were constructed and situated at Red Sands, Shivering Sands and the Nore.

Following an initial recce in a light aircraft by both David and Briant, the decision was made that the best platform to film around would be that at Red Sands, which had been vacated by the pirate radio station, Radio 390, the previous year.[14]

Michael Briant: 'It was very difficult from a fixed-wing aircraft which had height flying restrictions to see the fort properly, so it was necessary for me to do another recce. So I went down to Denham, got into a Hughes 300 helicopter with the pilot, Mike Smith, flew out to Margate and we navigated our way out into the Thames Estuary to the Red Sands fort and landed on the top. It was quite a risky thing to do because these World War II gun installations were very rusty with lots of rotten wood and rusty metalwork. The walkways between the legs were in a considerable state of disrepair. So Mike landed rather gingerly and he was horrified when I told him I wanted to walk round all six of the platform tops. So he shut the helicopter down and the two of us explored all six tops of the fort. What we were looking for was one of the platforms that was flat, safe, secure on which we could use the foam-making machine. So we looked around and decided which platform to use. We then climbed down inside it and there were the remnants of Radio 390. So we climbed down to the bottom of the fort and there was a trapdoor which led to a steel ladder going right down the leg, so it theoretically meant I could get the water up through that trap-door to the foam machine.

'On getting back to base however, our visual effects man, Peter Day, told me that you could only pump water to a certain height. After that, it didn't matter what size the pump was, it would always pump dry. Unfortunately, the height of the lowest workable platform for a pump down to sea level was something like 35-40 feet. So whether the tide was in or not, it was going to be far too high above sea level. So I had a problem, because for the amount of foam Hugh wanted to cover the top of this fort, I was going to need to get several hundred gallons of water up to the platform. The other problem was that these foam machines don't really work very well with salt water. You really need fresh water. We could use sea water, but it meant that we had to use double the quantity because of the salt's effect on the foam. So instead of needing to pump up 200-300 gallons, I would need 600 gallons of salt water. So now we had a structure that looked like a rig, it had got a safe flat top that we could put the foam machine on and we were surrounded by salt water, which I couldn't pump up anyway because it was too high. I had a big problem.'

Several options were considered. Briant contacted a local tug company who suggested that if several inflatable plastic swimming pools were placed on the top of the platform, they could fill them from the tugs at sea level using their high-pressure hoses. The costs involved in this method were deemed too high and the idea was abandoned.

Briant then booked a BBC scene crew and, together with a supply of fresh water in five-gallon containers, took them out from Whitstable in a fishing boat to the leg of the sea fort. However, when they arrived, the sea swell around the fort made climbing onboard too hazardous. 'I explained my dilemma to the fishermen who had taken us out to the fort and they said, "That's not a problem. We'll take the fishing boat out on a calm day and carry the drums up there. You just leave us all the containers and we'll take up the fresh water for you." And we did a deal that was quite financially favourable.'

The other main location required for the story was a deserted stretch of beach, which was found at Botony Bay, Kingsgate, two miles east of Margate.

The day after recording Episode 4 of The Web of Fear at Lime Grove, filming began on Sunday 4 February 1968 amidst freezing temperatures and rain.

Margot Hayhoe (assistant floor manager): 'I remember that it was bitterly cold. I don't think I've ever been so cold and there was a very heavy wind blowing as well. When I arrived on the first day there was a hut that was supposed to have been erected,[15] and every single time they tried to put it up, the wind blew it straight down again!'

One of the first scenes to be completed was that of the Doctor, Jamie and Victoria arriving at the beach in a rubber dinghy. Once again, however, things did not go exactly as planned.

Michael Briant: 'Hugh wanted the TARDIS to land at sea. He said, "Why does it always arrive conveniently on land? Why doesn't it land on the sea? And if it lands on the sea, of course it will float. And then they'll have to come ashore in a rubber boat." And I was going, "Rubber boats! Oh no, not rubber boats!" "Yes, that's great," Hugh said. "Pat's a sailor, he knows about boats. We'll have an outboard motor and Pat can drive the rubber dinghy."

'Hugh asked if we could see the boat inflate in the studio. Having owned a few dinghys, I knew that they don't inflate very quickly. You stand there with a foot pump and it takes about 15 minutes – not very Doctor Who. So I got onto Avon Dinghys and said, "Listen, we need to arrange for a dingy to inflate in about 15 seconds. Can it be done with compressed air?" And they said, "If you inflate it at that speed, the compressed air will turn it all to ice."

Above: The miniature TARDIS prop on the Kingsgate clifftop with the attached hanging wires (running from the lamp to the two reels) used to suspend it from the helicopter.

'So we said goodbye to that idea and it was decided that it would be too slow for Pat to row, so we thought we'd get an outboard motor. Avon was still providing us with the dinghy but the outboard motor was going to come from another company. It was arranged that it was all going to be delivered, brand-new, to the location for us, and we were going to operate it ourselves. So come the day of filming, there was the dinghy, there was the motor, but Avon had forgotten to pack the outboard motor bracket, so we couldn't attach the two together. So we had to have Pat row the dinghy ashore anyway!'

One person who made his mark on the cast and crew early in the production was Captain Mike Smith, a helicopter pilot from Gregory Air Services at Denham Aerodrome, who had been employed as an extra at six guineas a day to fly the helicopters used during the filming.

Margot Hayhoe: 'He had such a character! I well remember the first time that I met him, which was at the bar of the hotel[16] we were staying at in Margate. Mike had this party trick whereby he would eat a wine glass. I remember Victor Maddern [who played Chief Robson] sitting at the bar and asking "Who is that man who's eating the glass?" and Michael Briant telling him, "Oh, that's Mike Smith. He's the pilot of the helicopter." And Victor went rather pale and very quiet because the next day he was due to fly in the helicopter with Mike Smith…'

Above: The Hughes 300 helicopter escapes from the foam-covered rig in Episode 6.

Above right: Victoria (Deborah Watling) waves goodbye to the Doctor and Jamie at the end of Fury from the Deep.

To accomplish the TARDIS' landing on the sea, a small three-foot model of the police box was suspended from the bottom of the Hughes 300 helicopter that would be seen on-screen in the later episodes.

Michael Briant: 'Mike took off in his helicopter, flew 100 yards out to sea, and lowered the TARDIS on the end of its piano wire which kept the helicopter out of the top of the frame. But as it landed on the sea, it flopped straight onto its side. Although the baby TARDIS was made of wood, we hadn't worked out that it wasn't going to float upright. So what Mike had to try and do was hover the helicopter, keeping the piano wire taught, but it simply didn't work. So he flew back and said, "Look, I need someone to talk me down." So I foolishly said, "I'll do that." So I climbed in the helicopter with Mike, sat in the seat beside him and flew out there. The problem was that from the seats you couldn't see the model TARDIS suspended by wire from the centre of the helicopter. So I said, "Mike, I can't see it." So he said, "Right, take off the seat belt, climb out onto the skid and talk me down from there." So I said, "Okay, right you are." So I climbed out, hovering at 300 feet, stood on the skid of the helicopter and talked him down! And I suddenly realised where I was. Connected to the helicopter by only a headset, standing on the skid, holding on with one hand, 300 feet above sea level. Madness! But Mike was a great guy and a great pilot. He knew I was perfectly safe, he would have never asked me to do anything…What am I saying? The guy was out of his tree! He was the craziest pilot I've ever met! Nicest guy, brilliant pilot! So we got the shot and, with rather hot, clammy palms, because I'm really terrified of heights, we flew back and landed!'

To show the Doctor's rather uncertain mastery in flying the helicopter as he escapes from the gas rig in Episode 6, pilot Mike Smith was asked to perform some rather dangerous stunts. According to Michael Briant, 'What we asked Mike Smith to do was fly the Hughes 300 – which had, say, a 20-foot wing span – in between the legs of a fort which were about 30 feet apart, meaning he had a clearance of something like five or six feet on either side. Madness! Absolute madness! Very dangerous and totally against the aviation laws. I remember discussing this with Mike and saying, "Look, we're not forc-

ing you to do this. It's very much optional." And he said, "No, no, no. That's all right. I can do it." Mike was nervous though. He told me later that it was about the most dangerous thing he'd ever done in his life. So he flew out and Hugh filmed the sequence from the other helicopter and they landed back, having achieved everything they wanted to achieve. Mike was on a real adrenaline high.

'We finished filming that day and we went back to the hotel in Margate and Mike was in an amazing mood. Hugh had gone back to London but most of the production people were still there for the night and Mike Smith came into the lounge of this rather elegant hotel, a beautiful chandelier in the middle of the ceiling, nice club armchairs, quite a dignified place. Mike came in and ordered a bottle of brandy and a crate of champagne and said, "This is all on me. We're going to celebrate the achievement of flying a 20-foot wing span helicopter through a 30-foot gap." The champagne and brandy arrived, so we all had a mixture of champagne and brandy. We finished it and then he said, "Right, another crate of champagne and another bottle of brandy." I was sitting in my armchair thinking, "I am a BBC production manager, I have some responsibility for this…" That said, it was a great evening, a lot of laughter, a lot of fun. But none the less we were all getting quite high on this mixture of brandy and champagne. At that point, Mike pulled me over backwards in my armchair, splashed me on the floor and thrust another glass in my hand saying, "Drink this." I said, "Mike, thanks very much but I really think…" He said, "Michael, don't be so BBC! You've got to live a little, you've got to risk a little, you've got to enjoy life a little."

'And then he said, "You know, Michael, there's something I've never done. I've never swung like Errol Flynn from a chandelier, but tonight…" And he leapt up on the table, this tall guy with a little goatee beard, jumped in the air, grabbed the chandelier, swung across the room and the chandelier came out of the ceiling and three-quarters of the ceiling came down on top of him. What a laugh! There was Mike, covered in white plaster, sitting in the middle of this lounge floor. He wasn't hurt, which was the main thing, and I was left with the slightly embarrassing situation where I had to apologise to the hotel. But they didn't seem to mind. And it had been a great evening.'

Another 'victim' of Mike Smith's flying was Margot Hayhoe. 'While we were on location, Hugh David wanted some props that were up on the top of the cliff brought down to the beach. And the quickest way to get them down was in the helicopter. So I got in this helicopter with Mike Smith and when it took off, I screamed so loud! I'd never been in a helicopter before and, of course, it had one of those little bubble cockpits, so as it took off the earth disappeared from beneath your feet. I screamed and Mike thought this was terribly funny, so he started to wave the helicopter around and by the time I got down to the beach I was a shaking jelly. Everybody else found it terribly amusing, though!'

No doubt due to the eccentric antics of Mike Smith, Patrick Troughton refused to fly in the helicopter himself and, as a result, a single day's filming was completed on 12 February at Air Gregory's base, Denham Aerodrome in Buckinghamshire. With the helicopter on the ground and its blades rotating, low angle shots of the Doctor, Jamie and Victoria were accomplished which would be intercut later with the footage of the helicopter in flight.[17] Also on this day, an insert sequence of burning gas being vented from the beach pipeline was filmed.

Comment

It really is a great pity that Fury from the Deep no longer exists in the BBC's archives, as it seems that Hugh David planned and shot some spectacular material around Botony Bay and the Red Sands Sea Fort. The complexities of filming around the fort with two helicopters is, in itself, quite surprising, as visual effects designer Peter Day had already suggested to David that the shots could be accomplished by using a miniature. But the director was obviously committed to producing something both real and visually exciting.

THE DOMINATORS
(tx 10 August to 7 September 1968)

The Story

Seeking radioactive fuel for their space fleet, two Dominators, Rago and Toba, land on the pacifist planet of Dulkis. Using their robotic servants, the Quarks, the Dominators begin to drill through the crust of the planet with the purpose of dropping an atomic seed capsule into the heart of Dulkis, turning it into a radioactive mass that the Dominators can exploit. As the seeding device is dropped, the Doctor manages to intercept it and places the device inside the Dominators' spaceship. It duly explodes, destroying the invaders and saving the planet.

The Locations

1. Gerrards Cross Sand and Gravel Quarry, Wapsey's Wood, Oxford Road, Gerrards Cross, Buckinghamshire
2. Olley (Wrotham) Sand Pit, Trottiscliffe, Kent.

Shooting Schedule

EPISODE 1
▸▸ Dominator's spaceship lands

Above: Two Quarks in the sandpit at Gerrards Cross.

Olley Sand Pit // 28 April 1968
▸▸ Wahed, Etnin and Tolata run from Cully and die
Olley Sand Pit // 28 April 1968
▸▸ TARDIS materialises
Olley Sand Pit // 28 April 1968
▸▸ Quarks destroy Cully's ship
Gerrards Cross Quarry // 25 April 1968
▸▸ Doctor and Jamie discover Dominator's ship
Olley Sand Pit // 28 April 1968
▸▸ Toba and Quarks spot the Doctor and Jamie
Gerrards Cross Quarry // Date Unknown

EPISODE 2
▸▸ Balan, Kando and Teel outside Dominator ship
Gerrards Cross Quarry // 25 April 1968
▸▸ Toba, Rago and Quarks
Gerrards Cross Quarry // 25 April 1968
▸▸ Toba orders the Quarks to recharge
Gerrards Cross Quarry // Date Unknown
▸▸ Quarks begin to destroy Survey Unit
Gerrards Cross Quarry // 25 April 1968

EPISODE 3
▸▸ Rago stops Toba destroying Survey Unit
Gerrards Cross Quarry // 25 April 1968
▸▸ Rago orders Toba to bring survivors to him
Gerrards Cross Quarry // 25 April 1968
▸▸ Quarks herd prisoners up hillside
Gerrards Cross Quarry // 25 April 1968
▸▸ Quark explodes and Toba orders museum destroyed
Gerrards Cross Quarry // 25 April 1968

Above: The Doctor was played by Chris Jeffries for the location filming of The Dominators.

EPISODE 4

▸ Jamie and Cully observe the Quarks
  Gerrards Cross Quarry // 25 April 1968
▸ Jamie and Cully attack a Quark
  Olley Sand Pit // 28 April 1968

EPISODE 5

▸ Jamie and Cully chased by the Quarks
  Gerrards Cross Quarry // 25 April 1968
▸ Jamie and Cully attack the Quarks
  Gerrards Cross Quarry // 25 April 1968
▸ Quarks injure Cully
  Olley Sand Pit // 28 April 1968
▸ Doctor runs to Dominator ship with seed device
  Olley Sand Pit // 28 April 1968

▸▸ To complete scenes not finished on 25 and 28 April[18]
  Gerrards Cross Quarry // 29 April 1968
▸▸ Scenes with Jamie, Cully and Quarks[19]
  Gerrards Cross Quarry // 2 May 1968
▸▸ Scenes with Toba, Rago and Quarks[20]
  Gerrards Cross Quarry // 3 May 1968

The Facts

It had originally been intended that Thursday 2 May would be used for filming insert sequences on Stage 2 at Ealing Film Studios. However, due to various scenes not being completed during the original location shoot, two extra days at Gerrards Cross had to be included in order to finish all the required exterior scenes.

Although the Doctor appears briefly in a number of the location scenes for The Dominators, he is not actually played by Patrick Troughton. For these scenes, shot on 25 and 28 April, Troughton was doubled by Chris Jeffries. The scenes featuring Jeffries show the Doctor and Jamie finding the Dominators' spaceship for the first time (for which Troughton provided dubbed dialogue), the Doctor being forced to join the prisoners as the Quarks lead them across the island and the Doctor running to place the seed device in the Dominators' spaceship before take-off.

The opening shots of the story feature the landing of the Dominators' spaceship on Dulkis. For these scenes, the spaceship was painted onto a sheet of glass and positioned in front of the camera as it tracked over the landscape.

On 3 May 1968, a small article appeared in the Bucks Free Press, headlined 'Dr Who at the Dragon'. This article is something of a mystery. According to the report, on Saturday 27 April Patrick Troughton and an accompanying film crew, who had been filming in the hills around Princes Risborough, Buckinghamshire, called in for lunch at the George and Dragon pub located in the village. Also with the unit was actress Frances Bennett, who was well known at the time for playing Mary Augusta 'Gussie' Brown in the BBC soap opera Compact. The article concluded by stating that, later that same day, the crew visited the Red Lion pub in Whiteleaf[21] at the conclusion of filming.

However, there is no record of any filming for Doctor Who being done on that date, falling as it does between the recording of Episode 4 of The Wheel in Space on the Friday and the second day of location filming for The Dominators on the Sunday. Neither is there any indication in the BBC's files that either Troughton or Bennett was ever contracted to work on another production that day.

The vast majority of the Olley sand pit no longer exists, as the junction of the M20/M26 has been built over the top of it. However, Westfields Farm, which was used as the production base during the day, still stands next to the London-bound carriageway while Buckland Olley still operate a small sand excavation on the other side of the motorway.

Ouch!

During the filming of his last scene on location at Gerrards Cross, Arthur Cox who played the rebel Cully, twisted his ankle jumping over a sandhill, badly damaging his ligaments. This resulted in his ankle being in plaster for several weeks. As a consequence, director Morris Barry had to ensure that Cox was shot only from the waist up during the scenes set aboard Cully's ship in the first episode, filmed in advance at Ealing on 30 April and 1 May. By the time Episode 1 was recorded on 17 May, Cox had had the plaster removed and was able to walk normally again.

Comment

Having so successfully used the Gerrards Cross quarry for the filming of The Tomb of the Cybermen the year before, Morris Barry chose to return to the location in order to film large sections of The Dominators. And once again he makes a sterling job of it. Especially worthy of note is the destruction of Cully's ship, which is gloriously huge and spectacular. Why Barry felt it necessary to also spend a day shooting material at Olley's pit in Kent is unclear and in many ways the scenes shot there are the least satisfactory of the location filming, as the ground is covered in the tracks of the various heavy vehicles using the quarry.

THE MIND ROBBER

(tx 14 September to 12 October 1968)

The Story

Trying to avoid being engulfed by lava on Dulkis, the Doctor is forced to take the TARDIS out of time and space. Arriving in a white void, the Doctor, Jamie and fellow travelling companion Zoe come under mental attack. Just as they think that they are about to escape, the TARDIS disintegrates. The travellers then find themselves in a strange land populated by fictional characters and creatures such as unicorns, Lemuel Gulliver, Rapunzel and Medusa. The land of fiction is under the control of the 'Master', an English writer from 1926, who himself is under the control of a Master Brain computer. The computer wishes to conquer the Earth, so the Doctor engages it in a battle of wills, fought out by various fictional characters. During the battle, the Master Brain is destroyed, freeing the Master and returning the travellers to the reformed TARDIS.

The Locations

1. Harrison's Rocks, Birchden Wood, Groombridge, Tunbridge Wells, East Sussex.
2. Kenley Aerodrome, Kenley, near Croydon, Surrey.

Shooting Schedule

EPISODE 2

▸▸ **Doctor, Jamie and Zoe encounter the Unicorn (2/3)**
Kenley Aerodrome // 9 June 1968

EPISODE 3

▸▸ **Jamie climbs cliff to escape Toy Soldier**
Harrison's Rocks // 9 June 1968

The Facts

The short sequence of Jamie escaping from the Toy Soldier was filmed at Harrison's Rocks, a popular climbing venue owned in 1968 by the Bowles Outdoor Pursuits Centre. Apart from Frazer Hines, the only other actor required for the filming was his cousin, Ian Hines, playing the soldier.

To realise the charging unicorn required for the cliffhanger to Episode 2, the production team contacted Essex-based horse trainer Joan Rosaire, who agreed to supply her experienced stage and television palomi-

Left: Goldy the Wonder Horse, complete with horn and beard, at Kenley Aerodrome on 9 June 1968.

no, Goldy the Wonder Horse. As the focus was to be on the unicorn rather than the background, the decision was taken to film the sequence at night in an open and deserted area for which the RAF aerodrome at Kenley proved ideal.

On arriving at Kenley, director David Maloney realised that he had a potential problem on his hands. The horse, which he assumed would be white, was actually a mixture of cream and brown. In a bid to lighten the horse's appearance, Rosaire and the make-up department covered Goldy in white blanco, obtained from the local RAF station. Whiskers were then stuck to its chin as well as a polystyrene horn on its forehead, which the horse objected to and tried to shake off at every opportunity.

Joan Rosaire: 'Filming commenced at Kenley at midnight. The cameraman, his assistant and myself all stood on a very small platform fastened to the back of a vehicle with a huge spotlight attached to it. The idea was for the 'unicorn' to gallop alongside, appearing to chase after the Doctor. After one practise run we then went for a take – it was perfect. Goldy was a super showman! It was only then that we discovered they hadn't loaded the camera! So we did another two takes and it was in the can. I then had to let him loose to gallop off, turn around, gallop back and do several rears. This was done in two takes and then we wrapped. I had thought that Goldy was a little restless at the end and discovered that, during the filming in the pitch black, a riding school that rented some of the land had turned a dozen or so horses out to graze. My horse was aware of this, even though the rest of us were not, but, professional as he was, he had performed as asked although he would dearly have loved to go and visit the other horses. And, as he was totally free, he could well have done so.'

Comment

Once again, The Mind Robber is a Doctor Who story featuring an absolute minimum of location material. While

Right: Patrick Troughton and Frazer Hines are filmed on the railway tracks surrounding the Guinness Brewery at Park Royal on 11 September 1968.

The Locations

1. RAF Fairford, Fairford, Gloucestershire
2. Williamstrip Farm, Coln St Aldwyn, Gloucestershire
3. Hatherop Road, Coln St Aldwyn, Gloucestershire
4. Kingston Minerals, Kempsford Road, Kempsford, Gloucestershire
5. Associated British Maltsters, Wallingford, Oxfordshire
6. 18 St James' Gardens, Kensington, London, NW11
7. Peter's Hill, City, London, EC4
8. Knightrider Street, City, London, EC4
9. Moor Lane, City, London, EC2
10. Distaff Lane, City, London, EC4
11. St Nicholas Cole Abbey, Queen Victoria Street, City, London, EC4
12. Queen Victoria Street, City, London, EC4
13. Fore Street, City, London, EC2
14. TCC Condensers, Wales Farm Road, Ealing, London, W3
15. Princedale Road, Notting Hill, London, NW11
16. Heathfield Street, Notting Hill, London, NW11
17. Walmer Road, Notting Hill, London, NW11
18. Millbank Tower, Millbank, London, SW1
19. Guinness Brewery, Park Royal, London, NW10
20. Maida Hill Tunnel, Regent's Canal, Lisson Grove, London, NW8
21. Cumberland Terrace, Regent's Park, London, NW1
22. St Paul's Churchyard, City, London, EC4
23. Australia House, Strand, London, WC2
24. Denham Aerodrome, Tilehouse Lane, Denham Green, Buckinghamshire

the story could have lent itself to more exterior work had David Maloney wished, the only material that actually needed to be shot on location were the scenes featuring the unicorn, which would have proved difficult, if not impossible, to achieve within the confines of the studio.

THE INVASION

(tx 2 November to 21 December 1968)

The Story

The TARDIS narrowly misses being struck by a missile fired from the moon and lands in England. The Doctor, Jamie and Zoe make their way to London in order to see Professor Travers, only to discover that both he and his daughter Anne are now in America. They meet Isobel Watkins, whose uncle appears to have gone missing while working for the giant electronics company International Electromatics. The Doctor discovers that Tobias Vaughn, the company's managing director, is in league with the Cybermen and together they are planning an invasion of Earth which will begin when people are rendered helpless by a hypnotic signal emanating from a micro-circuit inside all IE equipment. But Vaughn is also planning to double-cross the Cybermen in a bid to seize power for himself. The Doctor convinces Vaughn that the Cybermen must be defeated and while the United Nations Intelligence Taskforce (UNIT) battle against the invading forces, a missile destroys the orbiting Cyberman spaceship.

Shooting Schedule

EPISODE 1

▸▸ **TARDIS materialises in field**
Williamstrip Farm // 3 September 1968
▸▸ **Field and cows on TARDIS scanner**
Williamstrip Farm // 3 September 1968
▸▸ **Panorama of countryside**
Williamstrip Farm // 3 September 1968
▸▸ **Doctor, Jamie and Zoe exit TARDIS**
Williamstrip Farm // 3 September 1968
▸▸ **Doctor, Jamie and Zoe get lift in lorry**
Hatherop Road // 4 September 1968
▸▸ **Doctor's party dropped in London**
Princedale Road // 11 September 1968
▸▸ **Patrolman kills lorry driver**
Hatherop Road // 4 September 1968
▸▸ **Doctor and Jamie arrive at IE offices**
Millbank Tower // 7 September 1968
▸▸ **Benton and Tracy on roof**
Millbank Tower // 7 September 1968

➤➤ Benton and Tracy ready to obtain Doctor
Millbank Tower // 7 September 1968

➤➤ Doctor and Jamie leave IE offices
Millbank Tower // 7 September 1968

EPISODE 2

➤➤ UNIT car follows Doctor and Jamie
Walmer Road // 11 September 1968

➤➤ Doctor and Jamie cornered by UNIT cars
Heathfield Street // 11 September 1968

➤➤ UNIT car arrives at plane
RAF Fairford // 3 September 1968

➤➤ Zoe and Isobel arrive at IE offices
Millbank Tower // 7 September 1968

➤➤ Doctor and Jamie return to IE
Millbank Tower // 7 September 1968

➤➤ Doctor and Jamie in goods yard
Guinness Brewery // 11 September 1968

EPISODE 3

➤➤ Doctor, Jamie and Vaughn watch train leave
Guinness Brewery // 11 September 1968

➤➤ Doctor and company leave in car
Millbank Tower // 7 September 1968

➤➤ Car arrives at IE factory
Location Unknown // Date Unknown

➤➤ Helicopter tracks Vaughn's car
Kingston Minerals // 5 September 1968

➤➤ Doctor and company enter IE factory
Guinness Brewery // 11 September 1968

➤➤ Doctor and Jamie on roof and down fire escape
Associated British Maltsters // 6 September 1968

➤➤ Doctor and Jamie climb into goods van
Guinness Brewery // 11 September 1968

EPISODE 4

➤➤ IE guards take crates into building
Guinness Brewery // 11 September 1968

➤➤ Doctor and Jamie on roof are hailed by Vaughn
Associated British Maltsters // 6 September 1968

➤➤ Doctor and Jamie see Zoe and Isobel
Associated British Maltsters // 6 September 1968

➤➤ Jamie climbs down rope ladder
Associated British Maltsters // 6 September 1968

➤➤ Roof escape with helicopter
Associated British Maltsters // 6 September 1968

➤➤ Doctor's party climbs ladder into helicopter
Denham Aerodrome // Date Unknown

➤➤ Doctor and Jamie in canoe
Regent's Canal // 13 September 1968

EPISODE 5

➤➤ Doctor and Jamie in canoe

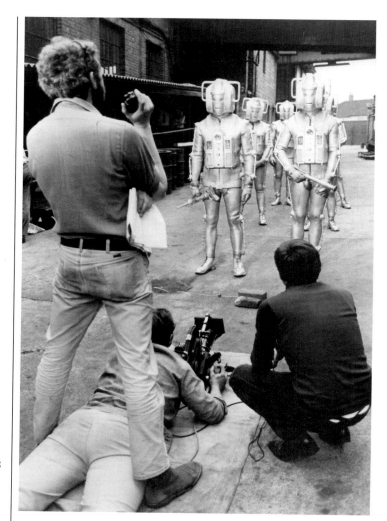

Regent's Canal // 13 September 1968

➤➤ Benton drops off Jamie, Zoe and Isobel
Moor Lane // 8 September 1968

➤➤ Policeman follows Isobel to manhole
Fore Street // 8 September 1968

EPISODE 6

➤➤ Turner arrives at manhole
Fore Street // 8 September 1968

➤➤ Jamie rescued from sewer
Fore Street // 8 September 1968

➤➤ Establishing shot – Peaceful London
Cumberland Terrace // 8 September 1968

➤➤ Establishing shot – Peaceful London
St Paul's Churchyard // 8 September 1968

➤➤ Establishing shot – Peaceful London
Australia House // 8 September 1968

**Above: Director
Douglas Camfield,
straddling camera-
man Alan Jonas,
prepares a further
shot at TCC
Condensers for
The Invasion.**

Above: Filming of the Cybermen's battle with UNIT at TCC Condensers is watched over by director Douglas Camfield and scriptwriter Derrick Sherwin.

➤➤ **Londoner collapses against grille**
Distaff Lane // 8 September 1968

➤➤ **Businessman clutches head**
St Nicholas Cole Abbey // 8 September 1968

➤➤ **Window cleaner hears Cyber-signal**
College of Arms // 8 September 1968

➤➤ **Cybermen burst from sewer**
Queen Victoria Street // 8 September 1968

➤➤ **Cybermen march down steps (6/7)**
St Peter's Hill // 8 September 1968

➤➤ **Cybermen march along pavement (6/7)**
Knightrider Street // 8 September 1968

EPISODE 7

➤➤ **Sergeant Walters arrives at Watkins' home**
St James' Gardens // 11 September 1968

➤➤ **Packer arrives at Watkins' home**
St James' Gardens // 11 September 1968

➤➤ **Doctor leaves Hercules in Land Rover**
RAF Fairford // 3 September 1968

EPISODE 8

➤➤ **UNIT battle Cybermen**
TCC Condensers // 9, 10 and 12 September 1969

➤➤ **TARDIS departs**
Williamstrip Farm // 3 September 1968

The Facts ➤➤

From The Invasion onwards, a week of shooting was allocated for each story in its own right, rather than overlapping to the previous story. This practice allowed for better use of the regular cast.

With a massive location shoot in front of him, the last thing that director Douglas Camfield needed was to have problems on his first morning of filming – but that's exactly what he faced. The plan had been to film

a number of scenes utilising the helicopter during the morning at RAF Fairford,[22] but when insurance difficulties arose and the helicopter didn't arrive, these scenes had to be postponed and the filming schedule for the day rethought.

One major piece of equipment made available to the production by the Royal Air Force was a Hercules transporter aircraft, which would be used to represent the exterior of UNIT's mobile HQ.

Geoffrey Cheshire (Tracy): 'I found Douglas to be one of those rare directors with whom one immediately felt both at ease and confident. As an illustration of this, we were filming at an RAF aerodrome, where one of my scenes required me to drive a Jaguar at top speed from one side of the airfield to the other, timed to arrive at the tailgate of a transport aircraft just as the ground crew positioned the ramps, so that the Jaguar could speed into the aircraft without slowing down, then stop within the length of the fuselage. You can imagine the tension, considering the possible financial and human consequences of bad timing or judgment. Of all people, Douglas should have been very, very worried, but at the end of each take, as I stopped the car literally within about 18 inches of the fuselage bulwark, I would see him smiling at me from where he had positioned himself, right on the spot where the car came to a halt. I will always remember his smiling face, which hid, so superbly, his undoubted concern.'[23]

With filming at RAF Fairford completed, the production team moved a few miles north to Williamstrip Farm at Coln St Aldwyn. For a fee of £30, farmer Clem Barton permitted the use of one of his fields in which all the TARDIS scenes were filmed. One sequence filmed during the day was the Episode 1 scene of the TARDIS becoming invisible, an effect that Camfield tried unsuccessfully to repeat while directing Terror of the Zygons in 1975.

Sue Willis (assistant floor manager): 'We were in a field miles from anywhere when lunchtime came. We'd arranged to have lunch in the farmhouse down the lane, but someone had to look after all the equipment, so I elected to stay behind. Shortly after, it started to rain and the only place I could shelter was actually in the TARDIS, so I put the camera equipment inside and sat down, listened to the rain on the roof and started to read a book. After a while, I heard something outside and thought it was one of the crew coming back. The TARDIS opened and this little man put his head round, and the look on his face as he saw this lady sitting in a telephone box in the middle of nowhere was wonderful!'

The last location outside London to be used for The Invasion was situated in Wallingford at the main building and grounds of Associated British Maltsters, which doubled for the country offices of International

Electromatics. The location was chosen primarily because it provided the production team with a tall, modern industrial block out in the countryside together with a set of railway sidings nearby which provided a visual link with the offices/railway scenes that would be filmed at the Guinness Brewery in London the following week.

The main sequences to be shot were the Doctor and Jamie's escape from the building along the roof in Episode 3 and their subsequent rescue of Zoe and Isobel in Episode 4. Filming was interrupted, however, by the Royal Air Force flying their old propeller-engined Argosies over the site, en route to the nearby airbase at RAF Benson.

As reported in the Oxford Mail,[24] during the lunch break Patrick Troughton and Wendy Padbury (who played Zoe) spent their time playing table tennis in the works canteen while Frazer Hines amused himself on the billiards table.

Douglas Camfield made an appearance in his own production during the filming of Episode 1 as the driver of the car that picks up the Doctor's party en route to London.

One location that the production team reputedly enjoyed visiting was the Guinness Brewery at Park Royal in London. Use was made of the director's entrance to the building and of the goods railway line running through the site.

Frazer Hines: 'We had a great Guinness lunch. Luckily, Patrick and I only had one thing to do after lunch. We had to do one look around a corner, and we couldn't manage it because every time we looked around the corner, we fell over. We'd had too much falling-over water, but it was only because we had no dialogue, that's the only reason we did it.'[25]

Several months later, Guinness sent Patrick Troughton a Christmas pudding filled with their famous product, but before he was able to enjoy it, it exploded in his agent's office!

Unused Locations

BBC Villiers House – The original three-page location breakdown for The Invasion indicates that an early contender for the IE laboratories seen in Episodes 3 and 4 was the BBC office building, Villiers House in Ealing, which Barry Letts had used the previous year in The Enemy of the World. The same document also indicates that it had originally been intended to use the exterior of two unnamed London Underground stations during the course of Episode 2.

Comment

Third Doctor Jon Pertwee would often say that there was nothing more frightening than finding a Yeti sitting on your loo in Tooting Bec, the point being that finding monsters in familiar surroundings was potentially far more frightening than encountering them on alien planets. This point is vividly illustrated in The Invasion, as the image of the Cybermen bursting out of the London sewers and appearing outside St Paul's Cathedral seems to have become ingrained in the memories of those viewers who watched Doctor Who in the 1960s. Likewise, the major battle sequence between UNIT and the Cybermen in the final episode is very satisfyingly handled. After seeing precious little of the Cybermen in the previous seven episodes, it's good that Camfield rewards his audience with some great action sequences at the end of the story.

THE KROTONS

(tx 28 December 1968 to 18 January 1969)

The Story

The TARDIS lands on the planet of the Gonds. The peaceful Gonds are ruled by the Krotons, alien creatures who exist in suspended animation in the form of a crystalline slurry within their spacecraft, the Dynotrope. Needing vast amounts of mental energy in order to reconstitute themselves, the Krotons have been educating the Gonds so that they can periodically take their two brightest students and drain them of their intelligence before disposing of their bodies. Registering the highest scores on the Krotons' learning machines, the Doctor and Zoe are ordered to enter the Dynotrope, where their mental energy finally reanimates the Krotons. Discovering they are made of tellurium, the Doctor works with the Gond scientist Beta in creating a form of sulphuric acid which ultimately dissolves the creatures.

The Locations

1. West of England Quarry, Malvern, Hereford and Worcestershire
2. Tank Quarry, North Malvern Road, Malvern, Hereford and Worcestershire

Shooting Schedule

EPISODE 1

▸▸ TARDIS arrives and travellers explore
Tank or West of England Quarry // 10-11 November 1968

EPISODE 2

▸▸ Monitor shot – Doctor and Zoe run from the Dynotrope
Tank or West of England Quarry // 10-11 November 1968

Above: A Kroton (Miles Northover) attempts to destroy the TARDIS in an abandoned location sequence.

The sequence of the Kroton attempting to destroy the TARDIS in Episode 3 was originally filmed in Malvern on Sunday 10 November. The footage was judged unsatisfactory and the scene was restaged in the studio when the final episode was recorded in Lime Grove D on 6 December.

Comment

The vast majority of the location material filmed for The Krotons was ultimately destined to be seen only on the Dynotrope monitors, which is rather a pity as the brief opening scenes showing the Doctor's party leaving the TARDIS and heading towards the Gond city are rather impressive, with the grey, rainy November day blending in rather well with the bleak granite quarry.

EPISODE 3

▸▸ Monitor shot – Doctor and Zoe walking
   Tank or West of England Quarry // 10-11 November 1968
▸▸ Doctor decided to go to the TARDIS
   Tank or West of England Quarry // 10-11 November 1968
▸▸ Monitor shot – Doctor and Zoe walking
   Tank or West of England Quarry // 10-11 November 1968
▸▸ Monitor shot – Doctor and Zoe enter the TARDIS
   Tank or West of England Quarry // 10-11 November 1968
▸▸ Kroton's POV in wasteland
   Tank or West of England Quarry // 10-11 November 1968
▸▸ Kroton's POV in wasteland
   Tank or West of England Quarry // 10-11 November 1968
▸▸ Monitor shot – Kroton in wasteland
   Tank or West of England Quarry // 10-11 November 1968
▸▸ Kroton's confused POV in wasteland
   Tank or West of England Quarry // 10-11 November 1968
▸▸ Kroton moves off as TARDIS appears
   Tank or West of England Quarry // 10 November 1968

The Facts

The two Malvern quarries used in The Krotons were owned by PYX Granite Co Ltd and, while the West of England Quarry had fallen into disuse by the time of the filming, the larger Tank Quarry was still a working site until its closure in 1970.

THE SEEDS OF DEATH
(tx 25 January to 1 March 1969)

The Story

Arriving on 21st century Earth, the Doctor discovers that T-Mat, a vital transmat system used for transporting both humans and freight around the world, has broken down. Travelling via rocket to the malfunctioning T-Mat relay station on the moon, the Doctor discovers that it has been overrun by Martian Ice Warriors. In preparation for an invasion, the Ice Warriors use the T-Mat to transport Martian seed pods around the world, which then release a deadly fungus which draws the oxygen out of the atmosphere. Using the T-Mat to return to Earth, the Doctor finds that water can destroy the seed pods and uses the weather control bureau to create enough rain to end the menace. Returning to the moon the Doctor misdirects the Ice Warrior fleet, taking them into orbit around the sun, while dispatching the remaining Ice Warriors at the relay station.

The Locations

1. Hampstead Heath (West Heath), West Heath Road, Hampstead, London, NW3

Shooting Schedule

EPISODE 4

▸▸ Ice Warrior walks through foam
   Hampstead Heath // 19 December 1968
▸▸ Ice Warrior attacks the technicians
   Hampstead Heath // 19 December 1968
▸▸ Ice Warrior attacks guard on radio
   Hampstead Heath // 19 December 1968
▸▸ Ice Warrior comes over the hill
   Hampstead Heath // 19 December 1968

EPISODE 6

▸▸ **Rain destroys the fungus**
  Hampstead Heath // 19 December 1968

The Facts

Brian Hayles' original scene breakdown for The Seeds of Death had specified the location for the film sequences as being Hyde Park in London.

Only a single day's filming, accomplished on the western extension to Hampstead Heath (for which the Greater London Council were paid £26 5s 0d) was required to film the journey of the lone Ice Warrior from the T-MAT Centre to the Weather Control building in Episode 4.

The car park outside Jack Straw's Castle public house, North End, formed the rendezvous point for the cast and crew. A total of five artists were required: Steve Peters as the Ice Warrior, Jimmy Haswell, Derek Chafer and Alan Chuntz as technicians and Derrick Slater as the guard who reports the Ice Warrior's progress on the walkie-talkie before getting killed.

As the location sequences were also to feature the advance of the de-oxygenating fungus, a water tanker was on hand to fuel the foam-making machine supplied by specialist props and equipment suppliers, Bill King's Trading Post, which had been used so effectively during the previous season's Fury from the Deep. The tanker also supplied water for the rain effects used during the final episode as the fungus is destroyed.

Comment

Brief as it is, the location footage shot by director Michael Ferguson for The Seeds of Death is wonderfully photographed and very dramatic, especially the scene showing the back-lit Ice Warrior making its way over the brow of a hill. The Ice Warrior costume looks impressive in daylight and it's a pity that this was the one and only time that they would be seen in a location setting.

THE WAR GAMES

(tx 19 April to 21 June 1969)

The Story

The TARDIS in the middle of No Man's Land during World War I, but the Doctor soon discovers that all is not as it seems. A race of alien creatures have captured humans from many Earth war periods, intent on developing a super-army with which they can take over the galaxy. With the help of resistance fighters from the different time zones who have shaken off their conditioning, the war games are closed down. However, unable to get the human soldiers back to their own time zones, the Doctor calls upon the Time Lords for their help. Now in their hands, the Doctor is put on trial for his continual interference in the affairs of other beings. Found guilty, he is exiled to Earth and forced to regenerate once more.

The Locations

1. Sheepcote Rubbish Tip, Wilson Avenue, Brighton, East Sussex
2. Seven Sisters Country Park, Exceat, Seaford, East Sussex
3. Bridle Path, Underhill Lane, Clayton, West Sussex
4. Eastbourne Waterboard Road, West Dean, East Sussex
5. Westdean and Church Only Road, West Dean, East Sussex
6. High Park Farm, Ditchling Road, Exceat, Seaford, East Sussex
7. Birling Manor Farm, East Dean, East Sussex

Shooting Schedule

EPISODE 1

▸▸ **Doctor's party met Lady Jennifer, capture by Germans**
  Sheepcote Rubbish Tip // 24 March 1969
▸▸ **Ambulance recaptured by Carstairs**
  Sheepcote Rubbish Tip // 25 March 1969
▸▸ **Doctor faces the firing squad (1/2)**
  Birling Farm // 1 April 1969

EPISODE 2

▸▸ **Firing squad is attacked; Zoe rescues Doctor**
  Birling Farm // 1 April 1969
▸▸ **Doctor and Zoe spy on the prison**
  Westdean and Church Only Road // 30 March 1969
▸▸ **Doctor's POV through recorder/telescope**
  Birling Farm // 1 April 1969
▸▸ **Doctor tells chauffeur to take them to the prison**
  Westdean and Church Only Road // 30 March 1969
▸▸ **Jamie and Redcoat come under fire**
  Birling Farm // 1 April 1969
▸▸ **Jamie is dragged away by British soldiers**
  Birling Farm // 1 April 1969
▸▸ **Doctor's party escape in the ambulance**
  Eastbourne Waterboard Road // 30 March 1969
▸▸ **Ambulance drives along the road**
  Westdean and Church Only Road // 30 March 1969
▸▸ **Ambulance caught in barrage**
  Sheepcote Rubbish Tip // 25 March 1969
▸▸ **Ambulance drives out of WWI Zone**
  Sheepcote Rubbish Tip // 25 March 1969

Above: The Romans attack near the River Cuckmere. One of the 'mundane' location photographs that producer Derrick Sherwin was so disappointed with.

▸▸ **Ambulance appears and is attacked by Romans (2/3)**
Seven Sisters Country Park // 27 March 1969

EPISODE 3

▸▸ **Ambulance escapes from Roman Zone**
Seven Sisters Country Park // 27 March 1969

▸▸ **Ambulance reappears in WWI Zone**
Sheepcote Rubbish Tip // 26 March 1969

▸▸ **Ambulance is captured by German soldiers**
Sheepcote Rubbish Tip // 26 March 1969

▸▸ **Ambulance passes an American Civil War soldier**
Westdean and Church Only Road //
30 March 1969

▸▸ **Ambulance is shot at by American Civil War soldier**
Westdean and Church Only Road //
30 March 1969

▸▸ **Ambulance blocked by tree, Carstairs in gunfight**
Bridle Path, Underhill Lane // 31 March 1969

▸▸ **Horsemen gallop down the road**
High Park Farm // 31 March 1969

▸▸ **Ambulance runs out of petrol**
Eastbourne Waterboard Road // 30 March 1969

EPISODE 4

▸▸ **Jamie fights with Confederate horseman**
Bridle Path, Underhill Lane // 28 March 1969

▸▸ **Jamie rescues Lady Jennifer but they are recaptured**
Bridle Path, Underhill Lane // 28 March 1969

EPISODE 7

▸▸ **Doctor, Jamie and Carstairs attacked by Romans**
Seven Sisters Country Park // 27 March 1969

▸▸ **Doctor, Jamie and Carstairs arrive in WWI Zone**
Sheepcote Rubbish Tip // 26 March 1969

▸▸ **Doctor, Jamie and Carstairs in machine gun attack**
Sheepcote Rubbish Tip // 23 March 1969

▸▸ **German gun nest attacked by resistance men and Zoe**
Sheepcote Rubbish Tip // 26 March 1969

EPISODE 8

▸▸ **Resistance men blow up building**
Birling Farm // 1 April 1969

EPISODE 9

▸▸ **Doctor, Jamie and Zoe struggle back to the TARDIS (9/10)**
Sheepcote Rubbish Tip // 23 March 1969

EPISODE 10

▸▸ **Jamie returns to Scotland**
Sheepcote Rubbish Tip // 26 March 1969

The Facts

Following the completion of the location filming, a dispute broke out between producer Derrick Sherwin and the BBC's photographic department over the stills taken during the filming in West Sussex.

'Enclosed are the stills taken on location filming of 'Dr Who' serial 'Z.Z.'

'I must say that looking through this rather sad and sorry lot of photographs I can't help wishing I'd taken my 'brownie' along with me!

'As this is the last of Patrick Troughton's Dr Who serials I do think a little more effort might have been made to secure some exciting action shots. Goodness knows, it was all there just begging to be put on celluloid – the sequences we shot were jam packed with action.

'I can find not one print that arouses anything but utter despair out of the entire 18! Perhaps there are another few rolls the photographer forgot to develop!? After all, he was with us for two days – I find it difficult to believe this is the result of his labours.'

Derrick Sherwin to Maureen Dormer and Ian Wyles –
10 April 1969

Eleven days later, Ian Wyles replied to Sherwin's memo, indicating that the pictures were only a reflection of what was going on during the two days that the photographer was on location.

'The first day consisted of filming mainly explosions with a request from the director to our photographer not to take any pictures that might give away the storyline. After lunch the cast was dismissed and explosion filming continued.

'The second day consisted of one Roman chariot and seven Roman soldiers. After lunch the cast stood around a First World War ambulance with no action of any sort.

'Although I was not present myself at this shooting,

I think it is fair to say that although you may have a dramatic storyline, as in this case, it just does not make dramatic still pictures.'

Sherwin duly responded on the 24th, completely disagreeing with Wyles' assumption that the filming did not provide adequate opportunities for dramatic photographs.

'If this is so, how come we shot what have been called some of the most exciting dramatic sequences ever seen in 'Dr Who'? Surely the dramatic composition of a still depends on the expertise and creative ability of the man behind the camera?

'Indeed, you were not there at the shooting and I find it a little distressing that you are prepared to refute the observations of one who was! I specifically chose these days for still photography because they provided the dramatically exciting sequences.

'I have to try and maintain audience interest in a ten-week show and consequently feel justified in showing a little displeasure that photographs which could provide exciting press material are of inferior quality! Can you honestly say that any of the stills are anything more than mundane snapshots?'

The Sheepcote Rubbish Tip had already doubled for No Man's Land some months earlier during the filming of Richard Attenborough's film Oh! What a Lovely War. Interestingly, at the same time as The War Games was being shot, Brighton Council were investigating mysterious 'subsidences' that had appeared on the tip. As the Evening Argus reported on Saturday 29 March, 'The battle of the Somme was responsible for subsidence on Sheepcote Valley Tip, Councillor Stanley Fitch told Brighton Council. Not the real thing exactly, but the recreation of the World War I battle by the film crew engaged on Oh! What a Lovely War last year. Councillor Fitch said film men had made dug-outs to a depth of 20 feet. The holes were these, not natural subsidence.'

Comment

With a number of war zones to represent, director David Maloney did well to find locations that were different enough to represent the areas needed for the story within such a relatively small area. While the location work, on the whole, is excellent, it's a shame that it virtually peters out after the first three episodes, only leaving the odd exterior sequence here and there over the remaining seven instalments. ■

FOOTNOTES

1. Associated Portland Cement Manufacturers Ltd were subsequently paid £25 for the use of the Dunstable quarry.

2. At the time of filming, Grim's Dyke House was used as a rehabilitation centre.

3. Mistakenly referred to as Lanse Traverse in the BBC documentation.

4. The name was later changed from Leatherbarrow to Leatherman.

5. The Frame #23 and 24 p.45

6. Although this location is now largely spelt 'Climping', this form of the name was in use during 1967.

7. Contrary to popular belief, although director Barry Letts had been in the Royal Navy, he had never met Mr Morgan before.

8. Judging by the helicopter's colour scheme, it was almost certainly operated by Bristow Helicopters where UH-12's were used for training at Redhill, Surrey and Middle Wallop, Hampshire.

9. The same piece of footage would later be used in The Dæmons (1971).

10. Mistakenly referred to as 'P J Poupart' on several of the production documents for The Web of Fear. The area is now known as Old Brewers Yard.

11. Doctor Who Magazine #72, p.28

12. Callum Jones was still paid his £26-5s-0d for the cancelled filming.

13. Gwenlyn had asked permission to film from '10.30am – 3.30pm (or times when Aldwych Station is closed to the public).'

14. Radio 390 closed down on 28 July 1967. Out of the three forts, Red Sands was the only complete structure, the other two having been damaged by shipping collisions in 1953 and 1963.

15. The Sea Entrance to the ESGO base, used during Episode 5

16. The Nayland Rock Hotel, Margate

17. Photographs taken on location by scriptwriter Victor Pemberton seem to indicate that several shots were taken of Troughton in the helicopter cockpit while it was situated on the cliff tops at Botony Bay. It also appears from Pemberton's pictures that dummies of Jamie and Victoria were placed in the helicopter for some of these scenes.

18. This was always planned as an over-run day, requiring the services of Arthur Cox (Cully), Kenneth Ives (Toba), Ronald Allen (Rago) and the three Quarks.

19. As this was an unplanned filming day on location, it is unclear as to what scenes were committed to film. Hand-written notes in film schedule indicate that Arthur Cox and the three Quarks were required in the morning, with Frazer Hines joining them in the afternoon, indicating that it was probably Jamie and Cully's attack on the Quarks in Episodes 4 and 5. As a result of this, all the film sequences known to have been completed at Gerrards Cross for the story are listed under the filming on 25 April 1968, the date when they were originally scheduled to be done.

20. As with 3 May, this was also an unscheduled day of location work at Gerrards Cross, for which Ronald Allen, Kenneth Ives and the three Quarks were called. As above, the scenes completed during this day are included in the 25 April listing.

21. A small village next to Princes Risborough. Both villages are situated approx 16 miles NW of the Gerrards Cross location.

22. Probably the Episode 4 scenes of the Doctor, Jamie, Zoe and Isobel climbing up the helicopter's rope ladder to escape from the IE factory.

23. Douglas Camfield – A Tribute, p.11/12

24. Oxford Mail, 7 September 1968

25. Doctor Who Magazine #243, p.10

PART THREE

'I'm pretty sure that's Cromer...'
The Brigadier – *The Three Doctors*

JON PERTWEE

SPEARHEAD FROM SPACE

(tx 3 January to 24 January 1970)

The Story

As the newly regenerated Doctor arrives on Earth, a wave of meteorites also lands in the English countryside. After convincing Brigadier Lethbridge-Stewart of his credentials, the Doctor begins an examination of one of the meteorites and discovers it to be, not only hollow, but also made of plastic. The meteorites house the Nestene Consciousness, a gestalt alien intelligence planning to invade Earth by means of the Autons, deadly humanoid weapons made of plastic. An advanced Auton, Channing, takes over production at a plastics factory, mass-producing other Autons disguised as shop window mannequins. At a pre-arranged time the mannequins come to life, wreaking havoc across the country. The Doctor, aided by Cambridge scientist Liz Shaw, develops a machine which defeats the Nestene intelligence. The link with Earth broken, the Autons become lifeless.

The Locations

1. Favourite Doll Factory, Georges Road, Holloway, London, N7
2. Junction of Euston Road and Midland Road, London, NW1
3. National Car Parks, Rear of St Pancras Station, Midland Road, London, NW1
4. John Sanders Ltd, The Broadway, Ealing, London, W5[1]
5. Lancaster Road, Ealing, London, W5[2]
6. High Street, Ealing, London, W5
7. Royal Horticultural Society, Wisley, Surrey
8. Hatchford Park School, Ockham Lane, Hatchford, Surrey[3]
9. TCC Condensers, Wales Farm Road, Ealing, London, W3
10. Wood Norton Estate, Evesham, Hereford and Worcestershire
    - Wood Norton Hall
    - Duc d'Orleans' Bathroom
    - Underground Nuclear Bunker
    - Rose Garden
    - Auxiliary Building
11. Mansion House Hotel, Coopers Lane, Evesham, Worcestershire[4]
12. Wheelbarrow Castle Cottage, Radford, Worcestershire
13. Madame Tussauds, Marylebone Road, Marylebone, London, NW1
    - Great Hall

Shooting Schedule

EPISODE 1

▸▸ UNIT technician sees something strange on radar
Wood Norton – Bunker // 8 October 1969

▸▸ Technician notices their flying in formation
Wood Norton – Bunker // 8 October 1969

▸▸ Seeley sees meteorite land in Oxley Woods
Royal Horticultural Society //
15 or 16 September 1969

▸▸ Technician works out landing co-ordinates
Wood Norton – Bunker // 8 October 1969

▸▸ Seeley uncovers and recovers meteorite
Royal Horticultural Society //
15 or 16 September 1969

▸▸ Technician accepts they must have been meteorites
Wood Norton – Bunker // 8 October 1969

▸▸ Doctor collapses out of TARDIS
Royal Horticultural Society // 15 September 1969

▸▸ Liz Shaw driven in car
Euston Road/Midland Road // 13 September 1969

▸▸ Car turns into UNIT HQ
NCP – Midland Road // 13 September 1969

▸▸ Brigadier meets with Liz Shaw
Wood Norton – Bunker // 8 or 9 October 1969

▸▸ Doctor is carried into the hospital
Wood Norton Hall // 9 or 10 October 1969

▸▸ Brigadier tells Liz about UNIT
Wood Norton – Bunker // 8 or 9 October 1969

▸▸ Munro telephones Brigadier about man by
police box
Wood Norton Hall // 9, 10 or 11 October 1969

▸▸ Brigadier orders an armed guard for the police box
Wood Norton – Bunker // 8 or 9 October 1969

▸▸ Henderson looks at X-Ray and sees two hearts
Wood Norton – Aux Building // 8, 9 or
10 October 1969

▸▸ Henderson telephones Dr Lomax
Wood Norton Hall // 12 or 13 October 1969

▸▸ Mullins telephones Daily Chronicle
Wood Norton Hall // 13 October 1969

▸▸ Seeley collects meteorite and hears soldiers close by
Royal Horticultural Society // 16 September 1969

▸▸ Doctor tries to look for his shoes
Wood Norton – Aux Building // 8, 9 or
10 October 1969

▸▸ Brigadier and Liz arrive at Ashbridge
Cottage Hospital
Hatchford Park School // 17 September 1969

▸▸ Brigadier besieged by news reporters
Wood Norton Hall // 14 October 1969

▸▸ Brigadier orders guards to be issued with live ammo
Wood Norton Hall // 9 October 1969

▸▸ Brigadier doesn't recognise the Doctor
Wood Norton – Aux Building // 9 October 1969

▸▸ Wagstaffe talks to Channing in phone kiosk
Wood Norton Hall // 13 October 1969

▸▸ Forbes warns Seeley not to come back to the wood
Royal Horticultural Society // 15 September 1969

▸▸ Autons kidnap the Doctor and knock out Henderson
Wood Norton – Aux Building // 11 October 1969

▸▸ Doctor escapes and Channing drives
ambulance away
Hatchford Park School // 17 September 1969

▸▸ Guards hear something happening
Royal Horticultural Society // 15 September 1969

▸▸ Munro and soldiers chase after Doctor
Hatchford Park School // 17 September 1969

▸▸ Guards cock their guns
Royal Horticultural Society // 15 September 1969

▸▸ Munro finds empty wheelchair
Hatchford Park School // 17 September 1969

▸▸ Guard shoots Doctor as he come through trees (1/2)
Royal Horticultural Society // 15 September 1969

EPISODE 2

▸▸ Henderson says he can detect no brain activity
Wood Norton – Aux Building // 12, 13 or
14 October 1969

▸▸ Brigadier and Munro examine meteorite
Wood Norton – Rose Garden // 14 October 1969

Above: The conversation between the Brigadier (Nicholas Courtney) and Captain Munro (John Breslin) was filmed on 14 October 1969. The scene was originally intended to be shot in the hospital foyer.

▸ **Ransome is guided through the plastics factory**
Favourite Doll Factory // 13 September 1969

▸ **Ransome sees that his workshop has changed**
TCC Condensers // 18 September 1969

▸ **Ransome confronts Hibbert**
Wood Norton Hall // Date Unknown

▸ **Ransome stops by his workshop, watched by Channing**
TCC Condensers // 18 September 1969

▸ **Liz experiments on the broken sphere**
Wood Norton – Bunker // 13, 14 or 15 October 1969

▸ **Channing and Hibbert talk about missing energy units**
Wood Norton Hall // Date Unknown

▸ **Seeley checks the sphere**
Wheelbarrow Castle Cottage // 23 October 1969

▸ **Auton picks up signal from sphere**
Royal Horticultural Society // 16 September 1969

▸ **Meg Seeley is suspicious of her husband**
Wheelbarrow Castle Cottage // 23 October 1969

▸ **Auton looses the signal**
Royal Horticultural Society // 16 September 1969

▸ **Scobie visits the Brigadier enquiring about meteorites**
Wheelbarrow Castle Cottage // 23 October 1969

▸ **Munro collects Forbes from hospital car park**
Hatchford Park School // 17 September 1969

▸ **Doctor 'hides' in the shower and then look for clothes**
Wood Norton Hall – Bathroom // 12 October 1969

▸ **UNIT soldiers dig up a sphere in Oxley Woods**
Royal Horticultural Society // 16 September 1969

▸ **Auton picks up signal from second sphere**
Royal Horticultural Society // 16 September 1969

▸ **Doctor dodges Henderson and Beavis**
Wood Norton Hall // 12 October 1969

▸ **Doctor escapes in Beavis' car**
Hatchford Park School // 17 September 1969

▸ **Brigadier tries to open the TARDIS**
Wood Norton – Bunker // 13, 14 or 15 October 1969

▸ **Munro looks at sphere, orders it back to the laboratory**
Royal Horticultural Society // 16 September 1969

▸ **Forbes crashes UNIT jeep, Auton takes sphere**
Royal Horticultural Society // 15 or 16 September 1969

▸ **Hibbert tells Channing that Scobie will soon arrive**
Wood Norton Hall // Date Unknown

▸ **Doctor arrives at UNIT HQ**
NCP – Midland Road // 13 September 1969

▸ **Doctor talks to Brigadier and examines broken sphere**
Wood Norton – Bunker // 13 or 14 October 1969

▸ **Ransome climbs over factory wall**
TCC Condensers // 18 or 19 September 1969

▸ **Channing talks to Scobie about his waxwork**
Wood Norton Hall // 15 October 1969

▸ **Ransome breaks into factory door**
TCC Condensers // 18 or 19 September 1969

▸ **Ransome picks up crowbar and climbs staircase**
Location Unknown // Date Unknown

▸ **Ransome breaks into his old workshop**
TCC Condensers // 18 September 1969

▸ **Ransome enters the room and is attacked by an Auton (2/3)**
Wood Norton Hall // 15 October 1969

EPISODE 3

▸ **Auton chases Ransome onto landing**
TCC Condensers // 18 September 1969

▸ **Ransome escapes, Channing 'orders' Auton's return**
TCC Condensers // 18 September 1969

▸ **Channing shows Ransome's brain print**
Wood Norton Hall // Date Unknown

▸ **Ransome collapses in front of UNIT soldiers**
Royal Horticultural Society // 16 September 1969

▸ **Meg Seeley tells her husband about Forbes' death**
Wheelbarrow Castle Cottage // 23 October 1969

▸ **Ransome in deep shock, Munro orders him moved to HQ**
Wood Norton Estate // 30 October 1969

▸ **Liz agrees to get TARDIS key for Doctor**
Wood Norton – Bunker // 16 or 17 October 1969

▸ **Munro talks to Seeley about the meteorites**
Wood Norton Estate // 30 October 1969

▸ **Channing says that the Autons have lost Ransome**
Wood Norton Hall // Date Unknown

▸ **Liz steals the key while Brigadier questions Ransome**
Wood Norton – Bunker // Date Unknown

▸ **Doctor tries TARDIS but finds the codes have changed**
Wood Norton – Bunker // 16, 17 or 20 October 1969

▸ **Meg Seeley drags the old chest from the outhouse**
Wheelbarrow Castle Cottage // 23 October 1969

▸ **Ransome tells Brigadier and Doctor about Channing**
Wood Norton – Bunker // Date Unknown

▸ **Munro finds out that Seeley has seen a meteorite**
Wood Norton Estate // 30 October 1969

▸ **Meg opens chest and sees glowing sphere**
Wheelbarrow Castle Cottage // 23 October 1969

▸ Channing and Hibbert see signal
Wood Norton Hall // Date Unknown

▸ Auton begins to head towards the sphere
Royal Horticultural Society // 16 September 1969

▸ Channing sees through the Auton's eyes
Wood Norton Hall // Date Unknown

▸ Establishing shot – Seeley's cottage
Wheelbarrow Castle Cottage // 23 October 1969

▸ Auton comes through bracken
Royal Horticultural Society // 16 September 1969

▸ Brigadier and Doctor decide to go and collect sphere
Wood Norton Estate // 30 October 1969

▸ Meg replaces the sphere and shoots the Auton
Wheelbarrow Castle Cottage // 23 October 1969

▸ Channing senses that the signal is muffled
Wood Norton Hall // Date Unknown

▸ Auton searches for sphere, attacked by UNIT
Wheelbarrow Castle Cottage // 23 October 1969

▸ Channing recalls the Auton
Wood Norton Hall // Date Unknown

▸ Auton runs from the cottage
Wheelbarrow Castle Cottage // 23 October 1969

▸ Channing tells Hibbert that UNIT have the swarm leader
Wood Norton Hall // Date Unknown

▸ Doctor examines the sphere
Wheelbarrow Castle Cottage // 23 October 1969

▸ Auton cuts its way into the UNIT tent
Wood Norton Estate // 30 October 1969

▸ Channing orders Ransome's total destruction
Wood Norton Hall // Date Unknown

▸ Auton kills Ransome
Wood Norton Estate // 30 October 1969

▸ Brigadier orders a cordon around the plastics factory
Wheelbarrow Castle Cottage // 23 October 1969

▸ Doctor examines the rip in the tent
Wood Norton Estate // 30 October 1969

▸ Doctor, Brigadier and Liz walk through factory
Location Unknown // Date Unknown

▸ Brigadier sees Channing through glass door
TCC Condensers // 18 September 1969

▸ Hibbert talks to Doctor and Brigadier
Wood Norton Hall // 16 or 17 October 1969

▸ Doctor detects an intelligence in the sphere
Wood Norton – Bunker // 16 or 17 October 1969

▸ Scobie talks to Brigadier and meets his Auton replica (3/4)
Evesham Hotel // Date Unknown

EPISODE 4

▸ Doctor, Liz and Brigadier talk about the intelligence
Wood Norton – Bunker // 22 or 23 October 1969

▸ Auton Scobie telephones Brigadier

Wood Norton Hall // Date Unknown

▸ Brigadier tells Doctor about Scobie's waxwork
Wood Norton – Bunker // 22 or 23 October 1969

▸ Doctor and Liz examine the waxwork of Scobie
Madame Tussauds – Great Hall //
5 November 1969

▸ Munro tells Doctor that Brigadier is unavailable
Wood Norton – Bunker // Date Unknown

▸ Doctor tells Liz they'll have to wait until closing time
Madame Tussauds // 5 November 1969

▸ Channing talks to Hibbert about sphere's recovery
Wood Norton Hall // Date Unknown

▸ Auton Scobie collects the sphere from Munro
Wood Norton – Bunker // 23 October 1969

▸ Channing releases the Autons from the waxworks
Madame Tussauds – Great Hall //
5 November 1969

▸ Doctor tells Brigadier that they must move on the factory
Wood Norton – Bunker // 21, 22 or
23 October 1969

▸ Channing places the swarm leader in the machine
Wood Norton Hall // Date Unknown

▸ Doctor and Liz work on their machine
Wood Norton – Bunker // 21, 22 or
23 October 1969

▸ Autons come to life and break out of shop front
John Sanders // 14 September 1969

▸ Policeman hears breaking glass and runs to see
Lancaster Road // 14 September 1969

▸ Autons gun down policeman and pedestrians
High Street // 14 September 1969

▸ Doctor tells Brigadier he needs to gain access to factory
Wood Norton – Bunker // Date Unknown

▸ Hibbert begins to break free from Channing's hold

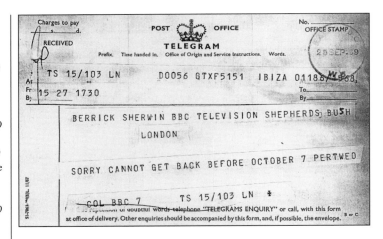

Above: Jon Pertwee's telegram from Ibiza, informing producer Derrick Sherwin of his arrival date.

Wood Norton Hall // Date Unknown

▶▶ **Cars begin to leave UNIT HQ**
NCP – Midland Road // 13 September 1969

▶▶ **Auton destroys Hibbert**
Wood Norton Hall // Date Unknown

▶▶ **Doctor opens outer perimeter door to the factory**
TCC Condensers // 18 or 19 September 1969

▶▶ **Channing hears that there are intruders
at the factory**
Wood Norton Hall // Date Unknown

▶▶ **Liz sees General Scobie and his men**
TCC Condensers // 19 September 1969

▶▶ **Channing watches events on his screen**
Wood Norton Hall // Date Unknown

▶▶ **Doctor uses machine to destroy Auton Scobie**
TCC Condensers // 19 September 1969

▶▶ **The real Scobie comes back to life**
Madame Tussauds – Great Hall //
5 November 1969

▶▶ **Brigadier commandeers troops as Doctor
enters factory**
TCC Condensers // 19 September 1969

▶▶ **Doctor and Liz destroy another patrolling Auton**
Location Unknown // Date Unknown

▶▶ **Autons and soldiers battle outside the factory**
TCC Condensers // 19 September 1969

▶▶ **Channing tells Doctor that he cannot defeat them**
Wood Norton Hall // Date Unknown

▶▶ **Autons and soldiers battle outside the factory**
TCC Condensers // 19 September 1969

▶▶ **Nestene creature attacks Doctor**
Wood Norton Hall // Date Unknown

▶▶ **Autons suddenly become lifeless**
TCC Condensers // 19 September 1969

▶▶ **Nestene is destroyed, as is Channing**
Wood Norton Hall // Date Unknown

▶▶ **Doctor agrees to stay and help UNIT**
Wood Norton – Bunker // 21, 22 or
23 October 1969

The Facts

Spearhead from Space was originally intended to be produced as a normal part-location, part-studio story and was very much scripted and pre-planned as such.

To ensure an impressive opening story for Jon Pertwee's Doctor, the production was allocated a total of seven days' worth of filming on location as opposed to the four that would have usually been permitted for a story of this length. Work began on Saturday 13 September 1969 and continued through to Friday the 19th, staying within the confines of London and Surrey.

In his original storyline, Robert Holmes had envisaged the entrance to UNIT HQ as being concealed behind a 'shabby run-down shop' in a London street. This was duly revised in his final script as being accessed via a barrier marked 'Private – Service Vehicles Only' at the top of a multi-storey car park. In the end, the decision was taken to utilise a car park owned by NCP, off Midland Road and situated just behind St Pancras Station in London, for which a £20 facility fee was paid. The scenes were scripted to feature a security attendant and an actor was duly hired, but his place was ultimately taken by producer Derrick Sherwin.

Derrick Sherwin: 'The actor we originally cast couldn't act! So I said, "Get that uniform off – I'll do it myself!" It was a stupid little part which didn't even have a line, but the guy couldn't get it right, so I threw him off the set.'[5]

The final part of the car park scene in Episode 4, showing both the Brigadier and the Doctor leaving UNIT, was removed in editing. As scripted, once the cars had left, the camera was due to zoom in for a close-up of the attendant, revealing that he has been replaced by an Auton.

The exterior of Auto Plastics was represented by the old TCC Condensers factory, which had appeared previously in *The Invasion*; indeed, the climactic battle between UNIT and the Autons was filmed in exactly the area that Douglas Camfield had used for a similar battle with the Cybermen.

At this time in *Doctor Who's* production, studio recording was still being done on an episode by episode basis, with one complete 25-minute segment being committed to tape each week. As planned, the recording of Episode 1 of *Spearhead from Space* was due to go into studio at Television Centre on Monday 13 October.[6]

It was only after initial location work had been completed that it became evident that strike action by the union ABS[7] (Association of Broadcasting Staff) would seriously affect the production of the story. Shortly after finishing the initial block of location work, Jon Pertwee left on a planned holiday to Club Nautico in Ibiza, still unsure as to what the status of his first story as the Doctor actually was. Within days it became apparent that the production team had indeed lost their studio allocations, so Sherwin immediately decided to complete *Spearhead* by shooting it entirely on film and almost entirely on location – a task which had to be accomplished without any further increase in budget.

As all the required exteriors had already been shot, all that remained was to find a suitable location to complete the interiors that would have been done in the studio. The ideal site was found at Wood Norton near Evesham, a large BBC owned premises used for the training of Corporation engineering personnel, where most of the required sets could be erected. Originally the home of the Duke of Orleans, and later a private school, Wood Norton was acquired by the BBC shortly before World War II for use as an emergency broadcast centre. New film schedules and actors' contracts were drawn up and filming was programmed to be conducted for three weeks between 7 and 28 October.

With details rapidly becoming finalised, Sherwin telegrammed Pertwee on 25 September, confirming the change of plan and requesting that, if possible, he should return to England on Sunday 5 October so that he could participate in the two-day read-through and rehearsal the following Monday and Tuesday, just prior to the first day of filming at Evesham on the Wednesday. Pertwee duly telegrammed Sherwin back on 28 September – 'SORRY CANNOT GET BACK BEFORE OCTOBER 7 PERTWEE' – and Sherwin replied, confirming that he would have to see Pertwee on his return on the 7th and inform him then of the details of the new filming schedule.

One area at Wood Norton that was utilised for the tracking station, the Brigadier's office and the UNIT laboratory was the substantial underground nuclear bunker that had been built in the late 1960s, designed to control a network of 20 underground radio stations that would broadcast a secret schedule of morale-boosting comedy, drama and religious programmes (along with Julie Andrews' 1965 hit, *The Sound of Music*) to the survivors of a nuclear conflict for up to 100 days.[8] Also used was one of the smaller pre-fabricated auxiliary buildings, in which the hospital ward set was constructed.

The Episode 1 scene of the Brigadier getting caught by the press in the foyer of the Ashbridge Cottage Hospital featured the on-screen use of one of the production's 16mm cameras (taking footage actually seen in the finished episode), as well as one of the sound crew recording the dialogue with a boom microphone. In the episode, as the mobile camera pans around following Nicholas Courtney, it also briefly shows both the main static high-angle camera and next to it, Cicely Cawthorne, the director's assistant, holding a bound yellow script. Finally, as the scene ends, the main boom microphone also lowers itself into shot.

Although Wood Norton provided the vast majority of interior locations, two other filming sites were used during the three weeks at Evesham. All the scenes around the Seeleys' cottage had originally been scripted to be shot in a studio set. Rather than try to recreate a homely cottage interior at Wood Norton, the decision was taken to film all the required sequences around a real house. The chosen building was a cottage owned by Mrs Bragge, adjoining the Wheelbarrow Castle pub in Radford, a few miles north of Evesham. Scenes were filmed both inside and outside the cottage, while the pub itself provided the production catering for the day.

The other location used was the Manor House Hotel, which was in reality the hotel that the production team were based in during the filming at Evesham. Here, the scenes of General Scobie meeting his Auton facsimile at the end of Episode 3 were filmed.

The Episode 3 sequences set in the army tent were filmed in a real tent set in the grounds of Wood Norton, while the Episode 2 scene of the Brigadier talking to Munro and examining the broken sphere was moved from the hospital foyer to the rose garden in the grounds of the Hall.

On completion of the filming at Evesham, the production team returned to London where one additional location had been secured for the production – Madame Tussaud's. Again originally intended to be recorded in the studio, agreement had been reached that filming could be conducted in the Great Hall overnight, once the building had closed to the public for the evening. For this one night's work, Madame Tussaud's was paid £163 2s 0d.

One short scene that was scripted but probably never filmed showed the Doctor and Liz driving up to Madame Tussaud's. This then led directly into the scene of the Doctor examining the waxwork tableau.

The notion that *Spearhead from Space* was the first story to be shot entirely on location is in fact incorrect. On completion of the location work in London, Surrey and Evesham, two further days were spent at Van Arden Studios in Ealing on 3 and 4 November. It is unclear precisely what material was shot at Van Arden, although the list of designer's set dressing props indicates that it was probably inserts of the Nestene sphere in Oxley Woods and possibly the later death of Ransome in Episode 4. The requirement were:

A. Grass to cover area 21' x 21'
B. 24 x Clumps of marsh grass
C. 6 x 8' high pine trees
D. 1 x Sack of leaves
E. 24 x Clumps of heather
F 2 x Bags of peat
G. 1 x Trestle table – metal legs
H. 2 x 5' benches – metal legs

One further day of filming was also conducted on 22 November, when a number of scenes were reshot around the Nestene tank room. The filming was restaged in London and featured Jon Pertwee, John Woodnutt and Ivan Orton.[9]

A total of 23,735 feet of 16mm film was shot for *Spearhead from Space*, approximately five times more than was actually transmitted. In order to process all the footage, two film editors were used to cut the final episodes together.

Above: Timothy Combe directs the filming in the barn at Sheephatch Farm for *Doctor Who and the Silurians.*

Comment

The decision to film *Spearhead from Space* almost entirely on location was a very brave one. With only two and a half weeks to prepare between the end of the original block of exterior work and the start of filming at Evesham, it must have been a very fraught time, but fortunately Holmes' script didn't demand anything excessively unusual. The effort certainly paid off. The locations chosen within the grounds of Wood Norton are sensibly varied, using the main house with all its wood panelling for the hospital interiors, a separate building for the ward itself and the underground bunker for the UNIT locations. The end result is nothing short of superb, looking plush, polished and expensive. If only all *Doctor Who* could have been made this way.

DOCTOR WHO AND THE SILURIANS

(tx 31 January to 14 March 1970)

The Story

The Doctor and Liz visit the Wenley Moor research centre, which has been experiencing unexplained power drains from their new type of nuclear reactor. While there, the Doctor discovers that potholers have been attacked in the nearby caves, leaving the lone survivor traumatised. Exploring the caves, the Doctor finds an intelligent race of humanoid reptiles that have accidentally been awakened from their hibernation by the research centre's activities. Having ruled the Earth in the distant past, they wish to reclaim their planet. To that end, the new Silurian leader releases a deadly virus, designed to wipe out humankind. The Doctor manages to discover a cure for the disease and the Brigadier blows up the Silurian base.

The Locations

1. Marylebone Station, Melcombe Place, Marylebone, London, NW1
2. Melcombe Place, Marylebone, London, NW1
3. Dorset Square/Balcombe Street, Marylebone, London, NW1
4. Walkway by Swanscombe House, Edward Woods Estate, corner Queensdale Crescent and St Ann's Road, Shepherd's Bush, London, NW11
5. Sheephatch Farm, Sheephatch Lane, Tilford, Surrey
6. Hankley Common, Rushmoor, Surrey
7. Milford Chest Hospital, Tuesley Lane, Milford, Surrey
8. High Street, Godalming, Surrey
9. Hog's Back Transmitter Station, Hog's Back, Guildford, Surrey

Shooting Schedule

EPISODE 1

▸▸ **Doctor and Liz in Bessie**
Godalming High Street // 20 November 1969

▸▸ **Doctor and Liz arrive at the research centre**
Hog's Back Transmitter Station // 20 November 1969

▸▸ **Doctor and Liz meet guard (cut)**
Hog's Back Transmitter Station // 20 November 1969

EPISODE 2

▸▸ **Injured Silurian emerges**
Hankley Common // 17 November 1969

▸▸ **Injured Silurian enters barn**
Sheephatch Farm // 13 November 1969

▸ **Squire attacked by Silurian**
Sheephatch Farm // 13 November 1969
▸ **Doctor, Liz and Brigadier at farm**
Sheephatch Farm // 13 November 1969
▸ **Silurian attacks Liz in barn (2/3)**
Sheephatch Farm // 14 November 1969

EPISODE 3

▸ **Liz found, UNIT begin their search**
Sheephatch Farm // 14 November 1969
▸ **Doctor, Liz, Quinn and Brigadier look at map**
Sheephatch Farm // 14 November 1969
▸ **UNIT search Wenley Moor**
Hankley Common // 17/18 November 1969
▸ **Quinn searches for Silurian**
Hankley Common // 17/18 November 1969

EPISODE 5

▸ **Doctor and Brigadier arrive as Baker dies (5/6)**
Milford Chest Hospital // 19 November 1969

EPISODE 6

▸ **Masters arrives at Platform 2**
Marylebone Station // 12 November 1969
▸ **Masters gets taxi**
Melcombe Place // 12 November 1969
▸ **Masters leaves taxi as police go by**
Dorset Square/Balcombe Street //
12 November 1969
▸ **Ticket inspector begins to fall ill**
Marylebone Station // 12 November 1969
▸ **Passengers begin to collapse and die**
Marylebone Station // 24 November 1969
▸ **Masters collapses and dies**
Edward Woods Estate // 12 November 1969
▸ **Masters dead on walkway**
Edward Woods Estate // 12 November 1969

EPISODE 7

▸ **Doctor and Liz see explosions**
Hog's Back Transmitter Station //
20 November 1969

The Facts

A location scene that was filmed on 20 November but edited from the first episode showed the Doctor and Liz arriving at the entrance to the Wenley Moor research centre. Liz shows their UNIT passes to a security guard (played by Brian John) and gives the codeword 'Cloudburst'.

The single brief scene showing the Doctor and Liz driving up Godalming High Street in the Doctor's vintage car Bessie was filmed from the first floor window of the Sun Hotel (for which the proprietors were paid a fee of £5), while two rooms at the Lake Hotel, also in Godalming, were used for wardrobe and make-up.

All the farm sequences were shot in and around the barn of Sheephatch Farm, owned by Dr Gordon Carter and his wife Estelle. During the 1960s, the barn had been awarded a blue plaque by Surrey County Council due to its special historical nature. The two days spent at the farm did cause one unforeseen problem for the production team, as recalled by Estelle Carter. 'One thing I do remember vividly was the 'Great Toilet Trouble'! At that time, we only had a hole in the ground and all those extra people trying to use it spelled disaster. I think we were blacklisted, never to be used again!'

A major problem occurred when the 16mm camera negative from the first day's filming at Marylebone Station was ruined by the processing laboratory,[10] necessitating a remount of the affected scenes on 24 November at a cost of £441 7s 0d. With the exception of Richard King and three vehicle drivers, all the actors used for the reshoot were different to those who had originally appeared on Wednesday the 12th.

In order to fill the railway station with more people, assistant script editor Trevor Ray contacted some of his acting friends as well as appearing in the footage himself, along with script editor Terrance Dicks and director Timothy Combe. Along with the three vehicles (taxi, ambulance and police car) that needed to be rehired, designer Barry Newbery also listed a number of other props that would be required for the shoot at Marylebone – two blankets, four suitcases, 12 newspapers (including four copies of *The Times*) and 20 fully practical tipped cigarettes.

Unused Locations

Wookey Hole – Director Timothy Combe's original intention had been to film *Doctor Who and the Silurians* around Wookey Hole in Somerset, shooting inside the famous caves in the area, rather than try to recreate them in the studio. A letter, dated 23 September 1969 and sent directly to Combe at his home in Richmond,[11] indicated the three possibilities open to the director.

1. *You go to Wookey + unit and shoot your exteriors (about two days) and the rest of the time get what you can in the caves – remembering that such a journey involves losing two days off your seven film days in travelling.*
2. *Ignore Wookey – move all cave sequences into studio and shoot your exteriors within daily reach of London.*
3. *Send unit to Wookey for filming as 1. YOU direct second unit here in London on 1st unit's travel day getting half day London exteriors, half day model shots. Move to Wookey in the evening and continue as in 1.*

Above: **The clapper-board is readied to begin the filming of shot 317 at Blue Circle Cement on 3 February 1970.**

If you have anything to pick up – race back to London day 7 (unit's return day) and work with second unit again.
Whatever happens you do have one to one-and-a-half days on model shots/London exteriors to fit in.

Comment

One can only feel sorry for Timothy Combe. It must have been hard enough to film the plague scenes in the middle of a London mainline station once, never mind having to do it all a second time when the footage was damaged. Nevertheless, Combe manages to create some fine imagery in his exterior scenes – the effects of the plague are well handled, as is the hunt on Wenley Moor. (But exactly why does the Brigadier find it necessary to fire his flare gun?) Perhaps the only part that could have been better were the final explosions seen by the Doctor and Liz as they leave the research centre. They all seem too far away and, being concentrated all in one place, somehow just too small to convey the destruction of the entire Silurian base.

THE AMBASSADORS OF DEATH

(tx 21 March to 2 May 1970)

The Story

When Mars Probe 7 blasts off from the red planet and no communications are received in the intervening seven months, rescue ship Recovery 7 sets off to investigate. On its return, the three 'astronauts' are kidnapped by a mercanery called Reegan. The Doctor soon realises that what returned in Recovery 7 wasn't human and that the real astronauts are still in space. In an attempt to discover the truth, the Doctor pilots another rocket into space and finds the humans on board a huge alien space-craft. Informed that it was three alien 'ambassadors' that returned in Recovery 7, the Doctor returns to find that it is General Carrington, a former astronaut on Mars Probe 6, who is holding the aliens hostage. Convinced that they are a threat, Carrington plans to create world panic that will end in the Martians' destruction. UNIT arrest Carrington and plans are made for the ambassadors' safe return.

The Locations

1. Southall Gas Works, White Street, Southall, Middlesex
2. White Street, Southall, Middlesex
3. TCC Condensers, Wales Farm Road, Ealing, London, W3
4. Claycart Bottom, off Rushmoor Road, Aldershot, Hampshire
5. Puckeridge Hill Road Bridge, Basingstoke Canal, Aldershot, Hampshire
6. Royal Engineers Driving Circuit, Farnborough Airfield, Aldershot, Hampshire
7. Wycombe Air Park, Clay Lane, High Wycombe, Buckinghamshire
8. Folley's Gravel Pit, Spade Oak, Little Marlow, Buckinghamshire
9. Gossmore Lane, Marlow, Buckinghamshire
10. Marlow Weir, Mill Road, Marlow, Buckinghamshire
11. Beacon Hill, Beacon Hill Road, near Ewshot, Hampshire
12. Little Marlow Sewage Treatment Works, Church Road, Little Marlow, Buckinghamshire
13. Blue Circle Cement, Northfleet, Kent

Shooting Schedule

EPISODE 1

▸▸ **Doctor and Liz arrive at Space Control**
Blue Circle Cement // 3 or 4 February 1970
▸▸ **Establishing shots – abandoned warehouse**
TCC Condensers // 28 January 1970
▸▸ **UNIT drive to and enter warehouse**
White Street // 27 January 1970
▸▸ **UNIT arrive at the warehouse**
TCC Condensers // 28 January 1970
▸▸ **Collinson's men gather and the first shot is fired**
TCC Condensers // 28 January 1970
▸▸ **UNIT and Collinson's men battle**
TCC Condensers // 28 January 1970

EPISODE 2

▸▸ **Recovery 7 is checked and loaded onto lorry**
Claycart Bottom // 30 January 1970
▸▸ **Recovery 7 convoy drives over bridge**

Puckeridge Hill Road Bridge // 30 January 1970
➤➤ **Recovery 7 convoy on main road**
Fleet Road // 30 January 1970
➤➤ **Convoy is attacked and hijacked**
Royal Engineers Driving Circuit // 31 January 1970
➤➤ **Doctor recovers the hijacked lorry**
Claycart Bottom // 30 January 1970

EPISODE 3

➤➤ **Reegan drives astronauts away**
Wycombe Air Park // 29 January 1970
➤➤ **Reegan hides dead bodies in gravel**
Folley's Gravel Pit // 23 January 1970
➤➤ **Crane drive spots something in the gravel**
Folley's Gravel Pit // 23 January 1970
➤➤ **Liz leaves Space Control in Bessie**
Blue Circle Cement // 4 February 1970
➤➤ **Liz begins to be pursued**
Wycombe Air Park // 29 January 1970
➤➤ **Liz leaves Bessie and runs across field**
Gossmore Lane // 29 January 1970
➤➤ **Liz is chased across the weir and caught (3/4)**
Marlow Weir // 29 January 1970

EPISODE 4

➤➤ **Liz escapes from the bunker**
Beacon Hill // 2 February 1970
➤➤ **Liz recaptured by Taltalien**
Beacon Hill Road // 2 February 1970
➤➤ **Astronaut arrives at Space Control**
Blue Circle Cement // 4 February 1970

EPISODE 5

➤➤ **Reegan watches Brigadier going to Quinlan's office (cut)**
TCC Condensers // 28 January 1970
➤➤ **Reegan attacks guard and technician at Space Control**
Southall Gas Works // 26 January 1970
➤➤ **Reegan alters the M3 Variant**
Southall Gas Works // 26 January 1970
➤➤ **Brigadier arrives and checks fuel bay**
Southall Gas Works // 27 January 1970

EPISODE 6

➤➤ **Reegan drives into Space Control**
Blue Circle Cement // 4 February 1970
➤➤ **Reegan connects gas line at Decontamination Area**
Southall Gas Works // 26 January 1970
➤➤ **Reegan turns on the gas cylinder**
Southall Gas Works // 26 January 1970
➤➤ **Reegan turns off the gas cylinder**
Southall Gas Works // 26 January 1970

➤➤ **Reegan's van drives away**
Southall Gas Works // 26 January 1970
➤➤ **Reegan leaves Space Control**
Blue Circle Cement // 4 February 1970

EPISODE 7

➤➤ **Reegan and astronauts gain entry to Isotope Factory**
Sewage Treatment Works // 23 January 1970
➤➤ **Reegan steals isotopes as police arrive**
Sewage Treatment Works // 23 January 1970
➤➤ **Brigadier escapes from Space Control**
Blue Circle Cement // 3 February 1970
➤➤ **Brigadier and soldiers fight and access the bunker**
Beacon Hill // 2 February 1970
➤➤ **Doctor's part gains entry to Space Control**
Blue Circle Cement // 3 February 1970

The Facts

Reegan's van had originally been scripted to have two interchangeable signs reading 'Progressive Launderers Ltd' and 'Masons Bakery'. For the production, these were changed to read 'Hayhoe Launderers Ltd' and 'Silcock Bakeries' named after Margot Hayhoe and Pauline Silcock, the assistant floor manager and the director's assistant respectively.

The climactic chase sequence at the end of Episode 3 between Liz and Reegan's men had to be carefully planned. At the time, Caroline John didn't possess a driving licence and so couldn't drive Bessie on the public roads. As a result, all shots of John actually driving the car had to be done on the private ground of Wycombe Air Park. Long shots of the character driving Bessie on the public roads around Marlow had to be completed with stuntman Roy Scammell dressed in Liz's dress and hat.

Above: **Reegan (William Dysart) begins to bury his dead henchmen at Folley's Gravel Pit, Spade Oak.**

The subsequent chase across the rather precarious path of Marlow Weir was mainly done by Caroline John (who hadn't informed the production team that she was pregnant at the time), while the stunt fall across the side of the weir was again performed by Scammell.

Filming at the Blue Circle Cement plant in Northfleet took place during a time of industrial dispute at the works over wet weather working clothes. However, the employees enjoyed the BBC's visit so much that the industrial action was called off. As a result, the £25 facility fee payable to Blue Circle was cancelled and the manager, Pat Ward, supplied the cast and crew with barrels of beer to thank them.

Actor Robert Cawdron was only required on location to film a single scene as Taltalian, but it is noticeable that, at the time of filming the scene, the decision had not been made to give Taltalian an accent.

For the third time in 18 months, a *Doctor Who* production team had elected to use the deserted TCC Condensers (Telegraphic Condenser Co Ltd) factory at Wales Farm Road, Ealing as a filming location. Following its use in both *The Invasion* and *Spearhead from Space*, the BBC had purchased the site and would, in time, demolish the building and create a new centre to house some of the corporation's many departments.

Ouch!

The whole of Saturday 31 January was dedicated to filming the hijacking of the low-loader carrying the Recovery 7 capsule, in a sequence that involved the use of several motorbikes and an Alouette helicopter (which had previously been used in *Doctor Who and the Silurians*). One sequence required a stunt rider to fall from his motorbike, apparently having been gassed by Reegan and his gang. However, when the scene was enacted, instead of falling over, the motorbike stayed upright and ploughed straight into the camera crew, hitting both the Assistant Cameraman (who was protected by the thick sheepskin jacket he was wearing) and the director's assistant, Pauline Silcock. With one leg gashed through to the bone, Silcock had to be taken to hospital, escorted by assistant floor manager, Margot Hayhoe. As a result, Silcock couldn't continue with the location work and a replacement, Michael Jackley, had to join the production.

Comment

The Ambassadors of Death certainly features a wide variety of different locations, but of all of them it's probably the footage shot at Marlow Weir that is the most impressive, as a chase sequence is conducted in which Caroline John runs along a precariously narrow path across the fast-flowing weir, following a backwards-running cameraman. Dangerous stuff.

INFERNO

(tx 9 May to 20 June 1970)

The Story

A massive drilling site is established with the aim of penetrating the Earth's crust and releasing energy source 'Stahlman's Gas', named after the arrogant director of the project. The Doctor, using energy from the project's reactor, accidentally transports himself into a parallel world where the drilling is further advanced and is being guarded by a fascist military regime that governs England. Despite computer warnings, the drilling continues and, as a result, disaster ensues when the crust is finally penetrated. As the Earth begins to break apart, the Doctor narrowly escapes death and returns to his original dimension, where he is finally able to shut the drilling down with only seconds to spare, thus averting a similar disaster.

The Locations

1. Berry Wiggins and Co Ltd, Hoo St Werburgh, Kent

Shooting Schedule

EPISODE 1

▸▸ **Doctor drive to Project in Bessie**
Berry Wiggins // 31 March 1970
▸▸ **Slocum arrives on his bicycle**
Berry Wiggins // 2 April 1970
▸▸ **Slocum kills technician**
Berry Wiggins // 2 April 1970
▸▸ **Doctor arrives at hut**
Berry Wiggins // 3 April 1970
▸▸ **Slocum enters nuclear switchroom**
Berry Wiggins // 2 April 1970

EPISODE 2

▸▸ **Doctor and Brigadier on walkway**
Berry Wiggins // 1 April 1970
▸▸ **Doctor confronts Wyatt**
Berry Wiggins // 31 March 1970
▸▸ **Dead Wyatt and soldiers**
Berry Wiggins // 1 April 1970
▸▸ **Liz walks to control watched by Bromley**
Berry Wiggins // 2 April 1970

EPISODE 3

▸▸ **Doctor opens door and looks around**
Berry Wiggins // 3 April 1970
▸▸ **Doctor is shot at by Latimer**
Berry Wiggins // 31 March 1970
▸▸ **Doctor escapes from RSF in Bessie**
Berry Wiggins // 3 April 1970
▸▸ **Doctor hides from RSF**

Berry Wiggins // 31 March 1970
▸▸ **RSF search while Doctor meets Primordial Bromley**
Berry Wiggins // 1 April 1970
▸▸ **Wyatt's fall from gasometer**
Berry Wiggins // 3 April 1970
▸▸ **Doctor meets Section-Leader Shaw**
Berry Wiggins // 31 March 1970

EPISODE 4

▸▸ **Doctor hides in Land Rover**
Berry Wiggins // 31 March 1970
▸▸ **Doctor finds disaster suit in Land Rover**
Berry Wiggins // 2 April 1970
▸▸ **Land Rover stops at disaster crew**
Berry Wiggins // 2 April 1970
▸▸ **Doctor joins the disaster crew**
Berry Wiggins // 2 April 1970

EPISODE 5

▸▸ **Benton emerges and sees soldiers**
Berry Wiggins // 2 April 1970
▸▸ **Benton drills soldiers**
Berry Wiggins // 2 April 1970
▸▸ **Benton returns to control**
Berry Wiggins // 2 April 1970

EPISODE 6

▸▸ **Brigade-Leader, Liz and Petra emerge from control**
Berry Wiggins // 2 April 1970
▸▸ **Petra sees Doctor and Sutton emerge**
Berry Wiggins // 2 April 1970
▸▸ **Doctor's party enter nuclear switchroom**
Berry Wiggins // 2 April 1970
▸▸ **Primord emerges from control**
Berry Wiggins // 2 April 1970
▸▸ **More Primords emerge**
Berry Wiggins // 2 April 1970
▸▸ **Brigade-Leader's party pursued by Primords**
Berry Wiggins // 2 April 1970
▸▸ **Brigade-Leader, Liz and Petra run to hut**
Berry Wiggins // 2 April 1970
▸▸ **Panic as eruptions take place**
Berry Wiggins // 2 April 1970

EPISODE 7

▸▸ **Doctor evades soldiers and encounters Bromley**
Berry Wiggins // 1 April 1970

The Facts

Although it appears that the story was produced under its transmitted title, *Inferno*, the film diary also makes mention of one of the story's earlier titles, *Project Inferno*, indicating that it changed very close to the location dates.

Left: **Stuntman Roy Scammell throws himself from the top of one Berry Wiggins' gasometers.**

Berry Wiggins and Co were paid £100 for the use of their premises. From the outset, director Douglas Camfield made it clear to his cast and crew that he expected them to adopt a professional attitude to the location filming and the environment that they would be working in.

'Between 31st March and 3rd April we shall be filming at Messrs BERRY WIGGINS of Rochester, oil refiners and manufacturers of bitumen. Because of the extreme fire hazard, this firm enforces the most stringent fire regulations. In fact, any employee found smoking on the premises is dismissed without question.

'We have secured permission to film on this excellent location, subject to the unconditional understanding that smoking is absolutely forbidden in any circumstances – except in our allocated vehicle area. The Management have made it clear that if any member of this production unit is found smoking within the plant area, filming permission will be revoked immediately, and the whole unit will be ordered to leave the location forthwith.

'I DO NOT have to stress what a tragedy this would be for the serial, bearing in mind the amount of filming involved. I would urge that all smoking materials, including matches, are left behind in transport to avoid any risk of forgetfulness. Apples, sweets and chewing gum will be available from the two Sues[12] as a comfort for habitual smokers! We must have 100 per cent co-operation in this matter. We cannot afford a moment's thoughtlessness. YOU HAVE BEEN WARNED.

Above: **The Doctor (Jon Pertwee) in Bessie. In the background is Kingsnorth Power Station, the site originally considered as the filming location for *Inferno*.**

'As you will see from the location filming script and schedule, we have a monumental amount to shoot in the time available – a daily average of 40-45 set-ups over a four-day period. If we are to complete our filming to standard, the whole operation must go like clockwork. I must ask your fullest and most professional co-operation in carrying through our schedule. To be blunt – no woolly thinking, no late risings, no incomprehension, no going to the wrong location etc etc – in fact, no hang-ups of any kind please. We have worked out a very detailed schedule. From it you will see exactly what, when and how we will shoot. Please study the schedule carefully and work out exactly what your contribution is. If you have any problems or are in any doubt about anything at all – CONTACT ME NOW. Contact me while there is time to sort things out and time for consultation. DO NOT WAIT UNTIL WE GET ON LOCATION. Once filming starts, we must go like the clappers.'

Douglas Camfield's letter to the Production Team – Film Diary

Fire prevention also extended to other areas of the production. Everyone was asked to make certain that their shoes did not contain steel studs, caps or heels in order to ensure that no sparks were created, and a number of guns used during the filming were non-firing fibreglass mock-ups.

The second day of filming fell on 1 April and Jon Pertwee decided to play a joke on stuntman Derek Martin.

Derek Martin: 'At that time, my pride and joy was a 1964 Jaguar 2.8 in mint condition. I put it in the hotel car park and we all left on a coach to go to the location.

Just after lunch, I received a message that the brewery had delivered at the hotel and had reversed into my car, smashing all the front in, and had left without saying anything. Naturally, I was fuming and couldn't wait to get back to the hotel. When the coach arrived back with the cast and crew aboard, they let me off first. There was the car, the front covered in canvas and crates all over it. I walked slowly over to the car, absolutely devastated. When I pulled back the canvas and removed the crates, there was no damage at all. I turned round and there was Jon and everybody laughing and chorusing, "April Fool!"'

The filming schedule required Jon Pertwee, who suffered from vertigo, to perform several scenes on top of a number of high gasometers. To help him get used to the heights that he would be working at, stuntmen Terry Walsh and Alan Chuntz walked him around the top of the gasometers to acclimatise him prior to the commencement of filming. But Pertwee wasn't the only member of the cast to have problems with the heights involved while filming at Berry Wiggins.

Ian Fairbairn (Bromley): 'I was on all these high catwalks, and I suffered desperately from vertigo at the time. Douglas would say, "Let go! For goodness' sake, let go of that rail!" And I said, "I can't, Douglas! I must hold on with one hand!" I was all this way up, and I was terrified. And then Pertwee had to shoot me with a fire-extinguisher – and, with me being a non-drinker, I wouldn't take the brandy that they were issuing – which was freezing!'[13]

Ouch!

On the morning of Friday 3 April, a scene was filmed showing the Doctor escaping from the RSF soldiers in Bessie. The sequence required Pertwee to drive the car at stuntman Alan Chuntz, who intended to throw himself clear at the appropriate moment. Unfortunately, the stunt was mistimed and Chuntz's left leg was hit by the car's bumper, causing a severe gash which needed several stitches at the local hospital.

Unused Locations

Kingsnorth Power Station – The discovery of Berry Wiggins as the ideal location to film Don Houghton's tale came quite by chance. Looking for suitable industrial-type premises, the BBC were initially planning to investigate Kingsnorth Power Station on the Isle of Grain. But as they made their way to the site, they passed Berry Wiggins on the approach road to the station and decided that they need look no further. Kingsnorth Power Station can be clearly seen in many of the location scenes in *Inferno*, however, most notably when the Doctor climbs onto the top of the gasometer to be confronted by Wyatt in Episode 3.

Comment

For a tale of industrial disaster, the production team could not have found a better place to stage it than Berry Wiggins Ltd, with its vast estate full of pre-fabricated buildings, gasometers and pipework. But Douglas Camfield uses it to add an extra dimension to his story-telling, as the location doesn't just become a pretty backdrop to the unfurling events. Rather, it becomes almost integral to the plot itself, with major sequences and chases being set among and indeed on top of the gasometers. The scenes set after 'Penetration Zero' in the parallel world are very well handled, instilling a genuine sense of heat and global disaster into the story.

TERROR OF THE AUTONS

(tx 2 January to 23 January 1971)

The Story

The Doctor's old enemy, the Master, arrives on Earth and steals the Nestene energy unit. He uses it to reopen a channel with the alien intelligence by connecting the sphere to the nearby Beacon Hill Radio Telescope. Taking over production at a plastics factory, the Master creates a new army of Autons, which begin to distribute the Nestene Autojets, plastic daffodils that spray a suffocating film onto their victims' faces. As the Nestenes begin to materialise above the radio telescope, the Doctor convinces the Master as to the foolishness of his alliance, and together the two Time Lords break the connection, flinging the Nestenes back into space.

The Locations

1. St Peter's Court, Chalfont St Peter, Buckinghamshire
2. Car Park, Church Lane, Chalfont St Peter, Buckinghamshire
3. Hodgemoor Woods, Chalfont St Giles, Buckinghamshire
4. Queen's Wharf, Queen Caroline Street, Hammersmith, London, W6
5. Robert Brothers Circus, Lea Bridge Road, Leyton, London, E10
6. Totternhoe Lime and Stone Co Ltd., Totternhoe, Dunstable, Bedfordshire
7. GPO Relay Station, Zouches Farm, Caddington, Bedfordshire
8. Thermo Plastics Ltd, Luton Road, Dunstable, Bedfordshire[14]

Shooting Schedule

EPISODE 1

▸▸ **Rossini meets the Master**
Robert Brothers Circus // 18 September 1970
▸▸ **Philips climbs the radio telescope**
GPO Relay Station // 22 September 1970
▸▸ **Radio telescopes begin to move**
GPO Relay Station // 22 September 1970
▸▸ **Doctor and Jo arrive at telescope in Bessie**
GPO Relay Station // 22 September 1970
▸▸ **Master and Farrel discover Jo**
Thermo Plastics Ltd // 23 September 1970
▸▸ **Philips' car is found** (cut)
Hodgemoor Woods // 17 September 1970

EPISODE 2

▸▸ **Bomb explodes**
Queen's Wharf // 17 September 1970
▸▸ **Master bids Farrel Snr. farewell**
Thermo Plastics Ltd // 23 September 1970
▸▸ **Doctor arrives at circus and begins investigation**
Robert Brothers Circus // 18 September 1970
▸▸ **Doctor is curious about Master's horse box**
Robert Brothers Circus // 18 September 1970
▸▸ **Jo sees Philips climb into Master's horsebox**
Robert Brothers Circus // 18 September 1970
▸▸ **Brigadier's car turns into woods**
Hodgemoor Woods // 17 September 1970
▸▸ **Master sees Doctor and Jo on monitor**
Robert Brothers Circus // 18 September 1970
▸▸ **Doctor and Jo attacked and rescued**
Robert Brothers Circus // 18 September 1970

EPISODE 3

▸▸ **Autons hunt Doctor and Jo in quarry**
Totternhoe Lime and Stone Co Ltd // 21 September 1970
▸▸ **Autons hand out daffodils**
St Peter's Court // 17 September 1970
▸▸ **Autons return to coach**
Church Lane Car Park // 17 September 1970
▸▸ **Doctor and Brigadier arrive at plastics factory**
Thermo Plastics Ltd // 23 September 1970
▸▸ **Doctor and Brigadier go through front entrance**
Thermo Plastics Ltd // 23 September 1970
▸▸ **Police car stops coach** (cut)
Hodgemoor Woods // 17 September 1970

EPISODE 4

▸▸ **Motorcycle policeman trails coach**
Hodgemoor Woods // 17 September 1970
▸▸ **Coach waits in quarry**
Totternhoe Lime and Stone Co Ltd // 21 September 1970
▸▸ **Doctor, Jo and Master arrive at coach in Bessie**
Totternhoe Lime and Stone Co Ltd //

Above: Katy Manning as Jo Grant is filmed approaching the plastics factory for Episode 1 of *Terror of the Autons.*

21 September 1970

▸▸ **Brigadier's car follows coach**
Hodgemoor Woods // 17 September 1970

▸▸ **Coach arrives at Beacon Hill**
GPO Relay Station // 22 September 1970

▸▸ **Doctor and Jo jump from coach**
GPO Relay Station // 22 September 1970

▸▸ **Coach comes to a stop**
GPO Relay Station // 22 September 1970

▸▸ **Master climbs telescope followed by Doctor**
GPO Relay Station // 22/23 September 1970

▸▸ **UNIT battle with Autons**
GPO Relay Station // 22/23 September 1970

▸▸ **Autons deactivate**
GPO Relay Station // 22 September 1970

▸▸ **Master escapes in coach**
GPO Relay Station // 22 September 1970

The Facts

All the location filming for *Terror of the Autons* was done under the story's original title, *The Spray of Death.*

Two scenes that included material filmed at Hodgemoor Wood on 17 September were edited from the story prior to transmission. The first, from Episode 1, was a continuation of the scene where UNIT's Sergeant Benton tells Captain Yates that the abandoned car belonging to Professor Philips, one of the workers at the radio telescope, has been discovered, complete with the zinc box in which the Nestene energy unit had been taken. The end of this scene was cut after recording but would have continued with Yates telling Benton to

bring the box back. The Doctor snaps out of his thoughts and suggests that they keep a watch on the car for an hour or two first, just in case Philips or the Master return for it. This then led into a cut film sequence with armed UNIT soldiers lying out of sight in a hedge. The soldiers, led by Benton, keep watch on a rather shabby car standing alone in the centre of the field.

The second deleted scene from Episode 3 was more extensive, although only the opening part involved any location work. The five-page scene was intended to immediately follow the 'Auton in the safe' sequence and would have begun with a police car driving up to the stationary coach in the woods. The scene would then have continued inside the coach (recorded in the studio) and featured the PC being told that the driver had got lost on the next stop of the promotions tour. The Master explains that the now terrified Farrel, the managing director of the plastics factory, has been overworking and is under strain. The policeman's interest is drawn to the carnival-masked Autons and he removes the false head of the Auton leader to see the blank face underneath. The Auton shoots him, to Farrel's dismay.

Although Max Diamond drove the police car for the location part of the scene, in the studio the policeman was actually played by Bill McGuirk, who received a credit at the end of the episode, even though his performance was never broadcast.

Barry Letts (director): 'I remember that we had a great deal of trouble with those scenes, because we did it in the studio, with backgrounds put in with CSO. Unfortunately the chrome window frames reflected the blue, and consequently disappeared. I think it likely that we decided on viewing it in editing that it wasn't acceptable and took it out.'

Episode 3 featured an impressive stunt fall filmed in the Totternhoe quarry, as the Auton policeman, played by Terry Walsh, is knocked over the edge of a precipice by Yates in the UNIT car.

Barry Letts again: 'On the recce that I did with Terry, I proposed that we should fake the fall, cutting away to Yates in the middle of it. But Terry said, "No, no! It's a lovely stunt. Let me do the whole thing." I pointed out that he would only get the same money, but he said that that wasn't the point. He just wanted to have a go. And he did, beautifully.'

One of the main filming locations chosen for *Terror of the Autons* was Zouches Farm, near Caddingdon, just south of Dunstable. Located on the farm was (and, indeed, still is) the GPO's Dunstable Relay Station, consisting of two transmitter towers which were used to simulate the radio telescope structure of the Beacon Hill Research Establishment. As several artistes were required to climb the steps leading up the tower, formal permission was required from the London office of the GPO for which the BBC paid £36. Although the intention had been to film only on the one day, it seems that the work overran and so arrangements were made to return the following afternoon to complete the scenes of the Master throwing a technician off the tower.

As well as the transmitter towers, a cut cornfield at Zouches Farm was used to stage the final battle between the Autons and the UNIT troops at the end of Episode 4. The scene featured a number of pyrotechnic effects, one of which was so powerful that it blew a hole in the straw hat worn by a masked Auton, played by stuntman Terry Walsh.

With the first two days of location filming around London completed, the cast and crew broke for the weekend, intent on beginning the scenes around the Dunstable locations on Monday morning. It was during this break that Nicholas Courtney began to suffer a sudden and unexpected attack of depression and insecurity. Having received an injection from his doctor to help him sleep, Courtney duly reported to Television Centre the next day, and boarded the coach taking the crew up the M1.

Nicholas Courtney (Brigadier Lethbridge-Stewart): 'Ken Trew [costume designer] accompanied me and chatted about the day's filming that lay ahead. I was unable to reply to anything he said. I was just dreading going to work. This was all the more extraordinary as I had hardly anything to do. Three or four lines at the most. We arrived at the location and when it was time for my first piece of work I was unable to stop shaking. Jon Pertwee noticed my distress, as indeed did Barry Letts. It was soon quite obvious that I was in no state to do any work that day. I was taken to the nearest hospital and then sent home. The next morning I went to see my own doctor who gave me a sedative and told me to rest that day as well. I had now missed two days' filming out of a tight schedule and no-one was any the wiser about what the trouble was – least of all myself.'[15]

Barry Letts: 'Nick felt that he couldn't go on when we were still at the quarry, so we asked one of the crowd artistes who was more or less the same size as Nick to double for him for the rest of the location. There's one shot of the Brig running away from camera where it's quite clear that he's wearing very un-Briggish white socks!'

Courtney's absence from the filming meant that the final scenes at Zouches Farm shot on 22 September had to be carefully orchestrated so that the Brigadier was either seen from behind, was obscured by another character or was strategically positioned just out of frame. The script was also duly adjusted, dropping Holmes' original ending where the Brigadier uses a loudhailer to give the Master several chances to escape before he,

Yates and UNIT shoot the running figure. The Brigadier was to have answered the Doctor's protests by saying 'How many deaths has he caused? How many more if he escapes?' – before the Doctor pulls off the mask to reveal that the figure is actually an Auton.

Courtney returned to the production on the last day of filming, where he was required for just two shots of the Doctor and the Brigadier visiting the plastics factory in Episode 3.

The establishing shots of Beacon Hill were actually achieved on location by photographing a foreground model of the two radio telescope dishes in front of the real transmitter masts on Zouches Farm.

All the scenes depicting Rossini's Circus were shot at the Robert Brothers Circus while it was pitched for its two-week stay at the playing fields on Lea Bridge Road in Leyton, East London, with many of the circus' resident clowns being booked and paid as extras for Episode 2. Tommy and Bobby Roberts[16] were paid £100 for the use of the circus and its facilities. *Doctor Who* wasn't the only BBC programme to make use of the circus during this period. One week prior to the filming of *Terror of the Autons*, location filming was carried out at Robert Brothers for two *Z-Cars* stories, *Talking to an Elephant* and *Off with the Motley*, shown in October 1970.[17]

Ouch!

Terror of the Autons was the debut story for Katy Manning, who played the Doctor's new assistant Jo Grant. On only her second day of filming, the myopic

Above: **The Master (Roger Delgado) reveals his plans to Rex Farrel (Michael Wisher). This scene was filmed at the Thermo Plastics factory on 23 September 1970.**

Manning slipped on a stone while running across the Totternhoe quarry, spraining her right ankle in the process. She was taken to the local hospital where she was X-rayed, but as the injury wasn't serious she was able to continue filming at Zouches Farm the following day. However, a line was added to Katy's dialogue following the jump from the coach, stating that she'd twisted her ankle in the leap, helping to explain away any stiffness of movement on her part.

Comment

With the first story of *Doctor Who's* eighth season featuring not only a new regular character but also the return of an old enemy, Barry Letts bravely decided to take on the role of director himself and produces a story which forms an excellent showcase for both the Autons and the Master. Particularly noteworthy is the excellent cat and mouse hunt in Totternhoe Quarry between the Auton policemen and the Doctor and Jo at the beginning of Episode 3, resulting in the spectacular stunt fall by Terry Walsh.

THE MIND OF EVIL

(tx 30 January to 6 March 1971)

The Story

At Stangmoor Prison, the Doctor witnesses a demonstration of the Keller machine, a device that can remove the evil impulses from the minds of hardened criminals. In reality, the machine is designed by the Master and houses an alien mind parasite. Using the evil impulses stored within the machine, the Master incites a riot at Stangmoor and uses the prisoners to hijack a Thunderbolt Nerve Gas Missile being transported by UNIT to a destruction site. With the missile in his possession, the Master plans to destroy a delicate peace conference being held between the major powers. The Doctor manages to turn the mind parasite against the Master and, unable to prevent his escape, the missile is set to explode, destroying the Keller machine with it.

The Locations

1. Dover Castle, Castle Hill, Dover, Kent
   A. Constable's Gate
   B. Outer Courtyard
   C. Inner Bailey
   D. Fitzwilliam's Gate
   E. King's Gate
2. Archers Court Road, Whitfield, Kent
3. Hanger, Alland Grange, RAF Manston, Manston, Kent
4. RAF Swingate, Dover, Kent
5. Pineham Road, Pineham, Kent

6. Cornwall Gardens, London, SW7
7. Commonwealth Institute, Kensington High Street, London, W8

Shooting Schedule

EPISODE 1

▸▸ **Doctor and Jo arrive at Stangmoor**
Dover Castle – A // 26 October 1970
▸▸ **Yates leaves peace conference (cut)**
Commonwealth Institute // 3 November 1970
▸▸ **Yates arrives at UNIT HQ (cut)**
Cornwall Gardens // 3 November 1970
▸▸ **Chin Lee burns papers**
Cornwall Gardens // 2 November 1970
▸▸ **Doctor returns to Stangmoor (cut)**[18]
Dover Castle – A // 26 October 1970

EPISODE 2

▸▸ **Chin Lee mentally attacks Benton**
Cornwall Gardens // 3 November 1970
▸▸ **Benton searches for Chin Lee, enters UNIT HQ**
Cornwall Gardens // 3 November 1970
▸▸ **Benton leaves UNIT HQ / Master bugs telephone**
Cornwall Gardens // 2 November 1970
▸▸ **Master listens to telephone conversation in hut**
Cornwall Gardens // 2 November 1970
▸▸ **Master listens to telephone conversation in car**[19]
Cornwall Gardens // 2 November 1970
▸▸ **Master instructs Chin Lee to kill**
Cornwall Gardens // 2 November 1970
▸▸ **Doctor and Brigadier with Fu Peng (cut)**
Commonwealth Institute // 3 November 1970

EPISODE 3

▸▸ **Motorcycle passes research station (cut)**[20]
RAF Swingate // 30 October 1970
▸▸ **Doctor and Chin Lee leave UNIT HQ**
Cornwall Gardens // 2 November 1970
▸▸ **Jeep fails to start (cut)**[21]
RAF Swingate // 30 October 1970
▸▸ **Master's car leaves for Stangmoor**
Cornwall Gardens // 2 November 1970
▸▸ **Master arrives at Stangmoor**
Dover Castle // 26 October 1970
▸▸ **Doctor drives off in Bessie (cut)**
RAF Swingate // 30 October 1970
▸▸ **Doctor captured on return to Stangmoor**
Dover Castle // 26 October 1970
▸▸ **Yates on telephone, convoy moves off (partially cut)**[22]
RAF Swingate // 30 October 1970
▸▸ **Doctor is shot at by prisoners**
Dover Castle // 27 October 1970

EPISODE 4

▶▶ **Convoy underway (cut)**[23]
Pineham Road // 30 October 1970

▶▶ **Master speaks to prisoners**
Dover Castle – A // 27 October 1970

▶▶ **Ambush of missile**
Archers Court Road // 28 October 1970

▶▶ **Yates follows missile**
Archers Court Road // 28 October 1970

▶▶ **Prisoners arrive at hanger, Yates caught**
Alland Grange // 29 October 1970

▶▶ **Prisoners return to Stangmoor (cut)**
Dover Castle – A // 27 October 1970

▶▶ **Aftermath of ambush**
Archers Court Road // 28 October 1970

▶▶ **Master leaves Stangmoor**
Dover Castle – C // 27 October 1970

EPISODE 5

▶▶ **Helicopter shots**[24]
Dover Castle – C // 28 October 1970

▶▶ **Prisoners move Doctor inside (cut)**[25]
Dover Castle – C // 28 October 1970

▶▶ **Master leaves (cut)**[26]
Alland Grange // 29 October 1970

▶▶ **Yates escapes (cut)**[27]
Alland Grange // 29 October 1970

▶▶ **Brigadier's van gets into Stangmoor**
Dover Castle – A/B/C/D // 26 October 1970

▶▶ **UNIT storm the prison and battle commences**
Dover Castle – C/D/E[28] // 27 October 1970

▶▶ **UNIT and prisoners battle (remount)**
Dover Castle – C // 31 October 1970

▶▶ **Prisoners give up (cut)**[29]
Dover Castle // 27 October 1970

EPISODE 6

▶▶ **Master watches as missile is readied**[30]
Alland Grange // 29 October 1970

▶▶ **Prisoners gassed (cut)**[31]
Alland Grange // 29 October 1970

▶▶ **Doctor, Jo and Barnham leave for hanger (cut)**
Dover Castle – A // 26 October 1970

▶▶ **Doctor and Master meet at the hanger**[32]
Alland Grange // 29 October 1970

▶▶ **Helicopter lands at hanger**[33]
Alland Grange // 29 October 1970

▶▶ **Doctor and Jo leave in helicopter**[34]
Alland Grange // 29 October 1970

▶▶ **Shots involving a car**
Location Unknown // 4 November 1970

The Facts

One of the main problems facing director Timothy Combe as he approached the production of *The Mind of Evil* was an overlong script. As a result, a number of scenes which had been scripted and shot had to be abandoned later in order to bring the finished episodes within the running time specified. One of the main casualties of this was nearly all the material shot at RAF Swingate on Friday 30 October. The location was used to represent the missile centre in Episode 3 where the Thunderbolt warhead begins its journey guarded by UNIT troops. Once the required five scenes were completed, the production team relocated to the Pineham Road, situated between the villages of Pineham and Guston, to shoot a scene for Episode 4 of the missile convoy moving along.

Timothy Combe: 'There were constant script problems on this series, especially in making the end feasible and having to use a helicopter on more occasions than originally envisaged. Probably there would have

Above: **Jon Pertwee poses with the Bloodhound missile and Sergeants Herridage and Talbot, Bombardiers Graham, Hall, Thompson and Lamb, Lance Bombardier Berkley and Gunner Davenport.**

been no overspend if pruning of the scripts had been done at the outset, and savings made accordingly – for example, all those Episode 3 scenes at RAF Swingate which added up to a whole day's filming wasted.'

While problems caused by shooting too much material wouldn't reveal themselves until later in the production, an immediate problem arose concerning the footage shot on Tuesday 27 October of the battle between the UNIT troops and the prisoners at Dover Castle. As usual, the day's footage was dispatched to London to be processed and then reviewed by Barry Letts. On viewing the rushes, Letts immediately contacted Combe to inform him that a proportion of the footage he had shot had been ruined due to a damaged negative. Letts also noted that much of the fight sequence had been filmed in long shot and that more close-ups were going to be needed.

Timothy Combe: 'We had been up against time and bad light when we first did the wide shots and I had to compromise my shooting script accordingly. I had planned to pick up these close-ups on another day and probably at another location where there were some stone walls which would pass as a prison. I did tell Barry this but, fortunately, the neg scratch on one roll of film allowed me to have an extra day's filming and the opportunity to reinstate some of my original ideas.'

The authorities at Dover Castle were immediately approached and agreed to a further day of filming being carried out at the location on Saturday 31 October, the total cost of which would amount to a further £436 10p

Timothy Combe: 'The producer wouldn't allow me very many extras, walk-ons or stuntmen on the Saturday, so there was a lot of inventive photography. It was a very small unit and fortunately we had a very good team spirit. The union members present turned a blind eye and I bought everyone a large drink after our morning's filming! I don't think that would be allowed nowadays.'

Only permitted a total of four walk-ons for the reshoot, Combe decided to don the prisoners' overalls himself in an attempt to swell the numbers.

As well as losing virtually everything shot on 30 October, all the material filmed at the Commonwealth Institute on 3 November was also destined to end up on the cutting-room floor. Following the completion of an early afternoon's work at Cornwall Gardens, the production team moved to the Institute in Kensington. A scene depicting Yates leaving the conference in the first episode was shot, after which the main reception of the Institute was lit for the final sequence of the day, the Doctor and the Brigadier's meeting with the Chinese peace delegate, Fu Peng, which would be filmed during the course of the evening.

For the role of the Chinese delegate, Combe had cast Oriental actor Andy Ho. However, when filming began, Combe discovered that he was deeply unhappy with Ho's performance. 'The actor I used had done a lot of work, so I don't know if it was my direction or what, but he was awful! He was a very precise person, there was no variation in the tone of his voice level, no lightness or freshness in him. I remember seeing the rushes and thinking, "Oh God, he's just as bad as I thought he was."'

Ho was paid in full on 10 November for his performance and duly released from his contract. Two days later, replacement actor Kristopher Kum was cast in the role. However, as the location budget had already escalated due to the extra, unplanned day of filming done at Dover Castle on 31 October, it was decided that a return to the Commonwealth Institute was not practical and the scene was performed as part of the studio recording for Episode 2 on Friday 20 November.

The Thunderbolt rocket used in *The Mind of Evil* was a genuine Bloodhound missile, which had been loaned to the production by the 36th Heavy Air Defence Regiment, based at Horseshoe Barracks in Shoeburyness, Essex. Unwilling to let untrained personnel handle either the missile or its transporter, the regiment supplied eight of its own men to look after the weapon. A line was duly inserted into the script to explain that some of the prisoners were posing as 'fake troops'.

Following the completion of location filming on *The Mind of Evil*, production assistant John Griffiths wrote a memo to Gavin Campbell, the BBC's Properties Manager, on 6 November, explaining concerns that he had about the services supplied to the production by Kingsbury Motors, the company regularly used to provide on-screen vehicles for *Doctor Who*. Throughout the location filming, a number of different vehicles had been used and most of them had caused problems at one stage or another. Griffiths recommended that Kingsbury's initial quotation of £695 be reduced by 75 per cent in compensation. Following his investigations, Campbell concluded on 18 December that, 'In the circumstances, I do not consider these complaints as justification for a reduction of at least 75 per cent,' but agreed that specific problems relating to the milk float and Black Maria supplied by Kingsbury's constituted an issue 'which I have to settle amicably and may involve the question of reducing the original charge of these vehicles.'

Prior to filming at Dover Castle, the cast and crew were warned that permission to film at the location had been very difficult to obtain and it was essential that members of the public who would be visiting the castle be 'unrestricted as much as humanly possible'.

On submitting his final episode to the BBC, scriptwriter Don Houghton had suggested that the climax of the story be played out in a quarry setting, but one that would be mocked up in the studio. In his accompanying letter to Terrance Dicks, he indicated that he was open to other suggestions as to how this could best be achieved.

'I suspect the director will be worried about our INT. FOR EXT. disused quarry. Matching is going to be problematic anyway. I only chose the quarry setting because, logically, it would help to isolate the explosion. I've been wracking my brains for an alternative – but none come readily to mind. It would be great if the whole sequence could be done on TK[35] – but that would well and truly overload your exterior shooting schedules. Maybe a compromise with a deserted barn, or an old railway shed, or a building of some sort, might be the answer. Depends very much on how the director and the producer feel.'

Don Houghton to Terrance Dicks – 28 August 1970

Comment

If Timothy Combe thought he'd had difficulties with the station scenes in *Doctor Who and the Silurians*, he certainly couldn't have envisaged the problems he would face when trying to get his location scenes for *The Mind of Evil* in the can. Watching the finished episodes, however, the problems he experienced are not at all apparent. The footage shot at Dover Castle is more than adequate, but the real coup must lie in the acquisition of a genuine missile to double as the Thunderbolt. As a result of this, the story takes on an edge of reality that would not have been present if a rather obvious BBC prop had been used.

THE CLAWS OF AXOS

(tx 13 March to 3 April 1971)

The Story

A large alien vessel crashes to Earth and the inhabitants, the golden-skinned humanoid Axons, request time to replenish their ship's energy banks. In return, the Axons offer the gift of Axonite, an organic compound. It soon becomes apparent that the Axons, Axonite and their ship are all part of one parasitic organism, intent on bleeding the Earth dry of all its energy resources. Risking his own life, the Doctor joins the Axos organism to the TARDIS circuitry and removes it from Earth, placing it in a perpetual time loop.

The Locations

1. Dengemarsh Road, Lydd, Kent
2. Dungeness Road, Dungeness, Kent
3. St Martin's Plain Camp, Cheriton High Street, Shorncliffe, Kent
   • Railway Bridge
   • Training Grounds

4. Dungeness 'A' Nuclear Power Station, Dungeness, Kent

Shooting Schedule

EPISODE 1

▸▸ **Pigbin Josh by boats**
   Dungeness Road // 5 January 1971
▸▸ **Pigbin Josh finds bicycle on rubbish tip**
   Dengemarsh Road // 4 January 1971
▸▸ **Pigbin Josh rides bicycle**
   Dengemarsh Road // 4 January 1971
▸▸ **Pigbin Josh falls into the water**
   Dengemarsh Road and Sewer // 4 January 1971
▸▸ **Pigbin Josh is pulled into Axos**
   Dungeness Road // 5 January 1971
▸▸ **Filer in car**
   Dengemarsh Road // 4 January 1971
▸▸ **Filer finds Josh's bicycle**
   Dungeness Road // 5 January 1971
▸▸ **Filer captured as UNIT arrives**
   Dungeness Road // 5 January 1971
▸▸ **Doctor's party enters Axos**
   Dungeness Road // 5 January 1971
▸▸ **Benton runs to UNIT mobile HQ**
   Dungeness Road // 5 January 1971
▸▸ **Yates and Benton examine Josh's body**
   Dungeness Road // 5 January 1971
▸▸ **Jo exits UNIT mobile HQ and enters Axos**
   Dungeness Road // 5 January 1971

EPISODE 2

▸▸ **Doctor's party exits Axos**
   Dungeness Road // 6 January 1971
▸▸ **Master and Filer leave Axos**
   Dungeness Road // 6 January 1971
▸▸ **Master jumps onto UNIT lorry**
   St Martin's Plain Camp – Bridge // 7 January 1971

EPISODE 3

▸▸ **TARDIS driven to Nuton Complex**
   Dungeness Nuclear Power Station // 8 January 1971
▸▸ **Axon attacks soldiers en route to reactor**
   Dungeness Nuclear Power Station // 8 January 1971

EPISODE 4

▸▸ **Doctor and Jo escape from Axos**
   Dungeness Road // 6 January 1971
▸▸ **Yates sets up video camera**
   Dungeness Road // 6 January 1971
▸▸ **Benton and Yates leave after Axos rises**
   Dungeness Road // 6 January 1971
▸▸ **Axons attack Land Rover**

Above: **Stuart Fell is dressed as the Axon monster in the grounds of Dungeness Power Station.**

St Martin's Plain Camp – Grounds //
7 January 1971
▸▸ **Evacuation of Nuton Complex**
Dungeness Nuclear Power Station // 8 January 1971
▸▸ **Brigadier's party arrive/leave safe distance point**
Dungeness Road // 6 January 1971
▸▸ **TARDIS arrives back**
Dungeness Road // 6 January 1971

The Facts

All the location work for *The Claws of Axos* was filmed under the story's original title, *The Vampire from Space*, as indeed was the first studio recording session held on 22 January 1971, during which the opening titles bearing the *Vampire* legend were recorded.[36] The decision to change the title to *The Claws of Axos* wasn't made until a week later, on 28 January.

As well as featuring all the scenes recorded at Television Centre that evening, the existing recording of the first studio day also features the full-length location film inserts required for Episode 1 and provides an excellent example of how location scenes can often be trimmed during the editing process. The following is a listing of all the film sequences transferred to the tape, showing the difference between the location scenes' original lengths and the transmitted lengths (italics indicate transmitted segment):

Pigbin Josh by boats – (Transmitted: 17" / Studio Tape: 55")
The sequence begins with a camera looking at the sea after which it pans left as the local tramp, 'Pigbin' Josh appears from between the boats. *He runs towards the camera and rides off on his bicycle.*

Pigbin Josh finds bicycle on rubbish tip – (Transmitted: 34" / Studio Tape: 1'25")
Josh cycles out of the fog and stops by the rubbish tip. *He wanders over and finds another bike. He dismisses it and throws it away.* On his way back, he finds a single shoe. He compares it with his own and stuffs it into his pocket. He gets back onto his bicycle and rides off into the fog again.[37]

Pigbin Josh rides bicycle – (Transmitted: 9" / Studio Tape: 20")
Josh rides his bicycle down the road. The camera cuts to a close-up with Josh muttering 'They won't find nothing on me…'

Pigbin Josh is pulled into Axos – (Transmitted: 52" / Studio Tape: 1'01")
As well as a few extra seconds before Josh sees Axos, the original sequence is slightly longer at the end and shows Josh being pulled all the way into the spaceship.

Filer captured as UNIT arrives – (Transmitted: 1'04" (total) / Studio Tape: 1'36" and 25")
The transmitted version of this scene is spilt into two with the insertion of a studio shot of Josh being rejected by Axos. In the original filmed version, the Washington agent, Filer, makes his way across the shingle from Josh's bicycle to Axos. Also cut from the transmitted version is a shot of Filer screaming just before the Axon tentacle attaches itself to him. At the conclusion of the sequence, the Doctor's party fully enters the mobile UNIT HQ and the door is shut behind them. The subsequent shot of the arrival of the car belonging to the government minister, Chinn, was filmed as a separate scene and likewise originally showed all the characters in the party entering the mobile HQ.

Doctor's party enters Axos – (Transmitted 31" / Studio Tape: 57")
The mobile HQ door opens and the Doctor, the Brigadier, Chinn exit together with Hardiman and

Winser, the two representatives from the Nuton Power Complex. They walk across the shingle to Axos. *The spaceship doors open and the Doctor's party enters the ship, the door closing behind them.*
Yates and Benton examine Josh's body –
(Transmitted 24" / Studio Tape: 36")
Essentially, the sequence is much the same as transmitted except that there is no flare to white as Josh's body disintegrates. Two brief reaction shots of Yates and Benton are deleted, as is a longer shot of Josh's face collapsing.

On Sunday 3 January, director Michael Ferguson and a small group of his production team travelled to their base hotel in Hythe, together with the BBC's scenery and props van, to prepare for the first day of filming on *The Claws of Axos* the following morning. When Ferguson woke up on Monday, he found that there had been an overnight fall of snow and a heavy sea fog had closed in around the coastline. Undaunted, he dispatched the scenery crew to the Dungeness Road to begin setting up the embedded entrance to the Axon spaceship which would be used the following day, while he and the rest of the crew began filming some early sequences for the story on the Dengemarsh Road a few miles away.

During the first day of filming on the Dungeness Road on Tuesday, the crew were visited by Patrick Welland, a reporter from the *Kentish Express*, who later commented on the cold working conditions that were having to be endured. 'The time is the present (near enough); the place, somewhere in England near the nation's power complex; the action, the arrival of 'something' from outer space together with some rather unpleasant organisms with an uncanny ability to change their form and known as Axon Monsters. And why must Dungeness be chosen as the site for this threatening interruption to our lives? "We wanted to find this sort of area where it's rather bleak and where there is a power station in the background, the prime reason we came here," explained producer Barry Letts, clad in a well-used fur maxi coat borrowed from the BBC wardrobe.

'No doubt Dungeness' wide open spaces and its power station went down well on film,' Welland continued. 'The weather was a different matter altogether. Actor Jon Pertwee, elegantly armed against the cold in a flowing cape, looked cheerfully around the barren prospect of Dungeness on a winter's afternoon and chortled: "If you

told me I was in Latvia, I'd believe you." Technicians and hangers-on could do nothing but make feeble jokes about Siberia and bear it; Jon Pertwee escaped to a large Ford Galaxie (JON 8E); the army, brought in from Shorncliffe as extras, opened up the bonnets of the Land-Rovers to get the warmth from the engines, while director Michael Ferguson had plenty of exercise anyway.'[38]

The second day on the Dungeness Road was spent filming all the scenes around Axos for Episodes 2 and 4. The weather had improved and the general temperature had risen some ten degrees, causing much of the surrounding snow to melt. By this time, script editor Terrance Dicks had returned to the production office and on Wednesday the 6th he wrote to the scriptwriters, Bob Baker and Dave Martin, to thank them for the rewrites that had been delivered during his absence. Commenting on the work in progress, Dicks wrote, 'Went down to Dungeness to see the filming. Everything is going very well. It's a fine, eerie location, but bloody cold! Feeling is only now returning to my lower extremities!' As the five days of location filming had been conducted in such an extraordinary variety of weather conditions, Dicks added an extra explanatory line to be spoken by Corporal Bell prior to the first location sequence in Episode 1 which would help explain the inconsistent film sequences:

Bell: A report in from the Met Office, Sir. There are freak weather conditions over the whole area.
Yates: Explain.
Bell: Sudden snow storms, Sir. Dense fog's covering the area.

Pertwee arrived at the location after getting back home in the early hours of that morning following an exhausting and chaotic trip from Ibiza, which cost him three nights without sleep.

Comment

Denge Marsh is an eerie place. For as far as the eye can see, it's just a flat plain of seemingly never-ending pebbles, occasionally punctuated by small, ramshackle little buildings. As such, it's an excellent location for a programme like *Doctor Who*, as it has a slightly unnatural, otherworldly quality to it, especially in the freezing and foggy conditions experienced during the *Axos* filming.

Naturally enough, the site was chosen primarily because of the nuclear power station at Dungeness, but having the Axos landing site nearby provided a superb opportunity to frame the two key elements of the story in a single shot. It's somewhat unfortunate that the Axos prop never really looks as if it's buried itself into the earth rather than just resting on top of it, but that's a minor gripe.

COLONY IN SPACE
(tx 10 April to 15 May 1971)

The Story
Discovering that the Master has stolen the file on a deadly weapon, the Time Lords send the Doctor to the barren world of Uxarieus in the year 2472 to retrieve it. On the planet, the Doctor finds a group of human colonists who have been struggling to survive, together with a survey team from IMC (the Interplanetary Mining Corporation) who are seeking to plunder the planet of its mineral wealth. To settle the dispute over the planet, the colonists send for an Earth Adjudicator who arrives in the form of the Master. The weapon is in the hands of the planet's original inhabitants and both they and their world have been affected by its radiation emissions. The Doctor convinces them to destroy the weapon rather than let it fall into the Master's hands.

The Locations
1. Old Baal Clay Pit, B3374, Carclaze, near St Austell, Cornwall

Shooting Schedule

EPISODE 1
▸▸ TARDIS materialises as robot goes past
Old Baal Clay Pit – A // 10 February 1971
▸▸ Doctor and Jo leave TARDIS watched by primitive
Old Baal Clay Pit – A // 10 February 1971
▸▸ TARDIS is dragged away by primitives
Old Baal Clay Pit – A // 10 February 1971

EPISODE 2
▸▸ Doctor and Caldwell leave Leeson's dome
Old Baal Clay Pit – A // 10 February 1971
▸▸ Doctor sees that the TARDIS has gone
Old Baal Clay Pit – A // 10 February 1971
▸▸ Monitor – Doctor and Caldwell drive to spaceship
Old Baal Clay Pit – A // 10 February 1971
▸▸ Doctor fights the primitives
Old Baal Clay Pit – E // 16 February 1971
▸▸ Morgan and Doctor arrive at Leeson's dome
Old Baal Clay Pit – A // 10 February 1971

EPISODE 3
▸▸ Caldwell save Winton from IMC guards
Old Baal Clay Pit – C // 12 February 1971
▸▸ Primitives take Jo into their city (3/4)
Old Baal Clay Pit – C // 12 February 1971

EPISODE 4
▸▸ Doctor arrives at the city and talks to primitives
Old Baal Clay Pit – C // 12 February 1971
▸▸ Doctor and Jo leave primitive's city
Old Baal Clay Pit – C // 12 February 1971

EPISODE 5
▸▸ Monitor – IMC landing
Old Baal Clay Pit – A // 10 February 1971
▸▸ Primitives attack Doctor and Master
Old Baal Clay Pit – D // 15 February 1971

EPISODE 6
▸▸ Rogers talks to Dent
Old Baal Clay Pit – C // 12 February 1971
▸▸ Rogers watches colonists ship
Old Baal Clay Pit – C // 12 February 1971
▸▸ Winton and Rogers fight
Old Baal Clay Pit – B // 11 February 1971
▸▸ Jo and Caldwell watch the colonists ship explode
Old Baal Clay Pit – D // 15 February 1971
▸▸ Jo and Caldwell enter the city
Old Baal Clay Pit – C // 12 February 1971
▸▸ Battle between IMC and colonists
Old Baal Clay Pit – B // 11 February 1971
▸▸ Monitor – Doctor and Jo approach Master's TARDIS
Old Baal Clay Pit – A // 10 February 1971
▸▸ Doctor and Jo watch Master's TARDIS dematerialise
Old Baal Clay Pit – A // 10 February 1971

The Facts
The IMC robot was constructed by outside contractor Magna Models at a cost of £450. Having transported the prop to Carclaze, it was discovered that two of the robot's four castors had completely jammed. Unable to free them, visual effects assistant Ian Scoones, who operated the robot on location, had no choice but to improvise.

Bernard Wilkie (visual effects designer): 'Those of us watching behind the camera knew nothing of Ian's problem. I realised that something was wrong when instead of the machine moving forward as planned, it began reeling from side to side. The director accepted the shot, assuming that the machine's drunken stagger was due to the uneven terrain. When the take was completed, I went over to help Ian out of the prop and found him red-faced and gasping for breath. Unable to manoeuvre the machine as planned, he had literally carried it by grasping two wooded struts on the inside.'[39]

Immovable castors were not the only problem surrounding the robot prop. One evening, the robot was accidentally pushed out of its protective shed and left overnight in the rain, damaging its plywood and heavy card construction. This necessitated the mechanism and cowling being rebuilt at a cost of around £100 to make it ready for the first block of studio recording. On 10 March 1971, visual effects manager Jack Kine informed Letts that he agreed with the report made by Bernard Wilkie, that the damage was due to 'bad handling'.

Hired for the production were two Steyr-Daimler-Puch Haflinger cross-country vehicles, which, after suitable dressing with extra front and rear circular bumpers, were to be used as the IMC patrol vehicles. However, during the course of the filming at Carclaze, the two vehicles sustained damage and had to be repaired at a total cost of £74.40.[40] Having had the two Haflingers repaired, G H Pettican, the BBC's Senior Properties Assistant, wrote to Michael Briant on 17 May 1971 informing him that the charge would need to come out of the budget assigned to *Colony in Space*. This was felt to be reasonable, as a nominal hire charge of £10 had initially been made for the vehicles, which Pettican pointed out could well have been £200 to £300 had full hire charges been made. Barry Letts duly agreed to the charge and authorised the payment.

Originally, a small garden was to have been seen outside the colonist dome belonging to the Leeson family. Prior to filming, small vegetable patches had been planted, but the heavy rain experienced during the week turned the garden into a mud patch. Aware that Nicholas Pennell and Terry Walsh would only wish to perform the Episode 6 mudfight once, Michael Briant elected to film it using both 16mm cameras to ensure that he obtained all the footage he required in one go.

As usual, Jon Pertwee decided to make his way to the location in his own car, by that time a Lancia GT, instead of taking advantage of the coach being laid on to transport personnel from Television Centre. After the filming at Carclaze, Pertwee took his vehicle to be cleaned, only to find that the slurry from the pit had splashed over the underside of his car and hardened due to the heat of the engine. As a result, the chassis, exhaust and engine were coated in a fine layer of fired china, which had to be carefully chipped off.

For the duration of the filming, the cast and crew stayed at the Edgcumbe Hotel, Narrowcliff in Newquay, whose staff proved very hospitable to the production team, heating up the outdoor swimming pool for their use and keeping the hotel bar open till late.

Graeme Harper (assistant floor manager): 'On one particular evening, some of the crew and most of the stuntmen decided to get completely plastered, and at about two o'clock in the morning, when all the sane ones among us were fast asleep in bed, some bright spark got up on a barstool and shouted, "Let's go for a swim!" Clothes started flying in all directions, and in a matter of seconds, there were 20 alarmingly pale, naked bodies standing there, wondering what to do next. The bit of my brain that was still sober managed to deduce that the next logical step involved submerging ourselves in water, so I bellowed for everybody to follow me, as I knew where the pool was, and our gang of merry streakers proceeded to charge through the hotel corridors, shouting and screaming with limbs and other various bits flailing all over the place. Now, I knew that the doorway leading to the water was on the left-hand side of the dead end that we were heading towards, but for some reason, my mouth betrayed me and started shouting that we should head through the doorway on the right…'[41] As a result of Harper's wrong direction, the group accidentally charged straight into the hotel room allocated to production assistant Nicholas John, who at that precise moment was sharing a few moments of intimacy with his wife

Comment

The grey bleakness of the china clay quarry sets it apart from the usual sand or chalk pits used in other stories, helping subliminally to reinforce the desperation and failure of the colonists' efforts. Out of all the footage shot at Carclaze though, the finest sequence has to be the fight between Winton, the man from the colony and Rogers, the man from the company. It seems as if director Michael Briant deliberately chose the wettest and dirtiest place in the entire quarry to film the sequence and full marks go to both Nicholas Pennell and Terry Walsh for entering into the spirit of the scene with such gusto.

THE DÆMONS

(tx 22 May to 19 June 1971)

The Story

Worried by the televised opening of an ancient burial chamber near the village of Devil's End, the Doctor and Jo arrive just as the final excavation occurs. A massive force is released, which results in a deadly heat barrier settling over the village, cutting it off from the outside world. At the church, the Master, in the guise of the new vicar, Mr Magister, is attempting to raise and control Azal, the last of the Dæmons, an alien race that visited Earth in its ancient past. Azal, determined to bequeath his powers to a worthy being or destroy the Earth as a failed experiment, finally chooses the Master. Seeing the Doctor as disruptive, Azal tries to kill him, but when Jo offers herself as a replacement, her act of self-sacrifice confuses Azal who subsequently destroys himself.

The Locations

1. Aldbourne, Wiltshire
   - St Michael's Church
   - Village Green
   - The Blue Boar Public House
   - 3 Crooked Corner
2. Four Barrows, Aldbourne, Wiltshire
3. Campbell Aircraft Company, Membury Airfield, Membury, Wiltshire
4. Lane by Oaken Coppice, Knighton, Wiltshire
5. Old Airfield, Darrells Farm, Ramsbury, Wiltshire
6. Airfield, Darrells Farm, Ramsbury, Wiltshire

Shooting Schedule

EPISODE 1

▸▸ **During a thunderstorm a man is killed in churchyard**
The Green/Church/Pub // 20 April 1971

▸▸ **Miss Hawthorne discusses death with Dr Reeves**
The Green // 20 April 1971

▸▸ **Furgus looks for Professor Horner**
Four Barrows // 21 April 1971

▸▸ **Doctor, Jo and Yates in Bessie's garage**
Campbell Aircraft Company // 19 April 1971

▸▸ **Furgus records TV link and goes inside barrow**
Four Barrows // 21 April 1971

▸▸ **Miss Hawthorne gives her warning of disaster**
Four Barrows // 21 April 1971

▸▸ **PC Groom nearly attacks Miss Hawthorne**
3 Cooked Corner // 22 April 1971

▸▸ **Sign spins sending the Doctor and Jo the wrong way**
Crossroads by Airfield // 19 April 1971

▸▸ **Miss Hawthorne meets Garvin and Master**
Churchyard // 20 April 1971

▸▸ **Miss Hawthorne is upset by Master and leaves**
Churchyard // 20 April 1971

▸▸ **Lost, the Doctor realises Jo has map upside-down**
Lane by Oaken Coppice // 19 April 1971

▸▸ **Harry talks to Horner about opening Devil's Hump**
Four Barrows // 21 April 1971

▸▸ **Furgus begins his midnight broadcast**
Four Barrows // 21 April 1971

▸▸ **Bessie speeds to the Devil's Hump**
Lane by Oaken Coppice // 19 April 1971

▸▸ **Road blocked by a tree, the Doctor and Jo run on**
Lane by Oaken Coppice // 19 April 1971

▸▸ **Midnight strikes and Doctor shouts to stop the dig**

Four Barrows // 21 April 1971

▸▸ **The site is blasted as barrow is opened**
Four Barrows // 21 April 1971

▸▸ **Jo enters the Devil's Hump**
Four Barrows // 21 April 1971

EPISODE 2

▸▸ **Jo asks Harry to get a doctor**
Four Barrows // 22 April 1971

▸▸ **PC Groom alone at the dig is watched**
Four Barrows // 22 April 1971

▸▸ **PC Groom is killed by something large**
Four Barrows // 22 April 1971

▸▸ **Benton and Yates spot and examine hoofprints**
Airfield by Darrells Farm // 26 April 1971

▸▸ **Helicopter lands on village green**
The Green // 28 April 1971

▸▸ **Jo goes to meet Yates and Benton**
The Green/Pub // 28 April 1971

▸▸ **Benton hears Miss Hawthorne's cries for help**
Churchyard // 20 April 1971

▸▸ **Garvin walks through graveyard**
Churchyard // 20 April 1971

▸▸ **Benton and Hawthorne escape as Garvin is killed**
Churchyard // 20 April 1971

▸▸ **Van explodes at heat barrier forms**
Airfield by Darrells Farm // 26 April 1971

▸▸ **Brigadier examines van and heat barrier**
Airfield by Darrells Farm // 26 April 1971

▸▸ **Doctor and Jo move tree and recover Bessie**
Airfield by Darrells Farm // 27 April 1971

▸▸ **Brigadier throws stick at heat barrier**
Lane by Oaken Coppice // 19 April 1971

▸▸ **Brigadier talks to Yates on radio**
Airfield by Darrells Farm // 27 April 1971

▸▸ **Doctor and Jo find Groom dead at dig**
Four Barrows // 22 April 1971

▸▸ **Bok makes his way over the Devil's Hump**
Four Barrows // 22 April 1971

▸▸ **Bok enters the Devil's Hump (2/3)**
Four Barrows // 22 April 1971

EPISODE 3

▸▸ **Girton climbs into the UNIT helicopter**
The Green // 28 April 1971

▸▸ **Girton and Yates fight and helicopter takes off**
The Green // 28 April 1971

▸▸ **Helicopter flies over Bessie**
Airfield by Darrells Farm // 26 April 1971

▸▸ **Brigadier watches helicopter and warns Doctor**
Old Airfield by Darrells Farm // 23 April 1971

▸▸ **Doctor misses heat barrier but helicopter explodes**
Airfield by Darrells Farm // 26 April 1971

Left: Cameraman Fred Hamilton checks a light reading before the filming of Bok at the Four Barrows.

➤ **Master sees plume of smoke from explosion**
Churchyard // 20 April 1971

➤ **Doctor and Yates tend Jo**
Airfield by Darrells Farm // 26 April 1971

➤ **Doctor arrives at heat barrier and talks to Brigadier**
Old Airfield by Darrells Farm // 23 April 1971

➤ **Earthquake at the heat barrier (3/4)**
Old Airfield by Darrells Farm // 23 April 1971

EPISODE 4

➤ **Doctor tells Osgood to get a move on**
Old Airfield by Darrells Farm // 23 April 1971

➤ **Jo leaves through bedroom window**
Pub // 20 or 28 April 1971

➤ **Doctor tells Osgood to reverse the polarity**
Old Airfield by Darrells Farm // 23 April 1971

➤ **Jo is attacked by ivy in the churchyard**
Churchyard // 20 or 28 April 1971

➤ **Doctor tells Osgood that he'll explain again**
Old Airfield by Darrells Farm // 23 April 1971

➤ **Yates hides as Bert leaves the church**
Churchyard // 28 April 1971

➤ **Jo faints in churchyard**
Churchyard // 20 or 28 April 1971

➤ **Doctor shows diagram on windshield and drives away**
Old Airfield by Darrells Farm // 23 April 1971

➤ **Jo awakens and runs to church**
Churchyard // 20 or 28 April 1971

➤ **Bert shoots at the Doctor**
Airfield by Darrells Farm // 27 April 1971

➤ **Osgood tests the machine, which explodes**
Old Airfield by Darrells Farm // 23 April 1971

➤ **Morris dancers enter the village green**
The Green // 24 April 1971

➤ **Doctor caught by the Morris dancers**
The Green // 24 April 1971

➤ **Doctor is tied to the maypole**
The Green // 24 April 1971

➤ **Bert encourages the villagers to burn the Doctor**
The Green // 24 April 1971

➤ **Miss Hawthorne and Benton save the Doctor**
The Green // 24 April 1971

➤ **'Magic' effects and Bessie remote movements**
The Green/Church // 28 April 1971

EPISODE 5

➤ **Brigadier gives Osgood five minutes to succeed**
Old Airfield by Darrells Farm // 23 April 1971

➤ **Villagers get up from ground after earthquake**

The Green // 24 April 1971
- ▸▸ **Doctor tells the truth about the Master**
  The Green // 24 April 1971
- ▸▸ **Yates runs from church and Doctor calls Brigadier**
  The Green // 28 April 1971
- ▸▸ **Brigadier on radio, tells Osgood to start machine**
  Old Airfield by Darrells Farm // 23 April 1971
- ▸▸ **Doctor hopes the Brigadier will hurry**
  The Green // 28 April 1971
- ▸▸ **Machine begins to smoke**
  Old Airfield by Darrells Farm // 23 April 1971
- ▸▸ **Doctor tells villagers to spread out**
  The Green // 29 April 1971
- ▸▸ **Bok appears in churchyard and kills Bert**
  The Green/Churchyard // 29 April 1971
- ▸▸ **Brigadier switches on the booster**
  Old Airfield by Darrells Farm // 23 April 1971
- ▸▸ **Hole forms in barrier and vehicles pass through**
  Old Airfield by Darrells Farm // 23 April 1971
- ▸▸ **Bok begins to weaken**
  The Green // 29 April 1971
- ▸▸ **Machine comes through barrier but explodes**
  Old Airfield by Darrells Farm // 23 April 1971
- ▸▸ **Doctor runs past Bok into church**
  The Green/Churchyard // 29 April 1971
- ▸▸ **Brigadier arrives and soldier shoots at Bok**
  The Green // 29 April 1971
- ▸▸ **UNIT unsuccessfully attack Bok**
  The Green // 30 April 1971
- ▸▸ **Bok destroyed by bazooka, but reforms**
  Churchyard // 30 April 1971
- ▸▸ **Bok suddenly returns to being a stone gargoyle**
  Churchyard // 30 April 1971
- ▸▸ **Everyone runs as church explodes and Master captured**
  Churchyard/The Green // 30 April 1971
- ▸▸ **Dancing begins as Brigadier and Yates go for a pint**
  The Green // 24 April 1971

The Facts

As scripted, *The Dæmons* provided director Christopher Barry with a very specific set of locations to look for, first and foremost an ancient barrow at which the story would begin.

Christopher Barry: 'We started with Ordnance Survey maps and reference books that I had because of my interest in archaeology. We ringed practically every long barrow in Britain, visited them and took photographs of them. There were hundreds of long barrows, and in the end we didn't use a long barrow at all, we settled for a couple of bell barrows. We settled for that because there they were, just up a track from Aldbourne. It was a quiet village, had a lovely church,

a village green where we could land a helicopter and the main road was down the other end of the village so we wouldn't interrupt traffic. It was lovely and ideal.'[42]

On Tuesday 27 April, several days into the location work, the Aldbourne Parish Council considered the filming that was being conducted in the village at a special meeting, as reported in the *Wiltshire Gazette Herald*[43]: 'Filming of 'Dr Who' on the village green by the BBC was discussed and the meeting decided that any donations to the church and parish council should go to the scheme for pond drainage. The clerk reported that he had received no official reply to a letter sent to the BBC and it was agreed that the vicar and clerk should seek an interview with the deputy producer concerning any donation to the parish council.' Agreement was duly reached with both the Parish Council (responsible for the use of the village) and the Church Parochial Council (who looked after St Michael's Church), each of them receiving a £50 facility fee.

Even though the story had been allocated twice the normal amount of location filming time for a production of this size, the sheer amount of exterior footage needed required that not one but three 16mm film cameras be pressed into service, thus emulating the multi-shoot capability of the recording studio. This meant that a single take could be shot from several different angles at once rather than having to perform the same scene over and over again with a single camera, repositioning it each time to capture a different angle.

Christopher Barry: 'There was such a lot of dialogue to get through that the whole thing had to be done television-style using our three cameras. Fred Hamilton was the overall lighting cameraman and under him were three operators, all with headphones on so they could follow my directions as in an OB situation, with me telling them whenever they were 'in shot'. Each camera was 'crystal locked' so that you could start and stop all three simultaneously by remote control.'[44]

The filming of the opening scene of the story, showing the short-lived character Jim leaving the village pub in the midst of a thunderstorm, was filmed on the evening of Tuesday 20 April. To provide the rain effects, arrangements were made with the Ramsbury Fire Brigade to come to the village and provide a downpour with their hoses, for which they were paid £90.

For the most part, the weather during the ten-day shoot was fine and dry. As Christopher Barry went to bed in his Marlborough hotel in the early hours of Friday 23 April after his fourth day of filming, he didn't have any idea of what awaited him the following morning. 'I woke up and it was very quiet that morning, and as I opened my eyes I realised that it was very bright. So I went to the window, opened the curtains and looked out, and there were these dirty great snowflakes coming down and everything was covered in about three inches of snow. I couldn't believe it!"[45]

What made matters worse was the fact that on the day of the snowfall, the production team were due to shoot all the scenes surrounding UNIT's attempt to break through the heat barrier at the old airfield by Darrells Farm in Ramsbury, a location which was now covered in snow. Fortunately, the weather forecast for the day indicated that a rapid thaw was likely, so, with little option, Barry called an early lunch and postponed any attempt to film until the afternoon. As forecast, the snow melted relatively quickly and what didn't was brushed away from the filming site as far as possible. The script had originally specified that the circuit diagram of the heat exchanger drawn by the Doctor was to be on what was now soaking wet ground, but fortunately the decision had already been made in pre-production that the diagram's location should be changed to the motorbike's windshield.

Somewhat irritated by the day's problems and delays, Pertwee's temper began to fray and, after being calmed down by Nicholas Courtney, he decided to take off for a ride around the airfield on the motorbike, much to the consternation of Christopher Barry, who was already trying to commit as many shots to film as possible during the shortened filming day.

To show the effect of the heat barrier, sacks of coal dust were obtained from the local coal yard and spread in a line to indicate the charring effect of the intense heat supplemented by the planting of burnt twigs in the ground. To foreshorten the background and negate the need to extend the 'barrier' any further than necessary, the blackened line was seen running up and over a strategically placed hump on the far side of the road.

The visual effect of a hole forming in the heat barrier was achieved on location, rather than being added on electronically in post production.

Peter Day (visual effects designer): 'To rig up the heat barrier, we fixed a semi-circular metal frame from one side of the road to the other. Onto this we fixed shredded, silver, reflective plastic, similar to the tinsel used in Christmas decorations. We placed a sheet of glass between the camera and the heat barrier and smeared the glass with Vaseline along the line of the metal frame. The result when viewed through the camera was an angry haze, caused by the plastic moving in the wind.'[46] This effect was supplemented by the use of butane gas heaters, which were placed under the camera lens to distort the air, adding to the impression of intense heat.

The exploding rock and twig thrown at the barrier by the Doctor and Brigadier respectively were dummies packed with explosives, the detonator of which was attached to the end of a fixed piece of nylon line. When the prop reached the correct distance, the taut line activated the detonator and the explosive triggered.

The script for *The Dæmons* required Captain Mike Yates to once again ride a motorbike, as he had done in *The Mind of Evil*. Actor Richard Franklin often rode a small 50cc scooter to rehearsals, but felt considerably less confident handling a larger, more powerful motorbike. For the long shots, Franklin was doubled by Peter Diamond, while for the close-ups, where Franklin needed to deliver lines of dialogue, the motorbike was placed onto the low-loader that had brought the exploding baker's van to the airfield.

The Hughes 300 helicopter used in the production was hired once again from Gregory Air Services at Denham Aerodrome and was piloted, as in *Fury from the Deep*, by Captain Mike Smith. The first day the helicopter was required was Monday 26 April, when all the sequences of the villager Girton, trying to drive the Doctor and Jo into the heat barrier were shot at the airfield by Darrells Farm, just south of Ramsbury.

For the destruction of the helicopter, it had originally been intended to film the explosion using a model, but in the end, the effect was achieved by using the same James Bond model explosion test shot that was seen in the opening episode of *The Enemy of the World*. In order for the helicopter to land two days later on the village green, it was necessary to gain official permission to remove the telephone lines that radiated out to all the local houses from a telegraph pole situated on the green.

Saturday 24 April was allocated as the day on which all the shots involving the maypole in Episodes 4 and 5 would be completed. For these sequences, a professional troupe of Reading-based Morris dancers, the Headington Quarry Men, were hired at a cost of £90. Christopher Barry had originally hoped that the entire day's filming could be moved to the Sunday (which had been allocated as a day off), thus allowing him to attend his sister's wedding. However, Pertwee had already made prior arrangements to perform a cabaret in Portsmouth on the Saturday evening, which meant that the dates could not be altered. As a result, Barry sent a telegram which was read out at the wedding – 'Sorry, but *Doctor Who* prevents me from attending!'

During the morning of Thursday 29 April, the production teams were visited by Dennis Hooper, the editor of *Countdown*, together with a photographer, in order to gain material for a two-page article entitled 'A Day with Dr Who' that would appear in the comic's 1972 annual.

At least two separate colour 8mm ciné films were taken during the filming of *The Dæmons*. One reel, shot on Wednesday 28 April, shows the fight by the helicopter between Yates and Girton, while a separate reel, lasting approximately six minutes, was shot on Friday 30 April and contains many shots of the filming work in progress.

Right: **The Daleks and Ogrons are filmed emerging from the railway tunnel during Episode 4 of** *Day of the Daleks.*

Ouch!

After filming a take of the Doctor riding the motorbike on the perimeter track around Darrells Airfield, Jon Pertwee began to turn the vehicle when it skidded on a patch of mud, causing it to fall on top of him, resulting in a bruised left knee and right shin. He duly blamed the faulty adjustment of the front brakes for the accident.

Comment

If you didn't know better, you'd swear that someone had discovered the village of Aldbourne first and then had gone away and decided to write a *Doctor Who* story around it. It's amazing just how well the northern end of the village fits in with so many of the story's requirements, with the church, pub and houses all facing directly onto a sizeable green. Indeed, the fact that Christopher Barry elected not to film any of the village outside the area of the green adds much to the atmosphere, making it feel friendly and inviting but strangely isolated at the same time.

DAY OF THE DALEKS
(tx 1 January to 22 January 1972)

The Story

A band of guerrillas from the 22nd century travel back in time to assassinate Sir Reginald Styles, the diplomat whom they believe was responsible for slaughtering the delegates at a peace conference, causing a world war which led to the eventual conquest of Earth by the Daleks. Transported to the future, the Doctor realises that the murders were actually caused by Shura, a member of the guerrilla team, trying to fulfil his mission. The Doctor returns to the 20th century pursued by the Daleks, who are intent that the

future should not be changed. The Doctor saves the delegates, evacuating them from Styles' mansion, and convinces Shura who is hiding in the cellar about the time paradox that he is responsible for. Shura waits until the Daleks enter the empty house before exploding his bomb.

The Locations

1. United States International University, Dropmore Park, Burnham, Buckinghamshire
2. Bull's Bridge,[47] Hayes, Middlesex
3. Harvey House, Green Dragon Lane, Brentford, Middlesex

Shooting Schedule

EPISODE 1

» **Guerrilla appears in house grounds**
Dropmore House // 13 September 1971
» **Guerrilla attacked by Ogrons**
Bulls Bridge // 14 September 1971
» **Guerrilla found by UNIT**
Bulls Bridge // 14 September 1971
» **Benton and guerrilla in ambulance**
Bulls Bridge // 15 September 1971
» **Guerrilla vanishes in ambulance**
Bulls Bridge // 15 September 1971
» **Auderly House at dusk**
Dropmore House // 13 September 1971
» **Benton reports to Yates**
Dropmore House // 13 September 1971
» **Time tunnel begins to activate**
Bulls Bridge // 15 September 1971
» **Guerrillas appear in tunnel**
Bulls Bridge // 15 September 1971
» **UNIT soldiers shot**
Bulls Bridge // 15 September 1971
» **Shura sees the Doctor inside the house**
Dropmore House // 13 September 1971
» **Guerrillas run to house**
Dropmore House // 13 September 1971

EPISODE 2

» **Benton reports missing men to Yates**
Dropmore House // 13 September 1971
» **Shura runs back to the tunnel**
Dropmore House // 13 September 1971
» **Shura attacked by Ogron**
Bulls Bridge // 15 September 1971
» **Ogrons approach the house**
Dropmore House // 13 September 1971
» **Anat shoots Ogrons**
Dropmore House // 13 September 1971
» **Doctor, Brigadier and Ogrons**

Dropmore House // 13 September 1971
➤➤ **Doctor follows Anat and Boaz into tunnel**
Bulls Bridge // 16 September 1971

EPISODE 3

➤➤ **Doctor exits the manhole**
Bulls Bridge // 15 September 1971
➤➤ **Doctor evades Ogron patrol**
Bulls Bridge // 15 September 1971
➤➤ **Doctor walks past security camera**
Bulls Bridge // 15 September 1971
➤➤ **Doctor approaches and enters building**
Harvey House Flats // 16 September 1971
➤➤ **Monia walks to hideout**
Bulls Bridge // 15 September 1971
➤➤ **Doctor sees slaves and attacked by Ogron**
Harvey House Flats // 14 September 1971
➤➤ **Doctor and Jo escape on bike**
Harvey House Flats // 14 September 1971
➤➤ **Ogrons chase Doctor and Jo from building (cut)**
Harvey House Flats // 16 September 1971
➤➤ **Ogrons chase bike**
Bulls Bridge // 15 September 1971

EPISODE 4

➤➤ **Guerrillas attack Ogrons and Dalek**
Harvey House Flats // 14 September 1971
➤➤ **Brigadier tells Yates to extend the search**
Bulls Bridge // 15 September 1971
➤➤ **Shura enters house**
Dropmore House // 13 September 1971
➤➤ **Doctor and Jo re-enter the tunnel via manhole**
Bulls Bridge // 16 September 1971
➤➤ **Doctor and Jo emerge from tunnel**
Bulls Bridge // 15 September 1971
➤➤ **Delegates arrive at Auderly House**
Dropmore House // 14 September 1971
➤➤ **Jeep arrives with Doctor and Jo**
Dropmore House // 14 September 1971
➤➤ **Daleks and Ogrons emerge from tunnel**
Bulls Bridge // 15 September 1971
➤➤ **Benton on radio**
Bulls Bridge // 15 September 1971
➤➤ **Daleks advance on Auderly House**
Dropmore House // 13 September 1971
➤➤ **Delegates leave**
Dropmore House // 14 September 1971
➤➤ **Daleks enter the house**
Dropmore House // 13 September 1971
➤➤ **Doctor tells Brigadier to allow Daleks in**
Dropmore House // 14 September 1971
➤➤ **Doctor and Styles watch house explode**
Bulls Bridge // 16 September 1971

The Facts

For the scene of the peace delegates arriving and departing from Auderly House, the production team hired a Rolls-Royce (MWF 435F) and a Daimler (AWP 633H) from Kingsbury Motors. To make them look more like diplomatic vehicles, small adhesive insignia were attached to the two front doors on both cars. However, once the filming was complete, attempts to remove the insignia resulted in the paintwork of both cars being scratched and, in the case if the Rolls-Royce, several small pieces of paint (seven coats' thick) had come away.

On seeing the damage, Kingsbury Motors complained to the BBC, whereupon G H Pettican, the Corporation's Senior Properties Assistant responsible for loss and damages, asked the company to bring the two cars to Television Centre so that they could be inspected by Barry Letts, who was warned that the production office would likely have to bear a large proportion of the claim. On 28 October, Kingsbury Motors duly sent an invoice to the BBC for the repair of the two vehicles. The Rolls-Royce had cost £45 to restore, while the Daimler had come in at £34. However, Kingsbury also charged the BBC for the loss of use they incurred while the vehicles were undergoing their four-day repair, totalling another £80 for each car. Agreement that the production office would pay the bill of £239 was finally accepted by Letts on 20 December 1971.

The railway bridge location running next to the River Crane was hired from the Central Electricity Board for a fee of £160.[48] As well as providing the ideal location for the time tunnel entrance, the wasteground adjoining the site also provided the derelict buildings and manholes required for the scenes set in the 22nd century. However, due to the uneven ground around the site, wooden boards had to be laid to ensure that the Daleks could move smoothly around the location. The same problem also faced director Paul Bernard when filming the Daleks moving across the lawn at Dropmore House. To hide the wooden duckboards, Bernard was forced to film at ground level or with various foreground objects strategically placed to obscure the view.

Unused Locations

Osterley Park House – The original location chosen to represent the home of Sir Reginald Styles was Osterley Park House in Osterley, Middlesex, situated only three miles east of the canal tunnel and wasteland being used near Bulls Bridge. The reasons why Osterley Park wasn't used are unknown, although the decision to change the venue seem to have been taken less than a week before location filming was due to begin. Curiously, although the fictional name for the mansion in the story was Auderly House, the original rehearsal scripts for *Day of* *the Daleks* had referred to it as Austerley House (as did Terrance Dicks' subsequent novelisation of the story).

Comment

The original filming schedule for the story lists the Episode 4 scene of the Daleks advancing on Auderly House in the following manner: *LS Grounds rear – see the seven DALEKS appear across the lawns. In front of them a dozen UNIT men fall back.* The notation for seven Daleks has been duly crossed through and amended to three. And there's the real problem with the story – the Daleks just don't have enough of a presence. The time paradox script written by Louis Marks is a sound one by and large, but with only three Dalek casings to play with, there's no conviction that the Daleks pose any real threat and this is especially felt in the final location scenes as they close in on Styles' mansion. Even with the excellent Ogrons to back them up, the whole attack feels very spartan and unconvincing, a feeling reinforced by the very casual way the delegates are evacuated from the building. The filming around the railway bridge is far better, providing a very memorable location and some suitably dramatic shots of the Daleks and Ogrons emerging from the tunnel – giving the impression that there are more than three Daleks after all.

THE SEA DEVILS

(tx 26 February to 1 April 1972)

The Story

A seemingly imprisoned Master manages to make contact with a colony of undersea reptiles related to the Silurians, who have been systematically sinking various craft in the English Channel. With the aid of Trenchard, his misguided prison governor, the Master steals equipment from a naval base in order to construct a machine that will revive the remaining Sea Devils from hibernation. Following an attack on the naval base, the Doctor is kidnapped and taken to the underwater shelters, where he is forced to help the Mater complete the machine. The Doctor sabotages the device, however, causing the destruction of the Sea Devils' base. The Doctor and the Master are rescued from the sea, but the Master escapes in a naval hovercraft.

The Locations

1. Fraser Gunnery Range, HMS St George, Eastney, Southsea, Portsmouth, Hampshire
2. HMS Reclaim, Portsmouth Harbour, Hampshire
3. No Man's Land Fort, the Solent
4. Red Cliff, Sandown, Isle of Wight
5. Whitecliff Bay, Isle of Wight
6. Bembridge Sailing Club, Bembridge, Isle of Wight
   • Bembridge Harbour
7. Norris Castle, East Cowes, Isle of Wight
8. Priory Bay, Seaview, Isle of Wight

Shooting Schedule

EPISODE 1

▸▸ **Doctor and Jo approach in boat**
Bembridge Harbour // 28 October 1971

▸▸ **Doctor and Jo arrive in boat**
Bembridge Sailing Club // 28 October 1971

▸▸ **Doctor and Jo arrive at prison**
Norris Castle // 29 October 1971

▸▸ **Doctor and Jo leave the prison**
Norris Castle // 29 October 1971

▸▸ **Doctor Robbins' borrows boat**
Bembridge Sailing Club // 28 October 1971

▸▸ **Establishing shot – HMS Seaspite**
Fraser Gunnery Range // 21 October 1971

▸▸ **Doctor arrives on the beach**
Fraser Gunnery Range // 21 October 1971

▸▸ **Doctor examines charred lifeboat**
Fraser Gunnery Range // 21 October 1971

▸▸ **Jo borrows Robbins' motorbike**
Bembridge Sailing Club // 28 October 1971

▸▸ **Establishing shots – Sea Fort**
No Man's Land Fort // 26 October 1971

▸▸ **Doctor and Jo climb sea fort ladder**
No Man's Land Fort // 26 October 1971

▸▸ **Sea Devil hand on boat**
No Man's Land Fort // 26 October 1971

▸▸ **Boat smokes**
No Man's Land Fort // 26 October 1971

▸▸ **Boat wreckage**
No Man's Land Fort // 26 October 1971

EPISODE 2

▸▸ **Trenchard arrives in car at HMS Seaspite**
Fraser Gunnery Range // 25 October 1971

▸▸ **Jo's POV – Master walks through base**
Fraser Gunnery Range // 25 October 1971

▸▸ **Doctor's POV of empty courtyard**
Fraser Gunnery Range // 25 October 1971

▸▸ **Trenchard leaves HMS Seaspite in car**
Fraser Gunnery Range // 25 October 1971

▸▸ **Doctor and Jo arrive back at the prison**
Norris Castle // 29 October 1971

EPISODE 3

▸▸ **Jo overpowers the guards**
Norris Castle // 29 October 1971

▸▸ **Jo hides from guards, she heads for the prison**

Norris Castle // 29 October 1971
➤ Jo hides from more guards, tries rear door
Norris Castle // 29 October 1971
➤ Jo finds the right window
Norris Castle // 29 October 1971
➤ Jo enters the prison and searches inside
Norris Castle // 29 October 1971
➤ Doctor and Jo escape, spotted by guard
Norris Castle // 29 October 1971
➤ Doctor and Jo absail down cliff
Red Cliff // 27 October 1971
➤ Sea Devil emerges, Doctor and Jo through minefield (3/4)
Whitecliff Bay // 27 October 1971

EPISODE 4

➤ Doctor and Jo hide behind bush
Norris Castle // 29 October 1971
➤ Sea Devils come ashore[49]
Whitecliff Bay // 27 October 1971
➤ Doctor, Jo and Hart arrive at the prison
Norris Castle // 29 October 1971
➤ Doctor, Jo and Hart board HMS Reclaim
HMS Reclaim // 26 October 1971
➤ Doctor enters diving bell
HMS Reclaim // 26 October 1971
➤ Empty diving bell raised (4/5)
HMS Reclaim // 26 October 1971

EPISODE 5

➤ Admiral gives message to sailor
HMS Reclaim // 26 October 1971
➤ Admiral and 1st Officer on bridge
HMS Reclaim // 26 October 1971
➤ Admiral orders commencement of attack
HMS Reclaim // 26 October 1971
➤ Admiral watches through binoculars
HMS Reclaim // 26 October 1971
➤ 1st Officer spots dead Sea Devils
HMS Reclaim // 26 October 1971
➤ Admiral calls cease fire
HMS Reclaim // 26 October 1971
➤ Sea Devils begin to attack HMS Seaspite
Fraser Gunnery Range // 21 October 1971
➤ Sea Devils capture Doctor, Jo, Hart and sailors (5/6)
Fraser Gunnery Range // 25 October 1971

EPISODE 6

➤ Jo escapes and finds the Doctor
Fraser Gunnery Range // 21 October 1971
➤ Jo runs from the Sea Devils
Fraser Gunnery Range // 21 October 1971
➤ Jo and Hart escape and leave in hovercraft

Fraser Gunnery Range // 22 October 1971
➤ The battle for HMS Seaspite begins
Fraser Gunnery Range // 22 October 1971
➤ Hart fires the Bofors Gun
Fraser Gunnery Range // 22 October 1971
➤ Doctor chases the fleeing Master
Fraser Gunnery Range // 25 October 1971
➤ Doctor chases Master to speedboats
Priory Bay // 28 October 1971
➤ Sea Devils return to the sea
Fraser Gunnery Range // 22 October 1971
➤ Doctor chases Master in speedboats
Bembridge Harbour // 28 October 1971
➤ Sea Devils capture the Doctor
Priory Bay // 28 October 1971
➤ Doctor and Master rescued from sea
HMS Reclaim // 26 October 1971
➤ Doctor watches underwater explosion
Fraser Gunnery Range // 22 October 1971
➤ Master escapes in hovercraft
Fraser Gunnery Range // 22 October 1971

The Facts

As the *Doctor Who* production office had secured some major success in previous years utilising the assistance of both the Army (*The Invasion*) and the RAF (*The Mind of Evil*), Barry Letts decided that it was time to see if the Royal Navy would be as willing to co-operate in the production of a *Doctor Who* story as the other armed forces had been.

One of the main requirements for *The Sea Devils* was the use of the Navy's diving and salvage vessel, HMS Reclaim. An application to view the ship was favourably received and on 10 September 1971 the vessel's Lieutenant Commander, K G Less, wrote to Letts offering him the opportunity to look over the Reclaim on either 20 or 21 September, as they were due to be sailing to Falmouth and then Scotland between 22 September and 15 October. In response to the letter, Letts and Terrance Dicks visited HMS Vernon, the Royal Navy's Diving School in Portsmouth, enjoyed a conducted tour of the Reclaim and then entered into discussions as to whether it could be used in the programme. As a result, a week later, on 27 September, the Ministry of Defence officially wrote to the BBC giving their permission for the filming of both diving operations on board the Reclaim and an air/sea rescue.

Michael Briant: 'The locations sort of scouted themselves. The big thing to get from the Navy was HMS Reclaim and she was based at Portsmouth at this time. So there was no question of going anywhere but Portsmouth to film aboard her, and so once you were stuck there you really had to find all your other locations

Right: Jon Pertwee, together with the 'six-inch metal tube' that injured him, attempts to defuse a land mine made from an upside-down plant pot!

within that vicinity. HMS Fraser – the Naval base on the coast between Southsea and Langston Harbour was perfect, except that it didn't have a harbour as required by the script. So Jon had to run his motorboat up onto the beach in Episode 1 in quite a big surf. There is a cutaway if you look carefully. You see the boat chugging in, then you cut to Edwin Richfield (Captain Hart) saying, "What the hell's he doing here?", then you cut back to Jon walking along the beach. Between those shots the waves were five feet high, and though Jon was quite happy to drive the boat up onto the shore, the guy who owned it wasn't and declined to let him, fearing, possibly quite rightly, the consequences if it had turned over on top of him. As it was, we had half a dozen Naval ratings up to their waists in water, pulling the boat in whenever we finished filming a take.'[50]

With the Royal Navy on board, the production office began to draw up a list of all the material requirements needed for the story. Among the equipment requested was a large helicopter, which was planned to be used to rescue the Doctor and the Master at the end of Episode 6. While the Navy was able to acquiesce in virtually all the BBC's needs, it became evident early on that it would not be possible to use one of the Navy's helicopters. Instead, the Navy offered the use of an IHU hovercraft, which not only could be used for the rescue scene but also other action sequences as well.

For the rescue sequence, the BBC requested the loan of two sets of fully practical submarine escape suits, which would be required not only on location but also for the studio sequences to be recorded on 14 December. In a memo sent by production assistant Colin Dudley to Jennie Betts, the BBC's Television Administration Facilities Assistant, the planned sequence, due to be filmed with the material involving HMS Reclaim, was described thus:

'One artist will be floated in the sea alongside, wearing a Naval escape suit, another artist, similarly clad, will 'pop-up' alongside him, having exited from the decompression chamber[51] at a depth of six feet. The cameraman may be in a 'Gemini' inflatable boat at the time.'
Colin Dudley to Jennie Betts – 6 October 1971

Michael Briant: 'Originally, Jon was going to do that sequence himself – swim out of the diving bell in the free-ascent costume and float to the surface. Quite rightly, I think now, the Navy wouldn't let him do it because with the ship being so close, there was a very real danger that the guy could come up and crack his head on the hull of HMS Reclaim. Two Naval divers did those shots for us instead, but the trouble then was that we never knew exactly where they were going to come up. The camera could pick up an area as wide as a living room – which is pretty large for a television long shot – but it took six or seven runs at it before we finally got them surfacing in the area we were photographing. Before that they were either left of frame, right of frame, or out of shot altogether.'[52]

In the end, the desired shots proved so problematic to achieve that the opening of the sequence, showing the men surfacing, was abandoned and the televised version begins with them both already floating on the surface.

One sequence planned and filmed but subsequently removed during editing was the opening to Episode 1, due to be seen as a precursor to the Doctor and Jo sailing towards the Master's prison which opening the transmitted episode. As originally conceived, following the opening titles a close-up of a speedboat's wake (filmed from the craft itself) would have been seen, before the camera panned up to reveal the Doctor water-skiing behind. On the beach, the boat-owner, Robbins was to have been talking to Jo:

Robbins: *Well, do you want to go to the island or not? Mr Trenchard doesn't like to be kept waiting.*
Jo: *Well yes…but you see, he said he'd meet me here…*
Doctor: *(OOV) Jo!*

At this point, the Doctor was to have let go of the speedboat tow-rope and ski straight up onto the beach, saying 'Ready, Jo? Time we were off.' As Pertwee was an accomplished water-skier, it's not difficult to imagine that this was an embellishment to the script he had personally suggested. Several internal memos refer to the planned sequence and it duly appears on the first two pages of the shot list. However, notations made by the director's assistant, Pauline Silcock, on her copy of the schedule indicate that a modified version of the scene was filmed on 28 October, deleting both the speedboat and water-skiing Doctor.

Due to the potentially dangerous nature of many of the sequences in *The Sea Devils*, regular stuntmen, Stuart Fell and Terry Walsh, were much in demand over the location filming dates.

Following the bulk of the filming aboard HMS Reclaim on 26 October, the motor launch Vera Lynn (which appears as Robbins' boat) came alongside the ship at around 2.30 pm while another small vessel, Horne's Launch, collected Len Hutton (Visual Effects), Terry Walsh, Stuart Fell and another stuntman, Mike Stephens, from Ryde on the Isle of Wight and conveyed them to the Reclaim. Both boats then left HMS Reclaim to film scenes around No Man's Land Sea Fort in the Solent. Horne's Launch acted as the camera platform while Jon Pertwee and Katy Manning performed the scene of the Doctor and Jo approaching the fort aboard the Vera Lynn. The subsequent shots of the Doctor and Jo climbing up the ladder into No Man's Land Fort were deemed to be too dangerous for the actors to perform, so the scene was completed with Walsh doubling for the Doctor while the rather stocky Fell donned Katy Manning's white

trouser suit to double for Jo. Mike Stephens' performance for the day was as the Sea Devil hand that appears over the side of Robbins' boat before it's destroyed.

Two days later, Stuart Fell was required to don Katy Manning's costume once again for the scene of her riding Robbins' motor scooter off the jetty. Once this shot was completed, Fell then changed out of Jo's clothes and into those of the Master for the Episode 6 chase sequence involving the small Buccaneer craft that had been hired from Brealy Smith Speedboats. Again, these sequences were filmed from Horne's Launch and, while Jon Pertwee and Roger Delgado were required to ride the boats for various close-ups (with Pertwee getting noticeably drenched at one point), the majority of the chase was performed by Fell and Walsh. However, as much of the chase was filmed from in front of the Master's boat looking back at the Doctor following, it required Stuart Fell to ensure that his face was kept out of shot as much as possible.

For the climactic scenes in Episode 3, showing the Doctor and Jo making their way to the beach where they are subsequently confronted by a Sea Devil, the plan had originally been to film the two characters as they abseiled their way down the cliff face. This was to have been achieved by using two qualified Royal Marine abseilers from R Company at RMB Eastney, as confirmed on 15 October by Lieutenant Commander Rose, the BBC's liaison at HMS Excellent. However, the film shot list for *The Sea Devils* seems to indicate that this part of the scene was never actually filmed.

The Sea Devils featured many shots of various ships, submarines, helicopters and explosions. This footage was not filmed on location but was supplied by the Admiralty's own film archive from such documentaries as *Where No Breezes Blow*, *The Navy is a Ship* and *Defence in Depth*. Some six months after production of *The Sea Devils*, the Navy's Director of Public Relations contacted the BBC, informing them that the Navy considered the publicity deriving from the story was sufficient for them to waive any royalty fees payable for the footage used.

Ouch!

While filming the escape from the Sea Devil at Whitecliff Bay at 3.00 pm on 27 October, Pertwee was required, as part of the action, to throw himself down onto a coil of specially blunted barbed wire, which marked the perimeter of the minefield. When the wire didn't support his weight in the way the production team had thought it would, Pertwee managed to bruise his ribs on a 'six-inch metal tube' (ie the sonic screwdriver) in his breast pocket.

Comment

Doctor Who always received good support from the armed forces and when the Royal Navy were asked to

Above: Christopher Barry prepares to direct Ky (Garrick Hagon) and Jo (Katy Manning) entering the caves at Stone House Farm, Frindsbury.

the planet's 500-year seasons and that the mutations are actually a natural part of the Solonian life cycle. Using a thaesium radiation crystal from the mine, Ky is quickly transformed from humanoid to a mutant and then to an ethereal super-being – the final stage. Ky kills the Marshal, finally allowing Solos to gain its independence.

The Locations

1. Western Quarry, Bean Road, Northfleet, Kent
2. Stone House Farm, Lower Rochester Road, Frindsbury, Kent
3. Chislehurst Caves, Old Hill, Chislehurst, Kent

Shooting Schedule

EPISODE 1

➤ **Old Solonian chased**
 Western Quarry // 7 February 1972
➤ **Marshal kills Old Solonian**
 Western Quarry // 8 February 1972

EPISODE 2

➤ **Ky and Jo chased by guards, Jo collapses**
 Western Quarry // 7 February 1972
➤ **Ky attacks guard and steals oxymask**
 Western Quarry // 7 February 1972
➤ **Stubbs, Cotton and attacked guard**
 Western Quarry // 7 February 1972
➤ **Ky and Jo enter cave, Ky revives Jo**
 Stone House Farm // 10 February 1972
➤ **Ky tells Jo about the mutants**
 Stone House Farm // 10 February 1972

EPISODE 3

➤ **Ky and Jo watch firestorm, Mutt appears**
 Stone House Farm // 9 February 1972
➤ **Ky hides Jo in the cave and wards of mutants**
 Chislehurst Caves // 11 or 12 February 1972
➤ **Doctor and Varan enter caves and save Ky**
 Chislehurst Caves // 11 or 12 February 1972
➤ **Ky opens the Time Lord container**
 Chislehurst Caves // 10-12 February 1972
➤ **Doctor and Ky begin to search for Jo**
 Chislehurst Caves // 10-12 February 1972
➤ **Varan hides in cave mouth as guard passes**
 Stone House Farm // 9 February 1972
➤ **Varan runs from cave**
 Stone House Farm // 9 February 1972
➤ **Guards chase Varan**
 Western Quarry // 8 February 1972
➤ **Doctor and Ky continue search**
 Chislehurst Caves // 10-12 February 1972
➤ **Marshal sends Stubbs and Cotton into caves**

lend a hand, they responded in tremendous fashion. Fortunately, Michael Briant didn't squander the opportunities presented to him and made sure that everything offered by the Navy is seen on screen. He also managed to capture some superbly memorable footage. 'I have never forgotten the scene where the Sea Devils came out of the sea. It was so eerie, the costumes so well made, it has to be one of the finest moments of *Doctor Who*,' wrote contributor Gareth Howard-Payne in *Doctor Who Magazine* #133. The only pity is that the Sea Devils' emergence in Episode 4 is done as a very grainy day-for-night shot, which doesn't provide quite as much impact as it should.

THE MUTANTS

(tx 8 April to 13 May 1972)

The Story

The Time Lords send the Doctor on a mission to deliver a sealed container to an unknown recipient. The TARDIS lands on Skybase, a space station orbiting the planet Solos, which is soon to gain its independence. Determined to prevent this is the Marshal, the controller of Skybase, who insists that Solos should be used for colonisation. To further his aims, he instructs Professor Jaeger to transform the poisonous atmosphere of the planet into one fit for human consumption. In the thaesium mines on Solos, the Doctor meets Sondergaard, who is seeking a cure for the 'disease' that is causing the native Solonians to mutate. The mysterious container opens in the hands of Solonian rebel leader Ky and the contents are revealed – four inscribed tablets. The Doctor deduces that the tablets represent

Stone House Farm // 9 February 1972
▸▸ **Varan reaches the village**
Western Quarry // 8 February 1972
▸▸ **Doctor and Ky find Jo**
Chislehurst Caves // 10-12 February 1972
▸▸ **Marshal sets explosives**
Stone House Farm // 9 February 1972
▸▸ **Gas seeps through caves**
Chislehurst Caves // 10-12 February 1972
▸▸ **Stubbs gets no response to radio**
Chislehurst Caves // 10-12 February 1972
▸▸ **Mutts collapse as Jo recounts her story**
Chislehurst Caves // 11 or 12 February 1972
▸▸ **Marshal watches cave mouth explosion**
Stone House Farm // 9 February 1972
▸▸ **Stubbs informs others they are trapped (3/4)**
Chislehurst Caves // 10-12 February 1972

EPISODE 4

▸▸ **Doctor's party follow silver-suited figure**
Chislehurst Caves // 10-12 February 1972
▸▸ **Marshal orders caves sealed**
Stone House Farm // 9 February 1972
▸▸ **Ky's party walk through passages, Jo sees mutant**
Chislehurst Caves // 11 or 12 February 1972
▸▸ **Ky's party attacked by guard**
Chislehurst Caves // 10 February 1972
▸▸ **Ky's party find exit shaft**
Chislehurst Caves // 10 February 1972
▸▸ **Ky's party make their way to surface**
Chislehurst Caves // 10-12 February 1972
▸▸ **Doctor and Sondergaard enter thaesium cave**
Chislehurst Caves // 10-12 February 1972
▸▸ **Doctor and Sondergaard reach the exit**
Chislehurst Caves // 10-12 February 1972

EPISODE 5

▸▸ **Doctor and Sondergaard leave the caves**
Western Quarry // 8 February 1972
▸▸ **Doctor and Sondergaard arrive at village**
Western Quarry // 8 February 1972
▸▸ **Doctor leaves Sondergaard**
Western Quarry // 8 February 1972
▸▸ **Marshal orders Doctor hunted**
Western Quarry // 8 February 1972
▸▸ **Sondergaard enters caves**
Stone House Farm // 9 February 1972
▸▸ **Sondergaard speaks to Mutants**
Chislehurst Caves // 11 or 12 February 1972

The Facts

The entrances to the Solonian caverns were all filmed using a small series of cave mouth openings found in one of the fields belonging to Stone House Farm in Frindsbury, for which the owner, James Castle, was paid £20. One problem that the production team hadn't foreseen was the amount of noise coming from the nearby road, carrying lorries and tankers to and from the Medway towns.

During filming, the production team were regularly visited by the two animals out grazing in the field, namely, a pony called Cheddar and a llama. During a filming break, Jon Pertwee also discovered a small field mouse that he decided to name 'Solos'.

For the filming at Chislehurst Caves, the production team applied a mixture of wallpaper paste and glitter to the walls, as well as painting various Solonian symbols throughout the caves to match those seen on the tablets given to Ky. After the filming was over, the symbols were left on the cave walls, where they remain to this day.

The map of the Solonian caves used by the Marshal in Episode 4 was actually part of a genuine map showing the layout of Chislehurst Caves.

To create the alien landscape of Solos, director Christopher Barry arranged to have vast quantities of buddleia sprayed silver and placed around the quarry and Stone House Farm locations.

Described by Jon Pertwee as 'taking coals to Newcastle', the production team brought along to the Chislehurst location two fake Jabolite rocks, the largest being that used in Episode 4 for the cover to the thaesium cave. The 'rocks', together with a quantity of smaller pieces to simulate rock falls, were supplied to the production at an extra cost of £36.

The early 1970s were marked by serious industrial disputes, particularly involving British miners, which in turn had an effect upon the country's power supply, resulting in sudden power cuts. While filming was being conducted in Chislehurst, one such power cut hit the area, plunging the caves into darkness.

Ouch!

Filming on *The Mutants* got off to a bad start when at 9.15 am on the morning of 7 February, Katy Manning fell while shooting her first scene in the Associated Portland Cement Quarry in Northfleet, straining the ankle she'd already weakened while filming *Terror of the Autons* 16 months earlier.

Comment

'Slag, ash and clinker' is how the planet of Solos is described in the story, and, to that end, all the location material for *The Mutants* seems deliberately crafted to appear grey, foggy and somewhat bland. However creative it might be, this effect does have a rather negative effect, as much of the resultant footage just looks dull

Above: **The Doctor (Jon Pertwee) rescues the Brigadier (Nicholas Courtney) from the time distortion.**

and uninteresting. However, the use of two separate locations to represent the caves of Solos does work rather well, the footage shot in the cave mouths at Frindsbury seamlessly blending in with the later filming done in Chislehurst Caves.

THE TIME MONSTER

(tx 20 May to 24 June 1972)

The Story

At the Newton Institute, the Master has constructed TOMTIT, a device to ostensibly provide instantaneous travel but which has really been put together to summon Kronos, a creature that lives outside time. The Master uses TOMTIT to bring Krasis, an Atlantian high priest, to the future to help him with Kronos. Still unsuccessful, the Master and Krasis travel back to Atlantis to steal the Crystal of Kronos, with which they can tame the creature. Kronos destroys Atlantis and, in the vortex, the Doctor time-rams the Master's TARDIS to prevent his escape. Now released, Kronos agrees to let the Doctor go but chooses to punish the Master for all eternity. The Doctor pleads for the Master and the renegade Time Lord escapes.

The Locations

1. Swallowfield Park, Swallowfield, Berkshire
2. Stratfield Saye Park, Stratfield Saye, Hampshire
3. Roads near Stratfield Saye, Hampshire
4. Mortimer Lane, Mortimer, Berkshire
5. School Lane, Heckfield Heath, Hampshire
6. Road near Old Church Farm, Hartley Wintney, Hampshire

Shooting Schedule

EPISODE 1

▸▸ **Master crosses courtyard**
Swallowfield Park // 4 April 1972

▸▸ **Window cleaner climbs up ladder**
Swallowfield Park // 4 April 1972

▸▸ **Institute clock strikes 11.00am**
Swallowfield Park // 4 April 1972

▸▸ **Window cleaner falls**
Swallowfield Park // 4 April 1972

▸▸ **Window cleaner found by visitors**
Swallowfield Park // 4 April 1972

▸▸ **Brigadier examines window cleaner**
Swallowfield Park // 4 April 1972

▸▸ **Doctor and Jo in Bessie, device registers**
Road nr. Old Church Farm // 7 April 1972

▸▸ **Institute clock reads 1.45pm**
Swallowfield Par // 4 April 1972

▸▸ **Doctor and Jo in Bessie**
Road nr. Old Church Farm // 7 April 1972

▸▸ **Doctor and Jo arrive in Bessie**
Swallowfield Park // 4 April 1972

▸▸ **Doctor and Jo stopped by cows (cut)**
Road nr. Old Church Farm // 7 April 1972

EPISODE 2

▸▸ **Doctor and Jo arrive as time slows down**
Swallowfield Park // 4 April 1972

▸▸ **Cook leaves the Institute**
Swallowfield Park // 4 April 1972

▸▸ **Benton crosses courtyard**
Swallowfield Park // 4 April 1972

▸▸ **Benton re-enters via a window**
Swallowfield Park // 4 April 1972

▸▸ **The Master and Percival head to the lab**
Swallowfield Park // 4 April 1972

EPISODE 3

▸▸ **Old Stuart is wheeled out to courtyard**
Swallowfield Park // 5 April 1972

▸▸ **Time begins to change in courtyard**
Swallowfield Park // 5 April 1972

▸▸ **Doctor rescues Ruth from time distortion**
Swallowfield Park // 5 April 1972

▸▸ **Doctor rescues Brigadier from time distortion**
Swallowfield Park // 5 April 1972

▸▸ **UNIT convoy underway**
School Lane // 6 April 1972

▸▸ **Master watches convoy on wrist monitor**
School Lane // 6 April 1972

▸▸ **UNIT convoy attacked by knight**
Stratfield Saye Park // 6 April 1972

▸ **Yates on radio**
Stratfield Saye Park // 6 April 1972

▸ **UNIT convoy attacked by Roundheads**
Stratfield Saye Park // 6 April 1972

▸ **Doctor, Jo and Brigadier leave Institute**
Swallowfield Park // 5 April 1972

▸ **Bessie en route to convoy**
Road near Stratfield Saye // 7 April 1972

▸ **Battle between UNIT and Roundheads**
Stratfield Saye Park // 6 April 1972

▸ **Roundheads vanish**
Stratfield Saye Park // 6 April 1972

▸ **Doctor, Jo and Brigadier listen to V1 rocket (3/4)**
Road near Stratfield Saye[53] // 7 April 1972

▸ **UNIT convoy attacked by V1 rocket (3/4)**
Mortimer Lane // 6 April 1972

EPISODE 4

▸ **UNIT convoy after V1 explosion**
Mortimer Lane // 6 April 1972

▸ **TARDIS is pulled upright by tractor**
Mortimer Lane // 6 April 1972

▸ **Doctor and Jo leave in TARDIS**
Mortimer Lane // 6 April 1972

▸ **TARDIS dematerialises**
Mortimer Lane // 6 April 1972

▸ **Benton, Ruth and Stuart creep around courtyard**
Swallowfield Park // 5 April 1972

▸ **Brigadier and UNIT troops arrive**
Swallowfield Park // 5 April 1972

▸ **Brigadier and UNIT troops frozen**
Swallowfield Park // 5 April 1972

▸ **Brigadier and UNIT troops frozen – Lab POV x 3**
Swallowfield Park // 5 April 1972

EPISODE 6

▸ **Brigadier and UNIT troops begin to unfreeze**
Swallowfield Park // 5 April 1972

▸ **Brigadier and UNIT troops restored to normal**
Swallowfield Park // 5 April 1972

The Facts

A scene planned but ultimately cut from Episode 1 featured the Doctor and Jo's journey to the Newton Institute being held up by a herd of cows. The animals were provided by Mr Hewitt, the owner of Old Church Farm in Hartley Wintney, but as the film diary noted, 'This sequence will be after lunch to time in with milking time!'

It is not known why the scene was dropped. The filming on 6 April had been attended by a reporter from the *Basingstoke Gazette*, who indicated in his article that the sequence with the cows was still being planned for the following day. Certainly the later camera scripts indi-

cate that this scene was never transferred to videotape for relaying into studio during recording, indicating that either the sequence was abandoned as the crew tried to film it or dropped due to time or quality constraints.

Mortimer Lane, located between the villages of Stratfield Saye and Beech Hill, was the location chosen to portray the explosion of the World War II V-1 rocket dropped on the UNIT convoy by the Master. To forewarn the residents, the *Reading Evening Post* ran a front page article about the filming being done in the area.

'Some time tomorrow, residents of the village of Stratfield Saye are going to be disturbed by one of the loudest explosions they are ever likely to hear. There is, however, no cause for alarm.

'Everyone's worst fears will go unrealised, for the explosion will be nothing more than members of the *Doctor Who* team working on a new television series. They will themselves withdraw half a mile before setting off the explosion, which is expected to be large enough to leave a crater behind in the ground.

'A particularly deserted site has been specially selected, and the local police have already been warned what to expect.'[54]

Ouch!

The main sequence to be filmed at Stratford Saye Park on Thursday 6 April was the attack on the UNIT convoy by the knight on horseback for Episode 3. The sequence called for the knight to charge at the three UNIT vehicles, which would all veer off of the road in different directions, allowing the knight to ride through the middle and off down the road. At 10.45 am, while the sequence was being filmed, the stunt went wrong, resulting in the horse colliding with the third vehicle and throwing stuntman

Above: **Jon Pertwee, Katy Manning and Ian Collier rehearse a scene outside Swallowfield Park on 5 April 1972.**

Greg Powell though the air. As a result, Powell was taken to Basingstoke Hospital where he was examined by Dr Motivola and an X-ray taken of his left shoulder and right arm. At some point during the day, a further shot of the same sequence was successfully attempted.

Comment

One of the principal location requirements for *The Time Monster* was a building which could not only double for a Cambridge research centre but that had a clock tower, in order to emphasise the time distortions occurring during the activation of TOMTIT. The buildings around Swallowfield Park proved ideal. For the most part, the Wootton Institute scenes are well handled, as are the various UNIT sequences shot around Stratfield Saye, so it's difficult to pinpoint exactly why the story doesn't work as well as it should. The observation that this is very much a four-part story padded out to six episodes seems valid; there's a reasonable story at the heart of *The Time Monster* and, with a little more pace, it could have been so much better.

THE THREE DOCTORS
(tx 30 December 1972 to 20 January 1973)

The Story

At UNIT HQ, the Doctor comes under attack from a strange organism found in the instrumentation affixed to a weather balloon. The Doctor calls on the Time Lords for assistance, but they are themselves helpless against a power-draining black hole. Breaking the temporal laws, the Time Lords send the Doctor's two earlier incarnations to help him. Trapped in a time eddy and only able to advise, the First Doctor deduces that the creature is a time bridge. Crossing the bridge, all three Doctors are transferred through the black hole to an anti-matter world created by Omega, a Time Lord stellar engineer who originated the power source that made time travel possible. Omega wants to be free of his world and needs the Doctor to take his place in order to stabilise the anti-matter. However, Omega's physical body has been corroded, leaving only the force of his will remaining. Omega is taunted into touching the Second Doctor's recorder, which, having fallen into the TARDIS' force field generator, remains unconverted matter. Omega's world is destroyed and everyone is returned home.

The Locations
1. Summerfield Bungalow, Springwell Lane, Rickmansworth, Hertfordshire
2. Springwell Quarry,[55] Springwell Lane, Rickmansworth, Hertfordshire
3. Springwell Reservoir, Springwell Lane, Rickmansworth, Hertfordshire
4. Halings House, Halings Lane, off Tilehouse Lane, Denham Green, Buckinghamshire

Shooting Schedule

EPISODE 1
▶▶ Ollis finds balloon
Springwell Reservoir // 7 November 1972
▶▶ Tyler meets Mrs Ollis
Summerfield Bungalow // 7 November 1972
▶▶ Tyler arrives and Ollis vanishes
Springwell Reservoir // 7 November 1972
▶▶ Doctor and Jo speak to Mrs Ollis
Springwell Reservoir // 7 November 1972
▶▶ Doctor and Jo arrive at UNIT and see organism
Halings House // 10 November 1972
▶▶ Gell Guards attack UNIT HQ
Halings House // 10 November 1972
▶▶ Gell Guards attacked with bazooka
Halings House // 10 November 1972
▶▶ Doctor Two on Time Lord screen
Springwell Quarry // 9 November 1972
▶▶ Doctor One (Hartnell) on screen[56]
Summerfield Bungalow // 9 November 1972

EPISODE 2
▶▶ Doctor and Jo arrive in anti-matter world
Springwell Quarry // 7 November 1972
▶▶ Doctor and Jo recover
Springwell Quarry // 7 November 1972
▶▶ Doctor and Jo find lab equipment and Bessie
Springwell Quarry // 8 November 1972
▶▶ Doctor and Jo find Tyler
Springwell Quarry // 8 November 1972
▶▶ Doctor, Jo and Tyler on Omega's screen
Springwell Quarry // 8 November 1972
▶▶ Doctor's group captured by Gell Guards
Springwell Quarry // 8 November 1972
▶▶ UNIT HQ vanishes (2/3)
Halings House // 10 November 1972

EPISODE 3
▶▶ Brigadier meets Ollis
Springwell Quarry // 9 November 1972
▶▶ Brigadier and Ollis decide on frontal attack
Springwell Quarry // 9 November 1972
▶▶ Brigadier's group flee towards UNIT HQ
Springwell Quarry // 9 November 1972

EPISODE 4
▶▶ Brigadier's group drives off in Bessie

Springwell Quarry // 9 November 1972
➤➤ **Bessie drives through explosions**
Springwell Quarry // 9 November 1972
➤➤ **Doctor and Doctor Two escape and look for Bessie**
Springwell Quarry // 9 November 1972
➤➤ **Brigadier's group arrive at UNIT HQ**
Springwell Quarry // 9 November 1972
➤➤ **Ollis reappears by reservoir**
Springwell Reservoir // 7 November 1972
➤➤ **Ollis returns home**
Summerfield Bungalow // 7 November 1972

The Facts

This story was filmed under the working title, *The Black Hole.*

Before being allowed to film at Springwell Reservoir, production assistant David Tilley had to visit Mr Mackett of the Rickmansworth and Uxbridge Valley Water Company in order to explain the filming and also gain the permission of the North Harrow Waltonians Angling Association.

The original intention had been to fully integrate Hartnell's Doctor into the story, giving him an equal share of the action with Troughton and Pertwee. After Hartnell accepted the invitation to appear in the anniversary story, his wife, Heather, contacted Barry Letts warning him that her husband was in very poor health. She added that her husband would not be able to endure any location work and would be unlikely to recall anything but the simplest lines of dialogue. The scripts were subsequently rewritten, drastically pruning down Hartnell's involvement, removing virtually all the requirements to have him either out on location or on the studio floor. In the end, with the exception of one brief shot of the First Doctor in a garden, all of Hartnell's scenes were filmed at Stage 3A, Ealing Film Studios on 6 November 1972.

The extensive list of location shots planned for this story went through some modification, with many being abandoned either prior to or during the filming. Most of those abandoned were simply remounts of existing shots filmed from alternative angles, but some did feature new material. One of these unfilmed sequences was originally written for Episode 4 and had been intended to follow directly on from the scene where the Brigadier's party, fleeing from the Gell Guards, use Bessie to return to UNIT HQ. In the unshot sequence, Jo activates the car's 'Super Drive' (used in the previous story, *The Time Monster*), allowing the Brigadier to drive at high speed through Omega's Gell Guard creatures before finally crashing into a sand dune. Tyler's shocked reaction of 'We nearly broke our necks' was to have been answered by Jo's comment, 'Nothing to worry about, Professor.

Invisible inertial safety belts…' – once again referring to a similar comment of the Doctor's in *The Time Monster.*

Comment

Visualising Omega's anti-matter world was always going to be something of a problem for the production team and it's a pity that the decision was taken to fall back on the use of a chalk quarry. Omega is portrayed as a powerful being who is in control of his world. Perhaps the bleakness of his creation was supposed to convey something about his own state of mind. If that was the case, then it doesn't come over very clearly.

Above: **John Levene, Katy Manning, Rex Robinson, Laurie Webb and Nicholas Courtney on location in Rickmansworth.**

CARNIVAL OF MONSTERS
(tx 27 January to 17 February 1973)

The Story

The TARDIS lands aboard the SS Bernice, a ship sailing across the Indian Ocean, in 1926. Jo and the Doctor are held as stowaways, and the Doctor is amazed when a plesiosaur attacks the ship. Suddenly, time appears to jump back and events being to play themselves out again. The Doctor discovers that they're on board a live exhibit inside a Miniscope, a banned device storing miniaturised life forms. Things become dangerous when vicious carnivores, Drashigs, break out of their swamp environment and invade the inner workings of the scope. The Doctor manages to leave the machine and, with the help of its owner, returns all the collected exhibits to their proper places in time and space.

The Locations

1. Tillingham Marshes, Howe Farm, Tillingham, Essex
2. Carwoods Quarry, Asheldham, Essex
3. RFA Robert Dundas, Chatham Dockyard to Sheerness Docks, Kent

Shooting Schedule[57]

EPISODE 1
▸▸ Doctor and Jo make their way from hold to cabin
RFA Robert Dundas // 2 June 1972

EPISODE 2
▸▸ Doctor and Jo hide from Andrews and Claire
RFA Robert Dundas // 1 June 1972

▸▸ Reaction as plesiosaur appears
RFA Robert Dundas // 2 June 1972

▸▸ Andrews and Daly pursue Doctor and Jo
RFA Robert Dundas // 1 June 1972

▸▸ Doctor and Jo emerge from cave
Carwoods Quarry // 31 May 1972

▸▸ Doctor and Jo begin to explore the marshes
Tillingham Marshes // 30 May 1972

▸▸ Doctor senses something wrong
Tillingham Marshes // 30 May 1972

▸▸ Doctor and Jo watch Drashig appear (2/3)
Tillingham Marshes // 30 May 1972

EPISODE 3
▸▸ Doctor and Jo cross marshes back to cave
Tillingham Marshes // 31 May 1972

▸▸ Doctor and Jo run into cave
Carwoods Quarry // 31 May 1972

▸▸ Andrews and Captain discuss the monster
RFA Robert Dundas // 2 June 1972

▸▸ Daly machine guns the Drashig
RFA Robert Dundas // 2 June 1972

EPISODE 4
▸▸ Jo watches Andrews and Daly
RFA Robert Dundas // 2 June 1972

The Facts
This story was filmed under the working title, *Peepshow*. And, due to the watery nature of the locations, it was a necessity to ensure that all members of the cast and crew were issued with life jackets while at the Tillingham Marshes and onboard the Robert Dundas.

Once the production was over, however, a dispute arose over the return of the life jackets to the BBC's Property Department. On 5 June 1972, the Property Master, Frank Holland, wrote to Barry Letts, informing him that a total of 33 life jackets had been issued to the production and had been signed for by the assistant floor manager, Karilyn Collier. Once the filming was completed, only 25 jackets had been returned to the Property Stores. Holland informed Letts that unless the missing eight life jackets were returned within a week, there would be no alternative but to charge the *Doctor Who*

production office the £62.40 for their replacement.

To achieve the sequences set on board the SS Bernice, production assistant Christopher D'Oyly John managed to secure the use of the Royal Fleet Auxiliary ship, Robert Dundas, one of two coastal storage tankers owned by the Royal Navy (the other being the Robert Middleton) until the early 1970s. By June 1972, the vessel had been sold to the Sheffield company Thomas W Ward Ltd, who were about to break it down for scrap. On 24 May, a deal was agreed with Wards that would allow the BBC to film onboard the Robert Dundas a week later, on 30 and 31 May. However, for reasons unknown, the filming dates had to be shifted to 1 and 2 June. Ward's accommodated this change of plan, but when they found it left them out of pocket they wrote to Jennie Betts of the BBC's Facilities department with a suggestion.

'Due to the alteration in the original date from the 30th and 31st May to the 1st and 2nd June, we have been involved in extra costs, over and above those allowed for under the agreement of 24th May, of approximately £218. This figure is made up due to the fact that our tug contractors had to supply two men during the movement from Chatham to Sheerness and then overtime rates were involved on 3rd June due to this being a Saturday movement, and I wondered whether you would be prepared to meet this cost on a 50/50 basis, which would involve a further cost to you of £109.'

T W Gray (Thomas W Ward Ltd) to Jennie Betts –
3 July 1972

On 13 July, Betts replied, agreeing to pay half of the money incurred by Ward's due to the 'confusion caused by the change of filming dates.'

With all the artists made-up and costumed, the cast and crew left the St George's Hotel, Rochester at 9.30 am on the morning of 1 June and were conveyed the short distance to the Royal Naval Dockyard in Chatham, where the Robert Dundas was berthed. For the first two hours after arrival, scenes were rehearsed and the ship itself was dressed with various items to take on its role as the SS Bernice. Following lunch, the ship was boarded at 12.45 pm and then, towed by a tug, it moved off down the River Medway while filming commenced. To avoid showing the banks of the Medway or any other river traffic, Letts had to choose his camera angles carefully, usually opting for high-angle shots looking down on the action, or very low-angle shots on the deck floor. After two hours, the ship arrived at Sheerness and berthed, but work continued on board for another three hours, until 6.00 pm. With the filming wrapped for the day, the cast and crew returned to Chatham on the tug, eating their evening meal en route. The following morning, having returned to Sheerness via the tug, filming continued for two and a half hours before a cold lunch was served (due to the fact that there was no power on board the Robert Dundas). The Friday afternoon was declared a standby period in order to complete any scenes not finished during the morning.

Due to the dampness of the Tillingham Marshes, all in attendance were advised to wear either waders or boots and, with high tide expected at 3.26 pm on Tuesday and 3.56 pm on Wednesday, ample safety equipment was also shipped to the location in the form of life jackets (see above), lifelines and a small boat.

While filming commenced on the marshes on Tuesday the 30th, designer Roger Liminton and a number of the BBC scene crew travelled to the small pit in Asheldham to prepare the cave mouth entrance of the Drashig world.

Comment

Carnival of Monsters features a rare excursion by a *Doctor Who* production team to East Anglia. Considering its closeness to London, it seems very peculiar that the programme made so little use of locations in Norfolk, Suffolk and Essex. In creating the worlds within the Miniscope, director Barry Letts certainly manages to secure some fine locations, especially the marshes at Tillingham, which provide a real sense of never-ending barren nothingness, ideal for the Drashig world. Finding a real ship to double for the SS Bernice is also a real blessing, as one can imagine how inadequate it might have looked had it been recreated in the studio. The only times that the effect is blown is when we actually see the water, the slow-flowing murkiness of the Medway looking nothing like the Indian Ocean thousands of miles away.

FRONTIER IN SPACE

(tx 24 February to 31 March 1973)

The Story

The TARDIS lands on an Earth freighter at a time of great tension between the powers of Earth and Draconia, each side believing that they are under unprovoked attack from the other. When the freighter is attacked, the Doctor and Jo realise that the real perpetrators are the Ogrons acting under the control of the Master. Accused of helping the Draconians, the Doctor is taken to an Earth prison, but he is captured during an assault by the aliens, who in turn accuse the Doctor of working for Earth. Escaping their embassy, the Doctor is recaptured by Earth soldiers and sentenced to life in a lunar penal colony. Managing to convince both Earth and Draconia that it is the Master who is provoking war between them, the Doctor travels to the Ogron home planet with the Draconian Prince and General Williams

from Earth. There he discovers that the Master is in league with the Daleks, who have masterminded the whole plot. In the confusion that follows, the Doctor is wounded. The Daleks leave for their base and the Doctor sends a telepathic message to the Time Lords...

Above: **The Daleks arrive on the Ogron homeworld. This scene from** *Frontier in Space* **was filmed at Beachfields Quarry on 12 September 1972.**

The Locations

1. Hayward Gallery, Belvedere Road, Lambeth, London, SE1
2. 8A Fitzroy Park, Highgate, London, N6
3. Beachfields Quarry, Cormongers Lane, Redhill, Surrey

Shooting Schedule

EPISODE 2

▸▸ **Doctor and Jo are taken to the prison**
    Hayward Gallery // 10 September 1972
▸▸ **Draconians attack and capture the Doctor**
    Hayward Gallery // 10 September 1972
▸▸ **Doctor escapes from the Draconian embassy**
    8A Fitzroy Park // 13 September 1972
▸▸ **Ogrons attack the prison**
    Hayward Gallery // 10 September 1972

EPISODE 3

▸▸ **Doctor and Jo are recaptured**
    Hayward Gallery // 10 September 1972

EPISODE 5

▸▸ **Master leads Jo across the Ogron planet**
    Beachfields Quarry // 11 September 1972

EPISODE 6

▸▸ **Doctor's party attacked by Ogrons**
    Beachfields Quarry // 11 September 1972
▸▸ **Doctor's party confronts the Master and Daleks**
    Beachfields Quarry // 12 September 1972

Right: **The Thals drag a Dalek to its doom at Beachfields Quarry.**

The Facts

This story was filmed under the title *Frontiers in Space*.

8a Fitzroy Park was at that time the home of BBC director Naomi Capon.

The main problem facing director Paul Bernard's team when filming around the Hayward Gallery was dealing with the large number of homeless people that had taken up residence in the concrete walkways since the building first opened in 1968. Bernard's solution was to get the fully costumed actors playing the Ogrons to ask the tramps to move on, figuring that their imposing size alone would persuade the vagrants to move without any trouble.

Comment

When Paul Bernard looked for an imposing and futuristic building at which to film the scenes around the Earth prison, it seemed that the newly constructed Hayward Gallery with its 'brutalist' architecture, concrete walls and high-level walkways was ideal. Unfortunately, what might have looked futuristic in the early 1970s now looks laughably dated. On the other hand, the all too brief use of the strange architecture and gardens of 8A Fitzroy Park is rather inspired and it represents the noble Draconian empire rather nicely.

PLANET OF THE DALEKS

(tx 7 April to 12 May 1973)

The Story

In pursuit of the Daleks, the TARDIS lands on Spiridon, where the Doctor and Jo meet a group of Thals attempting to destroy a small band of Daleks. They're apparently there to study the invisibility of the Spiridon natives but a second Thal mission lands with the news that, in reality, the Daleks have a base on the planet containing a 10,000-strong army. Entering the base, the Doctor discovers the Dalek army is held in suspended animation in the ice caverns of Spiridon. Together, the Doctor and the Thals explode a bomb which weakens the cavern walls, burying the Daleks in super-cold liquid ice.

The Locations

1. Beachfields Quarry, Cormongers Lane, Redhill, Surrey

Shooting Schedule

EPISODE 5

▶ Doctor shows Taron the ice pool
Beachfields Quarry // 2 January 1973
▶ Doctor and Taron attack a Dalek

Beachfields Quarry // 2/3 January 1973
- ▸▸ **Two Daleks pushed into ice pool**
  Beachfields Quarry // 3 January 1973

The Facts

As had been experienced on *Day of the Daleks*, the Dalek casings proved difficult to move over the uneven surface of the quarry and so sheets of blockboard had to be laid to ensure smooth movement.

The lakes in the quarry were converted into 'ice-pools' by the use of copious amounts of dry ice, which was thrown into the water causing it to bubble and be covered by a heavy layer of dense mist. Thirty blocks of dry ice were originally taken to the location, but by the end of the first day, a further 20 had to be ordered so that the shots could be completed.

In order to facilitate the filming around the lake, a six-metre scaffolding rostra was constructed in the water on which the camera could be placed.

Comment

Planet of the Daleks features only a few brief location scenes in Episode 5 but, short as they are, they are well worthwhile as they set up the notion that the Daleks can be rendered immobile or even killed by extreme cold, an important plot point for later in the adventure. Fortunately, the production of the story fell during a cold and damp January, further reinforcing the idea of freezing liquid ice pools.

THE GREEN DEATH

(tx 19 May to 23 June 1973)

The Story

Following the strange death of a miner at Llanfairfach, the Doctor, the Brigadier and Jo travel to Wales to investigate the colliery, discovering that bright green toxic waste has seeped into the mine. The source of the waste, a by-product of a new, reputedly clean oil-refining technique, is tracked to the nearby Global Chemicals, who have been disposing of the poisonous slime by pumping it into the mine. The waste also causes animal mutations, infesting the mine with giant maggots which eventually burrow to the surface and begin pupating into poison-spitting flies. The Doctor discovers by accident that the fungus cultivated by ecologist Professor Clifford Jones as an alternative food supply is lethal to the maggots and counteracts the poisonous effects of the toxic waste. Infiltrating Global Chemicals, the Doctor finds that the company is run by a supercomputer, the BOSS, who controls the director, Stevens. Freed by the Doctor from the computer's hold, Stevens causes the destruction of the plant.

The Locations

1. Ogilvie Colliery, Deri, near Bargoed, Glamorgan
2. Colliery Quarry, Deri, near Bargoed, Glamorgan
3. Troed-y-Rhiw-Jestyn, Deri, near Bargoed, Glamorgan
4. RCA International, Brynmawr, Powys

Shooting Schedule

EPISODE 1

- ▸▸ **Arial shot of Llanfairfach Colliery**
  Ogilvie Colliery // 15 March 1973
- ▸▸ **Closed signs on colliery**
  Ogilvie Colliery // 12 March 1973
- ▸▸ **Stevens arrives at Global Chemicals, talks to crowd**
  RCA International // 16 March 1973
- ▸▸ **Jones confronts Stevens and the crowd**
  RCA International // 16 March 1973
- ▸▸ **Brigadier drives Jo to Wholeweal**
  Troed-y-Rhiw-Jestyn // 12 March 1973
- ▸▸ **Doctor arrives on Metebelis and is attacked**
  Quarry // 13 March 1973
- ▸▸ **Doctor runs and sees snake**
  Quarry // 13 March 1973
- ▸▸ **Doctor traverses ledge in snowstorm**
  Quarry // 13 March 1973
- ▸▸ **Doctor spots the crystal cluster**
  Quarry // 13 March 1973
- ▸▸ **Something large flaps its way towards the Doctor**
  Quarry // 13 March 1973
- ▸▸ **Doctor dodges huge talons**
  Quarry // 13 March 1973
- ▸▸ **Doctor escapes in the TARDIS**
  Quarry // 13 March 1973
- ▸▸ **Evans goes to pit lift**
  Ogilvie Colliery // 13 March 1973
- ▸▸ **Evans descends in pit lift**
  Ogilvie Colliery // 13 March 1973
- ▸▸ **Doctor arrives at Global Chemicals**
  RCA International // 16 March 1973
- ▸▸ **Jo approaches the mine**
  Troed-y-Rhiw-Jestyn // 12 March 1973
- ▸▸ **Doctor and Brigadier approach mine in Bessie**
  Ogilvie Colliery // 12 March 1973
- ▸▸ **Jo and Bert begin to descend into the mine (1/2)**
  Ogilvie Colliery // 13 March 1973
- ▸▸ **Doctor and Brigadier see lift machinery working (1/2)**
  Ogilvie Colliery // 12 March 1973

EPISODE 2

- ▸▸ **Brigadier returns to his car and uses radio**
  RCA International // 16 March 1973
- ▸▸ **Wholeweal community make a diversion**

Above: A puppet maggot is filmed on the Ogilvie Colliery slag heap.

RCA International // 16 March 1973

▶▶ **Doctor makes his way into Global Chemicals**
RCA International // 19 March 1973

▶▶ **Security camera activates**
RCA International // 19 March 1973

▶▶ **Monitor – Doctor in grounds**
RCA International // 19 March 1973

▶▶ **Doctor makes his way through the plant**
RCA International // 19 March 1973

▶▶ **Doctor is apprehended**
RCA International // 19 March 1973

▶▶ **Doctor fights guards and meets Stevens**
RCA International // 19 March 1973

▶▶ **Brigadier arrives with cutting gear**
RCA International // 12 March 1973

▶▶ **Cable is cut and Doctor's party descends in lift**
Ogilvie Colliery // 13 March 1973

EPISODE 3

▶▶ **Ambulance leaves the mine**
Ogilvie Colliery // 12 March 1973

▶▶ **Guards rush to Fell's body**
RCA International // 20 March 1973

EPISODE 4

▶▶ **UNIT preparing to destroy mine, talk with milkman**
Ogilvie Colliery // 13 March 1973

▶▶ **Doctor asks for time to visit Global Chemicals**
Ogilvie Colliery // 13 March 1973

▶▶ **Jo anxious for the Doctor's return to mine**

Ogilvie Colliery // 13 March 1973

▶▶ **Countdown to explosion**
Ogilvie Colliery // 13 March 1973

▶▶ **Maggot emerges on slag heap next to soldier**
Ogilvie Colliery – Slag Heap // 14 March 1973

▶▶ **Brigadier observes the maggots**
Ogilvie Colliery – Slag Heap // 14 March 1973

▶▶ **UNIT tries to attack the maggots**
Ogilvie Colliery – Slag Heap // 14 March 1973

▶▶ **Milk float drives past window**
Ogilvie Colliery // 13 March 1973

▶▶ **Doctor disguised as milkman at Global Chemicals**
RCA International // 16 March 1973

▶▶ **Jo talks to Benton at the slag heap**
Ogilvie Colliery – Slag Heap // 14 March 1973

▶▶ **Brigadier tells Benton about the RAF strike (4/5)**
Ogilvie Colliery – Slag Heap // 14 March 1973

EPISODE 5

▶▶ **Cliff sees Jo on the slag heap**
Ogilvie Colliery – Slag Heap // 14 March 1973

▶▶ **Helicopter bombs maggots as Jo and Cliff flee**
Ogilvie Colliery – Slag Heap // 15 March 1973

▶▶ **Helicopter flies away and burning maggots**
Ogilvie Colliery – Slag Heap // 15 March 1973

▶▶ **Doctor escapes from Global leaving Yates behind**
RCA International // 20 March 1973

▶▶ **Doctor smashes through the barrier in milk float**
RCA International // 16 March 1973

▶▶ **Doctor arrives back at slag heap**
Ogilvie Colliery – Slag Heap // 14 March 1973

▶▶ **Doctor drives off with Benton**
Ogilvie Colliery – Slag Heap // 15 March 1973

▶▶ **Bessie approaches the cave**
Ogilvie Colliery – Slag Heap // 15 March 1973

▶▶ **Doctor holds of maggots as Cliff and Jo are rescued**
Ogilvie Colliery – Slag Heap // 15 March 1973

EPISODE 6

▶▶ **Benton arrives with chrysalis**
Troed-y-Rhiw-Jestyn // 12 March 1973

▶▶ **Bessie is loaded with sacks of fungus and drives off**
Ogilvie Colliery – Slag Heap // 14 March 1973

▶▶ **Maggots begin to eat the fungus and die**
Ogilvie Colliery – Slag Heap // 15 March 1973

▶▶ **Doctor and Benton drive past giant fly**
Ogilvie Colliery – Slag Heap // 15 March 1973

▶▶ **Giant fly attacks Doctor and Benton**
Ogilvie Colliery – Slag Heap // 15 March 1973

▶▶ **Yates escapes from Global Chemicals**
RCA International // 20 March 1973

▶▶ **Yates runs through countryside**
Ogilvie Colliery – Slag Heap // 15 March 1973

➤ **Yates finds Brigadier and Benton**
Ogilvie Colliery – Slag Heap **//** 15 March 1973
➤ **Doctor arrives at entrance to Global Chemicals**
RCA International **//** 16 March 1973
➤ **Guard is affected by processing and Doctor enters**
RCA International **//** 16 March 1973
➤ **Brigadier waits for Doctor**
RCA International **//** 16 March 1973
➤ **Doctor runs from factory and everyone
takes cover**
RCA International **//** 16 March 1973
➤ **Doctor leaves Wholemeal and climbs into Bessie**
Troed-y-Rhiw-Jestyn **//** 12 March 1973
➤ **Doctor drives away as the sun sets**
Troed-y-Rhiw-Jestyn **//** 12 March 1973

The Facts

The primary location requirement for *The Green Death* was a real coalmine. The production team approached the National Coal Board in Swansea for permission to film at a working pit and were given authorisation to shoot at Ogilvie Colliery in Deri, which was subsequently closed down in 1975.

Receiving a payment of £125, the NCB permitted the BBC to film as required around the site, as well as shooting material of various characters using the caged pit-lift to enter and exit the mine. However, due to the high risk of explosions, no filming was allowed to be done in the underground passages, although several of the cast and crew, including Jon Pertwee and director Michael Briant, were allowed to visit the coalface to see real mining operations.

Due to the large amount of filming that Briant hoped to achieve while in Wales, it was decided to operate two separate film units while on location. The first, headed by Briant and Chief Cameraman Bill Matthews, concentrated on all the main sequences, while the second unit was overseen by Assistant Cameraman Ken Lowe. For this reason, two production assistants were also employed: John Harris, who oversaw the entire production, and Michael McDermott, who attended the location filming only. The filming was originally planned to begin on 8 March 1973, but this was later revised to a start date of the 12th.

All the Episode 1 scenes of the Doctor landing on Metebelis 3 were filmed in a small quarry connected to the colliery, where the mine kept its supply of explosives. The quarry was decorated with pieces of tinsel and silver paper and lit by blue arc lamps.

Michael Briant: 'We did several low-angle takes of Jon climbing along what appeared to be a cliff edge, looking as though he's clinging on for grim death

when in fact he was only three inches above the ground. He hated every second of that because there were coachloads of kids there who'd arrived to watch the filming, all sitting on the edges of the quarry, watching Jon maniacally acting away, falling over with laughter.'[58]

Colin Mapson (visual effects assistant): 'Our team simulated the hostile weather environment using a wind machine and bits of polystyrene for snow. We had great fun attacking Jon Pertwee with a large pair of prop bird talons (held from above by us), and by throwing lightweight rocks and spears at him as he ran for the safety of the TARDIS.'[59]

The Hughes 300 helicopter used in the production was the same aircraft that had appeared in *Fury from the Deep* five years earlier, although by this time it had apparently become the property of Twyford Moors Helicopters, based in Weston Super Mare. For the second unit shots of footage taken from the helicopter, a camera mount was used which had originally been constructed for an episode of *Z-Cars* in September 1972.

To supplement the puppet maggot models, the slag heap was covered with water-filled condoms to give the illusion of hundreds of maggots burrowing their way out of the mine.

The RCA International factory had been empty for 16 months by the time that *The Green Death* was filmed there.

Episode 6 featured the roof escape of Mike Yates from Global Chemicals. The long shot of Yates jumping from the roof was actually performed by Terry Walsh, with Richard Franklin resuming the role for the final close-up. The brief shot required Franklin to jump up in the air so that the film could be cut together from his descent. However, when Franklin landed, he split the seat of his trousers.

Comment

As with his previous work on *The Sea Devils*, Michael Briant makes the most of his chosen location for *The Green Death*. The mine workings and slag heaps are used to tremendous effect, as is the small farm building which appears as the "Nuthutch", whose rough and muddy exterior immediately befits the back-to-nature ethics of Professor Jones and his environmentalist colleagues at the Wholeweal community. Particularly outstanding are the closing moments of the story, when the Doctor leaves Jo for the last time and returns to Bessie alone, pausing for a moment before he drives away as the sun sets. The subdued lighting and the lack of dialogue emphasise the Doctor's sense of loss.

Right: Jon Pertwee and Elisabeth Sladen talk with Kevin Lindsay between takes outside Peckforton Castle.

THE TIME WARRIOR

(tx 15 December 1973 to 5 January 1974)

The Story

Investigating the mysterious disappearance of several scientists, the Doctor travels back to the 13th century and discovers that a Sontaran officer, Linx, has been bringing them back in time to repair his crashed spaceship. Hiding on board the TARDIS, journalist Sarah Jane Smith is captured by the local robber chief, Irongron, in whose castle Linx is working, providing him advanced weapons in payment for shelter. Helping the neighbouring Wessex Castle to resist attack from Irongron, the Doctor, Sarah and Hal, a Wessex archer, return to Irongron's castle. The Doctor frees the kidnapped scientists and returns them home as Linx prepares to leave. Hal shoots the Sontaran in the probic vent, killing him, and the three manage to escape just as Linx's spaceship explodes, destroying the castle.

The Locations

1. Peckforton Castle, Stone House Lane, Peckforton, Cheshire

Shooting Schedule

EPISODE 1

▸▸ Irongron and Bloodaxe meet Linx
Peckforton Castle // 7 May 1973

▸▸ TARDIS materialises, Doctor and Sarah exit
Peckforton Castle // 7 May 1973

▸▸ Irongron and Bloodaxe on battlements
Peckforton Castle // 8 May 1973

▸▸ Sarah disturbs Hal
Peckforton Castle // 7 May 1973

▸▸ Irongron is nearly hit, Hal spotted
Peckforton Castle // 8 May 1973

▸▸ Sarah is caught, watched by Doctor
Peckforton Castle // 7 May 1973

▸▸ Sarah and Hal dragged into castle,
Doctor sees Linx (1/2)
Peckforton Castle // 8 May 1973

EPISODE 2

▸▸ Hal faces the robot knight
Peckforton Castle // 9 May 1973

▸▸ Doctor shoots arrow at robot knight
Peckforton Castle // 8 May 1973

▸▸ Sarah and Hal enter Irongron's castle
Peckforton Castle // 9 May 1973

▸▸ Doctor battles with Irongron's men (2/3)
Peckforton Castle // 9 May 1973

EPISODE 3

▸▸ Doctor 'rescued' by Sarah and Hal
Peckforton Castle // 10 May 1973

▸▸ Irongron's men attempt to attack
Wessex Castle

Peckforton Castle // 10 May 1973
▸▸ **Doctor and Sarah enter Irongron's castle as monks**
Peckforton Castle // 8 May 1973

EPISODE 4

▸▸ **Doctor and Sarah escape from Irongron's castle**
Peckforton Castle // 8 May 1973
▸▸ **Doctor leaves the TARDIS with his 'shield'**
Peckforton Castle // 7 May 1973
▸▸ **Guards fall asleep watched by Doctor, Sarah and Hal**
Peckforton Castle // 8 May 1973
▸▸ **Doctor, Sarah and Hal run from Irongron's castle**
Peckforton Castle // 8 May 1973
▸▸ **Doctor and Sarah say goodbye to Hal**
Peckforton Castle // 7 May 1973

The Facts

Linx's spaceship was a Jabolite construction, which cost a total of £840 to produce.

As several scenes featured Hal the Archer firing arrows, actor Jeremy Bulloch had to be taught to correctly fire a longbow by armourer Doug Needham. However, to protect the crew from any stray arrows, wooden boards were erected around the camera.

Location Facts

Peckforton Castle was not in reality a castle at all, but a Victorian folly built in the style of a 12th century castle by John Tollermach, the MP for Cheshire (1841-1872) between 1844 and 1851. At the time of filming *The Time Warrior*, Peckforton was a private home owned by G W Barratt, but by the end of the 1980s the building had gone into receivership and was purchased for just over £1m by Evelyn Graybill. The building was extensively refurbished but Graybill's plan to turn Peckforton into a hotel never materialised for lack of further funds.

Since *The Time Warrior*, Peckforton Castle has also featured in two 1991 productions, Granada Television's *The Casebook of Sherlock Holmes: The Boscombe Valley Mystery* and the film *Robin Hood* starring Patrick Bergin.

Comment

One of the biggest problems with the filming at Peckforton Castle is that it just looks too, well, nice. Irongron and his men are represented as a band of cut-throat slobs and yet they appear to be living in a very well-kept and agreeable building. You just get the feeling that if everything had been a bit more rough and ready it might have created the illusion better.

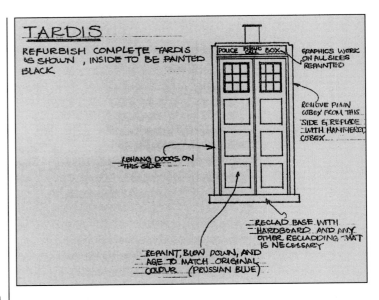

Above: **Plans for the TARDIS refurbishment prior to the location filming of *Invasion of the Dinosaurs*.**

INVASION OF THE DINOSAURS

(tx 12 January to 16 February 1974)

The Story

The TARDIS lands in a strangely deserted London. Wrongly arrested by the Army as looters, the Doctor and Sarah escape when their military transport is blocked by the appearance of a tyrannosaurus rex. Meeting up with UNIT, they learn that London has been evacuated following the strange appearance and disappearance of various prehistoric monsters. The creatures have been brought back by Professor Whittaker in order to clear the capital. Looking to return to a cleaner, less corrupt and less polluted Earth, Whittaker and his cohorts plan to use a timescoop to roll time back to a 'Golden Age' before any technological progress. The Doctor manages to enter the secret base situated under Moorgate Underground Station and alters the timescoop settings. When activated by the misguided politician, Sir Charles Grover, the timescoop only manages to send itself, Grover and Whittaker into the prehistoric past.

The Locations

1. Albert Embankment, London, SE11
2. Westminster Bridge, Westminster, London, SW1
3. Whitehall, London, SW1
4. Trafalgar Square, London, SW1
5. Margaret Street, London, W1
6. Haymarket, London, SW1
7. Billingsgate Market, Lower Thames Street, London, EC3
8. Covent Garden, Strand, London, WC2
9. Outer Circle (by Cambridge Gate), Regent's Park,

London, NW1

10. Clayponds Avenue, Brentford, Middlesex
11. Wilmer Close, Kingston-upon-Thames, Surrey
12. Canbury Gardens, Lower Ham Road, Kingston-upon-Thames, Surrey
13. Lower Ham Road, Kingston-upon-Thames, Surrey
14. Southall Gas Works, White Street, Southall, Middlesex
15. Moorfields, London, EC2
  • Phillips Jewellers, 125 Moorfields
  • Moorgate Underground Station
16. New Union Street, London, EC2
17. Northfields School, Balfour Road, London, W13
18. GPO Sorting Office, Orchard Road, Kingston-upon-Thames, Surrey
19. Palmer Crescent, Kingston-upon-Thames, Surrey
20. Pickfords Depositories, Brownlow Road, Ealing, London, W13
21. Kingston Meat Market, The Bittoms, Kingston-upon-Thames, Surrey
22. South Lane, Kingston-upon-Thames, Surrey
23. The Straight, Southall, Middlesex
24. Chamberlain Road, Ealing, London, W13
25. Central Electricity Generating Board Sub Station, Elderberry Road, Ealing, London, W5
26. White Street, Southall, Middlesex
27. Parkfields Road, Kingston-upon-Thames, Surrey
28. Long Lane, Smithfield, London, EC1
29. Wimbledon Common, Wimbledon, London, SW19
30. Lindsay Street, Smithfield, London, EC1
31. Riverside Drive, Ham, Middlesex

Shooting Schedule

EPISODE 1

▸▸ **Deserted London**
Albert Embankment // See Footnote[60]

▸▸ **Deserted London**
Westminster Bridge // See Footnote

▸▸ **Deserted London**
Whitehall // See Footnote

▸▸ **Deserted London**
Trafalgar Square // See Footnote

▸▸ **Deserted London**
Margaret Street // See Footnote

▸▸ **Deserted London**
Haymarket // See Footnote

▸▸ **Deserted London**
Billingsgate Market // See Footnote

▸▸ **Deserted London**
Long Lane // See Footnote

▸▸ **Deserted London**
Covent Garden // See Footnote

▸▸ **Deserted London**
Outer Circle // See Footnote

▸▸ **Dog sniffs around car**
Clayponds Avenue[61] // 27 September 1973

▸▸ **Looter attacked near milk float (partially cut)**
Wilmer Close // 26 September 1973

▸▸ **TARDIS materialises, Doctor and Sarah leave**
Canbury Gardens // 27 September 1973

▸▸ **Doctor tries telephone and they walk to bus stop**
Lower Ham Road // 27 September 1973

▸▸ **Phillips hides as patrol passes**
Southall Gas Works // 25 September 1973

▸▸ **Doctor and Sarah nearly run down by Phillips**
Lower Ham Road // 27 September 1973

▸▸ **Phillips enters jewellers, followed by Doctor and Sarah**
Moorfields // 23 September 1973

▸▸ **Doctor and Sarah run to Phillips crushed car**
New Union Street // 23 September 1973

▸▸ **Doctor and Sarah at closed police station**
GPO Sorting Office // 26 September 1973

▸▸ **Looter's Land Rover passes by**
Palmer Crescent // 26 September 1973

▸▸ **Doctor and Sarah follow vehicle**
GPO Sorting Office // 26 September 1973

▸▸ **Doctor and Sarah discover looters and Pterodactyl**
Pickfords Warehouse // 24 September 1973

▸▸ **Doctor and Sarah are caught as looters**
Kingston Meat Market // 26/27 September 1973

▸▸ **Soldiers fight off Tyrannosaurus Rex**
The Straight // 25 September 1973

▸▸ **Doctor and Sarah try to escape**
Northfields School // 24 September 1973

▸▸ **Land Rover drives to detention centre**
Chamberlain Road // 24 September 1973

EPISODE 2

▸▸ **Doctor and Sarah escape from soldiers**
The Straight // 25 September 1973

▸▸ **Soldiers realise that their prisoners have gone**
The Straight // 25 September 1973

▸▸ **Doctor observes Stegosaurus**
Kingston Meat Market // 27 September 1973

▸▸ **Stegosaurus disappears in a time eddy**
Kingston Meat Market // 27 September 1973

▸▸ **Doctor tries to stun Apatosaurus (2/3)**
Central Electricity Generating Board // 29 September 1973

EPISODE 3

▸▸ **Yates rescues the Doctor and stuns Apatosaurus**
Central Electricity Generating Board // 29 September 1973

▸▸ **Doctor drives in Land Rover back to warehouse**
White Street // 25 September 1973
▸▸ **Doctor drives in Land Rover back to warehouse**
Parkfields Road // 26 September 1973
▸▸ **Doctor rescues Sarah from Tyrannosaurus**
Central Electricity Generating Board //
24 September 1973

EPISODE 4

▸▸ **Doctor leaves UNIT HQ in Whomobile**
Northfields School // 24 September 1973
▸▸ **Doctor stops and checks readings against his map**
Long Lane // 23 September 1973
▸▸ **Doctor stops and takes more readings**
South Lane // 27 September 1973
▸▸ **Doctor tracks signal to Underground station**
Moorgate Station // 23 September 1973
▸▸ **Doctor leaves Underground and drives off**
Moorgate Station // 23 September 1973
▸▸ **Doctor and Brigadier arrive at the
Underground station**
Moorgate Station // 23 September 1973

EPISODE 5

▸▸ **Doctor evades army patrol**
White Street // 25 September 1973
▸▸ **Doctor is pursued by army patrol**
Wimbledon Common // 26 September 1973
▸▸ **Doctor cornered by Tyrannosaurus and
Apatosaurus (5/6)**
Lindsey Street // 23 September 1973

EPISODE 6

▸▸ **Doctor runs as the two dinosaurs fight**
Lindsay Street // 23 September 1973
▸▸ **Brigadier and Finch stand-off over the Doctor**
Central Electricity Generating Board //
29 September 1973
▸▸ **Doctor and Brigadier drive under Apatosaurus**
Riverside Drive // 27 September 1973
▸▸ **Brigadier throws hand grenade at Stegosaurus**
Moorgate Station // 23 September 1973
▸▸ **Brigadier radios for reinforcements**
Moorgate Station // 23 September 1973

The Facts

After being assigned to the story, director Paddy (Patricia) Russell immediately decided that, in order to create the right atmosphere, she would need to show, not merely empty side-streets, but several central London landmarks deserted and devoid of life.

For reasons which are not entirely clear, Russell elected to film these opening sequences unofficially, separate-

Above: **A cut sequence from Episode 3, showing Captain Yates (Richard Frankin) lying next to an out-of-proportion dinosaur leg.**

ly from the main location shoot and without either BBC or police permission. Instead, she set up her own film unit consisting of herself, cameraman Tony Leggo and his assistant, Fred Bagwell. Using a BBC camera and film stock, the trio set off at 4.00 am one Sunday morning, filming around some of the capital's major landmarks – Westminster Bridge, Albert Embankment, Whitehall and Trafalgar Square. Due to the lack of police permission, the silent filming had to be done at speed with the camera crew trying to look like tourists. However, when the footage was processed at Ealing Film Studios the following week and the unauthorised filming was discovered, Russell was duly reprimanded for her actions.

Barry Letts (producer): 'If there was any telling off done, it certainly wasn't by me. I didn't know about it beforehand but when I was told I was as gleeful as Paddy herself that she'd been so enterprising. Maybe the Organiser (nowadays called the Manager) of our department got a frisson of horror if she/he found out. We certainly would have got into bad trouble if they'd been caught.'

Although a 26-page film diary and a 75-page film shot list had been drawn up and issued to the production team for the main six-day location shoot, the filming evidently was done very much on-the-fly, with various scenes being shot at different locations to those originally scouted (see *Unused Locations*).

By the time of the film diary's assembly, locations had still not been finalised for the vast majority of scenes which would need to be filmed on Tuesday 25 September, including the beginning of the major chase sequence between the Doctor and the Army in Part 5. Eventually, and with very little time to spare, production assistant George Gallaccio arranged for the scenes to be filmed in and around Southall Gas Works.

Part 1 lost an additional brief sequence in the opening 'deserted London' montage sequence, which was intended to appear after the shot of the abandoned milk float and money bag, described so:

LOOTER comes cautiously round the corner, spots the money and runs to it. He bends, a big shadow falls over him. Zoom in as he cowers away.

For these shots, the looter was played by Leslie Noyes while the visual effects requirement for the scene was a 'Pterodactyl shadow'.

Another sequence shot, but ultimately edited out of the broadcast version of Part 3, showed Mike Yates rushing to rescue the Doctor, stunned by the explosion from a UNIT grenade. The missing sequence showed Yates flinging himself next to the tyrannosaurus' leg and firing his service pistol at the creature before reaching for the Doctor's sabotaged stun gun. The shots were ultimately removed from the sequence because it was obvious that the prop dinosaur's leg was conspicuously out of proportion with the other model footage.

The first shots to be completed on Sunday 23 September involved the use of the Doctor's new vehicle. Called 'The Alien', but unofficially known as the Whomobile, the three-wheeled vehicle had been commissioned by Jon Pertwee after meeting designer Peter Farries, chairman of the Nottingham Drag and Custom Club, at a motor exhibition and asking him to construct a space car that he could use for personal appearances. Pertwee convinced Barry Letts to make use of the vehicle in the programme, although by the time filming began the windshield, required to make the vehicle legal for use on the roads, had not been completed and fitted. As a result, a temporary replacement had to be attached. The use of the Whomobile in Part 4, as the Doctor tries to trace the source of the timescoop emissions, replaced the motorbike that had been the Doctor's scripted mode of transport.

Unused Locations

The production's film shot list indicates a number of locations that were going to be used for various scenes throughout the story, but which were evidently changed when something easier or more suitable was found. The list below indicates the locations originally considered, the first being the typewritten location, followed by others which were handwritten onto the list when the original was crossed out.

1 – Looter attacked near milk float
Brackley Terrace, Brentford // Park Road,
Kingston-upon-Thames
1 – Phillips hides as patrol passes
Willoughby Arms, Willoughby Road, Kingston-upon-Thames[62] // Swanscombe Road, Chiswick
1 – Doctor and Sarah caught as looters
Park Road, Kingston-upon-Thames
1 – Soldiers fight off tyrannosaurus rex
Coombe Road, Chiswick // Park Road,
Kingston-upon-Thames

2 – Doctor and Sarah escape from soldiers
Brackley Terrace, Chiswick // Park Road,
Kingston-upon-Thames
2 – Soldiers realise that their prisoners have gone
Brackley Terrace, Chiswick // Park Road,
Kingston-upon-Thames
2/3 – Doctor tries to stun Apatosaurus
Hearn St, Back of Liverpool Street Station
3 – Doctor drives back to warehouse
Swanscombe Road, Chiswick // Willoughby Road,
Kingston-upon-Thames // Loughborough Rd
4 – Doctor stops and takes more readings
Ropemaker Street
5 – Doctor evades army patrol
Swanscombe Road, Chiswick // Willoughby Road,
Kingston-upon-Thames // Loughborough Rd

Comment

Invasion of the Dinosaurs is something of a curate's egg. Certainly, the location material showing the deserted London in the first episode is quite spectacular and manages to conjure up the desired impression of an evacuated capital very well. This effect may not have posed so much of a problem with the outlying locations, but it must have been that much harder with those scenes set around the inner London locations and it's a testament to Paddy Russell and her team that the scenes work so well. The main let-down of the story is often identified as the model dinosaurs but most of them work reasonably well. The only one which doesn't is the one that unfortunately appears the most – the tyrannosaurus rex.

DEATH TO THE DALEKS
(tx 23 February to 16 March 1974)

The Story

Aiming for the planet of Florana, the TARDIS lands on Exxilon and immediately has all power drained from its energy banks. The Doctor meets up with a party from Earth who have travelled to Exxilon to obtain Parrinium, a cure for a devastating plague that is spreading throughout the galaxy. A Dalek taskforce arrives to also collect Parrinium, but suffers from the same total power loss as the TARDIS and the Earth ship. The source of the power drain is the futuristic living city built centuries ago by the Exxilons, which turned against its creators shortly after completion, sending them down a path of savagery. Pursued by the Daleks, the Doctor enters the city and destroys it. With power restored, the Daleks leave the planet, believing that they have stolen all the mined

Left: The Exxilons attack on the Daleks, filmed with a cylindrical tube over the camera lens from within the Dalek casing itself.

Parrinium. But they are destroyed by one of their own bombs, detonated by Galloway, one of the humans who has smuggled himself on board their spacecraft.

The Locations

1. ARC Sand Pit, Puddletown Road, Gallows Hill, Dorset
   - Area A - Mining Area Pit
   - Area B - Boulder Pit
   - Area C - Ambush Pit

Shooting Schedule

EPISODE 1

▸▸ **Spaceman killed**
Gallows Hill - A // 16 November 1973
▸▸ **TARDIS materialises**
Gallows Hill - A // 16 November 1973
▸▸ **Exxilon attacks Doctor**
Gallows Hill - A // 16 November 1973
▸▸ **Sarah finds lamp and runs back to TARDIS**
Gallows Hill - A // 16 November 1973
▸▸ **Doctor and Exxilons fight**
Gallows Hill - A // 16 November 1973
▸▸ **Doctor activates boulder trap**
Gallows Hill - B // 14 November 1973

EPISODE 2

▸▸ **Exxilon ambush**
Gallows Hill - C // 15 November 1973

EPISODE 3

▸▸ **Galloway talks to Dalek**
Gallows Hill - A // 13 November 1973
▸▸ **Root attacks miners and Daleks**
Gallows Hill - A // 13/14 November 1973
▸▸ **Daleks make new plans**
Gallows Hill - A // 14 November 1973

The Facts

The Amey Roadstone Company was due to be paid £150 for the use of the ARC sand pit but, on completion of the filming, they requested that the BBC pass on their facility fee to the Wool and Bovington Scout Services Group.

Once again, the production team faced the problem of the Daleks being able to negotiate the rough terrain that would be encountered while out on location. As an alternative to laying down sheets of wood, as had been done for *Day of the Daleks* and *Planet of the Daleks*, a set of elemac camera dolly rails were laid into the sand. For the Part 2 sequence of the Exxilons ambushing the Doctor and the Daleks, a total of 90 feet of track was laid. The Dalek casings themselves were then mounted on dolly bases to fit the track. However, this meant that it was no longer possible for the Dalek operators to propel the castings by pushing them along with their feet. The only way around the problem was for the Daleks to be pushed along the track prior to the commencement of the shot. But this was to create its own problems.

Michael Briant (director): 'For the major scene you had five or six people walking down this path with the Daleks, all chatting. This was the longest track I think I've ever seen and I had it on a bit of a slope. Jon was in the lead and it was his job to set off the first Dalek, then set off the second Dalek, and John Abineri (Railton) was to push the third. I was on top of this sand dune with the camera and shouted "Action!", and dear old Jon gave the first Dalek a hell of a push and got it running down the track. Then he got the second one going, and started walking, and from up there looking down, all I could see were these three Daleks vanishing at a hundred miles an hour down the tracks, and these figures following slowly behind! Then the front Dalek started shaking from side to side and a little voice from the inside was shouting "Help!" and of course they couldn't get their feet down because of this elemac track. I fell down laughing as John Scott Martin careered off the end of the track at about 30 miles an hour and crashed! I shouted, "Are you okay?", and before he could say anything the next two Daleks came catapulting into him! He was fine, but we soon decided that Daleks on elemac tracks going downhill aren't terribly safe!'[63]

The living, snake-like root of the Exxilon city, which rises up out of a small lake in the quarry and attacks both a Dalek and an Exxilon, was controlled by visual effects designer Jim Ward, along with his two assistants, Peter Pegrum and Colin Mapson, using wires slung across the high banks surrounding the lake. The controlling wires are clearly visible in a number of shots.

Comment

Death to the Daleks may not be one of the best scripts that the programme has ever boasted, but the location material shot by Michael Briant and cameraman Bill Matthews is highly effective. The scenes from Part 1 of the darkened surface of Exxilon, shot using a day-for-night filter, are remarkably eerie as the Doctor's attackers are seen initially only as shadowy figures. As well as using Gallows Hill, several scenes set on the exterior surface of the planet were also recorded in the studio. And there lies part of the problem with *Death to the Daleks*. The difference between the location filming and the studio planet sets is just too jarring – one looks great, the other looks horribly fake. The overall effect of the story would have been much better if an extra day could have been budgeted for at Gallows Hill.

PLANET OF THE SPIDERS
(tx 4 May to 25 May 1974)

The Story

Suspicious about events at the meditation centre he's attending, Mike Yates calls in Sarah to investigate and together they discover that the group leader, Lupton, and his associates have made contact with the giant spiders of Metebelis III. Under the control of a spider, Lupton steals the Doctor's blue Metebelis crystal from UNIT HQ and, despite a chase across land, air and water, Lupton escapes when he is transported to the spiders' home world. The Doctor discovers that K'anpo, the meditation centre's abbot, is in reality his Time Lord guru, and at his bidding he travels to Metebelis III to confront the Great One, a giant mutated spider which needs the Doctor's crystal to increase its mental capacity to infinity. But the plan is flawed and the Great One is killed by the power overload. Riddled with the radiation from the Great One's cave, the Doctor begins to regenerate…

The Locations

1. Tidmarsh Manor, Tidmarsh, Berkshire
2. Mortimer Railway Station, Stratfield Mortimer, Berkshire
3. Bloomfieldhatch Lane / Mereoak Lane,[64] near Stratfield Mortimer, Berkshire
4. Le Marchant Barracks, London Road, Devizes, Wiltshire
5. Membury Airfield, Membury, Wiltshire
6. River Severn, near Westbury-on-Severn, Gloucestershire

Shooting Schedule

EPISODE 1

▸▸ **Yates walks through countryside**
Tidmarsh Manor // 11 March 1974
▸▸ **Yates approaches the meditation centre**
Tidmarsh Manor // 11 March 1974
▸▸ **Yates collects Sarah from the station**
Mortimer Railway Station // 11 March 1974
▸▸ **Yates tells Sarah about meditation centre**
Bloomfieldhatch / Mereoak Lane // 11 March 1974
▸▸ **Yates and Sarah continue conversation**
Bloomfieldhatch / Mereoak Lane // 11 March 1974
▸▸ **Yates' car forced off road**
Bloomfieldhatch / Mereoak Lane // 11 March 1974
▸▸ **Yates and Sarah leave the meditation centre**
Tidmarsh Manor // 11 March 1974

EPISODE 2

▸▸ **Lupton attacks soldier in UNIT carpark**

▸▸ Le Marchant Barracks // 13 March 1974

▸▸ **Lupton escapes in the Whomobile**
Le Marchant Barracks // 13 March 1974

▸▸ **Doctor takes off in Autogyro**
Membury Airfield // 12-13 March 1974

▸▸ **Lupton chased by Autogyro, Bessie and Police**
Membury Airfield // 12-13 March 1974

▸▸ **Air-to-air shots**
Membury Airfield // 12 March 1974

▸▸ **Lupton escapes by boat, Doctor follows in hovercraft**
River Severn // 14-15 March 1974

The Facts

The scene of Sarah's arrival at the station and subsequent collection by Mike Yates needed some careful setting-up as only two trains were due to pass through the station during the hour allocated to the filming.[65]

The MGB, hired from Kingsbury Motors, needed to have its boot lid removed for some scenes in order to mount a camera in the rear of the vehicle. Stuntman Terry Walsh took over the driving of the MGB for the sequence where the car swerves off the road as it tries to avoid the tractor, although this piece of farm machinery, driven by J R Balsdon of Barn Elms Farm, Bradfield, was itself a late substitute for the road blockage originally intended – a cow.

Filming at Le Marchant Barracks, the home of the 1st Battalion of the Wessex Regiment, was continually held up by heavy rain, which started only 30 minutes after filming had begun.

Membury Airfield, which had been used three years previously during the filming of *The Dæmons*, formed the backdrop for the opening half of the chase sequence featured in Part 2. The ground-based chase sequences between Bessie, the Whomobile and the police panda car were filmed on the roads surrounding the airfield, some shot with an undercranked camera to give the illusion that the vehicles were travelling at a greater speed than they actually were.

Pride of place over the two days at Membury Airfield went to the one-man Cricket gyroplane, a new aircraft being developed by Campbell Aircraft Ltd (who had been the owners of the airfield garage used in the opening episode of *The Dæmons*). Approaches had been made to the company, who were very responsive to the possibility of using the programme as the Cricket's debut appearance. Close-up shots, filmed at a low angle against the sky, were taken of both Pertwee and John Dearth (Lupton) in the pilot's seat to give the impression that the two characters were actually flying the gyroplane, although, in the long shots, the flying was performed by A M W Curzon-Herrick.

As well as the gyroplane, a Bell Jet Ranger helicopter was hired from Alan Mann Helicopters at Fairoaks Airport in Chobham. The helicopter was used to film the aerial shots of the autogyro in flight, as well as CSO backgrounds used for the flying Whomobile. In pre-production, consideration had been given to hiring a professional Wescam helicopter camera mount to achieve the required shots, which would have been fixed to one of Gregory Air Services' helicopters, a company that had experience of working with Wescam equipment. When the equipment hire was costed, it transpired that the Wescam mount alone, supplied complete with a two-man crew, would cost £350 per day. On top of this would have to be added the travel costs for the support vehicle and the hire of the helicopter. Deeming the costs involved as being too high, the decision was made to go with Alan Mann Helicopters, who were able to supply a Jet Ranger complete with an external mini-tyler camera mount for £90 per flying hour.

The last two full days of location work on *Planet of the Spiders* were dedicated to the filming of the final four and a half minutes of Part 2's river-bound chase sequence. For the two days, the production unit based themselves along a narrow lane in Westbury-on-Severn leading to the Strand on the banks of the river, while the chase itself was filmed downstream, between Westbury, Newnham and Frampton-on-Severn.

Having spotted a newspaper article about the Skima two-man hovercraft in the *Southern Evening Echo* during pre-production of *Invasion of the Dinosaurs* in August 1973, the production team made approaches to the Teddington-based manufacturers, Pindair. The company's owner, Michael Pinder, proved to be very enthusiastic about the use of his hovercraft and, as the other locations had not been confirmed by this point, he promised to think about possible locations near London where the vehicle could be used to perform some 'spectacular manoeuvres'.

Knowing that a speedboat would also be required for the chase sequence, Pinder suggested an acquaintance of his by the name of Mike Kirk, who had supplied various boats for stunt situations in the past. In the end, the boat stolen by Lupton was a Hamilton Jet Boat, built in New Zealand and supplied by another friend of Pinder's, Geoffrey Kenyon-May of Bristol Channel Yachts in Lydney. The propellerless design of the boat ensured that filming could continue even at low tide when there was only four inches of water in the Severn. Very much a lover of water craft, Jon Pertwee was so impressed with the boat that he immediately purchased one from Kenyon-May, which was dispatched to him via the company's branch in southern France.

Kenyon-May was on hand for both days filming on

Right: Jon Pertwee and Elisabeth Sladen wait for their next scene on the banks of the River Severn in *Planet of the Spiders.*

the Severn, acting as double for John Dearth during the filming of long shots while Michael Pinder was cast as Hopkins, the original pilot of the hovercraft who is attacked by Lupton at the beginning of the sequence. As well as the small two-man Skima seen on-screen, a larger four-man hovercraft was also hired to act as a filming platform during the chase.

One sequence planned with the Skima was for the hovercraft, piloted by Pertwee, to leave the river and to drive over the top of a sleeping tramp, played by stunt-man Stuart Fell.

Jon Pertwee: 'Barry had positioned his cameras at the left-hand side of the bank we were using for the sequence. I was to drive up the bank and go straight over the top of Stuart who was lying just over a grassy knoll out of my vision. I powered up the hovercraft and on "Action" drove it up and over the bank. Unfortunately, I was caught by a gust of wind which took me off course and I wiped out the entire camera crew. This was somewhat fraught as there were two barely protected propellers on the craft. The machine was then retrieved from the chaos and repositioned back up the river. The hovercraft's owner came up level with me and shouted, "You've gotta make allowances for the wind." So on the next take, I zoomed down the river, over the grass bank

and, allowing for the wind, steered to the right. Unfortunately, by now there was no wind, and, unknown to me, Barry had taken the opportunity to move his camera to the right side of the bank. Unhappily, I ploughed straight into the hapless camera crew once more. On the third take I got it right!'[66]

The filming of the chase sequence on the Severn was attended by a small unit from the BBC's *Points West* news programme.

Ouch!

While filming at Membury Airfield on Tuesday 12 March, things went seriously wrong during the scene of Lupton's theft of the gyroplane.

Graeme Harper (assistant floor manager): 'The gyroplane was held by wooden chocks, although the blades were going round so that he [John Dearth] could get in it and start off. As he approached the gyroplane, it suddenly came to life and trundled away. The camera crew, which it was approaching rapidly, fled just as it toppled over and went 'bang', bits flying everywhere. Naturally, all hell broke loose. Everyone was running around hoping that no one was hurt – which they weren't – although John Dearth was stunned and shocked. He was lying flat on the floor, panicking because bits were flying everywhere, and when he got up, the costume people, who got to him first, found that a piece of the rotor blade had sliced through his jacket, missing him by half an inch! They sewed the coat up and we redid the scene with another gyroplane. The owners were none too pleased as it wasn't insured, being a prototype, but they brought in the other one.'[67]

Comment

With the exception of a few brief scenes in the first episode, the location filming done for *Planet of the Spiders* was almost entirely devoted to Lupton's theft of the Metebelis crystal from UNIT HQ and the subsequent chase sequence, which takes up nearly 12 minutes of the 25' 02" second episode.

FOOTNOTES

1. John Sanders Ltd ceased trading in the late 1980s and the shop has since been taken over by Marks and Spencer.

2. Lancaster Road was formally a side street coming off from Ealing High Street. When the Ealing Broadway Shopping Centre was built, Lancaster Road was converted into an alley, which ran alongside John Sanders Ltd.

3. At the time of filming, Hatchford Park, a Grade II listed building, was a special needs school. Following the school's closure in 1990, it was purchased by Countryside Residential and Latchmere Properties and began to be converted into 13 luxury flats at a cost of £11 million. The conversion was nearly complete, when arsonists struck the premises in September 2000, destroying 95 per cent of the building.

4. The hotel was renamed 'The Evesham Hotel' in the early 70s. The internal doorway through which Scobie walks towards the front door has now been filled in.

5. *Doctor Who Magazine* #166, p.17

6. Episode 2 was due to be recorded on 23 October, Episode 3 on 30 October and Episode 4 on 6 November.

7. The strike action, which began in October 1969, was over a pay dispute.

8. The radio stations, equipped with iron rations, table-tennis tables and bunk beds were maintained until 1993.

9. It is likely that Orton appeared as Channing in the brief shot where he turns the dial on the side of the Nestene tank before running away, just prior to the attack upon the Doctor in Episode 4. Slow motion examination of this scene reveals that Hugh Burden was not playing Channing in this scene.

10. This information hails from a production file document dated 5 March 1970. Barry Letts' recollection was that the can of film containing both the negative and the viewing print went missing, either at the processing laboratory or at Ealing Studios, where hundreds of other reels of BBC film were also sent.

11. The copy of the letter in the *Doctor Who and the Silurians* production file is unsigned, although due to its nature, it probably was written by Barry Letts.

12. Assistant floor manager Sue Hedden and director's assistant Sue Upton.

13. *Douglas Camfield – A Tribute* – p.19

14. The building is now owned by Linpac Automotives

15. *Five Rounds Rapid!*, Nicholas Courtney, p.59

16. Bobby Roberts actually appeared in Episode 3, being questioned by the Doctor about Phillips' disappearance as he leads the elephants from the big top.

17. The filming of *Z-Cars* was likely done at the circus' previous venue at Borehamwood rather than at Lea Bridge Road.

18. The front of each camera script contains a sequential list of all the studio scenes and filmed inserts that make up the episode. This is referred to as the running order. This scene does not appear in the running order for Episode 1.

19. This scene appears in the film schedule but is placed in the script's running order after the Doctor and the Brigadier's visit to Fu Peng.

20. This scene does not appear in the running order for Episode 3 (see footnote 17).

21. This scene does not appear in the running order for Episode 3 (see footnote 17).

22. This film sequence appears as two telecine sequences in the script. TK6, lasting eight seconds appears in the finished episode and features Yates on the telephone to the Brigadier informing him that they are going to be driving through the night. The second part, TK6A, which was to have lasted fourteen seconds, was to have shown a jeep driving off with the convoy.

23. This scene does not appear in the running order for Episode 4 (see footnote 17).

24. A total of four helicopter shots are listed in the film schedule. The script running order only features two.

25. Although listed on the film schedule to be shot at Dover Castle, the transmitted version of the scene was in fact recorded in Studio 3 on 19 December 1970.

26. This scene does not appear in the running order for Episode 5 (see footnote 17).

27. This scene does not appear in the running order for Episode 5 (see footnote 17).

28. It appears that any material filmed in Area E at Dover Castle appears to have been edited out of the transmitted episode.

29. This scene does not appear in the running order for Episode 5 (see footnote 17).

30. This sequence appears to have been originally intended to form part of the latter half of Episode 5. It was actually transmitted as part of Episode 6.

31. This scene does not appear in the running order for Episode 6 (see footnote 17).

32. This transmitted scene appears in the running order, but not in the film schedule.

33. This transmitted scene appears in the running order, but not in the film schedule.

34. This transmitted scene appears in the running order, but not in the film schedule.

35. Telecine filmed insert.

36. As such, this is the earliest surviving studio recording.

37. At the very end of this sequence on the transmitted version of the episode, a single flash frame exists from the later part of the scene, just prior to his find the shoe.

38. *Kentish Express*, 8 January 1971, p.2

39. *The Doctor's Effects*, Steve Cambden, p.32

40. Visual effects assistant Ian Scoones also recalls that the Halfingers were also used to transport some of the crew to and from the production hotel at Narrowcliffe, Newquay – *The Doctor's Effects*, Steve Cambden, p.91

41. *Classic Who: The Harper Classics*, Adrian Rigelsford, p.20

42. *The Frame* #2, 1987, p.5

Despite its action-packed nature, the whole thing seems too indulgent and over-the-top, with various exotic chase vehicles being changed every few minutes. The scenes surrounding the UNIT airstrip fare the worst, with speeded-up car chases, unconvincing CSO work and weather conditions which evidently changed significantly between the two Membury filming days. The latter half, played out on and around the river Severn, looks far better, all the more so because Pertwee piloted the hovercraft himself for much of the time. The chase also has a superb cliffhanger ending as the Doctor jumps onto Lupton's boat only to find that he's completely vanished. ∎

43. *Wiltshire Gazette Herald*, 29 April 1971, p.4

44. *An Adventure in Space and Time* #59, 1985, p.12

45. *Return to Devils End*, Reeltime Pictures

46. *The Doctor's Effects*, Steve Cambden, p38

47. 'Bull's Bridge' is the term referred to in the BBC's documentation for the location. However, the location used is a tunnel situated a short distance north from Bull's Bridge.

48. This wasn't the only cost to be incurred for filming at the location around Bulls Bridge. Payments also had to be made to the London Borough of Hounslow (£50.00) and the British Waterways Board (£78.75).

49. The film shot list indicates that this sequence was filmed either at Whitecliff Bay or at Red Cliff, Sandown. Of the two, Whitecliff Bay is more likely as the film diary specifies that a caravan in the park above the bay was to be used for costume changes, and that three Sea Devil costumes would be placed therein.

50. *An Adventure in Space and Time* (CMS) – *The Sea Devils*, p.9-10

51. Another name for the Reclaim's diving bell.

52. *An Adventure in Space and Time* (CMS) – *The Sea Devils*, p.10

53. Possibly Trowe's Lane, Stratfield Saye.

54. *Reading Evening Post*, 5 April 1972, p.1 – 'Look Who's Here – Stratfield Saye is about to be Exterminated'

55. Referred to as 'Harefield Lime Works' in the production documentation.

56. Neither the film diary or the film shot list for the story make any mention of the film sequences showing the first and second Doctor's on the Time Lord's screen. However, the BBC photographs of Hartnell, Troughton and Pertwee standing together in an exterior location state that they were taken on 9 November, which seems to indicate that Hartnell was brought down to the Rickmansworth location and the production team took the opportunity to film a short sequence with him while he was there.

57. There is a great deal of confusion between the film sequences listed in the script, those in the film diary and those seen on screen. For instance, the Episode 1 sequence of the Doctor and Jo making their way along the deck of the SS Bernice doesn't appear in the film diary at all, while others set in the marshes are not present in the script. The shooting schedule listed is the best possible interpretation of the available information.

58. *An Adventure in Space and Time* (CMS) – *The Green Death*, p.10

59. *The Doctor's Effects*, Steve Cambden, p.114

60. Paddy Russell has for many years indicated that this opening sequence pre-filming was achieved over two separate dates prior to the official late September location work. Her memory is that the scenes around Westminster Bridge, Albert Embankment, Whitehall and Trafalgar Square were filmed one Sunday morning around 20 June 1973 (making it either 17 or 24 June). However, BBC documentation indicates that Malcolm Hulke was not originally commissioned to write the scripts for *Timescoop* until 2 July 1973 (following two submitted storylines delivered on 10 February and 15 June 1973), with the first two episodes not being delivered until 29 July. This would seem to indicate that either Russell's memory is at fault or that she was commissioned to direct the story at the same time as the submission of Hulke's second storyline, prior to any scripts being available and that the pre-filming was conducted on the basis of the storyline only – a set of circumstances which seem unlikely.

Russell also refers to the remainder of the pre-filming, which she recalls was done officially, as being conducted on Sunday 2 September. There is no indication in the BBC production file for this story of any sanctioned location work being performed on this date. However, given when the scripts were actually delivered, this is a much more likely date for the unauthorised filming excursion conducted by Russell, Leggo and Bagwell.

61. This scene was originally supposed to have been filmed on Tuesday 25 September at either Burford Road, Brentford (according to the film diary) or the nearby Clayponds Avenue (as per the film shot list, which refers to it as 'Clayponds Lane'). However, the slate number attributed to the scene on the film shot list is 165, indicating that it was actually filmed on Thursday 27 when the production team were filming between Kingston Meat Market and various roads in Ham. It is unknown whether the crew travelled to Brentford to film this single scene or whether an alternative location was found in the Kingston/Ham area. As the Clayponds Avenue remains unaltered in the production's film shot list, this has been taken as the likely final location for this sequence.

62. This would have undoubtedly made use of the metal fire escape coming from the rear of the pub which would have been used in the same manner as that at Southall Gas Works, where the scene was eventually shot.

63. *Doctor Who Bulletin* #31 p.10

64. The film diary does not actually name the roads used to film the driving sequences featuring Yates and Sarah. However, the hand-drawn map in the diary does have arrows pointing to roads which correspond to Bloomfieldhatch Lane/Mereoak Lane to the north-east of Mortimer Station and other roads heading in the direction of Burghfield.

65. Trains were scheduled to pass through Mortimer at 10 and 36 minutes past the hour.

66. *I Am The Doctor*, Pertwee and Howe, p.110 and 111

67. *Doctor Who Magazine* #90, p.17

PART FOUR

> 'Do you have a season in South Croydon… ?'
> The Doctor – *The Hand of Fear*

TOM BAKER

THE FOURTH DOCTOR

ROBOT
(tx 28 December 1974 to 18 January 1975)

The Story
The newly regenerated Doctor is called to assist an investigation into the theft, by something unusually large and heavy, of the plans and equipment needed to construct a newly developed disintegrator gun. Meanwhile, Sarah visits Thinktank, an organisation devoted to the frontiers of scientific research. There, she discovers that the K-1 robot constructed by Thinktank's former robotics expert, Professor Kettlewell, is still active. The Doctor soon discovers that the robot has been used by Hilda Winters, the director of Thinktank and head of the Scientific Reform Society, to obtain information on the disintegrator gun. With the gun, the robot steals the control codes to all the nuclear weapons held by the world powers. With these, SRS can threaten the nations, forcing them to accept their way of life. Managing to gain control of the disintegrator gun, the Brigadier tries to destroy the robot, but instead it grows to a gigantic size. The Doctor manages to deactivate the nuclear codes which have been set into operation and infects the robot with a metal virus, reversing its growth and corroding it to dust.

The Locations
1. BBC Engineering Training Centre, Wood Norton Hall, Wood Norton, Evesham, Worcestershire

Shooting Schedule

PART 1
▸▸ **Robot breaks into research centre**
Wood Norton Hall // 1 May 1974
▸▸ **Robot breaks through electric fence**
Wood Norton Hall // 5 May 1974
▸▸ **Doctor and Brigadier discuss the fence**
Wood Norton Hall // 5 May 1974
▸▸ **Sarah arrives and enters Thinktank**
Wood Norton Hall // 2 May 1974

▸▸ **Sarah meets Winters and Jellicoe**
Wood Norton Hall // 28 April 1974
▸▸ **Doctor and Brigadier discuss the theft**
Wood Norton Hall // 5 May 1974
▸▸ **Sarah, Winters and Jellicoe enter Kettlewell's laboratory**
Wood Norton Hall // 28 April 1974
▸▸ **UNIT preparations at Emmett's Electronics**
Wood Norton Hall – Bredon Wing // 2/5 May 1974
▸▸ **Sentry outside vault door (cut)**
Wood Norton Hall // 2 May 1974
▸▸ **Doctor indicates the one unguarded route**
Wood Norton Hall // 2 May 1974
▸▸ **Sentry shoots at Robot, others run to assist**

Wood Norton Hall // 1/2 May 1974
⏩ Sarah leaves Kettlewell's house in car
Wood Norton Hall // 2 May 1974
⏩ Sarah examines her Thinktank pass
Wood Norton Hall // 28 April 1974
⏩ Doctor, Brigadier and Benton examine hole[1]
Wood Norton Hall // 30 April 1974
⏩ Sarah arrives at Thinktank and re-enters laboratory
Wood Norton Hall // 28 April/2 May 1974

PART 2

⏩ Doctor visits Thinktank and enters laboratory
Wood Norton Hall // 28 April 1974
⏩ Harry arrives at Thinktank
Wood Norton Hall // 28 April 1974
⏩ Doctor driving in Bessie to Kettlewell's house
Wood Norton Hall // 1 May 1974

PART 3

⏩ Sarah arrives at Kettlewell's house
Wood Norton Hall // 2 May 1974
⏩ Robot exits house as soldiers fire
Wood Norton Hall // 2 May 1974
⏩ Robot is loaded into van and is driven away
Wood Norton Hall // 2 May 1974
⏩ UNIT arrives at bunker entrance
Wood Norton Hall // 1/5 May 1974
⏩ Monitor shot – Soldiers approaching bunker
Wood Norton Hall // 1 May 1974
⏩ Automatic machine gun activates
Wood Norton Hall // 5 May 1974
⏩ Brigadier speaks to Winters on the radio
Wood Norton Hall // 5 May 1974
⏩ Brigadier orders Benton to knock out machine guns
Wood Norton Hall // 5 May 1974
⏩ Guns and mines destroyed and Doctor works on lock
Wood Norton Hall // 5/6 May 1974
⏩ Monitor – Doctor and UNIT outside bunker
Wood Norton Hall // 6 May 1974
⏩ Robot appears at doors and destroys tank (3/4)
Wood Norton Hall // 1/6 May 1974

PART 4

⏩ Monitor – Robot outside bunker
Wood Norton Hall // 1 May 1974
⏩ Doctor tells Brigadier he'll have to continue work on lock
Wood Norton Hall // 6 May 1974
⏩ Robot kills Kettlewell and collapses
Wood Norton Hall // 6 May 1974
⏩ Doctor learns that robot and Sarah have vanished
Wood Norton Hall // 29 April 1974
⏩ Benton remembers the metal virus

Wood Norton Hall // 29 April/6 May 1974
⏩ UNIT soldier runs out of the bunker
Wood Norton Hall // 6 May 1974
⏩ Brigadier talks to Harry on the radio
Wood Norton Hall // 29 April 1974
⏩ Brigadier shoots robot with disintegrator gun
Wood Norton Hall // 6 May 1974
⏩ Robot picks Sarah up and places her on roof
Wood Norton Hall // 28 April/1 May 1974
⏩ UNIT open fire with bazooka and grenades
Wood Norton Hall // 29 April 1974
⏩ Doctor and Harry drive back in Bessie
Wood Norton Hall // 28 April 1974
⏩ Robot attacks UNIT who fall back
Wood Norton Hall // 29/30 April/1 May 1974
⏩ Doctor and Harry look in amazement at robot
Wood Norton Hall // 30 April 1974
⏩ Robot infected, shrinks and disintegrates
Wood Norton Hall // 30 April/1 May 1974

The Facts

Up to this point in *Doctor Who's* history, all the location work done for the programme had been achieved with the use of either 16mm or 35mm film cameras. The production of *Robot* marked another first in the history of the show, as it was the first story to have its location material shot on electronic outside broadcast video equipment, a decision made by producer Barry Letts.

The reason for the use of OB cameras was simple. The conclusion of the story required the robot to grow to gigantic size and the use of location material shot on videotape would theoretically make the illusion, achieved by the use of CSO, more successful than the unstable film/video mix that had marred many of the effects sequences in *Invasion of the Dinosaurs* and, to a lesser extent, *Carnival of Monsters*.

Barry Letts: 'I feel the *Carnival* experiment was more successful than the dinosaur one, largely because everything in the frame was in movement, so the movement of the filmed image (due to the mechanics of the camera and the telecine machine) was not so noticeable. As the eye tends to compensate for the movement of the background, those horrible dinosaurs look as if they're floating. With the absolutely stationary video image in *Robot* the problem was solved. Also, the contrast between the lack of definition in the 16mm picture and the pin-sharpness of the video image was avoided.'

Unfortunately, many of the shots of the giant robot were not as successful as they might have been due to the fact that the yellow CSO background used to key the costume onto the location footage would often reflect off the aluminium body parts, causing the robot to become 'transparent' in places.

One of the principal reasons for choosing the BBC's premises at Wood Norton as a location was the fact that it possessed an underground bunker[2] that had been used during the filming of *Spearhead from Space* in October 1969. But four years on, the BBC's attitude towards it had changed.

Christopher Barry (director): 'Suddenly, somebody at the BBC said, "Sssh, you can't have that seen, it's secret," despite the fact that if you drive down the road you can see it. But we couldn't show it on television. So we had to build a rather unconvincing entrance into the side of a hill, rather similar to the way that we'd done with the tumulus in *The Dæmons*.'[3]

On 16 April, the head of the visual effects department, Jack Kine, wrote to Barry Letts concerning the requirement to use various pyrotechnics during the location recording at Wood Norton.

'I checked with Mr Duncan Enoch, Head of Engineering Training, Tech Ops, to see that no high power transmissions would be taking place during our filming period. I took these steps because should such a transmission occur while we were using pyrotechnics there is a chance that a charge could be activated and fired. He assures me that no high power transmissions would take place during the visit of the Dr Who team.'
Jack Kine to Barry Letts – 16 April 1974

The conclusion to the third episode showed the robot using the gun to disintegrate a tank. Christopher Barry had indicated a desire to get the Army involved in the production of *Robot* and procure a full-sized tank for the scene, but the allocated budget wouldn't stand for the extra expense. Intrigued by the use of models, Barry Letts suggested the use of an Action Man toy tank as a suitable substitute. Although the shot ultimately remained in the finished production, Christopher Barry hated the use of something which looked so fake.

Barry Letts: 'I take full responsibility for that horrible toy tank in the foreground of one of the *Robot* shots. Chris objected strongly, but I insisted, being fascinated by the use of models in the blue-screen (CSO) process. It would have worked if we had had a finely made scale model. As it was, Chris was right and I was utterly wrong.'

Following the completion of recording at Wood Norton, actor Michael Kilgarriff, who had endured his first experience of acting inside the full robot costume, suffered nightmares of about being locked inside a midget submarine.

Comment

As *Robot* marked the use on *Doctor Who* of outside broadcast cameras for the first time, the decision to

record all the exterior material at the BBC's Wood Norton establishment was a sound one and, by and large, it pays off. The only real problem is that it becomes obvious to the viewer early on that only one location was used, as the style of the buildings and grounds are very much the same from one set-up to the next.

THE SONTARAN EXPERIMENT
(tx 22 February to 1 March 1975)

The Story
Arriving on an apparently desolate Earth, the Doctor discovers a group of survivors from a crashed GalSec spacecraft, lured to the planet by a fake distress call. Also on Earth is Field Major Styre, a Sontaran, who is conducting experiments on the humans in order to collect data for a proposed invasion of the planet. When the Doctor challenges Styre to a duel, the Sontaran becomes quickly exhausted due to his unfamiliarity with Earth's gravity and has to return to his ship to recharge. But the Doctor's new travelling companion, Harry Sullivan, removes a vital piece of equipment causing Styre to be drained of all his remaining energy, which kills the Sontaran and destroys his ship.

The Locations
1. Hound Tor, near Manaton, Dartmoor, Devon
2. Headland Warren, near Postbridge, Devon

Shooting Schedule

PART 1
▶▶ **Doctor, Harry and Sarah arrive at matterbeam area**
Headland Warren – A // 26 September 1974
▶▶ **Sarah thinks she sees something**
Headland Warren – B // 26 September 1974
▶▶ **The Doctor is watched by Zake and Erak**
Headland Warren – A // 26 September 1974
▶▶ **Harry falls into the pit**
Headland Warren – D // 27 September 1974
▶▶ **Erak tells Krans about the Doctor**
Headland Warren – F // 28 September 1974
▶▶ **Harry recovers and Sarah sees that the pit is a trap**
Headland Warren – D // 27 September 1974
▶▶ **Zake pursued is by robot and falls to his death**
Headland Warren – B/C // 26 September 1974
▶▶ **Doctor hears scream and runs to help**
Headland Warren – A // 26 September 1974
▶▶ **Erak and Krans think the Doctor has killed Zake**
Headland Warren – C // 26 September 1974
▶▶ **Sarah returns to the matterbeam, but the Doctor is gone**

Right: The inflatable Sontaran head has make-up applied before the recording of the final scenes at Hound Tor.

Headland Warren – A // 26 September 1974
➤ **Harry crawls into tunnel**
Headland Warren – E // 27 September 1974
➤ **Sarah calls for the Doctor**
Headland Warren – A // 26 September 1974
➤ **Doctor is dragged along by Krans and Erak**
Headland Warren – C // 26 September 1974
➤ **Sarah finds the pit empty**
Headland Warren – D // 27 September 1974
➤ **Krans questions the Doctor**
Headland Warren – E // 28 September 1974
➤ **Sarah drags a branch to the pit**
Headland Warren – D // 27 September 1974
➤ **Harry crawls out of the tunnel**
Hound Tor – I // 29 September 1974
➤ **Roth grabs Sarah as robot approaches**
Headland Warren – D // 27 September 1974
➤ **Vural questions the Doctor**
Headland Warren – F // 28 September 1974
➤ **Doctor on Sontaran monitor**
Hound Tor – N // 30 September 1974
➤ **Robot activates and moves off**
Headland Warren – B // 26 September 1974
➤ **Harry walks past rocks**
Hound Tor – K // 29 September 1974
➤ **Vural, Krans and Erak consider Doctor's story**
Headland Warren – F // 28 September 1974
➤ **Roth tells Sarah his suspicions about Vural**
Headland Warren – B // 26 September 1974

➤ **Sarah rescues the Doctor**
Headland Warren – F // 28 September 1974
➤ **Roth, Sarah and Doctor run away**
Headland Warren – B // 26 September 1974
➤ **Vural, Krans and Erak search**
Headland Warren – F // 28 September 1974
➤ **Doctor fall down the pit just as the robot arrives**
Headland Warren – D // 27 September 1974
➤ **Harry climbs the rocks**
Hound Tor – K // 29 September 1974
➤ **Harry sees spacecraft**
Hound Tor – O // 1 October 1974
➤ **Doctor recovers consciousness**
Headland Warren – E // 27 September 1974
➤ **Robot arrives and Styre appears from spacecraft (1/2)**
Hound Tor – O // 1 October 1974

PART 2

➤ **Vural, Krans and Erak find Doctor in pit**
Headland Warren – E // 27 September 1974
➤ **Harry finds prisoner**
Hound Tor – G // 29 September 1974
➤ **Robot captures Vural, Krans and Erak**
Headland Warren – D // 27 September 1974
➤ **Harry brings prisoner water**
Hound Tor – G // 29 September 1974
➤ **Doctor finds tunnel**
Headland Warren – E // 27 September 1974
➤ **Styre questions Sarah**
Hound Tor – H // 29 September 1974
➤ **Harry avoids Styre**
Hound Tor – J // 29 September 1974
➤ **Doctor exits tunnel**
Hound Tor – I // 29 September 1974
➤ **Harry finds Sarah imprisoned**
Hound Tor – H // 29 September 1974
➤ **Styre reports to Sontaran Marshal**
Hound Tor – N // 30 September 1974
➤ **Sarah is tested and the Doctor is shot**
Hound Tor – H // 29 September 1974
➤ **Robot brings prisoners to Styre**
Hound Tor – O // 1 October 1974
➤ **Harry returns to Sarah and finds Doctor**
Hound Tor – H // 29 September 1974
➤ **Styre files report on dead prisoner**
Hound Tor – G // 29 September 1974
➤ **Doctor decides to find out what Styre is doing**
Hound Tor – L // 30 September 1974
➤ **Styre begins gravity bar experiment**
Hound Tor – M // 30 September 1974
➤ **Doctor destroys robot**
Hound Tor – N // 30 September 1974
➤ **Styre halts the gravity bar experiment**

Hound Tor – M // 30 September 1974
▸▸ **Doctor watches Styre report to the Marshal**
Hound Tor – N // 30 September 1974
▸▸ **Doctor tells Harry and Sarah his plan**
Hound Tor – H // 29 September 1974
▸▸ **Doctor and Styre fight and Styre dies**
Hound Tor – N/O // 1 October 1974
▸▸ **Doctor talks to Sontaran Marshal**
Hound Tor – N // 30 September 1974
▸▸ **Doctor, Harry and Sarah leave via the transmat**
Headland Warren – A // 26 September 1974
▸▸ **Over-run material recorded**
Hound Tor // 2 October 1974

The Facts

The story was originally written by Bob Baker and Dave
Martin under the title *The Destructors* and the production's outside broadcast schedule was duly assembled
using that title. However, the story changed its name to
The Sontaran Experiment shortly before recording began.

Following the delivery on 14 July 1974 of the first
draft script for the opening episode, producer Philip
Hinchcliffe wrote a memo to his predecessor, Barry
Letts, asking for his advice concerning the potential
costings involved in constructing the sets specified by
the scriptwriters. Among these were a ruined priory
(complete with a courtyard, corridor and two dungeons), a lean-to hut set against a rock face that would

be used by Vural, the leader of the GalSec survivors,
and a working interior to the Sontaran spacecraft,
which would be situated in the priory courtyard.

The request for costings was passed to Raymond
Cusick, then the Acting Chief Assistant (Drama) to the
Head of Design, and Cusick duly made his reply on 29
July, remarking that it would be difficult to cost accurately as so much would depend on 'what the exact
needs are after seeing the locations'. At this point, it was
assumed that the pit into which Harry and the Doctor
fall would need to be specially excavated by local contractors and that a location would be found to mimic
the ruined priory which would then have to be suitably
dressed to add dungeons and trap doors.

Instead of shooting *The Sontaran Experiment* on
film, the decision was made to record the entire story
using the Outside Broadcast video cameras that had
first been used during production of *Robot*. However,
the logistics of the two recordings were vastly different.
Robot had been shot on location at the BBC's engineering training centre at Wood Norton, so if any
extra facilities and expertise were required, everything
was readily to hand. *The Sontaran Experiment* however, would be shot in the middle of nowhere.

Ian Rutter (OB VT editor): 'The on-site recording
facility consisted of one TR70 2" VT machine temporarily installed in a very old BBC OB truck which
had been rescued from vehicles about to be scrapped. To

give you an idea of its age, the video cables were all lead-covered. The TR70 had been installed by OB engineer Perry Mitchell, who was then sent on an engineering course to learn how to look after this beast of a machine. It was known as the 'Mighty Wurlitzer' on account of the incredible number of controls, flashing lights and alarm sounds the control panel contained. There were two complete operating positions, one on the left hand side to record and one on the right for playback. The whole machine weighed nearly a ton and needed an air compressor to run the air bearings on the head drum. One cameraman had his family down with him and I let his little lad start the machine to record daddy's pictures. When he hit the start button and the lights flashed and the mighty wheels turned, his eyes opened wide and his mouth literally dropped at what he had done. Apparently he could talk about nothing else for days.

'The first day of the shoot on Dartmoor was incredibly wet, with the whole site nearly awash, but we were trying our best to record. I had never seen the TR70 before but operation was pretty obvious. Unfortunately, the machine just would not rotate the head drum. Out came the manuals, AVO multimeter and scope. Technology in those days was soldering iron-friendly. I soon collected several 'helpful' engineers and one cameraman who kept wanting to know how long it would take to fix. I had the quite large motor servo tray of the machine extended and the said cameraman was peering into it pretending to know what was what, when a capacitor exploded with a loud bang and shot vertically upwards just missing his ear. It rose gracefully to the ceiling, trailing smoke and bits of brown paper. When the smoke cleared the cameraman was quite white-faced and left very quietly, leaving us to fix the fault – not easy as there were no mobile phones then, so getting advice was difficult.'

Ouch!

On Sunday 29 September, the production moved from the moorland of Headland Warren to the rocks of Hound Tor. Around 5.00 pm, the scene of Styre knocking the Doctor to the ground (just prior to him getting shot) was rehearsed. When the time came to actually record the scene, Tom Baker rushed forward and, prior to his making contact with Kevin Lindsay, slipped on the wet grass, falling heavily on his left shoulder. Baker was immediately relayed to Torquay Hospital where he was X-rayed and diagnosed with a fractured left clavicle. Meanwhile, recording continued, shooting all the scenes that could be managed that day which didn't require the Doctor.

The injury necessitated that Baker wear a sling in order to take the weight off his shoulder and, as a result, the shooting schedule had to be slightly altered. As the Doctor was wearing a large overcoat as well as his scarf,

which would cover up the bandages, close-ups of Baker could still be recorded, provided the actor remained stationary. All the remaining long shots and fight sequences involving the Doctor were accomplished by dressing stuntman Terry Walsh in the Doctor's costume.

Location Facts

In December 1995, Hound Tor – the inspiration for Sir Arthur Conan Doyle's *The Hound of the Baskervilles* – was vandalised when a gang of youths deliberately pushed over one of the 30-ton granite 'fangs' on the top of the Tor.

Comment

Some brave decisions had to be made about the production of *The Sontaran Experiment*. It was the first story to be intentionally shot entirely on location and the first to be realised using OB equipment. The result is a superb little two-parter. Dartmoor gives exactly the right feeling of natural desolation that the story required and everything works so well because the script doesn't demand more than the chosen location can provide.

GENESIS OF THE DALEKS
(tx 8 March to 12 April 1975)

The Story

The Doctor, Harry and Sarah are sent by the Time Lords to the wastelands of Skaro at a time when the Daleks are first being created by the crippled Kaled scientist, Davros. Promised as a survival machine for the future of the Kaled race, Davros intends to use the Dalek's powers for evil, not only to win the war against their enemies, the Thals, but also to begin the conquest of other worlds. The Doctor manages to entomb the Daleks in the Kaled bunker and the Daleks exterminate Davros, having no further use for him.

The Locations
1. Betchworth Quarry, Pebblehill Road, Betchworth, Surrey

Shooting Schedule

PART 1
➠ **Soldiers are shot and Doctor appears**
Betchworth Quarry // 9 January 1975
➠ **Doctor meets Time Lord, Sarah and Harry**
Betchworth Quarry // 6 January 1975
➠ **Doctor, Sarah and Harry caught by explosions**
Betchworth Quarry // 7 January 1975
➠ **Doctor stands on land mine, watched by Muto**
Betchworth Quarry // 8 January 1975

▸ **Model of dome**
Betchworth Quarry // 8 January 1975
▸ **Doctor and Harry escape and are recaptured**
Betchworth Quarry // 9 January 1975
▸ **Sarah pursued by Muto**
Betchworth Quarry // 9 January 1975
▸ **Sarah chased to wrecked building**
Betchworth Quarry // 9 January 1975

The Facts

One of the props taken on location to show the variation in war technology on the planet was one of the Drahvin guns used during the production of *Galaxy 4* in 1965.

At the end of one of the filming days at Betchworth, producer Philip Hinchcliffe arrived at the location to see how director David Maloney was progressing with the work.

Philip Hinchcliffe (producer): 'All the girls from the make-up and wardrobe department were grouped around the camera, standing about ten yards back. Their concentration was solely on the artistes. I was chatting to David, checking that everything was on schedule and that he'd get all his shots done before the light faded, and suddenly I caught sight of these enormous rats. They were hopping around in the litter, directly behind the girls. I said to David, "Have you seen what I've seen?" And he said, "Yes, don't say a word. The girls will run off and we'll never get the shots in the can." So we kept going, half expecting a chorus of screams at any second, but they never noticed what was going on.'[4]

Comment

Genesis of the Daleks is a good example of how time-consuming location shooting on film can be. Four full days were allocated at Betchworth Quarry, netting a total of just over ten minutes of footage, all which was seen in the first episode. As a location, Betchworth works well as the battle-scarred surface of Skaro and its limited use provides a scene-setter for the rest of the story, which is set almost entirely within the Kaled and Thal bunkers, helping to emphasise the nature of the war which has been raging for aeons.

REVENGE OF THE CYBERMEN

(tx 19 April to 10 May 1975)

The Story

The time ring transports the Doctor, Harry and Sarah back to Nerva at a point thousands of years before its use as a survival ark, a time when it is being used as beacon to warn space traffic away from a new asteroid named Voga. The Doctor finds that the deaths of the beacon's crew, apparently caused by a so-called 'space plague', are actually due to a poison injected into the victims by deadly cybernetic creatures called Cybermats. The Cybermats are being controlled by surviving crewman Kellman, who is in turn working for the Cybermen, who plan to destroy the asteroid because the gold it carries becomes a threat to their survival. The Cybermen board the beacon and force the Doctor and two of the Nerva crew to carry cobalt bombs into the heart of Voga. Kellman, however, is a double-agent. He's really working for the Vogans, who are intent on destroying both the beacon and the Cybermen with their Skystriker rocket. The Doctor manages to return to Nerva as the Cybermen leave the beacon but the rocket is redirected and destroys their spacecraft.

The Locations

1. Wookey Hole Caves, Wookey Hole, Wells, Somerset
   A. Cathedral Cave
   B. Passageway between Cathedral Cave and Witch's Parlour
   C. Stairs near entrance to Witch's Parlour
   D. Witch's Parlour Cave
   E. Passageway between Witch's Parlour and Witch's Kitchen
   F. Witch's Kitchen Cave

Shooting Schedule

PART 1

▸ **Radio operator killed**
Wookey Hole – F // 20 November 1974

PART 2

▸ **Sarah and Harry arrive on Voga**
Wookey Hole – D // 19 November 1974
▸ **Vogan Hawks arrive in boats, Harry and Sarah captured**
Wookey Hole – E/F // 20 November 1974
▸ **Sarah and Harry transported along tunnel**
Wookey Hole – B // 18 November 1974
▸ **Vogan Hawks pursue Sarah and Harry**
Wookey Hole – A // 18 November 1974
▸ **Vogans Hawks capture Harry and Sarah, Vogan Doves appear**
Wookey Hole – F // 20 November 1974

PART 3

▸ **Cybermen and prisoners arrive, battle with Vogans**
Wookey Hole – D/E // 19 November 1974
▸ **Vogan Doves second assault on Cybermen**
Wookey Hole – F // 20 November 1974
▸ **Sarah watches battle and makes for boat**
Wookey Hole – F // 20 November 1974

Right: Terry Walsh as a Vogan Dove in Wookey Hole, complete with restraining rope to stop him plummeting down the rock face.

▶▶ Sarah dematerialises
Wookey Hole – D // 19 November 1974

▶▶ Doctor's party down rock face
Wookey Hole – A // 18 November 1974

▶▶ Cybermen continue battle with Vogan Doves
Wookey Hole – F // 20 November 1974

▶▶ Commander tires and discussion about bombs
Wookey Hole – C // 19 November 1974

▶▶ Harry and Kellman in passage (cut)
Wookey Hole – C // 19 November 1974

▶▶ Doctor caught up in rockfall (3/4)
Wookey Hole – C // 19 November 1974

▶▶ Harry begins to undo Doctor's buckle (3/4)
Wookey Hole – C // 19 November 1974

PART 4

▶▶ Two Cybermen wait as countdown ticks
Wookey Hole – F // 21 November 1974

▶▶ Doctor, Harry and Lester ambush Cybermen
Wookey Hole – F // 21 November 1974

▶▶ Aftermath of Lester's death
Wookey Hole – D/E // 19 November 1974

▶▶ Aftermath of Lester's death, Doctor undoes his buckle
Wookey Hole – F // 20 November 1974

▶▶ Doctor dematerialises
Wookey Hole – D // 19 November 1974

The Facts

Prior to filming, the cast and crew were reminded that the caves boasted the title 'The Oldest Stately Home in England' and were warned to be careful both where they sat and where they placed equipment, not to break any rocks in the caves and not to touch the two stone formations known as 'The Witch' and 'The Witch's Dog'.

Technically, the filming at Wookey Hole required a lot of forward planning, in order to complete all the desired scenes.

Elmer Cossey (film cameraman): 'Because of the amount we had to do, we had four film cameras on it – which is unusual. Normally you just work with one. But the special effects were done in the caves. We had people running, and the cameras picked them up one after the other, which made it a lot easier to do. We had to shoot nearly 13 minutes a day, which was very unusual. Normally on something like that, you're talking about five minutes maximum. But because we were using multiple cameras, we were able to do things very much quicker than we normally would. There was a lot more planning involved than normal. With one camera, you can busk it a bit. As soon as you have more than one, you've really got to have everything planned. I had three other cameras being operated, and one that I was using myself as a sort of spare, if we suddenly saw a shot we wanted. So you have to plan well, otherwise you're wasting the multiple cameras.

'The chase sequence was done going back along the caves, starting at the top and gradually working down. That was one of the reasons why we were using more than one camera. Because of the nature of the place, you could hide cameras behind rocks, and in some cases, built an artificial rock and hide a camera behind that. So you could actually do a chase in one go, rather than have to keep going backwards and forwards. It made that particular shoot different from everything else.'[5]

For the scene in Part 2 where the Vogan Hawks[6] pursuing Harry and Sarah are ambushed by the Doves, stuntman Terry Walsh took on the role of the speaking Vogan who appears on the high ledge. As the ledge was slippery and ended in a sheer drop, Walsh was held in place by a rope held by his colleague, Alan Chuntz.

Actor Jeremy Wilkin (Kellman) was only required on location for a single scene of Kellman and Harry making their way along the narrow passage in Part 3. Due to the finished episode overrunning, the filmed sequence was cut and reshot during the later studio session.

For the final day of filming at the caves, the production team was joined by a film crew from the BBC's local news programme, *Points West*. During the 4'54" item, broadcast on Friday 22 November, Tom Baker was interviewed by Gwyn Richards before taking two fully dressed Cybermen to a local pub.

Ouch!

Revenge of the Cybermen was probably more accident-prone than any other story in the history of the programme. As director Michael Briant later astutely noted, having a full film crew of 40 to 50 people in the claustrophobic caves may well have rapidly used up the available air, causing oxygen starvation, thus contributing to many of the incidents over the four-day filming period.

Armourer Jack Wells fell ill during the filming, an electrician fell from a ladder while erecting some lights, breaking his leg, and assistant floor manager Rosemary Hester began to suffer from panic attacks, necessitating that she be driven home and replaced by another AFM, Russ Karel.

By far the most serious incident involved Elisabeth Sladen and Terry Walsh. At 3.20 pm on Wednesday 20 November, filming was being conducted in Chamber 2, known as the Witch's Kitchen. The scene required Sladen to climb on board one of the Sizzla boats and power across the lake. However, Sladen soon lost control of the boat and, to avoid crashing into the cave wall, she jumped into the water, whereupon she began to be pulled down by the strong undercurrents created by the submerged caverns. Walsh, who was standing by in case of an emergency, immediately dived into the lake and rescued Sladen, but in doing so he swallowed quantities of the lake water and subsequently had taken to hospital for a check-up.

Comment

Viewing *Revenge of the Cybermen*, you can certainly appreciate the production team's wisdom in filming as many of the Vogan interiors as possible at Wookey Hole, rather than trying to achieve them in the studio. Visually, Wookey Hole provides a much more interesting location than the Chislehurst Caves used by Christopher Barry in *The Mutants*, as it contains large multi-level caverns, tight little crevices and underground lakes and streams making the choice of shots much more varied. Wookey Hole was originally a location considered by Timothy Combe when planning *Doctor Who and the Silurians* and, viewing *Revenge*, one can get a sense of how different that story would have looked had the location been used back in 1970.

TERROR OF THE ZYGONS

(tx 30 August to 20 September 1975)

The Story

When several oil rigs situated off the Scottish coast collapse under mysterious circumstances, the Brigadier recalls the Doctor to Earth to help. Arriving in the village of Tullock, the Doctor discovers that the rigs have been destroyed by the mythical Loch Ness Monster, which is in reality a Skarasen cyborg controlled by a small group of shape-changing Zygons from their spacecraft at the bottom of the loch. With their home planet destroyed by a steller explosion, the Zygons aim to take over Earth and convert it into a replica of their home world, but the Doctor defeats the Zygons, allowing the Skarasen to return to its home in the loch.

The Locations

1. Climping Beach, Climping, West Sussex
2. Ambersham Common, South Ambersham, West Sussex
3. Hall Aggregates Quarry, Storrington, West Sussex[7]
4. Charlton, West Sussex
5. Furnace Pond, Mill Lane, Crabtree, West Sussex
6. Millbank Tower, Millbank, London, SW1

Shooting Schedule

PART 1

▶▶ **TARDIS arrives (cut)**
Ambersham Common // 17 March 1975
▶▶ **Doctor's party finds the road and meets the Duke**
Ambersham Common // 18 March 1975
▶▶ **Benton arrives at Fox Inn**
Charlton – Inn // 20 March 1975
▶▶ **Duke drops of Doctor's party**
Charlton – Inn // 20 March 1975
▶▶ **Munro in sea**
Climping Beach // 17 March 1975
▶▶ **Munro and Harry are shot by the Caber**
Climping Beach // 17 March 1975
▶▶ **Open sea**
Climping Beach // 17 March 1975
▶▶ **Doctor examines the wreckage outside the hospital**
Storrington Quarry // 18 March 1975

PART 2

▶▶ **Soldier in the mist**
Ambersham Common // 19 March 1975
▶▶ **Benton examines the soldier's body**
Ambersham Common // 19 March 1975
▶▶ **Doctor examines the soldier's body**
Ambersham Common // 19 March 1975
▶▶ **Sarah chases the Zygon Harry**
Charlton – Inn/Barn // 20 March 1975
▶▶ **Zygon dematerialises**
Charlton – Barn // 20 March 1975
▶▶ **Doctor drives away from village**
Charlton – Inn // 20 March 1975
▶▶ **Land Rover breaks down and Doctor runs from Skarasen**
Ambersham Common // 19 March 1975

Right: Part of the deleted opening scene for *Terror of the Zygons*, filmed on Ambersham Common on 17 March 1975.

```
HARRY
You know, I've a feeling that a herd of
slithy toves and a jabberwoch are
likely to appear any minute.

SARAH
Me too.  We could be almost anywhere -
eastern Europe, western Europe,
Scandinavia ...

HARRY  (hopefully)
Perhaps even Britain, eh?

SARAH
Perhaps.

THEY both turn on hearing a strange "Tardis
becoming visible" noise

/CAMERA LOCKED OFF/
MS TARDIS appears in Forest  (THEIR P.O.V.)
```

▶ Doctor with Skarasen towering over him (2/3)
Ambersham Common // 19 March 1975

PART 3

▶ Doctor drops the target reciprocator
Ambersham Common // 19 March 1975
▶ Brigadier and Sarah find the Doctor
Ambersham Common // 18 March 1975
▶ Benton and soldiers hear Angus' scream
Charlton – Inn // 20 March 1975
▶ Soldiers pursue Zygon through the woods
Furnace Pond // 21 March 1975
▶ Fake Sister Lamont attacks soldier
Furnace Pond // 21 March 1975
▶ Doctor and Brigadier in Land Rover
Ambersham Common // 18 March 1975
▶ UNIT depth charges the Loch
Furnace Pond // 21 March 1975
▶ Second depth charge fired
Furnace Pond // 21 March 1975
▶ Spaceship leaves the Loch (3/4)
Furnace Pond // 21 March 1975

PART 4

▶ Brigadier on radio
Furnace Pond // 21 March 1975
▶ Brigadier leaves with Harry and Sarah
Furnace Pond // 21 March 1975
▶ Spaceship descends (Background plate)
Storrington Quarry // 18 March 1975
▶ Fake Duke leaves the spaceship
Storrington Quarry // 18 March 1975
▶ UNIT arrives and the spaceship explodes
Storrington Quarry // 18 March 1975
▶ Establishing shot – Stanbridge House
Millbank Tower // Date Unknown
▶ TARDIS departs
Ambersham Common // 19 March 1975

The Facts

Following the destruction of Charlie Rig at the beginning of the story, the next scene was originally intended to begin with the TARDIS materialising invisibly due to a faulty fusion plate. As Sarah and Harry wonder where they've landed, the Doctor fixes the TARDIS and steps from the now-visible police box wearing a tam o'shanter and carrying a compass that will guide them to the Brigadier.

To achieve the effect of the Doctor and his companions exiting and entering the invisible police box, the scene had to be shot in two halves. However, the natural light changed so radically during the afternoon of 17 March that the various sequences did not convincingly match when the final scene was cut together.

Douglas Camfield (director): 'It was technically below standard. We couldn't shoot it again, so in the end we had to abandon it. The problem was that to make someone appear out of nowhere you have to mask off half the celluloid and film the actors coming out. Then you mask off that half and film the background without the actors, so that when the two halves run together, the crew seems to be coming out of nowhere. There was only 20 minutes between the two shots, if that, but the light had changed so much that you could clearly see the dividing line between the two halves.'[8]

As a result, it was decided to abandon the sequence entirely and join the Doctor and his companions already making their way through the countryside. It is interesting to note, however, that a remnant of the missing scene remains in the broadcast version of the episode: a brief snatch of the TARDIS' materialisation noise can be heard as the picture fades up on the Doctor striding his way through the bracken.

As had been achieved many times before, the shots showing characters leaving the Zygon spaceship were achieved by placing the Plasticard and wood model, constructed by effects assistant Steve Bowman, close to the camera and having the actors moving on the other side of the quarry.

The film diary indicates that the story was shot under one of its original titles, *Secret of Loch Ness,* a name which also appears in two of the local press reports of the filming.[9] However, two other local newspapers[10] refer to the story by its on-screen title, *Terror of the Zygons* (or 'Zugons' as the *Bognor Regis Observer* called it), indicating that the change of name took place around the time that filming began on location.

Comment

Putting the rather weak Skarasen effects to one side, *Terror of the Zygons* is an excellent adventure, which is helped by some truly stunning location work. Filming in Scotland may have proved to be a practical impossibility, but you'd be hard pushed to tell that it *wasn't* shot in the Highlands. Douglas Camfield handles all his location material well: the chase across Tullock Moor is fast and exciting, Sarah's pursuit and confrontation with the Zygon Harry is both scary and thrilling, and the depth-charging of Loch Ness is, as you'd expect from Camfield, powerful and loud.

PYRAMIDS OF MARS

(tx 25 October to 15 November 1975)

The Story

While excavating a tomb in Sekkara, Egyptologist Marcus Scarman is killed by Sutekh, the last of the alien race of Osirians[11], who has been imprisoned in the Egyptian pyramid by Horus for his crimes. Reanimating Scarman's body, Sutekh returns him to his home in England so that, with the aid of service robots in the form of mummies, he can build a missile to destroy the power source on Mars that is holding him prisoner. The Doctor destroys the missile but is forced to transport Scarman to Mars in the TARDIS, where Scarman deactivates the power supply. With time fast running out, the Doctor traps Sutekh in a time corridor and propels him into the far future to his death.

The Locations

1. Stargrove Manor, East End, Hampshire

Shooting Schedule

PART 1

▸▸ **Doctor and Sarah climb out of window**
Stargrove // 29 April 1975
▸▸ **Doctor and Sarah approach Organ Room**[12]
Stargrove // 29 April 1975
▸▸ **Doctor, Sarah and Warlock chased by Namin**
Stargrove // 30 April 1975

PART 2

▸▸ **Ernie spots Mummy in trap**
Stargrove // 2 May 1975
▸▸ **Ernie hits force field**
Stargrove // 2 May 1975
▸▸ **Ernie follows Scarman and Mummy from Lodge**
Stargrove // 30 April 1975
▸▸ **Ernie running from window**
Stargrove // 2 May 1975
▸▸ **Two Mummies hunt Ernie**
Stargrove // 2 May 1975
▸▸ **Ernie killed by Mummies outside Lodge**
Stargrove // 30 April 1975

PART 3

▸▸ **Doctor and Sarah watch pyramid missile**
Stargrove // 1 May 1975
▸▸ **Doctor and Sarah dismantle the deflection barrier**
Stargrove // 29 April 1975
▸▸ **Completing the dismantling**
Stargrove // 29 April 1975
▸▸ **Doctor and Sarah approach and enter hut**
Stargrove // 29 April 1975
▸▸ **Doctor and Sarah find gelignite in hut**
Stargrove // 29 April 1975
▸▸ **Scarman at barrier**
Stargrove // 30 April 1975
▸▸ **Doctor and Sarah hide the gelignite**
Stargrove // 1 May 1975
▸▸ **Doctor plants gelignite, Sarah fires**
Stargrove // 1 May 1975
▸▸ **Mummy moves to remove gelignite**
Stargrove // 1 May 1975

The Facts

The first task faced by production manager Peter Grimwade was to find a location to portray the house and grounds belonging to Marcus Scarman. One of the locations he scouted was Stargrove Manor in Hampshire, which was owned at the time by the Rolling Stones' lead singer, Mick Jagger, who had purchased the house and its 37 acres of land in 1965 at a cost of £14,000.

Paddy Russell (director): 'The [production] manager went and searched, and I saw about four different houses before I settled on Stargrove. This was greatly to his chagrin, because he'd had a lot of problems getting in touch with Mick Jagger. "I knew you'd do that," he told me. "I wish I hadn't told you!" But it was the right location – stable buildings, woods and so on. He knew me and he knew that was the house I'd choose. But he showed me the others in the hope I might not!'[13]

Stargrove was subsequently sold in 1993 to Formula One racing team boss Frank Williams for almost £2 million. Five years later it would change hands once again, going to rock star Rod Stewart for £2.5 million. However, as a tax exile based mainly in Beverly Hills and Palm Beach Florida, it was estimated that Stewart would only be able to spend around 90 days a year in the mansion.

The original intention had been to film the explosion of the Osirian war missile as a full-sized visual effect on Thursday 1 May, once all the scenes utilising the prop had been successfully completed. When it was realised that the resultant explosion might possibly damage the Grade II listed building, it was decided to achieve the effect using a model of the pyramid next to a photographic blow-up of the courtyard.

Right: George Tovey
waits to film his
death scene at the
hands (or chests!)
of two mummies in
the grounds of
Stargrove Manor on
30 April 1975.

Ian Scoones (visual effects designer): 'I had a stills photographer take a series of pictures of the background of the spaceship scene, and had enlargements made – about six to eight feet long. We cut these out and painted them because the colour wasn't strong enough. We matched the trees and built up the model set, including the figures of the mummies.'[14]

As it hadn't been planned to take the missile prop away from the location, Tom Baker decided to dispose of it himself…

Baker and Sladen's final day of filming had been on Thursday 1 May, shooting all the sequences involving the use of the pyramid in the courtyard at Stargrove. During the day, they had been visited by children from nearby East Woodhay Primary School, who had watched Baker filming his scenes dressed in full mummy costume. The following day, both Baker and Sladen were on stand-by in case any outstanding scenes needed to be completed, but by 12.30 pm both artists had been released, so Baker decided he'd pay a surprise visit to the school, as recounted by the then-headmistress, Margaret Jones:

'He walked into the office with that long scarf on and said, "You came to see me at work yesterday and so today I've come to see you."' But Tom Baker had not come alone, and during his hour-long visit to the school he presented the children with something to remember him by – the ten-foot high Osirian war missile prop that they'd finished with the previous day. As Margaret Jones told the reporter of the *Newbury Weekly News*, 'We don't quite know what we will use it for, but it will probably be for imaginative outside plays!'[15]

Paddy Russell: 'The people I was sorriest for were the unfortunate mummies. The costumes were fairly rigid with just an eye slit which had a narrow bandage over it. The costumes were in quite a few pieces – two for the body, two for the legs, and the head separate. During the design, I can remember Barbara Kidd (costume designer) ringing me up on several occasions, saying "Come and have a look." I put the head on and tried moving about. One of my advantages as a drama director has been that I started out as an actress, so I'm very aware of the problems that actors can have.

'We got one of the boys in at a fairly early stage and tried the basic costume on him. We experimented to find out how much he could see and how well he could move. Barbara made a lot of alterations then for movement. We'd got the sight about right, except for looking down which was the one thing they really couldn't do.

'It was all right in the studio, because that was a smooth floor and the scenes are rehearsed. But when filming a scene with the mummies chasing some unfortunate through the woods, I was shooting on a fairly steep slope. Those two poor boys! Woods are woods, so the ground wasn't even. We had to find them a path that was reasonable, so we got them to walk the ground slowly where I needed them for the shot and we watched very carefully to make sure that there was nothing in the way that would trip them up when they tried to put a bit of speed on. They were very brave and they earned every miserable penny we paid them!'[16]

For the scenes where the Doctor disguises himself as one of the mummies in order to plant the gelignite on the war missile, Paddy Russell insisted, much to Baker's annoyance, that he, rather than a stand-in, should wear one of the mummy costumes as his body language would still be distinguishable even though none of his features would be visible.

The camera scripts for *Pyramids of Mars* indicate that a number of location scenes were slightly trimmed in the final editing of the episodes:

Doctor and Sarah approach Organ Room (Part 1): The originally filmed scene was almost halved in length for the transmitted episode. Prior to their hearing the voices of Warlock and Namin, the Doctor and Sarah were to have been seen moving through the shrubbery by the side of the house, with the following dialogue taking place:

Sarah: *Where are we going?*
Doctor: *I'm rather interested to see what this fearsome Egyptian looks like, aren't you?*

Doctor, Sarah and Warlock chased by Namin (Part 1): Lost about 1'20" of material.

Ernie hits force field (Part 3): At the end of the sequence, poacher Ernie Clements was to look about worriedly and then sidle off into the bushes beside the drive.

Ernie running from window (Part 3): This sequence was substantially shortened from the scene's original 1'02" running time. As Ernie runs from the house, one of the Mummies was to have picked up his dropped shotgun and broken it like a twig before following him into the woods.

Comment

Pyramids of Mars is a stunning piece of *Doctor Who* in almost every respect and the high regard it's held in among fans of the series is an honour justly deserved. Only one location was required for the story and the house and grounds of Stargrove made an ideal setting, perfectly conjuring up the Edwardian period in which the story is set. But it's the mummies that are one of the real triumphs in this story. Fortunately, the costumes look as impressive in the daylight as they do in the studio and their massive bulk, relentlessly chasing after poor Ernie Clements, is an image well remembered in the minds of many.

THE ANDROID INVASION

(tx 22 November to 13 December 1975)

The Story

The TARDIS apparently lands near the village of Devesham, whose inhabitants, like the people at the nearby Defence Station, behave in an exceedingly odd manner. The Doctor and Sarah discover that the village is in fact a fake populated by lifelike androids, created by the Kraals on their barren world of Oseidon as a training ground for their forthcoming invasion of Earth. The Doctor and Sarah manage to arrive on Earth with the first wave of

androids, which are programmed to release a virus created by the Kraal scientist, Styggron. Reaching the Defence Station, the Doctor manages to jam the androids' operating signal using the centre's radio telescope dish. The Doctor then reprogrammes his android double to attack Styggron, who becomes infected by his own virus.

Above: **Sarah (Elisabeth Sladen) is filmed sneaking around the defence station on 21 July 1975.**

The Locations

1. National Radiological Protection Board, Harwell, Oxfordshire
2. Worsham Quarry, Witney, Oxfordshire
3. Tubney Wood, Tubney, Oxfordshire
4. East Hagbourne, Oxfordshire

Shooting Schedule

PART 1

▸▸ **TARDIS arrives, attacked by mechanics**
Tubney Wood // 23 July 1975

▸▸ **Doctor and Sarah examine 'dead' Adams**
Worsham Quarry // 22 July 1975

▸▸ **Doctor and Sarah arrive in village**
East Hagbourne // 24 July 1975

▸▸ **Corp. Adams and mechanics arrive in village**
East Hagbourne // 24 July 1975

▸▸ **Villagers arrive on lorry**
East Hagbourne // 24 July 1975

▸▸ **Sarah sees faceless mechanic**
East Hagbourne // 25 July 1975

▸▸ **Doctor arrives at Defence Station**
NRPB // 21 July 1975

▸▸ **Sarah attacked by man in canister**
Tubney Wood // 22 July 1975

▸▸ **Doctor's escape and recaptured by mechanics**
NRPB // 21 July 1975

Above: Tom Baker and his stunt double Terry Walsh at the National Radiological Protection Board.

PART 2

▸▸ **Doctor and Sarah escape Defence Station**
NRPB // 21 July 1975

▸▸ **Soldiers pursue Doctor and Sarah**
Tubney Wood // 23 July 1975

▸▸ **Doctor emerges from pond**
Tubney Wood // 22 July 1975

▸▸ **Doctor returns to the village and
tries telephone**
East Hagbourne // 24 or 25 July 1975

▸▸ **Doctor runs to Post Office**
East Hagbourne // 25 July 1975

▸▸ **Doctor watches patrolling mechanics**
East Hagbourne // 25 July 1975

▸▸ **Doctor confronts fake Sarah (2/3)**
Tubney Wood // 24 July 1975

PART 3

▸▸ **Villagers depart on lorry**
East Hagbourne // 24 July 1975

▸▸ **Doctor captured by Styggron and rescued
by Sarah**
East Hagbourne // 25 July 1975

PART 4

▸▸ **Doctor emerges from pod**
Worsham Quarry // 22 July 1975

▸▸ **Sarah meets fake Doctor at TARDIS**
Tubney Wood // 22 July 1975

▸▸ **Doctor and Sarah run from station**
NRPB // 21 July 1975

▸▸ **Doctor and Sarah hide**
NRPB // 21 July 1975

▸▸ **Doctor and Sarah depart in TARDIS**
Tubney Wood // 23 July 1975

The Facts

One noticeable difference between the location filming for *The Android Invasion* and the studio material, which began to be recorded on Monday 11 August, is Tom Baker's voice. When the filming began on 21 July, Baker had developed a bad throat, causing him to sound rather hoarse in the sequences shot that week.

Despite his illness, it was Baker himself who suggested that he should do the scene of the Doctor surfacing from under the pond water in Tubney Woods. Director Barry Letts' original plan was to shoot the scene using Terry Walsh, filming him from behind.

Comment

Just as *The Dæmons* had done back in 1971, *The Android Invasion* presents us with another quaint and memorable English village setting for a *Doctor Who* story and it's one that, like its predecessor, works extremely well. Director Barry Letts makes good use of the setting, centring events around the village pub, the post office and the war memorial, although it's interesting that he doesn't decide to utilise the church that's seen a short distance away in a number of shots. The scene in Part 1 of Sarah almost stumbling over the edge of the quarry is also well handled when compared with a similar scene in the later *The Five Doctors*. Even though the slope of Worsham Quarry was not that steep, at least Letts made some effort with his camera angles to make the sequence seem dramatic – which is more than can be said for its counterpart in the 20th anniversary special.

THE SEEDS OF DOOM
(tx 31 January to 6 March 1976)

The Story

In the Antarctic, a research team uncovers two frozen seed pods in the ice. Later, in England, the Doctor recognises the pods as belonging to the Krynoid, a voracious form of alien plant life. Flying to the Antarctic base, the Doctor finds that one of the pods has opened and infected Winlett, a member of the team. As Winlett rapidly begins to transform into a Krynoid, two mercenaries sent by the millionaire botanical collector, Harrison Chase, arrive and steal the second pod, before destroying the base and the first Krynoid. At Chase's mansion, the pod infects one of its liberators who, within hours, turns into a gigantic monster, enveloping the mansion. Realising that the Krynoid is about to release thousands of new pods, the Doctor orders an air strike, which destroys the Krynoid and Chase's mansion.

The Locations

1. Buckland Sand and Silica Co Ltd, Reigate Road, Buckland, Surrey
2. Athelhampton House, Athelhampton, Dorset
3. BBC Television Centre, Wood Lane, Shepherd's Bush, London, W12

Shooting Schedule

PART 1

▸▸ **Winlett finds the first pod**
Buckland Sand and Silica Co Ltd // 8 December 1975

▸▸ **Establishing shot – Chase's Mansion**
Athelhampton House // 1 November 1975

▸▸ **Doctor and Sarah arrive at base camp**
Buckland Sand and Silica Co Ltd // 8 December 1975

▸▸ **Doctor finds second pod**
Buckland Sand and Silica Co Ltd // 7 December 1975

PART 2

▸▸ **Krynoid's feet walk past in snow**
Buckland Sand and Silica Co Ltd // 7 December 1975

▸▸ **Krynoid reaches power unit**
Buckland Sand and Silica Co Ltd // 8 December 1975

▸▸ **Doctor, Sarah and Stevenson reach unit**
Buckland Sand and Silica Co Ltd // 7 December 1975

▸▸ **Doctor's party leave unit watched by Krynoid**
Buckland Sand and Silica Co Ltd // 7 December 1975

▸▸ **Doctor's party return to base camp**
Buckland Sand and Silica Co Ltd // 7 December 1975

▸▸ **Scorby, Keeler and Sarah leave for power unit**
Buckland Sand and Silica Co Ltd // 8 December 1975

▸▸ **Doctor leaves camp looking for Sarah**
Buckland Sand and Silica Co Ltd // 8 December 1975

▸▸ **Doctor watches aeroplane leave**
Buckland Sand and Silica Co Ltd // 8 December 1975

▸▸ **Doctor sees power unit**
Buckland Sand and Silica Co Ltd // 8 December 1975

▸▸ **Krynoid follows Doctor to power unit**
Buckland Sand and Silica Co Ltd //
8 December 1975

▸▸ **Doctor and Sarah run from power unit**
Buckland Sand and Silica Co Ltd //
8 December 1975

PART 3

▸▸ **Doctor and Sarah found by Dr Chester**
Buckland Sand and Silica Co Ltd //
8 December 1975

▸▸ **Doctor and Sarah get into car**
Ext. Studio 8 – Television Centre //
16 December 1975

▸▸ **Doctor fights chauffeur and examines car**
Buckland Sand and Silica Co Ltd //
7-8 December 1975

▸▸ **Doctor and Sarah arrive in Daimler**
Athelhampton House // 30 October 1975

▸▸ **Doctor and Sarah run into Scorby**
Athelhampton House // 31 October 1975

▸▸ **Doctor beats up Scorby and runs with Sarah**
Athelhampton House // 31 October 1975

▸▸ **Doctor gives Sarah piggy-back across stream (cut)**
Athelhampton House // 31 October 1975

▸▸ **Doctor and Sarah on terrace**
Athelhampton House // 1 November 1975

▸▸ **Scorby and security guards by statue**
Athelhampton House // 1 November 1975

▸▸ **Doctor hides rope and runs towards house**
Athelhampton House // 1 November 1975

▸▸ **Guards catch Sarah**
Athelhampton House // 2 November 1975

▸▸ **Sarah taken into house by Scorby**
Athelhampton House // 31 October 1975

PART 4

▸▸ **Doctor hides Sarah under arch**
Athelhampton House // 1 November 1975

▸▸ **Sarah watches guards go past**
Athelhampton House // 1 November 1975

▸▸ **Keeler helped from house**
Athelhampton House // 2 November 1975

▸▸ **Keeler taken to cottage**
Athelhampton House // 1 November 1975

▸▸ **Sarah emerges from hiding**
Athelhampton House // 30 October 1975

▸▸ **Sarah watches Chase leave cottage**
Athelhampton House // 1 November 1975

▸▸ **Ameila Ducat and guard at main gate**
Athelhampton House // 30 October 1975

▸▸ **Ameila talks to Sir Colin and Dunbar**
Athelhampton House // 30 October 1975

Right: Map of the Athelhampton estate, highlighting the various filming areas.

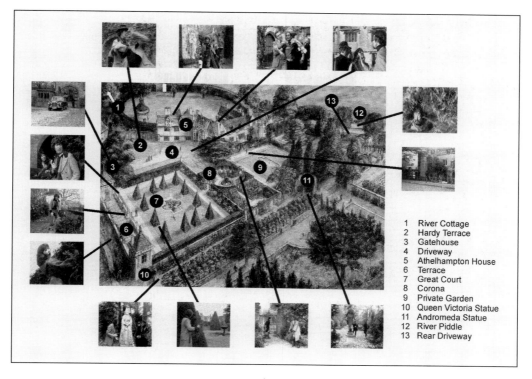

1   River Cottage
2   Hardy Terrace
3   Gatehouse
4   Driveway
5   Athelhampton House
6   Terrace
7   Great Court
8   Corona
9   Private Garden
10 Queen Victoria Statue
11 Andromeda Statue
12 River Piddle
13 Rear Driveway

▸▸ Dunbar runs from the house
   Athelhampton House // 30 October 1975
▸▸ Dunbar runs through the woods
   Athelhampton House // 31 October 1975
▸▸ Krynoid kills Dunbar, confronts Doctor and Sarah (4/5)
   Athelhampton House // 31 October 1975

PART 5
▸▸ Chase sees the Krynoid, Doctor runs from cottage
   Athelhampton House // 1 November 1975
▸▸ Doctor runs to car and escapes
   Athelhampton House // 31 October 1975
▸▸ Chase sees Krynoid and takes photographs
   Athelhampton House // 2 November 1975
▸▸ Doctor rushes inside building
   Ext. Studio 8 – Television Centre // 16 December 1975
▸▸ Chase lying on the ground
   Athelhampton House // 2 November 1975
▸▸ Chase meets Scorby and Sarah
   Athelhampton House // 2 November 1975
▸▸ Doctor and Henderson arrive at gates
   Athelhampton House // 3 November 1975
▸▸ Doctor and Henderson get out of car
   Athelhampton House // 2 November 1975

▸▸ Doctor and Henderson break into house
   Athelhampton House // 2 November 1975
▸▸ Move plants outside
   Athelhampton House // 2 November 1975
▸▸ Doctor's party locked outside house (5/6)
   Athelhampton House // 2 November 1975

PART 6
▸▸ UNIT troops attack with laser gun
   Athelhampton House // 2 November 1975
▸▸ UNIT troops run from woods
   Athelhampton House // 2 November 1975
▸▸ Beresford with Sir Colin meet by main gate
   Athelhampton House // 3 November 1975
▸▸ Scorby flees through side door (cut)
   Athelhampton House // 31 October 1975
▸▸ Scorby attacked by foliage as he flees
   Athelhampton House // 31 October 1975
▸▸ Scorby dies in pond
   Athelhampton House // 3 November 1975
▸▸ UNIT watches the Krynoid
   Athelhampton House // 3 November 1975
▸▸ Beresford and Sir Colin talk to Doctor on RT
   Athelhampton House // 3 November 1975
▸▸ Beresford confirms air strike
   Athelhampton House // 3 November 1975
▸▸ Beresford and Sir Colin watch the house

Athelhampton House // 3 November 1975
▸▸ **Doctor and Sarah flee attacked by foliage**
Athelhampton House // 31 October 1975
▸▸ **UNIT troops under cover**
Athelhampton House // 3 November 1975
▸▸ **TARDIS arrives in Antarctica**
Buckland Sand and Silica Co Ltd //
8 December 1975

▸▸ **CSO backgrounds for Parts 5 & 6**
Athelhampton House // 30 October /
1 November 1975

The Facts

Director Douglas Camfield decided to record all the required location work for *The Seeds of Doom* using electronic outside broadcast cameras in order to facilitate the later CSO work that would be added onto the footage. As a result, the finished images of the giant Krynoid towering over Chase's mansion are far more convincing than the unsteady film and CSO mix used for *Invasion of the Dinosaurs*.

When recording scenes over the two days at Buckland Sand and Silica Co Ltd, the cast had to make do with fairly basic facilities…

Michael McStay (Moberley): 'The entire cast had one bus which served as a general dressing room, and the sight of our leading lady (Elisabeth Sladen) struggling around the central aisle in her underclothes, trying to ignore the presence of four or five healthy young men, always started the day well and remains a warm memory!'

Unusually, the two location recording blocks were separated by over a month, with the first four episodes, including all the interior scenes using the Antarctica base sets, having been completed in the studio by the time exterior work began at Buckland Sand and Silica Co Ltd.

Michael McStay: 'I was living in Devon at the time and my wife had come down to London to watch the studio recording. On the way back to the flat that I was borrowing, I had a serious car smash that left my wife on crutches for a year and myself with head injuries including a suspected fractured skull. The first person into the hospital in the early hours of the morning was Sheila, the director's wife, bringing new toothbrushes, toothpaste, flannels, towels and all those toilet things that we would need immediately.

'The second person into my ward was Dougie [Camfield], hovering over me and asking anxiously, not "How are you?" and "Thank goodness you're alive", but "Will you be all right for the filming in the sandpits?" Douglas was always a man who had his priorities right. Actors were ten-a-penny, but not when they had just completed two weeks in studio and continuity demanded their

Left: **Production assistant Graeme Harper prepares a scene, watched by actor Tony Beckley.**

presence in front of the cameras for a further two days!

'I must say that hope of sympathy of any kind was quickly dispelled when John Challis, another member of the cast (and, it is necessary to add, a good friend) was told the news of my accident. He recoiled in genuine horror and gasped, "Oh no! Not that beautiful Opel Manta!"

'The day of filming arrived. Fortunately, make-up had supplied me with a pretty full beard, as worn by any regulation Antarctic explorer. It would not have been very effective in disguising the scars under the studio lights, but given the blizzards whipped up in the sandpit by the BBC technicians, and a hooded anorak, we got away with it. I shall always remember the sound operator complaining that with the wind effect and my battered lips, he was having difficulty hearing what I was saying. Dougie's response was that he couldn't give a damn about what I was saying, as long as I looked all right!'

McStay wasn't the only actor, however, subject to Camfield's sense of priorities.

John Gleeson (Winlett): 'I was due to have a double hip replacement and Dougie later confessed to having cast me as Winlett because he could visualise – due to my rather weird gait – that I could very easily turn into a horrible green vegetable! Of course, it didn't work quite so well on location, as I had an awful job getting up while holding the actual Seed of Doom!'

The coach trip to the production hotel in Horley on Saturday 6 December was interrupted by Tom Baker in a fashion he would repeat several times during his time on

Right: **Make-up assistant Janet Gilpin receives a hug from a friendly Krynoid in the grounds of Athelhampton House.**

the programme. During the journey, Tom arranged for the coach to stop in a village, whereupon he, Elisabeth Sladen and John Challis all disembarked, knocked on a cottage door and went in to watch the episode that was airing that evening (*The Android Invasion*, Part 3) with the family that owned the property.

Long-serving stuntman Alan Chuntz was awarded a rare few lines of dialogue in his role as Chase's chauffeur.

Alan Chuntz (Chauffeur): 'I said a line and stopped. Douglas Camfield said, "Well?" And I said, "Well, what?" He said, "You've got more dialogue…" I said, "Where?!" I'd forgotten to turn the page of my script over!'[17]

The death of Chase's mercenary hard man, Scorby, in Part 6 was filmed at the back of the Athelhampton estate around the charmingly named River Piddle, but shooting the scene was far from straightforward.

John Challis (Scorby): 'I had to wade across a lake and be drowned by some rampant weed on the other side. As this was shot in December you can imagine how cold this was. Also, the lake was quite deep – up to the chest, but two-thirds of it was mud. At the end of this shot I was supposed to swim underwater out of camera range. On the first take, the weed failed to rise, on the second the camera slipped down the bank, and on the third I got stuck in the mud. The fourth time, mercifully, it worked. I was plunged into a hot bath by my concerned dresser, given a tumbler full of Dettol and then presented with a bottle of brandy by the programme for doing my own stunt!'

Athelhampton House, which had famously been used as a central location in *Sleuth*, the 1972 film starring Michael Caine and Laurence Olivier, was owned at the time by former MP Sir Robert Cooke and his wife Jenifer, who, several years later, still clearly remembered the work done around the estate.

Lady Jenifer Du Caan: 'The whole thing got madder and madder and we got more and more weird. They were trying out so many special effects that things overtook us all. Tom Baker was meant to run to the big oak door of the wine cellar and open it with a great flourish, which indeed he did, but we had left the key in by mistake. It's about eight inches long, a really heavy, metal key. He was trying to break into the house by kicking the door down, but he kicked with such strength that he broke the key, which we were all amazed by.' In the final episode, the Krynoid finally reaches such proportions that only a missile attack from the RAF can deal with it. This aspect of the storyline somewhat alarmed the gardeners at Athelhampton. 'The gardeners got very worried that this was for real so I had to do quite a lot of calming in that direction. It was shown in January and February when it was very cold, and somebody sent us a postcard saying, "It's a cold time of year to be homeless!"'

During the recording of the cliffhanger to Part 5, John Challis found that the door, supposedly locked by Chase, was in fact open, causing him to curse. The outtake was subsequently screened during the summer of 1976 as part of *Festival 40*, a retrospective season shown by the BBC celebrating television's Ruby anniversary.

On 12 December 1975, the *Dorking Advertiser* published a report by Rosheen Payne on the recording carried out at the Buckland sand quarry, entitled, 'Who's in Town? The Time Doctor'.

'The wind whistled round the Antarctic base camp. Snow drifted relentlessly as three hunched figures struggled on, seeking the comfort of the light glowing from the camp window. Suddenly they became recognisable – it was Dr Who and Sarah accompanied by a man armed with a gun! Just then someone called out: "Cut, we'll have to do it again, loves, the wind's not strong enough. And keep the snow down." The tension eased and we were transformed back to a cold, dark and damp Sunday afternoon in a sand pit at Buckland Sand and Silica Co in Reigate, watching the BBC filming for the February series of 'Dr Who' starring Tom Baker and Elisabeth Sladen.

'It was freezing cold. Fifty or more members of the BBC outside broadcasting unit shuffled though the mud and sand in big coats, wellingtons and bobble hats. Even Dr Who and Sarah, togged up for Antarctic conditions, felt the need to hover over a charcoal brazier while technicians fixed a hitch. The BBC operation sprawled immodestly everywhere. Vans, coaches and lawnmowers littered the sand hills and massive cables snaked their way through puddles and lakes. A make-shift canteen steamed in the night air and children ran excitedly up and down the hills oblivious of the cold and wet.

'But under the glare of the television lights we were in the world of icebergs and glistening snow. Set against a sand cliff, special effects men had certainly done their job of creating a South Pole with icebergs, snow drifts and crevices. On the monitor it looked just like the real thing … Never let it be said that a film star's life is an easy one. The short sequences involving the base camp looked, on the face of it, simple. But what price perfection, if they did the scene once, they must have done it a dozen times before everything synchronised. An enormous fan standing six feet high whirred away. A special effects man tipped a box of snow into its path and, hey presto, we had a snow storm. Busy and worried production assistant Graham [sic] Harper let forth a string of filmy phrases and called everyone "love" – it was great. With clapper board in hand he worried about timing, whether the actors had the right stance against the 'wind' and whether the snow was right.

'Just as they were approaching the stage when everything looked good and they might have taken the final shot, a voice was heard: "We've got a technical hitch." "Okay everybody, let's break for tea," said Graham, looking remarkably calm. "We'll never get finished at this rate," someone told the producer Philip Hinchcliffe. Dr Who and Sarah joined the queue for tea in plastic cups and biscuits. "We'll be half-an-hour late but there's a grill laid on for you at 8.00 pm," Graham cajoled the Doctor who was thawing out on the brazier.

'Earlier in the day the sand hills were used for a dramatic chase in which Dr Who is pursued after breaking away from his captors – but this time he is back in England. Filming on the two days they were in the area started at eight in the morning and went on until 8 or 9.00 pm. And then it was back to the comfort and warmth of the Post House Hotel, Horley, where Dr Who and his entourage stayed. With hours like that and in weather like this, who'd be a film star?'

Comment

One of the clever techniques employed by Douglas Camfield while shooting at Athelhampton was the very careful selection of his camera angles – clever because they have the effect of making the grounds appear very much larger than they actually are. The gatehouse, for instance, is only situated a short distance away from the main house, but in the transmitted episodes it appears that there is a long winding driveway leading up to the front of the building. Camfield makes some excellent use of the Dorset location, especially with his very effective night shoot that makes up the thrilling climax to Part 4.

Above: **Tom Baker and Terry Walsh pose next to the Gloriette in Portmeirion during the filming of** *The Masque of Mandragora.*

THE MASQUE OF MANDRAGORA
(tx 4 September to 25 September 1976)

The Story

Drawn off course by the Mandragora Helix, the TARDIS accidentally brings part of it to Earth when the Doctor lands in San Martino in 15th century Italy. There, the evil Count Federico, aided by his astrologer Hieronymous, is trying to forcibly gain the dukedom from his nephew, Giuliano. Having secretly revived the ancient Cult of Demnos, Hieronymous is taken over by Mandragora, intent on using him to bring the rest of the helix energy to Earth. Using a metal breastplate and a length of copper wire, the Doctor manages to drain the small amount of helix energy on Earth before the bridgehead is opened.

The Locations

1. Portmeirion, Penrhyndeudraeth, Gwynedd

Shooting Schedule

PART 1

▶▶ **Federico and soldiers harass the peasants**
Portmeirion – A // 3 May 1976

▶▶ **Federico enters the gates of San Martino**
Portmeirion – Bridge Hs // 4 May 1976

▶▶ **Federico and entourage ride towards the palace**
Portmeirion – Walkway // 6 May 1976

▶▶ **TARDIS materialises and Doctor and Sarah exit**
Portmeirion – B/1 // 3 May 1976

▶▶ **Sarah picks an orange**
Portmeirion – B/2 // 3 May 1976

▶▶ **Sarah is abducted by brethren**
Portmeirion – B/3 // 3 May 1976

▶▶ **Helix energy passes through trees and undergrowth**
Portmeirion – B/4 // 3 May 1976

▶▶ **Doctor sees Helix kill peasants by the lake**
Portmeirion – B/5 // 3 May 1976

▶▶ **Rossini tries to capture Doctor but he escapes**

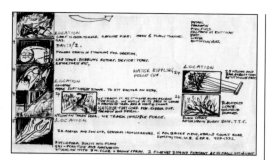

Right: **Storyboards created by visual effects designer Ian Scoones outlining the effects needed for the filming at Portmeirion.**

Portmeirion – E/1 // 5 May 1976
▶ **Doctor runs into another troop and is captured**
Portmeirion – E/2 // 5 May 1976
▶ **Helix kills gate soldier**
Portmeirion – Bridge Hs // 4 May 1976
▶ **Doctor is taken for execution (1/2)**
Portmeirion – Gloriette/Piazza // 4 May 1976

PART 2

▶ **Doctor dismounts horse and vaults over balustrade**
Portmeirion – Hercules Hall // 6 May 1976
▶ **Doctor runs down past 2 guards with dead body**
Portmeirion – Pantheon/Buddha // 4 May 1976
▶ **Doctor hides in market square**
Portmeirion – Battery Square // 6 May 1976
▶ **Doctor runs down steps to evade pikemen**
Portmeirion – Watch House // 6 May 1976
▶ **Two pikemen talk about where the Doctor has gone**
Portmeirion – G // 6 May 1976
▶ **Doctor watches the pikemen searching**
Portmeirion – F // 5 May 1976
▶ **Giuliano leads the Doctor and Sarah out of palace**
Portmeirion – Bristol Colonnade // 6 May 1976
▶ **Giuliano leads the Doctor and Sarah down steps**
Portmeirion – Cascade // 6 May 1976
▶ **Giuliano, Doctor and Sarah to temple ruins**
Portmeirion – F // 5 May 1976
▶ **Giuliano and Sarah attacked by guards (2/3)**
Portmeirion – F // 5 May 1976

PART 3

▶ **Doctor and brethren join in the fight**
Portmeirion – F // 5 May 1976

PART 4

▶ **Giuliano says goodbye to Doctor and Sarah**
Portmeirion – B/1 // 3 May 1976

The Facts

This story was filmed under its original title, *Secret of the Labyrinth*. Wanting to introduce another story with a historical setting, producer Philip Hinchcliffe

asked Louis Marks to write a four-part adventure set in and around 15th century Renaissance Italy. Marks' scripts specified a number of exterior settings, including a city gate and street, palace gardens, an execution yard, a field and country road and a ruined temple.

In suggesting the Italian setting, Hinchcliffe already had a fairly good idea of where they could film the exterior material. During the mid 1960s, he had acted as a guide to a group of American tourists and one of the stop-off points had been Portmeirion, a picturesque village created by Sir Clough Williams-Ellis and based on the Italian harbour town of Portofino. Opening the site in 1926, Williams-Ellis added many further buildings to his creation over the next 50 years in all manner of different styles – Georgian, Baroque, Jacobean etc. Hinchcliffe duly took his chosen director, Rodney Bennett, on a recce of the village and soon managed to convince him that it would be an ideal location in which to film Marks' story.

It was soon realised that the location scenes would need to be very carefully planned and shot to ensure that none of the buildings in other architectural styles or any other modern features would be seen. As a result, designer Barry Newbery had to cover up any non-period details using drapes, shutters and foreground props. A good example of this can be seen in the Part 2 chase sequence set in the market square, where hanging foreground and background props conceal the modern windows of Battery House as well as the antiques shop situated next door.

One of the central requirements for the story was the entrance to the catacombs used by Hieronymous and his brethren.

Barry Newbery (designer): 'I remember I walked all through the woodlands around Portmeirion searching for a suitable place to film this. Eventually, we came to a little hollow by a lake, with a tree-lined path leading down to it, and I decided that this was the only place it could be done. I reasoned that if I built a wall at the bottom of the hollow and put some black drapes behind it, this would look reasonably like a secret entrance.

'The catacombs were supposed to be part of some old Roman ruins. To help reinforce that impression I also had a couple of classical columns set up by the edge of the lake, with the remains of the entablature across the top of them. Sir Clough Williams-Ellis saw these columns and liked them so much that he asked if we could leave them there when we finished. Unfortunately we had to say no as they were made of Jabolite – lightweight polystyrene – and would have blown away the next time there was a strong breeze.'[18]

Marks' original script had specified a vineyard for the TARDIS' landing site. With no vineyard available at Portmeirion, the specification was changed (as per the film diary) to peach trees before becoming an orange grove in the finished version, the fruit being connected by wires to an available tree for Sarah to pick shortly after she leaves the TARDIS.

Visual effects played a limited part in the filming of *The Masque of Mandragora*, being confined to the appearances of the Helix as it makes its way from the TARDIS to the underground temple.

Ian Scoones (visual effects designer): 'The ball itself was a sparkler that was superimposed over the film in the studio. Where it hit the lake, I timed a huge explosion to go off in the water. You then saw it zig-zag towards us. It was a sort of electronic fuse, a firework that goes underwater. When this waterproof fuse goes off underwater it produces extraordinary effects, such as bubbles and smoke. It was about 20 feet long and all I did was tape a bit of rock to one end and lob it out into the water. I saw where it fell and put our main explosion just above it. By setting them off both at the same time you get the explosion and the fuse coming towards you. Stuntman Stuart Fell was dressed as a peasant who tries to fight off this unearthly thing as it comes towards him. His pitchfork had to catch fire. Later on somebody else has a sword that also has to catch fire. Both were done by gas with the pipe going away from the handle which you could not see. We had a little fuse that would ignite the gas on cue.'[19]

As a previous film crew had caused some problems for the Portmeirion management, the cast and crew were asked to be on their best behaviour during their week's stay. However, each evening a party was held in the room of Chris D'Oyly John, the production unit manager, who knew that if he confined the merry-making to his apartment, then the BBC would only have to make good any damage caused in one room. On occasions, the crew would move to the bar at the central hotel, where Tom Baker and Ian Scoones could often be found at four o'clock in the morning.

On 3 March 1976, the management at Portmeirion contacted the BBC asking if they could receive an on-screen credit for the use of the village when the programme was transmitted. The request was denied.

Comment

Like Douglas Camfield before him, Rodney Bennett manages to make his chosen location look much larger than it really is. Somewhat restricted by the architectural styles in Portmeirion, Bennett and designer Barry Newbery made an excellent job of convincing us that we really are in Renaissance Italy as opposed to north-west Wales, and the whole illusion is helped enormously by the warm and sunny weather that the production team seem to have enjoyed during their filming week.

THE HAND OF FEAR

(tx 2 October to 23 October 1976)

The Story

Landing in a quarry on Earth, the Doctor and Sarah are caught in an explosion as a rock face is blasted away by workers. When Sarah is recovered, she is found to be clutching a fossilised hand. Possessed by voices in her head, she takes the hand into the fission room of the Nunton Research Complex and, as the radiation level increases, the fossil begins to transform itself into living matter. The Doctor rescues Sarah but soon the hand possesses one of the workers, who takes it into the very heart of the reactor, sending it critical. When the reactor explodes, the hand absorbs all the energy emitted, finally regenerating the original creature, a Kastrian criminal called Eldrad. The Doctor returns Eldrad to Kastria, but finds that the Kastrian civilisation has ended over the intervening 150 million years. Eldrad's plans to return to Earth as ruler are foiled by the Doctor when Eldrad falls to his death. When the Doctor receives a call to return to Gallifrey, he finally takes Sarah back to Earth.

The Locations

1. Cromhall Quarry, Cromhall, Wotton-under-Edge, Gloucestershire
2. Oldbury Power Station, Oldbury Naite, Thornbury, Gloucestershire
3. Stokefield Close, Thornbury, Gloucestershire

Shooting Schedule

PART 1

▸ **Workers prepare quarry for blasting**
Cromhall Quarry // 15 June 1976
▸ **TARDIS materialises, Doctor and Sarah talk**
Cromhall Quarry // 14 June 1976
▸ **Explosion and Sarah discovered**
Cromhall Quarry // 15 June 1976
▸ **Sarah discovers Eldrad's hand in rocks**
Cromhall Quarry // 14 June 1976
▸ **Sarah taken away by ambulance**
Cromhall Quarry // 15 June 1976
▸ **Doctor searches the quarry**
Cromhall Quarry // 14 June 1976
▸ **Sarah attacks gate guard while Doctor and Carter drive**
Oldbury Power Station // 16 June 1976
▸ **Sarah crosses the Turbine Hall**
Oldbury Power Station // 17 June 1976
▸ **Doctor and Carter pass signpost**
Oldbury Power Station // 16 June 1976
▸ **Sarah climbs staircase**

Oldbury Power Station // 17 June 1976
▸▸ Doctor and Carter arrive and are surrounded
Oldbury Power Station // 16 June 1976
▸▸ Sarah attacks technician at pile cap
Oldbury Power Station // 17 June 1976

PART 2
▸▸ Technician climbs down as Director speaks
Oldbury Power Station // 17 June 1976
▸▸ Doctor and Carter walk through the station
Oldbury Power Station // 17 June 1976
▸▸ Doctor and Carter climb, Carter picks up spanner
Oldbury Power Station // 17 June 1976
▸▸ Carter attacks Doctor and falls to his death
Oldbury Power Station // 17 June 1976
▸▸ Driscoll crosses the station pursued by Doctor
Oldbury Power Station // 17 June 1976
▸▸ Director goes back, Sarah follows Doctor
Oldbury Power Station // 17 June 1976

PART 3
▸▸ Doctor, Sarah, Director and guards leave the plant
Oldbury Power Station // 16 June 1976
▸▸ Vehicle stops and they take cover
Oldbury Power Station // 16 June 1976
▸▸ Station doesn't explode, vehicle begins to return
Oldbury Power Station // 16 June 1976
▸▸ Doctor and Sarah re-enter the station

Oldbury Power Station // 16 June 1976
▸▸ Doctor, Sarah and Eldrad walk to TARDIS
Cromhall Quarry // 14 June 1976
▸▸ TARDIS dematerialises
Cromhall Quarry // 14 June 1976

PART 4
▸▸ TARDIS materialises
Stokefield Close // 17 June 1976
▸▸ Sarah leaves the TARDIS and it dematerialises
Stokefield Close // 17 June 1976

The Facts

Bob Baker and Dave Martin originally submitted their story outline for *The Hand of Fear* on 29 May 1975. However, their original vision was markedly different from the final broadcast, featuring a post-revolutionary Earth, two giant silicon-based Omegan life forms and the eventual death of a 70-year old Brigadier.

Following a meeting with Philip Hinchcliffe and Robert Holmes, the two writers were formally commissioned on 19 June to produce a set of six scripts which would conclude the thirteenth season. Eight days later, on 27 June, Hinchcliffe contracted director Douglas Camfield to helm the new story.

Central to the writer's storyline was the use of a nuclear power station. From their office, the writers could see the Oldbury Power Station and they made tentative enquiries about touring the plant and gaining accurate information on internal safety procedures. The management welcomed them with open arms. Official permission to film at Oldbury was subsequently granted by the Central Electricity Generating Board on 1 July.

By the time of the production meeting for *The Hand of Fear* on 18 August, two other specific locations had been pencilled in for use in the story – Titherington Quarry, where the Omegan hand would be found, and Bristol Zoo, which would feature heavily in the final half of the adventure.

Camfield actually joined the production on Monday 1 September, the day before Baker and Martin delivered the scripts for the final three episodes. By the time Robert Holmes was able to fully direct his attention to them some two weeks later (after extensively rewriting Terrance Dicks' *The Brain of Morbius*), it was evident that the scripts, as they stood, would be unworkable. Despite rewrites, *The Hand of Fear* was dropped from the production schedule on 14 October, only two weeks before the story was due to go on location. In the end, Robert Banks Stewart's hastily written *The Seeds of Doom* took the place of Baker and Martin's story.

Realising that there was still a good story at the heart of Baker and Martin's scripts, Holmes roughed out a simplified version of the adventure which was sent to the writers on 9 February 1976, hoping that they could develop it into a four-part story for the fourteenth season. Agreeing to the changes, the writers redrafted the scripts and a new director, outspoken Australian Lennie Mayne, was assigned to the project. On 5 May, the management at Oldbury were contacted again and a new reconnaissance visit was arranged for 13 May.

Examining the scripts for the new version of *The Hand of Fear*, the Oldbury management contacted the BBC on 18 May to let them know (a) that there was no such thing as a 'fission room' in a nuclear facility such as theirs and (b) that they were not keen for aircraft to fly directly over the power station as seen towards the conclusion of Part 3, as the RAF attempt to blow up the facility. In the event, the attacking aircraft would be represented by stock footage obtained from World Backgrounds and the BBC's own *Tomorrow's World*.

With plans for filming at Oldbury becoming finalised, a second recce of the station was conducted on 8 June. On this visit, Max Faulkner was in attendance to plan the stunt fall that would he would perform, doubling for actor Rex Robinson, as his character, Dr Carter tumbles off the stairway to his death on the pile cap below.

As originally scripted, the nuclear power station was named Nuton by Baker and Martin, using the same name they'd given to the power station in *The Claws of*

Axos back in 1971. For the production, this was changed to the Nunton Research and Development Complex.

The other main location needed for the production was a quarry in which the TARDIS would land in Part 1. However, the most important requirement was that the quarry would need to be a fully active one in which real blasting operations could be filmed. The production team found the ideal location a few miles east of Oldbury at the Amey Roadstone Company quarry at Cromhall and a formal approach to film at the site was made on 18 May, with a recce being conducted on Wednesday 2 June.

In order to gain a dramatic close-up of the blasting, a protected, locked-off camera was placed on the quarry floor and filmed the quarry face as the explosives were detonated.

Colin Mapson (visual effects designer): 'The guys who blew up the rock face were fantastic, real experts. They told us within ten feet where the blast debris would reach, allowing us to set up the camera for a spectacular low shot. They were spot-on with their prediction and it looked wonderful. I've heard a rumour that the remote camera was destroyed in the blast, but this is not my recollection at all. The rocks and debris did reach the camera as planned, but it was well protected inside a reinforced steel box. Somebody who was oblivious to the protective steel box probably saw that the camera had been buried and assumed that it had been destroyed.'[20]

The roadside location for the final sequence showing Sarah leaving the Doctor was evidently not chosen until the production team were actually filming in Gloucestershire; the respective shots being listed in the film diary as to be done 'at a location to be arranged for a later day'. The eventual road chosen was Stokefield Close, a small cul-de-sac situated in Thornbury, the town in which director Lennie Mayne was staying for the duration of the filming. Elisabeth Sladen's leaving scene had to be shot a number of times, however, when takes were ruined by people leaving their homes at the wrong moment or by aircraft flying overhead.

Comment

Throughout the location filming for *The Hand of Fear*, Lennie Mayne managed to produce some powerful images for this, his final *Doctor Who*. From the dramatic close-up of the quarry wall exploding through to the clever use of a fish-eye lens to subtly distort the images of those taken over by Eldrad, Mayne showed his inventiveness behind the camera throughout. The whole story is a great exit for Elisabeth Sladen, allowing her to show all the wit and warmth that has made her such a favourite among *Doctor Who* fans. Her final scene, left in the middle of a quiet cul-de-sac as the TARDIS gradually dematerialises, is the perfect way for her to go.

THE DEADLY ASSASSIN

(tx 30 October to 20 November 1976)

The Story

After receiving a premonition that the Time Lord president is about to be assassinated, the Doctor travels to his home world but is unable to stop the murder from happening. Framed for the crime, the Doctor is put on trial but soon realises that his old enemy, the Master, is behind everything. In a bid to track the Master down, the Doctor mentally enters the APC Net, a computer holding the accumulated wisdom of the Time Lords through the ages. Once attached, the Doctor finds himself in a nightmarish dreamscape, pursued by the Master's henchman, Chancellor Goth. When the Doctor defeats Goth, the Master seizes the presidential emblems, intent on using the power they hold to regenerate his wizened body. The plan is foiled by the Doctor and the Master manages to escape.

The Locations

1. Betchworth Quarry, Pebblehill Road, Betchworth, Surrey
2. Royal Alexandra and Albert School, Rocky Lane, Merstham, Surrey
3. Wycombe Air Park, Clay Lane, High Wycombe, Buckinghamshire

Shooting Schedule

PART 2

▸ **Doctor appears in Matrix dreamscape**
Betchworth Quarry // 26 July 1976

▸ **Crocodile snaps at the Doctor's feet**
Royal Alexandra School // 29 July 1976

▸ **Doctor attacked by Samurai warrior**
Betchworth Quarry // 26 July 1976

▸ **Operating table and soldier/horse sequences (2/3)**
Betchworth Quarry // 26 July 1976

▸ **Doctor is trapped on railway line (2/3)**
Betchworth Quarry // 27 July 1976

PART 3

▸ **Doctor steps into egg and clown sequences**
Betchworth Quarry // 26 July 1976

▸ **Doctor sees plane, runs and is wounded**
Betchworth Quarry // 27 July 1976

▸ **Biplane flies and shoots at the Doctor**
Booker Aerodrome // 30 July 1976

▸ **Scanner – moving trough foliage**
Royal Alexandra School // 28 July 1976

▸ **Hunter shoots at the Doctor who hides in a cave**
Betchworth Quarry // 27 July 1976

▸ **Hunter poisons the water hole**
Royal Alexandra School // 28 July 1976

▸ **Hunter walks into Doctor's grenade trap**
Bethchworth Quarry // 28 July 1976

▸ **Doctor realises the hunter is still alive**
Royal Alexandra School // 28 July 1976

▸ **Hunter is injured but not dead**
Betchworth Quarry // 28 July 1976

▸ **Doctor sees that the water hole is poisoned**
Royal Alexandra School // 29 July 1976

▸ **Injured hunter sets off**
Betchworh Quarry // 28 July 1976

▸ **Doctor's water hole and blowpipe sequences**
Royal Alexandra School // 29 July 1976

▸ **Doctor staggers through the marsh**
Royal Alexandra School // 29 July 1976

▸ **Doctor reaches the swamp and smells marsh gas**
Royal Alexandra School // 29 July 1976

▸ **Goth reveals his identity at the swamp**
Royal Alexandra School // 29 July 1976

▸ **Goth sets gas alight and falls into swamp**
Royal Alexandra School // 30 July 1976

▸ **Goth and the Doctor fight to the death (3/4)**
Royal Alexandra School // 30 July 1976

PART 4

▸ **Doctor clubs Goth in the swamp**
Royal Alexandra School // 30 July 1976

▸ **Doctor disappears from the Matrix dreamscape**
Betchworth Quarry // 26 July 1976

The Facts

Even though five days were allocated to the location work for *The Deadly Assassin*, director David Maloney still had to film at a frantic pace, with Tuesday 27 July being the biggest challenge – no less than 60 separate shots were scheduled to be completed during the day.

Originally, the ending to Part 2 was intended to be the Doctor falling down the cliff after the attack of the Samurai warrior.

Although both Tom Baker and Bernard Horsfall were used for the close-ups of the fight sequence in the swamp, most of the action was performed by stuntmen Terry Walsh and Eddie Powell. With the pond water adjudged to be too murky, the cliff-hanger freeze-frame shot of the Doctor drowning under the surface of the swamp was actually achieved in the swimming pool of the Royal Alexandra and Albert School.

Unused Locations

To film the biplane sequences, it had originally been intended to travel to Redhill Aerodrome and use the facilities of the Tiger Club based there. For reasons unknown, a late change was made and the flying shots were rescheduled to be completed at Wycombe Air Park (also known as Booker Aerodrome), using a 1946 Stampe biplane (G-AWXZ) hired from Personal Plane Services, a company run by the famous Bianchi family, suppliers of aircraft to the film and television industry.

Prior to its use in *Doctor Who*, the biplane had undergone a major cosmetic conversion to alter it from a 1940s training aircraft into a World War I Vickers SE5 single-seat fighter, complete with machine gun, for the film *Aces High*. Since then, the biplane, believed to be the most used aircraft in the history of filmmaking, has been employed in over 70 other productions, such as *Indiana Jones and the Last Crusade* and the 1999 version of *The Mummy*, for which it was completely overhauled.

Comment

When fans talk about *The Deadly Assassin*, one of the aspects most often mentioned is the Matrix dreamscape sequence which forms nearly 20 minutes of the third episode. And rightly so, for it makes up one of the finest pieces of location material ever filmed for the programme. With only two principal actors and five full days of exterior filming available, David Maloney put together a truly exciting and visceral game of cat and mouse between the Doctor and Goth. Aided by the gloriously hot summer of 1976, the sequence is designed to look as if it's set in the tropics, complete with a jungle and swamp, and succeeds beautifully. Both the Doctor and Goth become sweaty, tired, dirty and injured as the chase progresses, lending the sequence a gritty realism sadly lacking in the Matrix scenes that were to appear at the end of *The Trial of a Time Lord* ten years later.

THE TALONS OF WENG-CHIANG

(tx 26 February to 2 April 1977)

The Story

The TARDIS materialises in Victorian London in order that the Doctor can take his new companion, the young savage Leela, to the theatre. After being attacked by the Chinese sect, the Tong of the Black Scorpion, and learning about the recent disappearances of several young women, the Doctor investigates and soon becomes suspicious of Li H'sen Chang, a Chinese magician appearing at the nearby Palace Theatre. The Doctor, assisted by Henry Gordon Jago, the theatre manager, and Professor Litefoot, the Limehouse coroner, soon discover that the women have been killed so that their life essence can feed the ravaged body of Chang's master Weng-Chiang, who in reality is Magnus Greel, a war criminal from the 51st century. After locating his time machine in the hands of Professor Litefoot, Greel attempts to return to

his own time but meets his end when he falls into his own life-force extraction machine.

The Locations

1. Northampton Repertory Theatre, Swan Street, Northampton
2. St Crispin's Hospital, Duston, Northampton
3. Empty Rates Office, Fish Street, Northampton
4. Wapping Pier Head, Wapping High Street, London, E1
5. Clink Street, London, SE1
6. St Mary Overy's Wharf, Cathedral Street, Southwark, London, E1
7. East Dock/Centre Basin, St Katherine's Dock, East Smithfield, London, E1
8. Ivory House, St Katherine's Dock, East Smithfield, London, E1
9. Bankside, Southwark, London, E1
10. Bridewell Place, Wapping, E1
11. Broad Oak, 24 Cambridge Park, Twickenham, Middlesex

Shooting Schedule

PART 1

▶▶ **Chang finishes act and talks to Jago backstage**
Northampton Rep Theatre // 9 January 1977
▶▶ **Buller accuses Chang of his wife's disappearance**
Northampton Rep Theatre // 11 January 1977
▶▶ **Chang talks to Buller in his dressing room**
St Crispin's Hospital // 12 January 1977
▶▶ **Establishing shot – Riverside**
Wapping Pier Head // 16 December 1976
▶▶ **TARDIS materialises, Doctor heads off**
Clink Street // 14 December 1976
▶▶ **Jago talks to a frightened Casey**
Northampton Rep Theatre // 10 January 1977
▶▶ **Tong attack Buller, Doctor and Leela**
Clink Street // 14 December 1976
▶▶ **Doctor pursues Tong to sewer entrance**
Ivory House // 17 December 1976
▶▶ **Chang perform levitation trick**
Northampton Rep Theatre // 9 January 1977
▶▶ **Doctor and Leela at police Station**
Fish Street // 8 January 1977
▶▶ **Bullers body discovered in the river**
Wapping Pier Head // 16 December 1976
▶▶ **Chang comes to the police Station**
Fish Street // 8 January 1977
▶▶ **Chang in carriage urges driver to go faster**
St Mary Overy's Wharf // 14 December 1976
▶▶ **Jago talks to Casey about the missing girls**
Northampton Rep Theatre // 10 January 1977

▸▸ Jago investigates Chang's dressing room
St Crispin's Hospital // 12 January 1977
▸▸ Doctor and Leela arrive at the Limehouse
Mortuary Wapping Pier Head // 16 December 1976
▸▸ Doctor meets Professor Litefoot
St Crispin's Hospital // 12 January 1977
▸▸ Doctor leaves the Mortuary
Wapping Pier Head // 16 December 1976
▸▸ Leela kills the axe-carrying Coolie
Bridewell Place // 16 December 1976
▸▸ Doctor and Leela enter the sewers
Ivory House // 17 December 1976

PART 2

▸▸ Doctor and Leela exit the sewers
Ivory House // 17 December 1976
▸▸ Doctor and Leela return to the police Station
Fish Street // 8 January 1977
▸▸ Chang returns to theatre
Northampton Rep Theatre // 11 January 1977
▸▸ Chang hypnotises Jago in his dressing room
St Crispin's Hospital // 12 January 1977
▸▸ Chang goes to the theatre cellar
Northampton Rep Theatre // 10 January 1977
▸▸ Litefoot tells the Doctor his findings
St Crispin's Hospital // 13 January 1977
▸▸ Litefoot's cab moves down the street
Clink Street // 14 December 1976
▸▸ Doctor leaves Litefoot's cab
Bankside // 14 December 1976
▸▸ Doctor meets Jago and de-hypnotises him
Northampton Rep Theatre // 11 January 1977
▸▸ Greel searches the streets in his cab
Wapping Pier Head // 16 December 1977
▸▸ Greel and Chang arrive at Litefoot's house
24 Cambridge Park // 15 December 1976
▸▸ Doctor chases Greel through the theatre
Northampton Rep Theatre // 10 December 1976
▸▸ Litefoot patrols the gardens
24 Cambridge Park // 15 December 1976

PART 3

▸▸ Doctor approaches Litefoot's house
24 Cambridge Park // 15 December 1976
▸▸ Leela through window, Chang shoots at Doctor
24 Cambridge Park // 15 December 1976
▸▸ Chang and Mr Sin leave chased by Leela
24 Cambridge Park // 15 December 1976
▸▸ Chang captures Teresa
Wapping Pier Head // 16 December 1976
▸▸ Chang leaves Teresa in his dressing room
St Crispin's Hospital // 12 January 1977
▸▸ Chang heads towards theatre cleaners
Northampton Rep Theatre // 10 January 1977
▸ Leela sees Teresa in Chang's dressing room
St Crispin's Hospital // 13 January 1977
▸ Chang hypnotises cleaner
Northampton Rep Theatre // 10 January 1977
▸ Chang pulls Leela from dressing room
St Crispin's Hospital // 13 January 1977
▸ Chang takes to girls towards the cellar
Northampton Rep Theatre // 12 January 1977
▸ Doctor and Litfoot in row boat
St Katherines Dock // 17 December 1976
▸ Laundry basket is changed at Litefoot's house
24 Cambridge Park // 15 December 1976
▸ Litefoot waits in the boat for the Doctor
St Katherines Dock // 17 December 1976
▸ Casey finds Teresa in theatre
Northampton Rep Theatre // 12 January 1977

PART 4

▸▸ Chang returns to the theatre
Northampton Rep Theatre // 12 January 1977
▸▸ Jago and Casey walk across the stage
Northampton Rep Theatre // 10 January 1977
▸▸ Jago and Casey talk backstage
Northampton Rep Theatre // 12 January 1977
▸▸ Chang loads pistol in his dressing room
St Crispin's Hospital // 13 January 1977
▸▸ Doctor and Leela heave Litefoot's house for theatre
24 Cambridge Park // 15 December 1976
▸▸ Jago and Casey see the Doctor in theatre box
Northampton Rep Theatre // 10 January 1977
▸▸ Jago crawls into the Doctor's box
Northampton Rep Theatre // 11 January 1977
▸▸ Policeman walks around Litefoot's house
24 Cambridge Park // 15 December 1976
▸▸ Doctor and Leela watch singer
Northampton Rep Theatre // 9 January 1977
▸▸ Chang begins his magic act and does card trick
Northampton Rep Theatre // 9 January 1977
▸▸ Policeman is attacked
24 Cambridge Park // 15 December 1976
▸▸ Chang performs 'Cabinet of Death' trick
Northampton Rep Theatre // 9 January 1977
▸▸ Casey falls dead from Chang's cabinet
Northampton Rep Theatre // 9 January 1977
▸▸ Greel's cab drives away with the Time Cabinet (4/5)
24 Cambridge Park // 15 December 1976

PART 5

▸▸ Doctor and Leela discover policeman's body
24 Cambridge Park // 15 December 1976
▸▸ Litefoot and Jago outside Greel's hideout
Clink Street // 14 December 1976

The Facts

The story was filmed under its original title, *The Talons of Greel*.

Prior to filming, letters had been posted to all the residents along the various London streets that would be used for filming, asking them not to park their vehicles outside their houses. However, on the evening of Thursday 16 December, it was discovered that someone had parked a car next to the houses at Wapping Pier Head, where the scene of Greel's carriage searching the streets was to be filmed. When the owner of the vehicle couldn't be located, it was up to designer Roger Murray-Leach to improvise, which he did by covering the car in tarpaulin and a large pile of hay.

The stunt of Leela crashing through the window of Litefoot's house was achieved by Stuart Fell, dressed in Louise Jameson's costume. For the sequence, a window of 24 Cambridge Park was exchanged for one made of fragile toffee-glass. Fell was also responsible for choreographing the Tong's attack upon the cab driver, Buller and later, the Doctor and Leela in the opening episode. However, with no Chinese stuntmen available in the country, Fell called in two of the colleagues that he'd worked with on the programme over the years, Max Faulkner and Alan Chuntz.

Alan Chuntz: 'We waited for the early hours of the morning to do that scene. It was freezing cold. All we wore were flimsy cotton suits, which meant that our muscles were stiffening up. It was very painful when we hit the ground.'[21]

Comment

The general high regard for this story is partly due to the highly atmospheric location work accomplished by David Maloney and his crew. The scenes set on the fogbound streets of Victorian London play up to all the clichés, but as that's precisely what the audience expects, no one feels cheated. Maloney wisely elected to shoot all the exterior footage on film, leaving his second block of location work, recorded on videotape, solely for the interiors of the theatre, Chang's dressing room and the mortuary. So effective is the use of the videoed interiors that it's remarkably difficult to tell what was done on location and what was shot in the studio.

IMAGE OF THE FENDAHL

(tx 29 October to 19 November 1977)

The Story

Detecting a time disturbance, the Doctor lands the TARDIS near to Fetch Priory, where Doctor Fendelman has been using his invention, the sonic time scanner, to study a 12 million-year-old skull excavated by his archaeologist colleagues. The skull, an ancient artefact of the Fendahl, a creature from Time Lord mythology that feeds on life itself, is activated by the power from the time scanner and begins to take over Thea Ransome. Ransome transforms into the Fendahl and as the creature's power begins to grow, the Doctor programmes the time scanner to cause an implosion that destroys both the Fendahl and the Priory.

The Locations

1. Stargrove Manor, East End, Hampshire

Shooting Schedule

PART 1

▸▸ **Hiker in woods**
Stargrove – Set-up 4 // 3 August 1977
▸▸ **Hiker begins to panic and run**
Stargrove – Set-up 4 // 3 August 1977
▸▸ **Hiker comes to a standstill**
Stargrove – Set-up 4 // 3 August 1977
▸▸ **Hiker is killed**
Stargrove – Set-up 4 // 3 August 1977
▸ **Colby finds hiker's body**
Stargrove – Set-up 3 // 1 August 1977
▸ **TARDIS in cow field**
Stargrove – Set-up 5 // 4 August 1977
▸ **Doctor and Leela meet Ted Moss**
Stargrove – Set-up 6 // 1 August 1977
▸ **Doctor and Leela by Priory gates**
Stargrove – Set-up 1 // 1 August 1977
▸ **Doctor and Leela in woods**
Stargrove – Set-up 4 // 2 August 1977
▸ **Doctor, Leela and hooded figure in woods**
Stargrove – Set-up 4 // 2 August 1977
▸▸ **Leela arrives at the cottage (1/2)**
Stargrove – Set-up 2 // 4 August 1977
▸▸ **Something approaches the Doctor (1/2)**
Stargrove – Set-up 4 // 2 August 1977

PART 2

▸▸ **The Doctor runs for his life**
Stargrove – Set-up 4 // 2 August 1977
▸ **Leela attacks security guard**
Stargrove – Set-up 1 // 3 August 1977

PART 3

▸▸ **Tyler watches van arrive at Priory**
Stargrove – Set-up 1 // 1 August 1977
▸▸ **Doctor and Leela head back to the Priory**
Stargrove – Set-up 4 // 2 August 1977
▸▸ **Doctor and Leela at Priory gates**
Stargrove – Set-up 1 // 3 August 1977

PART 4

⇒ **Doctor and Leela run from the Priory**
Stargrove – Set-up 1 // 3 August 1977
⇒ **Doctor and Leela run for cover**
Stargrove – Set-up 7 // 4 August 1977
⇒ **Doctor and Leela run for cover**
Stargrove – Set-up 4 // 2 August 1977

The Facts

For the second time in just over two years, the *Doctor Who* production team employed Mick Jagger's Berkshire home, Stargrove, the use of which was only confirmed on 26 July, six days before filming was due to begin. A total of seven different areas were used in the grounds as outlined in the film diary:

Set-Up 1: *Gates (Mock-up) by tree on Cam. R. of House, on path to country lane*
Set-Up 2: *Cottage, back of stable block*
Set-Up 3: *Dog shot, by wood pile below mock gate*
Set-Up 4: *Woods through rose garden*
Set-Up 5: *TARDIS field at back of the house*
Set-Up 6: *Country Lane – Gateway and opposite*
Set-Up 7: *Explosion area*

It had originally been planned that the explosion of the Priory at the end of the story would be an effect carried out on location during the evening of Thursday 4 August. In the end, the visual effects filming was abandoned, probably due to the same restriction about having explosions going off near a Grade II listed building that had reduced the destruction of the Osiran war missile in *Pyramids of Mars* to a model effect. For *Image of the Fendahl* the destruction of the Priory was achieved using 57 feet of 35mm stock explosion footage obtained from EMI's Elstree Studios.

Following the location work, the BBC received a letter from local residents complaining about the noise created by the filming personnel and their vehicles during the two periods of night work on 2 and 3 August.

Of the four days location work allocated to the production, only the first was spent filming entirely during daylight hours. In order to power the exterior filming lights, a generator was brought to the location.

Elmer Cossey (film cameraman): 'We got all ready to go, and one of the dressers came up to the chief electrician and said, "Your generator's on fire." … Over the top of this hill was a red glow and smoke. Suddenly there was a bang, and all the lights went out. There were frantic phone calls back to London to the lighting company – a little difficult a two o'clock in the morning. But by about 4.00 am we had another generator down, and fortunately there was still plenty of darkness.'[22]

A number of location sequences in the transmitted episodes were shortened from those originally planned and shot. The Doctor and Leela's meeting with Ted Moss in the first episode lost approximately 30" of material from the end of the scene, of Moss taking from his shirt a square charm with a pentagram design which he presses to his forehead.[23] At the climax of the same episode, prior to Leela's arrival at the Tylers' cottage, the Doctor was to have made mention of the paralysis of his legs just before the Fendahl begins to approach. The conclusion of Part 4, showing the Doctor and Leela running from the Priory, was also trimmed from 1'42" down to the transmitted 13".

Comment

Normally, one might have assumed that reusing the same location within two years would not have been a good idea. It's unknown whether director George Spenton-Foster ever viewed *Pyramids of Mars* to see how Paddy Russell utilised the location, but he certainly manages to avoid filming in the same areas of Stargrove as his predecessor and he doesn't duplicate any of Russell's set-ups. Somewhat surprisingly, neither director made much use of the house itself, preferring to concentrate on the surrounding gardens and woodland. But when the building is seen, Foster chose to use the front of the house instead of the rear, as used by Russell.

THE SUN MAKERS
(tx 26 November to 17 December 1977)

The Story

The TARDIS lands on Pluto at a time in the far future when the planet is run by an all-controlling business venture, simply known as the Company. The Doctor and Leela rescue Cordo, who tries to commit suicide knowing that he can never repay the extortionate taxes imposed upon him. Together, they join forces with a band of subterranean dissidents and discover that the Company is subduing the populace by means of PCM, a pacifying chemical pumped into the air supply. When the PCM is turned off, the workers revolt and kill Gatherer Hade, the Company's chief tax collector, while the Doctor deals with the profiteering Usurian at the head of the Company, the Collector.

The Locations

1. WD and HO Wills Tobacco Factory, Hartcliffe Way, Hartcliffe, Bristol, Avon
2. Camden Town Deep Tube Shelters, Stanmore Place, Camden Town, London, NW1

Shooting Schedule

PART 1

▸ TARDIS arrives and Cordo is saved
WH and HO Wills Factory **//** 15 June 1977

▸ Doctor, Leela and Cordo hide as Hade examines TARDIS
WH and HO Wills Factory **//** 15 June 1977

▸ Cordo calls the lift to escape
WH and HO Wills Factory **//** 13 June 1977

▸ Hade tells Marn about Kandor
WH and HO Wills Factory **//** 15 June 1977

▸ Doctor, Leela and Cordo in descending lift
WH and HO Wills Factory **//** 13 June 1977

▸ Hade talks to Marn about the smuggling conspirators
WH and HO Wills Factory **//** 13 June 1977

▸ Cordo tells of his plans to go to the undercity
Camden Deep Shelters – A **//** 16 June 1977

▸ Doctor, Leela and Cordo walk down steps
Camden Deep Shelters – F **//** 17 June 1977

▸ Doctor, Leela and Cordo caught by the rebels
Camden Deep Shelters – G **//** 17 June 1977

▸ K9 emerges from TARDIS
WH and HO Wills Factory **//** 15 June 1977

▸ Scanner – K9 leave the TARDIS
WH and HO Wills Factory **//** 15 June 1977

▸ K9 descends in the lift
WH and HO Wills Factory **//** 13 June 1977

▸ K9 makes his way down the passage
Camden Deep Shelters – B **//** 16 June 1977

▸ Scanner – K9 moves down passage
Camden Deep Shelters – B **//** 16 June 1977

▸ K9 at junction (cut)
Camden Deep Shelters – H **//** 17 June 1977

▸ K9 arrives at the ladder
Camden Deep Shelters – C **//** 16 June 1977

▸ Doctor and Cordo meet K9
Camden Deep Shelters – C **//** 16 June 1977

▸ Scanner – Doctor, Cordo and K9 by ladder
Camden Deep Shelters – C **//** 16 June 1977

PART 2

▸ Cordo avoids Megro guards in long passage (cut)
WH and HO Wills Factory **//** 14 June 1977

▸ Leela tells K9 to come with her and Cordo
Camden Deep Shelters – C **//** 16 June 1977

▸ K9 tells Leela about airborne chemical inhibitor
Camden Deep Shelters – I **//** 20 June 1977

▸ K9 attacks guard (remounted)
Camden Deep Shelters – J **//** 20 June 1977

▸ Scanner – Doctor leaves Hade
WH and HO Wills Factory **//** 15 June 1977

▸ Doctor and two Megro guards (cut)
WH and HO Wills Factory **//** 15 June 1977

▸ Doctor makes his way back to the undercity
Camden Deep Shelters – D **//** 17 June 1977

▸ Scanner – Doctor going to undercity
Camden Deep Shelters – D **//** 17 June 1977

▸ Guard revives (remounted)
Camden Deep Shelters – A **//** 20 June 1977

▸ Leela finds stunned guard has gone (remounted)
Camden Deep Shelters – A **//** 20 June 1977

▸ Leela's party hijack guard vehicle and battle (2/3)
WH and HO Wills Factory **//** 14 June 1977

PART 3

▸ Doctor records himself walking past camera (remounted)
Camden Deep Shelters – E **//** 17 June 1977

▸ Doctor's party make their way to rescue Leela
WH and HO Wills Factory **//** 15 June 1977

▸ Scanner – Doctor walking up and down (remounted)
Camden Deep Shelters – E **//** 17 June 1977

▸ Hade and Marn examine camera (remounted)
Camden Deep Shelters – E **//** 17 June 1977

PART 4

▸ Goudry and workers attack guard
Camden Deep Shelters – H **//** 17 June 1977

▸ Veet and workers throw Hade from the roof
WH and HO Wills Factory **//** 14 June 1977

▸ Doctor says goodbye to everyone
WH and HO Wills Factory **//** 14 June 1977

The Facts

When director Pennant Roberts saw the script's need to represent various areas of the Megropolis underworld, he immediately thought of returning to a location he had used during the 1976 filming of the second part of the *Survivors* story, *Lights of London* – Camden Town deep tube shelters. Following the heavy bombing of London in 1940, the government made the decision in October of that year to build a number of specially designed deep-level bomb shelters under existing Underground stations, each of which could hold up to 8000 people in two parallel 1200ft tunnels. The Camden Town shelter, along with seven others of the ten planned,[24] were constructed by London Transport to their usual design specifications, as it was thought that they could be joined together after the war to form an express tube line. In the end, this idea was never acted upon.

Pennant Roberts: 'We'd always supposed that the tunnel scenes would be shot on film due to the length of tunnel required. I remembered a suitable tunnel complex in Camden Town after directing *Survivors* there a few years before [sic], but then I remembered their access was difficult at Camden, and we needed to take a three-man buggy into the tunnels for the end of part two.'[25]

Although the Camden Deep Shelters would prove useful for many of the subterranean shots, a suitably long and accessible corridor was still required. Fortunately, an ideal example would be discovered at the other main location chosen for the story.

One of the main requirements of the script was a flat roof to represent the high Megropolis building on which the TARDIS lands in the first episode. Producer Graham Williams had originally intended that the roof scenes would be done using a studio set and CSO.

Pennant Roberts: 'I wasn't too happy. The roof scenes were my only chance to show the scale of the Company's operations. A roof set would have taken up almost the whole studio space, and the scenes themselves were too long for me to be able to vary my shooting without complicating my overlay set-ups disproportionately. Plus the problem of the Gatherer's death plunge in the final episode.'[26]

As Roberts had already decided to make use of the deep shelter in Camden, an effort was naturally made to try and keep all the locations within the London area. A number of tall buildings in the city were investigated, including the recently built Barbican building, but all of them proved unsatisfactory due to the fact that the London skyline could still be seen to some degree.

While searching for a suitable location, production assistant Leon Arnold showed Pennant Roberts a copy of *The Architectural Review* containing photographs of the Wills Tobacco Factory in Bristol. Although the building was not a particularly high one, it did cover an enormous area, making it ideal for the shots that Roberts needed to accomplish.

Pennant Roberts: 'The penny dropped that we didn't need a high roof, we needed a large one – then all you could see would be roof.'[27]

Permission was duly granted to film on the roof of the Wills factory, but the management warned the production team of its fragile nature and this information was duly passed on to the rest of the cast and crew in the production film schedule. 'The roof in Bristol is completely suspended and without column supports, and therefore very vulnerable to damage. So please don't run, jump, hop or prance unless requested by your director. Please do not stand in large groups, thus putting strain on one area. Please note – should you fall through, the ground is approx three floors below and we are only taking Elastoplasts!'

The Wills factory also fulfilled another important location requirement – the long corridor needed for the scene with the guard vehicle at the close of Part 2.

The building contained a massive 300-foot tunnel linking two halves of the factory together, down which the buggy could easily be driven.

The filming at the Wills Factory was also covered by a camera crew from the regional BBC news programme, *Points West*. The 45" report was broadcast on Tuesday 14 June with a commentary by Graham Purches.

Comment

London is a city full of interesting hidden places, so it's a pity that, having gained access to the restricted Camden Town deep shelters, more use wasn't made of them. The large staircase used in the first episode seems to suggest that the travellers are heading deep beneath Megropolis, and it's a shame that more wasn't made of this sort of feature.

THE INVASION OF TIME
(4 February to 11 March 1978)

The Story

After striking a with a group of unseen telepathic aliens, the Doctor returns to Gallifrey and claims the vacant position deal of Lord President. Behaving in a seemingly erratic fashion, the Doctor banishes Leela from the capital and orders K9, the Doctor's new mobile dog-shaped computer, to disable the planet's protective transduction barriers. The aliens known as Vardans proceed to invade Gallifrey but the Doctor, who is in reality working to banish the aliens to their home world, uses K9 to trace their planet of origin and place a time loop around it, removing the Vardans from Gallifrey. Celebrations are curtailed, however, when the Sontarans appear, who have used the Vardans to gain access to the planet. Using the knowledge gained from the matrix, the Doctor arranges for the forbidden Demat gun to be constructed, with which he destroys the Sontaran invasion force.

The Locations

1. St Anne's Hospital, Redstone Hill, Redhill, Surrey
   - Room C12, First Floor (OB)
   - Room D8, Second Floor (OB)
   - Room D11, Second Floor (OB)
   - Room D14A, Second Floor (OB)
   - SFC – Second Floor Corridor (OB/Film)
   - Metal Workshop by Boiler House (OB)
   - Boiler House (Film)
   - Basement (OB)
   - Lift Shaft Staircase
   - Location A – 'Gasometer'
   - Location B – 'Tunnel'
2. British Oxygen, Blacks Road, Hammersmith

Left: Rodan (Hilary Ryan) and two of Gallifrey's Outsiders on location at Beachfields Quarry.

Broadway, London, W6
3. Beachfields Quarry, Cormongers Lane, Redhill, Surrey

Shooting Schedule

PART 1

▸▸ Leela talks to K9 in console room
St Anne's Hospital // Date Unknown

▸▸ Doctor returns to the TARDIS
St Anne's Hospital // Date Unknown

▸▸ Andred tells Kelner about unauthorised time vessel
St Anne's Hospital – D8 // 7 December 1977

▸▸ Doctor hears the amber alert
St Anne's Hospital // Date Unknown

▸▸ Kelner gives his orders concerning the time vessel
St Anne's Hospital – D8 // 7 December 1977

▸▸ Doctor asks K9 where Leela is
St Anne's Hospital // Date Unknown

▸▸ Leela in swimming pool
British Oxygen // 18 November 1977

▸▸ Andred decides to take charge of the situation himself
St Anne's Hospital – D8 // 7 December 1977

▸▸ Doctor and guards walk to Chancellor's office
St Anne's Hospital – SFC // 13 December 1977

▸▸ Doctor claims the presidency
St Anne's Hospital – C12 // 6 December 1977

▸▸ K9 talks to TARDIS console
St Anne's Hospital // Date Unknown

▸▸ Doctor talks to Borusa about his presidential claim
St Anne's Hospital – C12 // 6 December 1977

▸▸ Borusa and Kelner are summoned by the Doctor

St Anne's Hospital – D8 // 7 December 1977

▸▸ Doctor requests an office of his own
St Anne's Hospital – C12 // 6 December 1977

▸▸ Doctor talks to Kelner about redecoration
St Anne's Hospital – D14A // 6 December 1977

▸▸ Leela looks through costumes for induction
St Anne's Hospital – D14A // 6 December 1977

▸▸ Borusa talks to the Doctor about the Matrix
St Anne's Hospital – C12 // 6 December 1977

▸▸ Doctor talks to Borusa about the power he will get
St Anne's Hospital – C12 // 6 December 1977

▸▸ Andred asks Leela not to kill anyone
St Anne's Hospital – D14A // 6 December 1977

PART 2

▸▸ Doctor wakes and orders Leela's banishment
St Anne's Hospital – C12 // 6 December 1977

▸▸ Leela escapes from guards
St Anne's Hospital – SFC // 13 December 1977

▸▸ Leela is chased past two Time Lords
St Anne's Hospital – SFC // 12 December 1977

▸▸ Borusa wonders what the Doctor is playing at
St Anne's Hospital – C12 // 6 December 1977

▸▸ Leela hides as guards run past
St Anne's Hospital – SFC // 13 December 1977

▸▸ Doctor dresses and makes for the door
St Anne's Hospital – C12 // 6 December 1977

▸▸ Guard coughs outside the door
St Anne's Hospital – SFC // 13 December 1977

▸▸ Doctor finds Borusa's secret door
St Anne's Hospital – C12 // 6 December 1977

▸▸ Andred speaks to guards outside Chancellor's office

▸▸ **Doctor tries sonic screwdriver on door**
St Anne's Hospital – SFC // 13 December 1977

▸▸ **Guards look at each other**
St Anne's Hospital – C12 // 6 December 1977

▸▸ **Doctor manages to open the secret door**
St Anne's Hospital – SFC // 13 December 1977

▸▸ **Leela follows Doctor as he makes his way down passage**
St Anne's Hospital – C12 // 6 December 1977

▸▸ **Andred informs Kelner that Leela has been traced**
St Anne's Hospital – SFC // 13 December 1977

▸▸ **Leela follows the Doctor**
St Anne's Hospital – D8 // 7 December 1977

▸▸ **Kelner calls Borusa and asks about the Doctor**
St Anne's Hospital – SFC // 12 December 1977

▸▸ **Leela follows the Doctor**
St Anne's Hospital – D8 // 7 December 1977

▸▸ **Kelner orders Andred to get after Leela**
St Anne's Hospital – SFC // 13 December 1977

▸▸ **Doctor and Leela walk past guards**
St Anne's Hospital – D8 // 7 December 1977

▸▸ **Guards follow Andred to the Panopticon**
St Anne's Hospital – SFC // 13 December 1977

▸▸ **Kelner watches Leela outside the TARDIS**
St Anne's Hospital – SFC // 13 December 1977

▸▸ **Andred and the guards continue on their way**
St Anne's Hospital – D8 // 7 December 1977

▸▸ **Doctor blocks his ears to Leela's efforts**
St Anne's Hospital -SFC // 13 December 1977

▸▸ **Kelner watches Andred outside the TARDIS**
St Anne's Hospital // Date Unknown

▸▸ **Doctor talks to K9 about his plans**
St Anne's Hospital – D8 // 7 December 1977

▸▸ **Leela hears footsteps approaching**
St Anne's Hospital // Date Unknown

▸▸ **Leela meets Rodan**
St Anne's Hospital – SFC // 13 December 1977

▸▸ **Doctor orders K9 to destroy the transduction barriers**
St Anne's Hospital – D8 // 5 December 1977

▸▸ **Kelner observes the Doctor and Andred**
St Anne's Hospital // Date Unknown

▸▸ **Andred almost enters Rodan's office but walks away**
St Anne's Hospital – D8 // 7 December 1977

▸▸ **Kelner tells Borusa to rouse the Doctor**
St Anne's Hospital – SFC // 13 December 1977

▸▸ **Borusa and Kelner see the Doctor**
St Anne's Hospital – D14A // 6 December 1977

▸▸ **K9 heads towards transduction barriers**
St Anne's Hospital – C12 // 6 December 1977

▸▸ **Rodan registers ship heading towards Gallifrey**
St Anne's Hospital – Basement // 5 December 1977

▸▸ **K9 blasts guard and barrier controls**
St Anne's Hospital – D8 // 5 December 1977

St Anne's Hospital – Boiler Hs // 15 November 1977

▸▸ **Rodan says she must speak to the Castellan**
St Anne's Hospital – D8 // 5 December 1977

▸▸ **Rodan reports that they are being invaded (2/3)**
St Anne's Hospital – D8 // 5 December 1977

PART 3

▸▸ **Leela is sure that the Doctor has a plan**
St Anne's Hospital – D8 // 5 December 1977

▸▸ **K9 returns from destroying the barriers**
St Anne's Hospital – Basement // 5 December 1977

▸▸ **Leela and Rodan decide to leave the citadel**
St Anne's Hospital – D8 // 5 December 1977

▸▸ **Doctor returns to President's office**
St Anne's Hospital – SFC // 14 December 1977

▸▸ **Borusa confirms redecoration work is complete**
St Anne's Hospital – D14A // 8 December 1977

▸▸ **Leela and Rodan confronted by Andred**
St Anne's Hospital – SFC // 14 December 1977

▸▸ **Doctor and Borusa talk about the Vardans**
St Anne's Hospital – D14A // 8 December 1977

▸▸ **Andred agrees to let Leela and Rodan go**
St Anne's Hospital – SFC // 14 December 1977

▸▸ **Borusa asks why Leela was to be banished**
St Anne's Hospital – D14A // 8 December 1977

▸▸ **Leela and Rodan in cloaks run along the corridor**
St Anne's Hospital – SFC // 14 December 1977

▸▸ **Doctor talks about Leela's banishment**
St Anne's Hospital – D14A // 8 December 1977

▸▸ **Leela and Rodan leave the citadel and are surrounded**
Beachfields Quarry // 15 November 1977

▸▸ **Kelner gives guard his orders**
St Anne's Hospital – D8 // 8 December 1977

▸▸ **Leela and Rodan are taken to Nesbin**
Beachfields Quarry // 15 November 1977

▸▸ **Doctor and Borusa leave the President's office**
St Anne's Hospital – D14A // 8 December 1977

▸▸ **K9 returns to the TARDIS**
St Anne's Hospital // Date Unknown

▸▸ **Doctor gives his orders to Kelner**
St Anne's Hospital – D8 // 8 December 1977

▸▸ **K9 communicates with TARDIS console**
St Anne's Hospital // Date Unknown

▸▸ **Kelner brings lists and Doctor orders expulsions**
St Anne's Hospital – D8 // 8 December 1977

▸▸ **Nesbin explains who they are**
Beachfields Quarry // 15 November 1977

▸▸ **K9 communicates with TARDIS console**
St Anne's Hospital // Date Unknown

▸▸ **Kelner orders Gomer's expulsion**
St Anne's Hospital – D8 // 8 December 1977

▸▸ **Andred tells Gomer of their plan to resist**
St Anne's Hospital – SFC // 14 December 1977

▸ Leela and the outsiders agree to fight
Beachfields Quarry // 15 November 1977

▸ Doctor and guard make their way to Panopticon
St Anne's Hospital – SFC // 14 December 1977

▸ Andred plots against the President
St Anne's Hospital – SFC // 14 December 1977

▸ Doctor enter TARDIS and talks to K9
St Anne's Hospital // Date Unknown

▸ Andred enters TARDIS and tries to kill
the Doctor (3/4)
St Anne's Hospital // Date Unknown

PART 4

▸ Kelner talks to Vardans about a minor infringement
St Anne's Hospital – D8 // 8 December 1977

▸ Andred recovers but is unable to shoot the Doctor
St Anne's Hospital // Date Unknown

▸ Doctor decides to leave TARDIS for a few moments
St Anne's Hospital // Date Unknown

▸ Doctor tells Andred his plan
St Anne's Hospital // Date Unknown

▸ Vardans tells Kelner they suspect the Doctor
St Anne's Hospital – D8 // 8 December 1977

▸ Doctor takes Andred's helmet
St Anne's Hospital // Date Unknown

▸ Kelner reports that Andred has evaded capture
St Anne's Hospital – D8 // 8 December 1977

▸ Leela shows off her archery skills
Beachfields Quarry // 14 November 1977

▸ Doctor decides he has to dismantle the force field
St Anne's Hospital // Date Unknown

▸ Leela formulates a plan of attack
Beachfields Quarry // 14 November 1977

▸ Andred tries to work out a calculation
St Anne's Hospital // Date Unknown

▸ Doctor begins work on force field
St Anne's Hospital – Boiler Hs // 15 November 1977

▸ Raiders move towards citadel
Beachfields Quarry // 14 November 1977

▸ Force field begins to disappear
St Anne's Hospital – Boiler Hs // 15 November 1977

▸ TARDIS shakes
St Anne's Hospital // Date Unknown

▸ Doctor successfully dismantles force field
St Anne's Hospital – Boiler Hs // 14 November 1977

▸ K9 and Andred leave for President's office
St Anne's Hospital // Date Unknown

▸ K9 and Andred head towards the President's office
St Anne's Hospital – SFC // 14 December 1977

▸ Rebels divide and head for the citadel
Beachfields Quarry // 14 November 1977

▸ Doctor, Vardan, K9 and Andred head for the office
St Anne's Hospital – SFC // 14 December 1977

▸ Andred and K9 arrive at Preident's office
St Anne's Hospital – D14A // 8 December 1977

▸ Doctor decides to pop into his office
St Anne's Hospital – SFC // 14 December 1977

▸ Doctor locks his office doors
St Anne's Hospital – D14A // 8 December 1977

▸ Vardan dematerialises
St Anne's Hospital – SFC // 14 December 1977

▸ Doctor tells Andred about lead insulation
St Anne's Hospital – D14A // 8 December 1977

▸ Kelner orders the Doctor to be shot on sight
St Anne's Hospital – D8 // 8 December 1977

▸ Doctor puts sash, rod and circlet onto K9
St Anne's Hospital – D14A // 8 December 1977

▸ Guards are attacked as rebels arrive
St Anne's Hospital – SFC // 14 December 1977

▸ Andred lets the rebels into the office
St Anne's Hospital – D14A // 9 December 1977

▸ K9 traces the Vardan's home planet
St Anne's Hospital – D14A // 9 December 1977

▸ K9 confirms that the Vardans have been expelled
St Anne's Hospital – D14A // 9 December 1977

PART 5

▸ Borusa leaves his office via the secret door
St Anne's Hospital – C12 // 7 December 1977

▸ Borusa tests the shielding in the President's office
St Anne's Hospital – D14A // 9 December 1977

▸ Borusa returns to his office and continues listening
St Anne's Hospital – C12 // 7 December 1977

▸ Borusa switches on the Panopticon amplifier
St Anne's Hospital – C12 // 7 December 1977

▸ Doctor and the rebels spilt
St Anne's Hospital – SFC // 14 December 1977

▸ Leela kills a Sontaran
St Anne's Hospital – SFC // 15 December 1977

▸ Borusa continues to listen
St Anne's Hospital – C12 // 7 December 1977

▸ Doctor tells Leela he has an appointment at his office
St Anne's Hospital – SFC // 15 December 1977

▸ Borusa listens
St Anne's Hospital – C12 // 7 December 1977

▸ Doctor's party followed by Sontarans
St Anne's Hospital – SFC // 15 December 1977

▸ Borusa pulls a staser on Doctor's party
St Anne's Hospital – D14A // 9 December 1977

▸ Stor orders his troops to break down office doors
St Anne's Hospital – SFC // 15 December 1977

▸ Doctor persuades Borusa to put down the staser
St Anne's Hospital – D14A // 9 December 1977

▸ Stor changes his tactics
St Anne's Hospital – SFC // 15 December 1977

▸ Doctor's party leave for Borusa's room

Right: Article from the *BOC Pennant*, British Oxygen's internal newspaper.

Dr Who gets in the swim

DON'T tell any marauding Daleks but Dr Who has his bathroom in the basement of Hammersmith House.

The BOC swimming pool recently spent over six hours hurtling through deepest interstellar space as part of the intimate domestic arrangements of the police box-cum-spaceship Tardis.

It was all very idyllic with groves of potted palms until director Gerald Blake yelled "Action". Then some very nasty things happened. Two evil and very alien Sontarans — described by Gerald Blake as a cross between an egg and a potato — chased Dr Who (Tom Baker) and the shapely Leela (Louise Jameson — pictured right) across the side of the pool.

Despite the discharge of deadly rayguns and some debris in 7ft 3ins of water it all ended amicably over lunch. And another episode of the Dr Who adventure "Invasion of Time" was in the can. It is expected to be screened on BBC1 in February.

St Anne's Hospital – D14A // 9 December 1977
▸▸ Stor finds the door has opened
St Anne's Hospital – SFC // 15 December 1977
▸▸ Stor enters the empty office
St Anne's Hospital – D14A // 9 December 1977
▸▸ Doctor sends Leela and rebels to the TARDIS
St Anne's Hospital – C12 // 7 December 1977
▸▸ Stor tells Kelner he may be of use
St Anne's Hospital – D14A // 9 December 1977
▸▸ Doctor asks Borusa about the Great Key
St Anne's Hospital – C12 // 7 December 1977
▸▸ Rebels are attacked by Sontarans
St Anne's Hospital – SFC // 16 December 1977
▸▸ Borusa accidentally reveals that he has the Great Key
St Anne's Hospital – C12 // 7 December 1977
▸▸ Doctor ask Borusa which key is the correct one
St Anne's Hospital – C12 // 7 December 1977
▸▸ Borusa finally give the Doctor the Great Key
St Anne's Hospital – C12 // 7 December 1977
▸▸ Kelner is threatened and submits to Stor
St Anne's Hospital – D14A // 9 December 1977
▸▸ Doctor and Borusa evade and run from Sontarans
St Anne's Hospital – SFC // 16 December 1977
▸▸ Kelner examines the damaged equipment
St Anne's Hospital – Boiler Hs // 16 November 1977
▸▸ Doctor gives key to Leela and requests Rodan's help
St Anne's Hospital // Date Unknown
▸▸ Stor gets impatient and threatens Kelner

St Anne's Hospital – Boiler Hs // 16 November 1977
▸▸ Rodan works on the TARDIS console
St Anne's Hospital // Date Unknown
▸▸ Kelner reports the by-pass and Stor gets angry
St Anne's Hospital – Boiler Hs // 16 November 1977
▸▸ Doctor reflects on the Sontaran's aims
St Anne's Hospital // Date Unknown
▸▸ Kelner decides to by-pass the safety circuits
St Anne's Hospital – Boiler Hs // 16 November 1977
▸▸ Rodan complete her work as Sontaran fleet approach
St Anne's Hospital // Date Unknown
▸▸ Kelner switches on his by-pass
St Anne's Hospital – Boiler Hs // 16 November 1977
▸▸ TARDIS is in danger, Doctor throws the fail-safe (5/6)
St Anne's Hospital // Date Unknown

PART 6

▸▸ Stor orders Kelner to bring entrance probe for TARDIS
St Anne's Hospital – Boiler Hs // 16 November 1977
▸▸ Inner door is barricaded as Sontarans enter TARDIS
St Anne's Hospital // Date Unknown
▸▸ Doctor, Leela and Rodan walk through TARDIS
St Anne's Hospital – A/B // 16 November 1977
▸▸ Doctor arrives at conservatory and taps sundial
St Anne's Hospital – D8 // 12 December 1977
▸▸ Sontaran begins to cut through TARDIS door
St Anne's Hospital // Date Unknown
▸▸ Doctor decides to set off and find K9
St Anne's Hospital – D8 // 12 December 1977
▸▸ Andred comments about K9
St Anne's Hospital – Workshop // 5 December 1977
▸▸ Leela is convince that they are going in circles
St Anne's Hospital – A // 16 November 1977
▸▸ Stor realises that a stalemate exists
St Anne's Hospital // Date Unknown
▸▸ Doctor realises that the Sontarans have broken through
St Anne's Hospital – Workshop // 5 December 1977
▸▸ Stor leaves the control room
St Anne's Hospital // Date Unknown
▸▸ Doctor hypnotises Rodan and give her the Great Key
St Anne's Hospital – Workshop // 5 December 1977
▸▸ Doctor, Leela and Andred head down stairs to bathroom
St Anne's Hospital – Lift Shaft // 16 November 1977
▸▸ Stor detects a biological barrier
St Anne's Hospital – Corridor // 17 November 1977
▸▸ Rodan works on the D-Mat gun
St Anne's Hospital – Workshop // 5 December 1977
▸▸ Doctor, Leela and Andred walk down corridor
St Anne's Hospital – Corridor // 17 November 1977

▸ **Kelner, Stor and Sontaran head down the stairs**
St Anne's Hospital – Lift Shaft // 16 November 1977

▸ **Doctor meet Borusa in bathroom as Sontarans arrive**
British Oxygen // 18 November 1977

▸ **Doctor's party hide in sick bay as Sontarans enter**
St Anne's Hospital – D11 // 17 November 1977

▸ **Doctor tells Leela to take Andred and Borusa to workshop**
St Anne's Hospital – D8 // 12 December 1977

▸ **Leela gets lost**
St Anne's Hospital – A // 16 November 1977

▸ **Sontaran get eaten by plant**
St Anne's Hospital – D8 // 12 December 1977

▸ **Doctor begins to lose his way**
St Anne's Hospital – A // 12 December 1977

▸ **Kelner and Stor enter the conservatory**
St Anne's Hospital – D8 // 12 December 1977

▸ **Doctor walks through TARDIS**
St Anne's Hospital – B // 16 November 1977

▸ **Stor releases his trapped trooper**
St Anne's Hospital – D8 // 12 December 1977

▸ **Doctor meets up with Leela, Stor advances**
St Anne's Hospital – Corridor // 17 November 1977

▸ **Kelner turns of power source in art gallery**
St Anne's Hospital – Basement // 5 December 1977

▸ **Doctor collects and arms the D-Mat gun**
St Anne's Hospital – Workshop // 5 December 1977

▸ **Doctor follows Stor**
St Anne's Hospital – Corridor // 17 November 1977

▸ **Doctor comes back to the workshop, knowing nothing**
St Anne's Hospital – Workshop // 5 December 1977

▸ **Doctor says he will miss Leela**
St Anne's Hospital // Date Unknown

▸ **Doctor pushes out cardboard box**
St Anne's Hospital // Date Unknown

▸ **The box is marked 'K9 Mk II', Doctor laughs**
St Anne's Hospital // Date Unknown

The Facts

To conclude the fifteenth season, the original intention was to put into production a six-part script by David Weir entitled *Killers of the Dark*,[28] dealing with a race of Gallifreyan cat people. The storyline was accepted and Weir was duly commissioned to begin writing the scripts. As Weir was writing, the production team began to be assembled and pre-production work began based on the storyline and the scripts for the first five episodes, which were delivered on 15 August 1977. On reading the finished scripts, however, it rapidly became apparent that Weir's style was completely unsuited to the programme and so, reluctantly, *Killers of the Dark* had to be formally abandoned.

With time rapidly running out, Graham Williams and Anthony Read contacted Robert Holmes and sought his advice. Holmes suggested writing a standard four-part story appended with a two-part coda. With this information, Williams and Read visited the BBC club and discussed their options over some stiff drinks. Williams duly drafted a storyline on 25 August and Read then spent the next fortnight writing the scripts, which were then revised and rewritten by Williams into the final story. A provisional production schedule was drawn up on Tuesday 13 September, with the final scripts being distributed to the cast on 10 October.

However, as Blake began his pre-production work on *The Invasion of Time*, another serious problem arose in the shape of a technical strike by the props and electricians departments at the BBC. By the time the dispute was over, a sizeable backlog of Christmas programmes waiting to go into production had accumulated. As a result, the production office were informed that they could only be allocated a single three-day studio block as well as the five days of location filming already scheduled. Two alternatives were proposed to Williams – either abandon the production and use the money elsewhere or use an outside broadcast unit to complete the story on location. Reluctant to curtail the season, Williams decided to push on with the production and utilise the OB unit offered him. The unusual situation also necessitated an unusual production order for the programme. The studio scenes would be completed first, followed by the film location work. Then, two and a half weeks later, the ten days of OB work would be recorded.

The three-day studio block was given over to all the scenes featuring the production's largest set, the Panopticon meeting hall. This meant that all the smaller sets would need to be realised by designer Barbara Gosnold on location.

One of the principal locations chosen for the filming was St Anne's Hospital in Redhill. As the hospital was an empty, disused building with a number of sizeable rooms, the decision was taken to utilise the premises for all the OB work, due to be conducted in the opening half of December.

As most of the rooms that would house the sets were based on the second floor, Gosnold dressed the entire length of the floor's linking corridor, which would feature throughout the story. Several rooms were used more than once to represent different locations. Room D8 was initially dressed as the transaction barrier control room, before being stripped and redressed as Castellan Kelner's office and later as the TARDIS' conservatory, complete with the Sontaran eating plant. Room D14A also required redressing, showing both the plain and lead-lined President's office, as well as being used for two brief scenes from Part 1 set in the

Gallifreyan dressing room. Another main set which had to be accommodated at St Anne's was the TARDIS console room. Although the hospital rooms were large, they were not sizeable enough to allow the full dimensions of the normal TARDIS studio set, which resulted in the console room appearing smaller than normal.

Lighting also proved to be a problem. With the sets erected, the hospital ceilings were not tall enough to allow any primary overhead illumination, so the majority of the set lighting had to come from the front and sides, casting unfamiliar shadows on the rear walls of the console set. Strangely, however, no attempt was made to disguise the hospital's brick walls, complete with pipework, situated just outside the internal doors of the TARDIS, revealing the true nature of the OB location. It is unknown, however, precisely when this material was recorded as the outside broadcast schedule contains no information on the recording of any of the console room scenes.

In designing the sets to fit the hospital rooms, Gosnold arranged them so that the entrance doors of the various sets opened directly onto the adjoining corridor. This unfortunately resulted in production personnel opening the doors and walking directly onto the sets while sequences were actually being recorded.

As originally scripted, the location material shot at Beachfields Quarry should have featured two separate glass shots showing the exterior of the Time Lord capital, the first relating to Leela and tranduction barrier controller Rodan's excursion into the wastelands, the second, a cut sequence of Leela and the outsiders advancing to attack.

'A fairly bleak stretch of open country. On the horizon (glass shot) can be seen the distant helical towers of the Time Lords' citadel.'
The Invasion of Time – Camera Script – Part 3, pages 23 and 24

'We see the citadel towering in front of them (glass shot).'
The Invasion of Time – Camera Script – Part 6, page 38

Due to its location, it proved difficult to shoot scenes at Beachfields Quarry without extraneous noise reaching the soundtrack from aeroplanes using Gatwick Airport, trains running to the nearby Redhill station or nearby roadworks. This meant that scenes were kept fairly short and often had to be shot in small bursts.

In writing the scripts, Read and Williams made a number of suggestions as to the possible types of locations that could be sought for certain sequences. For the scenes of the Doctor, Leela and Rodan seemingly walking through the same parts of the TARDIS over and over again, the script had specified:

'Inside an (empty) gasometer? Anyway, a vast well with stairs and handrail down.'
The Invasion of Time – Camera Script – Part 6, page 8

Although all this material was shot on location at St Anne's, the film diary still retained the use of the term 'gasometer' to tie in with the script (hence its use in the location listing above).

The other main location suggested in the script was in connection with the TARDIS conservatory seen in Part 6, where the recommendation was made that it should be *'Preferably the tropical house at Kew, or Shepherds Bush Green…'*

Comment

The problems facing *The Invasion of Time* over the loss of allocated studio space were not far removed from those facing Derek Martinus when shooting Jon Pertwee's debut, *Spearhead from Space*. In performing a location remount, the one advantage that *Spearhead* had was its modern day setting. Not so with *The Invasion of Time*, which required that designer Barbara Gosnold turn an old empty hospital into the technological splendour of Gallifrey's capital. Understanding the problems faced by the team, it's amazing that the programme carries off the illusion as well as it does – that is, until we get out of the console room and start to explore the deeper recesses of the TARDIS. Then it becomes apparent that there simply was no money left to dress the various areas of the hospital.

THE PIRATE PLANET

(tx 30 September to 21 October 1978)

The Story

The locator traces the second segment of the Key to Time to the planet Calufrax, but when the TARDIS lands, the Doctor discovers that he's arrived on Zanak instead, ruled over by a cybernetic Captain on his mountainside bridge. Aided by the telepathic Mentiads, the Doctor discovers in the mines that Zanak is really a hollow planet that uses giant transmat engines to rematerialise around other smaller worlds before mining all the mineral wealth and energy from them. Realising that the plundered energy is required to keep alive the wizened body of Zanak's original ruler, Queen Xanxia, until she can stabilise a new, younger projection of herself, the Doctor manages to thwart the planned jump to Earth. With both Xanxia and the Captain dead, the bridge is finally destroyed and the Doctor obtains the second piece of the key – the mined remains of Calufrax.

The Locations

1. Disused Railway Tunnel, Daren-felen, Gwent, Wales
2. Big Pit, Blaenavon, Gwent, Wales
3. Coity Mountain, Gwent, Wales
4. Monmothshire Golf Course, Llanfoist, Gwent, Wales
5. Bwlch y Garn, Ebbw Vale, Gwent, Wales

6. Cathedral Cave, Dan-yr-Ogof Showcaves, Dan-yr-Ogof, Powys, Wales

7. Berkeley Power Station, Berkeley, Gloucestershire

Shooting Schedule

PART 1

▶▶ **Mentiads cross the countryside**
Coity Mountain // 2 May 1978

▶▶ **Mentiads cross the countryside**
Coity Mountain // 2 May 1978

▶▶ **Monitor – Mentiads cross the countryside**
Coity Mountain // 2 May 1978

▶▶ **Guards attempt to attack Mentiads**
Bwlch y Garn // 2 May 1978

PART 2

▶▶ **Mula and K9 cross the countryside**
Monmouthshire Golf Club // Date Unknown

▶▶ **Kimus and Doctor gain entry to transporter tunnel**
Daren-felen // 5 May 1978

▶▶ **Kimus waits outside tunnel**
Daren-felen // 5 May 1978

▶▶ **Doctor and Romana examine Zanak's engine rooms**
Berkeley Power Station // 1 May 1978

▶▶ **Kimus hears guard approaching tunnel**
Daren-felen // 5 May 1978

▶▶ **Kimus shoots the guards as Doctor exits tunnel**
Daren-felen // 5 May 1978

▶▶ **Doctor, Romana and Kimus enter the mine**
Big Pit // Date Unknown

▶▶ **In the mine, the Doctor realises the truth about Zanak (2/3)**
Dan-yr-Ogof Caves // 4 May 1978

PART 3

▶▶ **Romana and Mentiads cross the countryside**
Coity Mountain // 2 May 1978

▶▶ **Mentiads reach the bottom of the mountain**
Coity Mountain // 2 May 1978

PART 4

▶▶ **Mentiads open transporter tunnel door**
Daren-felen // 5 May 1978

▶▶ **Mentiads realise that their power has gone**
Daren-felen // 5 May 1978

▶▶ **The engine room explodes**
Berkeley Power Station // 1 May 1978

▶▶ **Kimus, Mula and Mentiads come down the mountain**
Coity Mountain // 2 May 1978

▶▶ **Doctor lays cable and Meniads destroy the bridge**
Daren-felen // 5 May 1978

The Facts

While visiting a pub in late April 1978 during the final stages of production on the preceding story, *The Ribos Operation*, Tom Baker had attempted to befriend a small dog by offering it a sausage. Getting too close, the dog leapt at Baker, biting him on the left side of the mouth. As a result, Baker wore a large sticking plaster during his photocall with Mary Tamm and K9 on 25 April. As most of *The Ribos Operation* had been completed, the injury was disguised as much as possible; however, for *The Pirate Planet*, a short alteration was made to the opening TARDIS scene (recorded on 5 June, by which time the wound had healed), showing the Doctor hurting his face on the console, thus explaining the marks that were evident during the earlier location filming.

The decision to shoot around south Wales was made jointly by director Pennant Roberts, who had shot material around Callow Hill near Monmouth while directing three episodes of the second series of *Survivors*,[29] and by production assistant Michael Owen Morris, who had been brought up in Abergavenny.

Pennant Roberts: 'Circumstances dictated that we needed to shoot the 'spanner in the works' sequence (with accompanying exploding filing cabinet) on the actual pilecap of the nuclear reactor itself. The station manger, a

Above: Pennant Roberts directs Tom Baker and Mary Tamm at Berkeley Power Station on 1 May 1978.

likeable but rather concerned Welshman from Llanelli called Mr Rees, was worried that we could somehow be responsible for triggering a chain reaction. During the camera recce, we staged a rehearsal to reassure him of the scale of the special effect we intended to use – outside in the open air, perfectly safe, and actually extremely tame. Come the day, the effects designer popped just a bit more explosive into the cabinet to preserve his professional reputation and give additional oomph to the sequence. I'm glad to say that we all survived the experience!'

Due to K9's inability to travel on grass, the brief sequence from Part 2 showing K9 crossing the countryside was filmed at the Monmouthshire Golf Course near Llanfoist, where the camera was placed in one of the fairway bunkers. This allowed the scene to be filmed at ground level, thus disguising the wooden boards along which K9 was travelling.

The scenes around the entrance to the transporter tunnel leading to the Bridge were all filmed around a disused railway tunnel at the east end of the Clydach railway tunnel near the village of Daren-felen, the entrance of which was covered by a large scenic flat.

During the single day of filming at the Dan-yr-Ogof showcaves, Tom Baker was asked to open the new Jubilee Passage, an extension to the cave system that had cost £20,000 to prepare.

Comment

In order to highlight one of the key scenes in the story, where the Doctor realises the truth about the planet Zanak, Pennant Roberts decided that the scene needed to be shot in a real cave – and he really couldn't have chosen better that the Cathedral Cave at Dan-yr-Ogof. The size of the cave lends great weight to the scene and is visually far more impressive than the real cave interiors seen in *The Mutants,* and even *Revenge of the Cybermen.* On the other hand, the let-down has to be the exterior of the mine workings which looks like exactly what it is – a run-down Welsh colliery.

THE STONES OF BLOOD

(tx 28 October to 18 November 1978)

The Story

Searching for the third segment to the Key to Time, the TARDIS lands near an ancient stone circle known as the Nine Travellers, where the Doctor and Romana meet archaeologist Professor Emilia Rumford and her assistant Vivien Fay. The circle is the ritual meeting place for a local group of druids who worship the Cailleach. Narrowly avoiding becoming a sacrifice, the Doctor discovers that Vivien Fay is the latest guise of an ancient being who has

been on Earth for 4000 years after escaping from a prison ship travelling in hyperspace. Together with two of the stones from the circle, which are really blood-sucking silicon-based lifeforms called Ogri, 'Vivien' kidnaps Romana and takes her to the spaceship. Following, the Doctor accidentally releases two justice machines called the Megara. He eventually manages to expose Vivien Fay as Cessair of Diplos, the criminal whom the Megara were en route to try. Having been sentenced, Fay is transformed into a new stone in the circle, but not before the Doctor obtains her necklace – the third segment.

The Locations

1. The King's Men, Rollright Stones, Little Rollright, Oxfordshire
2. Reed College, Little Compton, Warwickshire
3. Field belonging to Manor Farm, Oakham Road, Little Rollright, Oxfordshire
4. Little Rollright Quarry, Oakham Road, Little Rollright, Oxfordshire

Shooting Schedule

PART 1

▸▸ **Doctor and Romana leave TARDIS and see marks**
Manor Farm // 14 June 1978
▸▸ **Doctor and Romana meet Emilia at stone circle**
Rollright Stones // 13 June 1978
▸▸ **Doctor heads back to TARDIS**
Manor Farm // 14 June 1978
▸▸ **Romana helps Emilia and Vivien with the survey**
Rollright Stones // 13 June 1978
▸▸ **Doctor arrives at De Vries' house**
Reed College // 12 June 1978
▸▸ **Emilia and Vivien go, leaving Romana alone**
Rollright Stones // 13 June 1978
▸▸ **Romana hears the Doctor call**
Rollright Stones // 13 June 1978
▸▸ **Romana falls over the edge of the cliff**
Little Rollright Quarry // 15 June 1978

PART 2

▸▸ **Romana struggles on the side of the cliff**
Little Rollright Quarry // 15 June 1978
▸▸ **Emilia approaches stone circle with bike**
Manor Farm // 14 June 1978
▸▸ **Romana on cliff side calls for help**
Little Rollright Quarry // 15 June 1978
▸▸ **Doctor meets K9 on moorland**
Manor Farm // 14 June 1978
▸▸ **Doctor rescues Romana from cliff**
Little Rollright Quarry // 15 June 1978
▸▸ **Romana tries the tracer again**

Left: Tom Baker and Beatrix Lehmann prepare to record a scene at the Rollright Stones for *The Stones of Blood*.

Manor Farm // 14 June 1978
▸▸ **Doctor and K9 approach De Vries' house**
Reed College // 12 June 1978
▸▸ **Romana exits TARDIS to see two crows perched on top**
Manor Farm // 14 June 1978
▸▸ **Approaching the circle, Romana meets Vivien Fay (2/3)**
Manor Farm // 14 June 1978

PART 3
▸▸ **Doctor and Emilia run from De Vries' house**
Reed College // 12 June 1978
▸▸ **Doctor sends Ogri over the cliff**
Little Rollright Quarry // 15 June 1978

PART 4
▸▸ **K9 tells Emilia that she must rebuild the projector**
Rollright Stones // 13 June 1978
▸▸ **Emilia readies the new projector**
Rollright Stones // 13 June 1978
▸▸ **Romana and Ogri appear in circle**
Rollright Stones // 13 June 1978
▸▸ **Romana, Emilia and K9 return to the circle**
Rollright Stones // 13 June 1978
▸▸ **A weakening K9 holds off Ogri**
Rollright Stones // 13 June 1978
▸▸ **Vivien is sentenced and Megara vanish**

Rollright Stones // 13 June 1978
▸▸ **Doctor and Romana say goodbye**
Manor Farm // 14 June 1978

The Facts

Presented with a script centring on a stone circle, director Darrol Blake immediately recalled a visit made with his wife many years earlier to the Rollright Stones in Oxfordshire, a 104-foot oolitic limestone circle dating back some 4000 years. Permission was duly gained from the site's trustees to film at the circle known as The King's Men, and preparations began for location work to be done on 13 June 1978. One of the main advantages of the site was the fact that it ran next to a minor road, which allowed easy access to the circle. For the day of the shoot, the road was closed off, allowing the recording to take place in relative peace. In order to give the site more substance, the centre of the circle was augmented with a number of extra fake stones carved from Jabolite.

One of the main concerns was how the Ogri would actually move and, on visual effects designer Mat Irvine's recommendation, any notion of having an actor in a monster suit was quickly dismissed. Instead, it was decided that the Ogri should be represented throughout the story in their 'solid' form. As a result, three fibreglass stones were built, all of which could be lit from within to show their 'living' status. For the scenes requiring the Ogri to move, the props were placed on a simple wooden trolley, which was pulled using a cable along a railed piece of blockboard. The trolley also proved useful for the scene showing K9 hurriedly moving off as he tracks the whereabouts of Romana.

Mat Irvine (visual effects designer): 'One scene required K9 to hurtle up the side of a field, do a right-angled turn and hurtle off into the distance at a far greater pace. Even if he had been fitted with a go-kart engine on a four-wheeled-drive chassis he would have had a bit of a problem … In the end the problem was solved by attaching a length of thick fishing nylon to his front end to assist him along the first part of the run. At the point where he stopped at the corner, uttered some lucid K9 remark and then turned, he was helped by a second nylon line to be pulled onto the Ogri trolley. This was hidden behind a low hedge and so the scene showed K9 apparently taking off at a turn of speed never seen before or since. It took five of us to do this one sequence – one on each nylon line, one on the radio control, one on the trolley rope and one flat on his back behind the hedge heaving K9 onto the trolley.'[30]

There was a brief moment of panic when the crew awoke one morning to discover that the TARDIS prop had been 'stolen'. Eventually, it was discovered that the business training students at Reed College, which had been used as the location for Callieach worshiper Leonard De Vries' home on the first day, had secretly run off with it and deposited it in the Little Rollright Quarry as a joke.

Although a number of scenes in the story were specified as being set at night, the budget would not extend to working during the hours of darkness, so a day-for-night filter was applied to the camera to create the appearance of night shooting.

Comment

Director Darrol Blake is quoted as saying how much he hated the look of what he termed 'piebald productions', dramas which feature location work shot on film while the studio work is all on video. It was for that reason that he elected to shoot *The Stones of Blood* entirely on video. The wisdom of his choice is clear from the effortless blending of the material shot at the Rollright Stones during the day with the night-time scenes set within the circle, which were all recorded on a smaller studio mock-up featuring only the larger inner stones.

THE ANDROIDS OF TARA

(tx 25 November to 16 December 1978)

The Story

Landing in the idyllic countryside of Tara, the Doctor decides to spend time fishing while Romana locates the fourth segment of the Key to Time. After tracking it

down, Romana falls into the clutches of Count Grendel, who carries Romana off to Castle Gracht, convinced that she's an android. Grendel, who seeks to usurp the Taran throne, is amazed to find that she is not only real but also identical to his prisoner, Princess Strella, the woman betrothed to the rightful heir of Tara, Prince Reynart. The Doctor is taken by Reynart's men and helps the Prince to repair his android double, which will be used as a decoy in expectation of an assassination attempt. When the Prince is captured by Grendel, the Doctor battles to stop the Count from taking over the Taran throne. With his castle stormed, his plans in ruins and following an epic swordfight with the Doctor, Grendel dives from his battlements and escapes to fight another day.

The Locations
1. Leeds Castle, Leeds, Kent

Shooting Schedule

PART 1
▸▸ **TARDIS Materialises**
   Leeds Castle – A // 24 July 1978
▸▸ **Scanner – Countryside**
   Leeds Castle // 28 July 1978
▸▸ **Doctor and Romana leave the TARDIS**
   Leeds Castle – A // 24 July 1978
▸▸ **Doctor starts fishing**
   Leeds Castle – B // 24 July 1978
▸▸ **Romana tracks segment and is rescued by Grendel**
   Leeds Castle – A/D // 24 July 1978
▸▸ **Grendel carries Romana to his horse**
   Leeds Castle – C // 24 July 1978
▸▸ **Doctor is captured by Farrah and Zadek**
   Leeds Castle – B // 24 July 1978
▸▸ **Grendel and Romana arrive at Castle Gracht**
   Leeds Castle – H // 28 July 1978
▸▸ **Doctor, Zadek and Farrah arrive at the lodge**
   Leeds Castle – E // 24 July 1978

PART 2
▸▸ **Doctor whistles for K9**
   Leeds Castle – E // 24 July 1978
▸▸ **Establishing shot – Castle Gracht**
   Leeds Castle // 28 July 1978
▸▸ **Doctor's party approach Tara, Farrah attacks guard**
   Leeds Castle – C // 25 July 1978
▸▸ **K9 watches guards at Castle Gracht**
   Leeds Castle – J // 28 July 1978
▸▸ **K9 locates Romana's presence in the castle**
   Leeds Castle – J // 28 July 1978
▸▸ **Grendel's guards move into the airshaft**
   Leeds Castle – C // 25 July 1978

Left: Director Michael Hayes instructs Tom Baker and Paul Lavers at Leeds Castle.

PART 3

▸▸ Doctor and K9 approach the pavilion
Leeds Castle – C // 27 July 1978

▸▸ Lamia and android Romana approach the pavilion
Leeds Castle – C // 27 July 1978

▸▸ Romana escapes from the castle
Leeds Castle – H // 26/27 July 1978

▸▸ Lamia takes android Romana into pavilion
Leeds Castle – C // 27 July 1978

▸▸ Guards attack the pavilion and Lamia is killed
Leeds Castle – C // 27 July 1978

▸▸ Grendel calls the Doctor out
Leeds Castle – C // 27 July 1978

▸▸ Shot at, the Doctor flies back into the pavilion
Leeds Castle – C // 27 July 1978

▸▸ Romana rescues the Doctor from the pavilion
Leeds Castle – C // 27 July 1978

▸▸ Grendel kidnaps Romana (3/4)
Leeds Castle – E // 25 July 1978

PART 4

▸▸ Doctor and K9 set off in boat while guard patrols
Leeds Castle – F/G // 25 July 1978

▸▸ K9 begins to cut the door down
Leeds Castle – F // 25 July 1978

▸▸ K9 continues to cut through the door
Leeds Castle – F // 25 July 1978

▸▸ Grendel leads Romana and Reynart out of the cell
Leeds Castle – Cellar // 27 July 1978

▸▸ Doctor breaks through into castle
Leeds Castle – F // 25 July 1978

▸▸ Castle gates open
Leeds Castle – H // 26 July 1978

▸▸ Zadek and Farrah run into castle, attacking guards
Leeds Castle – H // 26 July 1978

▸▸ Doctor and Grendel fight
Leeds Castle – Cellar // 26 July 1978

▸▸ Grendel looses and jumps from the battlements
Leeds Castle – G // 26 July 1978

▸▸ K9 drifting in boat
Leeds Castle – F // 25 July 1978

The Facts

Just prior to the BBC arriving to make use of the location, Leeds Castle had been used for an important Middle East conference between the Israelis, Americans and Egyptians which was organised with less than 24 hours notice from the Home Office. As the delegates were under threat of assassination, over 200-armed officers mounted a 24-hour guard around the estate.

The majority of the daytime shots around the castle and the building doubling as Reynart's lodge were filmed on Monday 24 and Friday 28 July, when the castle and grounds were closed to the public. Night shooting around the castle was then conducted on Tuesday the 25th and Wednesday the 26th after the building had closed for the evening. This left Thursday the 27th, when filming centred around the Pavilion of the Summer Winds in a secluded part of the estate. The Pavilion was a specially constructed building and does not actually exist in the grounds of Leeds Castle. And, in order to make Leeds Castle look even more exotic, long shots were filmed through a glass matte painting, which added extra turrets to the castle exterior.

One of the scenes shot on the first morning at Leeds Castle was of the Doctor fishing. The scene was shot using a valuable antique fishing rod which Tom Baker accidentally let go of while casting into the water, propelling the rod into the lake. Director Michael Hayes took his teenage son, Patrick, on location and used him to provide the rustling of the bushes caused by the Taran beast as well as getting him to row the boat carrying the lightweight K9 prop out into the middle of the castle moat for the final sequence.

Even though the castle was closed from 5.30 pm in the evening, the building was home to a number of residents who had to be considered during the night shoots, which weren't scheduled to finish until 2.30 am.

Paul Lavers (Farrah): 'Just before we were about to start, Michael Hayes came over with a bottle of whisky to give us all a shot, because it was quite cold by then, and coming across the car park, Simon Lack [Zadek] slipped and this bottle of whisky smashed all over the place. Michael came up to us and said, "Listen, I know you've got to storm this castle, but could you do it quietly because there are people sleeping!"'[31]

Comment

The Androids of Tara really makes the most of both its beautiful location and the glorious summer of 1978. The glass shot additions to Leeds Castle, adding some fairy tale-like spires to the upper part of the structure, seem rather unnecessary, and unfortunately they tend to appear somewhat darker than the rest of the building and therefore don't actually look as if they belong to it. The other major embarrassment is the Taran beast that attacks Romana at the beginning of the story. Truly hideous!

THE POWER OF KROLL

(tx 23 December 1978 to 13 January 1979)

The Story

Landing on the third moon of Delta Magna, the Doctor discovers a feud between the native green-skinned Swampies and the technicians working on a nearby methane refinery, situated in the swamp. Having received arms from the mercenary Rohm-Dutt, who is ostensibly delivering on behalf of the activist group the Sons of Earth, Romana is taken for sacrifice by the Swampies as a prelude to their attack upon the refinery. She is rescued by the Doctor, but soon the refinery's operations disturb Kroll, a gigantic squid worshipped as a god by the Swampies. The Doctor learns that Kroll's enormous size is due to its swallowing an ancient Swampie relic, in truth the fifth segment. When Kroll attacks the refinery, the Doctor plunges the tracer into Kroll, retrieving the segment and regenerating the organic matter into hundreds of ordinary squid.

The Locations

1. The Maltings, Snape, Suffolk
2. Iken Cliff, Iken, near Snape, Suffolk

Shooting Schedule

PART 1

▸▸ **TARDIS materialises, Doctor and Romana set out**
The Maltings – A1 // 18 September 1978

▸▸ **Thawn and Fenner set out in hovercraft**
The Maltings – A1 // 21 September 1978

▸▸ **Romana is captured by Swampies**
Iken Cliff // 22 September 1978

▸▸ **Doctor is captured and Romana taken in boat**
The Maltings – A1 // 18 September 1978

▸▸ **Romana is questioned by Rohm-Dutt**
Iken Cliff – B4 // 26 September 1978

▸▸ **Rohm-Dutt gives rifles to Swampies**
Iken Cliff – B4 // 27 September 1978

▸▸ **Romana is taken for sacrifice**
Iken Cliff – B4 // 25 September 1978

▸▸ **Rohm-Dutt watches the sacrificial dance**
Iken Cliff – B4 // 25 September 1978

▸▸ **Doctor pushes off in boat (cut)**
Iken Cliff // 26 September 1978

▸▸ **Doctor arrives by boat and follows Swampie (1/2)**
Iken Cliff – B6 // 26 September 1978

▸▸ **Gates are closed as Romana's sacrifice nears (1/2)**
Iken Cliff – B4 // 25 September 1978

▸▸ **Ranquin looks to the heavens as Romana screams (1/2)**
Iken Cliff – B4 // 25 September 1978

▸▸ **Doctor runs to Romana's rescue (1/2 – cut)**
Iken Cliff – B4 // 25 September 1978

PART 2

▸▸ **Ranquin and Varlik talk to Rohm-Dutt about attack**
Iken Cliff – B4 // 25 September 1978

▸▸ **Armed Swampies wait as Kroll surfaces**
Iken Cliff – B5 // 21 September 1978

▸▸ **Doctor, Romana and Rohm-Dutt captured by Swampies**
Iken Cliff – B4 // 27 September 1978

▸▸ **Doctor and Romana talk about the seven holy rituals**
Iken Cliff – B4 // 28 September 1978

▸▸ **Rohm-Dutt tries to convince Varlik of his innocence**
Iken Cliff – B4 // 28 September 1978

▸▸ **Ranquin delivers his verdict (2/3)**
Iken Cliff – B4 // 28 September 1978

▸▸ **Doctor realises he has less time than he thought (2/3)**
Iken Cliff – B4 // 28 September 1978

PART 3

▸▸ Varlik begins to doubt Kroll as storm begins
Iken Cliff – B4 **//** 28 September 1978

▸▸ Doctor, Romana and Rohm-Dutt jump across swamp
Iken Cliff – B7 **//** 19 September 1978

▸▸ Swampies pursue the escapees
Iken Cliff – B7 **//** 19 September 1978

▸▸ Rohm-Dutt is pulled under the swamp by Kroll (3/4)
Iken Cliff – C8 **//** 19 September 1978

▸▸ Doctor and Romana in boat as Kroll appears (3/4)
Iken Cliff – B5 **//** 19 September 1978

PART 4

▸▸ Kroll's tentacles break through Swampie village
Iken Cliff – B4 **//** 28 September 1978

▸▸ Ranquin decides to pursue dryfoots to pacify Kroll
Iken Cliff – B6 **//** 22 September 1978

▸▸ Doctor plunges tracer into Kroll revealing segment
The Maltings – A2 **//** 20 September 1978

▸▸ Doctor and Romana make their way across swamp
Iken Cliff – B3 **//** 20 September 1978

▸▸ TARDIS dematerialises
The Maltings – A1 **//** 18 September 1978

The Facts

Because much of the script would be very difficult to convincingly realise within the confines of the studio, it was decided that *The Power of Kroll* would be allocated a larger proportion of location filming time (nine days as opposed to the normal four days for this length of story) at the expense of one of the three-day studio sessions.

With Robert Holmes' script written expressly to include the largest monster ever seen in *Doctor Who*, Kroll (apart from the odd tentacle) was always going to have to be realised using a model, which would be matted into the live action work shot in Suffolk. To this end, as well as the usual 16mm equipment, a 35mm camera was also taken to the marshes so that the various pieces of location footage could be married up with the model footage, which would also be shot on 35mm. However, the film cameraman allocated to the story, Martin Patmore, had never been involved in creating these types of shots before and so sought advice as to how he should best shoot his location material. Instead of filming the relevant scenes full frame with the required action filling only part of the shot, Patmore was told that he should mask off the unused portion of the frame, leaving part of the film unexposed. As a result, when the location film came to be matted with the model effects shots, a harsh line was evident between the two pieces of footage, something which could have been avoided had the masking not been done.

Above: The Doctor (Tom Baker) and Romana (Mary Tamm) among the reed beds in *The Power of Kroll.*

Comment

On paper, *The Power of Kroll* had the potential to be a superb story – a Robert Holmes script, nine days location work using both 35mm and 16mm film stock and one of the largest monster models (12 feet from tentacle to tentacle) ever seen in the programme. But the result overall is rather disappointing and lacklustre. That said, Stewart makes good use of his chosen location, particularly with the TARDIS landing among the dense reed beds. It really is a shame, however, that the attempted matte shots of Kroll appearing on the skyline aren't better than they are.

DESTINY OF THE DALEKS

(tx 1 September to 22 September 1979)

The Story

Landing on a strangely familiar planet, the Doctor meets the Movellans, a race of humanoids who reveal that they are on Skaro and that their mission is to investigate why their enemies, the Daleks, are mining the ruins of the old Kaled city with the help of a group of prisoners. Investigating the ruins himself, the

Doctor's worst suspicions are confirmed when he realises that the Daleks are trying to locate their creator Davros, in the hope that he will help them win a long-standing war with the Movellans. The Doctor realises that the Movellans are themselves robotic and manages to deactivate them and destroy the Daleks. The prisoners leave Skaro in the Movellan spacecraft, taking Davros with them to stand trial for his crimes.

The Locations

1. Winspit Quarry, Worth Matravers, Dorset
2. Binnegar Heath Sand Pit, Puddletown Road, Wareham, Dorset

Shooting Schedule

EPISODE 1

▶▶ TARDIS materialises
Winspit Quarry // 11 June 1979

▶▶ Doctor and Romana leave the TARDIS
Winspit Quarry // 11 June 1979

▶▶ Doctor and Romana examine the ruins
Winspit Quarry // 15 June 1979

▶▶ Body is buried and Doctor examines the corpse
Winspit Quarry // 14 June 1979

▶▶ Doctor and Romana watch the spaceship land
Binnegar Heath // 12 June 1979

▶▶ Spaceship opens and all establishing shots
Binnegar Heath // 13 June 1979

▶▶ Doctor and Romana run as explosions begin
Binnegar Heath // 12 June 1979

▶▶ Doctor and Romana take cover in ruins
Winspit Quarry // 15 June 1979

▶▶ Romana heads back to the TARDIS
Winspit Quarry // 15 June 1979

▶▶ TARDIS is blocked off as Romana is followed by Tyssan
Winspit Quarry // 11 June 1979

▶▶ Romana returns to the ruins
Winspit Quarry // 15 June 1979

EPISODE 2

▶▶ Romana talks to Jall and Veldan in the excavations
Winspit Quarry // 14 June 1979

▶▶ Romana pretends to die
Winspit Quarry // 14 June 1979

▶▶ Romana is carried off at the end of the work shift
Winspit Quarry // 14 June 1979

▶▶ Doctor see another grave and meets Romana
Winspit Quarry // 15 June 1979

EPISODE 3

▶▶ Doctor's POV of landscape from underground room
Winspit Quarry // 11 June 1979

▶▶ Romana and Tyssan head back to spaceship
Winspit Quarry // 11 June 1979

▶▶ Tyssan acts a decoy to draw off the Dalek
Winspit Quarry // 15 June 1979

▶▶ Romana runs to the Movellan spaceship
Binnegar Heath // 13 June 1979

▶▶ Doctor prepares to explode the bomb
Winspit Quarry // 15 June 1979

▶▶ Doctor activates his sonic screwdriver
Winspit Quarry // 15 June 1979

▶▶ Doctor hides from Daleks and finds Kaled mutant
Binnegar Heath // 12 June 1979

▶▶ Dalek destroyed and Movellan deactivated
Binnegar Heath // 12 June 1979

▶▶ Lan tests the Nova Device
Binnegar Heath // 12 June 1979

▶▶ Doctor sees Romana in Nova Device and is captured (3/4)
Binnegar Heath // 12 June 1979

EPISODE 4

▶▶ Lan attacked and reprogrammed
Binnegar Heath // 13 June 1979

▶▶ Agella is attacked and reprogrammed
Binnegar Heath // 13 June 1979

▶▶ Lan, Agella and prisoners walk to spacecraft
Binnegar Heath // 13 June 1979

▶▶ Doctor leaves the spaceship (cut)
Binnegar Heath // 13 June 1979

▶▶ Doctor heads for ruins as armed Daleks pass
Winspit Quarry // 14 June 1979

▶▶ Daleks advance on the spaceship
Binnegar Heath // 13 June 1979

▶▶ Daleks continue to advance
Binnegar Heath // 13 June 1979

▶▶ Sharrel crawls to the Nova Device
Binnegar Heath // 12 June 1979

▶▶ Prisoners run from spaceship and are exterminated
Binnegar Heath // 13 June 1979

▶▶ Romana deactivates Sharrel
Binnegar Heath // 12 June 1979

▶▶ Daleks continue to advance (cut)
Binnegar Heath // 13 June 1979

▶▶ Daleks explode
Binnegar Heath // 13 June 1979

▶▶ Doctor and Romana run from spaceship
Binnegar Heath // 13 June 1979

▶▶ Doctor and Romana watch spaceship leave
Binnegar Heath // 12 June 1979

▶▶ Doctor and Romana clear the TARDIS and leave
Winspit Quarry // 11 June 1979

The Facts

Terry Nation's original script for *Destiny of the Daleks* specified that all the location sequences were intended to be filmed at night, with the TARDIS initially landing during a thunderstorm.

As with *The Savages*, two different quarry locations were used to represent the surface of the story's planet – one sandy and one rocky. The sand pit location chosen was the Amey Roadstone Company site at Binnegar Heath, near Wareham, next door to and part of the same quarry as Gallows Hill, where *Death to the Daleks* had been shot almost six years earlier. The second location was Winspit Quarry, situated near Swanage on the south coast, which featured a set of ruined and dilapidated buildings which would be used to represent the remains of the Kaled city. The same location had been previously used in 1966 for the filming of *The Underwater Menace*.

The site, which had been employed to quarry the Purbeck limestone used to construct several major buildings in London, had fallen into disuse in the late 1940s. Due to the potentially hazardous nature of the site, the quarry was visited in early May 1979 by the BBC's Assistant Safety Officer, Derek Short, together with two of his colleagues. Short subsequently reported his observations to production assistant Henry Foster on 22 May, recommending that all members of the production team should wear hard hats while near the quarry face. Short also commented that 'You are advised that the use of visual effects explosives should be used with extreme caution; if possible all such effects should be carried out after the completion of the use of this location as a working area.' This was a particular concern for the production, as a number of potentially large explosions needed to take place in the quarry, showing the Daleks' underground mining charges being detonated. To ensure that the explosions could be carried out safely, visual effects designer Peter Logan mixed the magnesium charges used with gunpowder, producing a visually effective but safe explosion.

With a pitifully small visual effects budget allocated to the production, problems arose when director Ken Grieve expressed a desire to see a large group of explosive-laden Daleks making their way to the Movellan spaceship in the final episode, where they would ultimately be destroyed. The visual effects team had pulled out of storage the remaining Dalek casings, all of which were in various states of disrepair, and had managed to assemble, after some renovation, four complete Daleks. The budget wouldn't stretch to any new Daleks being built for the climactic sequence, however, so the only option open to Peter Logan's team was to create five crude, vacuum-formed dummy casings which could be mounted on a simple wooden frame to strengthen them. These dummy Daleks were created without any castors or internal work-

Left: Dummy Daleks go for a walk across the surface of Skaro.

ings, so when they were required to move, the operators had to literally pick them up and carry them, resulting in a rather erratic unsteady movement on camera.

To increase the number of explosions seen at the end of the story, a simple 'cheat' was performed when filming the sequence showing a line of five Daleks being destroyed. Firstly, the five dummy casings were filmed together. The three casings furthest from the camera were then removed and explosive charges were placed in the sand where the Daleks had stood. Then the explosives packed into the two dummy Daleks, along with the three charges laid in the ground, were detonated. When the two pieces of footage were edited together, the impression was given that all five Daleks had been destroyed.

As with *The Dæmons*, the decision was taken to film *Destiny of the Daleks* using three film cameras. Two were conventional 16mm tripod-mounted cameras but the third marked another first for *Doctor Who*, the use of a Steadicam harness. The harness, worn by cameraman Fred Hamilton, was a complicated rig of dampers and counterweights designed by Panavision to produce wonderfully smooth shots using a hand-held camera.

The Kaled mutant discovered by the Doctor in the sand was a popular children's novelty of the late 1970s called 'Worms', although the intention had originally been to use the toy's green predecessor, 'Slime'.

Comment

It's a pity that Ken Grieve decided to shoot *Destiny of the Daleks* at two entirely different quarries as the difference between them is rather too stark, making it hard to suspend one's disbelief. Of the two, Winspit Quarry, with its rocks and ruins, is by far the more interesting. By the end of the story, the whole thing begins to become rather farcical when the vacuum-formed dummy Daleks start to wobble over the dunes towards the Movellan spaceship. While the crude shells are fine for the explosion shots, the rest of the footage involving them should never really have made it into the final edit.

CITY OF DEATH
(tx 29 September to 20 October 1979)

The Story
When a Jagaroth spaceship explodes on Earth in 400 million BC, its pilot Scaroth finds himself splintered throughout time. In Paris in 1979, the Mona Lisa is stolen from the Louvre and the Doctor, together with the English detective Duggan, discovers that it has been taken by one of Scaroth's splinters, which is posing as the wealthy Count Scarlioni. The Count is funding expensive temporal experiments in order to reverse time so that he can stop his spaceship from exploding. With Romana's unwitting aid, Scaroth is able to travel back to primeval Earth. Following in the TARDIS, Duggan knocks Scaroth unconscious and, pulled back to 1979, the last of the Jagaroth is killed when his time machinery explodes.

The Locations
1. Eiffel Tower, Parc du Champ de Mars, Paris, France
2. Dupleix Metro Platform (Line 6), Rue August Bartoldi, Paris, France
3. Trocadéro Metro Platform (Line 6), Place du Trocadéro, Paris, France
4. Avenue Kléber, Paris, France
   • Boissière Metro Platform (Line 6)
   • Boissière Metro Entrance
5. Rue de Rivoli, Paris, France
   • Louvre Museum
6. Le Notre Dame Brasserie, Place du Petit Pont, Paris, France
7. Place de la Concorde, Paris, France
8. Denise Rene Gallery, Boulevard St Germain, Paris, France
9. Avenue des Champs Elysées, Paris, France
10. 47 Rue Vieille du Temple, Paris France

Shooting Schedule

PART 1
▸▸ **Doctor and Romana looking from the Eiffel Tower**
Eiffel Tower // 2 May 1979
▸▸ **Train arrives at the station**
Rue August Bartoldi // 3 May 1979
▸▸ **Doctor and Romana depart train at Trocadéro**
Place du Trocadéro // 3 May 1979
▸▸ **Doctor and Romana run along platform and leave**

Boissière Metro Platform // 3 May 1979
▸▸ **Doctor and Romana exit Metro and cross road**
Avenue Kléber // 3 May 1979
▸▸ **Doctor and Romana pass poster on gate**
Rue de Rivoli // 3 May 1979
▸▸ **Doctor and Romana cross to the café**
Le Notre Dame Brasserie // 1 May 1979
▸▸ **Exterior of Scarlioni's chateau**
47 Rue Vieille du Temple // 2 May 1979
▸▸ **Doctor and Romana discuss the timeslip**
Le Notre Dame Brasserie // 1 May 1979
▸▸ **Doctor and Romana walk across road**
Location Unknown // Date Unknown
▸▸ **Doctor and Romana cross Place de la Concorde**
Place de la Concorde // 3 May 1979
▸▸ **Doctor and Romana head towards the Louvre**
Louvre Museum // 2 May 1979
▸▸ **Doctor and Romana followed by Duggan**
Rue de Rivoli // 3 May 1979
▸▸ **Doctor and Romana look at artwork outside shop**
Location Unknown // 3 May 1979
▸▸ **Doctor and Romana on walkway by the Seine**
Riverside Walk // 3 May 1979
▸▸ **Outside the café, Romana examines the bracelet**
Le Notre Dame Brasserie // 1 May 1979

PART 2
▸▸ **Doctor and Romana are brought to the chateau**
47 Rue Vieille du Temple // 2 May 1979

PART 3
▸▸ **Doctor leaves the gallery**
Denise Rene Gallery // 30 April 1979
▸▸ **Romana and Duggan run back to the chateau**
Location Unknown // 3 May 1979
▸▸ **Doctor heads back towards the Louvre**
Rue de Rivoli // 3 May 1979
▸▸ **Doctor talks to Gendarmes outside Louvre**
Louvre Museum // 2 May 1979
▸▸ **Doctor runs from the Louvre**
Louvre Museum // 2 May 1979
▸▸ **Doctor runs back to the chateau (3/4)**
Location Unknown // 3 May 1979

PART 4
▸▸ **Doctor, Romana and Duggan along Champs Elysées**
Avenue des Champs Elysées // 3 May 1979
▸▸ **Doctor tries to hail a taxi**
Location Unknown // 3 May 1979
▸▸ **Doctor and Romana arrive at gallery**
Denise Rene Gallery // 30 April 1979
▸▸ **Doctor and Romana say goodbye to Duggan**
Eiffel Tower // 2 May 1979

Left: **Tom Baker and Lalla Ward enjoy the programme's first overseas filming in** *City of Death.*

The Facts

City of Death was very much a last-minute script. Having successfully parodied many classic tales in previous years, it was decided to write a script based on the character of Bulldog Drummond. The chosen scriptwriter was David Fisher, who developed a storyline entitled *The Gamble with Time*, featuring a lone survivor of the alien Sephiroth, disguised as a wealthy aristocrat, who has been amassing a fortune via the casinos in Las Vegas in order to fund his time experiments. Rewrites moved the location of the action to Monte Carlo of the 1920s and, although the basic story was fine, there were too many elements of it that were deemed unworkable.

By this point, Fisher was facing personal problems which meant that he would not be able to perform any further work on the script. With production dates looming fast, producer Graham Williams and script-editor Douglas Adams had no alternative but to lock themselves away and concoct a new script based on Fisher's outline while the appointed director, Michael Hayes, sat in Williams' house waiting for them to finish.

The script they eventually developed was *The Curse of Sephiroth* (changed to *City of Death* shortly before filming commenced), in which the action had now been transferred from Monte Carlo to Paris. It was at this point that a new possibility presented itself.

Graham Williams: 'No sooner had we settled on Paris than I decided to cost out the script. I felt that we could actually go to Paris at no extra cost as long as we were clever about it. I gave John Nathan-Turner, then my pro-duction unit manager, the list of the cast that I intended taking over and the time we'd be there, and he returned to me a costing that was within £15 of what we'd spend going to Ealing Film Studios to shoot it. Thus I could guarantee, with my writer's hat on, that the producer, wearing my other hat, wouldn't need to take chippies, scene shifters, prop boys – any of the supernumeraries usually vital to a normal shoot. All the scenes in Paris were written with a view to taking the minimum crew across, yet making it virtually undetectable to the viewer the way in which we had done it.'[32]

Having decided that it would be financially viable to perform the programme's first foreign location shoot for *City of Death*, Michael Hayes and production assistant Rosemary Crowson visited Paris to search out suitable locations, taking with them a 16mm film camera with which they could shoot footage of any likely sites, as well as giving Hayes the option to test out various ideas while exploring the city. Prior to the recce, Hayes had decided that one of the opening shots he wanted to try was a close-up of the Doctor and Romana, with the camera then zooming back in a single shot to reveal them standing at the top of the Eiffel Tower.

Wanting to experiment with the scene while on his recce, Hayes got in contact with Samuelsons, a specialist supplier of television and film camera equipment, and arranged for their Paris office to supply the 600mm lens needed for the shot. With help from his son, Hayes managed to fix the lens to the camera and everything seemed to work fine. However, when the shot was attempted for real on Wednesday 2 May, it was discovered that the required lens wouldn't fit the mounting on the BBC film camera and the shot had to be scrapped.

Although the team travelling to Paris was as small as possible, it didn't stop the shoot being extremely problematic. At 12.00 pm on Monday 30 April, the cast and crew flew into Charles de Gaulle Airport where they were met by a minibus which took them to Café Vagenende, 142 Boulevard St Germain, for lunch. With time at a premium, work began at 3.00 pm, filming the scenes around the Denise Rene Art Gallery.

However, unbeknownst to the crew, the 1st of May is a public holiday in France and, because it fell on a Tuesday in 1979, many businesses had decided to close on the Monday as well. As a result, the gallery was locked and empty, meaning that the Doctor could not be seen physically entering the building as Hayes had wished. Improvising, Hayes elected to shoot what he could with the Doctor going right up to the door as if to open it.

John Nathan-Turner (production unit manager): 'After one particularly boisterous take where Tom shook the door a little too vigorously, the alarms went off. The crew hurriedly fled for the next location, while the PUM, armed only with A-level French, waited for the police. A large, elegant lady in black arrived with keys and turned off the alarm. I explained how sorry we were, and that we were the BBC, who had come to film as arranged. When she replied "Quelle BBC?" I began to worry about the other facilities which had supposedly been organised.'[33]

Problems were also encountered when filming outside the Louvre Museum, when the production team discovered that the needed permission to film in their grounds had been denied.

John Nathan-Turner: 'This was the only time that I have ever seen Michael Hayes swell with rage. I intervened, stopped him verbally strangling his production assistant and said he should proceed with the shoot at the Louvre and refer the gendarmerie and Louvre staff to me. Heaven knows what I would have said to them, but fortunately, Michael worked swiftly, aided and abetted by the camera assistant (as the film cameraman himself was throwing up in some bushes in the Louvre grounds at the time), and we were away to the next location before anyone realised what was happening.'[34]

The situation didn't get any better when the Part 1 scenes filmed at various points in the Paris Metro were shot.

Michael Hayes: 'In Paris, you put a camera tripod down at your peril unless you've got your official sheaf of paper. While we were filming in the Metro, a French policeman arrived and asked for our permit. I said, "I haven't got one, but you will be relieved to hear that there is no film in the camera," to which he responded, "You won't be relieved to hear that it doesn't make any difference. It's the tripod, not the camera." But he was quite nice about it. I said, "Well, in that case, you'll be relieved to hear that we've finished," so he went away.'[35]

Unused Locations

The May public holiday also meant that one location had to be changed entirely at short notice. The intention had been to film all the exterior café sequences outside Café Coquille St Jaques, situated on the Rue St Jaques. When the production team arrived at the location as agreed at 8.30 am on 1 May, they found it closed and boarded up for the holiday and no amount of persuasion would convince patron Monsieur Lebeau to open it. Instead, some quick negotiations were entered into with the owners of the Notre Dame Brasserie on Place du Petit Pont, who allowed the filming to be conducted outside their premises.

Comment

'If you've got it, flaunt it,' the saying goes. And Michael Hayes certainly makes the very best of the programme's first ever foreign location shoot. By the time of the Paris filming, Tom Baker and Lalla Ward were becoming closer in their personal relationship, which makes the extended sequence of them touring the capital especially charming.

THE LEISURE HIVE
(tx 30 August to 20 September 1980)

The Story

Missing the 1825 opening of the Brighton Pavilion, the TARDIS deposits the Doctor and Romana on the cold and windy beach of the seaside town many years later. A frustrated Romana suggests they visit the Leisure Hive on Argolis, a recreation centre constructed by the survivors of a massive nuclear war on the planet. There, the Argolins come under pressure from their Earth financier, Brock, to sell the Hive to their old war enemies, the reptilian Foamasi. Problems then begin to occur with the Hive's Tachyon Recreation Generator, which results in the death of one of the guests. Meanwhile, Argolin Pangol has been using Earth scientist Hardin to modify the machine so that he can duplicate himself into a mighty army with which he will destroy the Foamasi. Foamasi government agents arrive and expose the deal to gain control of the Hive as being the work of a renegade Foamasi group. The Doctor, meanwhile, sabotages the Generator, which reverts Pangol into a young baby.

The Locations
1. Brighton Beach, Fish Market Hard, Brighton, East Sussex

Left: **A poorly Tom Baker with a stricken K9 on the beach at Brighton for *The Leisure Hive.***

Shooting Schedule

PART 1

▸ **Romana and K9 on beach**
Brighton Beach // 20 March 1980

▸ **Beach shots involving the Doctor**
Brighton Beach // 21 March 1980

The Facts

The only location sequence required for *The Leisure Hive* was the opening of the first episode. However, on the first day at Brighton Tom Baker proved too unwell to film any material; the schedule was hastily reshuffled so that shots not featuring the actor were filmed first. By the second day, Baker was feeling well enough to begin filming his sequences, all of which were completed as planned.

Once the crew had arrived at Brighton, it became apparent that, even with the new front rollers that K9 had been fitted with only weeks earlier, the robotic dog was not going to be able to cope with the pebbles covering the beach. In the end, the only solution was to use the hollow dummy K9 and pull it along by means of two nylon lines attached to the front.[36]

Andy Lazell (visual effects designer): 'Footage of the dog going into the sea and exploding was achieved by our having hammered a wooden stake into the beach at low tide. When we came to do the shot at high tide, the dog's nylon line and pyrotechnics cable were led around the submerged stake to be pulled by Stuart [Brisdon] and Perry [Brahan] on the beach. The sequence worked well, but we had to sit in the pub for hours at the conclusion of filming, waiting for the tide to go out so that we could retrieve the wooden stake.'[37]

The final shot of the location sequence was filmed from the roof of the Queen's Hotel, which served as the production base while at Brighton.

Comment

Watching *The Leisure Hive* for the first time was a strange experience for *Doctor Who* fans – new opening titles, a new arrangement of the theme, a new costume for the Doctor and Radiophonic Workshop incidental music all combined to make it, initially, a rather unsettling experience. My overriding memory of the story's original transmission, however, is the lengthy opening pan across the beach huts to the familiar shape of the TARDIS. A highly inventive shot and a radical way for the programme to enter the 1980s.

FULL CIRCLE

(tx 25 October to 15 November 1980)

The Story

Attempting to return Romana to Gallifrey, the TARDIS falls through a Charged Vacuum Emboitment into E-Space and lands on Alzarius. There they meet the Terradonian inhabitants of a crashed Starliner who have been attempting to repair their spaceship for aeons. The community's elders, the Deciders, announce Mistfall, a

Above: **The Doctor surrounded by tropical foliage in** *Full Circle.*

time when humanoid creatures rise from the marshes, and they recall all the Terradonians back into the Starliner for their own protection. The Doctor discovers that the Terradonians are not the descendants of the original crew of the spacecraft, but are evolved Marshmen. The Deciders reveal that the Starliner has been ready to leave for centuries, but no one knows how to pilot it. With the Doctor's help, the spacecraft finally leaves Alzarius.

The Locations

1. Black Park, Fulmer, Buckinghamshire

Shooting Schedule

PART 1

▸▸ **Doctor and Romana exit the TARDIS**
Black Park // 25 July 1980
▸▸ **Outlers try to steal the riverfruit**
Black Park // 23 July 1980
▸▸ **Draith and Dexeter discuss the insect eggs**
Black Park // 23 July 1980
▸▸ **Mistfall begins and Draith chases Adric**
Black Park // 23/24/25 July 1980
▸▸ **Draith is dragged into the marsh**
Black Park // 24 July 1980
▸▸ **Running away, Adric discovers the TARDIS**
Black Park // 24/25 July 1980
▸▸ **Outlers run to the Starliner**
Black Park // 24 July 1980
▸▸ **Doctor and K9 watch mistfall**
Black Park // 25 July 1980
▸▸ **The Marshmen emerge (1/2)**
Black Park // 25 July 1980

PART 2

▸▸ **K9 follows Marshmen, Doctor sees Marshchild**
Black Park // 25 July 1980
▸▸ **K9 is unable to cross the brook**
Black Park // 25 July 1980
▸▸ **Doctor discovers that the TARDIS is missing**
Black Park // 25 July 1980
▸▸ **Doctor sees Starliner, followed by Marshchild**
Black Park // 25 July 1980
▸▸ **K9 tracks Marshmen to cave**
Black Park // 25 July 1980

PART 3

▸▸ **Marshmen move towards the Starliner**
Black Park // 25 July 1980

The Facts

Two days prior to the start of filming at Black Park, a location rehearsal was held at the lake in Black Park to test the effectiveness of the Marshman costumes.

To enhance the landscape and make it look more alien, coloured powder paint was sprinkled onto the foliage, adding red, orange and blue tinges to the vegetation. Various tropical plants were also placed in the foreground of shots, with their containing pots kept below the level of the camera lens. Finally, the powerful location arc lamps were fronted with coloured gels to make the ambient light look more exotic.

As with *The Leisure Hive*, K9 refused to operate over the uneven, soft and muddy ground at Black Park, so the same technique had to be employed as on Brighton beach, namely a nylon line attached to the front of the dog, being pulled by a willing volunteer.

For the scene showing K9's pursuit of the Marshmen being stopped by his arrival at a small brook, assistant K9 operator Steve Cambden, who was operating the controlling nylon line, had to position himself out of shot in the middle of a holly bush which was itself in the middle of a water-filled bog.

Comment

Watching *Full Circle*, you can appreciate how effective good lighting can be to a production. When people see film crews, they sometimes question the need for the huge arc lights that are often employed when filming daylight scenes. In this story, the extra tinted lighting adds tremendously to the early sequences, creating the impression of Alzarius being a warm, sunny and pleasant planet on which to live. That illusion is compounded by the tranquil scenes of the Terradonian community going about their business. And although the Marshmen are largely a return to the *Doctor Who* stalwart of a rubber-suited monster, the photography of them rising from the surface of the mist-covered lake is highly atmospheric.

Left: Tom Baker and Lalla Ward amid the trees at Burnham Beeches for *State of Decay.*

STATE OF DECAY

(tx 22 November to 13 December 1980)

The Story

The TARDIS lands on a seemingly medieval planet where the small group of inhabitants live in fear of the 'Three Who Rule' from a castle-like Tower – King Zargo, Queen Camilla and their councillor, Aukon. The Doctor and Romana join a group of rebels who are anxious to be free of this tyrannical rule. The Doctor discovers that Zargo, Camilla and Aukon are really servants of the Great Vampire, the last of a mighty race slain by the Time Lords. Feeding the Great Vampire with the blood of the villagers, the 'Three Who Rule' hope to raise the creature from its resting place under the Tower – in reality the spaceship that Zargo, Camilla and Aukon used to arrive on the planet in their pre-vampiric form. As the Great Vampire begins to rise, the Doctor uses one of the Tower's original shuttle craft to spear the creature through the heart, killing both it and its vampire servants.

The Locations

1. Burnham Beeches, Burnham, Buckinghamshire

Shooting Schedule

PART 1

▸▸ TARDIS materialises
Burnham Beeches // 30 April – 1 May 1980
▸▸ Doctor and Romana meet peasant

Burnham Beeches // 30 April – 1 May 1980
▸▸ **Doctor and Romana captured by rebels**
Burnham Beeches // 30 April – 1 May 1980
▸▸ **Doctor and Romana escorted by rebels to hideout**
Burnham Beeches // 30 April – 1 May 1980
▸▸ **Doctor and Romana attacked by bats (1/2)**
Burnham Beeches // 30 April 1980

PART 2

▸▸ **Doctor and Romana caught by guards**
Burnham Beeches // 30 April – 1 May 1980

PART 3

▸▸ **Doctor walks through the woods to the TARDIS**
Burnham Beeches // 30 April – 1 May 1980

The Facts

The footage of the bat swarm, as seen at the end of the first episode, was not achieved on location, but realised using a piece of stock footage taken from a 1975 documentary, *Animal Marvels: Frontiers of Life.* However, several static dummy bats, attached by nylon wires to poles, were used on location. Visual effects designer Tony Harding also adapted a toy flapping bird for the close-up of the Doctor being bitten.

Prior to visiting the location on 1 May, producer John Nathan-Turner went to Ealing Studios to watch the first day's film rushes, including the bat attack on the Doctor and Romana. On seeing that Tom Baker had insisted that the Doctor's blood should be blue when bitten, Nathan-Turner requested that the sequence be reshot, but when time ran out and the remount could not be achieved, the sequence was trimmed to remove the close-up shot of the Doctor's hand covered in blue blood.

Although transmitted fourth in the season, *State of Decay* was actually the second story to be made. Baker had still not fully recovered from the illness that had affected the filming of *The Leisure Hive* a month earlier, which left him looking somewhat drawn and made his naturally curly hair appear flat. This necessitated Baker having a perm before the filming at Burnham Beeches, in order to regain his trademark locks.

Comment

After such stories as *Pyramids of Mars*, *The Brain of Morbius* and *Image of the Fendahl*, *State of Decay* is yet another attempt to adopt the style of Hammer horror complete with dark and creepy woodland, and to that end Burnham Beeches provides a suitably foreboding backdrop. For many years, it was wrongly stated that the location used for this story was Black Park in Iver Heath and in many ways it's a pity that it wasn't. Backing onto Pinewood Studios, Black Park was often used as a location for many of the Hammer classics, which would have provided a circular logic.

WARRIORS' GATE

(tx 3 January to 24 January 1981)

The Story

The TARDIS is hijacked by the time-sensitive Tharil, Biroc and taken to a white void where a spaceship holding others of his race is stranded. In the void is a gateway, a passage between universes, which could lead the TARDIS back into N-Space. The Doctor learns that the Tharils were long ago cruel masters to their human slaves, who rebelled by constructing the deadly Gundan robots. Now they are held captive themselves and forced, using their unique powers, to navigate spaceships through time. The Doctor helps to release the Tharils and Romana and K9 choose to stay with Biroc and help liberate the other members of his race.

Photographed Locations

1. Powis Castle, Welshpool, Powys, Wales

Shooting Schedule

PART 3

▸▸ **Doctor follows Biroc behind the mirror**
Powis Castle // 1 September 1980

▸▸ **Doctor and female Tharil walk to banqueting room**
Powis Castle // 1 September 1980
▸▸ **Romana sees that injured Tharil has healed**
Powis Castle // 1 September 1980

PART 4
▸▸ **Romana and Biroc walk beyond the mirror**
Powis Castle // 1 September 1980

The Facts

To represent the world behind the mirrors, director Paul Joyce had wanted to shoot location sequences at Powis Castle near Welshpool, but when it became evident that the budget wouldn't stretch to sending a film unit to Wales, Joyce had to change his plans. What the budget *would* allow for was a stills photographer to be sent to the castle to take pictures of the location. These black and white photographs were then used as backgrounds onto which the colour images of the characters would be matted.

Comment

It may not have been Paul Joyce's first option, but the use of the black and white photographs seems a fittingly wierd way to represent what lay beyond the bounds of the gateway. A strange use of a location – but then it's a strange story.

LOGOPOLIS

(tx 28 February to 21 March 1981)

The Story

In an effort to repair the TARDIS' chameleon circuit, the Doctor plans to travel to Logopolis and use the skills of the mathematicians there to accomplish the work. The Doctor is haunted by a strange white figure that warns him of impending disaster. Arriving on Logopolis, the Doctor meets the Monitor, who reveals that the universe long ago passed the point of heat death. Using mathematics, the Logopolitans have opened up Charged Vacuum Emboitments, holes into an alternative universe, in order to drain away the excessive heat. The Master arrives on the planet and, by killing several Logopolitans, he accidentally disrupts the calculations, causing the CVEs to close. Realising the destruction of the universe is imminent, the Doctor and the Master join forces and travel to the Pharos radio telescope project on Earth in order to transmit a copy of the Logopolitan program which will reopen the CVEs. The Master seizes the opportunity to blackmail the universe but, in defeating his enemy's plans, the Doctor falls from the telescope gantry and is forced to regenerate.

The Locations

1. 43 Ursula Street, Battersea, London, SW11
2. Albert Bridge, Kensington and Chelsea, London, SW3
3. Cadogan Pier, Chelsea Embankment, London, SW3
4. BBC Receiving Station, Crowsley Park, Blounts Court Road, Sonning Common, Berkshire
5. Lay-By, Amersham Road (A413), Denham, Buckinghamshire

Shooting Schedule

PART 1

▸▸ Policeman pulled into police box
Amersham Road // 22 December 1980
▸▸ Tegan and Aunt Vanessa set off for airport
43 Ursula Street // 16 December 1980
▸▸ Car pulls into lay-by
Amersham Road // 22 December 1980
▸▸ Tegan examines flat tyre
Amersham Road // 22 December 1980
▸▸ Tegan prepares to change tyre
Amersham Road // 22 December 1980
▸▸ Doctor's TARDIS lands at lay-by
Amersham Road // 22 December 1980
▸▸ Scanner shot – Car in lay-by
Amersham Road // 22 December 1980
▸▸ TARDIS rematerialises around police box
Amersham Road // 22 December 1980
▸▸ Watcher observes Tegan and Aunt Vanessa
Amersham Road // 22 December 1980
▸▸ Tegan tries to change tyre
Amersham Road // 22 December 1980
▸▸ Doctor sees the Watcher
Amersham Road // 22 December 1980
▸▸ Tegan enters TARDIS
Amersham Road // 22 December 1980
▸▸ Aunt Vanessa checks the police box
Amersham Road // 22 December 1980
▸▸ Aunt Vanessa is attacked
Amersham Road // 22 December 1980
▸▸ Doctor meets police
Amersham Road // 22 December 1980
▸▸ Doctor tells police about the Master and escapes (1/2)
Amersham Road // 22 December 1980

PART 2

▸▸ Detective Inspector knocks on TARDIS door
Amersham Road // 22 December 1980
▸▸ Detective Inspector asks for key
Amersham Road // 22 December 1980
▸▸ Detective Inspector prepares to open police box
Amersham Road // 22 December 1980
▸▸ Detective Inspector opens police box

Amersham Road // 22 December 1980
▸▸ TARDIS lands on pier
Cadogan Pier // 16 December 1980
▸▸ Doctor sees the Watcher on bridge
Cadogan Pier // 16 December 1980
▸▸ Doctor goes to see the Watcher
Cadogan Pier // 16 December 1980
▸▸ Doctor talks to the Watcher
Albert Bridge // 16 December 1980
▸▸ TARDIS dematerialises
Cadogan Pier // 16 December 1980

PART 4

▸▸ Dawn breaks at Pharos Project
Crowsley Park // 18 December 1980
▸▸ Adric and Nyssa leave the TARDIS
Crowsley Park // 18 December 1980
▸▸ Adric and Nyssa break cover
Crowsley Park // 18 December 1980
▸▸ Doctor sees Watcher in the TARDIS
Crowsley Park // 18 December 1980
▸▸ Crossing over to the radio telescope
Crowsley Park // 18 December 1980
▸▸ Doctor climbs the telescope ladder
Crowsley Park // 18 December 1980
▸▸ Guards run across grounds
Crowsley Park // 18 December 1980
▸▸ Guards begin to climb telescope
Crowsley Park // 18 December 1980
▸▸ Guards climb the telescope
Crowsley Park // 18 December 1980
▸▸ Adric, Tegan and Nyssa run to telescope
Crowsley Park // 18 December 1980

The Facts

The original intention had been to film the location material for *Logopolis* over a four-day period from 16-19 December 1980, with the scenes shot at the Amersham Road lay-by being filmed on the 17th and 19th.

Problems arose, however, when a one-day strike was called on Sunday 23 November 1980, which had the effect of cancelling the final studio day planned for the preceding story, *The Keeper of Traken*. When the studio schedules were examined to see when the recording could be remounted, the only available date was Wednesday 17 December, the second planned date for location filming on *Logopolis*. As a result, the filming on the lay-by had to be postponed (from both 17 and 19 December), as both Tom Baker and Matthew Waterhouse (Adric) were required in studio to finish the remaining scenes from *Traken*. The lay-by scenes were all rescheduled and filmed on Monday 22 December.

Unused Locations

Jodrell Bank – As the latter half of the story centred around events at the Pharos Project radio telescope, one of the locations originally scouted by director Peter Grimwade and production assistant Margot Hayhoe was the huge radio telescope at Jodrell Bank in Cheshire.

Margot Hayhoe: 'We had a tour around the site to see whether we could use it as a location, because this big telescope dish was a vital part of the story. But the powers-that-be at Jodrell weren't keen for us to shoot there and it would have been too far for us to go anyway.'

In the end, the decision was taken to use the BBC's own Receiving Station at Crowsley Park, near Henley-on-Thames, which would provide the masts and steel ladders needed for the close-ups. As with *Terror of the Autons*, a model of the telescope dish was taken on location and carefully lined up with the background action to produce the effect of people running next to a real structure.

Barnet By-Pass – Knowing that one of the last surviving police boxes to be found in the south was situated in a lay-by on the A6 near South Mimms, it had been intended to use the location and the real police box to record all the scenes surrounding Aunt Vanessa's car.

Margot Hayhoe: 'We thought we might be able to go there, but of course I went for a recce and found that it had been demolished. So we went off to the A413, the dual carriageway that goes off up to Chalfont St Peter. There is a wonderful lay-by there, which meant that the unit could park and everything could be done safely. I have fond memories of thinking, "What a wonderful location, I could use this for something else." I went back a few years later to show somebody else and of course they'd built the M25 across it, so it was no longer a beautiful quiet lay-by, it had the great legs of an M25 support bridge going across it. A great shame.'

Comment

The location work in *Logopolis* is reasonably executed but, on the whole, not terribly exciting. However, to give Peter Grimwade credit, the various scenes with the Watcher are certainly eerie. As a distant, static figure, the Watcher's presence (especially when accompanied by Paddy Kingsland's excellent score) is genuinely unsettling, particularly during the unheard discussion on Albert Bridge between the figure and a clearly downcast Doctor. It's also worthy of note that during the scenes on Cadogan Pier, Chelsea Power Station (with its twin chimneys) can clearly be seen further up the river – the same building which is seen as derelict and destroyed in the 1966 film *Daleks – Invasion Earth 2150 AD*. ■

FOOTNOTES

1. This scene was originally recorded for inclusion in Part 2, but was pulled back into Part 1 during editing.
2. See *Spearhead from Space* for further details on the bunker.
3. *The Frame* #2, p.7
4. *Classic Who – The Hinchcliffe Years*, Adrian Rigelsford, p.39
5. *In-Vision* #6, p.6
6. The film diary for *Revenge of the Cybermen* differentiates the two Vogan factions seen in the story by using the terms 'Hawks' and 'Doves'. The 'Hawks' refer to those Vogans under the control of Vorus, whilst the 'Doves' are the longer haired faction ruled over by the elderly Tyrum.
7. Now Sandgate Park.
8. *Doctor Who Appreciation Society Yearbook 1978-79*, page 38
9. *West Sussex County Times* – 28 March 1975 and *Bognor Regis Post* – 22 March 1975
10. *Evening Argus* – 18 March 1975 and *Bognor Regis Observer*

– 21 March 1975
11. The camera script and promotional material issued at the time of broadcast all spell Sutekh's race as 'Osirian'. However, on a couple of occasions in the camera script, this was mis-typed 'Osiran' and it was this pronunciation which the cast adopted.
12. Not listed in film schedule.
13. *In-Vision* #9, p.3
14. *In-Vision* #14, p.6
15. *Newbury Weekly News*, 8 May 1975, p.1 – 'Look Who's Here!'
16. *In-Vision* #9, p.6; *Doctor Who Magazine* #127, p.10
17. *Doctor Who Magazine* #152, p.14
18. *The Frame* #23/24, p.12
19. *TARDIS* Vol.5 No.3/4, p.7/8
20. *The Doctor's Effects*, Steve Cambden, p.115
21. *Doctor Who Magazine* #152, p.15
22. *In-Vision* #26, p.11 – Although there's no information

stating when the incident with the generator occurred, it would seem likely that it was on the night of Wednesday 3 August on which only three of the eight planned scenes were shot.
23. Which explains why Moss uneasily pulls his shirt collar when the Doctor begins to ask about the ghosts of Fetchborough.
24. The other deep shelters were constructed at Belsize Park, Goodge Street, Stockwell, Clapham North, Clapham Common and Clapham South (all on the Northern Line) and Chancery Lane on the Central Line. Two others were started at Oval and St.Paul's but construction were halted before completion.
25. *Gallifrey* #10, p.9
26. *Gallifrey* #10, p.9
27. *Doctor Who Magazine* #246, p.37-8
28. This is the only known official title of Weir's submission which appears on the commissioning sheets. There is no documented evidence to support the often-quoted title for this adventure, *The Killer Cats of Geng Sengh* (spellings vary).
29. The unit base for *The Pirate Planet* was the White Hart Hotel in Monmouth, the same hotel that Roberts had used as his base for *Survivors*.
30. *Doctor Who Special Effects*, Mat Irvine, p.42/43
31. *Web Planet* #3
32. *Doctor Who Magazine Winter Special*, 1983, p.39/40
33. *Doctor Who Magazine* #233, 1995, p.9/10
34. *Doctor Who Magazine* #233, 1995, p.10
35. *Doctor Who Magazine*, #224, 1995, p.40
36. One of which can be clearly seen just in front of Lalla Ward's feet in the transmitted footage.
37. *The Doctor's Effects*, Steve Cambden, p.148

PART FIVE

'Is that supposed to be Heathrow... ?'
Tegan – *The Visitation*

PETER DAVISON

THE FIFTH DOCTOR

CASTROVALVA
(tx 4 January to 12 January 1982)

The Story

The Doctor's young travelling companion Adric helps him back to the TARDIS after his regeneration. On the way, however, Adric is captured by the Master, who uses a projection of the boy to set a trap. This sends the TARDIS back to Event One, the creation of the universe. After the destabilised Doctor manages to avoid destruction, his new companions, air-stewardess Tegan and the young Traken girl Nyssa, help to get him to the hillside capital, Castrovalva, a stable environment where he can recuperate. The Doctor discovers that Castrovalva is really an elaborate space/time trap set by the Master and created using Adric's advanced mathematical skills. As the capitol begins to fold in on itself, the Doctor and his companions break free, but the Master is trapped within Castrovalva as it disappears forever.

The Locations

1. Crowborough Wireless Telegraph Station, Duddleswell, East Sussex
2. Buckhurst Park, Withyham, Hartfield, East Sussex
3. Harrison's Rocks, Birchden Wood, Groombridge, Tunbridge Wells, East Sussex.

Shooting Schedule

PART 1

▸ Tegan and Nyssa get Doctor to the TARDIS
   Crowborough WT Station // 1 September 1981
▸ Master's TARDIS materialises
   Crowborough WT Station // 1 September 1981
▸ Master's TARDIS dematerialises leaving dazed Adric
   Crowborough WT Station // 1 September 1981
▸ The two TARDIS' dematerialise
   Crowborough WT Station // 1 September 1981

PART 2

▸ Tegan climbs out of the TARDIS
   Buckhurst Park // 2 September 1981
▸ Tegan climbs a tree and sees something
   Buckhurst Park // 2 September 1981
▸ Tegan and Nyssa carry Doctor as far as the stream
   Buckhurst Park // 2 September 1981
▸ Seeing Castrovalva, they camouflage the zero cabinet
   Buckhurst Park // 3 September 1981
▸ Tegan and Nyssa reach the rocks
   Harrison's Rocks // 4 September 1981
▸ Warriors talk and Doctor opens zero cabinet
   Buckhurst Park // 3 September 1981
▸ Tegan and Nyssa climb the rocks but the

doing anything at all dangerous, but I can remember Fiona Cumming [the director], who also doesn't like heights, being very brave and saying "Look Janet, I can do it" and taking a walk across rather a high rock. I think that's what persuaded Janet to do it in the end.'

Having found the main location requirement, it was necessary that the other exterior filming sites be found in the same area. For this reason, it was never a practical possibility to return to the BBC Receiving Station at Sonning Common (which had been used to represent the Pharos Project in *Logopolis*) in order to shoot the opening scenes.

A suitable replacement was found at the wireless telegraphy station at Duddleswell, which provided a similar landscape to the BBC's own property seen in Tom Baker's final story. To complete the illusion, the model of the radio telescope dish built for *Logopolis* was transported to Duddleswell and used as a background model, establishing that it was the same fictional location.

Looking for a scenic piece of woodland to film the bulk of the location material, the production team came across the estate of the Earl and Countess de la Warr at Buckhurst Park, Withyham. On the first day at the location, John Nathan-Turner mistakenly greeted someone he thought was the gardener only to discover that it was Earl de la Warr himself. His Lordship agreed to waive any fee for the use of his land, providing he could have a photograph of himself taken with the TARDIS. He was also well remembered by the production team because of the enormous gin and tonics he would treat them to.

Following the filming at Duddleswell, the cast and crew travelled to their production hotel, the Wellington at Mount Ephraim, Tunbridge Wells. During the course of the evening, Matthew Waterhouse (who played Adric) became rather drunk and awoke the next morning feeling unwell. Waterhouse was only required for the single scene of the Doctor's party jogging back to the TARDIS at the end of Part 4 and so wasn't required until later in the morning. By the time he arrived at Buckhurst Park, he still hadn't recovered.

Matthew Waterhouse: 'I was green and, before we began to shoot the scene, Peter looked at me and said, "Are you all right?" I said I was, so we were jogging along and suddenly I got the urge to throw up. So I ran behind this tree and threw up, but what I didn't know was that the man on the boom mic panned it to right above me, so even though it isn't on film, my throwing up is immortalised in sound. But I got my revenge because it turned out that I threw up over the sound box which was hidden behind the tree!'[1]

Above: Peter Davison and an unwell Matthew Waterhouse at the estate of Earl de la Warr in *Castrovalva*.

path runs out
Harrison's Rocks // 4 September 1981
▸▸ **They return to find Doctor gone and blood on ground (2/3)**
Buckhurst Park // 3 September 1981

PART 3

▸▸ **Tegan and Nyssa run and hide from the warriors**
Buckhurst Park // 3 September 1981
▸▸ **Doctor climbs the rocks and hears Nyssa call**
Harrison's Rocks // 4 September 1981
▸▸ **Warriors pass Tegan and Nyssa with zero cabinet**
Harrison's Rocks // 4 September 1981
▸▸ **Tegan and Nyssa begin to climb rocks**
Harrison's Rocks // 4 September 1981
▸▸ **Tegan and Nyssa continue climbing**
Harrison's Rocks // 4 September 1981
▸▸ **They stop for a rest and a rope ladder appears**
Harrison's Rocks // 4 September 1981

PART 4

▸▸ **Doctor's party sees that Castrovalva has vanished**
Buckhurst Park // 3 September 1981
▸▸ **Doctor's party arrive back at the TARDIS**
Buckhurst Park // 2 September 1981

The Facts

The primary location requirement for *Castrovalva* was a set of suitable rocks to represent the base of the citadel, which would be reasonably easy for the cast to climb. The ideal location was found at Harrison's Rocks, a popular sandstone climbing venue which had previously been used in the 1968 story *The Mind Robber*.

Margot Hayhoe (production manager): 'Janet Fielding [who played Tegan] was terrified of heights and had to be persuaded to climb the rocks. I'm not very good at

Comment

As a place of rest and relaxation, locations were required for *Castrovalva* that would evoke a sense of peace, calm and tranquillity – and director Fiona Cumming certainly hit the jackpot with the use of Buckhurst Park and Groombridge. Even the rocks on which the citadel is built are not sharp and harsh, but round and soft-looking, giving the place a very non-threatening feel. Also noteworthy is the extremely effective shot filmed at Duddleswell that incorporates the Pharos radio telescope model used in *Logopolis*. If you didn't know it was a visual effect, you'd swear it was real.

THE VISITATION

(tx 15 February to 23 February 1982)

The Story

The TARDIS lands on the outskirts of London in 1666. After meeting with an itinerant thespian, Richard Mace, and finding several futuristic artefacts, the Doctor becomes suspicious that a recently reported 'shooting star' is actually an alien vessel. Visiting the now deserted house of the local Squire, the Doctor's suspicions are proved correct when he meets one of three fugitive Terileptils. The creatures plan to wipe out humankind by means of rats carrying a virulent strain of the great plague. The Terileptils are traced to central London, where they are ultimately destroyed when a conflagration breaks out in their hideout in Pudding Lane, starting the Great Fire.

The Locations

1. Black Park, Fulmer, Buckinghamshire
2. Tithe Barn, Hurley High Street, Hurley, Berkshire

Shooting Schedule

PART 1

▸▸ **Open escape pod at dusk**
Black Park – 2A // 5 May 1981
▸▸ **Establishing shot – Manor gates**
Tithe Barn // 8 May 1981
▸▸ **Tegan and Doctor talk outside TARDIS**
Black Park – 4A // 7 May 1981
▸▸ **Villagers attack the Doctor's party**
Black Park – 1A/1B + 3A or 3B // 6 May 1981
▸▸ **Doctor's party meet Richard Mace**
Black Park – 2B // 5 May 1981
▸▸ **Doctor arrives and enters the Squire's house**
Tithe Barn // 8 May 1981
▸▸ **Nyssa lets Tegan, Adric and Mace into the house**
Tithe Barn // 8 May 1981

PART 2

▸▸ **Monitor – Doctor, Nyssa and Mace leaving house**
Tithe Barn // 8 May 1981
▸▸ **Mace says his farewells to Doctor and Nyssa**

Left: Peter Davison at Tithe Barn on 8 May 1981 for *The Visitation.*

Tithe Barn // 8 May 1981
▸▸ **Villager's bracelets begin to activate**
Black Park – 1A/3A // 6 May 1981
▸▸ **Doctor, Nyssa and Mace enter the pod**
Black Park – 2A // 5 May 1981
▸▸ **Controlled villagers approach pod**
Black Park – 2A // 5 May 1981
▸▸ **Mace tries to scare villagers with his pistols**
Black Park – 2A // 5 May 1981
▸▸ **Doctor runs back into pod**
Black Park – 2A // 5 May 1981
▸▸ **Doctor and Mace go to find the Miller**
Black Park – 3A // 6 May 1981

PART 3

▸▸ **Adric runs from the manor house**
Tithe Barn // 8 May 1981
▸▸ **Villagers approach the TARDIS**
Black Park – 4A // 7 May 1981
▸▸ **Adric is captured as he leaves the TARDIS**
Black Park – 4A // 7 May 1981
▸▸ **Adric is led through the woods**
Black Park – 3A // 7 May 1981
▸▸ **Mace and Tegan load the miller's cart**
Tithe Barn // 8 May 1981

PART 4

▸▸ **Terileptil leader instructs the android**
Tithe Barn // 8 May 1981

Above: Sarah Sutton, Peter Davison and Janet Fielding in Buckhurst Park during the filming of *Black Orchid*.

▸▸ Adric is led through the woods
Black Park – 1C // 6 May 1981
▸▸ Terileptil leader leaves the manor house
Tithe Barn // 8 May 1981
▸▸ Adric follows the android
Black Park – 3B // 6 May 1981
▸▸ Adric walks to the TARDIS
Black Park – 4A // 7 May 1981
▸▸ Android gains entry to the TARDIS
Black Park – 4A // 7 May 1981
▸▸ Terileptil leader drives along London street
Tithe Barn // 8 May 1981

The Facts

The main body of the escape pod was realised by the use of a glass matte painting supplementing a piece of scenery erected in Black Park, representing the entry ramp and the door rim.

Located on the flight path to Heathrow Airport, filming at Black Park was continually interrupted by the noise of aeroplanes flying overhead, causing the production to fall seriously behind schedule. Fortunately, towards the end of the filming period, a lightning strike by the Heathrow air-traffic controllers severely curtailed flights in and out of the airport, allowing the woodland filming to be completed within the three days allocated.

Tithe Barn had been chosen as the location for Squire John's manor house as it was 'a perfect example of 17th century architecture' set at the end of a cul-de-sac. During the filming, shots had to carefully framed to avoid any modern artefacts, such as the television aerial on the roof and the bomb shelter that was being constructed at the rear of the house. As with Black Park, the close proximity to Heathrow resulted in a number of takes being ruined by aircraft noise – and, on one occasion, by a neighbour mowing his lawn.

Comment

Trying to recreate the 17th century was never going to be an easy task, but Peter Moffatt achieved it extremely well in *The Visitation*. Having located a house of the proper period, it's a shame that it isn't seen more.

BLACK ORCHID

(tx 1 March to 2 March 1982)

The Story

Landing at Cranleigh Halt railway station in 1925, the Doctor is mistaken for a friend of Lord Cranleigh, who is due to be playing in a cricket match being held at Dalton Hall. Much to Cranleigh's delight, the Doctor wins the match and is invited to attend the Hall's fancy dress ball. When a murder is discovered and Cranleigh's fiancée, Ann, is attacked, the Doctor is blamed. But the perpetrator is revealed as Cranleigh's now deranged older brother, George – an explorer, hideously disfigured at the hands of an Amazonian tribe during his search for the black orchid. After starting a fire and climbing onto the roof of the Hall, George accidentally falls to his death.

The Locations

1. Buckinghamshire Railway Centre, Quainton, Buckinghamshire
2. Quainton Road, Quainton, Buckinghamshire
3. 99 Quainton Road, Quainton, Buckinghamshire
4. Buckhurst Park, Withyham, Hartfield, East Sussex

Shooting Schedule

PART 1

▸▸ TARDIS materialises on platform of Cranleigh Halt
Quainton Road Railway Station // 5 October 1981
▸▸ Scanner – Shot of station
Quainton Road Railway Station // 5 October 1981
▸▸ Doctor's party met by Tanner with Rolls Royce
Quainton Road Railway Station // 5 October 1981
▸▸ Conversation in Rolls Royce (cut)
Buckhurst Park // 9 October 1981
▸▸ Policeman discovers the TARDIS on the platform (cut)
Quainton Road Railway Station // 5 October 1981
▸▸ Doctor plays cricket at Dalton Hall
Buckhurst Park // 9 October 1981
▸▸ Dancing on the terrace
Buckhurst Park // 7 October 1981
▸▸ Nyssa and Ann try to confuse the guests
Buckhurst Park // 7 October 1981
▸▸ Latoni tells Lady Cranleigh of the Unknown's escape
Buckhurst Park // 7 October 1981

Left: **Jim Morris is filmed on the platform of Quainton Road railway station for the opening scenes of** *Black Orchid.*

▶▶ Dancing the Charleston
Buckhurst Park // 7 October 1981

▶▶ Unknown begins to dance with Ann
Buckhurst Park // 7 October 1981

▶▶ Unknown steers Ann into the house
Buckhurst Park // 7 October 1981

PART 2

▶▶ Tegan has a drink with Sir Robert
Buckhurst Park // 8 October 1981

▶▶ Adric eats as Cranleigh and Sir Robert leave
Buckhurst Park // 8 October 1981

▶▶ Adric, Tegan and Nyssa voice disbelief about Doctor
Buckhurst Park // 8 October 1981

▶▶ Doctor asks Police to stop at railway station
Quainton Road // 5 October 1981

▶▶ The TARDIS has gone from the station
Quainton Road Railway Station // 5 October 1981

▶▶ TARDIS is discovered at Police Station
99 Quainton Road // 5 October 1981

▶▶ Sir Robert and Sgt Markham enter TARDIS
99 Quainton Road // 5 October 1981

▶▶ TARDIS materialises outside Dalton Hall
Buckhurst Park // 6 October 1981

▶▶ Everyone enters the house
Buckhurst Park // 6 October 1981

▶▶ George takes Nyssa onto the roof
Buckhurst Park // 6 October 1981

▶▶ Nyssa is rescued and George falls from the roof
Buckhurst Park // 6 October 1981

▶▶ Lady Cranleigh gives the Doctor a copy of Black Orchid
Buckhurst Park // 8 October 1981

The Facts

Although working steam trains were kept at the Buckinghamshire Railway Centre, no actual locomotive was used for the scene of the train departing from Cranleigh Halt. Instead, the illusion was created with the use of a smoke gun and several seconds of stock footage from the BBC production, *God's Wonderful Railway*.

99 Quainton Road, the building used to represent the police station, was mostly derelict at the time of shooting and production staff were warned not to enter the premises.

For the second time in the 19th season, Buckhurst Park played host to the *Doctor Who* cameras, although on this occasion use would be made of the house and surrounding grounds as opposed to the woodlands used for *Castrovalva*. At the wish of the owner, Lord de la Warr, the cast and crew were instructed that no photography should be conducted in the grounds with the exception of continuity and publicity photographs.

Throughout the production, George Cranleigh was played by stuntman Gareth Milne, who would perform the character's fatal fall from the roof at the end of the story. Although every precaution had been taken to make the area safe, the production team were warned not to venture onto the roof unless specifically authorised to do so. Even so, the stunt did not go exactly as planned.

John Nathan-Turner (producer): 'Gareth Milne set out the usual supply of stunt mattresses and cardboard boxes at his estimated point of impact. Now, normally with a stunt everyone gathers around. Painters who have been sought for hours suddenly materialise, as everyone takes their place to admire the stuntman's work. There is nothing sinister about this; it's just that everyone watches and usually applauds. On this occasion the cameras were rolling, Ron [Jones] called action and Gareth took the fall… but part of his legs missed the boxes and he hit the ground with an almighty noise. No one applauded. People ran to see Gareth, who fortunately was not seriously injured, but the noise on the soundtrack is actually the noise made by part of his body landing on the cement. Within minutes he was back shinning up the drainpipe for another sequence.'[2]

Unused Locations

With the vast majority of location work surrounding the events within the grounds of Dalton Hall, a number of different properties were scouted during September 1981 in an effort to discover one that would provide all that the script required. Among the buildings looked at were:

Nether Winchendon House, Aylesbury, Bucks[3]
Taplow House Hotel, Berry Hill, Taplow, Berks
Berkshire College of Agriculture, Hall Place, Burchetts Green, Maidenhead, Berks
Pennyhill Park Hotel, London Road, Bagshot, Surrey
Missenden Abbey, Great Missenden, Bucks
New Lodge, Drift Road, Windsor, Berks

Comment

Set in June but filmed in a cold, wet and windy October, *Black Orchid* manages to convey the spirit of a 1925 summer's day with ease, no doubt helped by the fact that director Ron Jones elected to shoot the location footage using 16mm film rather than OB cameras, which would have given a colder, harsher feel to the footage. Best of all is the opening half of the first episode, which has a wonderfully relaxed pace, showing the Doctor and his companions simply enjoying themselves in the English countryside.

EARTHSHOCK

(tx 8 March to 16 March 1982)

The Story

Following the disappearance of a group of geologists and palaeontologists from an underground cave system, Professor Kyle calls upon the military to help find them. When the Doctor and his friends are discovered in the caves, they are immediately blamed for the dis-

appearances but are suddenly attacked by two guard androids controlled by the Cybermen, who are planning to destroy a peace conference that threatens their existence. The Doctor deactivates their bomb and follows its activation signal to an approaching space freighter, on board which a huge army of Cybermen are concealed. The Cybermen change their plan and decide to crash the freighter directly onto Earth. Left alone on the ship, Adric manages to send the freighter back in time 65 million years where it explodes, killing Adric and causing the destruction of the dinosaurs.

The Locations

1. Springwell Lock Quarry, Springwell Lane, Rickmansworth, Hertfordshire.

Shooting Schedule

PART 1

▸▸ **Walters begins to scan the cavern**
   Springwell Lock Quarry // 29 October 1981
▸▸ **Troopers prepare to enter cavern**
   Springwell Lock Quarry // 29 October 1981
▸▸ **Snyder sees the scanner flare**
   Springwell Lock Quarry // 29 October 1981
▸▸ **Walters on radio to Scott**
   Springwell Lock Quarry // 29 October 1981
▸▸ **Walters and Snyder spot three new traces**
   Springwell Lock Quarry // 29 October 1981
▸▸ **Walters on radio to Scott**
   Springwell Lock Quarry // 29 October 1981
▸▸ **Walters relates the co-ordinates**
   Springwell Lock Quarry // 29 October 1981
▸▸ **Snyder decides to enter cavern**
   Springwell Lock Quarry // 29 October 1981
▸▸ **Walters on radio to Snyder/Scott/Mitchell**
   Springwell Lock Quarry // 29 October 1981

The Facts

Although the only location sequences required for *Earthshock* were those filmed in the quarry at Springwell Lock, it was deemed necessary to open the first episode with a brief three-second piece of stock footage showing a sandy quarry face. The location had previously been used in December 1972 to represent Omega's anti-matter world in *The Three Doctors*.

Comment

The location filming for *Earthshock* is short and not terribly exciting, but certainly does its scene-setting job. In fact, it's one of those cases where the location work is actually rather unnecessary, as the scenes could have easily been rewritten for the studio.

TIME-FLIGHT

(tx 22 March to 30 March 1982)

The Story

The Doctor manages to return Tegan to Heathrow Airport just as a Concorde vanishes into thin air. The Doctor theorises that the aeroplane has flown through a time warp, and a second Concorde, with the TARDIS aboard, follows on the same flight path. It too disappears 140 million years back in time. The Doctor discovers that the Master is attempting to control the gestalt race, the Xeraphin, which has become divided into good and evil due to the Time Lord's meddling. The Doctor defeats the Master, imprisons him on the Xeraphin home world and returns one of the Concordes, with all the passengers and crew, back to Heathrow. In his rush to leave the airport, the Doctor accidentally leaves Tegan behind…

The Locations

1. Balcony, Terminal 1, Heathrow Airport, Hounslow, Middlesex
2. Roof Car Park, Terminal 3, Heathrow Airport, Hounslow, Middlesex
3. Concorde, BA Maintenance Area (Concorde Hangar), Heathrow Airport, Hounslow, Middlesex

Shooting Schedule

PART 1

▸▸ TARDIS materialises in Terminal 1
   Heathrow Terminal 1 // 6 January 1982
▸▸ Scanner – view of concourse
   Heathrow Terminal 1 // 6 January 1982
▸▸ Policeman sees TARDIS and radios in
   Heathrow Terminal 1 // 6 January 1982
▸▸ Police come to meet Doctor's party
   Heathrow Terminal 1 // 6 January 1982
▸▸ Doctor tells Andrews to contact UNIT
   Heathrow Terminal 1 // 6 January 1982
▸▸ Stapley and Bilton walk to Concorde
   BA Maintenance Area // 11 January 1982
▸▸ Doctor's party board Concorde
   BA Maintenance Area // 11 January 1982
▸▸ Everyone leaves the Concorde at 'Heathrow'
   BA Maintenance Area // 11 January 1982
▸▸ M4 motorway
   Car Park – Terminal 3 // 7 January 1982

PART 4

▸▸ TARDIS materialises on car park
   Car Park – Terminal 3 // 7 January 1982
▸▸ Police arrive as Master's TARDIS materialises

Car Park – Terminal 3 // 7 January 1982
▸▸ **Master's TARDIS is repelled**
Car Park – Terminal 3 // 7 January 1982
▸▸ **Tegan wanders through Terminal 1**
Heathrow Terminal 1 // 6 January 1982
▸▸ **Doctor says goodbye and leaves without Tegan**
Car Park – Terminal 3 // 7 January 1982

▸▸ **Ep.1/4 – All Concorde interior scenes:**
Flight Deck and Cabin
BA Maintenance Area // 11 January 1982

The Facts

Time-Flight had originally been submitted to the production office by Peter Grimwade as an idea for a Fourth Doctor story and script editor Christopher Bidmead was sufficiently intrigued by it to ask Grimwade to redevelop it for Peter Davison's new portrayal.

Central to getting the story produced was the co-operation of the British Airports Authority and also British Airways, the owner and operator of the Concorde aircraft running from Heathrow. Producer John Nathan-Turner met with representatives from both the BAA and BA in the Bridge Lounge of Television Centre to try and secure their agreement, and while the BAA seemed reasonable happy with the arrangements, British Airways were initially less so.

John Nathan-Turner: 'The lunch and meeting went reasonably well and both sets of executives requested approval of the script. I explained that the BBC were not prepared to part with editorial control, but that we would listen to any objections they might have. One of them was a bit off about this, so I simply whispered to my associate, just loud enough to be overheard, "What time are we seeing the Air France people?" Within a couple of days we had been granted full use of a British Airways Concorde on the ground, unlimited stock footage, as many Concorde models as we wanted and all for no charge.'[4]

As such, *Time-Flight* marked another first for *Doctor Who*, as it was the first time that permission had been granted for a television drama to be filmed within the airport.

The first two days of filming around Terminals 1 and 3 progressed without any major problems. The third day, Friday 8 January, had been allocated as the day when the production team would be allowed to film in and around Concorde. However, overnight, snow began to fall very heavily. Not only that, but one of British Airways' other Concordes began to experience technical problems, which necessitated the cancellation of Friday's filming as the aircraft put aside for the BBC had to be pressed into service instead.

Arrangements were made for a remount on Monday 11 January by which time the snow showers had stopped.

John Nathan-Turner: 'On the day we filmed, there was just a bit of snow on the ground, but on the day we *were* to have filmed there were raging blizzards, which would have wrecked it for us.'[5]

Comment

Strangely enough, considering the uniqueness of being allowed to film a drama at Heathrow as well as in and around Concorde, the whole thing falls rather flat. The use of Concorde was always there in Grimwade's original storyline, and yet it almost feels that the availability of the plane was the sole reason for doing the story, almost as if someone at British Airways had contacted the BBC and said, 'Hey, we've got a Concorde going spare for a day. Is there anything you can do with it?'

ARC OF INFINITY

(tx 3 January to 12 January 1983)

The Story

On Gallifrey, a member of the High Council illegally transmits the Doctor's bio-data to a mysterious robed figure, who then proceeds to use the information to try and physically bond himself to the Time Lord, thus giving the being access to the universe of matter. Alarmed by what has happened, the Time Lords recall the Doctor to Gallifrey, believing that executing him is the only way the creature can be stopped from fully crossing over from the anti-matter universe. Meanwhile, in Amsterdam, Tegan investigates the disappearance of her cousin, Colin Frazer, but is captured by the alien. The traitor is exposed as Counsellor Hedin, an old friend of the Doctor's, who reveals that the alien is really Omega. Entering the Matrix, the Doctor discovers that Omega has materialised in Amsterdam. Arriving in the city, the Doctor tracks down Omega's TARDIS and discovers that Omega's body has turned into a replica of himself. Fleeing from the Doctor, Omega's body begins to break down due to the incomplete bonding and when he tries to destroy everything in a huge anti-matter explosion, the Doctor has no alternative but to obliterate the Time Lord with a matter converter gun.

The Locations

1. Muntplein, Amsterdam, Netherlands
   • Flower Market
2. Frankendael House, 72 Middenweg, Amsterdam, Netherlands
3. Lijnbaansgracht, Amsterdam, Netherlands
   • Police Station (No.219)

4. Nieuwezijds Voorburgwal, Amsterdam, Netherlands
   • Bob's Youth Hostel (No.92)
5. Schiphol Airport, Amsterdam, Netherlands
6. Leidseplein, Amsterdam, Netherlands
   • Hoopman Bodega Café (No.4)
   • Telephone Boxes
7. Vondelpark Youth Hostel, 5 Zandpad, Amsterdam, Netherlands
8. Herenstraat, Amsterdam, Netherlands
9. Blauwburgwal, Amsterdam, Netherlands
10. Singel, Amsterdam, Netherlands
11. Amstelveld (Junction with Reguliersgracht), Amsterdam, Netherlands
12. Prinsengracht, Amsterdam, Netherlands
    • Junction with Reguliersgracht
    • Flower Stall, Junction with Utrechtestraat
13. Dam Square, Amsterdam, Netherlands
14. Damrak, Amsterdam, Netherlands
15. Sint Nicolaasstraat, Amsterdam, Netherlands
16. Amstel, Amsterdam, Netherlands
    • Amstel Sluize (Amstel Lock)
    • Junction with Kaizersgracht
    • Sarphati Kade (Skinny Bridge Approach)
17. Stationsplein (Central Station), Amsterdam, Netherlands

Shooting Schedule

PART 1

▶▶ **Colin telephones Tegan watched by Robin**
Muntplien // 3 May 1982
▶▶ **Robin shows Colin where they are staying for the night**
Frankendael House // 5 May 1982
▶▶ **Robin and Colin walk behind fountain**
Frankendael House // 5 May 1982
▶▶ **A shocked Robin by Frankendael steps**
Frankendael House // 5 May 1982
▶▶ **Robin enters the police station**
Police Station // 4 May 1982
▶▶ **Robin enters the youth hostel**
Bob's Youth Hostel // 4 May 1982

PART 2

▶▶ **Robin looks for Tegan Schiphol Airport**
Schiphol Airport // 3 May 1982
▶▶ **Robin meets Tegan at the Airport**
Schiphol Airport // 3 May 1982
▶▶ **Robin tells Tegan about Colin's disappearance (cut)**
Hoopman Bodega // 4 May 1982
▶▶ **Tegan decides that they need to go to the police (cut)**
Hoopman Bodega // 4 May 1982

▶▶ **Tegan and Robin decide to try and find Colin themselves**
Police Station // 4 May 1982
▶▶ **Tegan and Robin head towards Frankendael**
Lijnbaansgracht // 4 May 1982
▶▶ **Tegan and Robin arrive at Frankendael**
Frankendael House // 5 May 1982

PART 4

▶▶ **Scanner – view of Amsterdam streets**
Prinsengracht/Reguliersgracht // 5 May 1982
▶▶ **Doctor checks JHC reference in telephone box**
Leidseplein // 4 May 1982
▶▶ **Doctor decides to check the hostels on foot**
Leidseplein // 4 May 1982
▶▶ **Doctor and Nyssa leave the Vondelpark hostel**
Vondelpark Youth Hostel // 4 May 1982
▶▶ **Decision to check another hostel and then divide**
Singel // 4 May 1982
▶▶ **Doctor and Nyssa start off to Frankendael (cut)**
Bob's Youth Hostel // 4 May 1982
▶▶ **Doctor and Nyssa bump into woman with shopping**
Herenstraat // 4 May 1982
▶▶ **Doctor and Nyssa arrive at Frankendael**
Frankendael House // 5 May 1982
▶▶ **Doctor and Nyssa walk behind the fountain**
Frankendael House // 5 May 1982
▶▶ **Omega sees the gardener**
Frankendael House // 5 May 1982
▶▶ **Omega walks through flower market**
Flower Market // 3 May 1982
▶▶ **Doctor finds dead gardener and Omega's cloak**
Frankendael House // 5 May 1982
▶▶ **Omega listens to the barrel organ music**
Amstelveld // 5 May 1982
▶▶ **Doctor, Nyssa and Tegan follow though flower market**
Flower Market // 3 May 1982
▶▶ **Omega notices his hands**
Damrak // 7 May 1982
▶▶ **Doctor notes that Omega will soon revert to anti-matter**
Amstelveld // 5 May 1982
▶▶ **Passing couple notice Omega's face**
Amstel Sluize – Canal Siding // 6 May 1982
▶▶ **Omega spotted after frightening flower seller**
Prinsengracht // 5 May 1982
▶▶ **Nyssa spots Omega hiding, he runs off**
Blauwburgwal // 4 May 1982
▶▶ **Omega chased across NZ Voorburgwal**
Nieuwezijds Voorburgwal // 4 May 1982
▶▶ **Doctor's party run passed knocked down chef**
Sint Nicolaasstraat // 4 May 1982

▸▸ **Doctor's party chases after Omega in
Dam Square (cut)**
Dam Square // 7 May 1982

▸▸ **Omega runs through Dam Square**
Dam Square // 7 May 1982

▸▸ **Omega hides, runs and is chased by Doctor**
Amstel // 6 May 1982

▸▸ **Doctor disintegrates Omega**
Amstel Sluize // 6 May 1982

▸▸ **Tegan rejoins the Doctor and Nyssa**
Station Forecourt // 7 May 1982

The Facts

John Nathan-Turner: 'Graham Williams was the first producer to take *Doctor Who* on a foreign location shoot. I wanted to be the second.'⁶

Since 1981, the BBC had built up a good relationship with the Netherlands via the production of its midweek North Sea ferry-based soap, *Triangle*, so the choice of Amsterdam as a foreign filming destination for *Doctor Who* was a logical one. The task of writing the Amsterdam-based story went to Johnny Byrne, who decided to adapt an idea he'd developed about a time-shift in London caused by an alien entity. Script-editor Eric Saward duly sent a letter to Byrne on 1 October 1981, outlining the requirements for the story that he and Nathan-Turner has already agreed upon. The adventure was to be rooted in Amsterdam where Tegan was enjoying a holiday. There she was to become involved in some nefarious criminal activity, although anything involving drug smuggling, theft of Dutch Old Masters or diamonds, or anything political in nature was strictly vetoed.

Byrne's story outline, dated 15 December 1981, was entitled *The Time of Neman*, but when his proposal came to be reviewed, it was decided that the reasons for using Amsterdam needed to be more essential to the plot. It was at this point that the suggestion was made to change the main enemy of the piece from Neman to Omega, the Time Lord character that been established in the 1973 story, *The Three Doctors*.

John Nathan-Turner made an unscheduled appearance in the final episode (as the Doctor checks Tegan's JHC reference in the Amsterdam telephone directory) when he walked behind the telephone kiosk (in a brown sheepskin jacket), trying to keep members of the public away from the film camera.

One evening in Amsterdam, the cast and crew were walking around the area's red light district when someone approached Janet Fielding, believing her to be one of the city's hoertjes (prostitutes). Much to Peter Davison's amusement, Fielding had no idea what the man's real intentions were.

Comment

It seems odd that one of the criticisms made of Johnny Byrne's original outline by the production office was that the use of Amsterdam as a location was not essential to the plot. Although the reason given for Omega being in Amsterdam in the broadcast version is rather thin, one wonders why there needed to be a reason at all. Why couldn't the story be set in Amsterdam anyway? After all, there was never any logical reason given as to why most aliens spent their time invading London and the Home Counties in earlier adventures.

As with Michael Hayes before him, director Ron Jones obviously made an effort to ensure that the foreign location he'd been given was there on the screen as much as possible. It's interesting that he chose to achieve this largely by the use of a lot of very short, uncomplicated scenes which gave him the opportunity to continually move his camera to different locales.

MAWDRYN UNDEAD
(tx 1 February to 9 February 1983)

The Story

When the TARDIS instruments are jammed by a signal emanating from an apparently deserted spaceship, the Doctor discovers that the problem is caused by a still-active guidance beam for a transmat capsule. Realising that the beam emanates from the Earth of 1983, the Doctor travels in the capsule to shut off the signal, pre-setting the TARDIS so that it will travel to Earth once the beam is closed down. Things go wrong and the TARDIS ends up in the right place, only six years earlier, in 1977. There, Tegan and Nyssa discover a badly burned figure in the transmat who claims to be the Doctor, but who is in reality Mawdryn, one of a group of aliens cursed with perpetual regeneration after stealing and misusing a Time Lord device. In 1977, Tegan meets the Brigadier, as does the Doctor in 1983, where he is now teaching at nearby Brendan School. Back on the ship, Mawdryn's group blackmail the Doctor into giving them his remaining regenerations, finally allowing them to die. As the Doctor is about to make the sacrifice, the two Brigadiers meet and the resultant outpouring of energy provides the release that the aliens desire.

The Locations

1. Middlesex Polytechnic, Trent Park, Bramley Road, Cockfosters, London, N14

Shooting Schedule

PART 1

▸▸ 1983 – Establishing shot – Brendon School
Trent Park – A // 24 August 1982

▸▸ 1983 – Turlough drive car out of school gates
Trent Park – B/C // 24 August 1982

▸▸ 1983 – Turlough crashes car
Trent Park – D/E/F/G // 25 August 1982

▸▸ 1983 – Turlough looks down on crash site
Trent Park – H // 25 August 1982

▸▸ 1983 – Brigadier examines his car
Trent Park – H // 25 August 1982

▸▸ 1983 – Turlough recovers
Trent Park – H // 25 August 1982

▸▸ 1983 – Turlough and Ibbotson run to obelisk
Trent Park – J // 24 August 1982

▸▸ 1983 – Reaching the obelisk, Turlough
goes to the urn
Trent Park – K // 26 August 1982

▸▸ 1983 – Transmat capsule appears
Trent Park – K // 26 August 1982

▸▸ 1983 – Turlough goes into capsule and vanishes
Trent Park – K // 26 August 1982

▸▸ 1983 – Ibbotson rushes to the Brigadier
Trent Park – N // 24 August 1982

▸▸ 1983 – Brigadier and Ibbotson walk to the obelisk
Trent Park – K // 26 August 1982

▸▸ 1983 – Brigadier calls for Turlough (cut)
Trent Park – K // 26 August 1982

▸▸ 1983 – Capsule materialises
Trent Park – K // 27 August 1982

▸▸ 1983 – Doctor's sensor indicates the urn
Trent Park – K // 27 August 1982

▸▸ 1983 – Doctor removes box from urn
Trent Park – K // 27 August 1982

▸▸ 1983 – Turlough creeps up behind Doctor with rock
Trent Park – K // 27 August 1982

▸▸ 1983 – Turlough lifts rock and box explodes (1/2)
Trent Park – K // 27 August 1982

PART 2

▸▸ 1983 – TARDIS appears and then vanishes again
Trent Park – K // 27 August 1982

▸▸ 1977 – Scanner – The obelisk
Trent Park – K // 27 August 1982

▸▸ 1983 – Turlough tries to talk to Guardian
Trent Park – K // 26 August 1982

▸▸ 1977 – Tegan and Nyssa leave the TARDIS
Trent Park – K // 27 August 1982

▸▸ 1983 – Doctor meets the Brigadier
Trent Park – K // 26 August 1982

▸▸ 1977 – Capsule materialises next to Tegan and Nyssa

Trent Park – K // 27 August 1982

▸▸ 1983 – Brigadier begins to take boys back to school
Trent Park – K // 26 August 1982

▸▸ 1983 – Brigadier and Doctor walk to hut
Trent Park – L // 25 August 1982

▸▸ 1983 – Brigadier and Doctor arrive at hut
Trent Park – M // 25 August 1982

▸▸ 1977 – Tegan runs up school steps
Trent Park – P // 24 August 1982

▸▸ 1977 – Scanner – View of school from obelisk
Trent Park – K // 27 August 1982

▸▸ 1977 – Tegan asks boys where she can find a doctor
Trent Park – Q // 24 August 1982

▸▸ 1977 – Tegan meets the Brigadier
Trent Park – M // 25 August 1982

▸▸ 1977 – Brigadier tells Powell to get Dr. Runciman
Trent Park – Q // 24 August 1982

▸▸ 1983 – Turlough begins to run back to obelisk
Trent Park – R (cut) /P // 24 August 1982

▸▸ 1977 – Tegan and Brigadier head back to
the capsule
Trent Park – N // 24 August 1982

▸▸ 1977 – Nyssa waits outside the TARDIS
Trent Park – K // 27 August 1982

▸▸ 1977 – Brigadier, Nyssa and Tegan enter the
TARDIS (2/3)
Trent Park – K // 27 August 1982

PART 3

▸▸ 1983 – Turlough enters the capsule
Trent Park – K // 26 August 1982

▸▸ 1983 – Doctor and Brigdier reach the capsule
Trent Park – K // 26 August 1982

▸▸ 1983 – Doctor activates the box
Trent Park – K // 26 August 1982

▸▸ 1983 – The box explodes
Trent Park – K // 26 August 1982

▸▸ 1983 – Capsule dematerialises
Trent Park – K // 27 August 1982

PART 4

▸▸ 1977 – Doctor and Nyssa deposit Brigadier
at obelisk
Trent Park – K // 27 August 1982

▸▸ 1983 – Brigadier says goodbye to Doctor
Trent Park – K // 26 August 1982

The Facts

With over 45 different sequences to shoot over a four-day
period, director Peter Moffatt produced a 91-page shooting script outlining all the shots to be completed along
with a detailed plan showing camera positions, shooting
angles and cast movement for all the different set-ups.

Right: Peter Davison at Bodiam Castle, the location for *The King's Demons.*

Aided by all his pre-planning, Moffatt shot virtually everything that he'd intended to over the four days, almost all of which made it into the final edit. One of the only scenes to be truncated was that of the school-boy Turlough making his way back to the obelisk in Part 2, which had originally begun with his running away from a rope of knotted sheets hanging from the medical room window down which he had just escaped.

As Trent Park was an area of ground open to the public, designer Stephen Scott insisted that the TARDIS prop shouldn't be left unguarded overnight. As a result, a security man had to be hired to constantly watch over the police box during the time it was set up on the hillside location.

Comment

For a story set around a public school, it certainly made sense to film at a real educational establishment and the production team probably couldn't have found much better than the Middlesex Polytechnic at Trent Park, which fulfilled all the needs of Peter Grimwade's script. The hillside and obelisk are particularly well used, giving a sense of privacy for the various scenes that happen away from the school while affording a scenic view of the building half-a-mile away in the countryside.

THE KING'S DEMONS
(tx 15 March to 16 March 1983)

The Story

The TARDIS lands in 1215, in the middle of a jousting contest at fitz William Castle, being held in the presence of King John. The Doctor discovers that the King is actually an advanced shape-changing android called Kamelion, under the control of the Master, who is disguised as the King's Champion, Sir Gilles Estram. Planning to change the course of history by ensuring that King John is discredited and therefore cannot sign the Magna Carta, the Doctor manages to gain mental control of Kamelion in a battle of wills and, defeated, the Master flees.

The Locations
1. Bodiam Castle, Bodiam, East Sussex

Shooting Schedule

PART 1
▸ **The joust begins**
Bodiam Castle // 6 and 7 December 1982

➤ The Doctor meets King John and
watches joust
Bodiam Castle // 6 and 7 December 1982

➤ TARDIS carried inside fitz William Castle
Bodiam Castle // 5 December 1982

➤ Sir Giles arrests Sir Geoffrey de Lacey
Bodiam Castle // 5 December 1982

PART 2

➤ The Doctor finds the TARDIS gone
Bodiam Castle // 5 December 1982

➤ Turlough sends Sir Geoffrey off
Bodiam Castle // 7 December 1982

➤ Crossbowman shoots Sir Geoffrey
Bodiam Castle // 7 December 1982

The Facts

In his original script, Terence Dudley had suggested that the location for fitz William Castle should be Odiham Castle, near Basingstoke in Hampshire, a building which was historically correct for the story's setting and which had been visited by King John in 1216. It is likely, however, that Dudley hadn't actually seen any photographs of Odiham Castle when making his suggestion, as only ruins remain.

Filming on Monday 6 December was marred by heavy rain, which did nothing to help Peter Davison who was already suffering from a cold.

The final location sequence showing Sir Geoffrey de Lacey being shot by the crossbowman as he begins to ride back to London to expose the impostor posing as King John was substantially shortened in editing. As filmed, the wounded Sir Geoffrey is helped back to fitz William Castle by Turlough and the two are then surrounded by men at arms. Sir Geoffrey tries to defend them and draws his sword, but a guard plunges a sword into his stomach, killing him. Turlough is dragged away. In the transmitted episode, Turlough is captured as he re-enters the castle in a brief sequence shot in studio, the implication being that Sir Geoffrey is killed by the crossbow bolt.

Comment

Filmed in the middle of a very cold and damp December, the location work for *The King's Demons* fits the bleak 13th century setting very well. Bodiam makes an excellent location, as it features the classic turreted castle completely surrounded by a moat.[7] While the exterior of the castle is visually perfect, the production team had to avoid setting any scenes inside the building, as Bodiam Castle itself is nothing more than a shell.

THE FIVE DOCTORS

(tx 25 November 1983)

The Story

An unseen figure uses a forbidden timescoop to lift the first, second and third regenerations of the Doctor, together with a selection of his companions and enemies, out of their time streams, depositing them in an area of Gallifrey known as the Death Zone. With the Fourth Doctor trapped in a time eddy, the Fifth Doctor, detecting that his past is being altered, travels to Gallifrey to discover the cause. Meanwhile, the High Council, aware that power is being drained from the Eye of Harmony, summon the Master to help the Doctor, on promise of great reward. The Doctor discovers that Lord President Borusa is responsible for reactivating the Zone as well as the timescoop kidnappings, hoping that the various regenerations of the Doctor will penetrate the tomb of Rassilon and thus give him access to immortality. The promise of immortality is a trap however, and Borusa is condemned to eternal life as a static carving in the tomb.

The Locations

1. Plas Brondanw, Llanforthen, Penrhyndeudraeth, Gwynedd
2. Carreg Y Foel Grom, off B4407, Near Ffestiniog, Gwynedd
3. Manod Quarry, Cwt Y Bugail, Ffestiniog, Gwynedd
4. Cwm Bychan, near Llanbedr, Gwynedd
5. Tilehouse Lane, Denham Green, Buckinghamshire
6. Halings House, Halings Lane, off Tilehouse Lane, Denham Green, Buckinghamshire
7. 2 West Common Road, Uxbridge, Middlesex
8. Bus Stop, 15 North Common Road, Uxbridge,

Above: The joust that opens Part 1 of *The King's Demons* is filmed in the grounds of Bodiam Castle on 6 December 1982.

Middlesex
9. The Backs, River Cam, Cambridge (*Shada* location)
10. Blackmoor Head Yard, Cambridge (*Shada* location)

Shooting Schedule

▶▶ **Doctor, Turlough and Tegan talk about Eye of Orion**
Plas Brondanw // 5 and 11 March 1983

▶▶ **First Doctor caught in timescoop**
Plas Brondanw // 5 and 11 March 1983

▶▶ **Doctor feels there is something wrong**
Plas Brondanw // 5 and 11 March 1983

▶▶ **Establishing shot – UNIT Headquarters**
Halings House // 17 March 1983

▶▶ **Brigadier helps Second Doctor with coat**
Halings House // 17 March 1983

▶▶ **Second Doctor and Brigadier caught by timescoop**
Halings House // 17 March 1983

▶▶ **Feeling worse, the Doctor collapses**
Plas Brondanw // 5 and 11 March 1983

▶▶ **Third Doctor caught by timescoop**
Tilehouse Lane // 17 March 1983

▶▶ **Doctor helped to TARDIS by Tegan and Turlough**
Plas Brondanw // 5 and 11 March 1983

▶▶ **K9 warns Sarah of danger**
West Common Road // 17 March 1983

▶▶ **Fourth Doctor and Romana caught by timescoop**
River Cam // 15 October 1979

▶▶ **Sarah is caught by timescoop**
North Common Road // 17 March 1983

▶▶ **Second Doctor rescues Brigadier from Cyberman**
Manod Quarry // 9 March 1983

▶▶ **Third Doctor rescues Sarah**
Manod Quarry // 14 March 1983

▶▶ **First Doctor and Susan find TARDIS**
Carreg Y Foel Gron // 7 March 1983

▶▶ **Second Doctor tells Brigadier about Death Zone**
Carreg Y Foel Gron // 9 March 1983

▶▶ **Master arrives and sees corpse**
Cwm Bychan // 15 March 1983

▶▶ **Third Doctor and Sarah meet Master**
Cwm Bychan // 15 March 1983

▶▶ **With Bessie damaged, Third Doctor and Sarah walk**
Cwm Bychan // 15 March 1983

▶▶ **Second Doctor wonders if Rassillon has brought them**
Carreg Y Foel Gron // 9 March 1983

▶▶ **Third Doctor and Sarah see Cybermen**
Manod Quarry // 13 March 1983

▶▶ **Second Doctor and Brigadier enter caves**
Manod Quarry // 11 March 1983

▶▶ **Doctor meets Master, attacked by Cybermen**
Carreg Y Foel Gron // 7 March 1983

▶▶ **Master offers himself as servant to Cybermen**
Carreg Y Foel Gron // 8 March 1983

▶▶ **Master bargains with the Cybermen**
Carreg Y Foel Gron // 8 March 1983

▶▶ **Scanner – Cybermen outside TARDIS**
Carreg Y Foel Gron // 8 March 1983

▶▶ **Second Doctor and Brigadier hear something in caves**
Manod Quarry // 10 March 1983

▶▶ **Third Doctor and Sarah confront Raston robot**
Manod Quarry // 13 March 1983

▶▶ **First Doctor and Tegan head towards Tower**
Carreg Y Foel Gron // 8 March 1983

▶▶ **Second Doctor and Brigadier face the Yeti**
Manod Quarry // 10 March 1983

▶▶ **Scanner – Cybermen place bomb outside TARDIS**
Carreg Y Foel Gron // 8 March 1983

▶▶ **Raston robot massacres Cybermen**
Manod Quarry // 11/13 March 1983

▶▶ **Massacre VFX close-ups**
Manod Quarry // 10 March 1983

▶▶ **Sarah wonders how they will reach the top of the Tower**
Manod Quarry // 14 March 1983

▶▶ **Third Doctor and Sarah cross to the Tower**
Manod Quarry // 14 March 1983

▶▶ **Cybermen continue to work on the bomb**
Carreg Y Foel Gron // 8 March 1983

▶▶ **Cyberleader is informed that the bomb is ready**
Carreg Y Foel Gron // 8 March 1983

▶▶ **Scanner – Cybermen move away**
Carreg Y Foel Gron // 8 March 1983

▶▶ **Bombs detonate as TARDIS dematerialises**
Carreg Y Foel Gron // 8 March 1983

▶▶ **Fourth Doctor rushes to the TARDIS**
Blackmoor Head Yard // 19 October 1979

The Facts

Director Peter Moffatt's first thought on reading the script for *The Five Doctors* was to film all the Death Zone material in Scotland. Although the production had been given permission to find locations a little further afield than normal, Moffatt decided in the end that filming in Scotland would not be advisable, as the extra travelling distance would eat into the available shooting time.

Instead, all the locations needed for the Death Zone were discovered in North Wales by production manager Jeremy Silberston and were recced by the key members of the production team between 21 and 23 February 1983, at which time all the key locations were covered with a layer of snow. Although the snow had melted by the time filming began just over a week later,

Left: **Keith Hodiak as the Raston Robot dispatches a group of Cybermen in the bleak Manod Quarry.**

a bitingly cold wind was still blowing which often drained the colour from the actors' faces, something that Patrick Troughton tried to remedy by keeping a hip flask of whisky hidden in his voluminous coat.

In Terrance Dicks' original script, areas of the Death Zone were depicted somewhat differently than was ultimately visualised by Peter Moffat. Rather than just appearing on a misty moorland, the Second Doctor and the Brigadier were described as being deposited in *'An area of ruined, derelict, gutted buildings looming and sinister. A strange Dali-esque city-scape shrouded in heavy fog.'* In like manner, the Third Doctor and Sarah were to have met in a ruined street where they would have been attacked by a group of Autons. This was eventually substituted for Sarah's cheaper and far less dramatic tumble down a small hillside.

The location chosen to represent both the Eye of Orion and the garden from which the First Doctor is kidnapped was Plas Brondanw, the home of Lady Annabel Williams-Ellis, the widow of Sir Clough Williams-Ellis, who had created Portmeirion, the Italianate village used as the location for *The Masque of Mandragora* in 1976. The scenes filmed there had to be partially reshot on 11 March when it was discovered that the camera negative was damaged. This meant recalling Mark Strickson who, believing that his scenes had been completed, had gone away on holiday.

While Peter Moffat was directing the Second Doctor and the Brigadier being pursued by the Yeti in the caves, John Nathan-Turner was directing a second unit filming all the visual effects close-ups of the Raston robot massacring the Cybermen.

John Nathan-Turner (2nd unit director): 'The only real problem with the filming was that visual effects put some substance on one of the Cybermens' masks to make it smoke, but the smoke went inside the mask and we had to rip, and I mean rip, the helmet off as the actor was nearly suffocating. It was almost a very nasty accident.'[8]

The Yeti used at Manod Quarry on 10 March was an original costume from the 1968 story, *The Web of Fear,* which was discovered rolled up in a box and had to be laid out for two weeks in order to straighten it. The costume was duly fitted with new feet as only one of the originals had survived.

The only new monster in the production, the Raston robot, was played by dancer Keith Hodiak, who was employed to make the robot's various leaps and jumps look more convincing. The robot's egg-shaped head was made from vacuum-formed reflective plastic, which was just thin enough to allow Hodiak to see out. However, in the cold conditions the inside of the mask rapidly misted up, obscuring Hodiak's vision and meaning that he often had to be carefully led by the hand to and from the location. Hodiak's one-piece body suit also created another problem when filming was underway.

Peter Moffatt (director): 'At one point when he was inside the costume he had to go to the toilet. He ended up with this terrible stain on the costume which wouldn't dry and so someone had to hold a fan up against him to try and dry it off before the next take.'[9]

Of the three locations chosen close to London, two were situated in Denham. The first, Halings House, fulfilled the same function as it had done ten years earlier when it appeared as UNIT Headquarters in the tenth anniversary story, *The Three Doctors*. Also used was the nearby Tilehouse Lane for the scenes of the Third Doctor's timescoop kidnapping. As seen on the screen, the large field to the left of Tilehouse Lane is in fact Denham Aerodrome, which for many years was the base for the oft-used helicopter company, Gregory Air Services, and which had been used as a location in two stories, *Fury from the Deep* and *The Invasion*. Also worthy of note is the fact that White Plains, one of the first ever *Doctor Who* filming locations used in *The Reign of Terror*, is situated only a short distance from Denham Green Lane, where the Doctor spins Bessie around to avoid the Timescoop.

In 1995, BBC Video released an alternative special edition of *The Five Doctors*, augmented with both new and extended scenes, new visual effects and a stereo soundtrack. The new edition featured a number of extended location sequences, such as the Doctor emerging from the TARDIS at the Eye of Orion and a truly awful addition to the scene where the Third Doctor prepares to lasso the top of the Dark Tower. He asks Sarah to try and hold off the advancing Cybermen and she does so by feebly dropping a small rock down the slope, stating 'Doctor... missed!'

Originally, the Third Doctor was meant to have improvised a bow and arrow with the items taken from the Raston robot's cave in order to fire a line across to the top of the Dark Tower. On the day, Pertwee expressed dissatisfaction with the scripted idea and, following a conference with Moffatt and Nathan-Turner, it was mutually agreed to change the scene so that the Doctor fashioned a lasso instead.

Around mid-December 1982, Tom Baker decided not to take up the offer of appearing in *The Five Doctors*. To bridge the gap and at least have Baker appearing in some form, permission was sought and obtained to use two sections from the uncompleted 1979 production *Shada*.

Comment

Peter Moffatt certainly was wise in his decision to seek out wide empty spaces for his Death Zone footage and the cold weather and fog certainly make it look very inhospitable. The problem is that so much of the story's location material is set within the Death Zone that, after a while, one stretch of barren nothingness ends up looking very much like another. Far more satisfying is the re-use of Halings House as UNIT Headquarters. During the Pertwee years, UNIT never seemed to stay in one building for more than five minutes, so the return to Halings House forms a rather nice, subtle continuity link with the programme's past.

WARRIORS OF THE DEEP

(tx 5 January to 13 January 1984)

The Story

The TARDIS lands in Sea Base Four, a nuclear military establishment, in the year 2084. With two power-blocs on the brink of war, the Doctor, Tegan and Turlough are held as hostile intruders while the base comes under attack from a group of Sea Devils, who are being guided by a triad of Silurians. The reptiles plan to gain control of the base and launch the nuclear missiles, triggering a war to destroy mankind. The Doctor, much to his sorrow, helps the humans destroy the reptiles with deadly hexachromite gas and prevents the launch of the missiles.

The Locations

1. Royal Engineers' Diving Establishment, McMullen Barracks, Marchwood, near Southampton, Hampshire

Shooting Schedule

PART 2

▸ Doctor in Hydro tank
   Royal Engineers' Diving Est // 28 June 1983
▸ Doctor in airlock
   Royal Engineers' Diving Est // 28 June 1983
▸ Doctor begins to leave the airlock
   Royal Engineers' Diving Est // 28 June 1983

The Facts

As originally conceived, *Warriors of the Deep* was intended to be an entirely studio-bound story. The fact that the *Doctor Who* team had to travel to Southampton and use the facilities of the Royal Engineers' Diving Establishment was down to one person – Prime Minister Margaret Thatcher.

In mid-May 1983, with a year in office still left to her, Thatcher nevertheless decided that it would be a tactically good time to call a snap General Election, with her party riding high in the opinion polls following the recent victory in the Falklands War. The sudden announcement threw the BBC into turmoil as studio space needed to be found to enable the corporation to cover the impending election. Schedules were speedily altered and, as a result, the *Doctor Who* production office was informed that it would either have to pull the recording dates for *Warriors of the Deep* forward by two weeks to make use of what studio space was available, or abandon the recording block and, with it, the entire first story of the new season.

Unwilling to countenance such a move, John Nathan-Turner agreed to rush *Warriors* into production. There just wasn't enough time, however, to prepare for the filming scheduled at Ealing Film Studios from 15 to 17 June, utilising the water tank in Studio 3B. It was decided, therefore, to split the Ealing material over two different sites. Two days would be scheduled using the water tank in Studio A at Shepperton Studios, while scenes of the Doctor underwater would be recorded using the 15' glass-sided tank belonging to the Royal Engineers at their Diving Establishment at Marchwood, a top-security Ministry of Defence establishment near Southampton. Due to the military nature of the location, all BBC staff were instructed that no photographs, other than those essential to production work, should be taken on site.

In all, only three shots were filmed at Marchwood. For the close-up of the Doctor, Peter Davison briefly entered the tank before being replaced by stuntman, Gareth Milne, for the later sequence where the Doctor discovers an escape route. A very wet Davison was then filmed climbing into and out of the decompression chamber.

Comment

With three scenes making up just over a minute of the entire story, there's very little to say about the footage shot at Marchwood, except that the airlock used does sound reassuringly real and heavy, unlike the rest of the rather lightweight Sea Base set.

THE AWAKENING

(tx 19 January to 20 January 1984)

The Story

At Tegan's request, the Doctor takes her to the village of Little Hodcombe in 1984 so that she can visit her grandfather, Andrew Verney. The TARDIS lands in the crypt of the local derelict church at a time when the village is engaged in a war-game being controlled by the local magistrate, Sir George Hutchinson, commemorating the English Civil War battle that took place at Little Hodcombe in 1643. Tegan becomes worried when she learns that her grandfather has gone missing, while Jane Hampden, the local schoolteacher, is becoming concerned about the increasingly violent nature of the re-enactment. The Doctor discovers that the Malus, an ancient alien walled up in the church and discovered by Verney, has been using Hutchinson to stir up violent psychic energy in order to free itself. When Sir George is killed, the Malus self-destructs, causing the collapse of the church.

The Locations

1. Tarrant Monkton, Dorset
2. St Bartholomew's Church, Church Street, Shapwick, Dorset

- Village Cross
3. Bishops Court Farm, West Street, Shapwick, Dorset
4. Martin, Hampshire
   - Village Street
   - Ford
   - Village Green
5. Martin Down, Martin, Fordingbridge, Hampshire
6. Damers Farm, Martin, Fordingbridge, Hampshire

Shooting Schedule

PART 1

▸▸ **Jane searches the stables and sees horsemen**
Bishops Court Farm // 20 July 1983

▸▸ **Close up of horses hooves galloping**
Damers Farm // 22 July 1983

▸▸ **Willow takes Doctor's party taken to see Sir George**
St Bartholomew's Church // 20 July 1983

▸▸ **Distant shot of horseman on the hillside**
Martin Down // 21 July 1983

▸▸ **Turlough runs into the stable yard after Tegan (cut)**
Bishops Court Farm // 20 July 1983

▸▸ **Tegan runs into stable yard and has her bag snatched**
Bishops Court Farm // 20 July 1983

▸▸ **Doctor bumps into half-blind man and pursues him**
Martin – Village Street // 21 July 1983

▸▸ **Wolsey and Willow's search reaches village cross**
Shapwick – Village Cross // 19 July 1983

▸▸ **Doctor shows Will the church gravestones**
St Bartholomew's Church // 20 July 1983

▸▸ **Tegan and Turlough run out into the churchyard**
St Bartholomew's Church // 19 July 1983

▸▸ **Tegan and Turlough in village street by phone box**
Martin – Village Street // 21 July 1983

▸▸ **Tegan runs across the ford and is caught by Wolsey**
Tarrant Monkton // 19 July 1983

PART 2

▸▸ **Turlough is captured and Sir George locks him up**
Martin – Village Green // 21 July 1983

▸▸ **Turlough is taken to the stable**
Damers Farm // 22 July 1983

▸▸ **Will runs through meadow**
St Bartholomew's Church // 19 July 1983

▸▸ **Turlough plans to escape from the stable**
Damers Farm // 22 July 1983

▸▸ **Will hides by cottage near village green**
Martin – Village Green // 21 July 1983

▸▸ **Turlough and Verney take a rest**
Damers Farm // 22 July 1983

▸▸ **Tegan leaves in cart as Queen of the May**
Bishops Court Farm // 20 July 1983

Above: **Peter Davison, Mark Strickson and Janet Fielding wait by the fake lych-gate during a filming break for** *The Awakening* **on 20 July 1983.**

▸▸ **Doctor talks to Will and is captured by troopers**
Martin – Village Green // 21 July 1983

▸▸ **Wolsey arrives and rescues Doctor and Will**
Martin – Village Green // 21 July 1983

▸▸ **Turlough and Verney escape from the stable**
Damers Farm // 22 July 1983

▸▸ **Doctor's party arrive at the church**
St Bartholomew's Church // 20 July 1983

▸▸ **Sir George is affected by the Malus**
Martin – Village Green // 21 July 1983

The Facts

One of the important requirements for the actors in *The Awakening* was the ability to ride horses. Lack of horsemanship was the reason Clifford Rose (director Michael Owen Morris' third choice to play Sir George Hutchinson[10]) had to turn down the role when it was offered to him on 4 July 1983. Actor Jack Galloway, however, confidently accepted the role of Joseph Willow, claiming that he could indeed ride a horse. This was something the production team discovered wasn't quite true when he promptly fell off into the ford at Tarrant Monkton on the first morning of shooting.

The scene of the Doctor pursuing a half-blind man down the alley towards the church was actually filmed in Martin, as opposed to Shapwick, where the St Bartholomew's Church was actually located. The effect of the church in the distance was achieved by filming through a glass painting.

The final scene to be filmed at St Bartholomew's Church featured Glyn Houston (Colonel Wolsey) driving the horse-drawn cart carrying Peter Davison and Keith Jayne (Will Chandler) up to the lych-gate for Part 2. Initially, the horse was reluctant to approach the fake lych-gate (which had been erected by the scenic team the

previous day), being distracted by another horse in an adjacent field to the church. The decision was then taken to bring the horse into the churchyard itself in the hope that it might encourage the other to stop where required. When the shot was performed, the horse did indeed pull up at the gate, allowing Davison, Jayne and Houston to walk through. However, moments later, the horse, still attached to the cart, decided to make its own way into the churchyard, completely demolishing the lych-gate.

Ouch!

With several actors having turned down the central role of Sir George Hutchinson, Michael Owen Morris turned to New Zealander Denis Lill, an actor who had had previous experience of riding horses during the production of the third series of *Survivors*.

Denis Lill: 'I nearly crippled myself! The horse I was riding was quite spirited, and that was okay, I could handle that – but we had these 18th century saddles with a very high pommel in front and a very high cantle behind, and this damn horse squeezed me under a tree in the course of filming. I bent low, right over the sharp point in front of me, and the horse just pushed me up against a branch. My ribs just went crunch! I cracked a rib on that one. It was jolly difficult breathing for a while after that.'[11]

Comment

The real ingenuity behind Owen Morris' location work is the fact that no less than three separate villages were used to represent Little Hodcombe, and yet all three blend together seamlessly to create a unified whole. The Part 1 scene of Tegan and Turlough searching for the Doctor is a good example of this. One moment they're on the village street at Martin, but as soon as they turn the corner towards the ford, they're actually ten miles away at Tarrant Monkton. If you didn't know, you wouldn't be able to distinguish one area from another.

RESURRECTION OF THE DALEKS
(tx 8 February to 15 February 1984)

The Story

Caught in a time corridor, the TARDIS lands in London in 1984 where the Doctor discovers Stien, a sole-surviving fugitive who has used the Daleks' time corridor to escape from the far future. Meanwhile, the Daleks take control of the space station holding Davros in cryogenic suspension, wanting to use him to find a cure for a deadly anti-Dalek virus created by the Movellans. Stien is a duplicate, constructed by the Daleks to trap the Doctor so that they can replicate him and send him on a mission to destroy the High

Council on Gallifrey. The Doctor helps Stien to break free of his Dalek conditioning and, as Davros begins to become infected by the Movellan virus, Stien activates a self-destruct mechanism, destroying the Dalek ship and the space station.

The Locations

1. Curlew Street, Bermondsey, London, SE1
2. Shad Thames, Bermondsey, London, SE1
3. Lafone Street, Bermondsey, London, SE1
4. Butlers Wharf, Bermondsey, London, SE1

Shooting Schedule[12]

PART 1

▸▸ **Escapees and tramp shot by policemen**
Shad Thames // 11 September 1983

▸▸ **Galloway and Stein re-enter the warehouse**
Shad Thames // 11 September 1983

▸▸ **Stein watches soldiers enter the warehouse**
Shad Thames // 11 September 1983

▸▸ **TARDIS materialises**
Butlers Wharf // 12 September 1983

▸▸ **Doctor's party emerge from the TARDIS**
Butlers Wharf // 12 September 1983

▸▸ **Doctor's party meets Stein**
Shad Thames // 12 September 1983

▸▸ **Doctor's party enter warehouse**
Shad Thames // 12 September 1983

PART 2

▸▸ **Dalek pushed from warehouse and explodes**
Shad Thames // 12 September 1983

▸▸ **Archer meets policeman**[13]
Lafone Street // 12 September 1983

▸▸ **Policemen watch Doctor and Stein**
Shad Thames // 12 September 1983

PART 3

▸▸ **Tegan escapes from the warehouse**
Shad Thames // 12 September 1983

▸▸ **Tegan tries to escape policemen**
Butlers Wharf // 12 September 1983

▸▸ **Policemen escort Tegan**
Shad Thames // 12 September 1983

PART 4

▸▸ **Lytton and Policemen leave**
Shad Thames/Curlew Street // 11 September 1983

The Facts

Resurrection of the Daleks had originally been written to conclude the programme's 20th season, following

Above: **A Dalek packed with explosives is pushed from the warehouse door on 12 September 1983 in a scene from Part 2 of** *Resurrection of the Daleks.*

directly from the two-part adventure, *The King's Demons*. Peter Grimwade had been selected to direct Eric Saward's story, provisionally entitled *The Return*, and Michael Wisher had also agreed to reprise his role as the character of Davros. The two days that had been allocated to Grimwade for the location filming of *The Return* were Tuesday 4 and Wednesday 5 January 1983.

As had happened so many times in the past, the production of *The Return* was hit by an industrial dispute at the BBC, this time centring around EEPTU, the electricians' union. Problems started around October 1982, when the industrial action began to affect the production of *Terminus*, which lost one of its allocated studio days. The production of *Enlightenment* and *The King's Demons* was likewise seriously affected, with the former losing all its planned studio dates. By the time December arrived and the industrial action was over, it was clear that only two of the final three stories could be saved. The casualty would be *The Return*, which was officially abandoned on 3 January 1983. However, as the negotiations to produce a new Dalek story had been

Right: Sequence showing the exploding Dalek, as seen on-screen.

long and hard, John Nathan-Turner was determined to remount the production as part of Season 21, by which time the title had changed to *The Resurrection*.

The Dalek pushed from the warehouse loading bay door in Part 2 was specially constructed from expanded polystyrene, so that it could be easily blown apart by the small explosive device contained within it. To ensure that the explosives detonated at exactly the right moment, the internal electrical contacts were held apart by a breaker connected to a thin wire, which ran from the loading bay doors. With the dome section of the Dalek deliberately weighted to ensure that it would fall head first to the ground, the wire was shortened so that the breaker would be sharply pulled from the contacts, just as the Dalek made contact with the road. As the damage caused to the fragile Dalek was enough to render it useless had the explosives failed to detonate, a second back-up Dalek was also taken along to the location so that the sequence could be repeated if required.

Unused Locations

Wapping – The original intention had been to film the story at the location Eric Saward had specified in his script, namely, Wapping in East London. The main action had been envisioned as taking place in Wapping High Street with TARDIS landing at Wapping Pierhead, which would have also been used for the later shooting of the metal detector man.

Negotiations had been underway to use various premises in the Wapping area, but when the warehouse owners started to raise their fees, the decision was taken to transfer the action to the south side of the Thames and film in the visually similar area of Shad Thames, complete with the same warehouses and high-level, interconnecting walkways.

Comment

The evocative dereliction of the London docklands as seen in *Resurrection of the Daleks* certainly dates this particular story, as it was only a short time after filming took place that the empty warehouses began to be renovated into luxury apartments and penthouses. But it's a superb setting for a *Doctor Who* story and, for a change, it's actually improved by the miserable rainy days experienced during the shoot.

PLANET OF FIRE

(tx 23 February to 2 March 1984)

The Story

The TARDIS lands on Lanzarote after Kamelion reprogrammes the co-ordinates following his detection of a signal beacon. The signal comes from a Trion data-core, discovered in the sea during a wreck excavation. Planning to sell the artefact to fund a forbidden trip to Morocco, student Peri Brown has to be saved from drowning by Turlough. The Doctor connects the data-core to the TARDIS, which travels to the planet Sarn, where the natives are becoming divided over their belief in the fire god, Logar. It is discovered that Kamelion is being controlled by the Master, who has accidentally shrunken himself while experimenting with his Tissue Compression Eliminator and who needs the numismaton gas found on Sarn to restore his body. When Turlough realises that Sarn acts as a prison world for his own planet, Trion, and that the volcano is about to erupt, he contacts his own people for help. The Master is temporarily restored by the numismaton gas, but is then seemingly burned to death in the flames. A Trion ship arrives on Sarn and Turlough is informed that things have changed on their planet and that political prisoners are no longer persecuted. Turlough decides to return home while Peri travels on with the Doctor.

The Locations

1. Montañas del Fuego, Timanfaya National Park, Lanzarote
   A. Ridge
   B. Steep Hill
   C. Valley of Tranquillity
   D. High Area near Canal Path
   E. Cave of Doves
   F. Los Hornitos
   G. Yellow Area
   H. Volcano Mouth
   I. Asphalt Triangle
   J. Guides Cave
2. Mirador del Rio, Lanzarote
3. Papagoyo Bay, Lanzarote
4. Orzola, Lanzarote
   • Jetty
   • Fish Shop

Shooting Schedule

PART 1

▸▸ Amyand and Roskal climb the volcano
Montañas del Fuego – G // 19 October 1983

▸▸ Timanov and Malkon discuss faith
Mirador del Rio // 15 October 1983

▸▸ Amyand and Roskal reach top of volcano
Montañas del Fuego – H // 18 October 1983

▸▸ Trion artefact is retrieved from the sea
Papagoyo Bay // 14 October 1983

▸▸ Malkon is confused about his past
Mirador del Rio // 15 October 1983

▸▸ Amyand and Roskel descend the volcano
Montañas del Fuego – C // 18 October 1983

▸▸ Lookout observes Amyand and Roskel
through telescope
Montañas del Fuego – A // 17 October 1983

▸▸ Peri meets Howard and tell him of her plans
Orzola Jetty // 15 October 1983

▸▸ Peri examines Trion artefact on boat,
Howard leaves her
Papagoyo Bay // 14 October 1983

▸▸ Doctor examines the finds from the wreck
Orzola Jetty // 15 October 1983

▸▸ Peri sits on boat as Turlough returns to
TARDIS (cut)
Papagoyo Bay // 14 October 1983

▸▸ Peri looks at the Trion artefact again
Papagoyo Bay // 14 October 1983

▸▸ Peri jumps into the sea
Papagoyo Bay // 14 October 1983

▸▸ Monitor – Peri in trouble in the sea
Papagoyo Bay // 14 October 1983

▸▸ Turlough rescues Peri from the sea
Papagoyo Bay // 14 October 1983

▸▸ Doctor leaves alien currency at café
Orzola Fish Shop // 15 October 1983

▸▸ Turlough brings Peri ashore
Papagoyo Bay // 14 October 1983

▸▸ Doctor runs back to the TARDIS
Papagoyo Bay // 14 October 1983

▸▸ Lookout sees the TARDIS through his telescope
Montañas del Fuego – A // 17 October 1983

PART 2

▸▸ Lookout and Timanov discuss the new arrival
Mirador del Rio // 15 October 1983

▸▸ Peri runs and hides
Montañas del Fuego // 18 October 1983

▸▸ Doctor is anxious to get off of the volcano
Montañas del Fuego – I // 17 October 1983

▸▸ K-Master follows turn-of taken by Peri (cut)

Above: Peter Davison and Mark Strickson amid the volcanic landscape of Lanzarote during the filming of *Planet of Fire.*

Montañas del Fuego – J // 17 October 1983

▸▸ Peri sees the Doctor but is spotted by K-Master[14]
Montañas del Fuego – E // 17 October 1983

▸▸ Doctor and Turlough are captured by Amyand
Montañas del Fuego – F // 19 October 1983

▸▸ Peri arrives at the lookout's ridge
Montañas del Fuego – A // 17 October 1983

▸▸ K-Master confronts Peri who threatens to
drop circuit
Montañas del Fuego – A // 17 October 1983

▸▸ Peri climbs over ridge to escape from K-Howard[15]
Montañas del Fuego – A // 18 October 1983

▸▸ Timanov and Lookout see K-Howard
Montañas del Fuego – A // 18 October 1983

▸▸ Peri slides down the rocks to the bottom
Montañas del Fuego – A // 18 October 1983

▸▸ Timanov and Lookout greet K-Master
Montañas del Fuego – A // 17 October 1983

▸▸ Lost, Peri begins to despair
Montañas del Fuego – B // 18 October 1983

▸▸ Peri calls out in despair for the Doctor
Montañas del Fuego – B // 18 October 1983

▸▸ Peri sees the crashed Trion spaceship
Montañas del Fuego – C // 17 October 1983

PART 4

▸▸ Doctor talks to Amyand
Montañas del Fuego – D // 18 October 1983

▸▸ Turlough and Roskal approach spaceship
Montañas del Fuego – C // 17 October 1983

▸▸ Peri exits the cave
Montañas del Fuego – E // 18 October 1983

▸▸ Doctor and Amyand look for an entrance
Montañas del Fuego – B // 18 October 1983

▸▸ Peri on ridge, eyes streaming

Above: **Nicola Bryant's cuts and bruises are treated after she slides down the slopes of Montañas del Fuego on 18 October 1983.**

Montañas del Fuego – F **//** 19 October 1983
▸▸ **Doctor, Peri and Amyand escape as volcano erupts**
Montañas del Fuego – F **//** 19 October 1983
▸▸ **Amayand in silver suit (cut)**
Montañas del Fuego – A **//** 19 October 1983

The Facts

The idea of filming a *Doctor Who* story in the Canary Islands originated with Fiona Cumming, the person who ultimately directed the story. Cumming and her husband had gone on holiday to Lanzarote one Christmas in the early 1980s and immediately fell in love with the island. Cumming sent a postcard to John Nathan-Turner, jokingly making the suggestion that it would make an excellent filming location for the series. Revisiting the island the following year, Cumming spent some time photographing the landscape and sent the pictures to Nathan-Turner as a further inducement to use the island. Agreeing that it

would make a superb location, Nathan-Turner had the idea costed out and found that it would be possible.

The task of writing the scripts was given to Peter Grimwade, who was given the photographs that Cumming had taken as visual reference to work from. Initially, Grimwade set his story in two fictitious locations, the planet Sarn and the Greek island of Aeschyllos, but he was quickly instructed to change his Earth setting to Lanzarote in order to ensure that the island would receive some direct publicity, which would fulfil part of the financial agreement allowing the programme to use the island.

To assist with the preparations, the production team enlisted the help of Judy Grimshaw at Lanzarote Villas, a travel agency based in Horsham, West Sussex, who conducted much of the negotiations with various people on the island and who would also be on hand during the filming of the story.

The three-day pre-filming recce of the island was done in early September 1983 and was attended by Fiona Cumming, Judy Grimshaw, production manager Christina McMillan, production associate June Collins and script editor Eric Saward. On 7 September, shortly after the crew's return, Christine McMillan wrote to Judy Grimshaw, providing her with a four-page breakdown of the requirements for filming in Lanzarote, which would begin just over five weeks later.

A week after McMillan's letter, on 14 September, Grimshaw contacted Miguel Camera on Lanzarote who, having been given the schedule of required filming locations, was asked to contact the different authorities that oversaw the various sites in order to obtain official permission. As pyrotechnics were needed to simulate the exploding volcano, Camera was also asked to contact Juan Brito on the island, who would be able to source and supply the smoke and gunpowder needed by the visual effects designers during the filming.

To save space, the TARDIS used on Lanzarote was the small three-foot model version.

Friday 14 October marked Nicola Bryant's first day of filming as Peri, which was given over to the scenes involving the use of the boats. Three boats in total were used – Atoxa, used as the main exploration vessel, Flipper, a small powered inflatable that would be used to ferry personnel and equipment, and Gemini, the small boat that Peri's uncle, Howard, would use to leave her stranded. All three vessels were moored in Playa Blanca, a few miles west of Papagayo, where the scenes would be shot, and were sailed around the coast in time for the filming to begin at 9.15 am.

The first scene to be shot by Nicola Bryant was the Part 1 sequence of Peri starting to drown as she swims towards the shore. Unfortunately, Bryant's screams and cries for help were heard by a German tourist who, as Papagayo was a nudist beach, was completely naked. Unaware of the filming and believing Bryant's distress in the freezing Atlantic water to be real, the gentleman swam to her aid and brought her to shore. Once he realised that she was only acting, he reputedly became very incensed and later deliberately walked naked through the middle of a shot being filmed on the beach.

Although the Timanfaya National Park was open to the public, it was not open for general exploration. Visitors would be taken around the various areas of the park by coach. This also applied to the cast and crew for the three days of filming at the park; they were moved from one location to the next via two minibuses. It also meant that it was sometimes necessary to temporarily stop filming while other coach parties passed by.

The film diary provided the cast and crew with some timely reminders about what was and what was not acceptable in the park: *'Take great care if you have to leave the road. It is not always safe and we are not allowed to disturb some of the surfaces. Please do not take bits of rock as souvenirs. No one is to leave the path at the Valley of Tranquillity except Peri and visual effects.'*

Comment

Interviewed by *Doctor Who Magazine* in 1988, scriptwriter Peter Grimwade noted, 'Had I gone to Lanzarote, the story would have been utterly different – there are no two ways about it, something would have come out of that and it would probably have given me a much better story. I also think if you're using a location twice – for Sarn and Lanzarote – you've got to deliberately show the conflicting aspects.'

Certainly Fiona Cumming made a good go of showing two different sides of Lanzarote in *Planet of Fire* but it does, perhaps inevitably, look like it was all filmed in the same very hot and sunny place. It's also a pity that more of the island's stunning vistas (such as when the two religious dissenters, Amyand and Roskal, descend from the volcano in Part 1) weren't more readily used. In close-up, one piece of volcanic rock looks very much like another.

THE CAVES OF ANDROZANI

(tx 8 March to 16 March 1984)

The Story

Landing on the barren world of Androzani Minor, the Doctor and Peri find themselves caught up in a war between the disfigured madman, Sharaz Jek, and government troops working under the orders of Morgus,

Left: Peter Davison prepares to be filmed during the Part 4 chase sequence of *The Caves of Androzani*

a double-crossing industrialist based on Androzani Major. The war is over the control of Spectrox, a drug held by Jek that substantially prolongs life expectancy. The Doctor and Peri both contract Spectrox toxaemia, a fatal condition to which the only antidote is the milk of the Queen Bat that lives deep in the caves. The Doctor manages to obtain the bat's milk and a major battle ensues in which both Jek and Morgus are killed. Getting back to the TARDIS, the Doctor cures Peri but is forced to regenerate to save his own life.

The Locations

1. Masters Pit, Stokeford Heath, Gallows Hill, Wareham, Dorset

Shooting Schedule

PART 1

▸▸ **TARDIS materialises and Doctor follows tracks**
Masters Pit // 15 November 1983

▸▸ **Gunrunners discuss Jek and the Spectrox payment** (cut)
Masters Pit // 16 November 1983

PART 2

▸▸ **Stotz and Krelper argue**
Masters Pit // 16 November 1983

▶ Stotz taps out a call sign on his radio pack (cut)
Masters Pit // 16 November 1983
▶ Stotz talking to Jek on radio (cut)
Masters Pit // 16 November 1983
▶ Stotz dismantles radio and calls to gunrunners (cut)
Masters Pit // 16 November 1983

PART 3

▶ Gunrunners take the Doctor back to their spaceship (cut)
Masters Pit // 17 November 1983

PART 4

▶ Gunrunners chase after the Doctor
Masters Pit // 17 November 1983
▶ Doctor falls but is saved by the mudburst
Masters Pit // 17 November 1983
▶ Doctor gets Peri back to the TARDIS
Masters Pit // 15 November 1983
▶ TARDIS dematerialises
Masters Pit // 15 November 1983

The Facts

On reading Robert Holmes' scripts, director Graeme Harper envisaged that the surface of Androzani Minor should resemble Death Valley in Utah,[16] with its barren stretches of rocks, sand and mountains. Unable to duplicate his vision within the confines of England, Harper elected to use Masters Pit, a sand quarry in Wareham situated next door to those used for the filming of *Death to the Daleks* and *Destiny of the Daleks*.

To create the impression of a more desolate landscape, BBC artist John Peyre created two matte paintings that would later be electronically inserted into the footage shot at Wareham of the Doctor and Peri's arrival on Androzani Minor. The matte shots were not entirely successful, however, due to the slight movement present in film footage compared to the fixed matte background. For the later release of the story on DVD in 2001, the sequence was recomposed digitally, producing a far more stable join between the two pictures.

For reasons unknown, four of the five sequences planned for Wednesday 16 November involving the gunrunners were not filmed, leaving only the argument between the two gun-runners, Stotz and Krelper intact. The final day on location also lost a scene, showing the gradually weakening Doctor being tracked across the dunes by the gunrunners to their spaceship. This left only the main chase sequence between the Doctor, Krelper and another gunrunner to film for the final episode.

As Harper had deliberately decided to use real machine guns in the story as opposed to 'laser guns', it was necessary for the visual effects department to rig up the numerous small squibs that would simulate the bullets hitting the sand. During one particular set of explosions, Davison was temporarily blinded when sand was blown into his eyes.

Stuntman Gareth Milne doubled for Peter Davison performing the long tumble down the sand slope at the end of the chase sequence.

Comment

Graeme Harper is rightly praised for his work on *The Caves of Androzani*, and his location scenes certainly live up to the high standard set by the rest of the production. The exterior shots are never dull, the camera being positioned in unusual angles or kept on the move, which adds so much to the few scenes shot at Wareham. The tracking shot of the Doctor and Peri heading towards the caves in the first episode and the pacy and exciting chase sequence in the last are particularly noteworthy examples. ■

FOOTNOTES

1. *Panopticon VII*, Reeltime Pictures
2. *Doctor Who Magazine* #235, p.47
3. Later used as the main location for Chateau Anglais in Lenny Henry's sitcom *Chef*.
4. *Doctor Who Magazine* #235, p.48
5. *Ariel*, 1982
6. *Doctor Who Magazine* #236, 1996, p.36
7. The castle itself is actually of the wrong period for the story,

as it was actually built some 150 years after the 1215 date in *The King's Demons*.
8. *The Making of The Five Doctors*, DWAS, p.5
9. *The Fifth Doctor Handbook*, Howe, Stammers, Walker, p.249
10. Originally the character was named Sir John Hardiman and the role was initially offered to Anthony Valentine and then Charles Kay.
11. *Doctor Who Magazine*

#282, p.38
12. The shooting schedule is based on the four-part version of this story, originally prepared for transmission and used on the BBC Video release of the story.
13. This scene was originally scheduled to be filmed on 11 September but was postponed due to the rain.
14. The term 'K-Master' is used in both the film schedule and script to refer to the

Kamelion double of the Master, distinguished by his silver face.
15. The term 'K-Howard' is used in both the film schedule and script to refer to the Kamelion double of Professor Howard Foster, distinguished by his silver face.
16. A brief stock shot panning across Monument Valley, Utah, was inserted into the first location sequence to help establish the Androzani location.

PART SIX

> 'All right, I'll take you to... [Blackpool]'
> The Doctor – *Revelation of the Daleks*

COLIN BAKER

THE SIXTH DOCTOR

THE TWIN DILEMMA
(tx 22 March to 30 March 1984)

The Story
Destabilised by his regeneration, the Doctor decides to become a hermit and chooses the barren planet of Titan Three as his future home. On landing, he discovers a crashed spaceship and the body of Lieutenant Hugo Lang, who has been pursuing the kidnapped twin geniuses, Romulus and Remus. Exploring Titan Three, the Doctor realises that their kidnapper, Edgeworth, is in reality the former Master of Jaconda and Time Lord, Azmael. After escaping, the Doctor follows Azmael to Jaconda, which has become ravaged by the mythical giant Gastropods, who are using the twins to calculate a plan to spread their eggs throughout the universe. The Doctor destroys the Gastropods with Azmael's help, which costs the old man his life.

The Locations
1. Springwell Quarry, Springwell Lane, Rickmansworth, Hertfordshire
2. Gerrards Cross Sand and Gravel Quarry, Wapsey's Wood, Oxford Road, Gerrards Cross, Buckinghamshire

Shooting Schedule

PART 1
➤ TARDIS materialises on Titan Three (cut)
Springwell Quarry // 7 February 1984
➤ The Doctor discovers Lang's body
Springwell Quarry // 7 February 1984

PART 2
➤ Doctor and Peri find and enter the ventilation shaft
Springwell Quarry // 7 February 1984

PART 3
➤ TARDIS materialises on Jaconda

Wapsey's Wood Quarry // 8 February 1984
➤ **Doctor discovers the giant Gastropod trail**
Wapsey's Wood Quarry // 8 February 1984

The Facts
With the action taking place on Titan Three and Jaconda, director Peter Moffat elected to split his location work over two different quarry locations – the chalk quarries at Rickmansworth and the darker sand pits of Gerrards Cross, both of which had their limitations.

Peter Moffatt: 'They were both deep in mud when we did it and terribly limited, because pan the camera two inches the other way and you'd see the housing estates or trees.'[1]

the TARDIS to Telos. The Doctor discovers that the Cybermen have captured a time ship with which they plan to alter the web of time by diverting the course of Halley's Comet, crashing it into Earth and thus avoiding the destruction of their original planet Mondas. On Telos, the Doctor meets the native Cryons, for whom Lytton is *really* working. Flast, a dying and imprisoned Cryon, sacrifices her life, destroying the Cybermen's tombs, their central control and the stolen time vessel.

The Locations

1. Dartmouth Castle Public House, corner of Glenthorne Road and Overstone Road, London, W6
2. London Scrapyard, 161 Becklow Road, London, W12
3. Davis Road and Rear Alley, London, W12
   - Rear of 58 Davis Road
   - Rear Alley
4. Gerrards Cross Sand and Gravel Quarry, Wapsey's Wood, Oxford Road, Gerrards Cross, Buckinghamshire
5. Cameron Scrap Merchant, 36 Birkbeck Road, London, W3

Shooting Schedule

PART 1

▸▸ **Lytton's gang observe the diamond merchant**
Dartmouth Castle Public House // 29 May 1984

▸▸ **Lytton's gang arrive at garage and discuss plan**
36 Birkbeck Road // 1 June 1984

▸▸ **Lytton operates beacon as policemen watch garage**
36 Birkbeck Road // 1 June 1984

▸▸ **Lytton gets gun while Payne begins work on the sewer**
36 Birkbeck Road // 1 June 1984

▸ **TARDIS materialises and changes shape**
161 Becklow Road // 29 May 1984

▸▸ **Doctor traces signal to house and runs back to TARDIS**
Davis Road // 29 May 1984

▸▸ **Doctor returns to junkyard watched by t wo policemen**
161 Becklow Road // 29 May 1984

▸▸ **Two policemen approach the garage**
36 Birkbeck Road // 1 June 1984

▸▸ **TARDIS materialises and scuffle with policemen**
36 Birkbeck Road // 1 June 1984

▸▸ **Bates and Stratton escape work party**
Gerrards Cross Quarry – Area 1 // 30 May 1984

▸▸ **Bates is angry that Stratton didn't get the Cyber head**
Gerrards Cross Quarry – Area 1 // 30 May 1984

Above: **The model of Cyber-Control on location at Gerrards Cross, suspended from its metal armature.**

Moffatt had hoped to film the scenes of the devastated Jaconda using a burnt out forest location. When this proved impractical, the landscape had to be created using logs and tree stumps hired in from a props warehouse.

Comment

Like everything that makes up *The Twin Dilemma*, the location work is rather dull and uninspired and there's a definite feeling that by the time it came to the story's production, the season's budget had already been spent on rather more exciting ventures, leaving virtually nothing left in the kitty. Peter Moffat calls it, '...one of the worst ones I did, a terrible mish-mash. It didn't work.' True on virtually every level, it certainly wasn't the best way to introduce a new Doctor.

ATTACK OF THE CYBERMEN
(tx 5 January to 12 January 1985)

The Story

Intercepting a distress call, the Doctor lands in the Totters Lane scrapyard on Earth in 1985. The signal has been sent by Lytton who, under the pretence of robbing a London diamond merchant, makes contact with a group of Cybermen hiding in the sewers. The Cybermen capture the Doctor and Peri and travel in

▸ **Bates and Stratton observe the work party**
Gerrards Cross Quarry – Area 1 // 31 May 1984
▸ **Bates points to Cyber Control**
Gerrards Cross Quarry – Area 3 // 30 May 1984
▸ **Bates and Stratton make their way to Cyber Control**
Gerrards Cross Quarry – Area 2 // 30 May 1984
▸ **Bates and Stratton attack and decapitate Cyberman**
Gerrards Cross Quarry – Area 2 // 30 May 1984
▸ **Doctor, Peri and Russell make for the TARDIS**
36 Birkbeck Road // 1 June 1984

PART 2

▸ **TARDIS dematerialises**
36 Birkbeck Road // 1 June 1984
▸ **Stratton dresses as a Cyberman**
Gerrards Cross Quarry – Area 2 // 31 May 1984
▸ **Stratton needs a rest but Bates forces him to continue**
Gerrards Cross Quarry – Area 2 // 31 May 1984
▸ **Bates and Stratton see Lytton and Griffiths emerge**
Gerrards Cross Quarry – Area 3 // 30 May 1984
▸ **Lytton tries to convince Bates that he can help**
Gerrards Cross Quarry – Area 3 // 30 May 1984
▸ **Two Cybermen discover damaged grating** (cut)
Gerrards Cross Quarry – Area 3 // 30 May 1984

The Facts

Like all the stories in season 22, *Attack of the Cybermen* was produced in 45-minute instalments and therefore ran to fewer than the usual number of episodes.

On Monday 21 May 1984, one week before filming on *Attack of the Cybermen* was due to begin, director Matthew Robinson and key members of his production team embarked on a recce of the chosen locations for the four days of filming required for the story. At this stage, all the sites had been decided upon with the exception of the opening street location from Part 1, showing the exterior of the diamond merchants. During the course of the following week, the decision was taken to use the London headquarters of United International Pictures on Glenthorne Road as the building in question.

The use of the sand and gravel pit at Wapsey's Wood was suggested by the programme's unofficial adviser, Ian Levine, as it had been used to represent the surface of Telos in the 1967 story, *The Tomb of the Cybermen*, the adventure to which *Attack* was closely related. As with the original story, the Cybermen's control centre was realised by the use of a foreground miniature positioned not far from the camera, which was lined up with the top of the sand dunes. The actors in the background were then required to look and point at a specific spot which would create the illusion that the building was in the far distance.

Comment

In principle, going back to film in the same quarry that had been used for *The Tomb of the Cybermen* was a sound move. Sadly, what had looked impressive and mountainous in black and white back in 1967 looked decidedly less so in the colour of 1985. The footage wasn't helped by the fact that fog filters had been employed, which seemed to suck all the colour and contrast from the picture. A real disappointment.

THE MARK OF THE RANI

(tx 2 February to 9 February 1985)

The Story

Landing at the mining village of Killingworth in Northern England during the early part of the 19th century, the Doctor discovers that engineer George Stephenson has called an important meeting of many key industrial figures, a meeting which the Master intends to disrupt. Also present is another Time Lord known as the Rani, who has been extracting fluid from the brains of humans, leaving them unable to sleep and vastly increasing their aggression. Stealing the brain fluid, the Rani is forced into an uneasy alliance with the Master. The Doctor manages to outwit both the renegade Time Lords, flinging them to the far reaches of the galaxy in the Rani's TARDIS.

The Locations

1. Granville Colliery Spoil Heaps, Lodge Road, Donnington Wood, Donnington, Telford, Shropshire
2. Blists Hill Open Air Museum, Legges Way, Madeley, Telford, Shropshire
3. Coalport China Works, Coalport, Telford, Shropshire
4. Park Wood, Bury Street, Ruislip, Middlesex

Shooting Schedule

PART 1

▸ **Men head for the Tavern and Bath House**
Blists Hill Museum // 23 October 1984
▸ **Doctor and Peri leave the TARDIS**
Granville Colliery // 22 October 1984
▸ **Ward, Green and Rudge knock over peddler's tray**
Blists Hill Museum // 23 October 1984
▸ **Doctor and Peri watched by scarecrow**
Granville Colliery // 22 October 1984
▸ **Aggressors attack Drayman's cart**
Blists Hill Museum // 27 October 1984
▸ **Doctor and Peri hear commotion in the lane**
Granville Colliery // 22 October 1984

Right: Kate O'Mara and Anthony Ainley wait in the pouring rain during the ultimately abandoned woodland scenes for *The Mark of the Rani.*

▸▸ **Green and Rudge run off leaving Ward behind (cut)**
Blists Hill Museum // 27 October 1984

▸▸ **Green and Rudge run past Doctor and Peri**
Granville Colliery // 22 October 1984

▸▸ **Doctor and Peri help the Drayman**
Blists Hill Museum // 27 October 1984

▸▸ **Scarecrow watches the Doctor, Peri and Drayman (cut)**
Blists Hill Museum // 27 October 1984

▸▸ **Scarecrow climbs the style**
Granville Colliery // 22 October 1984

▸▸ **Doctor and Peri enter village, miners go to Bath House**
Blists Hill Museum // 23 October 1984

▸▸ **Master appears outside Bath House**
Blists Hill Museum // 26 October 1984

▸▸ **Master starts to follow the Doctor**
Blists Hill Museum // 26 October 1984

▸▸ **Doctor and Peri talk their way into the pit**
Blists Hill Museum // 23 October 1984

▸▸ **Master kills the dog and the guard**
Blists Hill Museum // 24 October 1984

▸▸ **Peri notices that the dog has stopped barking**
Coalport China Works // 29 October 1984

▸▸ **Master tells aggressors that Doctor is their enemy**
Blists Hill Museum // 24 October 1984

▸▸ **Doctor is attacked by the aggressors**
Blists Hill Museum // 25 October 1984

▸▸ **Master watches the attack**
Blists Hill Museum // 24 October 1984

▸▸ **Doctor is saved by Lord Ravensworth**
Blists Hill Museum // 25 October 1984

▸▸ **Master leaves the pit**
Blists Hill Museum // 24 October 1984

▸▸ **Miners begin to attempt to raise Rudge's body**
Blists Hill Museum // 25 October 1984

▸▸ **Doctor examines Rudge's neck**
Blists Hill Museum // 25 October 1984

▸▸ **Doctor dresses in old clothes ready for Bath House**
Coalport China Works // 29 October 1984

▸▸ **Master walks into disused mine**
Blists Hill Museum // 1 November 1984

▸▸ **Peri watches the Rani leave the Bath House**
Blists Hill Museum // 26 October 1984

▸▸ **Aggressors push the TARDIS on a cart**
Granville Colliery // 23 October 1984

▸▸ **Aggressors continue to push the TARDIS**
Granville Colliery // 23 October 1984

▸▸ **Scanner – Aggressors with TARDIS**
Blists Hill Museum // 27 October 1984

▸▸ **Doctor hears aggressors, Master confirms plan**
Blists Hill Museum // 26 October 1984

▸▸ **TARDIS is thrown down the pit**
Blists Hill Museum // 27 October 1984

▸▸ **Peri pushes the Doctor's trolley down the hill (1/2)**
Blists Hill Museum // 26 October 1984

▸▸ **Ward and the aggressors see the Doctor (1/2)**
Blists Hill Museum // 27 October 1984

▸▸ **Doctor is sent hurtling towards the pit shaft (1/2)**
Blists Hill Museum // 26 October 1984

PART 2

▸▸ **Stephenson rescues the Doctor**
Blists Hill Museum // 26 October 1984

▸▸ **Aggressors attack the guard**
Blists Hill Museum // 25 October 1984

▸▸ **Doctor and Peri follow Stephenson**
Blists Hill Museum // 26 October 1984

▸▸ **Ravensworth gives orders to guards**
Blists Hill Museum // 25 October 1984

▸▸ **Master hypnotises Luke**
Coalport China Works // 29 October 1984

▸▸ **Master tells Luke that the meeting must go ahead**
Coalport China Works // 29 October 1984

▸▸ **Doctor and Peri are attacked by quayside**
Blists Hill Museum // 24 October 1984

▸▸ **Luke lies to Ravensworth about Stephenson**
Coalport China Works // 29 October 1984

▸▸ **Doctor and Peri return to the Bath House**
Blists Hill Museum // 26 October 1984

▸▸ **Master walks through woods to find Stephenson (cut)**
Blists Hill Museum // 30 October 1984

▸▸ **Doctor leaves the mine workings**
Blists Hill Museum // 1 November 1984

▸▸ **Peri tells Doctor that Ravensworth wants to see him**
Blists Hill Museum // 26 October 1984

▸ **Rani begins to lay mines**
Park Wood // 8 November 1984

▸▸ **Rani continues to lay her mines**
Park Wood // 8 November 1984

▸▸ **Rani finishes with mines and Doctor stands alone (cut)**
Blists Hill Museum // 30 October 1984

▸▸ **Doctor hears aggressors and runs into woods**
Park Wood // 8 November 1984

▸ **Luke transformed and Peri rescued**
Blists Hill Museum // 30 October 1984

▸▸ **Peri takes Master and Rani, Doctor warns aggressors**
Blists Hill Museum // 31 October 1984

▸ **Aggressors have caught the Doctor**
Blists Hill Museum // 31 October 1984

▸ **Aggressors step on two mines leaving Doctor suspended**
Blists Hill Museum // 31 October 1984

▸ **Doctor frees himself**
Park Wood // 8 November 1984

▸▸ **Doctor and Peri run from the mine as it collapses**
Blists Hill Museum // 1 November 1984

▸▸ **Doctor and Peri head down the lane towards the pit (cut)**
Blists Hill Museum // 1 November 1984

▸▸ **Doctor gives brain fluid to Peri**
Coalport China Works // 29 October 1984

The Facts

Due to a chance mistake made within the BBC, John Nathan-Turner found that he was able to secure the use of a location film crew for two weeks for the cost of only one. Wanting to put the extra allocation to good use, the producer turned to Sarah Hellings, a director new to *Doctor Who*. Hellings had expressed an interest in working on the programme if she could shoot a story on film and, preferably, if it could have some historical content. Although the production office wasn't charged for the second week with the film crew, other sundry expenses involved in using them needed to be met (extra catering etc). In order to cover costs, the second two-day studio block allocated to the story was cancelled.

Trained as a film editor, Sarah Hellings had taken the BBC's director's course in the early 1980s, during which time she had contributed a number of film items to *Blue Peter* and its companion series, *Blue Peter Special Assignment*, one of which had involved spending three days at the Blists Hill museum. Knowing that the museum could provide much of what was required by the script, Hellings planned a recce of the site with her production manager, Tony Redston.

During the second week of filming, Nicola Bryant hurt her neck while sleeping and had to be taken to hospital. She was told that she would need to wear a padded neck support, which she could only take off while actually filming.

The weather remained reasonable during the filming of *The Mark of the Rani* until Tuesday 30 October, when shooting was due to begin in the wooded area next to the pit workings. A total of 18 scenes had been slated for completion during the day, showing the Rani placing her mines in Redfern Dell, Luke's transformation into a tree and Peri's subsequent rescue from danger. Only two short scenes had managed to be filmed in the morning when the rain began falling heavily – and continued to do so for the rest of the afternoon, necessitating the abandonment of the day's schedule. Fortunately, this was not immediately viewed as a problem, as a spare contingency day (Friday 2 November) had been programmed into the schedule, which could be used to shoot any unfinished material at the end of the two weeks.

Two days later, however, the problem was further compounded when more rain meant that scenes of the Doctor trying to escape from the pole to which he is tied also had to be postponed until the following day. Unfortunately, when the Friday dawned, it proved to be just as overcast and rainy as the previous days. Knowing that a large number of scenes still needed to be shot which couldn't be easily transferred to the studio, the cast and crew ventured out to try and complete what they could.

Sarah Hellings: 'It rained so hard that day that we

only got three shots in – which in the end proved unusable because not only could you see the rain, but also hear it on the mics.'[2]

On the team's return to London, John Nathan-Turner immediately applied for a one-day remount in order to shoot the missing scenes. The request was granted, but the time and money allocated would not permit a return to Shropshire. Fortunately, as all the scenes were set in woodlands, a suitable alternative was located at Park Wood in Ruislip, a location suggested by scriptwriters Pip and Jane Baker, who lived within a few minutes walk of the wood.

One of the hardest scenes to film was the runaway trolley onto which the Doctor is strapped at the end of Part 1. In order for the effect to be achieved, a trolley was designed which could hold one person hidden in the base who would lie on his front, steering with the front wheels and braking with the rear. The person chosen to 'pilot' the trolley was Visual Effects Assistant, Tom Davis.

George Reed (visual effects assistant): 'The trolley managed to get up quite a bit of speed as it rolled down the steep hill. Tom would be breaking as hard as he could when it reached the bottom, sometimes totally locking the wheels up, but the trolley just kept on going. So I had to grab the rear handle as it went past and get dragged along with it, which would finally bring it to a stop.'[3]

For the scenes of the Doctor visiting the Bath House, Colin Baker had to dress up in an old coat and dirty his face, although this simple scene did not go according to plan.

Colin Baker (The Doctor): 'When we actually recorded that scene, the very helpful prop man said, "Here's your pile of dirt, Mr Baker. That's our nice clean BBC dirt," and he put a pile of Fuller's Earth there for me to smear on my face. Unfortunately, in between the time he put it there and the time I came to use it, a dog had also thought, "That's a really nice piece of clean Fuller's Earth from the BBC, and I will avail myself of its propinquity." So when I smeared my face, it wasn't just Fuller's Earth that went on my face. I received much ribbing from the people standing around on that occasion. No one would come near me all day!'[4]

Comment

Although the story itself is rather preposterous (especially the ludicrous tree-making mines), Sarah Hellings' direction of the location work for *The Mark of the Rani* is superb. The opening sequence of the miners finishing their shift and making their way up the street to the tavern and bath house, leaving the camera to slowly pull up into the air, effortlessly draws you into the adventure. The real mark of Hellings' ability is that the finished programme never actually betrays how small the Blists Hill site really is, recalling Douglas Camfield's clever use of location at Athelhampton for *The Seeds of Doom*.

THE TWO DOCTORS

(tx 16 February to 2 March 1985)

The Story

Sent by the Time Lords to Space Station Camera to investigate unauthorised temporal experiments, the Second Doctor and Jamie find that the station head, Dastari, has been augmenting Androgums, a race of savages, with the aim of making them more intelligent. Chessene, a highly augmented Androgum woman, allies herself with the Sontarans, who invade the station, taking the Second Doctor with them to Earth where Dastari intends to dissect the Time Lord and find the symbiotic nuclei that makes safe time travel possible. Sometime later, the Sixth Doctor and Peri arrive on the ravaged station and rescue Jamie. Together, they trace the Second Doctor to a hacienda near Seville, where Chessene kills the Sontarans after double-crossing them, changes her plans and gets Dastari to turn the Second Doctor into an Androgum using genetic material taken from Shockeye, a voracious Androgum chef. The Sixth Doctor rescues the Second, who rejects the unstabilised transplant, while Chessene is killed as she attempts to use an unprimed time-travel capsule.

The Locations

1. Rio Guadiamar, SE521, between Gerena and Aznalcollar, Spain
2. Dehera Boyar, between Gerena and El Garrobo, Spain
3. Country Road between Gerena and El Garrobo, Spain
4. Seville Cathedral, Avenida de la Constitución, Seville, Spain
5. Various Streets in Santa Cruz District, Seville, Spain
   • Plaza de la Alianza

Shooting Schedule

PART 1 ▸▸

▸▸ **Doctor fishing for Gumblejack**
Rio Guadiamar // 16 August 1984
▸▸ **Chessene, Shockeye and Varl approach hacienda**
Dehera Boyar // 11 August 1984
▸▸ **Chessene tells Shockeye what she's learned**
Dehera Boyer // 11 August 1984
▸▸ **Varl watches Sontaran spaceship arrive**
Dehera Boyer // 9 August 1984
▸▸ **Oscar and Anita approach hacienda**
Dehera Boyer // 16 August 1984
▸▸ **Shockeye and Varl argue**
Dehera Boyer // 11 August 1984
▸▸ **Oscar and Anita see Sontaran spaceship**

Dehera Boyer // 16 August 1984
➤ Varl and Dastari carry Doctor 2 to hacienda
Dehera Boyer // 11 August 1984

PART 2

➤ Anita encourages Oscar to look for wreckage
Dehera Boyer // 16 August 1984
➤ Doctor meets Oscar and Anita
Dehera Boyer // 10 August 1984
➤ Doctor goes to scout the hacienda
Dehera Boyer // 9 August 1984
➤ Doctor furtively makes his way to the hacienda
Dehera Boyer // 10 August 1984
➤ Doctor hears Shockeye's voice and climbs to hear
Dehera Boyer // 11 August 1984
➤ Doctor falls from window
Dehera Boyer // 11 August 1984
➤ Doctor hides as Chessene looks through window
Dehera Boyer // 11 August 1984
➤ Doctor returns to the group, Anita remembers a way in
Dehera Boyer // 9 August 1984
➤ Shockeye watches Peri in the courtyard
Dehera Boyer // 11 August 1984
➤ Doctor and Jamie say goodbye to Anita at Icehouse
Dehera Boyer // 11 August 1984
➤ Shockeye chases and catches Peri (2/3)
Dehera Boyer // 12 August 1984

PART 3

➤ Doctor and Jamie slip into the hacienda
Dehera Boyer // 12 August 1984
➤ Stike orders Varl to set ship to self-destruct
Dehera Boyer // 9 August 1984
➤ Doctor, Peri and Jamie escape and discuss sabotage
Dehera Boyer // 12 August 1984
➤ Dastari tricks Stike and Varl into cellar
Dehera Boyer // 11 August 1984
➤ Shockeye and Doctor 2 leave the hacienda
Dehera Boyer // 11 August 1984
➤ Shockeye and Doctor 2 hijack lorry and drive off
Gerena/Garrobo Road // 16 August 1984
➤ Everyone searches for Doctor 2 and Shockeye
Santa Cruz Streets // 14/15 August 1984
➤ Stike staggers from hacienda as ship explodes
Dehera Boyer // 10 August 1984
➤ Doctor begins to feel the Androgum effect
Santa Cruz Streets // 14/15 August 1984
➤ Doctor's party avoids Chessene and Dastari
Santa Cruz Streets // 14/15 August 1984
➤ Doctor, Peri and Jamie find Las Cadenas
Santa Cruz Streets // 14/15 August 1984
➤ Chessene captures the Doctors

Santa Cruz Streets // 14/15 August 1984
➤ Group herded through courtyard by Chessene
Dehera Boyer // 11 August 1984
➤ Chessene gives into her Androgum side
Dehera Boyer // 11 August 1984
➤ Doctor kills Shockeye
Dehera Boyer // 12 August 1984

Unused Locations

Having decided to try and film one of season 22's productions abroad, John Nathan-Turner, recalling an enjoyable American holiday he'd spent in 1981, pitched the idea of setting a story in New Orleans. Knowing that such a trip could not be afforded on the programme's normal budget, discussions were begun with Lionheart, the BBC's American distributors, to see if they would be interested in a similar co-finance deal as had been arranged with ABC in Australia for *The Five Doctors*. Lionheart agreed to the proposal and Robert Holmes was formally commissioned to begin writing the scripts for a story set in America.

Robert Holmes: 'I had written the script to be set in New Orleans, not Seville. That's why I created the Androgums – I couldn't think of any reason why aliens should visit New Orleans and I recalled it was a jazz place – but not even I could envisage a race of aliens obsessed with jazz. And then I remembered it is the culinary centre of America, with lots of restaurants, so I invented the Androgums, who are obsessed with food – an anagram of gourmand. So they went to New Orleans for the food. They stayed, however, when it shifted to Seville because I couldn't think of anything else.'[5]

On 26 January 1984 a four-page document was drawn up entitled *6W – Cost of Filming in USA*, outlining the total finances required for ten days' planned filming in New Orleans.

Artistes' Expenses
8 Artistes to be flown out to New Orleans	£4384
8 Artistes overnight allowances	
(@ $121.60 per night) x 13 days	£8969
4 US artistes overnight allowances	
(@ $121.60 per night) x 13 days	£4484
Total for Artistes Expenses	*£17,837*

Production Travel
Preliminary Recce – Two weeks for Director,
Production Manager, Script Editor, Producer,
Designer and Production Unit Manager £10,532
Camera Recce – One week for Director, Production
Manager, Buyer, Designer, Production Unit
Manager, Cameraman, Sound and Lights £9213
Three people on production team to go out three weeks

Above: The cast and crew of *The Two Doctors* in the courtyard of Dehera Boyer.

beforehand and stay on for filming	*£5433*
Designer and Buyer to go out two weeks beforehand	
and stay on for filming	*£2414*
Two Visual Effects Designers to go out one week	
beforehand and stay on for filming.	*£1207*
42 staff x 13 overnight allowances for filming	*£47,087*
42 return flights to New Orleans @	
£548 per flight	*£23,016*
Total for Production Travel	*£98,902*
Rounded up to: -	***£100,000***

Overseas Production Facilities	
12 cars for two weeks	*£3404*
Bus for artistes	*£3475*
Van for costumes	*£425*
Van for make-up	*£425*
Van for props	*£425*
Van for visual effects materials	*£425*
Van for lighting equipment and generator	*£2000*
Cars for recces	*£1272*
Sub Total	*£12,000*
Rounded up in case of underestimate	*£15,000*
Location Catering – 50 x $20 a head for	
ten days	*£8000*
Contingency fund	*£5000*
Total for Overseas Production Facilities	***£28,000***

*Grand Total Required (**plus extra added to facilitate higher fees for US actors, extras and walk-ons and £1000 miscellaneous padding**)*   ***£208,985***

By this time, Gary Downie had been allocated to the story as production manager and was beginning to make plans for the initial recce to scout for locations that Holmes had specified, namely a plantation house and a bayou. Sometime shortly after, Lionheart decided to withdraw from the project. It appears from the existing documentation that efforts were made by Nathan-Turner around mid-February to secure extra funding from BBC

Enterprises for the trip; this evidently also fell through.

A review of the budget indicated that an overseas location could still possibly be afforded, provided it was kept within Europe. Nathan-Turner suggested Venice as a possible substitute, but the idea was discounted due to potential problems with tourists and unfavourable accommodation rates.

The Facts

With both New Orleans and Venice discounted, production associate Sue Anstruther suggested locating the story around Seville in Spain, based on an enjoyable holiday that she'd had there. Contact was duly made with travel firm Mundi Color, who were able to provide a favourable travel package for the production, confirming that the story could be filmed in Spain without any additional funding.

On that basis, production manager Gary Downie began arranging the recce visit to Spain for Sue Anstruther and himself by contacting the British Consulate in Seville, requesting a Spanish-speaking 'fixer' who could act as liaison during the visit. On arriving in Spain, however, the interpreter proved unavailable so Donald Carnegie, the Assistant British Consul, made himself available for three days before his aristocratic wife, Mercedes, volunteered for the role.

With no co-production money forthcoming, the finance on *The Two Doctors* was going to be especially tight and, if the filming in Spain was to be successful, all those involved would need to agree to a cut in their daily allowance. Having explained the situation to the cast and crew, John Nathan-Turner followed it up in the early part of July with a memo entitled *Travel and Duty*.

'*Doctor Who* is a low-budget show and so finds it very hard to do foreign filming. In order to go to Seville this year, we have spent much time and effort in finding a package that would make sure all the team members were well looked after, but would keep us within budget. We are glad that all of you we have spoken to have understood the spirit in which the arrangements have been made and accepted the deal, as this means the trip can take place.

'The arrangements made are that you will stay in a four star hotel, in sole occupancy, and a twin-bedded room with private bathroom, TV and air conditioning. Breakfast consists of both cooked breakfast and a choice of cold buffet. The hotel has an outdoor swimming pool and a choice of restaurants and bars as well as a coffee shop.

'The deal is that you will have your room and breakfast paid for direct by the programme and receive 2/5 of the daily allowance for Spain; approximately £22 per day. As location catering will be provided, the only meal you will need to pay for is dinner, which will cost an average of £5-£7 per head, either in the hotel or in town.

'If anyone now decides that they are not prepared to accept this deal, it may put our filming abroad in jeopardy. We therefore need final agreement to this deal by Thursday 19 July, in order not to risk having to cancel this trip.'

John Nathan-Turner to 'All the team filming in Seville'
— Undated

More Unused Locations

High on the list for Downie and Anstruther was finding a suitable hacienda, around which much of the story's action would ultimately take place. Venturing north-west of Seville, they eventually located a suitable one-storey building named Cortijos in the village of El Garrobo. The place was seemingly ideal, as it was covered by peeling white paint, suggesting the run-down appearance needed in the story, as well as being surrounded by olive groves. The owner was approached and permission was granted for a return visit by the director and designer at a later date.

Leaving the hacienda, the team headed back towards Seville down a country road joining El Garrobo and Gerena. Noting that the road would be suitable for the lorry hijack scene in Part 3, Downie was even more delighted when he spotted a second and even more suitable hacienda further down the road. Unlike the first, Dehera Boyar was an empty two-storey building, complete with overgrown courtyard, fountain, olive groves, a private bull-ring and chapel. On returning to London, Downie contacted the hacienda owner and made arrangements to visit during the director's recce a fortnight later.

When director Peter Moffatt saw the two buildings, he expressed a preference for Dehera Boyar and negotiations were immediately entered into to secure the building's use. However, the owner was somewhat reluctant to agree due to the fact that the hacienda was in the process of being sold. Discussions continued for the next fortnight but still a definite answer could not be gleaned, and with only a week to go before the cast and crew were due to fly to Spain and commence filming, a decision had still not been reached. It was for that reason that the film diary drawn up for the production ended up listing both Dehera Boyar and Cortijos as potential filming locations.

Eventually, the person selling the hacienda agreed to give the production team the details of the individual buying the building, namely Joanna Hearst, the aunt of Pattie Hearst, the notorious kidnap victim. Contact was made and agreement to use Dehera Boyar was quickly reached.

More Facts

With the cast and crew due to fly out on the morning of Wednesday 8 August, two days of rehearsals for the location material were held in Acton on Saturday 4 and Sunday 5 August. However, actress Elisabeth Spriggs, who had originally been cast as Chessene, refused to attend the location rehearsals. Peter Moffatt subsequently replaced her with Jacqueline Pearce at very short notice.

On arriving in Spain, a problem immediately arose when it was discovered that the case carrying some specialist make-up items, namely the wigs for Jacqueline Pearce and Laurence Payne, together with the bushy Androgum eyebrows, had gone missing. After frantic enquiries to the airline, it was discovered the case had somehow made its way to Germany. Unfortunately, the items in the missing case meant that none of the planned scenes featuring either Chessene, Dastari, Shockeye or the augmented second Doctor could be filmed early on in the schedule as planned. On the first day, this resulted in only two out of the six planned scenes being completed. However, anxious not to let the day go entirely to waste, John Nathan-Turner suggested to Peter Moffatt that two scenes from Part 1 (Chessene revealing what she has learned from the Dona Arana and Stockeye's argument with Varl), which had been planned for the studio, could be easily transferred to a location setting.

As the airline could not promise when the missing case would arrive in Seville, the schedule was rearranged for the second day but, with only a limited number of days available at the hacienda, Downie informed make-up artist Catherine Davies that if the case had not appeared by the end of the second day, then alternative arrangements would need to be made.

By the end of Friday 10 August, the case, despite many telephone calls, had still not arrived at Seville (and, reputedly, it never did), so Davies, together with her assistant Jane Buxton, took over the production hotel's hair-dressing salon, purchased some cheap Spanish wigs and started to create a new set of hairpieces to be used the following day. It is a credit to their inventiveness and hard work that Jacqueline Pearce actually preferred the substitute wig to her original.

Due to the strict regulations imposed upon airline baggage, the visual effects team were not permitted to take any of the pyrotechnics needed for their one main effect at the hacienda, the blowing-up of the Sontaran spacecraft. Arrangements were duly made for the team to collect a car on the first day in Spain and drive to Madrid, where they could obtain the required explosives from the main Spanish supplier. When the team arrived in the city, they found that the supplier couldn't complete the order until the following day. With the

When the rushes were duly processed and checked, it was discovered that the film negative of all the Part 1 scenes showing Oscar and Anita in the olive grove (originally shot on Thursday 9) had been damaged by a serious scratch. Reluctantly (because the production office would have to shoulder the full cost), Saxon and Gomez were recalled to Spain to reshoot the affected scenes, which were completed on the unit's final day in Spain, Thursday 16 August. John Nathan-Turner was apparently not at all pleased when he viewed the original damaged footage to discover that the so-called 'serious scratch' was barely noticeable.

During the Part 3 scene showing Dastari searching the Bar Hosteria del Laurel in Santa Cruz, a number of the production team make cameo appearances. Sitting in the corner table are director Peter Moffatt and costume designer Jan Wright, while the unit's Spanish 'fixer', Mercedes Carnegie, appears as the woman in the upper window who throws a rose to Dastari. In this scene, she also wears the costume that was originally intended for Anita, but which was changed at the last minute when the producer and director felt that it was to 'fussy' for the character.

Comment

Peter Moffatt has sometimes been criticised for his 'lacklustre' direction of *The Two Doctors*. In some respects, the criticism is a valid one, but considering the problems encountered while in Spain, it's amazing that the location footage turned out as well as it did. It's a pity that the fishing scene in Part 1 wasn't shot later back in England to get away from it looking like the rest of the Spanish footage. Scenes around the hacienda are well handled, as is the material shot in the streets of Seville. It is regrettable, though, that more use wasn't made of some of the main squares and sights of the city rather than the narrow avenues and closed-in passageways of the Santa Cruz district.

Above: **The Doctor (Colin Baker) alights from the TARDIS at the beginning of *Revelation of the Daleks*. Note the replacement lamp on the top of the police box.**

local Spanish fire brigade hired to be on stand-by during the explosion at the hacienda, the effect couldn't be postponed to a later date, so the decision was made to improvise. Visiting a gun shop, large quantities of neat gunpowder were purchased so that charges could be constructed to the effects team's own design. Returning to the hacienda, the improvised charges were placed in holes dug into the courtyard and surrounded by gallons of petrol. The resulting detonation resulted in a huge round of applause from the cast and crew.

With their location scenes complete, James Saxon (Oscar Botcherby) and Carmen Gomez (Anita) along with Sontaran actors Clinton Greyn and Tim Raynham, returned to London on the morning of Sunday 12 August along with Visual Effects Assistant Simon McDonald, who was entrusted with safely returning the unprocessed 16mm film stock from the first three days of location work to the BBC.

REVELATION OF THE DALEKS

(tx 23 March to 30 March 1985)

The Story

Tranquil Repose is a facility where the wealthy are able to have their dead bodies frozen until cures for their terminal diseases can be found. Landing on Necros to mourn the loss of his friend Arthur Stengos, the Doctor discovers that the company's mysterious 'Great Healer' is in reality Davros, who is using some of the bodies to create synthetic food while others are turned into a new army of Daleks. Davros' plans are foiled when Daleks loyal to the Dalek Supreme land on Necros and take him prisoner.

The Locations
1. Bolinge Hill Farm, Buriton, Petersfield, Hampshire
2. Butser Hill, Queen Elizabeth Country Park, Horndean, Hampshire
3. Queen Elizabeth Country Park, Gravel Hill, Portsmouth Road, Horndean, Hampshire
   A. Wooded Area, The Roman Site
   B. Benhams Bushes
1. IBM, North Harbour Building, Cosham, Portsmouth, Hampshire
2. Goodwood Estate, Halnaker, West Sussex
3. Tangmere Aerodrome, Tangmere, West Sussex

Shooting Schedule

PART 1
▸▸ TARDIS materialises next to pond
Bolinge Hill Farm // 7 January 1985
▸▸ Peri discovers Herba Baculum Vitae
Butser Hill // 7 January 1985
▸▸ Doctor tries to hypnotise the mutant
QE Country Park – A // 8 January 1985
▸▸ Doctor and the mutant fight
QE Country Park – A // 8 January 1985
▸▸ Doctor talks to mutant before he dies
QE Country Park – B // 8 January 1985
▸▸ Doctor and Peri climb over the wall
Goodwood Estate // 10 January 1985
▸▸ Doctor and Peri discuss Stengos as they walk
Tangmere Aerodrome // 10 January 1985
▸▸ Doctor and Peri see Dalek
IBM // 9 January 1985
▸▸ Doctor finds memorial statue which collapses (1/2)
IBM // 9 January 1985

PART 2
▸▸ Orcini unpacks his gun
Tangmere Aerodrome // 10 January 1985
▸▸ Orcini destroys a Dalek
Tangmere Aerodrome // 10 January 1985

The Facts
On reading the script, director Graeme Harper decided that his main location requirement for the story was to find a suitably surreal and futuristic building to double for Tranquil Repose. Production manager Michael Cameron located the ideal building during a recce in Hampshire a few days later: IBM's headquarters in Cosham. Negotiations were immediately entered into with IBM over the use of the heavily guarded building and suitable terms were eventually agreed. However, to comply with the company's high security, BBC staff were forbidden from taking any still photographs of the

Above: **Graeme Harper directs Colin Baker prior to his 'death' scene under the memorial statue, filmed at IBM, Cosham.**

premises without a pass and were told not to enter the building unless specific permission had been obtained.

Waking up in his bedroom at the Langrish Hotel, near Petersfield, on the first morning of filming, Graeme Harper received something of a shock. Overnight, it had begun to snow heavily, completely transforming the landscape he had planned to use. Harper chose to push on as best he could and set out to Buriton to shoot his first scenes around the large pond at Bolinge Hill Farm.

Visual effects designer John Brace, together with two trained divers from the same department, had visited the farm the previous day and submerged an effects rig into the pond housing a 'woofer', a compressed air device that would create the underwater explosion seen in the finished episode. But by the time they arrived on the Monday morning, the pond's surface had frozen over. Breaking the surface ice, stuntman Ken Barker, who was playing the mutant caused by Davros' experimentation, donned a wetsuit and waded into the freezing water to achieve one of the opening shots of the story. This involved Peri emerging from the TARDIS and throwing her breakfast roll into the icy lake, which is then grabbed by a hand emerging from under the water. However, as only a close-up of Barker's hand was needed, it meant that he didn't have to submerge any more than was necessary.

A further problem arose when the TARDIS was unloaded from the scenic van and it was discovered that the flashing police box light had been left behind in London. As there was no way of getting hold of it in time, a temporary replacement was constructed out of what materials were available on site.

The second day of filming proved to be the most problematic. On completion of the work at Bolinge Farm, the production team moved across the other side of the A3 to Butser Hill to film the dialogue about the Herba Baculum Vitae that Peri collects for her botany collection. Although the scene was completed as scheduled, more bad news awaited Graeme Harper. As the highest point in the South Downs, Butser Hill (using an area known as the Beacon) was due to be used the following afternoon to film an important showpiece scene of the story, showing for the first time that Daleks were capable of flight. To achieve the effect, John Brace had designed a powerful spring-loaded platform, capable of launching a lightweight explosive-laden Dalek into the air. However, due to the heavy snowfall, vehicular access up Butser Hill proved impossible and the whole effect had to be abandoned, along with another film sequence of a Dalek watching the Doctor and Peri as they head towards Tranquil Repose. Loath to lose the exploding Dalek sequence entirely, however, the scene was rewritten in a simplified form and later shot at the disused Tangmere Aerodrome.

IBM requested that the BBC donate their facility fee to the Cliffdale School in Cosham. This was agreed and Colin Baker took time out of his schedule to visit the school and present a cheque to the headmaster.

The long shot of the IBM building was augmented by the addition of two large black pyramids towering overhead, which were added in post-production.

The Doctor's memorial statue was a four-piece prop constructed from Jabolite, sculpted using a heated wire by Derek Howarth. As planned, the original ending to the first episode extended a little beyond the memorial's collapse, with Peri crying as blood seeps from under the fallen stones. This ending was vetoed by John Nathan-Turner and thus the episode concluded with a whiteout as the statue crashes down. For the beginning of Part 2, an alternative sequence was used, eliminating the flowing blood and showing Tranquil Repose's chief embalmer Jobel meeting Peri as she gets to the statue.

The climax of the story was also due to feature a film sequence which ended up being completely abandoned. The first half, due to be shot at IBM on 9 January, showed Peri, and the embalmers Takis and Lilt escaping from Tranquil Repose, followed by the Doctor and Peri walking off into the sunset, scheduled to be filmed on either Monday the 7th or Tuesday the 8th at Butser Hill. Ultimately, the scene was rescripted and recorded in the studio.

Comment

On the surface, the location filming for *Revelation of the Daleks* is nothing special. It's only when you understand the immense problems and pressures Graeme Harper experienced during the course of the week – when he virtually had to throw away all his plans and start from scratch – that you really appreciate exactly how much he achieved.

THE TRIAL OF A TIME LORD 1-4 (THE MYSTERIOUS PLANET)

(tx 6 September to 27 September 1985)

The Story

Taking the Doctor out of time and space, the Time Lords place him on trial for breaking the First Law of Time. As proof of the Doctor's interference in the affairs of others, the Valeyard, the Doctor's chief accuser, begins to show evidence by means of images projected from the Matrix. Exploring the planet of Ravolox in the distant future, the Doctor and Peri stumble across the remains of Marble Arch underground station and realise that the planet is really Earth. Deep beneath the ground, survivors of a firestorm are living in the tunnels, their lives governed by Drathro, a robot programmed to guard three 'sleepers' from Andromeda and protect the secrets they brought with them. Also on Ravolox, two mercenaries, Glitz and Dibber, are looking for the secrets, but when Drathro's power converter is destroyed, a chain reaction begins which threatens the universe. The Doctor manages to avert disaster, but the sleepers' secrets are destroyed along with Drathro.

The Locations

1. Queen Elizabeth Country Park, Gravel Hill, Portsmouth Road, Horndean, Hampshire
2. Butser Ancient Farm Project, Pidham Hill, East Meon, Hampshire

Shooting Schedule

PART 1

▸▸ **TARDIS materialises (cut)**
QE Country Park – A // 8 April 1986
▸▸ **Doctor and Peri explore pursued by Glitz and Dibber**
QE Country Park – B/C/E // 8 April 1986
▸▸ **Glitz and Dibber meet the natives**
QE Country Park – G // 9 April 1986
▸▸ **Glitz and Dibber are brought to the native camp**
Butser Ancient Farm // 10 April 1986
▸▸ **Glitz and Dibber's audience with Katryca**
Butser Ancient Farm // 10 April 1986
▸▸ **Katryca examines Glitz's gun**
Butser Ancient Farm // 10 April 1986
▸▸ **Peri is brought to the camp**
Butser Ancient Farm // 10 April 1986

PART 2

▸▸ **Katryca talks to Peri and imprisons her**
Butser Ancient Farm // 11 April 1986
▸▸ **Peri's POV of the light converter**

Butser Ancient Farm // 10 April 1986

▸▸ **Katryca tells Glitz he is to be sacrificed**
Butser Ancient Farm // 11 April 1986

▸▸ **Glitz, Dibber and Peri leave Katryca's hut**
Butser Ancient Farm // 10 April 1986

▸▸ **Broken Tooth tells Katryca of prisoners escape**
Butser Ancient Farm // 11 April 1986

▸▸ **Glitz, Dibber and Peri escape from the guard**
Butser Ancient Farm // 10 April 1986

▸▸ **Glitz and Peri run through the forest**
QE Country Park – D // 9 April 1986

▸▸ **Dibber blows up the light converter**
Butser Ancient Farm // 11 April 1986

▸▸ **Broken Tooth leads the natives**
QE Country Park – D // 9 April 1986

▸▸ **Glitz, Peri and Dibber run to the tunnel**
QE Country Park – D // 9 April 1986

▸▸ **Doctor's party enters the tunnel (2/3)**
QE Country Park – C/D // 8 April 1986

PART 3

▸▸ **Doctor's party and natives head back to camp**
QE Country Park – D // 9 April 1986

▸▸ **Katryca imprisons all except Balazar**
Butser Ancient Farm // 11 April 1986

▸▸ **L1 Robot's POV**
QE Country Park – A // 9 April 1986

▸▸ **L1 Robot arrives at camp**
Butser Ancient Farm // 10 April 1986

▸▸ **Broken Tooth and Balazar tell Katryca about robot**
Butser Ancient Farm // 11 April 1986

▸▸ **L1 Robot's POV of camp**
Butser Ancient Farm // 10 April 1986

▸▸ **Katryca and natives attack the L1 Robot**
QE Country Park – F // 9 April 1986

▸▸ **Natives leave and Peri tends to Doctor**
QE Country Park – F // 9 April 1986

▸▸ **Glitz and Dibber with multiblasters**
QE Country Park – C // 8 April 1986

The Facts

The Trial of a Time Lord marked a significant change in the production of *Doctor Who*. From this point on, the shooting of exterior scenes on either 16mm or 35mm film stock would make way for the exclusive use of Outside Broadcast video cameras.

With recording due to begin on Tuesday 8 April 1986, the cast and crew arrived at the Butser Ancient Farm on Monday 7 April and spent the day rehearsing all the scenes set within the farm project, which would be recorded on the Thursday and Friday. While rehearsals were going on, the tunnel entrance, which would be used the following day, was being prepared at Queen Elizabeth Country Park.

Left: **Colin Baker and Nicola Bryant at the Butser Ancient Farm Project during the photocall for the new** *The Trial of a Time Lord* **season.**

One of the visual effects requirements that had been specified for the first day's recording was that of rain, to be seen in the opening sequences of the TARDIS materialising (which would eventually be cut from the finished episode) and the Doctor and Peri's walk through the forest. However, the first morning of recording was cold, overcast and misty, rendering the effect redundant.

The production team were booked into three different hotels in the Midhurst area during the week's recording, during which a number of the cast indulged in a pudding-eating contest.

Colin Baker: 'My fluctuating girth, which has been the subject of many a sponsored slim over the last few years, was put under considerable pressure by a pudding-eating contest at our unit hotel. I cannot recall now which agent provocateur prompted this Androgum-mimicking activity, but it pains me to admit that I pipped Joan [Sims] and Tony [Selby] at the post by a steamed treacle pudding and three profiteroles. Nicola Bryant was left at the starting gate, staring in disbelief at an enormous flaming pear…'[6]

Comment

The 23rd season was a critical one in the history of the programme. Following internal criticism at the BBC over some of the content of the previous season, a warning shot across the bow was given when the production of the new series was suspended for a few extra months, causing the collapse of all the planned stories for Colin Baker's second full season. In order for the programme to ensure

Right: Cover of the OB schedule drawn up for Parts 1-4 of *The Trial of a Time Lord*, referring to the 18 month hiatus imposed on the programme after season 22.

it's continued survival, it needed to return in a revitalised and refreshed form. While the first instalment of *The Trial of a Time Lord* is pleasant enough, it doesn't really have the 'grab' factor that was desperately needed at this point in the programme's history, a point which applies just as much to the exterior recording as to the rest of the story. In short, director Nicholas Mallett's location work is adequate, but never really exciting or inventive.

THE TRIAL OF A TIME LORD 5-8 (MINDWARP)

(tx 4 October to 25 October 1985)

The Story

The Valeyard begins his second line of accusation. The Doctor and Peri land on the colourful world of Thoros-Beta to follow up some worrying reports that someone on the planet has been supplying advanced arms to a less developed civilisation. The planet is home to the Mentors and to an old acquaintance, Sil. Their leader Kiv has had his brain enhanced to the point where his body can no longer contain it and his neurosurgeon, Crozier, is looking for a suitable replacement into which to transplant the organ. Subjected to Crozier's experiments, the Doctor begins to behave in an irrational way, seeming willing to betray Peri for his own safety. Peri joins forces with the captive barbarian King Yrcanos, but she is soon captured and becomes the new host for Kiv's brain. Suddenly, the Doctor is taken out of time and is transported to the trial space station.

Appalled by events, Yrcanos kills Peri. Shocked by what he's seen, the Doctor begins to sense that all is not as it seems and that evidence has been tampered with.

The Locations

1. Telscombe Cliffs, Peacehaven, East Sussex

Shooting Schedule

PART 5

▸▸ **TARDIS materialises on Thoros Beta**
Telscombe Cliffs // 16 June 1986

▸▸ **Doctor and Peri discuss the Warlord of Thordon**
Telscombe Cliffs // 16 June 1986

▸▸ **Doctor and Peri enter cave**
Telscombe Cliffs // 15 June 1986

PART 6

▸▸ **Doctor demands that Peri tell him about the Alphans**
Telscombe Cliffs // 15 June 1986

▸▸ **Doctor tells Peri that she is expendable**
Telscombe Cliffs // 15 June 1986

The Facts

Having scoured the coastline for a location that featured a suitable cave entrance, the ideal place was discovered no more than a mile from producer John Nathan-Turner's Saltdean home. However, the only potential problem was that Telscombe Cliffs was a stretch of coastline used as an unofficial nudist beach, which meant that attempts had to be made to keep it clear of naked people.

In an effort, as per Philip Martin's script, to make the location material appear more alien, the footage was treated with a new piece of digital processing equipment developed in America called HARRY, which, when connected to a standard paintbox unit, allowed the sea to be turned bright pink, the sky green and the shoreline lilac.

The biggest problem faced by the production team involved the first sequence to be recorded on Monday 16 June – the TARDIS' materialisation followed by the Doctor and Peri leaving the ship. The plan had been for the TARDIS to appear on the dry shoreline but, unbeknownst to the production team, the times for high and low tide at Telscombe listed in the OB Schedule had become transposed. When the scenic crew began to assemble the police box at 8.30 in the morning, the tide had already turned and was rapidly creeping up the beach. By the time the long shot of the scene was ready to begin, the water outside the TARDIS was getting increasingly deep, causing Baker and Bryant some concern, especially as they were wearing electrically powered radio microphones with transmitters around their waists.

For the scene where the Doctor accidentally liquefies the rock, the original intention was for it to then explode. A small visual effects charge was detonated and this was recorded along with the Doctor and Peri's reaction. The material was subsequently cut from the transmitted sequence.

Comment

Ron Jones' use of the HARRY system on the location footage is a worthwhile attempt to make the Thoros-Beta seem truly 'otherworldly', but it's probably a great blessing that its on screen use was kept to a minimum, as the colours are extremely garish, making the exterior material quite difficult to watch comfortably.

THE TRIAL OF A TIME LORD 13-14 (TIME INC.)

(tx 29 November to 6 December 1985)

The Story

Now accused of genocide, the Doctor finds his defence collapsing when Mel and Glitz appear in the courtroom. The Doctor is alarmed to hear that they have been brought by the Master, who has been watching events from within the Matrix, ably demonstrating that it can be penetrated and altered. The Master reveals that the Valeyard is in fact a distillation of the Doctor's dark side, between his twelfth and final regeneration. The Valeyard escapes and enters the Matrix, followed by the Doctor, who finds himself in a dark, Victorian nightmare world created by his future self. The Doctor wins through and defeats the Valeyard, for which he is granted his freedom. However, as the Time Lords finally leave the courtroom, it is revealed that the Valeyard has escaped.

The Locations

1. Camber Sands (next to Rye Golf Links), Camber, near Rye, East Sussex
2. Gladstone Pottery Museum, Uttoxeter Road, Longton, Stoke-on-Trent, Staffordshire

Shooting Schedule

PART 13

▸▸ Doctor and Glitz arrive in Matrix dreamscape
Gladstone Pottery Museum // 30 June 1986
▸▸ Outside the Fantasy Factory, Glitz is harpooned
Gladstone Pottery Museum // 1 July 1986
▸▸ Doctor convinces Glitz to help him
Gladstone Pottery Museum // 1 July 1986
▸▸ Doctor and Glitz meet Mr Popplewick 1
Gladstone Pottery Museum // 30 June 1986

▸▸ Doctor and Glitz meet Mr Popplewick 2
Gladstone Pottery Museum // 30 June 1986
▸▸ Doctor appears on beach and is pulled under
Camber Sands // 23/24 June 1986

PART 14

▸▸ Doctor confronts the Valeyard
Camber Sands // 23/24 June 1986
▸▸ Doctor and Glitz enter the beach hut
Camber Sands // 23/24 June 1986
▸▸ Master's TARDIS materialises and Doctor is placed
Gladstone Pottery Museum // 3 July 1986
▸▸ Mr Popplewick 1 emerges onto balcony (cut)
Gladstone Pottery Museum // 30 June 1986
▸▸ Master and Valeyard attack and Doctor rescued
Gladstone Pottery Museum // 3 July 1986
▸▸ Doctor on tumbrel
Gladstone Pottery Museum // 2 July 1986
▸▸ Melanie appears in the Matrix
Gladstone Pottery Museum // 30 June 1986
▸▸ Melanie 'saves' Doctor from execution
Gladstone Pottery Museum // 2 July 1986
▸▸ Offices searched and Master catches Glitz
Gladstone Pottery Museum // 1 July 1986
▸▸ Mr Popplewick revealed as the Valeyard
Gladstone Pottery Museum // 2 July 1986
▸▸ Doctor tries to disconnect the machinery
Gladstone Pottery Museum // 3 July 1986
▸▸ Valeyard begins to untie himself
Gladstone Pottery Museum // 3 July 1986
▸▸ Doctor runs and building explodes
Gladstone Pottery Museum // 3 July 1986

The Facts

As decided by writer Robert Holmes and script editor Eric Saward, the concluding two episodes of *The Trial of a Time Lord* would once again feature a life-and-

Above: **Colin Baker and Nicola Bryant on the beach at Telscombe Cliffs during the filming of** *The Trial of a Time Lord* **Parts 5-8 on 16 June 1986.**

Above: **Colin Baker is helped from the specially constructed pit at Camber Sands by production manager Ian Fraser. They are watched over by director Chris Clough.**

With only a couple of weeks to go before the cameras would begin recording at Camber Sands, Nathan-Turner called in the services of his friends, Pip and Jane Baker, who had scripted the Vervoid segment of the season. At a witnessed and minuted meeting to ensure that no information was divulged about Saward's version of the final episode, the Bakers were informed of the two locations that had already been chosen, were handed the recce photographs that had been taken and were briefed on the cliffhanger to Part 13, to which they would have to provide a solution.

The main sequence to be shot at Camber Sands was the cliffhanger to Part 13, showing the Doctor being pulled under the surface. Prior to the recording, a six-foot-deep pit in the sand had been dug and subdivided into two separate chambers. The first contained two visual effects assistants who poked their arms through a rubber membrane covering their side of the pit, on which was scattered a light covering of coloured cork chippings, used to represent the sand. The main part of the pit was filled with water and contained a hydraulic lift topped by a flat platform, which again was covered with cork. When the scene was recorded, Baker (who performed the stunt himself) lay flat on the platform, which was then lowered down, taking him under the surface of the water. However, it was necessary for him to hold onto the sides and force his own head below the surface to stop him from floating to the top. The scene had to be recorded three times before Chris Clough obtained a take that he approved of.

The Camber beach hut, which doubled as the exterior of the Master's TARDIS, was not a prop but a real building situated on the sand. However, when the sequence of the Doctor and Glitz entering the hut came to be recorded, it was found that the hut was locked and the key couldn't be traced. Left with little option, the production team had to break the lock in order to make the scene work.

death struggle within the dreamscape world of the Matrix. As a variation on what had been achieved with *The Deadly Assassin*, it was decided to make the Matrix a confusing world which would send the Doctor around in endless bureaucratic circles. To emphasise this, director Chris Clough looked at locations that were literally circular in appearance, with gasometers, cooling towers and power stations all being considered, the main requirement being that they should have an internal circular walkway. Eventually, when no suitable building could be found, the production team decided to use the Gladstone Pottery Museum which had arisen as a possible location due to its circular bottle kilns.

On 24 May 1986, scriptwriter Robert Holmes died from Hepatitis B, having been admitted to hospital in the middle of the month. With only a rough draft of his script for Part 13 completed, Eric Saward took on the role of finishing the final two episodes for *The Trial of a Time Lord*, based on the discussions that he'd previously had with Holmes.

The strained relationship that had been developing between Saward and Nathan-Turner finally came to a head when the producer strongly disagreed to the downbeat and open-ended conclusion that Saward had written to Part 14, showing both the Doctor and the Valeyard falling into a time-vent from which it is unlikely they will escape. Saward resigned on the spot and immediately withdrew the rights for his script to be used.

Comment

Having been presented as a mysterious, brooding character throughout *The Trial of a Time Lord*, it seemed only fitting that the Valeyard's dreamscape conjured up within the heart of the Matrix should be a dark, cold, Dickensian image of bricks and cobbled streets. The location sequences would have greatly benefited, however, had they been shot on film rather than videotape. Compare the location sequences in this story to those of *The Talons of Weng-Chiang*. Both feature a similar Victorian setting, both are shot at night, and yet the visual subtlety afforded by the use of film in *Talons* is missing in these final segments of *Trial* – which come over as being too dark, too cold and, ultimately, too 'real'. ∎

FOOTNOTES

1. *Doctor Who Winter Special,* 1985, p15
2. *Doctor Who Magazine,* #103, p.28
3. *The Doctor's Effects,* Steve Cambden, p.159
4. *The Colin Baker Years,* BBC Video, 1994
5. *Doctor Who Magazine #100,* 1985, p.16
6. *Doctor Who Magazine* #206, p.13

PART SEVEN

'What's so terrible about Perivale... ?'
The Doctor – *Survival*

SYLVESTER McCOY

THE SEVENTH DOCTOR

TIME AND THE RANI
(tx 7 September to 28 September 1987)

The Story

Violently pulled off course by the Rani onto the planet Lakertya, the Doctor and his new companion Mel are knocked unconscious. The Time Lord is forced to regenerate once again. In her base, the Rani and her bat-like servants, the Tetraps, have kidnapped some of the universe's greatest geniuses, intent on harnessing their collective intellect to fuel a giant brain. The Rani hopes its amassed knowledge help her destroy an approaching asteroid composed of 'strange matter'. The resultant explosion will expand the brain to planet size, creating a time manipulator with which the Rani can recreate the universe. When the Doctor's intellect is added into the brain, the solution is discovered, but the launch of the missile, forcibly constructed by the native Lakertyans, is briefly delayed, causing it to miss the asteroid.

The Locations
1. Cloford Quarry, Cloford, Frome, Somerset
2. Whatley Quarry, Whatley, Frome, Somerset
3. Westdown Quarry, near Chantry, Frome, Somerset

Shooting Schedule

PART 1
▸▸ **Ikona watches multicoloured lights in the sky**
Cloford Quarry // 4 April 1987
▸▸ **TARDIS materialises**
Westdown Quarry // 8 April 1987
▸▸ **Ikona approaches the TARDIS (cut)**
Westdown Quarry // 8 April 1987
▸▸ **Establishing shot – Rani's laboratory**
Cloford Quarry // 6 April 1987
▸▸ **Ikona enters the TARDIS**
Westdown Quarry // 8 April 1987
▸▸ **Sarn runs from the laboratory**

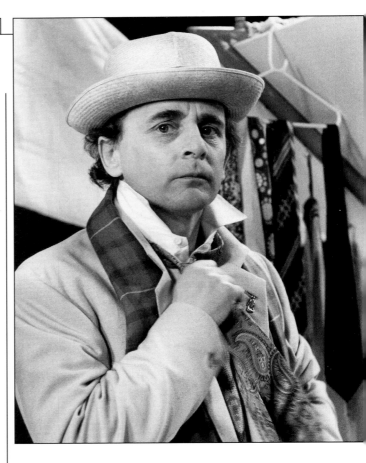

Cloford Quarry // 8 April 1987
▸▸ **Sarn runs from Mel and is killed in bubble trap**
Cloford Quarry // 7 April 1987
▸▸ **Angry, Ikona takes Mel hostage**
Cloford Quarry // 7 April 1987
▸▸ **Dragged along, Mel saves Ikona from bubble trap**
Cloford Quarry // 6 April 1987
▸▸ **Ikona and Mel run to hideout fearing pursuit**
Cloford Quarry // 7 April 1987
▸▸ **Ikona and Mel in hiding as Doctor and Rani find Sarn**
Cloford Quarry // 7 April 1987
▸▸ **Doctor and Rani enter TARDIS**
Westdown Quarry // 8 April 1987

Right: Ikona (Mark Greenstreet) and Mel (Bonnie Langford) witness the explosion in the lake during the filming of *Time and the Rani* at Whatley Quarry on 5 April 1987.

▸▸ Mel runs from hideout followed by Ikona
Cloford Quarry // 7 April 1987

▸▸ Urak watches as Mel runs
Whatley Quarry // 5 April 1987

▸▸ Hearing Urak, Mel gets caught in a bubble trap (1/2)
Whatley Quarry // 5 April 1987

PART 2

▸▸ Mel's bubble lands on lake, Ikona begins to disarm it
Whatley Quarry // 5 April 1987

▸▸ Ikona removes detonator, it explodes in the lake
Whatley Quarry // 5 April 1987

▸▸ Mel is attacked by Urak and is rescued by Ikona
Westdown Quarry // 8 April 1987

▸▸ Ikona shows Mel the Rani's laboratory
Cloford Quarry // 6 April 1987

▸▸ Faroon hears of Sarn's death
Cloford Quarry // 7 April 1987

▸▸ Rani leaves laboratory to go to her TARDIS
Cloford Quarry // 6 April 1987

▸▸ Ikona draws off Urak as Mel enters laboratory
Cloford Quarry // 6 April 1987

▸▸ Urak nets the Rani believing her to be Mel
Cloford Quarry // 4 April 1987

▸▸ Rani recovers and Urak follows
Cloford Quarry // 4 April 1987

▸▸ Rani enters her TARDIS leaving Urak outside
Cloford Quarry // 4 April 1987

▸▸ Rani orders Urak to find Mel
Cloford Quarry // 4 April 1987

▸▸ Rani returns to the laboratory
Cloford Quarry // 6 April 1987

PART 3

▸▸ Rani scans the grounds as Farron leaves Mel
Cloford Quarry // 7 April 1987

▸▸ Doctor runs from the laboratory
Cloford Quarry // 6 April 1987

▸▸ Mel is captured by Urak and Tetrap guard
Whatley Quarry // 5 April 1987

▸▸ Tetrap finds Doctor but is caught in bubble trap
Cloford Quarry // 4 April 1987

▸▸ Ikona and Doctor arrive at Centre of Leisure
Westdown Quarry // 8 April 1987

▸▸ Exchange takes place but Mel is a hologram
Whatley Quarry // 5 April 1987

▸▸ Doctor and Ikona walk along discussing Mel
Cloford Quarry // 4 April 1987

▸▸ Doctor considers Rani's plan but is captured
Cloford Quarry // 6 April 1987

PART 4

▸▸ Ikona escapes from Tetrap guard
Cloford Quarry // 4 April 1987

▸▸ Ikona carefully moves around
Cloford Quarry // 4 April 1987

▸▸ Tetraps swarm from laboratory watched by Ikona
Cloford Quarry // 6 April 1987

▸▸ Doctor and Mel leave laboratory and meet Ikona
Cloford Quarry // 6 April 1987

▸▸ Entrance to Centre of Leisure
Westdown Quarry // 8 April 1987

▸▸ Doctor's party run from laboratory
Cloford Quarry // 6 April 1987

▸▸ Rani sees countdown has stopped
Cloford Quarry // 4 April 1987

▸▸ Doctor tells Rani he's aborted the launch
Cloford Quarry // 4 April 1987

▸▸ Lakertyans and Mel watch the rocket launch
Westdown Quarry // 8 April 1987

▸▸ Rani dematerialises in her TARDIS
Cloford Quarry // 4 April 1987

▸▸ Doctor informs Lakertyans that the rocket will miss
Westdown Quarry // 8 April 1987

▸▸ Doctor gives tribute to Bayus, Ikona sorry Rani escaped
Westdown Quarry // 8 April 1987

▸▸ Doctor and Mel leave Lakertya
Westdown Quarry // 8 April 1987

The Facts

All the location recording for *Time and the Rani* was conducted under the story's original title, *Strange Matter*. Pip and Jane Baker's script had envisioned Lakertya as a woodland planet, but in early pre-production discussions designer Geoff Powell was among those who expressed concern that such a location could be too easily identified as rural England. As a result, the decision was taken to transpose the story to a treeless and rocky location.

An approach was duly made by production manager Tony Redstone to the Amey Roadstone Company, which in turn suggested using three of their quarries set around the Mendip Hills in Somerset. Of the three offered, only Whatley Quarry, which had the distinction of being the second biggest in Europe, was still actively being worked, the other two, Cloford and Westdown, having been closed some time earlier.

With all the dangers inherent in using a working pit, the decision to use Whatley was made on the basis of a large lake which had formed in one part of the quarry, which could be used to record the scenes of Mel's bubble trap landing on the water and subsequently being disarmed by the Lakertyan rebel, Ikona.

The main recording work for the story took place in Cloford Quarry where the scaffold and wood entrance to the Rani's laboratory, built by the Ealing-based set construction company Zircon, was erected against one of the quarry walls. To complete the illusion, a model of the upper rocket-launching gantry (based on a drawing that visual effects designer Colin Mapson had originally envisaged for the Bridge while working on *The Pirate Planet* in 1978) was transported to the quarry and hung as a foreground miniature in a number of shots.

The location work at Cloford Quarry on Tuesday 7 April was covered by an outside broadcast crew from the BBC's *Breakfast Time*. During the morning, 59 minutes of footage was recorded of work being done on the scenes of the young Lakertyan girl, Sarn, falling into the bubble trap, the subsequent explosions and both Ikona and the Doctor's reaction at seeing the skeleton. The final four and a half minute feature, complete with interviews with Sylvester McCoy, Bonnie Langford, Kate O'Mara and John Nathan-Turner conducted by Guy Mitchelmore, was transmitted on 5 May 1987.

Comment

The decision to transfer *Time and the Rani* from a woodland setting to a quarry may have been made with the best of intentions, but it certainly doesn't help to make Lakertya look either exciting or any less Earth-bound. *Doctor Who* is simply back in another quarry. That said, the superbly imposing entrance to the Rani's laboratory

Above: **Recording in Cloford Quarry on 7 April 1987, preparing to film the scenes around Sarn's skeleton.**

works extremely well, as do the high-powered explosions used for various sequences involving the bubble traps.

PARADISE TOWERS

(tx 5 October to 26 October 1987)

The Story

The TARDIS lands in Paradise Towers, a 304-storey building held as a great architectural achievement. In reality, it proves to be dilapidated and run-down, presided over by officious caretakers and their malevolent cleaning robots. The Doctor and Mel discover that the Towers are populated by rival gangs of girls called Kangs and cannibalistic old ladies. The Chief Caretaker is under the control of the disembodied architect of the Towers, Kroagnon, who is using the cleaning robots to dispose of the 'human flesh' that is polluting his creation by its presence. Kroagnon possesses the Chief Caretaker's body, but he is killed in an act of self-sacrifice by Pex, the only young male remaining in Paradise Towers.

The Locations

1. Elmswell House, Nightingales Lane, Chalfont St Giles, Buckinghamshire

Shooting Schedule

PART 1
➤ Scanner image of pool
   Elmswell House // 21 May 1987

PART 3
➤ Mel and Pex exit the lift and see the pool[1]
   Elmswell House // 21 May 1987
➤ Mel enthuses about the pool[2]
   Elmswell House // 22 May 1987

PART 4

▶ **Mel is attacked by pool cleaning robot**
Elmswell House // 22 May 1987

▶ **Mel destroys pool cleaning robot**
Elmswell House // 22 May 1987

▶ **Doctor and Kangs arrive**
Elmswell House // 21 May 1987

▶ **Pex is taunted and Rezzies arrive**
Elmswell House // 21 May 1987

▶ **Kangs and Rezzies unite**
Elmswell House // 21 May 1987

▶ **Plans are drawn to destroy cleaners**
Elmswell House // 21 May 1987

▶ **Pex offers to go to Kroagnon**
Elmswell House // 21 May 1987

The Facts

With all the main dialogue scenes having been completed on the first day of location filming, the second and final day was given over to the scenes of Mel (Bonnie Langford) and the Cleaning Robot in the swimming pool. The main problem, however, was that the swimming pool's heating unit had been turned off for some time and the water had dropped to a very low temperature.

Bonnie Langford: 'They hired a house which belonged to somebody like the Iranian Prime Minister, who was trying to sell it and didn't live in it. He had some staff who were living in a tiny portion of it. What they hadn't told us was that this pool had not been heated for about two years. The special effects boys were in the pool in wetsuits and couldn't stay in for longer than about half an hour. They said, "Right, we're going to do this little scene and then you're going to get into the pool, then we'll stop and do the other bit." They had warned me it was cold. And I said, "Can I ask a favour then, can we do it all in one go and get it over with – don't stop and leave me in this pool." I went in and was meant to say, "Oh, the water's lovely! Isn't it super?" I got in there and I could not speak! The cold! It was so cold! I got out of the pool and they got hairdryers to dry me off. Then I discovered the next day that the crew were all going into this sauna that they'd got working in the other room.'[3]

As Langford was not a strong swimmer, she was reticent about the required shots of her being pulled under the surface of the water. Ultimately, these were achieved by Ellie Bertram wearing a wig similar to Langford's hair.

As the swimming pool was supposed to be situated in the penthouse at the top of Paradise Towers, the shots of the pool looking from the patio needed to be treated in post-production, adding a false roof and thus disguising the trees surrounding Elmswell House.

The Pool Cleaning Robot, a prop controlled by the use of perspex rods, was supposed to feature a tentacle which emerged from the mouth and attached itself to Mel. When the mechanism failed to operate in a convincing manner, it was decided to abandon its use.

Comment

Given the freezing situation that Bonnie Langford found herself in, one has to admire her courage in enduring the difficult scenes. As the script had Mel constantly enthusing about how wonderful the pool would be and how much she was looking forward to her swim, Langford must have been hard-pressed to pull off the illusion that she was actually enjoying the experience. The crab-like Pool Robot itself is actually a far better construction than the other cleaning machines and works very well on screen.

DELTA AND THE BANNERMEN

(tx 2 November to 16 November 1987)

The Story

Having destroyed the Chimeron race, Gavrok and his mercenary Bannermen pursue the surviving Chimeron Queen, Delta. In a bid to escape, she joins a time-travelling group of Navarinos who are setting off for a holiday in the Disneyland of 1959. However, the spaceship hits a communications satellite, forcing it to crash-land outside the Shangri-La holiday camp in South Wales. The egg protected by Delta hatches and quickly develops into a new Chimeron Queen. Having tracked Delta to Earth, Gavrok kills the Navarinos and begins to pursue Delta. With the Doctor's help, the Bannermen are captured while Gavrok is killed by one of his own booby traps. Delta and her daughter are accompanied back to Chimera by Billy, a young mechanic, to help repopulate the planet.

The Locations

1. Springwell Quarry,[4] Springwell Lane, Rickmansworth, Hertfordshire
2. Majestic Holiday Camp, Friars Road, Barry Island, South Glamorgan
   A. Kitchen Service Tunnel
   B. Holiday Camp Entrance
   C. Yellow Chalet Area
   D. Mel and Delta / Billy's Chalet
   E. Dance Hall
   F. Dining Hall
   G. Laundry Store
   H. Storeroom
   I. Doctor's Surgery
   J. Gavrok / Hostages

Left: **Scenes around the TARDIS being recorded at the entrance on the Majestic Holiday Camp.**

3. British Tissues Hangar, Llandow Trading Estate, Llandow, South Glamorgan
4. Pysgodlyn Mawr Reservoir, Hensol Forest, near Welsh St Donats, South Glamorgan
5. Sutton Farm, Fort Road, Near Penarth, South Glamorgan
6. Coed Y Wallas, Near Castle Upon Alun, Mid Glamorgan

Shooting Schedule

PART 1

▸▸ **Loosing the battle, Delta and Chimeron run for ship**
Springwell Quarry // 24 June 1987

▸▸ **Gavrok is shot out of the spaceship**
Majestic Holiday Camp – A // 30 June 1987

▸▸ **Gavrok lands outside the ship**
Springwell Quarry // 24 June 1987

▸▸ **Chimeron gives Delta the orb**
Majestic Holiday Camp – A // 30 June 1987

▸▸ **Bannermen watch ship lift off**
Springwell Quarry // 24 June 1987

▸▸ **Doctor and Mel are told they've won a trip to Disneyland**
Llandow Trading Estate // 7 July 1987

▸▸ **Hawk and Weismuller gets film can from tree (cut)**
Hensol Forest // 26 June 1987

▸▸ **Hawk and Weismuller learn about satellite**
Hensol Forset // 26 June 1987

▸▸ **Tollmaster shows Doctor and Mel the bus**
Llandow Trading Estate // 7 July 1987

▸▸ **Delta and Gavrok on flight decks**
Majestic Holiday Camp – A // 30 June 1987

▸▸ **Delta lands the ship and boards the bus**
Llandow Trading Estate // 7 July 1987

▸▸ **Murray puts on some 50s music in the bus**
Majestic Holiday Camp – A // 30 June 1987

▸▸ **Hawk and Weismuller use radio and telescope**
Hensol Forest // 26 June 1987

▸▸ **Bus is hit by the satellite**
Majestic Holiday Camp – A // 30 June 1987

▸▸ **Weismuller learns that satellite is off course**
Hensol Forest // 26 June 1987

▸▸ **Bus violently shakes**
Majestic Holiday Camp – A // 30 June 1987

▸▸ **Bus lands at Shangri-La, passengers follow Burton**
Majestic Holiday Camp – B // 1 July 1987

▸▸ **Burton shows everyone to chalets**
Majestic Holiday Camp – C // 3 July 1987

▸▸ **Burton shows Mel and Delta their chalet**
Majestic Holiday Camp – D // 6 July 1987

▸▸ **Burton introduces Billy to Murray and Doctor**
Majestic Holiday Camp – C // 3 July 1987

▸▸ **Mel asks Delta if she wants to talk**
Majestic Holiday Camp – D // 6 July 1987

▸▸ **Work on bus engine, Murray breaks new crystal**
Majestic Holiday Camp – B // 1 July 1987

▸▸ **Delta pull her gun, Mel leaves for dinner**
Majestic Holiday Camp – D // 6 July 1987

▸▸ **Billy works on his bike, watched by woman**

tourist (cut)
Majestic Holiday Camp – H // 4 July 1987

▶▶ Gavrok interrogates and kills the Tollmaster
Llandow Trading Estate // 7 July 1987

▶▶ Mel talks to the Doctor in the dining hall
Majestic Holiday Camp – F // 30 June 1987

▶▶ At he dance, Billy sings and Ray dances with Doctor
Majestic Holiday Camp – E // 3 July 1987

▶▶ Hawk and Weismuller in tent
Majestic Holiday Camp // 6 July 1987

▶▶ Doctor follows Delta out of dance hall
Majestic Holiday Camp – E // 3 July 1987

▶▶ Doctor hears sobbing and enters laundry store
Majestic Holiday Camp – G // 6 July 1987

▶▶ Doctor and Ray hide as Keillor calls Gavrok (1/2)
Majestic Holiday Camp – G // 3 July 1987

▶▶ Orb breaks open and green baby emerges (1/2)
Majestic Holiday Camp – D // 6 July 1987

▶▶ Keillor threatens to kill Doctor and Ray (1/2)
Majestic Holiday Camp – G // 3 July 1987

PART 2

▶▶ Gavrok fires the beacon hunter
Majestic Holiday Camp – A // 30 June 1987

▶▶ Beacon explodes killing Keillor
Majestic Holiday Camp – G // 3 July 1987

▶▶ Billy arrives at chalet and Delta offers explanation
Majestic Holiday Camp – D // 6 July 1987

▶▶ Dawn breaks over Shangri-La
Majestic Holiday Camp // 6 July 1987

▶▶ Garonwy talks to Hawk and Weismuller
Sutton Farm // 27 June 1987

▶▶ Delta and Billy leave Mel to sleep
Majestic Holiday Camp – D // 6 July 1987

▶▶ Billy and Delta set off in the motorbike
Majestic Holiday Camp – H // 4 July 1987

▶▶ Doctor rouses Ray and they set off
Majestic Holiday Camp – G // 3 July 1987

▶▶ Vinny starts the day with a song
Majestic Holiday Camp – I // 4 July 1987

▶▶ Doctor explains the situation to Mel and Ray
Majestic Holiday Camp – D // 6 July 1987

▶▶ Billy and Delta stop by the lake
Hensol Forest – Lake // 26 June 1987

▶▶ Burton is sceptical, Doctor offers to take
him to TARDIS
Majestic Holiday Camp – I // 4 July 1987

▶▶ Mel tells Murray the Bannermen are on their way
Majestic Holiday Camp – C // 6 July 1987

▶▶ Burton is convinced after seeing the TARDIS
Majestic Holiday Camp – B // 2 July 1987

▶▶ Murray tells the tourists about the Bannermen
Majestic Holiday Camp – C // 3 July 1987

▶▶ Burton asks his staff to come to his office
Majestic Holiday Camp – I // 4 July 1987

▶▶ Doctor gives crystal to Murray and goes off
with Ray
Majestic Holiday Camp – B // 1 or 4 July 1987

▶▶ Burton orders his staff to pack
Majestic Holiday Camp – I // 4 July 1987

▶▶ Billy and Delta by the lake as the infant sings
Hensol Forest – Lake // 26 June 1987

▶▶ Doctor and Ray search, but to no avail
Coed Y Wallas // 29 June 1987

▶▶ Burton packs everyone into the coach
Majestic Holiday Camp – B // 1 July 1987

▶▶ Gavrok begins to scan the area
Majestic Holiday Camp – A // 30 June 1987

▶▶ Doctor talks to Hawk and Weismuller
Coed Y Wallas // 29 June 1987

▶▶ Murray takes out the crystal
Majestic Holiday Camp – B // 1 July 1987

▶▶ Doctor spots motorbike tracks and finds
Billy and Delta
Hensol Forest – Lake // 26 June 1987

▶▶ Murray does role call but Keillor is missing (cut)
Majestic Holiday Camp – B // 1 July 1987

▶▶ Keillor's scorched blue suede shoes and beacon (cut)
Majestic Holiday Camp – G // 3 July 1987

▶▶ Gavrok's trace is successful
Majestic Holiday Camp – A // 30 June 1987

▶▶ Bikes race past as Bannermen land
Coed Y Wallas // 29 June 1987

▶▶ Bus is destroyed, Gavrok takes Mel and
Burton hostage
Majestic Holiday Camp – B // 1 July 1987

▶▶ Delta hears Garonwy's bees
Coed Y Wallas // 29 June 1987

▶▶ Bannermen guard Hawk and Weismuller
Coed Y Wallas // 29 June 1987

▶▶ Doctor enlists Garonwy's help
Sutton Farm // 27 June 1987

▶▶ Doctor arrives for Mel and Burton (2/3)
Majestic Holiday Camp – J // 2 July 1987

PART 3

▶▶ Ray unlocks Hawk and Weismuller
Coed Y Wallas // 29 June 1987

▶▶ Bannermen shoot tracer dart into sidecar
Coed Y Wallas – Ford // 29 June 1987

▶▶ Garonwy shows Billy and Delta bees
Sutton Farm // 27 June 1987

▶▶ Garonwy shows Billy and Delta the honey store
Sutton Farm // 25 June 1987

▶▶ Arrex and Callon on radio to Gavrok
Coed Y Wallas // 29 June 1987

▶▶ **Doctor unsure which way to go**
Hensol Forest // 26 June 1987

▶▶ **Gavrok places and tests the sonic cone**
Majestic Holiday Camp – B // 2 July 1987

▶▶ **Doctor, Burton and Mel drive through cow field**
Coed Y Wallas // 29 June 1987

▶▶ **Doctor drives motorbike to goat field**
Sutton Farm // 25 June 1987

▶▶ **Doctor arrives at Garonwy's cottage and runs to barn**
Sutton Farm // 27 June 1987

▶▶ **Establishing shot – Bannerman ship**
Coed Y Wallas // 29 June 1987

▶▶ **Gavrok gives the order for blast off**
Majestic Holiday Camp – A // 30 June 1987

▶▶ **Arrex and Callon watch Garonwy's cottage**
Sutton Farm // 25 June 1987

▶▶ **POV – Delta and child leave the cottage**
Sutton Farm // 27 June 1987

▶▶ **Child grows and Delta shoots at Bannermen**
Sutton Farm // 27 June 1987

▶▶ **Callon runs leaving Arrex dead**
Sutton Farm // 25 June 1987

▶▶ **Gavrok gives order to land**
Majestic Holiday Camp – A // 30 June 1987

▶▶ **Spacecraft lands in goat field**
Sutton Farm // 25 June 1987

▶▶ **Doctor prepares cottage, they all leave**
Sutton Farm // 25 June 1987

▶▶ **Gavrok finds tracer, Callon arrives**
Sutton Farm // 25 June 1987

▶▶ **Doctor's convoy in progress**
Hensol Forest // 26 June 1987

▶▶ **Bannermen arrive at cottage and prepare to storm it**
Sutton Farm // 25 June 1987

▶▶ **Hawk touches sonic cone around TARDIS**
Majestic Holiday Camp – B // 2 July 1987

▶▶ **Bannermen fire at cottage**
Sutton Farm // 25/27 July 1987

▶▶ **Doctor thinks how to disarm sonic cone**
Majestic Holiday Camp – B // 2 July 1987

▶▶ **Bannermen get covered in honey and attacked by bees**
Sutton Farm // 6 July 1987

▶▶ **Billy is caught eating Chimeron food**
Majestic Holiday Camp // 3 July 1987

▶▶ **Doctor traces circle on ground as Bannermen land**
Majestic Holiday Camp – B // 2 July 1987

▶▶ **Doctor tells other the Bannermen are coming**
Majestic Holiday Camp – F // 30 June 1987

▶▶ **Billy woks on the amplifier and is collected by Doctor**
Majestic Holiday Camp – I // 4 July 1987

▶▶ **Bannermen are defeated and Gavrok killed**
Majestic Holiday Camp – B/C/I // 4 July 1987

▶▶ **Doctor warns Billy about his course of action**
Majestic Holiday Camp – D // 6 July 1987

▶▶ **Garonwy tells Hawk about the bee's life-cycle**
Majestic Holiday Camp – F // 30 June 1987

▶▶ **Billy puts box in sidecar and drives off with Doctor (cut)**
Majestic Holiday Camp – H // 2 July 1987

▶▶ **Weismuller ties up Bannermen and says goodbye**
Majestic Holiday Camp – A // 30 June 1987

▶▶ **Billy arrives and enters ship**
Majestic Holiday Camp // 2 July 1987

▶▶ **Billy stows his gear on the ship**
Majestic Holiday Camp – A // 30 June 1987

▶▶ **Delta and Billy say goodbye and Ray leaves**
Majestic Holiday Camp // 2 July 1987

▶▶ **Delta and Billy take off**
Majestic Holiday Camp – A // 30 June 1987

▶▶ **Doctor and Mel leave as campers arrive**
Majestic Holiday Camp – B // 2 July 1987

The Facts

The story was recorded under the title *Flight of the Chimeron*.

The filming done at Sutton's Farm for the scenes in and around the cottage belonging to the Welsh bee-keeper Garonwy was constantly beset by rain, necessitating that the planned order of sequences be altered, which also required a third unplanned day at the farm on Monday 6 July.

One of the most problematic shots to film was the arrival at the cottage of the Washington agents, Hawk and Weismuller, in the Morris Minor. Unfortunately, the camera angle used meant that the traffic on the nearby main road was constantly in shot. After several attempts, the production's two assistant floor managers, Christopher Sandeman and Kim Wilcocks, were sent down to the road to stop any vehicles until the shot could be completed.

The Series C Vincent Rapide motorbike and Steib sidecar were loaned to the production by enthusiast Mick Roberts from Cardiff on condition that they took good care of it. At one point, however, McCoy took a corner a little too enthusiastically, tipping the bike over and dumping both the bike and its passengers into the undergrowth. One mistake that wasn't noticed until late in the day related to the Part 3 scenes of the Doctor, Camp Director Burton and Mel driving the Vincent to the goat field where, for two shots, Sylvester McCoy had forgotten to remove his glasses.

By the time of filming, the holiday camp had been sold by its original owners, Butlin's, and was the property of another holiday company, Majestic, who were in the process of renovating the site. In order to maintain the 1950s feel, and to segregate the production team from Majestic's paying guests, the BBC were allocated the blocks of chalets in Yellow section, which had not undergone any modernisation.

Endeavouring to save some money, some of the OB crew decided to sleep in the allocated chalets, but rapidly lost interest in the idea after the first night when they were woken by rats.

Burton's dog seen in the first episode was actually John Nathan-Turner's own pet, Pepsi.

As the Nostalgia Trips coach needed to be dropped a few feet onto the front entrance of the holiday camp to simulate its bumpy arrival, the BBC purchased an old, clapped-out vehicle for £300. On completion of filming, the bus was then sold to BBC Exhibitions for the same amount of money, with a view to using it as an outdoor exhibit at the *Doctor Who* exhibition in Longleat. Housed in temporary storage, the bus was later re-used for the location work on *The Greatest Show in the Galaxy*.

The recording of *Delta and the Bannermen* was followed by two separate BBC film crews. The first was a team from the BBC regional news programme, *Wales Today*, which followed the filming at the Majestic Holiday Camp on Friday 3 July. The 2'10" report, broadcast that evening, followed recording of the Part 1 cliffhanger in the laundry store, together with interviews with Sylvester McCoy and John Nathan-Turner. Later, on Tuesday 7 July, a crew from the children's morning show *But First This…* followed the work being done outside the British Tissues Hangar at Llandow Trading Estate. The 5'45" item was broadcast on Monday 31 August and featured rehearsals of the Doctor and Mel meeting the Tollmaster (Ken Dodd) as well as Gavrok's interrogation of the same. Interviews were also conducted with McCoy as well as Bonnie Langford and Ken Dodd.

During the fortnight on location, OB VT Engineer Martin Perrett and his assistant Gary produced a special 13'30" video of various out-takes and clips of the location work, strung together with 1960s songs like 'Leader of the Pack' and 'Surfin' USA'.

For the first time since *The Talons of Weng-Chiang*, the composer of the programme's incidental music got a chance to be seen on screen. Knowing that a scene had been scripted featuring the holiday camp's mechanic, Billy, singing at the camp's 'Getting to Know You' dance, John Nathan-Turner asked Keff McCulloch to make an appearance as a member of the band. McCulloch appeared as the guitar player while his girlfriend Tracey Wilson and her sister Jodie appeared as the backing singers.

Keff McCulloch: 'We had a big party at the end. John likes parties and they'd been trying to get one together to celebrate the new series for a while, so they thought, '"Well, when we've finished the day's filming, we may as well have a party here" – they'd hired this holiday camp hall for filming, and so they used that! So the band I'd put together accompanied everybody, and everyone did a cabaret! That was hysterical! Absolutely brilliant. Sylvester got up on stage, held up his hand and said, "I have in my hand a 12-foot piece of knicker elastic! And with the help of Mr Don Henderson [who then walked on stage] I'm going to put one end of this elastic in Mr Henderson's mouth, I'm then going to go to the back of the hall, stretch it to 24 feet, and then let go!" So, everybody roared at that! So, Don Henderson's standing there, with this elastic in his mouth, and Sylvester climbed all over the chairs, moved everyone out of the way and ended up standing on the stairs, right at the back of the hall. Then, he shouted out, "Right, are you ready, Mr Henderson?" and Don went "Yeah… !" – he opened his mouth – and the elastic shot to the back, and Sylvester literally flew off the stairs! I've never seen anything funnier in my life!'[5]

The scenes set on the bridges of the two Bannermen spaceships, as well as those on the Nostalgia Trips coach as it heads to Earth, were all recorded on location in a service tunnel which ran to the kitchens in the camp's entertainments block.

Unused Locations

In his submitted scripts, Malcolm Kohll had originally envisaged the picnic location that Billy takes Delta and her baby to in Part 2 as a seaside beach, with a location somewhere on the Gower Peninsula being suggested. This, and the idea that Billy's Vincent motorbike should first be seen at a boatyard, were both abandoned to avoid having to visit any more locations than were absolutely necessary.

Comment

Set the daunting task of recording the first all-location story (barring a few seconds' worth of TARDIS interiors, shot during the production of *Dragonfire*) since *The Sontaran Experiment* in 1975, Chris Clough did remarkably well, successfully conjuring up the look and the feel of his 1950s Welsh setting. Also worthy of note are the brief opening scenes shot at Springwell Quarry. With the electronically added blue colour wash over the picture and the large ringed planet in the sky, it does actually look like an alien world rather than the Rickmansworth chalk quarry it is. But the best shot of the entire story is the wonderful closing moment when Garonwy, framed by the Shangri-La sign, looks back as the TARDIS dematerialises and gives a knowing half-wink. Perfect.

REMEMBRANCE OF THE DALEKS
(tx 5 October to 26 October 1988)

The Story

The Doctor lands in London during November 1963 as two Dalek factions, the Imperial white and the Renegade black, are seeking to gain control of the Hand of Omega, a remote stellar manipulator left behind in London by the First Doctor. A Dalek shuttle lands in the playground of Coal Hill School and its platoon of Imperial Daleks, together with a powerful Special Weapons Dalek, captures the device and transports it to their orbiting spacecraft. By communicator, the Doctor pleads with the Imperial leader, the Emperor Dalek, who is revealed to be Davros, not to use the tremendous power of the Hand of Omega. Davros ignores the Doctor and activates the device, which proceeds to follow a predetermined course set by the Doctor. The device sends Skaro's sun supernova, destroying Skaro and then obliterating the Dalek craft.

The Locations

1. Theed Street, London, SE1
   * No 12 – Yard and Warehouse
   * Door opposite 12 Theed Street
2. Kew Bridge Steam Museum, Green Dragon Lane, Brentford, Middlesex
3. Old Oak Common Lane, East Acton, London, W3
4. Streets around Kendal Avenue, North Acton, London, W3
5. Willesden Lane Cemetery, Willesden Lane, London, NW6
6. Territorial Army Hall, Horn Lane, Acton, London, W3
7. John Nodes Funeral Service, 181 Ladbroke Grove, London, W10
8. St John's CE Juinor and Infants School, Macbeth Street, Hammersmith, London, W6
   * Playground
   * Covered Playground
   * Chemistry Laboratory
   * Stairwell
9. Macbeth Street, Hammersmith, London, W6
   * Alley off Macbeth Street
   * Junction Macbeth Street and Riverside Gardens
10. Windmill Walk, London, SE1
    * Railway Bridge, Junction with Wootton Street

Shooting Schedule

PART 1

▶▶ Doctor and Ace arrive, see van and girl
Macbeth Street – Alley/Street // 12 April 1988

▶▶ Doctor examines aerial on top of van

Macbeth Street // 12 April 1988

▶▶ Doctor examines burn marks, girl runs off
St John's School – Playground // 9 April 1988

▶▶ Doctor crosses to the van and climbs in
Macbeth Street // 12 April 1988

▶▶ Ace returns with Mike, they get in the van
Macbeth Street – Alley/Street // 12 April 1988

▶▶ Army and Doctor battle with Dalek at Totters Lane
Kew Bridge Steam Museum // 6/7 April 1988

▶▶ Ace drives under bridge and swaps seats
Old Oak Common Lane // 8 April 1988

▶▶ Doctor drives van around corner, heading for school
Macbeth Street/Riverside Gdns // 12 April 1988

▶▶ Establishing shot – Army HQ
Horn Lane TA Hall // 8 April 1988

▶▶ Doctor and Ace return to school, watched by girl
St John's School – Playground // 13 April 1988

▶▶ Ratcliffe's men collect Dalek remains
Kew Bridge Steam Museum // 7 April 1988

▶▶ Doctor and Ace look out of laboratory window
St John's School – Classroom // 9 April 1988

PART 2

▶▶ Doctor and Ace get Anti-Tank Gun from Land Rover
Macbeth Street // 12 April 1988

▶▶ Doctor signs for gun and runs back to school
Macbeth Street // 12 April 1988

▶▶ Establishing shot – Funeral Parlour
John Nodes Funeral Service // 8 April 1988

▶▶ Doctor and Rev. Parkinson walk to grave
Willesden Lane Cemetery // 8 April 1988

▶▶ Headmaster and Mike fight, Hand of Omega is buried
Willesden Lane Cemetery // 8 April 1988

▶▶ Establishing shot – Army HQ

Above: **The Dalek invasion is temporarily halted by the arrival of the fire brigade on 4 April 1988.**

St John's School – Playgrd/Class // 13 April 1988
▸▸ **Dalek shuttle lands, Gilmore is ready to co-operate (3/4)**
St John's School – Playgrd/Class // 11 April 1988

PART 4

▸▸ **Grey and White Daleks battle**
Windmill Walk – Railway Bridge // 4 April 1988
▸▸ **Special Weapons Dalek destroys Grey Daleks**
Windmill Walk – Railway Bridge // 4 April 1988
▸▸ **Doctor lassos shuttle and slides down rope**
St John's School – Playgrd/Class // 11 April 1988
▸▸ **Mike is caught by two Daleks at Ratcliffe's yard**
12 Theed Street // 4 April 1988
▸▸ **Doctor's party exits the Dalek shuttle**
St John's School – Playground // 11 April 1988
▸▸ **Dalek's battle in Ratcliffe's yard**
12 Theed Street // 5 April 1988
▸▸ **Daleks leave with Hand of Omega, Ace follows Mike**
12 Theed Street // 5 April 1988
▸▸ **Daleks return to shuttle with Hand of Omega**
St John's School – Playground // 11 April 1988
▸▸ **Shuttle takes off**
St John's School – Playground // 11 April 1988
▸▸ **Doctor watches shuttle take off**
Macbeth Street – Alley // 12 April 1988
▸▸ **Ace watches shuttle fly overhead, followed by girl**
Theed Street // 4 April 1988
▸▸ **Doctor finds Black Dalek**
Theed Street // 5 April 1988
▸▸ **Doctor talks to Black Dalek which destroys itself**
Theed Street // 5 April 1988
▸▸ **Doctor examines remains of Black Dalek**
Theed Street // 5 April 1988
▸▸ **Mike's funeral**
Willesden Lane Cemetery // 8 April 1988

The Facts

To cope with the rigours of recording on the streets of London, the Dalek casings were once again internally modified by visual effects designer Stuart Brisdon. The small castors on the base of the Daleks were replaced with three orange ball-shaped wheels, normally seen on wheelbarrows. Unfortunately, the redesign caused the Daleks to wobble alarmingly on the rough, cobbled ground around Theed Street, resulting in numerous retakes being required. Eventually, Brisdon had to replace the standard castors and move the Daleks on unseen running boards.

The Territorial Army Hall in Horn Lane used to represent the exterior of the temporary Army HQ was the same hall used between 10 and 20 May 1965 to rehearse the third and fourth episodes of *The Chase*.

Above: **The Dalek shuttle is lowered by crane into the playground of St John's School during the recording of *Remembrance of the Daleks* on 11 April 1988.**

Horn Lane TA Hall // 8 April 1988
▸▸ **Ace hears Dalek orders, Dalek fires at Ace**
St John's School – Class/Stair // 9 April 1988
▸▸ **Ace attacks Dalek and flees downstairs**
St John's School – Class/Stair // 9 April 1988
▸▸ **Ace surrounded by Daleks, rescued by Doctor (2/3)**
St John's School – Cov'd Playgrd // 13 April 1988

PART 3

▸▸ **Ratcliffe discovers new grave**
Willesden Lane Cemetery // 8 April 1988
▸▸ **Ratcliffe pokes grave and gets a shock**
Willesden Lane Cemetery // 8 April 1988
▸▸ **Ratcliffe's men exhume grave watched by girl**
Willesden Lane Cemetery // 8 April 1988
▸▸ **Ratcliffe's men continue to dig**
Willesden Lane Cemetery // 8 April 1988
▸▸ **Ratcliffe and men arrive back in yard**
12 Theed Street // 4 April 1988
▸▸ **Doctor and Ace return to school**
St John's School – Playground // 13 April 1988
▸▸ **Hand of Omega unloaded, Daleks advance on men**
12 Theed Street // 4 April 1988
▸▸ **Doctor and Ace dodge the Daleks as they near yard**
Theed Street – Door opp. No.12 // 4 April 1988
▸▸ **Doctor finds dead men and Hand of Omega in yard**
12 Theed Street // 4 April 1988
▸▸ **Doctor and Ace run from warehouse**
12 Theed Street // 4 April 1988
▸▸ **Doctor and Ace hide in workman's hut**
Windmill Walk // 4 April 1988
▸▸ **Doctor and Ace meet Mike, followed by Daleks**
Macbeth Street – Alley/Street // 12 April 1988
▸▸ **Daleks and Army battle in playground**
St John's School – Playground // 13 April 1988
▸▸ **Daleks receive order to retreat**

The entire scene of the Doctor and Ace driving in the Red IV van from Totters Lane back to Coal Hill School had to be redubbed due to the difference in sound levels experienced while driving along the roads. These second unit scenes were directed by John Nathan-Turner, who was sitting in the back of the van together with his small crew. One major difficulty emerged when the myopic McCoy was required to drive the van without his glasses, a problem further exacerbated by the fact that the camera mount strapped to the near side of the vehicle increased the width on one side by some degree. As a result, the camera nearly got smashed against various obstacles on more than one occasion.

The final shot of this scene, showing the van driving around the corner of Macbeth Street into Riverside Gardens, was originally meant to be the conclusion of the sequence where Mike, Rachel and Allison, all members of the team dealing with alien transmissions, are initially called to the activity in Totters Lane.

The securing of St John's School as a location occurred very late in the day, which meant that director Andrew Morgan's first visit to the site was on the date of the camera recce. Unfortunately, production manager Michael McDermott was rather hard of hearing and was unaware of the noise coming from the nearby Hammersmith flyover.

The prop Coal Hill School sign attached to the wall of St John's gives the name of the headmaster as 'H Parson', an in-joke referring to Hugh Parson, the production's videotape editor.

Scriptwriter Ben Aaronovitch had indicated in his original scripts that the Dalek shuttle could be achieved using miniatures electronically added to the picture. However, as various other activities were scripted around the spacecraft, Andrew Morgan decided to achieve the effect for real. The full-sized shuttle craft, constructed of fibreglass panels attached to a metal frame, was erected in the playground of St John's School on Sunday 10 April and duly attached to a large mobile crane in order to 'fly' the ship in and out of the playground.

The destruction of the prop gates at 12 Theed Street, as seen in Part 3, was so powerful that it managed to dislodge the top of the Special Weapons Dalek as well as blowing six of the hemispheres clean off the skirt of one of the Imperial Daleks. Some judicious editing of the scene meant that the damage to the Daleks was barely seen on screen. The explosion also managed to set off various car alarms in the area.

A rather more serious incident occurred on Monday 4 April when the scenes of the battle between the two Dalek factions was staged. The chosen location was the railway bridge running over Windmill Walk, only a short distance from Waterloo East railway station. Although the various authorities had been informed of the recording, they were seemingly unaware of the size of the explosions being employed. Believing it to be an IRA attack upon the station, the fire brigade, numerous ambulances and police cars all turned up at the location to discover a group of Daleks emerging from the smoke.

Simon Williams, who played Group Captain Gilmore, became renowned during the production for his ribald sense of humour.

Karen Gledhill (Allison Williams): 'When they did the big explosion in the chemistry lab, Simon told some terrible story, something very rude about hamsters! He told it as we were all crouching down, ready to go. We were desperately trying not to laugh!'[6]

To supplement the crowd of schoolchildren seen at the beginning of Part 1, several young relatives of the cast and crew appeared namely Tam Williams (son of Simon Williams), Hero Trew (son of Ken Trew, costume designer), Zoe Morgan (daughter of Andrew Morgan, director) and Tasmin Breaks (sister of Jasmine Breaks – 'The Girl').

For the third time in the series' history, scenes were scripted to be set in the junkyard at 76 Totters Lane. As set dressing, a large set of gates were painted and erected at the rear of the Kew Bridge Steam Museum. However, instead of signwriting the correct name of 'I M Foreman', the scenic team had inadvertently painted 'I W Forman', which then got altered to the equally incorrect 'I M Forman'.

Comment

The Daleks are finally back with a bang in *Remembrance of the Daleks*, undoubtedly one of the best stories of the programme's latter years with superb location work to match. The earth-shaking explosions in Part 4 and the excellent Dalek shuttle craft landing and taking off are the highlights, but many of the smaller scenes are just as effective in their own way. The Doctor's burial of the Hand of Omega assisted by the blind Reverend Parkinson shows how video effects can be successfully matted onto location work given stable OB images to work with.

SILVER NEMESIS
(tx 23 November to 7 December 1988)

The Story

A meteor containing a statue made of the living metal, validium, created by Rassilon as the ultimate defence for Gallifrey, crash-lands in Windsor in November 1988. The statue is rapidly pursued by three different factions – the Cybermen, a group of Nazis intent on beginning

Left: Sylvester McCoy and Dolores Gray promote *Silver Nemesis* outside Hiorne's Tower on the Arundel Estate.

the Fourth Reich and Lady Peinforte, an old adversary of the Doctor who has travelled from the 17th century to acquire the statue made in her image. All are intent on reuniting the statue with its two other validium components – a bow and arrow, which will activate the statue's power. Eventually, the Doctor appears to hand control of the completed validium statue to the Cyberleader, who orders that it be sent to join the orbiting Cyberfleet. However, the Nemesis statue completely destroys the fleet, fulfilling a trap set by the Doctor.

The Locations
1. Greenwich Gas Works, Tunnel Avenue, Greenwich, London, SE10
2. High Street, Arundel, West Sussex
3. Tarrant Street, Arundel, West Sussex
4. London Road, Arundel, West Sussex
5. Arundel Castle, Arundel, West Sussex
   - West Wing
   - Quadrangle
   - The Keep
   - Vault
6. Arundel Estate, Arundel, West Sussex
   - Hiorne's Tower
   - Shooting Range
7. 'Casa Del Mar', Aldsworth Avenue, Goring-by-Sea, West Sussex
8. St Mary's House, The Street, Bramber, West Sussex
9. Black Jack's Mill Restaurant, The Lodge, Black Jack's Mill, Harefield, Middlesex

Shooting Schedule[7]

PART 1
- **Karl checks computer and reports to De Flores**
  Casa Del Mar // 2 July 1988
- **Lady Peinforte shoots at birds, mathematician works**
  St Mary's House // 1 July 1988
- **Nazi's drink toast to Fourth Reich, leave with bow**
  Casa Del Mar // 2 July 1988
- **Mathematician calculates Nemesis' return**
  St Mary's House // 1 July 1988
- **Doctor and Ace listen to jazz and are shot at**
  Black Jack's Mill Restaurant // 5 July 1988
- **Human blood is needed as the final potion ingredient**
  St Mary's House // 1 July 1988
- **Doctor discovers Earth faces imminent destruction**
  Black Jack's Mill Restaurant // 5 July 1988
- **Lady Peinforte and Richard travel from 1638 to 1988**
  St Mary's House // 1 July 1988

▸▸ Doctor says he's known about destruction since 1638
Black Jack's Mill Restaurant // 5 July 1988

▸▸ TARDIS materialises in Windsor Castle vaults
Arundel Castle – Vault // 27 June 1988

▸▸ Lady Peinforte's arrow begins to pulsate
St Mary's House // 1 July 1988

▸▸ Comet crashes into the ground
Greenwich Gas Works // 22 June 1988

▸▸ Doctor admits he fired Nemesis into space
Arundel Castle – Vault // 27 June 1988

▸▸ Richard sees strange carriage outside
St Mary's House // 1 July 1988

▸▸ Police car arrives at landing site
Greenwich Gas Works // 22 June 1988

▸▸ Lady Peinforte throws chair through window
St Mary's House // 1 July 1988

▸▸ Bow is missing, lights go out
Arundel Castle – Vault // 27 June 1988

▸▸ TARDIS arrives in 1638, Doctor sees corpse
St Mary's House // 1 July 1988

▸▸ Policemen examine comet as Lady Peinforte watches
Greenwich Gas Works // 22 June 1988

▸▸ Doctor explains that Nemesis is made of validium
St Mary's House // 1 July 1988

▸▸ Policemen are gassed
Greenwich Gas Works // 22 June 1988

▸▸ TARDIS arrives at Windsor, Doctor chases Queen
Arundel Castle – West Wing // 27 June 1988

▸▸ Lady Peinforte plans revenge on Doctor
Greenwich Gas Works // 22 June 1988

▸▸ Doctor tries to convince security men
Arundel Castle // 27 June 1988

▸▸ Walkmen are reprogrammed (cut)
Greenwich Gas Works // 22 June 1988

▸▸ Ace sees a portrait of herself on the castle wall (cut)
Arundel Castle // 27 June 1988

▸▸ Nazis, TARDIS and Cybermen arrive at landing site (1/2)
Greenwich Gas Works // 22 June 1988

PART 2

▸▸ Cybermen battle as Doctor and Ace escape with bow
Greenwich Gas Works // 22/23 June 1988

▸▸ Lady Peinforte and Richard walk down back street
Tarrant Street // 30 June 1988

▸▸ Cybermen cut open the comet
Greenwich Gas Works // 23 June 1988

▸▸ Doctor burns some of the mathematician's papers (cut)
St Mary's House // 1 July 1988

▸▸ Cybermen carry Nemesis comet into their

Above: The Doctor (Sylvester McCoy) and Ace (Sophie Aldred) examine a familiar portrait in a scene cut from Part 1 of *Silver Nemesis.*

spaceship (cut)
Greenwich Gas Works // 24 June 1988

▸▸ Lady Peinforte and Richard watched by skinheads
High Street // 30 June 1988

▸▸ Cybership flies overhead
Arundel Estate – Near Hiorne's Tower // 28 June 1988

▸▸ De Flores sprinkles out some gold dust
Arundel Estate // 30 June 1988

▸▸ TARDIS materialises, Doctor begins to track statue
Arundel Estate // 26 June 1988

▸▸ Cybership lands
Arundel Estate – Near Hiorne's Tower // 28 June 1988

▸▸ Skinheads attempt to mug Lady Peinforte and Richard
London Road // 30 June 1988

▸▸ Doctor and Ace walk along whistling

Arundel Estate // 26 June 1988
▸▸ Cyberleader orders communications unit activated
Arundel Estate – Hiorne's Tower // 28 June 1988
▸▸ Skinheads hang from tree
Arundel Estate // 26 June 1988
▸▸ Doctor tries to jam Cyber signal with jazz tape
Arundel Estate // 28 June 1988
▸▸ Cyber Lieutenant objects to Cyberleader's orders
Arundel Estate – Hiorne's Tower // 28 June 1988
▸▸ Doctor and Ace listen to jazz on hillside
Arundel Estate // 28 June 1988
▸▸ Jazz music comes through Cybermen's equipment
Arundel Estate – Hiorne's Tower // 28 June 1988
▸▸ Doctor and Ace decide to leave
Arundel Estate // 28 June 1988
▸▸ Doctor finds skinheads
Arundel Estate // 26 June 1988
▸▸ Lady Peinforte, Richard and Cybermen at the crypt
Arundel Estate – Hiorne's Tower // 28 June 1988
▸▸ Karl tells De Flores he's seen Lady Peinforte
Arundel Estate // 30 June 1988
▸▸ Hiding, Doctor tells Ace to blow up Cybership
Arundel Estate – Near Hiorne's Tower //
28 June 1988
▸▸ Cyberleader agrees to withdraw
Arundel Estate – Hiorne's Tower // 28 June 1988
▸▸ Lady Peinforte realises statue is in her tomb
Arundel Estate – Hiorne's Tower // 29 June 1988
▸▸ Doctor distracts Watchmen, Ace destroys ship
Arundel Estate – Near Hiorne's Tower //
28 June 1988
▸▸ Karl and De Flores set off
Arundel Estate // 30 June 1988
▸▸ Cybermen kill Watchmen, Ace is horrified
Arundel Estate – Near Hiorne's Tower //
28 June 1988
▸▸ Tomb contains statue, but no bones
Arundel Estate – Hiorne's Tower // 29 June 1988
▸▸ Doctor tries to find out who's listening to signal
Arundel Estate // 26 June 1988
▸▸ De Flores offers alliance with Cybermen
Arundel Estate // 28 June 1988
▸▸ Scanner doesn't show anyone receiving signal
Arundel Estate // 26 June 1988
▸▸ Lady Peinforte and Richard flee from
De Flores and Karl
Arundel Estate – Hiorne's Tower // 29 June 1988
▸▸ Doctor alters settings and Cyberships become visible
Arundel Estate // 26 June 1988

PART 3
▸▸ Lady Peinforte and Richard exit secret passage
Arundel Estate – Firing Range // 26 June 1988

▸▸ Ace is scared but refuses to return to TARDIS
Arundel Estate // 29 June 1988
▸▸ Cybermen listen to jamming signal
Arundel Estate – Hiorne's Tower // 29 June 1988
▸▸ Doctor and Ace run to crypt, music ends
Arundel Estate – Hiorne's Tower // 29 June 1988
▸▸ Doctor activates statue and runs from crypt
Arundel Estate – Hiorne's Tower // 29 June 1988
▸▸ Lady Peinforte realises Nemesis is alive
Arundel Estate // 28 June 1988
▸▸ TARDIS dematerialises
Arundel Estate // 26 June 1988
▸▸ De Flores uses gold dust to escape
Arundel Estate – Hiorne's Tower // 29 June 1988
▸▸ Doctor moves chess pieces and Ace collects coins
St Mary's House // 1 July 1988
▸▸ Lady Peinforte and Richard watch a hitchhiker
Arundel Estate // 30 June 1988
▸▸ Cyberleader determines to stop Doctor
Arundel Estate – Hiorne's Tower // 29 June 1988
▸▸ TARDIS arrives inside hanger
Greenwich Gas Works // 23 June 1988
▸▸ Miss Remington offers a lift
Arundel Estate // 30 June 1988
▸▸ Statue returns to hanger, Doctor give it the bow
Greenwich Gas Works // 23 June 1988
▸▸ Miss Remington talks her passengers
Arundel Estate // 30 June 1988
▸▸ Ace talks to the statue
Greenwich Gas Works // 23 June 1988
▸▸ Miss Remington talks her passengers
Arundel Estate // 30 June 1988
▸▸ Ace destroys a Cyberman, Cyberleader orders
her death
Greenwich Gas Works // 23 June 1988
▸▸ Lady Peinforte knows Remington's ancestors
Arundel Estate // 30 June 1988
▸▸ Ace kills another Cyberman and is fired at
Greenwich Gas Works // 24 June 1988
▸▸ Doctor calculates while statue waits
Greenwich Gas Works // 23 June 1988
▸▸ Ace kills Cyberman, but drops her coins
Greenwich Gas Works // 24 June 1988
▸▸ Doctor sets rockets for Cyberfleet
Greenwich Gas Works // 23 June 1988
▸▸ Ace destroys Cybermen on high gantry
Greenwich Gas Works // 23 June 1988
▸▸ Orders to statue, Cybermen killed by test fire
Greenwich Gas Works // 24 June 1988
▸▸ Cyberleader pulls gold coin from chest panel
Greenwich Gas Works // 23 June 1988
▸▸ Final face-off, Nemesis launches for Cyberfleet
Greenwich Gas Works // 24 June 1988

▸ **Miss Remington watches the comet blast off (cut)**
Arundel Estate // 30 June 1988
▸ **Richard kills Cyberleader with gold arrow**
Greenwich Gas Works // 24 June 1988
▸ **Richard entertains the Doctor and Ace in 1638**
St Mary's House // 1 July 1988

The Facts

One of the main guest artists engaged for *Silver Nemesis* was Hollywood and Broadway star Dolores Gray, who was appearing at the time in *Follies* at the Shaftesbury Theatre. Having hired out a Lincoln Continental stretch limousine to the production, the owner of the company, on learning of its illustrious passenger, agreed not only to drove the vehicle himself but also to transport Dolores Gray from her apartment in Putney to the location at Arundel.

Gray had agreed to bring along a selection of her own furs and jewellery for the American tourist character of Miss Remington (formally Miss Hackensack in the original script), but when the car arrived at Arundel, the driver discovered that he'd forgotten to put Gray's cases into the car and had left them, containing some £25,000 in jewellery, on the pavement in Putney. Fortunately, the stray cases had been spotted by the caretaker of the apartments, who had placed them inside the building.

Further problems ensued with the car when it was discovered, after a lengthy period attaching camera mounts, lights and video machines to the vehicle, that the petrol tank was almost empty, necessitating that everything be de-rigged so that the car could travel into town to refuel.

The tourist party seen visiting the castle in Part 1 was primarily made up of various *Doctor Who* production members who had worked with John Nathan-Turner over the years, namely Ian Fraser (production manager), Fiona Cumming (director), Andrew Morgan (director), Peter Moffatt (director), Nicholas Courtney (actor), Kathleen Bidmead (production unit manager) together with scriptwriters Graeme Curry, Stephen Wyatt and Kevin Clarke. The group was led by veteran director/producer Vere Lorrimer, whose numerous credits included the final season of *Blake's 7* in 1981.

Clarke also managed to appear in both the second and third episode of *Silver Nemesis* as well. In Part 2, he played a passer-by who stares at Lady Peinforte and her companion, Richard Maynarde as they wander down the street, while in the final episode, he appeared as the driver of the red Escort who picks up the hitchhiker.

The stunt in Part 1 showing the Doctor and Ace falling into the river at Black Jack's Mill Restaurant was co-ordinated by Paul Heasman, doubling for Sylvester McCoy, who was suffering from a heavy cold at the time. Heasman had attempted to persuade Sophie Aldred not

Above: **Lady Peinforte (Fiona Walker) and the mathematician (Leslie French) are filmed in the cramped surroundings of St Mary's House on 1 July 1988.**

to attempt the fall herself and allow her stunt double, Tracey Eddon, to stand in for her. Aldred insisted on performing the stunt, so Heasman, fearing that the actress would hurt herself on the sharp rocks beneath the shallow water, insisted that she break her fall by holding onto one of the supports of the bridge as she went in.

As recording began at Greenwich, the decision was made that the silver colour on the Cybermen costumes was too light, necessitating them being resprayed. This, together with the constant repainting that was necessary in order to touch the costumes up, led to a bad case of what costume designer Richard Croft termed 'Cyber-crotch'; the suits became so caked with paint that the fabric would crack and split, inevitably around the crotch area. This meant that constant running repairs had to be made to the costumes during the two weeks of recording. The other problem was that the chrome paint used for the helmets and chest units tended to oxidise fairly rapidly, turning from silver to gold. Not good for a Cyberman!

On completion of recording, it was discovered that Clarke had quite drastically overwritten, requiring some fairly major editing in order to bring the story down to the required running time (Part 1 reputedly ran a full eight minutes overtime). One major scene recorded but deleted in the broadcast version involved a chase sequence through the castle involving the Doctor and Ace being pursued by the two security men. While running down a staircase, Ace comes across a portrait of herself hanging on a wall which she doesn't recognise. The Doctor informs her that she doesn't remember it as it's from an event in her future. The portrait, which Aldred was allowed to keep, was painted from a specially taken photograph of her in period costume.

The Cybership was only ever represented on location by the front panel containing the sliding doors around which any action would take place. The rest of the ship, in the form of a model created by Mike Tucker, was then electronically added to the picture in post-production.

In order to create the illusion of the down-draught caused by a large spaceship moving over Windsor Safari Park, a helicopter was hired for a short period on 28 June and was recorded flying at low altitude past a line of trees. The model Cybership was later superimposed over the helicopter, although the spinning rotor blades were still visible in some shots.

Other electronic effects achieved in post-production included the addition of background features to 'Casa Del Mer' to make its surroundings look more like South Africa and less like West Sussex The three dormer windows in the roof of St Mary's House were also electronically erased.

Recording at 'Casa Del Mer' was delayed when the parrot being used to convey the idea that the location was really near the equator proved to be uncooperative and refused to descend from the trees outside the property.

The production of *Silver Nemesis* was followed by a small American crew recording a 55-minute documentary on the making of the story for the New Jersey Network and Lionheart, the BBC's American distributors. As well as covering rehearsals and costume fittings, the crew also attended the first two days of recording at Greenwich as well as the first two days at Arundel.

BBC Video released an extended version of *Silver Nemesis* in 1993 which reinstated a number of scenes edited from the broadcast version (including the portrait scene mentioned above), as well as lengthening several of the transmitted scenes. In total approximately 11 minutes of extra footage was added.

Unused Locations

As scriptwriter Kevin Clarke's setting for *Silver Nemesis* was Windsor, an approach was made to the Royal residence of Windsor Castle through the OB Lighting Manager, Ian Dow, who had looked after the broadcast of many Royal events from the castle. The request was turned down by the Buckingham Palace press office, who informed the BBC that, while documentaries were allowed to be made at Windsor Castle, dramas were not. However, to set the scene, an establishing shot of Windsor Castle was used, gleaned from an edition of *Songs of Praise*.

The use of the hangar at Greenwich Gas Works was not the first choice of location for Silver Nemesis. Director Chris Clough had originally hoped to record material at Acton Lane Power Station in North Acton, the location that James Cameron had used a few years earlier while filming *Aliens*. All looked favourable, but the Central Electricity Generating Board decided to withdraw its permission. Attention was also focused on another derelict power station near Kingston-upon-Thames, but the idea was abandoned when the production team were informed that it would cost £30,000 to decontaminate.

Comment

While the story itself may have more holes than the proverbial Swiss cheese, there's no denying that, visually, *Silver Nemesis* works quite well. The trick of using a piece of stock footage of the real Windsor Castle before cutting to the action shot at Arundel succeeds in making you believe that it's the same building, while the footage of the jazz concert at Black Jack's Mill is a joy to behold. And however silly the idea of Cybermen behind killed by catapult-launched gold coins is, the footage of Ace's fight with the Cybermen recorded at the hangar in Greenwich comes off extremely well, especially the dizzying sequence along the rusty gantry at the top of the building. Sadly, however, *Silver Nemesis* is one of those cases where the parts are undoubtedly greater than the whole.

THE GREATEST SHOW IN THE GALAXY
(tx 14 December 1988 to 4 January 1989)

The Story

The Doctor and Ace arrive on Segonax in order to visit the Physic Circus, the self-proclaimed Greatest Show in the Galaxy. The Doctor finds that the once-happy circus has now changed and is watched over by the Chief Clown, aided by his robotic minions. Along with a varied group of visitors, the Doctor and Ace are enrolled in the circus' talent contest, which is being performed for the only audience, a strange family of three. The Doctor discovers that the spectators are really the three Gods of Ragnarok who are constantly seeking to be entertained and destroy all who fail in the task. The Doctor directs the Gods' own power against them, destroying the circus.

The Locations
1. Warmwell Quarry, Warmwell, Dorset
   - Landing Base
   - Blue Lagoon
   - Skinners Road
   - Sandpile
   - Stall
   - Golden Pond
   - Circus Site

Shooting Schedule

PART 1
▸▸ **Nord appears on the landing base**
Warmwell Quarry – Landing Base // 15 May 1988

Left: Ian Reddington as the Chief Clown at Warmwell Quarry during the recording of *The Greatest Show in the Galaxy.*

▶▶ **Bellboy and Flowerchild flee**
Warmwell Quarry – Blue Lagoon // 18 May 1988

▶▶ **Hearse stops and follows kites**
Warmwell Quarry – Skinners Rd // 15 May 1988

▶▶ **Bellboy sees Flowerchild's kites**
Warmwell Quarry – Sandpile // 15 May 1988

▶▶ **TARDIS materialises, Doctor sees stalls lady**
Warmwell Quarry – Skinners Rd // 14 May 1988

▶▶ **Nord races along and throws away burger**
Warmwell Quarry – Skinners Rd // 15 May 1988

▶▶ **Stalls lady thinks Doctor and Ace are weirdoes**
Warmwell Quarry – Stall // 14 May 1988

▶▶ **Flowerchild kisses Bellboy goodbye**
Warmwell Quarry – Blue Lagoon // 15 May 1988

▶▶ **Kites pick up scent again, Hearse follows**
Warmwell Quarry – Skinners Rd // 15 May 1988

▶▶ **Bellboy makes his way to the road**
Warmwell Quarry – Skinners Rd // 15 May 1988

▶▶ **Doctor and Ace eat their fruit**
Warmwell Quarry – Stall // 14 May 1988

▶▶ **Bellboy calls for the kites to follow him**
Warmwell Quarry – Skinners Rd // 15 May 1988

▶▶ **Flowerchild enters the bus**
Warmwell Quarry – Golden Pond // 17 May 1988

▶▶ **Nord's bike breaks down at stall**
Warmwell Quarry – Stall // 14 May 1988

▶▶ **Flowerchild is strangled by the bus conductor**
Warmwell Quarry – Golden Pond // 17 May 1988

▶▶ **Doctor and Ace almost run down by hearse**
Warmwell Quarry – Skinners Rd // 15 May 1988

▶▶ **Nord makes his way to the circus**
Warmwell Quarry – Skinners Rd // 15 May 1988

▶▶ **Walking along, Doctor and Ace meet Captain and Mags**
Warmwell Quarry – Blue Lagoon // 18 May 1988

▶▶ **Nord asks clown for directions**
Warmwell Quarry – Circus Site // 16 May 1988

▶▶ **Doctor and Captain drink tea, Ace smashes robot**
Warmwell Quarry – Blue Lagoon // 18 May 1988

▶▶ **Whizzkid appears on the landing base**
Warmwell Quarry – Landing Base // 15 May 1988

▶▶ **Captain and Mags drive off, Doctor and Ace walk (cut)**
Warmwell Quarry – Blue Lagoon // 18 May 1988

▶▶ **Jeep passes hearse (cut) Chief Clown controls kites**
Warmwell Quarry – Skinners Rd // 14 May 1988

▶▶ **Flowerchild's body is dragged off leaving earring**
Warmwell Quarry – Golden Pond // 17 May 1988

▶▶ **Doctor and Ace arrive at bus, Jeep already there (cut)**
Warmwell Quarry – Golden Pond // 17 May 1988

▶▶ **Bellboy is caught by Chief Clown**
Warmwell Quarry – Stall // 15 May 1988

▶▶ **Doctor and Captain examine bus, conductor appears**
Warmwell Quarry – Golden Pond // 17 May 1988

▶▶ **Bellboy lies in the hearse**
Warmwell Quarry – Skinners Rd // 15 May 1988

▶▶ **Hearse arrives at the circus (cut)**
Warmwell Quarry – Circus Site // 16 May 1988

▶▶ **Doctor destroys conductor**

Warmwell Quarry – Golden Pond // 17 May 1988
▸▸ **Bellboy is bundled out of the hearse (cut)**
Warmwell Quarry – Circus Site // 16 May 1988
▸▸ **Captain and Mags drive off, Ace finds earring**
Warmwell Quarry – Golden Pond // 17 May 1988
▸▸ **Captain and Mags arrive at circus**
Warmwell Quarry – Circus Site // 16 May 1988
▸▸ **Whizzkid asks Stalls lady for directions**
Warmwell Quarry – Stall // 15 May 1988
▸▸ **Doctor and Ace arrive at circus**
Warmwell Quarry – Circus Site // 16 May 1988
▸▸ **Doctor and Ace walk towards the tent**
Warmwell Quarry – Circus Site // 16 May 1988
▸▸ **Ace hears screaming (1/2)**
Warmwell Quarry – Circus Site // 16 May 1988
▸▸ **Doctor can't hear anything, thinks Ace is making excuses (1/2)**
Warmwell Quarry – Circus Site // 16 May 1988
▸▸ **Doctor asks if they're going in, Chief Clown beckons (1/2)**
Warmwell Quarry – Circus Site // 16 May 1988

PART 2
▸▸ **Ace insists she heard screaming**
Warmwell Quarry – Circus Site // 16 May 1988
▸▸ **Hearse arrives, clowns carry out bus conductor (cut)**
Warmwell Quarry – Circus Site // 16 May 1988
▸▸ **Whizzkid sees stilt-walking clown**
Warmwell Quarry – Circus Site // 16 May 1988

PART 3
▸▸ **Ace and Deadbeat escape from the tent**
Warmwell Quarry – Circus Site // 16 May 1988

PART 4
▸▸ **Clowns return the repaired conductor**
Warmwell Quarry – Golden Pond // 17 May 1988
▸▸ **Crystal Ball shots Ace and Deadbeat**
Warmwell Quarry – Skinners Rd // 14 May 1988
▸▸ **Ace finds the box in the bus**
Warmwell Quarry – Golden Pond // 17 May 1988
▸▸ **Ace attacked by conductor, robot destroyed**
Warmwell Quarry – Golden Pond // 17 May 1988
▸▸ **Mags runs from tent followed by clowns**
Warmwell Quarry – Circus Site // 16 May 1988
▸▸ **Stalls lady blocks road, Mags slips past**
Warmwell Quarry – Skinners Rd // 15 May 1988
▸▸ **Mags meets Ace and Deadbeat**
Warmwell Quarry – Skinners Rd // 14 May 1988
▸▸ **Robot kills the clowns**
Warmwell Quarry – Blue Lagoon // 18 May 1988
▸▸ **Ace, Mags and Kingpin get into hearse**
Warmwell Quarry – Blue Lagoon // 18 May 1988

▸▸ **Ace, Mags and Kingpin drive back to circus (cut)**
Warmwell Quarry – Blue Lagoon // 18 May 1988
▸▸ **Doctor leaves circus as tent explodes**
Warmwell Quarry – Circus Site // 16 May 1988
▸▸ **Ace, Mags and Kingpin arrive at circus**
Warmwell Quarry – Circus Site // 16 May 1988
▸▸ **Stalls lady comments on the maelstrom**
Warmwell Quarry – Skinners Rd // 15 May 1988
▸▸ **Kingpin and Mags decide to set up new circus**
Warmwell Quarry – Circus Area // 16 May 1988

The Facts

The 'fruit' that the Doctor and Ace eat to appease the Stalls Lady in Part 1 was actually a mixture of custard and sweetcorn. The look of disgust on the actors' faces in the scene was quite genuine!

Deeming the erection of a full-sized circus tent in Warmwell Quarry too expensive, the decision was taken to construct a full-sized entrance vestibule and realise the rest of the structure by means of a large model, constructed by Mike Tucker. In order to ensure a seamless match between the lifesize scenery and the miniature tent, the model was also transported to Warmwell to ensure that it was shot under the same lighting conditions.

The motor-tricycle driven by Daniel Peacock as Nord (one of the visitors to the Psychic Circus) was hired from a local pair of motorbike enthusiasts known by the names of Ferret and Bootsy. Visual Effects added a special device to the bike, controlled by Peacock, which made it appear that the vehicle was backfiring.

The story concludes with a very impressive shot of Sylvester McCoy calmly walking away from the entrance to the tent as a huge explosion suddenly erupts from the vestibule. Originally, to emulate Stephen Wyatt's scripted concept of a turbulent wind ripping through the tent, the visual effects department hired several large air mortars – but they discovered when they tried to set them up that they'd been given the hoses and fittings from a different type of mortar. Unable to use the planned equipment, visual effects designer Steve Bowman decided instead to achieve a comparable effect using standard pyrotechnics, which resulted in an explosion far larger than McCoy had been expecting.

Although wearing different costumes, all the skills-performing clowns (providing directions to the circus while on highwire, unicycle and stilts) were played by the same person, Alan Heap.

The hippy bus seen in the first two episodes was the same vehicle used the previous year in *Delta and the Bannermen*. Following *The Greatest Show in the Galaxy*, the bus was returned to BBC Exhibitions and placed in storage again. Around a year later, when no suitable exhibition venue could be found for the bus, the vehicle was scrapped.

Comment

One of the hardest tasks in *Doctor Who* was making the inevitable quarry location actually look like an alien planet, but director Alan Wareing pulled it off with great aplomb, aided by some superb casting and Mark Ayres' fabulous score. The idea of realising the circus tent itself using a full-sized entrance together with a false-perspective model works extremely well; unless you're aware of the technique being employed, there's really no way of knowing that a full-sized marquee wasn't erected at Warmwell.

BATTLEFIELD

(tx 6 September to 27 September 1989)

The Story

The Doctor and Ace land in Carbury where a UNIT-escorted nuclear missile convoy, under the control of Brigadier Winifred Bambera, has got into trouble near Lake Vortigern. Under the lake lies an ancient space-ship from another dimension, containing the body of King Arthur together with his famous sword, Excalibur. The evil sorceress Morgaine and her warrior son, Mordred, arrive on Earth from the other dimension, as does Ancelyn, a young knight who's come to protect the King, all of whom recognise the Doctor as Merlin. UNIT battle against Mordred and his troops while Morgaine summons the Destroyer, a powerful being capable of devastating worlds. Learning of the Doctor's return, Lethbridge-Stewart comes out of retirement and defeats the Destroyer. Morgaine plans to die by activating the nuclear device until the Doctor convinces her that its use lacks honour and that Arthur, with whom Morgaine had a romantic attachment, is in fact long dead. Defeated and broken, Morgaine and her son are taken into UNIT custody.

The Locations

1. Fulmer Plant Park, Cherry Tree Lane, Fulmer, Buckinghamshire
2. Little Paston, Fulmer Common Road, Fulmer, Buckinghamshire
3. Black Park, Black Park Road, Fulmer, Buckinghamshire
4. Dowager House, St Martin's Without, Stamford, Lincolnshire
5. Hambleton, Leicestershire
   - St Andrew's Church
   - Hambleton Old Hall

Left: **A good knight's rest is called for during a break in the recording of *Battlefield* on 15 May 1989**

   - Ridge
   - Excavation Site
6. Twyford Woods, Off A151, Near Colsterworth, Lincolnshire
7. Castle Cement Quarry, Ketton, Lincolnshire

Shooting Schedule[8]

PART 1

▸▸ **Brigadier and Doris at garden centre**
Fulmer Plant Park // 6 May 1989
▸▸ **Bambera tries radio but gets static**
Hambleton Ridge // 15 May 1989
▸▸ **TARDIS materialises**
Twyford Woods // 13 May 1989
▸▸ **Doctor and Ace picked up by Warmsley**
Twyford Woods // 13 May 1989
▸▸ **Warmsley talks to the Doctor in car**
Twyford Woods // 13 May 1989
▸▸ **Knight plummets into the ground and rises**
Castle Cement // 14 May 1989
▸▸ **Doctor and Ace dropped off and see missile convoy**
Hambleton Ridge // 15 May 1989
▸▸ **POV's of the missile convoy**
Hambleton – Excavation Site // 11 May 1989
▸▸ **Doctor arrives at excavation and finds UNIT passes**

Hambleton – Excavation Site // 16-17 May 1989

▸▸ **Knight walks away from crater**
Castle Cement // 14 May 1989

▸▸ **Doctor and Ace leave after seeing Bambera**
Hambleton – Excavation Site // 16-17 May 1989

▸▸ **Brigadier gets a phone call about the Doctor**
Little Paston // 6 May 1989

▸▸ **Knight hides as UNIT command car drives past**
Twyford Woods // 13 May 1989

▸▸ **Mordred sees 'MOD Firing Range' sign**
Castle Cement // 14 May 1989

▸▸ **Doctor, Ace and Shou Yuing arrive at hotel**
Hambleton Old Hall // 8 May 1989

▸▸ **Knights and Bambera battle outside TARDIS**
Twyford Woods // 13 May 1989

▸▸ **Bambera returns to vehicle, tyre burning**
Twyford Woods // 13 May 1989

▸▸ **Brigadier prepares to leave**
Little Paston // 6 May 1989

▸▸ **Knights fight and tree falls**
Twyford Woods // 13 May 1989

▸▸ **Bambera and Warmsley arrive at hotel**
Hambleton Old Hall // 8 May 1989

▸▸ **Helicopter lands, Brigadier gets swagger stick**
Little Paston // 6 May 1989

▸▸ **Knight is blown into the air by grenade**
Twyford Woods // 13 May 1989

▸▸ **Ace tells of home-made explosive and sees knight land**
Hambleton Old Hall // 8 May 1989

▸▸ **Brigadier leaves in helicopter**
Little Paston // 6 May 1989

PART 2

▸▸ **Brigadier talks to Lavel**
Black Park // 6 May 1989

▸▸ **Bambera and Ancelyn fight**
Hambleton Old Hall // 8 May 1989

▸▸ **Establishing shots – ruined building**
Dowager House // 7 May 1989

▸▸ **Helicopter approaches London, Brigadier asleep**
Black Park // 6 May 1989

▸▸ **Brigadier suddenly awakes**
Black Park // 6 May 1989

▸▸ **Doctor picks up Bambera's gun and hat**
Hambleton Old Hall // 8 May 1989

▸▸ **Helicopter takes off from London for Carbury**
Black Park // 6 May 1989

▸▸ **Ace blows a hole in the excavation**
Hambleton – Excavation Site // 16-17 May 1989

▸▸ **Brigadier asks Lavel to call Husak**
Black Park // 6 May 1989

▸▸ **Bambera and Ancelyn run through wood**

Twyford Woods // 13 May 1989

▸▸ **Brigadier tells Lavel to land the helicopter**
Black Park // 6 May 1989

▸▸ **Morgaine brings down the helicopter**
St Andrew's Church // 15 May 1989

▸▸ **Lavel tries to control the helicopter**
Black Park // 6 May 1989

▸▸ **Doctor and Ace enter the tunnel**
Hambleton – Excavation Site // 16-17 May 1989

▸▸ **Brigadier asks if Lavel can get the helicopter down**
Black Park // 6 May 1989

▸▸ **Brigadier and Lavel survive the explosion**
Hambleton – Excavation Site // 16 May 1989

▸▸ **Morgaine annoyed with Mordred, meets Brigadier**
St Andrew's Church // 15 May 1989

▸▸ **Bambera and Ancelyn arrive at excavation**
Hambleton – Excavation Site // 16-17 May 1989

▸▸ **Brigadier agrees to cease-fire with Morgaine**
St Andrew's Church // 15 May 1989

▸▸ **Morgaine leaves promising to kill Brigadier next time**
St Andrew's Church // 15 May 1989

▸▸ **Brigadier commandeers Shou Yuing's car**
Hambleton Old Hall // 8 May 1989

PART 3

▸▸ **Ace rises from the lake with Excalibur**
Hambleton Excavation Site // 16 May 1989

▸▸ **Doctor and Brigadier emerge from tunnel**
Hambleton – Excavation Site // 16-17 May 1989

▸▸ **Morgaine orders Excalibur's retrieval**
St Andrew's Church // 15 May 1989

▸▸ **Bambera and Ace take umbrage at Brigadier (cut)**
Hambleton – Excavation Site // 16-17 May 1989

▸▸ **Command car sets off and is attacked**
Twyford Woods // 13/14 May 1989

▸▸ **Bambera and Ancelyn are attacked**
Twyford Woods // 14 May 1989

▸▸ **Doctor hypnotises and Brigadier shows ordnance**
Hambleton Old Hall // 8 May 1989

▸▸ **Husak finds smouldering tyre and beret**
Twyford Woods // 13 May 1989

▸▸ **Bessie is unveiled**
Hambleton Old Hall // 8 May 1989

▸▸ **Ancelyn and knight fight, stopped by Bambera**
Twyford Woods // 14 May 1989

▸▸ **Doctor gives chalk to Ace, leaves in Bessie**
Hambleton Old Hall // 8 May 1989

▸▸ **Establishing shot – ruined building**
Dowager House // 7 May 1989

▸▸ **Morgaine's Globe – Doctor and Brigadier in Bessie**
Hambleton – Excavation Site // 16-17 May 1989

▸▸ **Doctor stops Bessie and observes battle**

Hambleton Ridge // 15 May 1989

➤➤ **Doctor's POV of battle**
  Hambleton – Excavation Site // 11 May 1989

➤➤ **UNIT battle, Mordred admits it's a diversion**
  Hambleton – Excavation Site // 11 May 1989

PART 4

➤➤ **Doctor threatens to decapitate Mordred**
  Hambleton – Excavation Site // 11 May 1989

➤➤ **Mordred calls Doctor's bluff, Brigadier appears**
  Hambleton – Excavation Site // 11 May 1989

➤➤ **Brigadier threatens Mordred's life**
  Hambleton – Excavation Site // 11 May 1989

➤➤ **Morgaine orders knights into action**
  Hambleton – Excavation Site // 11 May 1989

➤➤ **Battle between UNIT and knights recommences**
  Hambleton – Excavation Site // 11 May 1989

➤➤ **Mordred bundled into Bessie**
  Hambleton – Excavation Site // 16-17 May 1989

➤➤ **Morgaine's Globe – Bessie driving along**
  Hambleton – Excavation Site // 11 May 1989

➤➤ **Explosion at hotel, Mordred flees**
  Hambleton Old Hall // 8 May 1989

➤➤ **Ancelyn and Bambera among the dead**
  Hambleton – Excavation Site // 11 May 1989

➤➤ **Mordred comes out of hiding as soldiers pass**
  Dowager House // 7 May 1989

➤➤ **Brigadier is thrown out of the window**
  Dowager House // 7 May 1989

➤➤ **Brigadier begins to recover**
  Dowager House // 7 May 1989

➤➤ **Brigadier, Ace and Doctor escape from ruin**
  Dowager House // 7 May 1989

➤➤ **Brigadier knocks out Doctor and takes gun**
  Dowager House // 7 May 1989

➤➤ **Ace sees explosions from ruin**
  Dowager House // 7 May 1989

➤➤ **Doctor and Ace return to the ruin**
  Dowager House // 7 May 1989

➤➤ **Doctor and Ace head to exploded house**
  Dowager House // 7 May 1989

➤➤ **Mordred confronts Bambera**
  Hambleton – Excavation Site // 11 May 1989

➤➤ **Doctor and Ace find Brigadier**
  Dowager House // 7 May 1989

➤➤ **Ancelyn and Mordred fight as Doctor walks through**
  Hambleton – Excavation Site // 11 May 1989

➤➤ **Explosion in the lake**
  Hambleton – Excavation Site // 16 May 1989

➤➤ **Doctor saves Ancelyn**
  Hambleton – Excavation Site // 11 May 1989

➤➤ **Girls go for ride in Bessie, leaving men behind**
  Little Paston // 6 May 1989

The Facts

Location recording on *Battlefield* had run for a total of three days when strike action over pay by the Broadcasting and Entertainments Trades Alliance (BETA) and the National Union of Journalists (NUJ) hit the recording, completely closing down production on Tuesday 9 and Wednesday 10 May 1989. In order to complete the required location work, two additional days were added to the schedule, which meant that the cast and crew returned to Hambleton on Tuesday 16 and Wednesday 17 May (although half of the scenes originally scheduled for Tuesday the 9th were able to be shot on Monday the 15th). In order to pay for the two extra days on location, the production office was required to list all the expenses incurred for the additional time and then claim the money back from a central fund at the BBC allocated for just such emergencies.

Designer Martin Collins' conversion of Hambleton Old Hall into the Gore Crow Hotel was so convincing that, on arrival, actor James Ellis thought that it was a real hotel and so entered the building and began looking around. It was only when the owners found Ellis in one of their bedrooms that he realised, suitably embarrassed, his mistake.

Once again, problems were caused by Sylvester McCoy's short-sightedness, this time while driving Bessie. For the sequence in Part 3 where the Doctor observes the battle around the missile convoy, McCoy couldn't actually see the marker placed on the ground to ensure that the vehicle stopped in shot. After several failed attempts, it was decided that a bigger marker was going to be needed, which meant that a rather nervous member of the production team had to stand in the path of Bessie, just out of camera shot.

One of the scenes postponed by the strike action was the explosion in Rutland Water, depicting the destruction of the underwater spacecraft. The local police were in attendance during the recording and, deciding that they were likely to get wet during the sequence, they retreated from the lakeside to their police car situated some distance away. When the explosives were detonated, a large piece of mud from the lake bed was thrown into the air, missing the camera crew but landing squarely on the watching policemen.

The can of Nitro-9 explosive used by Ace in Part 2 to blast open the entrance to the tunnel featured a clockwork timer device. This addition had been made by the visual effects department and was originally supposed to have been seen in *The Curse of Fenric* (broadcast after, but recorded before, *Battlefield*). However, during the recording of *Fenric*, Sophie Aldred dropped the augmented prop and damaged the timer, necessitating the use of a standard prop can. The clockwork mechanism was duly repaired in time for *Battlefield*.

The majority of the explosions surrounding Dowager House in Part 4 had to be added in post-production as it was not certain that the ruined building would be safe if real visual effects explosions were set off around it.

BBC Video released an extended version of *Battlefield* in 1998 that reinstated almost two minutes of material from early edits of the story. The only additional location material in the extended version was a short extension of the scene where the Doctor and the Brigadier exit the underwater tunnel, together with a further scene where Bambera and Ace take umbrage at Lethbridge-Stewart's manner.

Comment

Monday 15 May was the second opportunity this author had to visit a *Doctor Who* location shoot, as the production team struggled to record not only the scheduled scenes, but also a number of those postponed due to the strike action the previous week. One of my enduring memories of the day was how dynamic director Michael Kerrigan was, endlessly seeking to motivate his team and get the best from them. When I left the location that evening, *Battlefield* seemed to promise so much – so it was strange that it ended up delivering so little. Once again, the culprit is an over-ambitious script coupled with some weak plotting and dialogue. For the most part, the location work is well handled, with both Hambledon and the ruins of Dowager House proving to be more than adequate for the story. The only real failure comes with the shots of the helicopter, flying endlessly over the same trees in Black Park, making it less than convincing in the scenes where it should be flying over London.

GHOST LIGHT
(tx 4 October to 18 October 1989)

The Story

In the year 1883, the Doctor takes Ace to Gabriel Chase, the house that she burned down in her youth, so that she can confront the evil she felt there. The house is built upon an ancient stone spaceship and run by Josiah Samuel Smith, a Victorian gentleman who has evolved from an alien creature brought to Earth in the ship. Ace accidentally releases the spaceship's true owner, a powerful alien being called Control, who travelled to Earth to survey all life on the planet. Disturbed to find that life has changed and that his catalogue is now redundant, Light decides to destroy all organic life in a fire-storm, but he disintegrates when the Doctor convinces him that life's progress is unstoppable.

The Locations
1. Stanton Court, 11 Greenhill, Weymouth, Dorset

Shooting Schedule

PART 1-3
▸▸ **Gabriel Chase – Establishing shots**
    Stanton Court // 21 June 1989

The Facts▸▸

As the only location material required for *Ghost Light* comprised a few brief establishing shots of the exterior of Gabriel Chase, director Alan Wareing took the opportunity, on the penultimate day of recording *Survival*, to travel the few miles west to Weymouth with a small OB team and shoot the exterior of Stanton Court. Later, in post-production, the images were treated to include a small observatory dome on the roof of the house, to tie in with the interior scenes.

Comment

It's difficult to fathom out the logic of sending a small second OB unit out to record the establishing shots of Gabriel Chase for *Ghost Light*. The house is mainly seen at night and it's not as if the chosen building was absolutely ideal for the purpose anyway, having to be electronically augmented later in post-production. One wonders if it wouldn't have just been easier to have used a few appropriately doctored photographs instead.

THE CURSE OF FENRIC
(tx 25 October to 15 November 1989)

The Story

Landing at a military naval base in northern England near the end of the Second World War, the Doctor and Ace meet Judson, the brilliant but crippled inventor of the Ultima machine, designed to break German war codes. Millington, the commander of the base, has booby trapped the core of the machine, knowing that a Russian commando force will try to steal its secrets. Dr Judson uses the Ultima to decode ancient Nordic runes carved into the crypt of the nearby St Jude's church, an act which eventually leads to the release of Fenric, an ancient evil trapped by the Doctor 17 centuries earlier. Fenric rouses the Ancient Haemovore, the last survivor of a pollution-ravaged Earth brought back in time from the far future, who has created more vampiric Haemovores from humans lost at sea. The Haemovores attack both the base and the church, but the Doctor convinces the Ancient Haemovore of the futility of Fenric's plan to pollute the Earth with a

deadly toxin. The Ancient Haemovore accordingly
sacrifices its life to destroy Fenric.

The Locations

1. Crowborough Training Camp, Uckfield Road,
   Crowborough, East Sussex
   A. Hut 43
   B. Hut 44
   C. Hut 45
   D. Hut 46
   E. Hut 47
   F. Hut 48
   G. Hut 49
   H. Assault Course
   I. Guard Post (BBC Scenery)
   J. Tunnel Entrance and Laboratory
      Entrance (BBC Scenery)
   K. Gun Nest
1. St Lawrence's Church, The Moor, Hawkhurst, Kent
2. Bedgebury Lower School, Hastings Road,
   Lillesden, Hawkhurst, Kent
3. Roses Farm, Slip Way Hill, Hawkhurst, Kent
4. Yew Tree Farm, Slip Way Hill, Hawkhurst, Kent
5. Lulworth Cove, Dorset

Shooting Schedule[9]

PART 1

▶ **Russians paddle to shore**
   Lulworth Cove // 18 April 1989
▶ **TARDIS materialises**
   Crowborough Camp – H // 3 April 1989
▶ **Leigh watches Doctor and Ace and reports (cut)**
   Crowborough Camp – I // 3 April 1989
▶ **Bates listens to Leigh's report**
   Crowborough Camp // 6 April 1989
▶ **Russians come ashore**
   Lulworth Cove // 18 April 1989
▶ **Petrossian afraid to go in cave, Gatev lies water (cut)**
   Lulworth Cove // 18 April 1989
▶ **Doctor and Ace walk across the camp**
   Crowborough Camp // 3 April 1989
▶ **Leigh reports that one of the 'guests' is a girl**
   Crowborough Camp – I // 3 April 1989
▶ **Bates reacts to Leigh's report**
   Crowborough Camp // 6 April 1989
▶ **Guards grab weapons**
   Crowborough Camp – I // 8 April 1989
▶ **Guards surround Doctor and Ace**
   Crowborough Camp – G // 3 April 1989
▶ **Prozorov spots Gayev's body (cut)**
   Lulworth Cove // 18 April 1989
▶ **Prozorov reports, Sorin tries to rouse Gayev**

Above: **Rev Mr Wainwright (Nicholas Parsons) stands next to the clock tower of St Lawrence's Church, Hawkhurst**

Lulworth Cove // 18 April 1989
▶ **Doctor and Ace meet Judson**
   Crowborough Camp // 4 April 1989
▶ **Sorin issues instructions to his men**
   Lulworth Cove // 18 April 1989
▶ **Seaweed drifts past dragon's head**
   Lulworth Cove // 20 April 1989
▶ **Petrossian finds sealed Russian orders**
   Lulworth Cove // 18 April 1989
▶ **Doctor leaves Ace in the bunk room**
   Crowborough Camp // 6 April 1989
▶ **Something approaches Petrossian, who runs off**
   Lulworth Cove // 18 April 1989
▶ **Doctor meets Perkins, Sorin times guards**
   Crowborough Camp // 3 April 1989
▶ **Petrossian is caught and screams**
   Lulworth Cove // 18 April 1989
▶ **Doctor meets Wainwright at end of service**

St Lawrence's Church // 12 April 1989
➤➤ **Millington looks at chess game**
Crowborough Camp // 4 April 1989
➤➤ **Wainwright and Doctor walk through nave (cut)**
St Lawrence's Church // 13 April 1989
➤➤ **Wainwright tells Ace about the Viking curse**
St Lawrence's Church // 13 April 1989
➤➤ **Petrossian's body on the shore**
Lulworth Cove // 19 April 1989
➤➤ **Doctor meets Judson in crypt**
St Lawrence's Church // 13 April 1989
➤➤ **Doctor and Ace examine gravestone**
St Lawrence's Church // 12 April 1989
➤➤ **Hardaker scolds the girls about Maiden's Point**
Roses Farm // 15 April 1989
➤➤ **Doctor and Ace find Russian orders**
Lulworth Cove // 19 April 1989
➤➤ **Judson and Millington talk about German ciphers**
Crowborough Camp // 4 April 1989
➤➤ **Jean, Phyllis and Ace descend the rocks (cut)**
Lulworth Cove // 19 April 1989
➤➤ **Wainwright shows Doctor the Viking translations**
St Lawrence's Church // 13 April 1989
➤➤ **Ace declines to swim with Jean and Phyllis**
Lulworth Cove // 19 April 1989
➤➤ **Jean and Phyllis' legs tread water**
Lulworth Cove // 20 April 1989
➤➤ **Doctor reads the translation**
St Lawrence's Church // 13 April 1989
➤➤ **Seaweed around dragons head**
Lulworth Cove // 20 April 1989
➤➤ **Runic inscriptions, silent**
St Lawrence's Church // 13 April 1989
➤➤ **Doctor compares translation to Russian orders**
St Lawrence's Church // 13 April 1989
➤➤ **Jean and Phyllis find object and go home**
Lulworth Cove // 19 April 1989
➤➤ **Doctor shows Judson the translation**
Crowborough Camp // 4 April 1989
➤➤ **Prozorov finds object and throws it into sea**
Lulworth Cove // 19 April 1989
➤➤ **Hand catches object, dead Russian**
Lulworth Cove // 20 April 1989
➤➤ **Doctor and Ace meet Kathleen and baby**
Crowborough Camp // 6 April 1989
➤➤ **Doctor decides to look in Millington's office (cut)**
Crowborough Camp // 3 April 1989
➤➤ **Doctor and Ace examine Millington's office**
Crowborough Camp // 4 April 1989
➤➤ **Millington reads the translation**
Crowborough Camp // 4 April 1989
➤➤ **Doctor and Ace are surrounded (1/2)**
Lulworth Cove // 18 April 1989

PART 2

➤➤ **Judson reads the translation**
Crowborough Camp // 4 April 1989
➤➤ **Hand touches dragons head, dead Russian**
Lulworth Cove // 20 April 1989
➤➤ **New inscriptions appear in the crypt**
St Lawrence's Church // 13 April 1989
➤➤ **Dead Russian opens eyes**
Lulworth Cove // 20 April 1989
➤➤ **Doctor talks to Gayev, Sorin agrees to wait**
Lulworth Cove // 18 April 1989
➤➤ **Judson copies the new inscriptions**
St Lawrence's Church // 13 April 1989
➤➤ **Jean and Phyllis giggle at passing Marines**
Lulworth Cove // 19 April 1989
➤➤ **Vershinin and Prozorov see Marines (cut)**
Lulworth Cove // 19 April 1989
➤➤ **Doctor feels something different about church**
St Lawrence's Church // 13 April 1989
➤➤ **Wainwright stands in front of gravestone (cut)**
St Lawrence's Church // 12 April 1989
➤➤ **Millington tells Judson to use Ultima machine**
Crowborough Camp // 4 April 1989
➤➤ **Doctor and Ace examine new inscription**
St Lawrence's Church // 13 April 1989
➤➤ **Wainwright speaks from pulpit**
St Lawrence's Church // 13 April 1989
➤➤ **Sorin and commandos attack the Marines**
Lulworth Cove // 19 April 1989
➤➤ **Millington shows Doctor the secret laboratory**
Bedgebury School // 14 April 1989
➤➤ **Vershinin revelling in success**
Lulworth Cove // 18 April 1989
➤➤ **Ace talks to a saddened Wainwright**
St Lawrence's Church // 13 April 1989
➤➤ **Millington shows Doctor the Ultima's secret**
Crowborough Camp // 4 April 1989
➤➤ **Hardaker is annoyed with Jean and Phyllis**
Roses Farm // 15 April 1989
➤➤ **Millington demonstrates the poison**
Crowborough Camp // 7 April 1989
➤➤ **Perkins and Leigh find flask**
Bedgebury School // 14 April 1989
➤➤ **Jean and Phyllis run into the water**
Lulworth Cove // 19 April 1989
➤➤ **Dragons head**
Lulworth Cove // 20 April 1989
➤➤ **Jean and Phyllis disappear in mist**
Lulworth Cove // 19 April 1989
➤➤ **Millington issues orders to Bates**
Crowborough Camp // 4 April 1989
➤➤ **Perkins relays Millington's orders**
Crowborough Camp – F // 6 April 1989

▸▸ **Ultima machine decodes the new inscription**
Crowborough Camp // 4 April 1989

▸▸ **Prozorov is pulled into the water**
Lulworth Cove // 19 April 1989

▸▸ **Ace tells Judson inscription is a logic diagram**
Crowborough Camp // 4 April 1989

▸▸ **Jean and Phyllis attack Hardaker**
Roses Farm // 15 April 1989

▸▸ **Prozorov's body floats in the water**
Lullworth Cove // 20 April 1989

▸▸ **Doctor find's Hardaker's body**
Roses Farm // 15 April 1989

▸▸ **Jean and Phyllis confront Wainwright**
St Lawrence's Church // 12 April 1989

▸▸ **Judson resets the Ultima machine**
Crowborough Camp // 5 April 1989

▸▸ **Flask glows**
Bedgebury School // 14 April 1989

▸▸ **Judson ready to start machine**
Crowborough Camp // 5 April 1989

▸▸ **Ace realises her mistake**
Crowborough Camp // 11 April 1989

▸▸ **Flask glows brighter**
Bedgebury School // 14 April 1989

▸▸ **Haemovores rise from the sea**
Lulworth Cove // 19 April 1989

▸▸ **Ultima churns out names at high speed**
Crowborough Camp // 5 April 1989

▸▸ **Haemovores come ashore**
Lulworth Cove // 19 April 1989

▸▸ **Doctor, Ace and Wainwright enter the Decrypt hut**
Crowborough Camp // 8 April 1989

▸▸ **Doctor tires to stop the machine (2/3)**
Crowborough Camp // 5 April 1989

PART 3

▸▸ **Perkins destroys the radios**
Crowborough Camp // 6 April 1989

▸▸ **Doctor explains about the Haemovores**
Crowborough Camp – B // 6 April 1989

▸▸ **Haemovores advance on Russians**
Lulworth Cove // 19 April 1989

▸▸ **Ace checks on Kathleen and her baby**
Crowborough Camp – F // 6 April 1989

▸▸ **Millington talks to Judson**
Crowborough Camp // 4 April 1989

▸▸ **Russians observe the Haemovores**
Lulworth Cove // 19 April 1989

▸▸ **Wainwright checks the parish records**
St Lawrence's Church // 13 April 1989

▸▸ **Ace finds the flask**
Bedgebury School // 14 April 1989

▸▸ **Wainwright finds names in parish records**

St Lawrence's Church // 13 April 1989

▸▸ **Ultima prints out names of Sundvik's descendants (cut)**
Crowborough Camp // 5 April 1989

▸▸ **Haemovores appear behind gravestones**
St Lawrence's Church // 12 April 1989

▸▸ **Haemovores attack the vestry**
St Lawrence's Church // 13 April 1989

▸▸ **Ace arrives at the top of the bell tower and throws ladder**
St Lawrence's Church // 12 April 1989

▸▸ **Doctor battles with Haemovores**
St Lawrence's Church // 13 April 1989

▸▸ **Ace attacked on roof, rescued by Sorin**
St Lawrence's Church // 12 April 1989

▸▸ **Doctor counters Haemovores, they go to the crypt**
St Lawrence's Church // 13 April 1989

▸▸ **Ace blows open the sealed entrance**
Bedgebury School // 14 April 1989

▸▸ **Sorin confronts the Haemovores**
St Lawrence's Church // 13 April 1989

▸▸ **Doctor finds Ace has the flask**
Yew Tree Farm // 15 April 1989

▸▸ **Sorin's faith protects him, Haemovores leave**
St Lawrence's Church // 12 April 1989

▸▸ **Haemovores enter the mineshaft**
Bedgebury School // 14 April 1989

▸▸ **Sorin tells his troops there is a storm coming**
Lulworth Cove // 19 April 1989

▸▸ **Doctor, Ace and Wainwright struggle through shaft**
Yew Tree Farm // 15 April 1989

▸▸ **Millington orders shaft sealed, Sorin through fence**
Crowborough Camp – J // 11 April 1989

▸▸ **Bates tells Millington that Sorin is outside**
Crowborough Camp // 5 April 1989

▸▸ **Sorin talks to Millington**

Above: Jean and Phyllis (Joann Kenny and Joanne Bell) confront Wainwright (Nicholas Parsons) in the graveyard of St Lawrence's Church on 12 April 1989.

Crowborough Camp – C // 8 April 1989

▶▶ Vershinin and commandos pull back
Crowborough Camp // 11 April 1989

▶▶ Doctor tells Millington that Haemovores can affect metal
Crowborough Camp – C // 8 April 1989

▶▶ Metal doors begin to melt
Crowborough Camp – J // 11 April 1989

▶▶ Ace comforts Kathleen in her loss
Crowborough Camp // 6 April 1989

▶▶ Ultima is still printing out names
Crowborough Camp // 5 April 1989

▶▶ Ace confronts the Doctor
Crowborough Camp – D // 6 April 1989

▶▶ Wainwright watches as door melts
Crowborough Camp – J // 11 April 1989

▶▶ Ace chats up Leigh while Doctor releases Sorin
Crowborough Camp – B/I // 3 April 1989

▶▶ Water around dragons head begins to boil
Lulworth Cove // 20 April 1989

▶▶ Ace runs from Leigh
Crowborough Camp – I // 3 April 1989

▶▶ Wainwright's faith holds Haemovores at bay
Crowborough Camp – J // 11 April 1989

▶▶ Ace catches up with Doctor and Sorin
Crowborough Camp – B // 8 April 1989

▶▶ Wainwright loses faith, Haemovores advance
Crowborough Camp – J // 11 April 1989

▶▶ Ultima prints final name, Judson is struck
Crowborough Camp // 5 April 1989

▶▶ Lightning over Maiden's Point
Lulworth Cove // 19 April 1989

▶▶ Wainwright lies dead as Heamovores move on
Crowborough Camp – J // 11 April 1989

▶▶ Fenric takes over Judson's body
Crowborough Camp // 5 April 1989

PART 4

▶▶ Kathleen sings to her baby
Crowborough Camp – F // 6 April 1989

▶▶ Fenric-Judson vanishes, Millington orders shootings
Crowborough Camp // 5 April 1989

▶▶ Fenric-Judson appears in mineshft
Crowborough Camp // 11 April 1989

▶▶ Doctor, Ace and Sorin rescued by Russians
Crowborough Camp – A // 8 April 1989

▶▶ Fenric-Judson asks for the Ancient One (cut)
Crowborough Camp // 11 April 1989

▶▶ Doctor questions Ace about shouting to her mum (cut)
Crowborough Camp – B // 8 April 1989

▶▶ Millington looks at his chess set
Crowborough Camp // 4 April 1989

▶▶ Doctor realises he must play a game of chess
Crowborough Camp – B // 8 April 1989

▶▶ Fenric-Judson sends girls for Ancient One (cut)
Crowborough Camp // 11 April 1989

▶▶ Millington decides to secure the laboratory (cut)
Crowborough Camp // 8 April 1989

▶▶ Ancient Haemovore is summoned from sea
Lulworth Cove // 19 April 1989

▶▶ Millington enters the laboratory
Crowborough Camp – J // 11 April 1989

▶▶ Fenric-Judson swears revenge on the Doctor
Crowborough Camp // 7 April 1989

▶▶ Doctor and Ace find explosives in Millington's office
Crowborough Camp // 4 April 1989

▶▶ Doctor and Ace run clear as office explodes
Crowborough Camp – F // 7 April 1989

▶▶ Fenric-Judson tells Ancient Haemovore to kill humans
Crowborough Camp // 11 April 1989

▶▶ Ace remembers that Kathleen has a chess set
Crowborough Camp – F // 7 April 1989

▶▶ Marines attacked by Haemovores
Crowborough Camp // 11 April 1989

▶▶ Wrens huddle petrified
Crowborough Camp // 6 April 1989

▶▶ Marines throw poison grenades
Crowborough Camp // 11 April 1989

▶▶ Gas kills soldiers
Crowborough Camp – K // 8 April 1989

▶▶ Vershinin tells Sorin to destroy Ultima machine
Crowborough Camp – K // 8 April 1989

▶▶ Millington sees the Great Haemovore
Crowborough Camp // 7 April 1989

▶▶ Bates and Sorin agree to join forces
Crowborough Camp – E // 8 April 1989

▶▶ Transformed Wrens advance on Leigh
Crowborough Camp // 6 April 1989

▶▶ Doctor gets chess set, Ace stays with Kathleen
Crowborough Camp – F // 6 April 1989

▶▶ Nurse Crane killed by Haemovores
Crowborough Camp // 4 April 1989

▶▶ Sorin's faith wards off Jean and Phyllis
Crowborough Camp // 6 April 1989

▶▶ Ace and Kathleen begin to barricade the quarters
Crowborough Camp – F // 6 April 1989

▶▶ Millington shoots Vershinin
Crowborough Camp // 5 April 1989

▶▶ Doctor sets up chess game
Crowborough Camp // 7 April 1989

▶▶ Wrens quarters attacked, Ace and Kathleen escape
Crowborough Camp – F // 6 April 1989

▶▶ Doctor tries to set chess pieces correctly
Crowborough Camp // 7 April 1989

➤ Ace sees Kathleen safely away
  Crowborough Camp – E // 8 April 1989

➤ Fenric-Judson give Ancient Haemovore its orders
  Crowborough Camp // 6 April 1989

➤ Jean and Phyllis collapse and disintegrate
  Crowborough Camp – E // 8 April 1989

➤ Ancient Haemovore open its eyes
  Crowborough Camp // 6 April 1989

➤ Doctor challenges Fenric-Judson to find solution
  Crowborough Camp // 7 April 1989

➤ Vershinin shoots Millington
  Crowborough Camp // 5 April 1989

➤ Doctor confronts the Ancient Haemovore
  Crowborough Camp // 11 April 1989

➤ Fenric-Judson begs Ace to tell him the solution
  Crowborough Camp // 7 April 1989

➤ Doctor talks to Ancient Haemovore
  Crowborough Camp // 11 April 1989

➤ Ace sudden understands the winning move
  Crowborough Camp // 5 April 1989

➤ Sorin is told that he was chosen by Fenric
  Crowborough Camp // 7 April 1989

➤ Bates helps Vershinin to his feet
  Crowborough Camp // 5 April 1989

➤ Ace tells Fenric-Sorin the winning move
  Crowborough Camp // 7 April 1989

➤ Lightening hits the laboratory building
  Crowborough Camp – J // 11 April 1989

➤ Fenric and Doctor play the final game, Fenric dies
  Crowborough Camp // 7 April 1989

➤ Doctor explain that he had to break Ace's faith
  Crowborough Camp – J // 11 April 1989

➤ Ace dives into the sea
  Lulworth Cove // 19 April 1989

➤ Ace swims through the water
  Lulworth Cove // 20 April 1989

➤ Ace surfaces, accepting her feelings for her mother
  Lulworth Cove // 19 April 1989

The Facts

The story was recorded under the title *The Wolves of Fenric*.

Originally, it had been planned to record *The Curse of Fenric* using the conventional mix of location work followed by several sessions in the studio, recording the interior scenes. It wasn't until the pre-production location recce was carried out at a Ministry of Defence training camp at Crowborough, that the suggestion was made that the entire story could be shot on location. That way, it was argued, the show could feature the interiors of the real army huts, rather than creating mock-ups in the studio.

With the central location at Crowborough found, efforts were made to find the other necessary locations

within the same area. One of the main challenges came in trying to find a suitable church. Ian Briggs' script had specified an action sequence featuring Ace climbing down the bell tower and encountering the Haemovores on the church roof, before being rescued by Captain Sorin and his men.

Finding churches with bell towers was the easy part. The real problem lay in finding a building that had a suitable area of flat roof that would support the weight of both the actors and the camera crew. Eventually, the production team placed an ad in the local newspapers seeking information on any suitable church. In response, a local historian pointed them in the direction of St Lawrence's in Hawkhurst.

The use of St Lawrence's also fitted the production in another, rather more obscure way. At 1.25 am on the morning of 3 August 1944, a German V-2 bomb fell in the grounds of the church, causing extensive damage both to the graveyard and to St Lawrence's itself. In the story, the vicar, Mr Wainwright, finds his faith beginning to fail as he questions the futility of war and the deaths caused by bombs being dropped by the opposing sides.

The weather during the week's recording at Crowborough was extremely changeable with both sun, heavy rain and (just as had been experienced during the filming of *The Daemons* and *Revelation of the Daleks*) snow showers. Fortunately, the snow was not heavy and was duly washed away with hoses from the recording areas before any scenes were actually shot. However, this did have the effect of worsening the mud that was being churned up in the waterlogged ground by the production team. One of the worst affected areas was the entrance to the tunnel that had been constructed on site by the BBC Scenic Department. Here, the mud became so thick that the structure began to sink, thus explaining the building's rather odd angle as seen in the transmitted episodes.

Unfortunately, the Part 3 scene showing the Doctor, Ace and Wainwright exiting the tunnel also revealed the wellington boots Sophie Aldred was wearing. To cover up the offending footwear, a strategically placed crate was electronically added to the picture in post-production.

The climactic Part 4 scenes of the endgame between the Doctor and Fenric leading up to the Ancient Haemovore's self-sacrifice were not broadcast in the way that director Nicholas Mallett had originally intended.

Nicholas Mallett: 'The worst experience I had on *Doctor Who* was the very difficult scene in the bomb factory where the Ancient Haemovore dies. It needed a lot of coverage to punctuate the drama. We were using two cameras, and when we started back the next day, the VT operator had cued up this second tape at the beginning, so we wiped all the material on camera two, a lot of these punctuating shots. We didn't know anything about it until the editing and I spent about three days just going through this material trying to find it. Someone had realised that an error had been made and tried to cover it up, very effectively, but we kept seeing two or three frames of distortion, and when we blew it up, it was of the shots that had been erased... I thought, "My God, I don't know how we're going to get out of this one," and I did get quite low and worried about it because I felt I was not going to be able to achieve anything like I had intended. We got around it by flipping shots and zooming in, but dramatically it was a wonderful scene, and I felt I hadn't done it justice.'[10]

The scenes of the new runic inscription ('Let the chains of Fenric shatter!') that burn themselves into the crypt were originally to have been achieved using specially prepared boards created by the visual effects department, which utilised a fast-burning fuse and gunpowder set into the pre-carved runes. Although the effect was duly shot on location, it produced too much smoke, somewhat obscuring the image. Judging the shot to be unusable, the entire effect was reproduced electronically in post-production.

BBC Video released an extended version of *The Curse of Fenric* in 1991, which reinstated just over six minutes of material, most of which was taken up with extensions to existing scenes. One scene which was not reinstated, however, was part of the action sequence set on the church roof in Part 3. As scripted, following the shooting of the Haemovores by Sorin and his men, they were to have taken out several wooden stakes from their backpacks and (unseen) driven them through the hearts of the Haemovores, reducing them to pools of green slime. This explains why Sorin is seen with a bag of wooden stakes when he first sees Ace in the graveyard, but the bag is subsequently empty when they cross the belfry. However, in the transmitted episode, the hammering of the stake can still be heard as Ace begins to reclimb the rope ladder.

For some of the scenes of the Haemovores in the tunnel in Part 4, Sylvester McCoy's two sons, Sam and Joe, who were visiting the location that day, were allowed to appear in full costume as the two smaller Haemovores seen behind Jean and Phyllis, the east-end evacuee girls who are transformed into vampires. Unfortunately, their scene was subsequently cut from the transmitted episode but was reinstated in the extended BBC Video version.

While at Crowborough, on 8 April the production team was visited by another BBC crew from the children's programme *Take Two*, who recorded an item on the making of the story. The 4'10" feature, transmitted on 19 April, showed the recording of the firing squad sequence as well as the preparations for Jean and Phyllis' demise in Part 4. Originally, the item was also to have featured interviews with Joann Kenny and Joanne Bell

(playing Jean and Phyllis), together with make-up assistants Helen Johnson and Wendy Harrison. However, time became so short recording the death scene that when the *Take Two* team walked into the make-up room, the crew were asked to put down their equipment and help with the preparations by holding hairdryers.

At Lulworth Cove, the actors playing the Haemovores had the same problems that had been experienced during the production of *The Sea Devils* in 1971 – namely, the buoyant latex masks refused to sink properly under water. Each actor had to hold onto a large stone in order to disappear under the surface. Raymond Trickett, who played the Ancient Haemovore, had an even greater problem due to the size of his mask and the extra tubing on his costume. As well as rocks, Trickett also had to have his costume filled with stage weights to ensure his emergence scene could be successfully shot.

The dead Russian seen floating underwater before coming back to life was actually one of the visual effects assistants, John van der Pool. However, as van der Pool was black, and no black Russians were in the army in 1940s, he had to be made up to look caucasian.

Unused Locations

In an effort to keep the locations as close together as possible, the production team sought a suitable piece of coastline to record all scenes set around Maiden's Point. The original location planned for this was the area around Covehurst Bay at the eastern end of Hastings in East Sussex. However, during the location recce, cameraman Alan Jessop had strong reservations about using the location, as anything less than an extremely calm day would render it impossible to get all the required shots.

The much more distant alternative, the secluded Lulworth Cove in Dorset, was agreed upon by Nicholas Mallett (who had filmed another production there) in conjunction with Alan Jessop and visual effects designer Graham Brown, both of whom had prior experience of diving in the cove.

Comment

The decision to transform *The Curse of Fenric* into an all-location production was one that paid off extremely well, giving the story a very polished and plush look. The training camp at Crowborough and the church at Hawkhurst provide two superb central locations which really help to reinforce the 1940s setting. The only thing that slightly mars the story is the one thing the production team had no control over – the weather. For the most part, it's not really noticeable, but there are a few scenes that were obviously shot at different times and in completely different weather conditions, making the end result look rather disjointed.

SURVIVAL

(tx 22 November to 6 December 1989)

The Story

The Doctor returns Ace to Perivale so that she can catch up with her old friends. However, she is mystified to discover that they've almost all vanished from the area over recent weeks. It transpires that they have been transported to an alien planet by the cat-like Kitlings, who have the ability to teleport themselves and others across space. On the planet, humans gradually mutate into humanoid Cheetah people, whose savagery is slowly causing the planet's destruction. The Doctor is also transported to the Cheetah world by the Master who is trapped on the planet and is himself being transformed. Ace and her surviving friends return to Earth and, as the planet finally disintegrates, the Doctor is also teleported back when he refuses to succumb to savagery and fight the Master.

The Locations

1. 3 Medway Drive, Medway Estate, Perivale, Middlesex
2. 2 Medway Parade, Perivale, Middlesex (Motor Cycles Unlimited)
3. 20 Medway Parade, Perivale, Middlesex (Londis Food Market)
4. 23 Medway Parade, Perivale, Middlesex
5. 63 Medway Parade, Perivale, Middlesex
6. Balcony outside 37/39 Medway Parade, Perivale, Middlesex
7. 4 The Avenue, London, W5
8. Drayton Court Public House, The Avenue, London, W5
9. Ealing Central Sports Ground, Horsendon Lane South, Perivale, Middlesex
10. Colwyn Avenue, Perivale, Middlesex
11. Bleasdale Avenue, Perivale, Middlesex
12. Woodhouse Avenue, Perivale, Middlesex
13. EYJ Martial Arts Centre, North Ealing Sports Centre, Greenford Road, Sudbury Hill, Middlesex
14. Horsenden Hill, Horsendon Lane North, Perivale, Middlesex
15. Warmwell Quarry, Warmwell, Dorset

Shooting Schedule

PART 1

▶▶ Car-washing man vanishes, TARDIS materialises
Colwyn Avenue/Bleasdale Ave // 12 June 1989

▶▶ Woman shoos cats from her garden
Colwyn Avenue // 12 June 1989

▶▶ Doctor finds hoof print, boys watched by kitling
Horsenden Hill // 15 June 1989

▶▶ Master watches boys through kitling's eyes

Above: **Sylvester McCoy is surrounded by Cheetah People extras during the recording of** *Survival* **at Warmwell Quarry.**

EYJ Martial Arts Centre // 14 June 1989

▶▶ Ace tries telephone, decide to go to youth club
Horsenden Hill // 15 June 1989

▶▶ Doctor and Ace enter youth club and meet Paterson
EYJ Martial Arts Centre // 14 June 1989

▶▶ Ace goes to the pub, Doctor enters shop
Drayton Court Pub/4 The Avenue // 11 June 1989

▶▶ Doctor gets cat food and cheese in shop
20 Medway Parade // 11 June 1989

▶▶ Len follows Doctor out asking for money
Drayton Court Pub/4 The Avenue // 11 June 1989

▶▶ Harvey discovers that something has eaten Tiger
20 Medway Parade // 11 June 1989

▶▶ Ange tells Ace about her disappearing friends
23 Medway Parade // 11 June 1989

▶▶ Master observes Stuart through kitling's eyes
EYJ Martial Arts Centre // 14 June 1989

▶▶ Stuart jogs down street and vanishes
Colwyn Avenue // 12 June 1989

▶▶ Doctor lays out cat food and waits in hiding
Woodhouse Avenue // 13 June 1989

▶▶ Karra appears and chases Ace through playground
Ealing Central Sports Ground // 12 June 1989

▶▶ Dog begins to eat cat food, Ace calls
Woodhouse Avenue // 13 June 1989

▶▶ Ace runs and disappears
Ealing Central Sports Ground // 12 June 1989

▶▶ Ace appears on planet and tumbles down hillside
Warmwell Quarry // 22 June 1989

▶▶ Doctor arrives in empty playground
Ealing Central Sports Ground // 12 June 1989

▶▶ Ace finds body and runs from Karra

Warmwell Quarry // 22 June 1989

▸▸ Paterson grabs Doctor as he's about to capture kitling
Woodhouse Avenue // 13 June 1989

▸▸ Close-ups – Karra pursues Ace
Warmwell Quarry // 22 June 1989

▸▸ Karra attacks Stuart, Ace meets Shreela
Warmwell Quarry // 18 June 1989

▸▸ Doctor pursues kitling, Paterson rides after him
Colwyn Avenue – Alley // 13 June 1989

▸▸ Ace meets Midge and Derek at the camp
Warmwell Quarry // 18 June 1989

▸▸ Doctor and Paterson vanish
Woodhouse Avenue // 13 June 1989

▸▸ Doctor and Paterson appear in Cheetah camp (1/2)
Warmwell Quarry // 19 June 1989

PART 2

▸▸ Ace and Shreela watch kitlings scavenging
Warmwell Quarry // 18 June 1989

▸▸ Paterson makes a run, Cheetahs play with him
Warmwell Quarry // 19 June 1989

▸▸ Ace decides to try and catch a Cheetah
Warmwell Quarry // 18 June 1989

▸▸ Doctor and Paterson escape the camp on horseback
Warmwell Quarry // 19 June 1989

▸▸ Cheetah cuts through Ace's trap
Warmwell Quarry // 18 June 1989

▸▸ Doctor explains about the planet and kitling to Paterson
Warmwell Quarry // 19 June 1989

▸▸ Kitling watches milkman
3 Medway Drive // 10 June 1989

▸▸ Doctor and Paterson get caught in Ace's trap
Warmwell Quarry // 18 June 1989

▸▸ Master feeds a Cheetah
Warmwell Quarry // 19 June 1989

▸▸ Doctor's party come across Cheetah pride
Warmwell Quarry // 20 June 1989

▸▸ Master sends kitling off to find Doctor
Warmwell Quarry // 19 June 1989

▸▸ Walking though pride, milkman appears, they fight
Warmwell Quarry // 20 June 1989

▸▸ Ace sees injured Karra, she goes to help
Warmwell Quarry // 21 June 1989

▸▸ Doctor searches for Ace but finds Master
Warmwell Quarry // 23 June 1989

▸▸ Midge is almost caught, another Cheetah appears
Warmwell Quarry // 21 June 1989

▸▸ Master says Cheetahs are fighting in the Dead Valley
Warmwell Quarry // 23 June 1989

▸▸ One Cheetah wins, watched by Midge
Warmwell Quarry // 21 June 1989

▸▸ Master tells Doctor that he needs his help
Warmwell Quarry // 23 June 1989

▸▸ Karra reaches out for Ace's badge
Warmwell Quarry // 21 June 1989

▸▸ Midge kills injured Cheetah with tooth
Warmwell Quarry // 21 June 1989

▸▸ Master tells Doctor that the planet will change them
Warmwell Quarry // 23 June 1989

▸▸ Pride of Cheetahs howl
Warmwell Quarry // 21 June 1989

▸▸ Midge rejoins the group
Warmwell Quarry // 18 June 1989

▸▸ Ace gives Karra water, Doctor warns of danger
Warmwell Quarry // 21 June 1989

▸▸ Midge sides with Paterson
Warmwell Quarry // 18 June 1989

▸▸ Master cuts hide from carcass
Warmwell Quarry // 20 June 1989

▸▸ Ace begins to feel the change
Warmwell Quarry // 21 June 1989

▸▸ Midge begins to change and runs away
Warmwell Quarry // 18 June 1989

▸▸ Midge runs watched by kitling
Warmwell Quarry // 19 June 1989

▸▸ Master smiles, seeing through kitling eyes
Warmwell Quarry // 20 June 1989

▸▸ Kitling POV – Midge runs
Warmwell Quarry // 19 June 1989

▸▸ Master has made a rope and noose
Warmwell Quarry // 20 June 1989

▸▸ Doctor's party follow Midge
Warmwell Quarry // 19 June 1989

▸▸ Midge and Master vanish, Ace's eyes have changed (2/3)
Warmwell Quarry // 19 June 1989

PART 3

▸▸ Ace runs off with Karra
Warmwell Quarry // 19 June 1989

▸▸ Ace and Karra run though the valley
Warmwell Quarry // 22 June 1989

▸▸ Master resists the change, decides to hunt Doctor
63 Medway Parade // 10 June 1989

▸▸ Ace sees her reflection, She and Karra go hunting
Warmwell Quarry // 22 June 1989

▸▸ Doctor follows and persuades Ace to come home
Warmwell Quarry // 22 June 1989

▸▸ Master tells Midge that he must trust him
63 Medway Parade // 10 June 1989

▸▸ Ace transports the group back to Earth
Warmwell Quarry // 19 June 1989

▸▸ Party separates, Doctor goes to track down Master
Bleasdale Avenue // 12 June 1989

▸ Midge steals motorbike watched by Master
2 Medway Parade // 11 June 1989

▸ Doctor and Ace look round flat, Squeak cries
63 Medway Parade // 10 June 1989

▸ Midge walks into self-defence class
EYJ Martial Arts Centre // 14 June 1989

▸ Doctor and Ace talk about Midge, Ace's eyes change
37/39 Medway Parade // 10 June 1989

▸ Master see's Ace with his cat eyes
EYJ Martial Arts Centre // 14 June 1989

▸ Ace 'sees' Master at the youth club
37/39 Medway Parade // 10 June 1989

▸ Master takes control, Paterson arrives
EYJ Martial Arts Centre // 14 June 1989

▸ Doctor and Ace arrive, find Paterson dead
EYJ Martial Arts Centre // 14 June 1989

▸ Motorbike confrontation, Master stabs Karra,
she dies
Horsendon Hill // 15 June 1989

▸ Doctor confronts Master outside the TARDIS
Bleasdale Avenue // 12 June 1989

▸ Doctor and Master appear back on planet, they fight
Warmwell Quarry // 19 June 1989

▸ Doctor reappears, woman complains about cats
Bleasdale Avenue // 12 June 1989

▸ Cheetah takes Karra and Midge
Horsendon Hill // 15 June 1989

▸ Doctor and Ace leave
Warmwell Quarry // 18-23 June 1989

The Facts

The main visual effects requirement for *Survival* was the animatronic cat that would appear in several scenes. Although the production team were not entirely happy with the end result, the cable-operated animal (nicknamed 'Sooty' by producer John Nathan-Turner) was pressed into service on virtually all the recording days. Due to the shortness of the operating cables, the visual effects assistants often had to be hidden from view. When the Kitling watches the boys in the park at the beginning of Part 1, assistant Mike Tucker had to lie on the ground covered in a pile of grass to ensure some basic movement in the animal. In like manner, when Ace sits on the park swing with the Kitling, no less than four assistants were crouched on the ground below her, just out of camera shot.

For the corpse of Len and Harvey's cat, Tiger, a dummy animal was made using the same moulds as the animatronic cat, which was then dressed with fresh butcher's offal. Although the scene was recorded with the dummy corpse, it was felt that the effect was too gory and a less gruesome shot was substituted in its place.

Once again, John-Nathan Turner's own dog, Pepsi, made an appearance, eating the cat food the Doctor lays down in the first episode.

The production team were given permission to film the motorbike explosion at Horsendon Hill on 15 June, on the proviso that both the turf and the water reservoir situated under the hill were not damaged. The final shot was achieved by amalgamating three pieces of footage. Separate shots were recorded of stuntman 'Tip' Tipping dressed as the Doctor, riding from left to right, while champion motorcycle racer and trainee stuntman Eddie Kidd doubled for the Master's servant, Midge, riding from right to left. The third piece of footage showed the mortars exploding. Added together, these three separate images combined to give the desired illusion.

It was on this day that a dispute arose between Tipping and John Nathan-Turner, seemingly over the use of trainee Eddie Kidd in the sequence. As a result, Tipping walked off the show and had to be replaced as stunt arranger by Paul Heasman.

Having directed *The Greatest Show in the Galaxy* at Warmwell Quarry the previous year, director Alan Wareing decided to return to the location for the final six days of the shoot in order to record all the scenes on the Cheetah planet. Due to the vastness of the quarry, the only area reused from the production of *Greatest Show* was Golden Pond. Where the hippy bus had been 13 months earlier, designer Nick Somerville created the Cheetah encampment where the Doctor first meets the Master.

To dress the alien landscape at Warmwell Quarry, Nick Somerville placed an order for a ton of animal bones from an abattoir. Although the request had been made that the bones be steam-cleaned for health and safety purposes, when they were delivered to the location, many of them still had various pieces of flesh attached. In the hot temperatures, the meat quickly began to putrefy and became riddled with maggots.

The effect of the moon's reflection in the lake in Part 2 was achieved using a large lamp on the far side of the water, which was then painted out in post-production. In the same scene, the glowing moon water that Ace scoops up in her hand was realised by placing a small insulated quartz bulb in Aldred's palm connected to wires running down the back of her arm.

Interviewed for *The Frame* while on location at the EYJ Martial Arts Centre on Wednesday 14 June, Alan Wareing had expressed his hope that the sunny weather enjoyed by the production team during the first week wouldn't last.

Alan Wareing: 'To be honest, when we get to the planet I want grey overcast skies, because shadows and sunlight are a problem. I'm going to paint a lot of heavy skies in anyway on the locked-off shots, because the planet itself is supposed to be very stormy, with volcanoes and the like.'[11]

Despite Wareing's hopes, the hot weather continued, causing problems for many of the cast. Worst off were the extras playing the Cheetah people, who were encased in their fur fabric costumes and masks for a large percentage of the time and who were only able to find relief from the heat by using small battery fans and umbrellas and by sipping orange squash through straws. At one point, the heat became so intolerable for one female extra that she tore off her mask, stating that she'd had enough for the day. She was promptly dismissed from the production and sent home.

Sophie Aldred suffered from dehydration and had to be supplied with salt tablets, while several of the cast who had to wear yellow contact lenses (supplied by Clulows in Earls Court) often found themselves in agony as sand and dust from the quarry was blown into their eyes.

The strike action between the NUJ and BETA that had affected two days of location work on *Battlefield* back in May, again threatened to disrupt the production of *Survival*. The strike had already caused the cancellation of a day's location recce for the story on Friday 26 May and, as the unit approached the completion of the work at Warmwell, news came through that another period of strike action, which would force the shutdown of the OB crew, had been called for the afternoon of Friday 23 June, the final day of recording.

Due to the fine weather, the recording in the quarry had gone well and, after discussing the situation, Alan Wareing agreed that there was a possibility of completing the shooting schedule before the strike hit the production, if everyone worked at maximum efficiency. With everyone dedicated to completing the production, the final scene of *Survival* was recorded only 20 minutes before the strike action began.

The final scenes of the story underwent some last-minute alterations from what had originally been scripted. The original intention had been for both Time Lords to return to Earth and for the Doctor to tell the Master that he had evolved into something more than a Time Lord. The other main change affected the very last scene. Originally, the final sequence of the Doctor meeting up again with Ace was to have been recorded at Horsendon Hill along with the rest of the scene. Unfortunately, time ran out and the final exchange could not be completed. The entire scene was remounted later using a suitable area of trees and grass at Warmwell Quarry.

In early September 1989, confirmation that the 27th season of *Doctor Who* would not be going ahead came though to the production office. Realising that it was unlikely that the BBC would produce the programme in-house again, John Nathan-Turner and script editor Andrew Cartmel decided that it would be fitting to change the closing words of *Survival*. McCoy duly returned to Television Centre on 23 November 1989, the programme's 26th anniversary, to record the lines that would eventually be redubbed over the shot of the Doctor and Ace walking back to the TARDIS.

'There are worlds out there where the sky is burning, and the sea's asleep and the rivers dream. People made of smoke and cities made of song. Somewhere there's danger, somewhere there's injustice, somewhere else the tea's getting cold. Come on, Ace. We've got work to do.'

The Doctor – Survival: Part 3

Comment

Once again, Alan Wareing chose to return to the Dorset location he'd used only a year before and, as with *The Greatest Show in the Galaxy*, he managed to make Warmwell Quarry look like a truly alien world, aided by some excellent video effects by Dave Chapman. The majority of the material shot in Perivale works equally well, and looks every bit the boring, suburban place that Ace had complained about during her travels with the Doctor. Without the rather unsuccessful animatronic cat and the silly motorbike duel on Horsendon Hill, *Survival* would have been a rather better conclusion to the season. ■

FOOTNOTES

1. This scene (completed the following day), was originally intended to appear at the beginning of Part 4.
2. This scene was originally intended to appear at the beginning of Part 4.
3. *Doctor Who Magazine*

#260, p8-9
4. Referred to as 'Sandwell Quarry' in the production documentation.
5. *TARDIS*, Autumn 1987, p.6
6. *Doctor Who Magazine* #271, p.29
7. The details listed in the

shooting schedule refer to the transmitted version of the story, as opposed to the extended video release.
8. The details listed in the shooting schedule refer to the transmitted version of the story, as opposed to the extended

video release.
9. The details listed in the shooting schedule refer to the transmitted version of the story, as opposed to the extended video release.
10. *Doctor Who Magazine* #230, p.8
11. *The Frame* #11, p.9

| PART EIGHT |

'Look at that! San Francisco when it was still inhabited! Amazing...'
The Doctor – *Doctor Who*

PAUL McGANN

THE EIGHTH DOCTOR

DOCTOR WHO – THE TELEVISION MOVIE

(tx 27 May 1996)
(BBC/Fox Television)

The Story

Returning the executed remains of the Master to Gallifrey, the TARDIS is pulled off course, landing in San Francisco during the last few days of 1999. Exiting the TARDIS, the Doctor is gunned down by a street gang who are attempting to kill Chang Lee, a Chinese youth and rival gang member. The Master is not dead, however, and transforming himself into a morphant snake-like creature e escapes from the TARDIS. The Doctor is helped to hospital by Chang Lee, but dies on the operating table under the auspices of cardiologist Dr Grace Holloway. In the morgue, the Doctor regenerates and later recovers his memory with the help of Grace and Chang Lee. He begins to track down the Master, who has now taken over the body of Bruce, one of the hospital paramedics. The Master plans to rob the Doctor of his remaining regenerations, but as he begins the process the Doctor breaks free and the Master gets sucked into the Eye of Harmony, the energy source of the TARDIS.

The Locations

1. 222 Keefer Street, Vancouver, British Columbia, Canada
2. Alley between East Georgia Street and Union Street, Vancouver, British Columbia, Canada
3. Waterfront Road, Vancouver, British Columbia, Canada
4. BC Children's Hospital, 4480 Oak Street, Vancouver, British Columbia, Canada
5. Rear of 218 East Georgia Street, Vancouver, British Columbia, Canada
6. Golden Crow Centre, 211 East Georgia Street, Vancouver, British Columbia, Canada
7. 1998 Ogden Street, Vancouver, British Columbia, Canada
8. Hadden Park, Vancouver, British Columbia, Canada
9. Junction of Carrall Street and Keefer Street, Vancouver, British Columbia, Canada
10. Pacific Space Centre, Vanier Park, Vancouver, British Columbia, Canada
11. Andy Livingston Park, Junction of Carrall Street and Keefer Street, Vancouver, British Columbia, Canada

Shooting Schedule

▸▸ **Chinese family prepare their food**
222 Keefer Street // 5 February 1996
▸▸ **Chang Lee's gang ambushed and Doctor shot**

Alley // 1/2 February 1996

▸▸ **Ambulance takes the Doctor to hospital**
Waterfront Road // 8 February 1996

▸▸ **Doctor taken into hospital, Morphant in ambulance**
BC Children's Hospital // 26 January 1996

▸▸ **Doctor is rushed down corridors**
BC Children's Hospital // 23 January 1996

▸▸ **Doctor X-rayed, bullets removed**
BC Children's Hospital // 30 January 1996

▸▸ **Grace gets beeped at opera**
BC Children's Hospital // 30 January 1996

▸▸ **Grace washes in Prep Room, Brian calls**
BC Children's Hospital // 30 January 1996

▸▸ **Doctor tries to stop Grace, Doctor dies**
BC Children's Hospital // 29 January 1996

▸▸ **Grace examines the Doctor's X-ray**
BC Children's Hospital // 24-28 January 1996

▸▸ **Wheeler gets Lee from waiting area**
BC Children's Hospital // 24 January 1996

▸▸ **Grace tells Lee the bad news, Lee runs away**
BC Children's Hospital // 25 January 1996

▸▸ **Lee runs down corridor, chased by Grace**
BC Children's Hospital // 24 January 1996

▸▸ **Pete puts the Doctor into the morgue**
BC Children's Hospital // 23 January 1996

▸▸ **Pete hears noises from the morgue**
BC Children's Hospital // 23 January 1996

▸▸ **Doctor smashes the door down, Pete faints**
BC Children's Hospital // 26 January 1996

▸▸ **Doctor wanders down corridor and sees clock**
BC Children's Hospital // 25 January 1996

▸▸ **Doctor sees his reflection in empty ward**
BC Children's Hospital // 26 January 1996

▸▸ **Grace sleeps in her office**
BC Children's Hospital // 24-28 January 1996

▸▸ **Doctor finds a new outfit**
BC Children's Hospital // 23 January 1996

▸▸ **Lee goes through the Doctor's possessions**
218 East Georgia Street // 1 February 1996

▸▸ **Grace and Pete look at damaged door**
BC Children's Hospital // 23 January 1996

▸▸ **Doctor sees Grace in corridor**
BC Children's Hospital // 24-28 January 1996

▸▸ **Grace gets angry with hospital administrator**
BC Children's Hospital // 24-28 January 1996

▸▸ **Doctor joins Grace in the lift**
BC Children's Hospital // 24 January 1996

▸▸ **Doctor and Grace in the lift**
BC Children's Hospital // 25 January 1996

▸▸ **Doctor and Grace in car park, Doctor pull out probe**
Golden Crow Centre // 5 February 1996

▸▸ **Master talks to Curtis about the Doctor's body**
BC Children's Hospital // 24 January 1996

▸▸ **At her flat, Grace examines the Doctor**
1998 Odgen Street // 15 January 1996

▸▸ **Lee enters the TARDIS**
Alley // 1 February 1996

▸▸ **Doctor tries on his new shoes**
1998 Odgen Street // 16 January 1996

▸▸ **Doctor begins to remember and he likes his shoes**
Hadden Park // 16 January 1996

▸▸ **Doctor regains his memory and kisses Grace**
Hadden Park // 16 January 1996

▸▸ **Doctor knows about Master and Eye of Harmony**
Hadden Park // 16 January 1996

▸▸ **Doctor reveals all to Grace, she runs away**
Hadden Park // 16 January 1996

▸▸ **Doctor talks to Grace through letterbox**
1998 Odgen Street // 15 January 1996

▸▸ **Doctor walks through the window**
1998 Odgen Street // 17 January 1996

▸▸ **Doctor loses weight as Grace waits for ambulance**
1998 Odgen Street // 17 January 1996

▸▸ **Policeman collects chickens in traffic jam**
Carrall Street/Keefer Street // 6 February 1996

▸▸ **Doctor commandeers police motorbike**
Carrall Street/Keefer Street // 6 February 1996

▸▸ **Doctor and Grace ride off, followed by ambulance**
Carrall Street/Keefer Street // 6 February 1996

▸▸ **Motorbike and ambulance head for ITAR**
Waterfront Road // 7/8 February 1996

▸▸ **Doctor arrives at ITAR and sees ambulance**
Pacific Space Centre // 18 January 1996

▸▸ **Grace picks up her invitation**
Pacific Space Centre // 18 January 1996

▸▸ **Doctor takes pass, steals chip and sees Master**
Pacific Space Centre // 19 January 1996

▸▸ **Doctor and Grace escape by fire hose**
Pacific Space Centre // 18 January 1996

▸▸ **Doctor and Grace head back to the TARDIS**
Waterfront Road // 7 February 1996

▸▸ **Doctor, Grace and motorbike cop outside TARDIS**
Alley // 2 February 1996

▸▸ **Costume party at the hospital**
BC Children's Hospital // 23 January 1996

▸▸ **Wagg prepares for the start of his clock**
Pacific Space Centre // 19 January 1996

▸▸ **Wagg is told the clock won't start**
Pacific Space Centre // 19 January 1996

▸▸ **Lightning hits the TARDIS**
Alley // 2 February 1996

▸▸ **Countdown at the hospital**
BC Children's Hospital // 23 January 1996

▸▸ **Countdown at ITAR**
Pacific Space Centre // 19 January 1996

▸▸ **TARDIS dematerialises from the alley**

Left: Daphne Ashbrook and Paul McGann prepare to film their farewell scene on a cold and rainy Vancouver night in Andy Livingston Park on 7 February 1996.

Alley // 2 February 1996
▸▸ **Establishing shot – Hospital**
BC Children's Hospital // 26 January 1996
▸▸ **Countdown again at the hospital**
BC Children's Hospital // 23 January 1996
▸▸ **Countdown again at ITAR**
Pacific Space Centre // 19 January 1996
▸▸ **Doctor says goodbye to Lee and Grace**
Andy Livingston Park // 7 February 1996

The Facts

A total of six days filming was done at the BC Children's Hospital, but in order to ensure that the production didn't disrupt the establishment's normal workings, a disused area of the building was used and dressed as appropriate. The morgue area was a specially constructed set built in the hospital's empty therapy swimming pool.

For the close-up dialogue shots of the Doctor and Grace on the motorbike, the vehicle was mounted on a trailer and towed along.

One of the most difficult sequences to shoot was the farewell scene in John Livingston Park. Intermittent but heavy showers were a constant problem, almost resulting in the entire scene being shot with the characters holding umbrellas. Although most of the scenes were ultimately shot in between downpours, the damp air took its toll on Daphne Ashbrook's hair and Paul McGann's wig.

In order to promote the film, Fox also produced an electronic press kit through their creative services department, a 53-minute package of clips, interviews and behind-the-scenes footage. The EPK included approximately three minutes of material showing the filming of the shooting scenes in the alley on Friday 2 February and the Doctor and Grace's encounter with the motorcycle policeman four days later.

Further behind-the-scenes footage also appeared in a 52-minute video documentary entitled *Bidding Adieu*, produced by BBV, which followed Sylvester McCoy's experiences in Vancouver.

Unused Locations

Early versions of the script for *Doctor Who* (those pre-Matthew Jacobs, who wrote the final version) had centred much of the action around wastelands of Gallifrey and Skaro, so producers Philip Segal and Peter V Ware made a trip to Utah to scout for possible locations. As well as looking at the outlying deserts, a number of buildings within Salt Lake City were also highlighted for possible use. The interior of the Utah State Capital Building was earmarked for either Borusa's home or as a 'Time Lord temple'. As the early scripts also featured scenes set in London, the City and County Building in Washington Square was selected as a possible 'English' backdrop.

Comment

Some people loved it, some people hated it – but there's no denying that the Paul McGann movie is beautifully shot and features some stunning location work, expertly directed by Geoffrey Sax. Never has an actor slotted so effortlessly into the role of the Doctor than McGann and his presence adds much to the scenes in and around Grace's home and the touching farewell sequence at the end. Conditions were not good during the shoot, with Vancouver suffering more than its fair share of rain and snow, so it's all the more impressive that it turned out as well as it did. ■

'I don't think we're quite where I expected. But never mind. This looks very interesting...'
The Doctor – *The Space Pirates*

THE OTHER DOCTORS

Earth ravaged by a Dalek invasion. They make their way to Bedfordshire, the centre of the Dalek operations, and discover that the Daleks plan to drop a gigantic explosive device down a fissure in the Earth's crust into the very centre of the planet. With the molten core destroyed the Daleks purpose to replace it with a drive device so that they can pilot the planet like a giant spaceship. Tom manages to divert the bomb, which explodes off-course, completely destroying the Daleks.

The Locations

1. Jetty (next to St Mary's Church), Battersea Church Road, Battersea, London, SW11
2. Bendy Toys Factory, Ashford Road, Ashford, Middlesex[1]
3. River Ash Footbridge, Littleton Park, Littleton, Middlesex
4. Shepperton Studios Backlot, Studios Road, Littleton, Middlesex

Shooting Schedule

▸ **Robbery and TARDIS dematerialises**
Shepperton Backlot // 31 January – 22 March 1966
▸ **Tom Campbell's POV of ruined factory**
Battersea Church Road // 31 January – 22 March 1966
▸ **Doctor and Tom find dead Roboman in warehouse**
Bendy Toys Factory // 31 January – 22 March 1966
▸ **Louise wets her handkerchief in the Thames**
Battersea Church Road // 31 January – 22 March 1966
▸ **Doctor and Tom examine helmet, hear noise**
Bendy Toys Factory // 31 January – 22 March 1966
▸ **Doctor and Tom rush for the exit**
Bendy Toys Factory // 31 January – 22 March 1966
▸ **Wyler and Louise watch the saucer land**
Shepperton Backlot // 31 January – 22 March 1966
▸ **Doctor and Tom confronted by Dalek in**

This section lists a number of miscellaneous *Doctor Who* productions between 1966 and 1993, all of which involved the actual or potential use of locations.

DALEKS – INVASION EARTH 2150AD

(Released 22 July 1966)
(feature film)

The Story

Following a robbery, policeman Tom Campbell stumbles into the TARDIS believing it to be a genuine police box. Ttansported forward in time to the year 2150, the Doctor, Louise, Susan and Tom find the

Left: **The Doctor (Peter Cushing) and Tom Campbell (Bernard Cribbins) are filmed by the River Thames at a jetty off the Battersea Church Road for** *Daleks – Invasion Earth 2150AD.* **Note the rope used to pull the Dalek out of the river.**

the Thames
Battersea Church Road // 31 January – 22 March 1966

▸▸ **Doctor and David escape into the sewers**
Shepperton Studios // 31 January – 22 March 1966

▸▸ **Doctor and David leave the station and see saucer**
Shepperton Backlot // 31 January – 22 March 1966

▸▸ **Wyler and Susan leave garage and crash cordon**
Shepperton Backlot // 31 January – 22 March 1966

▸▸ **Scanner – van on road**
Shepperton Backlot // 31 January – 22 March 1966

▸▸ **Van drives past monument in square**
Shepperton Backlot // 31 January – 22 March 1966

▸▸ **Van drives down muddy road and into field**
Shepperton Backlot // 31 January – 22 March 1966

▸▸ **Wyler and Susan run as van explodes**
Shepperton Backlot // 31 January – 22 March 1966

▸▸ **David shoots two Robomen on bridge**
Shepperton Backlot // 31 January – 22 March 1966

▸▸ **Tom and Louise arrive at the mine and hide in shed**
Shepperton Backlot // 31 January – 22 March 1966

▸▸ **Wyler and Susan arrive at the cottage**
River Ash Footbridge // 31 January – 22 March 1966

▸▸ **Doctor and David meet Brockley**
Shepperton Backlot // 31 January – 22 March 1966

▸▸ **Brockley, Doctor and David head towards the mine**
Shepperton Backlot // 31 January – 22 March 1966

▸▸ **Daleks capture Doctor and kill Brockley**
Shepperton Backlot // 31 January – 22 March 1966

▸▸ **Battle with the Daleks outside the mine**
Shepperton Backlot // 31 January – 22 March 1966

▸▸ **Tom leaves mine and is saved by workers**
Shepperton Backlot // 31 January – 22 March 1966

⟩ **Dalek pulled backwards into the mine**
Shepperton Backlot // 31 January – 22 March 1966
⟩ **Workers run from mine as saucer crashes**
Shepperton Backlot // 31 January – 22 March 1966
⟩ **Tom foils the robbers**
Shepperton Backlot // 31 January – 22 March 1966

The Facts

The second *Doctor Who* film benefited from an increased budget and, unlike *Dr Who and the Daleks*, was not restricted to studio filming. This more lavish sequel was produced under the title *Daleks Invade Earth 2150AD*.

The main location used, other than the backlot at Shepperton Studios, was the southern bank of the River Thames, not far from Battersea Bridge, used to recreate the shot of the Dalek rising from the water and cutting off the Doctor's escape.

Geoff Glover (first camera assistant): 'The work carried out had to start early in the morning when the tide was at its lowest. Tracks had to be laid to take the Dalek out of the river. We had to wait a couple of hours for high tide so that we could film the Dalek emerging. This I recall was a problem as the Dalek started to float. However, with extra weights attached we managed to achieve the shot – just.'

The same part of the river also provided the basic plate for the shot of the ruined factory seen by policeman Tom Campbell (Bernard Cribbins) as he first exits the TARDIS. The building, Chelsea Power Station on Lots Road, was then replaced by a painted version, complete with broken chimneys as well as damage to the nearby gasometers of Chelsea Gas Works.

The scene of freedom fighter Wyler and Susan, the Doctor's granddaughter, approaching the woodland cottage was filmed using the footbridge over the River Ash, joining the main Shepperton complex to the studio's backlot. The cottage itself was a piece of scenery constructed over a spur of the river.

Sheila Steafel (young woman): 'After the filming, the sound had to be completely redubbed due to its poor quality, and as I was unavailable, someone else 'voiced' me. It was very odd on seeing the film to hear another voice issuing from my mouth!'

Comment

Aside from the work done on the Shepperton backlot, there isn't much true location filming to speak of in *Daleks – Invasion Earth 2150AD*. However, the main riverside scene still provides the 'shock' revelation that London has been invaded by Daleks, even though the idea of a swimming Dalek is just as silly here as it was in the original. One can see the problems they had with the shot, though, as the Dalek casing begins to sway quite noticeably in the water towards the end of the scene.

SHADA

(Proposed tx 19 January to 23 February 1980)
(unfinished story)

The Story

The Doctor and Romana answer a call from Professor Chronotis, a retired Time Lord who now teaches at St Cedds College in Cambridge. Chronotis wants them to take a powerful book, *The Worshipful and Ancient Law of Gallifrey*, back to their home planet. Meanwhile, an alien scientist named Skagra arrives, also seeking the book, which will lead him to the Time Lord prison planet of Shada. There, Skagra wishes to steal the mind of one of the inmates, Salyavin, whose knowledge will allow Skagra to project his will into the minds of all living beings. The Doctor discovers that Chronotis is really Salyavin, who managed to escape from Shada long ago in his TARDIS, now disguised as his Cambridge study. The Doctor fights a battle of wills against Skagra, imprisoning him inside his own spaceship.

The Locations

1. King's Parade, Cambridge, Cambridgeshire
2. Emmanuel College, St Andrew's Street, Cambridge, Cambridgeshire
3. The Backs, River Cam (between Clare Bridge and King's Bridge), Cambridge, Cambridgeshire
4. Clare Bridge, River Cam, Cambridge, Cambridgeshire
5. St Edward's Passage, Cambridge, Cambridgeshire
6. Botolph Lane, Cambridge, Cambridgeshire
7. Silver Street, Cambridge, Cambridgeshire
8. Trumpington Street, Cambridge, Cambridgeshire
9. Garret Hostel Lane and Bridge, Cambridge, Cambridgeshire
10. Trinity Lane, Cambridge, Cambridgeshire
11. Portugal Place, Cambridge, Cambridgeshire
12. Portugal Street, Cambridge, Cambridgeshire
13. Bridge Street, Cambridge, Cambridgeshire
14. Blackmoor Head Yard, Cambridge, Cambridgeshire
15. High Street, Grantchester, Cambridgeshire
16. Grantchester Meadows, Grantchester, Cambridgeshire

Shooting Schedule

PART 1

⟩ **Chris Parsons cycles to St Cedds College**
King's Parade // 15 October 1979
⟩ **Parsons heads towards Chronotis' room**
Emmanuel College // 17 October 1979
⟩ **Doctor and Romana punt down the river**
River Cam // 15 October 1979

Left: The Doctor (Tom Baker) punts Romana (Lalla Ward) gently along the Backs of the River Cam during the filming of *Shada*. These scenes would eventually be transmitted as part of *The Five Doctors* in 1983.

▶▶ Skagra watches them from the bridge
Clare Bridge // 15 October 1979

▶▶ Doctor and Romana arrive and see Wilkin
Emmanuel College // 17 October 1979

▶▶ Skagra walks down road
King's Parade // 15 October 1979

▶▶ Skagra talks to Wilkin
Emmanuel College // 17 October 1979

▶▶ Skagra walks down passage
St Edwards Passage // 15 October 1979

▶▶ Skagra hijacks a car
King's Parade // 15 October 1979

▶▶ Skagra drives past St Cedds
Free School Lane // 17 October 1979

▶▶ Skagra drives down road
High Street // 16 October 1979

▶▶ Skagra parks car and enters his invisible ship
Grantchester Meadows // 16 October 1979

PART 2

▶▶ Doctor rounds corner on bike and rides up road
Botolph Lane (Junction) // 15 October 1979

▶▶ Parsons on bike
Silver Street // 15 October 1979

▶▶ Doctor and Parsons almost collide
Trumpington Street // 15 October 1979

▶▶ Skagra returns to St Cedd's
Emmanuel College // 17 October 1979

▶▶ Doctor encounters Skagra, he cycles away
Garret Hostel Lane/Bridge // 19 October 1979

▶▶ Doctor passes singers followed by sphere, loses book
Trinity Lane // 19 October 1979

▶▶ Doctor turns and cycles down side alley
Portugal Place // 19 October 1979

▶▶ Doctor abandons the bicycle
Portugal Street // 19 October 1979

▶▶ Doctor runs down street and into yard
Bridge Street // 19 October 1979

▶▶ Doctor runs into yard and is trapped by sphere (2/3)
Blackmoor Head Yard // 19 October 1979

PART 3

▶▶ Fisherman is attacked by sphere
Grantchester Meadows // 16 October 1979

▶▶ TARDIS arrives, Doctor's party enter ship
Grantchester Meadows // 16 October 1979

▶▶ Clare talks to Wilkin about the book
Emmanuel College // 17 October 1979

▶▶ Skagra leaves ship with Romana
Grantchester Meadows // 16 October 1979

▶▶ Skagra enters TARDIS with Romana
Grantchester Meadows // 16 October 1979

▶▶ Wilkin crosses courtyard to Chronotis' room
Emmanuel College // 17 October 1979

PART 4

▶▶ Skagra's spaceship leaves the field
Grantchester Meadows // 16 October 1979

PART 6

» **Wilkin talks to policeman about missing room**
Emmanuel College // 17 October 1979

The Facts

As had happened a number of times previously, *Shada* was disrupted by an industrial dispute within the BBC. Although this would eventually escalate to the point where the production could no longer be completed, the first problems came while the team were filming in Cambridge, affecting the original plans to film the sequence from Part 2 of the Doctor being chased by Skagra's sphere at night, with the crew working between 6.00 pm through to 4.00 am the next morning.

Pennant Roberts (director): 'This was the result of quite a long discussion between Graham Williams, the producer, and myself. Graham felt that it wouldn't be possible to stage the chase sequence during the daytime because of the reactions of the public. However, it was obviously going to cause enormous problems to shoot such an extended chase sequence at night, what with the change of locations and the need to re-rig the lighting set-ups and move the generators around Cambridge. So I felt that it would be much more effective to do it in the daytime.'

However, industrial action was called, which meant that the technical manager, Tony Bate (who would have been in charge of the lighting equipment), was told to return to London. The planned night shoot would no longer be possible. As nothing had been scheduled to be filmed during the daylight hours of Thursday 18 October, the team found themselves with a full day to spare, which they put to good use, replanning the chase sequence so that it could be shot the following day, which had originally been set aside as a pick-up day so that the team could complete any unfinished material.

With the filming being rescheduled on the fly, it allowed for the addition of one unplanned extra to the production.

Pennant Roberts: 'A student recognised Tom and asked what we were doing and then wondered if there was any chance of involving the St John's Choristers in the shoot. I couldn't think of a reason why not and I though it would give a little bit of local colour. So we said, "Yes, come along if you like. We should be outside Trinity Hall at about three o'clock tomorrow afternoon. If you can get your people there, then you can take part." Sure enough, he turned up with a substantial number of the St John's Choristers. We put them under a lamp post and filmed the scene with the Doctor riding past them on his bicycle, pursued by the sphere. They, meanwhile, sang 'Chattanooga Choo-Choo'. It was completely last minute and unplanned, but I think it added a characteristic Cambridge touch to the story.'

The filming around Emmanuel College on Wednesday 17 October was briefly covered by a crew from BBC East's *Weekend Extra* programme, transmitted on 20 October. On the morning of Wednesday 17, however, the driver sent to collect two of the actors from their hotel couldn't locate Victoria Burgoyne (playing Clare Keightley) and had to return to the location with only Christopher Neame. Sent back to the hotel to try and find the missing actress, it was discovered that she had been trapped inside a toilet cubicle with a broken latch and that her cries for help had not been heard.

With one of the studio recording sessions completed, further industrial action prevented the following two from taking place. Once the strikes were over several weeks later, other productions were deemed more important than the completion of *Shada*, and despite efforts to have it remounted, the project was finally abandoned in June 1980. Two small location sequences from the filming on the Cam and in Blackmoor Head Yard were amalgamated into *The Five Doctors* in 1983, when Tom Baker decided that he didn't wish to appear in the story. The rest of the material was subsequently released by BBC Video in 1992, with the missing sections narrated by Tom Baker.

Unused Locations

Cavendish Laboratory – One brief scene that was scheduled to be filmed at Cambridge, but which was ultimately abandoned, was of the Doctor arriving and entering Chris Parsons' physics laboratory. The scene was due to be filmed at the Cavendish Laboratory, Madingley Road as the final shot of the day on Tuesday 16 October.

Comment

Pennant Roberts' cameras explore Cambridge to the full, effortlessly conveying the town's atmospheric splendour. The punting scene has a gentle and relaxed quality, greatly aided, as was the Parisian filming for *City of Death*, by Baker and Ward's growing closeness. The chase sequence in Part 2 is also superbly handled, especially considering the last-minute changes that surrounded it – and the inclusion of the St John's Choristers is a stroke of improvisational genius.

K9 AND COMPANY: A GIRL'S BEST FRIEND

(tx 28 December 1981)
(BBC spin-off)

The Story

Sarah Jane Smith travels to the village of Morton Harwood to see her Aunt Lavinia, only to be told that she has suddenly had to go on a lecture tour of

America. Sarah collects Brendan, her aunt's ward, from the railway station and together they open a large chest that had been left for Sarah's attention some years previous. Inside Sarah discovers a new K9, a present from the Doctor. Due to the local crop failures, Brendan is kidnapped by a coven of superstitious villagers and held for sacrifice to the goddess, Hecate. Sarah and K9 manage to track Brendan down just in time and rescue him from a sacrificial death in a local churchyard.

The Locations

1. Ruined Church, North Woodchester, Gloucestershire
2. Crossroads, Sapperton, Gloucestershire
3. Barnsley House, Barnsley, Gloucestershire
4. Miserden Petrol Station, Miserden, Gloucestershire
5. Wishanger Farm, Wishanger, Gloucestershire
6. Miserden Park Estate, Miserden, Gloucestershire
   - Miserden Nurseries
   - Lodge
   - Road
7. St Andrew's Church, Miserden, Gloucestershire
8. Bisley, Gloucestershire
   - Police Station
   - Post Office
9. Daneway, Gloucestershire

Shooting Schedule

▸▸ **Coven hold their ceremony**
North Woodchester // 15 November 1981

▸▸ **Sarah drives into village (cut)**
Daneway/Bisley Villages // 12 November 1981

▸▸ **Sarah almost hits an old man on the road (cut)**
Sapperton Crossroads // 16 November 1981

▸▸ **Sarah arrives at the Manor and meets Tracey**
Barnsley House // 16 November 1981

▸▸ **Sarah picks up Brendan**
Miserden Village – Petrol Station //
16 November 1981

▸▸ **Sarah and Brendan talk while driving (cut)**
Wishanger Farm // 14 November 1981

▸▸ **Sarah's car passes crossroads (cut)**
Sapperton Crossroads // 16 November 1981

▸▸ **Sarah's car burns up the drive (cut)**
Barnsley House // 16 November 1981

▸▸ **Sarah and Lilly Gregson meet while Tracey watches**
Bisley Post Office // 17 November 1981

▸▸ **Brendan collects a soil sample**
Miserden Park Estate – Nurseries //
13 November 1981

▸▸ **K9 pursues Tracey though greenhouses**
Miserden Park Estate – Nurseries //
13 November 1981

▸▸ **K9 accidentally destroys greenhouse**
Miserden Park Estate – Nurseries //
13 November 1981

▸▸ **Pollock examines damage, Brendan tells of attack**
Miserden Park Estate – Nurseries //
13 November 1981

▸▸ **Sarah arrives at Tracey's cottage**
Miserden Park Estate – Lodge // 13 November 1981

▸▸ **Pollock offers to take Sarah to the police (cut)**
Miserden Park Estate – Nurseries //
13 November 1981

▸▸ **Sarah and Pollock leave Police Station**
Bisley Police Station // 17 November 1981

▸▸ **Sarah and Pollock return while Tracey watches**
Barnsley House // 16 November 1981

▸▸ **Sarah sees Sgt. Wilson leave Tracey's cottage**
Miserden Park Estate – Lodge // 13 November 1981

▸▸ **Sgt. Wilson cycles down the road**
Miserden Park Estate – Road // 14 November 1981

▸▸ **Sgt. Wilson dies and is found by Sarah**
Miserden Park Estate – Road // 14 November 1981

▸▸ **Tracey tells Peter he must be initiated**
North Woodchester // 15 November 1981

▸▸ **Peter is initiated**
North Woodchester // 15 November 1981

▸▸ **Sarah almost crashes into tractor**
Wishanger Farm // 14 November 1981

▸▸ **Howard Baker makes toward Police Station (cut)**
Bisley Police Station // 17 November 1981

▸▸ **Sarah and K9 search churchyard**
St Andrew's Church // 16 November 1981

▸▸ **Sarah and K9 search another churchyard**
St Andrew's Church // 16 November 1981

▸▸ **Sarah drives to final church**
Miserden Village – Road // 16 November 1981

▸▸ **Brendan brought to churchyard**
North Woodchester // 15 November 1981

▸▸ **Sarah and K9 arrive and save Brenden**
North Woodchester // 15 November 1981

The Facts

The opening title sequence of *K9 and Company*, designed by producer John Nathan-Turner as a mixture of *Hart to Hart* and *Hawaii Five-0*, was shot on Thursday 12 November, taking most of the day to complete due to several changes of location and several changes of costume for Elisabeth Sladen.

- *Sarah sitting reading newspaper – Sheepscombe*
- *Sarah typing and drinking wine – The Bear Inn Public House, Miserden*
- *Sarah jogging and sitting on wall – Sheepscombe*
- *Sarah in car – Wishanger Farm, Wishanger and Miserden Park Estate, Miserden*

While filming the climatic scenes at the ruined church in North Woodchester, the new differential installed into K9 for the story sheared, rendering the prop immobile. Once again, a length of nylon line had to be attached to the front so that K9 could be manually pulled along.

The cauldron which had been hired for the production from a prop house also caused problems when the fire underneath melted the solder holding the chain links together, causing it to crash to the floor.

Comment

K9 and Company features some pleasant location work around the small villages of Gloucestershire, but the whole thing is tainted by the hideous shots of Sarah jogging in the opening sequence and her kung-fu kicks at the end of the story which, quite frankly, make poor Lis Sladen look ridiculous.

THE NIGHTMARE FAIR

(unproduced story, 1985)

The Story

Looking for some much-needed recreation, the Doctor takes Peri to the Blackpool Pleasure Beach. However, hiding beneath the funfair's Space Mountain ride, the Doctor discovers his old adversary the Celestial Toymaker, an ancient being from another universe. The Toymaker forces to the Doctor to play a new video game which will finally bring an end to his weary life when the high score of 125,000 is reached. However, the Doctor realises that the Toymaker's death will also result in the destruction of part of the universe and so he manages to imprison him in a forcefield powered by the Toymaker's own everlasting will.

The Locations

1. Blackpool Pleasure Beach, Ocean Boulevard, Blackpool, Lancashire
2. Blackpool Tower, Blackpool, Lancashire

Shooting Schedule (no filming done)

PART 1

▸▸ **Kevin watches as man is killed by strange figure**
Blackpool Pleasure Beach // c. 1 April 1985
▸▸ **Doctor joyfully examining Blackpool through telescope**
Blackpool Tower // c. 1 April 1985
▸▸ **Doctor looks at mechanised Chinese Mandarin**
Blackpool Pleasure Beach // c. 1 April 1985
▸▸ **Peri is rather disappointed by Blackpool**
Blackpool Pleasure Beach // c. 1 April 1985
▸▸ **Doctor and Peri on rollercoaster**
Blackpool Pleasure Beach // c. 1 April 1985
▸▸ **Kevin walks through park avoiding policemen**
Blackpool Pleasure Beach // c. 1 April 1985
▸▸ **Woman searches amusement arcade for her son**
Blackpool Pleasure Beach // c. 1 April 1985
▸▸ **Doctor and Peri have enjoyed the rollercoster**
Blackpool Pleasure Beach // c. 1 April 1985
▸▸ **Doctor and Peri leave the Octopus ride**
Blackpool Pleasure Beach // c. 1 April 1985
▸▸ **Doctor hears voices in his head, enters arcade**
Blackpool Pleasure Beach // c. 1 April 1985
▸▸ **Doctor heads toward Space Mountain, Kevin follows**
Blackpool Pleasure Beach // c. 1 April 1985
▸▸ **Doctor distracted, Peri has to ride with Kevin**
Blackpool Pleasure Beach // c. 1 April 1985
▸▸ **Peri argues with attendant about Doctor's disappearance**
Blackpool Pleasure Beach // c. 1 April 1985

The Facts

The Nightmare Fair had its origin in a trip that Colin Baker and John Nathan-Turner made on Tuesday 21 August 1984 to Blackpool Pleasure Beach in order to officially open the park's new £1.2 million showpiece ride – Space Invader.

The visit had fostered good relations between the production office, the management of the Pleasure Beach and the town council. Keen to capitalise on the relationship, Nathan-Turner suggested the idea of filming a *Doctor Who* story at Blackpool and, when the idea was accepted, approaches were made to former producer Graham Williams to write a script specifically featuring both Blackpool Pleasure Beach and the return of the Celestial Toymaker. Following the delivery of the basic storyline, Williams was formally commissioned to write a detailed scene breakdown on 25 September 1984, which he delivered under the working title of *Arcade*, followed by a full commission to write two 45 minute scripts on 17 November.

Williams' final scripts, dated 7 February 1985, featured scenes set on the Pleasure Beach's 1930s wooden rollercoaster and on their Gold Mine ride.[2] The script also featured a ride called Space Mountain, from which the Doctor is kidnapped in the first episode. It was likely that the new Space Invader ride would have been used for these scenes.

The second scene of the story emulated a shot that had been hoped for during the filming of *City of Death* at the Eiffel Tower, but which couldn't be achieved for technical reasons, namely a close-up of the Doctor and

Peri before the picture slowly zooms out to reveal them standing at the top of the Tower.

'We have left the Doctor and Peri about a mile back, zooming out to reveal them having been standing in the observation dome of the Blackpool Tower. The pull-back has revealed the sea front, and settled with the amusement park in the foreground. Feature the joys the fairground has to offer – a whirling Carousel, the "Waltza" ride, the biggest of the switchback rides, the crowds enjoying themselves mightily.'

The Nightmare Fair, Part 1

By the end of February 1985, director Matthew Robinson had been assigned to the project and agreements had been reached with actor Michael Gough to recreate the character of the Toymaker for the first time since 1966. It was then that John Nathan-Turner was informed that the production of the 23rd season of *Doctor Who* was to be postponed by a year in a cost-cutting measure at the BBC. As a result, *The Nightmare Fair*, along with all the other plans for the season, including the return of old enemies Sil and the Ice Warriors, were dropped.

Comment

Looking at the scripts, one can imagine that the footage of the Doctor enjoying his time at the Pleasure Beach would have been rather fun to watch, especially a wonderfully amusing scene on the park's wooden rollercoaster, where, by the end of the ride, he is immobile, his face frozen in a smile of pure joy. The opening scene with the Doctor and Peri at the top of Blackpool Tower is also nicely scripted and, if it could have been achieved, the long zoom back to reveal the beach would have been very impressive. That said, the script itself is awful and would have wasted the opportunity to bring back the Celestial Toymaker.

YELLOW FEVER

(unproduced story, 1985)

The Story

No synopsis is available for *Yellow Fever*, as the story was never completed by scriptwriter Robert Holmes.

The Locations

1. Singapore

The Facts

Another of the planned stories for the original Season 23 was *Yellow Fever* by Robert Holmes, a three-part adventure featuring the return of the Autons.

Through his production colleagues working on *Tenko*, John Nathan-Turner had met a representative of the Singapore Tourist Board, a Mr Tan, who was keen that programmes which enjoyed healthy overseas sales should consider Singapore as a potential filming location. Following an invitation to visit the country and assess its suitability, Nathan-Turner requested that the BBC assign a production manager who could not only accompany him on the trip but who would also be available for the production itself, should it go ahead. The person assigned was *Doctor Who* stalwart, Gary Downie.

John Nathan-Turner: 'The tourist board couldn't have been more helpful and supplied us with a bevy of guides and a minibus. They took us everywhere; the tourist spots, the beauty spots, ruins of wartime forts and historical places, including the famous Raffles Hotel. Most evenings there were spent in meetings with people who could be helpful if the shoot went ahead: more Tourist Board officials, airline representatives and hotel managers. In the end, major hotels were competing with one another to offer me the cheapest price for our unit's stay. I left Singapore with the most wonderful deal: £300 per head for return flight, bed and breakfast accommodation in a top hotel and unlimited shipping for equipment. It was to be a ten-day trip, which worked out as a seven-day shoot because of a day off and time to recover from jet lag. We came back with a video of some of the locations and masses of photographs. I can assure you, though extremely enjoyable, a junket it most certainly was not!'[3]

Returning from the visit, Nathan-Turner began to formulate an opening to the story whereby Peri expresses a desire to return to America and, seeing the Statue of Liberty on the scanner, she makes the assumption that the Doctor has actually fulfilled her wishes. On exiting the TARDIS however, the Doctor and Peri would have found themselves in a massive cultural garden featuring architecture from all over the world – including a 12-foot model of the Statue of Liberty. Among the garden's many statues would have been some that moved – the Autons. Nathan-Turner had also suggested the inclusion of both the Master and the Rani, operating as members of a travelling street theatre.

Holmes was duly contracted to write the first episode (officially listed as *Yellow Fever and How To Cure It*) on 26 October 1984 with a further contract being issued (this time listing the title as just *Yellow Fever*) on 6 February 1985, just three weeks before the cancellation of the season came through.

Comment

Excellent as he was, the one thing Robert Holmes disliked was being forced to write a script which had to contain certain pre-specified elements. This was the very reason he withdrew from scripting *The Six Doctors*, as he felt too creatively constrained by what he was being asked to achieve, and it's easy to see that he might have ended up feeling the same way about *Yellow Fever*, with the requirement to write not only around a specific location but also to feature no less than three returning enemies.

DIMENSIONS IN TIME

(tx 26 November to 27 November 1993)
(BBC Children in Need)

The Story

The Rani plans to trap all the regenerations of the Doctor into a time-loop situated in London's East End. In Walford, time jumps back and forth, between 1973 and 2013, as different Doctors and companions pop in and out of existence. The Seventh Doctor and Ace, together with K9. manage to pull the Rani's TARDIS into her own time tunnel, which sends all his regenerations and the respective companions back to their own time-streams.

The Locations

1. Cutty Sark, Greenwich, London, SE10
2. Royal Naval College, Romney Road, Greenwich, London, SE10
3. National Maritime Museum/Queen's House, Romney Road, Greenwich, London, SE10
4. *EastEnders* Backlot, BBC Elstree Centre, Clarendon Road, Borehamwood, Hertfordshire.

Shooting Schedule

PART 1

▸▸ **1973 - Seventh Doctor and Ace land next to Curry Sark**
Cutty Sark // 24 September 1993

▸▸ **1993 - Sixth Doctor and Ace meet Sanjay and Gita**
Elstree Backlot // 22 September 1993

▸▸ **2013 - Third Doctor and Mel meet Pauline and Kathy**
Elstree Backlot // 23 September 1993

▸▸ **1973 - Sixth Doctor meets Susan**
Elstree Backlot // 22 September 1993

▸▸ **2013 - Third Doctor meets Sarah**
Elstree Backlot // 23 September 1993

▸▸ **1993 - Aliens attack Fifth Doctor, Peri and Nyssa (1/2)**
Elstree Backlot // 22 September 1993

PART 2

▸▸ **1993 - Liz Shaw attacks Rani but is thwarted by Mandy**
Elstree Backlot // 22 September 1993

▸▸ **1993 - Liz Shaw attacks Rani but is thwarted by**

Big Ron (cut)[4]
Elstree Backlot // 22 September 1993

▸▸ **1993 - Third Doctor climbs into UNIT helicopter**
Royal Naval College // 24 September 1993

▸▸ **1973 - Sixth Doctor and Brigadier get out of helicopter**
Royal Naval College // 24 September 1993

▸▸ **1993 - Phil and Grant Mitchell meet Romana in lock-up**
Elstree Backlot // 23 September 1993

▸▸ **1993 - Romana is pulled into the Queen Vic watched by Frank**
Elstree Backlot // 23 September 1993

▸▸ **1973 - Third Doctor and Victoria leave the Cutty Sark**
Cutty Sark // 24 September 1993

▸▸ **1993 - Leela leaves Rani's TARDIS and meets Seventh Doctor**
National Maritime Museum // 24 September 1993

▸▸ **1993 - Seventh Doctor, Ace and K9 expel Rani's TARDIS**
National Maritime Museum // 24 September 1993

▸▸ **1993 - Seventh Doctor and Ace head for TARDIS**
National Maritime Museum // 24 September 1993

The Facts

Dimensions in Time was a 13-minute adventure produced for the BBC's 1993 *Children in Need* appeal. The two episodes, shown on 26 and 27 November 1993, were specially recorded to take advantage of a phenomenon known as the Pulfrich Effect, which meant that anyone watching the episodes while wearing a pair of glasses with a darkened lens over the right eye would see the production in 3D. *Dimensions in Time* was one of a number of programmes that made up a special 3D week on BBC Television.

The vast majority of the filming was done on the *EastEnders* lot at Elstree Studios on 22 and 23 September, while the small amount of studio material was recorded at Fountain Television, New Malden on 21 September.

K9, who was operated for the production by Mat Irvine, stripped its gears shortly before the recording of the afternoon scenes and had to be moved along, as it had been many times over the years, by using a piece of nylon line attached to the casing.

In order to get the shot he wanted for the scene of the helicopter landing at the Royal Naval College, German cameraman Tommy Beier required Nicholas Courtney to sit on the edge of his seat looking out of the open cockpit as the helicopter descended. Although he hadn't told anyone previously, Courtney suffered from vertigo and reputedly needed a stiff drink to calm his nerves after the short flight was over.

The recording of *Dimensions in Time* was followed by a team from *Tomorrow's World* for a 2'44" item, broadcast on Friday 3 December 1993, which endeavoured to explain the problems of making a 3D drama. The item followed various scenes being shot around the Cutty Sark and the Royal Naval College. Several weeks earlier on 7 November, Noel Edmonds hosted a lead-up programme to *Children in Need* called *Pause for Pudsey*. This featured a 1'50" report on the making of *Dimensions in Time*, which mainly concentrated on the work done at the *EastEnders* lot, but which also featured some of the helicopter work at the Royal Naval College.

Comment

Dimensions in Time had to be put together in a remarkably short amount of time and was constructed so that the camera moves would give the desired 3D effect for those wearing the special glasses. The location material is short and sweet, but features the rather impressive use of a large helicopter at the Royal Naval College. A silly piece of *Doctor Who* history with an incomprehensible plot – but as it was all in aid of charity, no one really minds.

THE DARK DIMENSION

(unproduced story, 1993)

The Story

In the year 2525, the Seventh Doctor is killed attempting to help a team of eco-warriors rid the world of a powerful alien creature. The warriors open up a time tunnel and force the creature into it, but it escapes to the year 1936 where Professor Oliver Hawkspur is engaged in his own time travel experiments. The creature takes over Hawkspur's body and begins to search for the Doctor, finally tracking him down to the Pharos Project in 1980 (see *Logopolis*). There he prevents the Fourth Doctor from regenerating thus altering the future and creating an alternative dark dimension. By 1999, Hawkspur has become a powerful millionaire, and is running for Prime Minister under the platform of his Evolutionary Party. The Fourth Doctor finally breaks free from Hawkspur's conditioning and with the Brigadier and Ace's help, begins to fight back against the creature. The creature fashions various monsters to aid him, created from memories extracted from the Seventh Doctor's mind just before his death. The Doctor and the creature battle each other at Hawkspur's mansion where a new time tunnel is opened. With the last of his strength, the Doctor forces the creature into the tunnel throwing it back in time to its death. With the creature gone, the correct timeline is restored and the Fourth Doctor collapses and successively regenerates into his fifth, sixth and seventh incarnations.

The Locations

1. Battersea Power Station, Battersea, London
2. Royal Holloway and Bedford New College, Egham Hill, Egham, Surrey

Shooting Schedule[5]

Listed Exteriors »

Wasteland – 8 scenes
Deserted Shoreline – 1 scene
Deserted Street – 3 scenes
Deserted Alley – 1 scene
Hawkspur Mansion – 9 scenes
Hawkspur HQ – 2 scenes
Parkland – 1 scene
Railway Station – 3 scenes
Tillary House – 3 scenes
Pharos Centre – 1 scene
Country Road – 1 scene
Church/Graveyard – 15 scenes
Road to Church – 1 scene
Downing Street – 1 scene
London Street – 1 scene
White Void – 6 scenes

Listed Interiors

Derelict Car Park – 2 scenes
Casualty Dept – 2 scenes
Casualty Ward – 1 scene
Computer Library – 2 scenes
Television Newsroom – 5 scenes
Dorothy's Room – 1 scene
Hawkspur's Office – 2 scenes
Research Centre – 7 scenes
Brigadier's Study – 2 scenes
Library – 9 scenes
Catacombs – 2 scenes
Church Crypt – 6 scenes
Corridor – 1 scene
Trial Chamber – 2 scenes
Court Waiting Room – 1 scene
Hawkspur's Mansion – 3 scenes
Changing Room – 1 scene
TARDIS Control Room – 1 scene
Inside Church – 1 scene
Inside Car – 1 scene

The Facts

Although no new *Doctor Who* had been produced by the BBC since December 1989, the Corporation were keen to capitalise on the programme's 30th anniversary, due to arrive towards the end of 1993. One proposal put forward by producers David

Jackson and Penny Mills was for BBC Enterprises to produce a special anniversary story that could be released directly to video. Initial responses to the project appeared favourable so approaches were made to writer Adrian Rigelsford to script the adventure. Initial drafts were written by Rigelsford and reviewed by script editor Joanna McCaul, but by the time of the rewrites Rigelsford was working on his own.

With the plans for the project apparently being given the green light, a production office was set up at Woodlands, the BBC Enterprises building. To prevent the plans for *The Dark Dimension* from leaking out, the project was referred to under the internal cover name of *The Environment Roadshow*.

Early drafts of the script were entitled *Lost in the Dark Dimension*, although at one stage head of Enterprises Tony Greenwood had wanted to rename the story *Slaves of the Crimson Time*. By the time the final 200-page rehearsal script had been prepared on 21 June 1993, the title *The Dark Dimension* had been settled upon.

A formal announcement of the project was made by BBC Enterprises on 10 June, around which time the production team was being brought together, consisting of Graeme Harper as director, Kevan Van Thompson (1st assistant), Stanislaw Fus (locations manager), Nic Jagels (production manager), Chris Fitzgerald (creature design), Tony Harding (visual effects designer), Alan Marshall and Mike Tucker (VFX assistants), Dave Chapman (video effects) and Bridget Tudor Evans (costume designer).

By this time, however, BBC Television were already negotiating with Philip Segal over a possible production to be made by the US company Amblin, and it was partly due to this that the production of *The Dark Dimension* was finally vetoed. The project was officially announced as cancelled on 9 July 1993.

Although the production office was not running for long, an initial location recce had been made and plans were being drawn up to use the Royal Holloway College in Egham as the exterior of Hawkspur's mansion. Consideration was also seriously being given to making use of the old Battersea Power Station, probably for the wasteland scenes set in the year 2525.

Plans were also being made to shoot a number of sequences at Shepperton Studios. The trial sequences involving the Sixth Doctor and the Ice Warriors were to have been shot on Stage K, while the medieval village constructed on the studio backlot (and used for the American series *Covington Cross* and the *Red Dwarf* episode *Emohawk – Polymorph II*) was also in view.

Towards the end of the story, a montage sequence had been planned as Hawkspur's biomorphic clones, in the form of various creatures drawn from the Doctor's mind, begin destroying the population of London. This sequence would have recreated a number of classic location sequences from the programme's history.

92. EXT. MONTAGE SEQUENCE DAY.

We see HAWKSPUR'S culling in progress, with monsters at all points of the capital...
CYBERMEN appear on the horizon of the steps of St Paul's, all opening fire on PEOPLE as they run for their lives...
A J MANSON (VO) Casualties are high.... Many of the wounded are being moved from London Central, as that area's now been declared a danger zone...
DALEKS glide round the lions in Trafalgar Square, with guns blazing as they surge towards the running TOURISTS...
A J MANSON (VO) It's believed that Martial law will be put into operation within the hour...
We see a whole line of white DALEKS, gliding across Westminster Bridge, heading towards Parliament...
Finally, with their bases glowing, we see two white DALEKS swoop past the face of Big Ben, with guns blazing.

Comment

The basic idea behind *The Dark Dimension* is actually a very clever way of producing a multi-Doctor story without resorting to the idea of the available Doctors getting together to fight some evil force (à la *The Three Doctors* and *The Five Doctors*). That said, the script reads a little like a fan's dream, with various old monsters appearing and disappearing at a bewildering pace. ■

FOOTNOTES

. Now known as Stronalva House.
. Williams' script indicates that the scenes set within the Gold Mine ride were intended to be shot on film. However, due to the nature of the scenes

it isn't clear whether this would have been accomplished on location or on sets at Ealing Studios.
3. *Doctor Who Magazine* #240, p.49
4. Viewers of *Children in Need*

had the opportunity to take part in a charity telephone vote to decide which of two *EastEnders* characters would 'help the Doctor' in Part 2. In the end, the character of Mandy won with 22,484 votes over Big

Ron with 17,044 votes.
5. As it's unclear as to how many of the interior scenes would have also been shot on location, all the scripted exterior and interior sequences are listed.

APPENDIX

GEOGRAPHICAL GUIDE

ENGLAND

AVON
Bristol
  The Sun Makers

BEDFORDSHIRE
Caddington
  Terror of the Autons
Dunstable
  The Macra Terror
Dunstable
  Terror of the Autons
Totternhoe
  Terror of the Autons

BERKSHIRE
Hurley
  The Visitation
Mortimer
  The Time Monster
Sonning Common
  Logopolis
Strathfield Mortimer
  Planet of the Spiders
Swallowfield
  The Time Monster
Tidmarsh
  Planet of the Spiders

BUCKINGHAMSHIRE
Burnham
  Day of the Daleks
Burnham
  State of Decay
Chalfont St Giles
  Terror of the Autons
Chalfont St Giles
  Paradise Towers
Chalfont St Peter
  The Savages
Chalfont St Peter
  Terror of the Autons
Denham
  Logopolis
Denham Green
  The Reign of Terror
Denham Green
  Fury from the Deep
Denham Green
  The Three Doctors
Denham Green
  The Five Doctors
Ewshot
  The Ambassadors
  of Death

Fulmer
  Full Circle
Fulmer
  The Visitation
Fulmer
  Battlefield
Genham Green
  The Invasion
Gerrards Cross
  The Reign of Terror
Gerrards Cross
  The Tomb of the
  Cybermen
Gerrards Cross
  The Dominators
Gerrards Cross
  The Twin Dilemma
Gerrards Cross
  Attack of the
  Cybermen
High Wycombe
  The Ambassadors of Death
High Wycombe
  The Deadly Assassin
Little Marlow
  The Ambassadors of Death
Marlow
  The Ambassadors of Death
Quainton
  Black Orchid

CAMBRIDGESHIRE
Cambridge
  Shada
Cambridge
  The Five Doctors
Grantchester
  Shada

CHESHIRE
Peckforton
  The Time Warrior

CORNWALL
Carclaze
  Colony in Space
Church Cove
  The Smugglers
Grade
  The Smugglers
Helston
  The Smugglers
Nanjizel Bay
  The Smugglers
Trethewey
  The Smugglers

Newlyn Harbour
  The Smugglers

DEVON
Manaton
  The Sontaran Experiment
Postbridge
  The Sontaran Experiment

DORSET
Athelhampton
  The Seeds of Doom
Gallows Hill
  Death to the Daleks
Gallows Hill
  The Caves of
  Androzani
Lulworth Cove
  The Curse of Fenric
Shapwick
  The Awakening
Tarrant Monkton
  The Awakening
Wareham
  Destiny of the Daleks
Warmwel
  The Greatest Show in
  the Galaxy
Warmwell
  Survival
Weymouth
  Ghost Light
Worth Matravers
  The Underwater Menace
Worth Matravers
  Destiny of the Daleks

ESSEX
Asheldham
  Carnival of Monsters
Tillingham
  Carnival of Monsters

GLOUCESTERSHIRE
Barnsley
  K9 and Company
Berkeley
  The Pirate Planet
Bisley
  K9 and Company
Coln St Aldwyn
  The Invasion
Daneway
  K9 and Company
Fairford
  The Invasion

Miserden
  K9 and Company
North Woodchester
  K9 and Company
River Severn
  Planet of the Spiders
Sapperton
  K9 and Company
Sheepscombe
  K9 and Company
Thornbury
  The Hand of Fear
Wishanger
  K9 and Company
Wotton-under-Edge
  The Hand of Fear

HAMPSHIRE
Aldershot
  The Ambassadors
  of Death
Buriton
  Revelation of the Daleks
East End
  Pyramids of Mars
East End
  Image of the Fendahl
East Meon
  The Trial of a Time
  Lord 1-4
Fordingbridge
  The Awakening
Hartley Wintney
  The Time Monster
Heckfield Heath
  The Time Monster
Horndean
  Revelation of the Daleks
Horndean
  The Trial of a Time
  Lord 1-4
Marchwood
  Warriors of the Deep
Portsmouth
  The Sea Devils
Portsmouth
  Revelation of the Daleks
Southsea
  The Sea Devils
Stratfield Saye
  The Time Monster

**HEREFORD and
WORCESTERSHIRE**
Evesham
  Spearhead from Space

Evesham
  Robot
Malvern
  The Krotons
Radford
  Spearhead from Space

HERTFORDSHIRE
Borehamwood
  Dimensions in Time
Rickmansworth
  The Three Doctors
Rickmansworth
  Earthshock
Rickmansworth
  The Twin Dilemma
Rickmansworth
  Delta and the Bannermen

ISLE OF WIGHT
Bembridge
  The Sea Devils
East Cowes
  The Sea Devils
Sandown
  The Sea Devils
Seaview
  The Sea Devils
Whitecliff Bay
  The Sea Devils

KENT
Chatham
  Carnival of Monsters
Chislehurst
  The Mutants
Dover
  The Mind of Evil
Dungeness
  The Claws of Axos
Frindsbury
  The Mutants
Hawkhurst
  The Curse of Fenric
Hoo St Werburgh
  Inferno
Kingsgate
  Fury from the Deep
Leeds
  The Androids of Tara
Lydd
  The Claws of Axos
Manston
  The Mind of Evil
Northfleet
  The Ambassadors of Death